The Finance Act 2007

The Finance Act 2007

Contributors

Graham J Airs, LLB, MA
Mohammed Amin, MA, FCA, AMCT, CTA (Fellow)
Charles Barcroft, CTA
Rebecca Benneyworth, BSC, FCA
Michael Bird, BA (Hons), ACA, CTA
Lynette Bober, MA (Cantab), ACA, CTA
Sarah Bradford, BA(Hons), ACA, CTA (Fellow)
Patrick Cannon, LLB, BCL, CTA (Fellow), Barrister
Anthony Davis, MA, CTA (Fellow)
Mark Downey
Keith Gordon, MA (Oxon), ACA, CTA, Barrister
Dean M Harris, CTA
John Hayward
Andrew Hubbard, BMus, PhD, CTA (Fellow), ATT
Simon Jennings, MA (Oxon), FCA, TEP
Terry Jordan, TEP
Jacquelyn Kimber
David Klass, BA
Zigurds Kronbergs, MA, BSc, ARCS, ACA, FCCA
David O'Keeffe
David Oliver, LLB, FCA
Tracy Payton, MA, ACA, CTA
Juliet Phillips
Louise Pinfold, BA (Hons)
Gary Richards, MA, LLB, ATII, Solicitor
Chris Russell, FFA, CTA (Fellow), Actuary
Paul Stainforth, LLB (Hons), CTA
Bernard Sweet
Alastair Wilson
Martin Wilson, MA, FCA

LexisNexis® Tolley

Members of the LexisNexis Group worldwide

United Kingdom	LexisNexis Butterworths, a Division of Reed Elsevier (UK) Ltd, Halsbury House, 35 Chancery Lane, London, WC2A 1EL, and London House, 20–22 East London Street, Edinburgh EH7 4BQ
Argentina	LexisNexis Argentina, Buenos Aires
Australia	LexisNexis Butterworths, Chatswood, New South Wales
Austria	LexisNexis Verlag ARD Orac GmbH & Co KG, Vienna
Benelux	LexisNexis Benelux, Amsterdam
Canada	LexisNexis Canada, Markham, Ontario
Chile	LexisNexis Chile Ltda, Santiago
China	LexisNexis China, Beijing and Shanghai
France	LexisNexis SA, Paris
Germany	LexisNexis Deutschland GmbH, Munster
Hong Kong	LexisNexis Hong Kong, Hong Kong
India	LexisNexis India, New Delhi
Italy	Giuffrè Editore, Milan
Japan	LexisNexis Japan, Tokyo
Malaysia	Malayan Law Journal Sdn Bhd, Kuala Lumpur
Mexico	LexisNexis Mexico, Mexico
New Zealand	LexisNexis NZ Ltd, Wellington
Poland	Wydawnictwo Prawnicze LexisNexis Sp, Warsaw
Singapore	LexisNexis Singapore, Singapore

First published in 2007

Published by LexisNexis Butterworths

A CIP Catalogue record for this book is available from the British Library.

ISBN 9781405725811 (LNB)

Typeset by Letterpart Ltd, Reigate, Surrey

Printed in the United Kingdom by Polestar Wheatons Ltd

Visit LexisNexis Butterworths at www.lexisnexis.co.uk

CONTENTS

RELEVANT DATES AND ABBREVIATIONS

Budget statement	21 March 2007
Finance Bill published	29 March 2007
Royal Assent	19 July 2007

The following abbreviations are used in this book—

ACT = Advance Corporation Tax
BGDA = Betting and Gaming Duties Act
BPRA = Business Premises Renovation Allowances
CA = Companies Act
CAA = Capital Allowances Act
CEMA = Customs and Excise Management Act 1979
CCL = Climate Change Levy
CFC = Controlled Foreign Company
CGT = Capital Gains Tax
CRCA = Commissioners for Revenue and Customs Act 2005
CTSA = Corporation Tax Self-Assessment
Ch = Chapter (of a part of an Act)
EC = European Communities
ECJ = European Court of Justice (Court of Justice of the European Communities)
EIS = Enterprise Investment Scheme
ESOP = Employee Share Ownership Plan
EU = European Union
FA = Finance Act
F(No 2)A = Finance (No 2) Act
HMRC = Her Majesty's Revenue and Customs
IHTA = Inheritance Tax Act
ITA = Income Tax Act
ITEPA = Income Tax (Earnings and Pensions) Act 2003
ITMA = Income Tax Management Act
IT-TOIA = Income Tax (Trading and Other Income) Act 2005
OTA = Oil Taxation Act
para = paragraph (of a Schedule to an Act)
PCTA = Provisional Collection of Taxes Act 1968
PRT = Petroleum Revenue Tax
reg = regulation (of an SI)
s = section (of an Act)
SAYE = Save as you Earn
Sch = Schedule (to an Act)
SDTS = Simon's Direct Tax Service
SI = Statutory Instrument (since 1948)
SR&O = Statutory Rule and Order
ss = sections
sub-cl = subclause
sub-para = sub-paragraph
sub-s = subsection
SDTS = Simon's Direct Tax Service
SWTI = Simon's Weekly Tax Intelligence
TA = Income and Corporation Taxes Act 1988
TCGA = Taxation of Chargeable Gains Act 1992
T&IA = Tribunal and Inquiries Act 1992

TMA	= Taxes Management Act 1970
VATA	= Value Added Tax Act 1994
VCT	= Venture Capital Trust

ABOUT THE AUTHORS

Graham J Airs, LLB, MA
Graham J Airs is a partner in Slaughter and May. He is a member of the Law Society's Tax Law Committee and of its International Tax Sub-Committee.

Mohammed Amin, MA, FCA, AMCT, CTA (Fellow)
Mohammed Amin is a tax partner at PricewaterhouseCoopers, and has specialised in the taxation of Finance and Treasury transactions for over a decade. He leads the PwC Islamic Finance Taxation Network in the UK. Amin is the only person in the UK to hold his three professional qualifications, and was recently included in the 'Asian Power 100', a list of the hundred most influential Asians in the UK, compiled by the Institute of Asian Professionals.

Charles Barcroft, CTA
Charles Barcroft is a chartered tax adviser. He is currently a member of the Editorial Board of De Voil Indirect Tax Service, a contributor to Tiley & Collison: UK Tax Guide and a member of the Chartered Institute of Taxation's EU and Human Rights Working Group. He was the Consultant Editor of De Voil: Value Added Tax between 1977 and 1994 and a technical officer (indirect taxes) with The Chartered Institute of Taxation between 1997 and 2005.

Rebecca Benneyworth, BSC, FCA
Rebecca Benneyworth is a lecturer, writer and consultant on a variety of taxes. She lectures extensively throughout the UK, both to accountants and business people. She has a small accountancy practice based in Gloucestershire, with a variety of small business clients. Rebecca is also a member of the committee of the Tax Faculty of the ICAEW, and was recently named Best Tax Lecturer at the LexisNexis Taxation Awards.

Michael Bird, BA (Hons), ACA, CTA
Michael Bird is Director of International Corporate Tax at KPMG. He has over 15 years experience as a UK and international tax adviser and during that time has advised clients on a wide range of cross-border transactions, including reorganisations, financing structures and leasing arrangements. He is KPMG's leading specialist on the CFC legislation, advising widely on impact of the rules and related planning opportunities. Michael Bird also lectures internally and externally on international tax issues and has written a number of articles, including on the CFC rules.

Lynette Bober, MA (Cantab), ACA, CTA
Lynnette Bober is a Tax Manager at Rawlinson & Hunter. She is a Chartered Accountant and a member of the Chartered Institute of Taxation. She specialises in the field of personal taxation and trusts. She is a contributor to Tolley's Administration of Trusts and a member of the ICAEW Tax Faculty's Personal Tax and Finance and Inheritance Tax and Trusts sub-committees.

Sarah Bradford, BA (Hons), ACA, CTA (Fellow)
Sarah Bradford is the director of Writetax Ltd, a company providing technical writing services on tax and National Insurance contributions. She writes extensively and has contributed to a range of products and services, including various editions of the Finance Act Handbook and Simon's Direct Tax Service. She can be contacted by email at sarah.bradford@writetax.co.uk.

Patrick Cannon, LLB, BCL, CTA (Fellow), Barrister
Patrick Cannon is a barrister practising in the Chambers of GR Bretten QC at 15 Old Square, Lincoln's Inn specialising in tax advice and advocacy. He is the author of Tolley's Stamp Taxes 2006–07 and writes a tax and SDLT column for Property Week. His SDLT newsletter can be subscribed for at www.patrickcannon.net.

Anthony Davis, MA, CTA (Fellow)
Anthony Davis is a partner in the London office of the international law firm Gide Loyrette Nouel, advising on the UK and multi-jurisdictional taxation of financial transactions. He is a member of committees of the Law Society and the Chartered Institute of Taxation.

Mark Downey
Mark Downey is a life tax manager at a major listed UK insurance group where he specialises in all aspects of the taxation of life insurance companies, covering the spectrum from compliance issues to providing internal advice on transactions. He also has experience in the taxation of policyholder benefits and life insurance product design. Before taking on his current role, Mark previously spent four years as a senior consultant in the insurance tax group of a Big Four accountancy firm during which time he was a regular writer and conference speaker on issues affecting life insurance companies. Mark began his tax career in the Inland Revenue as was, spending 14 years as an inspector of taxes and specialising in the taxation of insurance companies, both life and general, for the final five years of his Revenue career.

Keith Gordon, MA (Oxon), ACA, CTA, Barrister
Keith Gordon is a Barrister practising from Atlas Chambers in London's Gray's Inn. Previously, he practised as a Chartered Accountant and a Chartered Tax Advisor (CTA). He is a well-known writer and lecturer on tax matters and was a runner-up in the tax writer of the year category at the 2006 LexisNexis *Taxation* Awards. He is a member of the Personal Taxes Sub-Committee of the Chartered Institute of Taxation (CIOT) and the Tax Law Rewrite's Consultative Committee.

Dean M Harris, CTA
Dean Harris is a Director at KPMG specialising in the taxation of privately owned businesses.

John Hayward
John Hayward is a self-employed pension consultant, well-known author and conference speaker. He has written for Pensions World and Tax Journal and is a member of the latter's Editorial Board. He has contributed to Butterworth's Tax Planning Service, Robin Ellison's Pensions Law and Practice, Simon's Direct Tax Service, Tolley's Finance and Law for the Older Client, the Finance Act Handbook 2004–2007 and to the ICAEW's TAXline. He is a past chairman of the former Association of Pensioneer Trustees and its first honorary life member. He is co-opted to the committee of its successor, the Association of Member Directed Pension Schemes.

Andrew Hubbard, B Mus, PhD, CTA (Fellow), ATT
Andrew Hubbard is a tax director in the Nottingham office of Tenon. His initial training was as a musician (he is one of the few tax advisors to have a PhD in musicology) but he moved into taxation when he became an Inspector of Taxes. He now specialises in the taxation of entrepreneurs. Andrew is a member of the Council of the Chartered Institute of Taxation and chairs its small business working group: he is a past president of the Association of Taxation Technicians. Andrew is well known as a writer and commentator on tax matters and received the Tax Writer of the Year award at this years LexisNexis Butterworths Taxation Awards.

Simon Jennings, MA (Oxon), FCA, TEP
Simon Jennings is a tax partner at the London office of Rawlinson & Hunter. He qualified at Deloitte & Touche, joined Rawlinson & Hunter as a senior manager in 1985 and became a partner in 1987. He specialises in trusts, tax planning (especially for foreign domiciliaries), UK residence, general technical tax advice, anti-avoidance, trust and land transactions and Inland Revenue investigations. He has experience in contentious matters including Special Compliance Office negotiations and as an expert witness. Simon Jennings lectures on tax matters both in the UK and abroad. He is the editor of Tolleys Administration of Trusts & Planning & Administration of Offshore & Onshore Trusts and is a contributor to several other reference books and journals. He is a Fellow of the ICAEW; a founder member of STEP and is on its Technical Committee and International Committee. He is also a member of the Trust Law Reform Committee; the ICAEW Trust and Inheritance Sub-Committee.

Terry Jordan, TEP
Terry Jordan joined the Inland Revenue in 1973 and having had spells in the Capital Taxes Office, Management and Policy Divisions, left the Revenue in 1988 as a Principal. Since 1996 he has been with Berg Kaprow Lewis LLP, a top 50 firm of Chartered Accountants based principally in Finchley, North London. Terry is a member of BKL Tax, the firm's tax consultancy business which, as well as advising the general practice partners at Berg Kaprow Lewis LLP, also gives independent tax consultancy advice to around 200 firms of accountants and solicitors. As well as consulting on inheritance tax and estate planning for owner-managed businesses and their proprietors, Terry presents at seminars both at the firm's quarterly 'Tax Advantage Club' and more widely. Terry is a member of the Society of Trust and Estate Practitioners (STEP) and is the press secretary of the City of London branch.

Jacquelyn Kimber
Jacquelyn Kimber is a qualified Chartered Tax Adviser with over ten years' experience advising corporate and non-corporate entrepreneurial clients on UK and international tax issues. After spending a number of years at one of the 'Big 4', Jacquelyn joined Chiltern in April 2002. She currently works as an Associate Director in the corporate tax department, where she continues to provide advice on both corporate and personal tax matters.

David Klass, BA
David Klass is an associate in the London office of the international law firm Gide Loyrette Nouel, advising mainly on the UK and multi-jurisdictional taxation of financial transactions.

Zigurds Kronbergs, MA, BSc, ARCS, ACA, FCCA
Zigurds G Kronbergs is International Tax Services Coordinator with BDO Global Coordination BV in Brussels. He is an experienced tax author and has contributed to professional and general publications on UK and international tax for over 20 years. He also reports regularly on Latvian tax developments for the International Bureau for Fiscal Documentation (IBFD) in Amsterdam and has been a member of a team of IBFD consultants advising the Latvian State Revenue Service.

David O'Keeffe
David O'Keeffe is a tax partner and head of KPMG's R&D Tax Relief Group in the UK. He is also a leading member of KPMG's global R&D network. He has been very closely involved in the consultation process that led up to the introduction of this relief. He continues to work closely with HMRC, DTI, the Treasury and other agencies to influence the ongoing development of the relief.

David Oliver, LLB, FCA
David Oliver is a tax director in the London office of Tenon where he provides taxation advice to entrepreneurs and media based clients. David originally qualified as a barrister before subsequently qualifying as a chartered accountant.

Tracy Payton, MA, ACA, CTA
Tracy Payton is a director in Deloitte's Real Estate Tax group where she specialises in advising companies and UK funds on M&A and property transactions. She is a Chartered Accountant and a member of the Chartered Institute of Taxation. Tracy has been a key member of the Treasury-appointed technical working group that has worked closely with the Government in connection with the development of the Real Estate Investment Trust legislation.

Juliet Phillips
Juliet Phillips is currently Head of Tax at Lloyd's of London and previously worked for Andersen specialising in international corporate tax.

Louise Pinfold, BA (Hons)
Louise Pinfold is a technical writer with LexisNexis Butterworths. After 10 years with the Inland Revenue, she spent some time as a tax manager and subsequently as a consultant with a tax software house. She has been an investigations consultant and writer for a number of years.

Gary Richards, MA, LLB, ATII, Solicitor
Gary Richards is a partner at Berwin Leighton Paisner LLP, advising on a wide range of international and domestic transactions. Gary is a member of the Law Society's Tax Law Committee, chairing the VAT & Duties sub-committee and participating in the Stamp Taxes working group. He is also a member of the editorial team for the British Tax Review. He was actively involved in the Inland Revenue's consultative group on the reform of taxation of intangibles and more recently on the introduction of SDLT including SDLT and partnerships.

Chris Russell, FFA, CTA (Fellow), Actuary
Chris Russell is a Tax Consultant at Russell Harman & Co. After a successful actuarial career, he qualified as a Fellow of the Institute of Taxation and turned his attention to the taxation of financial institutions, specialising in that of life offices and their products. With an increasing friendly societies clientele, in 1993 he began to advise the movement in its fiscal dealings with Government and has been tax consultant to the Association of Friendly Societies throughout its existence. He continues to sit on the tax sub-committee as technical adviser.

Paul Stainforth LLB (Hons), CTA
Paul Stainforth is a Chartered Tax Adviser on the staff of LexisNexis Butterworths. He is currently the Managing Technical Editor of Simon's Direct Tax Service – the leading reference service on UK direct taxes, relied on by thousands of practitioners. Other tax publications to which he contributes include Tolley's Yellow Tax Handbook and Tolley's Tax Digest. He was formerly a corporate tax adviser at KPMG.

Bernard Sweet
Bernard Sweet is a senior director within Chiltern's corporate tax team. His in-depth experience of many aspects of corporate tax work is based on a background within the Inland Revenue (as it was then), in industry and in a Big 4 firm. He has been closely involved in mergers and acquisitions, joint ventures, UK and international structures, group finance issues and transfer pricing. He also has years of experience in negotiating with HMRC at both a corporate and industry level (having been Chairman of the Tax Panel of the Association of British Insurers). He brings with him a depth of technical knowledge and over 25 years' experience of transactional work and day-to-day management of tax within a corporate environment.

Alastair Wilson
Alastair Wilson is a Senior Tax Manager in the Newcastle office of KPMG LLP. He became a member of the Association of Taxation Technicians in 1998 and a member of the Chartered Institute of Taxation in 1999. He advises companies and their shareholders on a broad range of taxation issues which include acquisitions, disposals and fundraising under the venture capital schemes.

Martin Wilson, MA, FCA
Martin Wilson is Chairman of the Capital Allowances Partnership LLP (www.cap-allow.com), specialists in all aspects of capital allowances and related reliefs. A Chartered Accountant, he is the author of numerous published works on the subject, including Tottel's Capital Allowances: Transactions & Planning.

FINANCE ACT 2007

INTRODUCTION

PART 1
CHARGES, RATES, THRESHOLDS ETC

Income tax. For the year 2007–08, the starting rate, basic rate and higher rate remain at 10 per cent, 22 per cent and 40 per cent, respectively (s 1). Nor is any change made to the lower rate for savings income (10 per cent) or to the dividend (formerly Schedule F) upper rate (32.5 per cent). The starting-rate limit was set at £2,230 and the basic-rate limit at £34,600 by the Income Tax (Indexation) Order 2007, SI 2007/943. The personal allowance was increased to £5,225; the blind person's allowance to £1,730; the personal allowance for those aged 65 or more was increased to £7,550 and for those aged 75 or more to £7,690, and the married couple's allowances for those aged 65 or more were all increased by the Income Tax (Indexation) (No. 2) Order 2006, SI 2006/3241. The Chancellor has, however, announced that in 2008–09, the starting rate will be abolished, and the basic rate reduced to 20 per cent.

Corporation tax. The main rate of corporation tax for the financial year 2008 is to be 28 per cent on profits other than oil taxation ring-fence profits and 30 per cent on ring-fence profits (s 2). The rate for 2007 was set at 30 per cent by FA 2006 s 24. The small companies' rate of corporation tax for the financial year 2007 is increased to 20 per cent for profits other than ring-fence profits but remains at 19 per cent for ring-fence profits. The marginal-relief fraction is accordingly $^{1}/_{40}$ for profits other than ring-fence profits but remains at $^{11}/_{400}$ for ring-fence profits. A formula is prescribed for computing small companies relief for companies any part of whose accounting periods falls in 2007 and whose profits consist partly of ring-fence profits and partly of other profits (s 3).

Inheritance tax. The nil-rate band for the year 2010–11 is set at £350,000 (s 4).

Alcohol and tobacco. The rates of excise duty on beer, wine and cider are increased by approximately 3.4 per cent, in line with retail price inflation, with effect from 26 March 2007. The rate of duty on spirits remains unchanged (s 5). The rates of excise duty on tobacco products are increased by approximately 3.4 per cent, in line with retail price inflation, with effect from 18:00 hrs on 21 March 2007 (s 6).

Gambling. Significant changes are made to the rates of gaming duty charged under FA 1997 ss 10–15. In addition to a revalorisation for inflation, there is an aggregation of the first two duty bands and the introduction of a new top rate of 50 per cent. The changes take effect for accounting periods beginning after 31 March 2007 (s 7). A new excise duty, remote gaming duty, chargeable under the Betting and Gaming Duties Act 1981 is introduced (from a date to be appointed) on the provision of facilities for remote gaming, which is defined as gaming in which participation is via the internet, telephone, television, radio or any other kind of electronic or other technology for facilitating communication. The duty is to be charged on the provision of facilities for remote gaming where either those facilities are provided under a remote operating licence or at least one piece of remote gambling equipment used in providing those facilities is situated in the UK. The rate of duty is to be 15 per cent of the operator's remote gaming profits for an accounting period (s 8 and Sch 1). The maximum prize that can be offered by a Category C gaming machine is increased from £25 to £35. Future amendments to maximum prizes and definitions of gaming machines in the Betting and Gaming Duties Act 1981 for the purposes of amusement-machine licence duty may be made by order (s 9).

Environment. Increases are made to the rates of excise duty under the Hydrocarbon Oil Duties Act 1979 on most categories of dutiable oils with effect from 1 October 2007 (s 10). Changes are made to the rates of vehicle excise duty under the Vehicle Excise and Registration Act 1994. Rates for the lowest polluting vehicles have been frozen or reduced; rates for other vehicles have been increased, notably for vehicles emitting over 225g/km. In particular, the premium rate, payable by vehicles using diesel fuel, has been abolished. The changes take effect with respect to licences taken out after 21 March 2007 (s 11). The rates of air passenger duty under FA 1994 s 30 are doubled with retroactive effect from 1 February 2007; by a separate order, the category of states other than EEA states in respect of which the lower rates apply is extended (s 12). Rates of climate change levy are increased in line with the rate of retail price inflation, with effect from 1 April 2008 (s 13). The rate of aggregates levy is increased by 21.9 per cent, with effect from 1 April 2008 (s 14). The standard rate of landfill tax is increased from £21 to £24 with effect from 1 April 2007; the standard rate is to be further increased to £32 (an increase of 33.33 per cent) from 1 April 2008 and the lower rate is to be increased from £2.00 to £2.50 from the same date (s 15). A mechanism is put in place for charges to be imposed on emissions trading in relation to specified greenhouse gases (s 16).

PART 2
ENVIRONMENT

Energy-saving: houses. Companies carrying on a Schedule A business including residential property may claim a deduction (under new TA 1988 ss 31ZA–31ZC) in respect of capital expenditure on the acquisition and installation of certain energy-saving items in the property. The capital expenditure must be incurred before 1 April 2015 and not qualify for capital allowances. A similar deduction (the Landlords' Energy-Saving Allowance, available under ITTOIA 2005 s 312) already exists in respect of income tax (s 17). The deadline for expenditure qualifying for the deduction under ITTOIA 2005 s 312 is extended from 31 March 2009 to 31 March 2015 and the definition of qualifying expenditure broadened to match that for the corporation-tax allowance introduced by s 17 (s 18). Regulations may be made under new FA 2003 ss 58B and 58C to introduce relief from stamp duty land tax in respect of the first acquisition of a dwelling that is a zero-carbon home, as defined in those Regulations. The relief is not to have effect until 1 April 2012 (s 19). Income arising to an individual from the sale of electricity generated by a domestic microgeneration system is to be exempt from income tax under a new ITTOIA 2005 s 782A, with effect from 6 April 2007 (s 20). Income arising from the receipt of a renewable obligation certificate is to be exempt from income tax under a new ITTOIA 2005 s 782B. Similarly, a capital gain arising from the disposal of such a certificate is to be exempt from capital gains tax under a new TCGA 1992 s 263AZA. Both exemptions have effect from 6 April 2007 (s 21).

Other measures. Aggregate removed from the ground along an existing or proposed rail, tram or monorail line is to be exempt from aggregates levy, from a day to be appointed (s 22). Detailed changes are made to the system of reliefs from climate change levy (s 23 and Sch 2). Regulations may be laid for HMRC to impose conditions relating to the approval of the regulatory body for the Landfill Communities Fund for the purposes of landfill tax (s 24).

PART 3
INCOME TAX, CORPORATION TAX AND CAPITAL GAINS TAX

Anti-avoidance. With effect from 6 April 2007, a new Chapter 9 (ss 61A–61J) is inserted into Part 3 of ITEPA 2003 to provide that payments received by persons in respect of services provided through a managed service company are to be treated as employment income (to the extent they are not so treated already) and taxed accordingly. Section 61A is an introductory section. Section 61B defines a 'managed service company', as one that satisfies four criteria. Broadly speaking, those criteria are (1) the business of the company consists wholly or mainly of directly or indirectly providing the services of an individual to other persons; (2) payments made by the company to such an individual or that individual's associates form the majority or the whole of the amounts received by the company in respect of the individual's services; (3) the way in which the payments are received by the individual or the individual's associates is such that the amount received is more than would have been received, after the deduction of income tax and national insurance contributions under PAYE, had the payments been received as employment income; and (4) the person whose business is that of promoting and facilitating the use of the managed service company is 'involved' (as defined) with the company. Section 61C supplements s 61B. Section 61D provides that payments or benefits received by the individual concerned or by that individual's associate and which can reasonably be taken to be in respect of the services provided by that individual and which are not earnings within the meaning of ITEPA 2003 Part 3 Chapter 1 received directly by the individual from the managed service company (MSC) are deemed to be earnings from employment paid by the MSC to the individual. Section 61E sets out a three-step process for calculating the deemed payment under s 61D. Section 61F provides a definition of the payment or benefit that section 61D requires the individual to have received and how the cash equivalent of such payments or benefits received in a form other than cash is to be calculated. Section 61G provides for the application of the Income Tax Acts to the deemed payment under s 61D. In particular, the individual is not to be charged to tax in respect of the payment if he or she would not have been so chargeable if the individual had been employed by the client (the person for whom the services were performed) and the deemed payment had been made by the client to the individual in respect of that employment. Section 61H provides relief where the MSC makes a distribution (by way of dividend or otherwise) and any part of that distribution has been treated as a deemed payment under s 61D. The relief is given (upon the making of a claim) by deduction of the payment from the amount of the distribution. Section 61I defines 'associate' for the purposes of these provisions and s 61J is an interpretation section. A new ITTOIA 2005 s 688A allowing for tax that ought to have been deducted by an MSC from relevant payments to be recovered from other persons is inserted, and other consequential amendments are made (s 25 and Sch 3).

Further restrictions are placed on the amount of 'sideways relief' and capital gains relief that may be claimed in respect of trading losses by a 'non-active partner' in a general partnership or by the limited partner in a limited partnership. 'Sideways relief' is the name given in ITA 2007 Part 4 Chapter 3 to the set-off under ss 64–70 of that Act of trading losses against general income and the set-off under ss 72–74 of that Act of trading losses of the first four years of trading against the taxpayer's income of the three preceding tax years. Capital gains relief for this purpose means the set-off under TCGA 1992 s 261B of trading losses against capital gains of the same tax year. The restrictions are contained in new ITA 2007 ss 103C and 113A. Section 103C provides that a cap is to be placed on the total amount of sideways relief and capital gains relief that an individual carrying on a trade or trades in partnership as either a non-active partner or a limited partner and incurring a loss in one or more of those trades may obtain by way of sideways relief and capital gains relief in any one tax year. The cap is to operate after all other restrictions placed on loss relief under ITA 2007 Part 4 Chapter 3 and is set at £25,000 (the amount may be varied by Treasury order). The cap is to apply from 2 March 2007 (the date on which these restrictions were announced) and provision is made for computing the trading loss for a tax year for which the individual's basis period straddles 2 March 2007. The effect of ITA 2007 Part 4 Chapter 3 is broadly to restrict the total loss relief that a partner may claim to the amount of capital that partner has contributed to the partnership. New ITA 2007 s 113A excludes capital contributed to the partnership by a non-active partner or a limited partner in the first four years of trading from account, where the contribution was made for a 'prohibited purpose'. A contribution is made for a prohibited purpose if the main purpose or one of the main purposes for which it is made is to obtain sideways relief or capital gains relief. Similar restrictions are imposed on an individual who is a partner in a limited-liability partnership (LLP) who does not devote a significant amount of time to the trade of the LLP in the tax year concerned. The restrictions apply solely to capital contributed after 1 March 2007. New ITA 2007 s 103A defines the expression 'limited partner' and new ITA 2007 s 103B defines what is meant by a 'non-active partner'. Losses from 'qualifying film expenditure' are excluded from the restrictions imposed by ITA 2007 ss 103C and 113A; new ITA 2007 s 103D defines 'qualifying film expenditure'. Consequential amendments are made (s 26 and Sch 4).

TCGA 1992 s 8, as amended by FA 2006 s 69, excludes relief for the purposes of corporation tax for capital losses arising from arrangements that have the securing of a tax advantage as their main purpose or one of their main purposes. That exclusion is now replaced (by amending TCGA 1992 s 8 further) by a more general exclusion from relief in respect of losses accruing to a company in circumstances such that had a gain accrued to the company instead, that gain would have been exempt from corporation tax. A new TCGA 1992 s 16A introduces what amounts to a general anti-avoidance rule in respect of capital losses. It provides that a capital loss accruing to any person is not to be an allowable loss for the purposes of capital gains tax where it accrues as a result of or in connection with 'arrangements' and the main purpose or one of the main purposes of such 'arrangements' is to secure a tax advantage. Both 'arrangements' and 'tax advantage' are defined. These provisions have retroactive effect from 6 December 2006 (s 27).

A similar general anti-avoidance rule is inserted in TA 1988 s 75 in respect of management expenses. As amended, that section now excludes a deduction for management expenses to the extent that any part of those expenses is incurred directly or indirectly in connection with arrangements the main purpose or one of the main purposes of which is to secure a deduction or increased deduction or any other tax advantage. 'Arrangements' is defined (the definition is identical to that in TCGA 1992 s 16A) and 'tax advantage' is defined by reference to TA 1988 s 840ZA. The provision has effect in relation to accounting periods beginning after 19 June 2007; where an accounting period straddles 20 June 2007, the part that falls on and after that date is treated as if it were a separate accounting period. Expenses paid before 20 June 2007 are, however, excluded from these provisions (s 28).

Where a commission in respect of certain life insurance policies, life annuities or capital redemption policies is rebated or reinvested in the policy or contract by an intermediary, the deduction for premiums paid when computing the gain on the occurrence of certain chargeable events with respect to those policies or contracts is reduced by the amount of the rebated or reinvested commission. The provisions apply only where the total premiums paid in the tax year in which the chargeable event occurs up to the point at which it occurs, and in the preceding three tax years, is more than £100,000. An anti-fragmentation rule prevents avoidance of the £100,000 threshold by using a number of linked policies. The provisions apply to policies or contracts made or varied after 20 March 2007 (s 29).

Schedule 5, introduced by s 30, contains provisions designed to frustrate a number of different avoidance schemes using financial products. In many cases, these involve fine tuning of relatively new but existing anti-avoidance provisions, as a result of disclosures made to HMRC. Schedule 5 paras 1 and 2 deals with amounts not forming part of a company's income. Paragraph 1 is concerned with schemes, apparently used by financial traders, which hinge around the provision in TA 1988 s 347A(1)(*b*) that certain types of annual payment shall not be within the charge to corporation tax. Traders purchasing the right to receive such payments claim a deduction for the purchase price under Schedule D Case I and then treat the receipt as exempt under s 347A, thus creating a trading loss. Accordingly, section 347A as it had effect before 6 April 2007 is amended by omitting sub-s (1)(*b*). On or after 6 April 2007, s 347A was to have effect as amended by ITA 2007. However, the section is now to be repealed altogether. The provisions have effect from 6 December 2006, but HMRC has given notice that it intends to contest claims for trading losses arising before that date under these circumstances.

Schedule 5 para 2 addresses the provisions charging the settlor of a settlement to income tax on the income of the settlement in circumstances under which the settlor retains an interest in the settlement (ITTOIA 2005 s 624) or the income is that of a minor child of the settlor (ITTOIA 2005 s 629). TA 1988 s 660C(4) provides that income so treated as being income of the settlor alone cannot be the income of any company for the purposes of corporation tax. It has come to the attention of HMRC that some companies have tried to take advantage of the exemption provided by TA 1988 s 660C(4) by entering into arrangements amounting to a settlement. Accordingly, s 660C(4) is to be repealed with effect for accounting periods ending after 5 March 2007.

Schedule 5 paras 3–8 deal with structured finance arrangements. These are arrangements as defined in TA 1988 s 774A (introduced by FA 2006 Sch 6 para 6). These essentially involve the receipt by a borrower of money or other assets from a lender, the transfer by the borrower or a person connected with the borrower to the lender or a person connected with the lender of an asset as security, and a series of payments in respect of the security to the lender or a person connected with the lender which reduce the borrower's financial liability in respect of the arrangement and also reduce the borrower's taxable income. The intention of TA 1988 ss 774A–774G was to ensure that the borrower was treated as still liable to tax on the income transferred to the lender which was applied in repaying the loan, but to give relief to the lender in respect of any finance charge recorded in its account in respect of the transaction. Under the disclosure rules of FA 2004 Part 7, the existence of schemes designed to sidestep this legislation has come to the attention of HMRC. Accordingly, it is now provided that the legislation is also to have effect where there is no alienation of the borrower's income but payments are received by the lender in respect of the asset transferred by the borrower and those payments are applied to reduce the borrower's liability in respect of the arrangement. Under TCGA 1992 s 263E, the disposal of a security under a structured finance arrangement is disregarded for capital gains purposes if one of two conditions is met. Both conditions require prospective knowledge of what is to happen to the security transferred under the arrangement (namely, whether it is subsequently reacquired by the borrower or is held by the lender or a person connected with the lender until it ceases to exist). The section is amended so that the intention that either of the conditions is to be satisfied is sufficient for the disposal to be disregarded. If, however, it subsequently transpires that the relevant condition is breached, a disposal at market value is to be regarded as taking place at that time.

Schedule 5 para 9 relates to manufactured payments made under arrangements having an unallowable purpose. TA 1988 Sch 23A para 7(1) currently provides that where a manufactured payment exceeds the amount of the payment that it represents, the excess is to be treated as a fee and not as a manufactured payment. Accordingly, the restriction under TA 1988 Sch 23A para 7A on relief for manufactured payments made under arrangements having an unallowable purpose has no effect on such an excess. With respect to payments made after 5 December 2006, however, such deemed fees are brought within the provisions of Sch 23A para 7A.

Schedule 5 para 10 deals with options and groups of companies. TCGA 1992 s 171 is amended to insert a further exception to the rule that assets transferred within a group of companies are transferred at neither a gain nor a loss. The new exception is for a disposal by the transferor company in fulfilment of an obligation under an option granted by the transferee company at a time when those companies were not members of the same group. It has effect for options exercised after 5 March 2007.

Schedule 5 paras 11–16 deal with loan relationships. Paragraph 11 amends FA 1996 s 85C, which was itself introduced into the loan-relationships legislation no less recently than 2006. It deals with situations where under generally accepted accounting principles a company has a creditor loan relationship matched with either a debtor loan relationship or issued share capital that is treated as a liability in its accounts, and at the same time, there is an amount that is not fully recognised in respect of both the creditor loan relationship and the debtor loan relationship or liability. The section requires amounts to be recognised in respect of both the creditor loan relationship and the matching debtor loan relationship or liability. The amendment now made extends the scope of the section to replace references to issued share capital by references to a capital contribution, which forms part of the company's capital (not necessarily share capital) and which falls to be treated as a liability. Paragraphs 12–14 amend FA 1996 ss 91A–91G (introduced by F(No 2)A 2005), which treat certain shares held as investments as if they were loan relationships. Paragraph 12 amends FA 1996 s 91A, which provides that shares subject to outstanding third-party obligations and having interest-like characteristics shall be treated as if they were rights under a creditor loan relationship. The amendment clarifies occasions when no debits are to be brought into account and excludes shares in a building society from the scope of the section. Paragraph 13 makes parallel amendments to FA 1996 s 91B, which applies to 'non-qualifying shares' in circumstances where FA 1996 s 91A does not apply. Paragraph 14 amends the definition of 'share' for the purposes of the loan-relationships legislation in FA 1996 s 103. Paragraph 15 amends FA 1996 Sch 9 para 11A, which essentially provides that exchange gains and losses in respect of loan relationships not on arm's length terms are disregarded to the same extent as the interest is disregarded. It applies whenever a company has a debtor loan relationship and either the whole of any interest or other distribution out of the company's assets is treated as a distribution for the purposes of the Corporation Tax Acts or the transfer pricing provisions of TA 1988 Sch 28AA require the company's taxable profits to be computed as if the loan had not been made. A scheme has been disclosed to exploit the opportunity under TA 1988 Sch 28AA para 6D for a company ('the guarantor company') that has guaranteed the issue of securities by another connected company to opt to be treated as if it had issued the securities itself in circumstances where the actual issuing company is obliged under the transfer pricing provisions to reduce the amount of interest in respect of those securities which it may deduct. This allows a compensating adjustment to be received. However, in the scheme disclosed to HMRC, the optional claim is exercised or not, as the case may be, to claim a deduction for exchange losses but not to take into account the corresponding exchange gain. The amendments made by para 15 essentially provide that where a claim under TA 1988 Sch 28AA para 6D could have been made in these circumstances it is deemed to have been made. Paragraph 16 amends FA 1996 Sch 10 para 4. This essentially provides that where a company holds investments in the form of rights under a unit trust scheme or offshore fund, and at any time in that period the trust or fund fails to satisfy the non-qualifying investments test of FA 1996 Sch 10 para 8, the investments are to be treated as if they were rights under a creditor loan relationship and the corresponding debits and credits that the company must take into account as a result are valued on the basis of fair-value accounting. The amendment made by para 16 provides that any debits or credits relating to such investments made with a 'relevant avoidance intention' are to be left out of account.

Paragraph 17 is intended to counter a scheme relating to plant and machinery subject to a lease and finance lease-back subject to the anti-avoidance provisions of CAA 2001 Part 2 Chapter 17. Within that Chapter, CAA 2001 s 228D (introduced by FA 2004) provides that where there is a sale and finance lease-back or where there is a lease and finance lease-back, certain amounts receivable in respect of the lessor's interest under the lease-back may be disregarded in calculating the lessor's income or profits. The amendment made by para 17 disapplies s 228D to a lease and finance lease-back arrangement, in respect of lease rentals paid after 5 December 2006.

Paragraphs 17 and 18 amend the derivative-contracts legislation of FA 2002 Sch 26. Paragraph 17 amends FA 2002 Sch 26 para 17A, which provides that amounts to be brought into account under the derivative-contracts legislation shall be computed according to generally accepted accounting practice. For periods of account ending after 5 March 2007, the amendment made by para 17 provides that in respect of contracts that are derivative contracts by virtue of their being treated as financial assets or liabilities, the amounts to be brought into account are to be computed on the basis of fair-value accounting. Finally, para 18 amends FA 2002 Sch 26 para 26, which deals with expired options that have been treated as derivative contracts. As the legislation currently stands, it provides that where there is a transfer of value between connected companies when such an option expires, and the transferee is not chargeable to corporation tax on the contract, the transferor must bring an appropriate amount into account. The amendment made by para 18 ensures that the legislation now applies where there has been a failure to exercise all the rights under an option, which until that failure has been treated as a derivative contract. It applies to failures taking place after 5 March 2007 (s 30 and Sch 5).

Section 31 and Sch 6 address schemes designed to circumvent the provisions in FA 2006 Sch 10 relating to the sale of lessor companies. The schemes in question are of two types – those that exploit different definitions of control in order to transfer assets free of tax and those that manipulate the accounting value of leased assets to reduce or eliminate the charge imposed by FA 2006 Sch 10. Paragraph 1 of Sch 6 amends TA 1988 s 343 and introduces a new s 343A. The effect of TA 1988 s 343, which allow company reconstructions without a major change of ownership to take place in a tax-neutral way, is made subject to the provisions of s 343A where businesses involving the leasing of plant or machinery are involved. Section 343A provides that s 343 is not to have effect where the trade being transferred from the predecessor to the successor is or forms part of a business of leasing plant or machinery unless the principal company or companies of the predecessor immediately before the transfer are the same as the principal company or companies of the successor immediately after the transfer. A parallel provision is made where the predecessor or successor carry on the trade in partnership. The effect is to ensure that transfers that are not 'qualifying changes of ownership' bringing the charge under FA 2006 Sch 10 into play may not benefit from the tax neutrality ensured by TA 1988 s 343.

Paragraph 2 amends FA 2006 Sch 10 itself. It inserts FA 2006 Sch 10 paras 38A and 38B. Para 38A applies where amounts that fall or would fall to be shown in a balance sheet in respect of plant or machinery would otherwise be reduced or increased as the direct or indirect result of arrangements of which the main purpose, or one of the main purposes, is to secure a 'relevant tax advantage'. 'Relevant tax advantage' is defined to mean a situation in which any company would otherwise not be regarded as carrying on a business of leasing plant or machinery and either the amount of any income that any company would under Sch 10 be treated as receiving would be reduced or any expense any company would be treated as incurring would be increased. Where this is the case, that reduction or increase is to be ignored (s 31 and Sch 6).

Sections 32 and 33 address themselves to schemes involving the purchase of capital losses or chargeable gains. TCGA 1992 s 184A (introduced by FA 2006 with the aim of further restricting the relief available for capital losses on a change of ownership) provides that a 'qualifying loss' accruing to a company that has undergone a change of ownership may only be deducted from a gain that accrues to the company on the disposal of an asset that it held before the change of ownership. A qualifying loss is a loss that accrues to the company on the disposal of an asset held before the change of ownership. Section 184B is a mirror-image section, which provides that a loss accruing to a company that has undergone a change of ownership may only be set against a 'qualifying gain' if that loss accrues to it on the disposal of an asset held before the change of ownership. A qualifying gain is a gain on the disposal of an asset held by the company before the change of ownership. Both sections apply only where there are arrangements to secure a tax advantage. Amendments are made to ss 184A and 184B to ensure that losses may not be deducted at all under either section unless new conditions inserted into FA 2006 s 70 apply. FA 2006 s 70(9) and (10) as enacted allow gains or losses arising on the disposal of assets held before the change of ownership by any other company that was a member of the same group as the company that undergoes the change of ownership to qualify for set-off as appropriate, provided that certain conditions are satisfied. These conditions aim to exclude gains and losses that are the subject of gain or loss-buying schemes. The amendments, including the insertion of new sub-ss (11)–(13) also allow the extended opportunity for set-off to include the set-off of qualifying losses against gains accruing to any company that was a member of the same group before the change of ownership as long as the company claiming the loss remains under the control of the parent company of the group (s 32).

Section 33, which inserts FA 1994 s 227A, is aimed at the purchase of losses from corporate members of Lloyd's. It provides that losses of the 'last active underwriting year' (as defined) of a company that is a corporate member of Lloyd's are not to be available for surrender as group relief unless a continuity condition is satisfied. The continuity condition requires that the surrendering company and the claimant company be members of the same group or consortium throughout a period beginning from the last day of the last active underwriting year of the surrendering company and ending on the first day of the first underwriting year in which the losses of the last active underwriting year are declared (s 33).

FA 2003 Sch 24 and ITTOIA 2005 ss 38–44 provide (for the purposes of corporation tax and income tax respectively) that employers may not claim a deduction in respect of 'employee benefit contributions' except to the extent that benefits are actually paid or transferred to employees within nine months of the end of the period in respect of which the deduction is claimed. An employee benefit contribution is defined in FA 2003 Sch 24 para 1 and ITTOIA 2005 s 39 as a transaction under which the employer transfers money or assets to a third party and that third party holds or uses the money or assets for the purposes of a scheme for providing benefits to employees or former employees. These definitions are amended such that they now refer to a transaction under which, as the result of any act or omission, property is held or may be used under such a scheme or there is an increase in the total value of property that may be so held or used. References elsewhere in the provisions to a 'third party' (the trustees of such a scheme, for example) are replaced by references to a 'scheme manager'. Other consequential amendments are made. The intention is to frustrate schemes designed to circumvent these provisions under which employers declare a trust over assets that they already control and subsequently claim a tax deduction to the value of that declaration (s 34).

TA 1988 s 804ZA (inserted by FA 2005 s 87) has effect to deny a foreign tax credit against UK corporation tax to the extent that there is a prescribed scheme or arrangement in place to make that credit available. Section 804ZA is now amended to apply also to any UK tax that is treated under TA 1988 s 801 as if it were foreign tax for the purposes of giving double tax relief (s 35).

Capital allowances. The Chancellor of the Exchequer announced in his Budget speech his intention to abolish industrial buildings allowances and agricultural buildings allowances over a four-year period ending on 1 April 2011. As a first step, no balancing adjustments are to be made under either CAA 2001 Part 3 (industrial buildings allowances) or CAA 2001 Part 4 (agricultural buildings allowances) in respect of balancing events occurring after 20 March 2007 ('post-commencement balancing events') unless they occur before 1 April 2011 in pursuance of certain contracts made in writing before 21 March 2007 ('relevant pre-commencement contracts'). For the purpose of calculating a purchaser's qualifying expenditure under CAA 2001 s 311 for industrial buildings allowances after a sale of the relevant building, the residual qualifying expenditure immediately after a sale that takes place after 20 March 2007 (except one taking place before 1 April 2011 pursuant to a relevant pre-commencement contract) will be deemed to be the same as it was immediately before the sale. The same provision is made in respect of the identical provision (CAA 2001 s 376) relating to agricultural buildings allowances (s 36). The temporary 50 per cent first-year allowance for capital expenditure on plant and machinery by small enterprises is extended for a further year from 1 April 2007 (corporation tax) or 5 April 2007 (income tax) (s 37).

Insurance and friendly societies. Sections 38 to 46 contain further provisions to reform the taxation of insurance companies and friendly societies. They are the result of consultation begun in May 2006.

Section 38 introduces Sch 7, which creates a new class of life-assurance business for tax purposes – 'gross roll-up business', which comprises five existing classes – pension business, overseas life-assurance business, life-reinsurance business, ISA business, and child trust-fund business. Schedule 7 also contains provisions relating to capital redemption business.

Schedule 7 paras 1–5 make consequential amendments. Paragraph 6 inserts definitions, including a definition of 'life-assurance business' (by references to insurance contracts in certain paragraphs in Regulations under the Financial Services and Markets Act 2000; a redefinition of 'capital redemption business' and a definition of 'PHI business' to mean all long-term business other than life-assurance business. Paragraphs 7–9 insert definitions of 'child trust-fund business' and 'individual savings account business' and amend the definition of 'overseas life-assurance business'. Paragraph 10 inserts a new TA 1988 s 431EA, containing the definition of 'gross roll-up business' as mentioned, which is effectively any life-assurance business that is not 'BLAGAB' (basic life-assurance and general annuity business). Paragraphs 11 and 12 make consequential amendments. Paragraph 13 amends TA 1988 s 432A, which allocates income, gains and losses among different classes of business of an insurance company. There are now to be only three such classes of business – gross roll-up business (GRB), BLAGAB and PHI business. Paragraphs 14 and 15 make minor amendments. Paragraph 16 amends TA 1988 s 432B, which, together with TA 1988 ss 432C–432F, deals with the apportionment of receipts brought into account under FA 1989 s 83 in computing Schedule D Case I profits. Paragraph 17 replaces the existing TA 1988 s 432C with a new identically numbered section, which allocates the net amount brought into account under FA 1989 s 83 for non-participating funds. Paragraph 18 repeals TA 1988 s 432D, which is now redundant. Paragraph 19 substantially amends FA 1989 s 83 for participating funds. Paragraph 20 makes consequential amendments to TA 1988 s 432F. Paragraph 21 substitutes a new TA 1988 s 432G, which provides for the allocation of amounts to a transferee company consequent on a 'transfer-in' of business. Paragraphs 22 and 23 make consequential amendments, and para 24 repeals TA 1988 s 436. Paragraph 25 inserts a new TA 1988 s 436A, which provides that profits from GRB are to be taxed under Schedule D Case VI as a deemed separate business and computed according to the rules of Schedule D Case I. Paragraph 26 makes consequential amendments, and paragraphs 27–30 repeal TA 1988 ss 438B, 438C, 439 and 439B respectively. Paragraphs 31–33 make consequential amendments. Paragraph 34 repeals TA 1988 s 441. Paragraphs 35–38 make consequential amendments. Paragraph 39 repeals TA 1988 ss 458 and 458A. Paragraphs 40–43 make consequential amendments to TA 1988 ss 460, 461, 461B and 466, relating to friendly societies. Paragraphs 44–54 make consequential amendments to other provisions of TA 1988, including those relating to claims by an insurance company for double tax relief. Paragraph 55 repeals TA 1988 Sch 19AA (determination of assets of an overseas life-assurance fund), which is now redundant. Paragraph 56 makes minor consequential amendments to the controlled foreign companies legislation. Paragraphs 57–59 amend FA 1989 ss 88 and 89. Paragraphs 60–64 make consequential amendments to TCGA 1992. Paragraphs 65–67 make consequential amendments to the loan-relationships legislation (FA 1996 Schs 9, 11). Paragraphs 68–71 make consequential amendments to CAA 2001. Paragraph 72 makes a consequential amendment to FA 2001 Sch 22 para 20 (remediation of contaminated land). Paragraphs 73–75 amend FA 2002 Sch 12 (relief for research and development expenditure) and FA 2002 Sch 26 (derivative contracts). Paragraphs 76–79 make consequential amendments to ITTOIA 2005.

Schedule 7 Part 2 (paras 80–84) makes transitional provisions. In particular, para 80 provides that losses incurred in a period of account beginning before 1 January 2007 ('pre-commencement losses') may not generally be set against profits of a period of account beginning after 31 December 2006 ('post-commencement profits'), subject to the exceptions provided (s 38 and Sch 7).

Section 39 and Sch 8 contain further reform of the taxation of insurance companies. Subject to transitional provisions in Sch 8 Part 2, the amendments have effect in respect of periods of account beginning after 31 December 2006. The provisions contained in Sch 8 have the effect of ending the so-called 'Crown option', under which the tax authorities could effectively choose whether to apply the Schedule D Case I basis or the 'I minus E' basis for computing the taxable profits of an insurance company.

Section 39 introduces Sch 8. Schedule 8 paras 1–3 make consequential amendments. Paragraph 4 replaces TA 1988 s 432 by new TA 1988 ss 431G and 431H. Section 432 merely provides that where an insurance company carries on life-assurance business in conjunction with any other category of insurance business, the life-assurance business shall be treated as a separate category of business for the purposes of the Corporation Tax Acts. This provided the tacit basis for applying the I minus E basis instead of the normal rules of computation of Schedule D Case I, but left it open for Schedule D Case I to prevail. Now, new TA 1988 s 431G provides that where an insurance company carries on life-assurance business (whether or not it also carries on any other insurance business) the profits of that business are to be charged to tax under the I minus E basis. As the I minus E basis was not previously anywhere explicitly defined in the legislation, a definition is inserted in TA 1988 s 431(2) by para 3. Two circumstances in which the I minus E basis is not to apply are specified. It is made explicit that where the I minus E basis is used, but a loss would have arisen had the profits been computed according to the rules of Schedule D Case I, that loss may be set off under TA 1988 s 434(A)(2), or used in a general loss claim under TA 1988 s 393A or group relief claim under TA 1988 s 403. New TA 1988 s 431H repeats the separate-business rule previously in TA 1988 s 432 and provides that non-life-assurance business is to be charged to tax under Schedule D Case I (except for mutual companies). Paragraphs 5 and 6 make consequential amendments. Paragraph 7 repeals TA 1988 s 439A. Paragraph 8 amends TA 1988 s 440. Paragraph 9 inserts new TA 1988 s 440C, which provides rules for occasions when the basis of computation (I minus E or Schedule D Case I) is changed. Paragraphs 10–13 make further consequential amendments. Paragraph 14 inserts new FA 1989 s 85A. The new section provides that where an insurance company is in any accounting period charged to tax under the I minus E basis, any 'excess adjusted Case I profits' are to be charged to tax under Schedule D Case VI. Provision is made for how to compute 'excess adjusted Case I profits'. Paragraphs 15–27 make consequential amendments. Part 2 (paras 28 and 29) makes transitional provisions (s 39 and Sch 8).

Section 40 and Sch 9 deal with the transfer of long-term insurance business from one company to another. Section 40 introduces Sch 9. Schedule 9 para 1 substitutes in TA 1988 s 431(2) a new definition of 'insurance-business transfer scheme' (IBTS), with the tax consequences of which the provisions deal. The current definition is limited to schemes under Financial Services and Markets Act 2000 s 105, the majority of which require court approval. The new definition also includes schemes where the transferee carries on the transferred business outside an EEA state. Paragraph 2 makes consequential amendments. Paragraphs 3–5 substitute new TA 1988 ss 444AA, 444AB, 444ABA, 444ABB, 444ABC and 444ABD for the existing TA 1988 ss 444AA, 444ABA and 444ABB. New s 444AA, as did its predecessor, determines when a period of account ends on the occasion of an IBTS. New s 444AB deals with the taxation of the transferor under the Schedule D Case I basis when the whole or substantially the whole of the transferor's business is transferred. It provides that where there are either 'relevant non-transferred assets' or 'retained assets', the 'relevant amount' in respect of those assets is to be treated as an additional trading receipt under FA 1989 s 83(2) to be taken into account in computing its taxable profits. New s 444AB defines the 'relevant amount' in relation to relevant non-transferred assets, and new s 444ABB provides that definition in relation to retained assets. New s 444ABC deals with the situation where part only of the long-term business is transferred, and defines the relevant amount in relation to the relevant non-transferred assets in that case. New s 444ABD provides that profits representing the amount by which the value of transferred liabilities exceeds the amount of transferred assets is a profit of the period that includes the transfer date. Paragraph 6 substitutes TA 1988 s 444AC and inserts new TA 1988 s 444ACZA. The new s 444AC deals with the taxation of the transferee under Schedule D Case I when the whole or substantially the whole of the transferor's business is transferred. It provides that the 'transferred surplus' (as defined) is to be excluded from the transferee's receipts taken into account under FA 1989 s 83(2). New s 444ACZA deals with the situation where part only of the long-term business is transferred, and similarly provides that the 'transferred surplus' is to be excluded from the transferee's receipts under FA 1989 s 83(2). Paragraph 7 repeals TA 1988 s 444AD. Paragraph 8 inserts new TA 1988 ss 444AEA–444AED, which are anti-avoidance provisions in relation to transfer schemes. Essentially, it is provided that where an IBTS takes place as part of 'transfer-scheme arrangements' and the main purpose or one of the main purposes of those arrangements is the obtaining of a 'Case I advantage', for transferor or transferee or both, that advantage is nullified by being treated as an increase in value of the assets of the long-term insurance fund. New s 444AEB defines what is a 'Case I advantage' for the transferor, and new s 444AEC a 'Case I advantage' for the transferee. New s 444AED provides for a clearance procedure. Paragraphs 9–13 make consequential amendments. Paragraph 14 amends TCGA 1992 s 211 (which provides that the transferee 'steps into the shoes' of the transferor) no longer requires the obtaining of a clearance under TCGA 1992 s 138. Paragraph 15 makes a consequential amendment; para 16 gives the Treasury to make provision by order in relation to transfer schemes. Paragraph 17 is a commencement provision (s 40 and Sch 9).

Section 41 and Sch 10 make miscellaneous other amendments to the insurance-company legislation. In particular, a substituted FA 1989 s 83XA provides that an increase or decrease in the value of structural assets held in a non-profit fund is to be tax-neutral except in abnormal circumstances; new TCGA 1992 s 210C provides that the restriction under TCGA 1992 s 18(3) on losses arising on disposals between connected persons is not to apply to a transfer by an insurance company of assets of an authorised investment fund to the fund manager; and FA 1989 s 83 is amended so as to clarify that amounts brought into account under subsection (2) of that section in taxing an insurance company are not also to be taken into account for any other purpose of corporation tax (s 41 and Sch 10).

Section 42 and Sch 11 deal with the treatment of 'technical provisions' made by general insurers. These are provisions made against claims arising from general insurance business. The existing rules in FA 2000 s 107 are repealed; new rules are to be made by regulation, and Sch 11 provides the framework for those regulations. The main provision to be made is that the amount of the provision may not exceed an 'appropriate amount' (s 42 and Sch 11).

Where a corporate member of Lloyd's (the successor) takes over the syndicate capacity of another corporate member (the predecessor), new FA 1994 s 227B provides that TA 1988 s 343 (company reconstructions without change of ownership) is to apply as if references to a trade included references to the underwriting business of the predecessor. It is a relieving provision (s 43).

Section 44 introduces Sch 12, which makes provision concerning the transfer of tax-exempt life or endowment business by a friendly society to an insurance company. Such business remains exempt from corporation tax on income and chargeable gains following its transfer to a company (which may take place on a conversion of the friendly society to corporate form; the business so transferred is to be treated as a separate business from any other business carried on by the company. Exemption is to be lost if the terms are varied so as to increase the premiums payable. The Treasury may by order modify the Corporation Tax Acts as they apply to the transferred business. Tax-exempt other business (e.g. permanent health insurance) is also to remain tax-exempt on transfer to an insurance company, as long as the benefits are not varied (s 44 and Sch 12).

TA 1988 s 462 is amended so that it refers to the tax-exempt business of an insurance company as well as that of a friendly society; tax-exemption is no longer to be lost in respect of a non-qualifying policy where the person holding the rights under the policy acquired them on an assignment (assignation) other than for money or money's worth or if it is held with a body other than a friendly society or insurance company (s 45).

The provisions in TA 1988 and ITTOIA 2005 requiring an officer of HMRC to determine the tax-exempt part of a purchased life annuity are repealed (s 46).

Repos. Section 47 and Schs 13 and 14 set out a new regime for taxing repos (agreements for the sale and repurchase of securities) and make consequential amendments. The new treatment is intended to match as far as possible the accounting treatment of these agreements, while at the same time minimising the opportunities that, in the government's opinion, the current system offers for tax avoidance. The Schedules are introduced, and it is provided that the Treasury may by order make such other amendments as are felt to be necessary. The new system is to have effect from a date to be appointed.

Schedule 13 contains the provisions relating to the new regime. Paragraph 1 is a purpose paragraph, which explains that the legislation is intended to ensure that where there is an arrangement that involves the sale and subsequent purchase of securities, and that arrangement amounts in substance to a loan at interest, the charge to corporation tax on the parties is to reflect that substance. Notwithstanding that general rule, paras 6 and 11, which deal with the capital gains consequences of repos, are still to have effect in the case of 'quasi-repos'. Paragraph 2 defines a 'debtor repo' for the purposes of the Schedule and para 3 defines a 'debtor quasi-repo'. Essentially, a debtor repo is a repo from the aspect of the company that sells the securities in return for money or other assets ('the advance') from 'the lender' (the purchaser) and under the arrangement either has the right or the obligation to repurchase those or similar securities at a later date. Five conditions must be satisfied if a debtor repo is to exist, and the company that has the repo is termed 'the borrower'. The borrower has a debtor quasi-repo on the other hand, if it does not have a debtor repo but five other conditions are satisfied. The essential difference between a debtor repo and a debtor quasi-repo, is that under the latter arrangement, any person other than the borrower may sell the securities, and that the right or obligation to repurchase may be conferred or imposed on a person other than the borrower. Paragraph 4 sets out the consequences for a borrower who has a debtor repo or a debtor quasi-repo. It also applies, broadly, where the borrower has a liability that is discharged under an arrangement under which the borrower or any other person sells securities and a right or obligation is imposed on the borrower or any other person subsequently to purchase securities, but where another person is involved, that money passes from the borrower to that other person or the borrower's liability under the arrangement is discharged – but only in the circumstances in which the main purpose or one of the main purposes of the arrangement is to obtain a tax advantage. Where this is the case, then during the duration of the arrangement, the borrower is to be taxed in respect of income as if it still held the securities that are initially sold, but any manufactured payment in respect of those securities that it actually receives is to be ignored. However, this treatment is to apply only if under generally accepted accounting practice (GAAP), the borrower is required to recognise or otherwise to take into account the income in question in determining its profit or loss. There is an exception in relation to double tax relief in the case of overseas securities. Paragraph 5 provides that while the borrower in a debtor repo or debtor quasi-repo is to be taxed on income as if the securities had not been sold (as provided by para 3) it may also claim a relief for any amount that it is required under GAAP to treat as a finance charge in respect of the advance. Such an amount is to be treated as interest under the loan-relationship rules and as interest in respect of which income tax is in principle deductible at source under ITA 2007 Part 15. Paragraph 6 provides that for the purposes of corporation tax on chargeable gains as regards the borrower, the sale and repurchase of the securities under a debtor repo are to be ignored. A disposal is to be regarded as taking place, however, if it becomes clear at any time during the currency of the arrangement that the repurchase is no longer to take place or the borrower ceases under GAAP to have to record a financial liability in respect of the advance.

Schedule 13 para 7 defines a 'creditor repo', which is a debtor repo seen from the point of view of the lender, and para 8 defines a 'creditor quasi-repo'. Essentially, a creditor repo is a repo from the aspect of the company that purchases the securities in return for money or other assets ('the advance') from 'the borrower' (the seller) and under the arrangement either has the right or the obligation to sell those or similar securities at a later date. The equivalent five conditions must be satisfied if a creditor repo is to exist, and the company that has the repo is termed 'the lender'. The lender has a creditor quasi-repo on the other hand, if it does not have a creditor repo but five other conditions are satisfied. The essential difference between a creditor repo and a creditor quasi-repo, is that under the latter arrangement, securities may be sold to any person other than the lender, and that the right or obligation to sell back the securities may be conferred or imposed on a person other than the lender. Paragraph 9 sets out the consequences for a lender who has a creditor repo or a creditor quasi-repo. Where this is the case, then during the duration of the arrangement, the lender is to be taxed in respect of income as if it did not hold the securities that are initially sold, and that any manufactured payment in respect of those securities that it actually makes had not been made. However, this treatment is not to apply if under GAAP, the lender is required to recognise or otherwise to take into account the income in question in determining its profit or loss. Paragraph 10 provides that while the lender is so treated under para 9, it must, however, recognise for tax purposes any amount that it is required under GAAP to treat as a finance return in respect of the advance. Such an amount is to be treated as interest receivable under the loan-relationship rules. Paragraph 11, as the mirror image of para 6, provides that for the purposes of corporation tax on chargeable gains as regards the lender, the purchase and subsequent sale of the securities under a creditor repo are to be ignored. An acquisition is to be regarded as taking place, however, if it becomes clear at any time during the currency of the arrangement that the subsequent sale is no longer to take place or the lender ceases under GAAP to have to record a financial asset in respect of the advance.

Schedule 13 para 12 is an anti-avoidance provision. It applies where under an arrangement a person receives an advance from a company or partnership of which the company is a member, in circumstances in which the company does not have a creditor repo or creditor quasi-repo, but would have one if an assumption held good. The assumption is that the accounts of the company or partnership are required under GAAP to record a financial asset in respect of the advance. Two further conditions must be satisfied – that the arrangement is designed to secure a tax advantage and to produce a return ('quasi-interest') to the company or partnership amounting in substance to interest on money. Where this is the case, para 10 is to apply as if the company had a creditor repo and the quasi-interest were a finance return. Paragraph 13 provides that tax is to be deducted at source from payments by the lender to the borrower in respect of a creditor repo as if they were manufactured payments, and that in respect of a debtor repo, the reverse-charge provisions of ITA

2007 Part 15 Chapter 9 are to have effect as if the lender were making manufactured payments to the borrower. Any actual manufactured payments are to be ignored for these purposes. Paragraph 14 is an interpretation paragraph and para 15 gives the Treasury power to modify the provisions of Sch 13 in respect of non-standard repos or redemption arrangements. Schedule 14 makes consequential amendments.

CFCs. Section 48 and Sch 15 amend the controlled foreign companies (CFC) legislation (TA 1988 Part XVII Chapter IV) as a response to the judgment of the European Court of Justice in *Cadbury Schweppes plc v IRC* (Case C-196/04). The Court held, essentially, that whereas the UK's CFC legislation was compliant in principle with Community law, it was disproportionate to the extent that it did not provide an exemption for companies that had genuine economic substance in their territory of residence. The judgment was based on the principle of freedom of establishment, and hence has no effect vis à vis third countries. The draft legislation, which these provisions follow very closely, was criticised as excessively restrictive and potentially still leaving the UK in breach of the EC Treaty. Section 48 introduces Sch 15.

Schedule 15 para 1 amends TA 1988 s 747 to make the CFC legislation (TA 1988 ss 747–756 and Schs 24–26) have effect subject to a successful application under new TA 1988 s 751A by a UK-resident company to which an apportionment of a CFC's profits has been made. Where a successful application has been made, it is to be further assumed that all persons connected or associated with the applicant company have also made successful applications. Paragraph 2 amends TA 1988 s 749 so that in determining whether persons have a 'majority assessable interest' in a CFC the effect of any application under s 751A is to be ignored. Paragraph 3 makes a similar amendment to TA 1988 s 749A, which deals with elections and designations under s 749. Paragraph 4 amends TA 1988 s 750(3) so that in determining for the purposes of the low-tax test what would be the amount of UK corporation tax chargeable on a CFC, the effect of any application under s 751A is to be ignored. Paragraph 5 inserts ss 751A and 751B. New s 751A provides for an application to be made by a UK company that has a 'relevant interest' in a CFC in respect of the profits of which an apportionment falls to be made on the UK company, where the CFC has a 'business establishment' in an EEA territory and there are individuals working for the CFC in that territory. The application is for a reduction (where appropriate to nil) of the CFC's chargeable profits. Where the application is granted, the CFC's chargeable profits are to be reduced by the amount specified in the application, but solely for the purpose of determining the amount (if any) chargeable on the UK company by the CFC rules. Any creditable tax of the CFC is correspondingly to be reduced. In order to grant the application, HMRC must be satisfied that the amount specified in the application does not exceed the amount that can "reasonably be regarded as representing the net economic value" arising to the 'appropriate body of persons' and created directly by 'qualifying work'. The 'appropriate body of persons' is the CFC and any persons with an interest in it; in the case where the CFC is a member of a group, it includes all other group members. 'Qualifying work' is work done directly by individuals working for the CFC in any EEA territory in which it has a business establishment. 'Business establishment' is defined by reference to TA 1988 Sch 25 para 7. Applications must be made in respect of each accounting period in which the conditions are satisfied. Section 751B prescribes how and when applications under s 751A are to be made, and allows for appeal against a refusal by HMRC to grant an application. Paragraph 6 is an interpretation section. Paragraph 7 amends the exempt-activities test in TA 1988 Sch 25 to the effect that the condition that the CFC's business affairs must be effectively managed in its home territory is not to be satisfied in respect of a CFC in an EEA territory unless there are sufficient individuals working for it there who have the competence and authority to undertake all or substantially all of the company's business. Paragraph 8 abolishes the public-quotation exemption for all CFCs. Paragraph 9 provides for discovery assessments. Paragraph 10 is a commencement provision. The amendments made by Sch 15 are to have effect in respect of CFC accounting periods beginning after 6 December 2006, with provision for straddling periods (s 48 and Sch 15).

R&D. Amendments are made to FA 2002 Sch 13 paras 14–16 to correct an error affecting the availability of vaccine research relief for small and medium-sized enterprises (s 49). The definition of a small and medium-sized enterprise (SME) for the purposes of research and development (R&D) relief is amended to double the limits applicable heretofore. Those limits are now to be 500 employees, turnover of EUR 100 million (approximately £67.5 million) and balance-sheet total of EUR 86 million (approximately £58.2 million). The new definition applies also for the purposes of vaccine research relief under FA 2002 Sch 13. However, larger SMEs (companies that qualify as SMEs only as a result of the new limits) claiming a payable tax credit for R&D relief may claim the enhanced 50 per cent deduction only in respect of expenditure that does not qualify for relief under FA 2000 Sch 20 (s 50).

Venture capital schemes etc. Section 51 introduces Sch 16, which makes amendments to the corporate venturing scheme, the enterprise investment scheme and the venture capital trust scheme. Paragraphs 1–3 insert new FA 2000 Sch 15 para 22A into the corporate venturing scheme, new ITA 2007 s 186A into the enterprise investment scheme and new ITA 2007 s 297A into the venture capital trusts scheme and make consequential amendments. The new legislation introduces a test for the maximum number of employees that an investee company may have under any of the schemes. In each scheme, the investee company may have no more than 50 full-time equivalent employees when the shares are issued. Paragraphs 4–6 (inserting new FA 2000 Sch 15 para 35A, ITA 2007 s 173A and ITA 2007 s 292A respectively) introduce a further new condition – namely that the total amount of capital that an investee company may raise under any of the three schemes in the year ending with the date on which the shares are issued is not to exceed £2 million. Paragraph 7 inserts the same condition in TCGA 1992 Sch 5B, in respect of reinvestment relief under the enterprise investment scheme. Paragraph 8 makes transitional provisions. Paragraphs 9–12 amend the definition of 'relevant intangible assets' (with reference to trades that are not excluded trades merely by reason of substantially consisting of the receipt of royalties or licence fees) to limit them to those created by the investee company or a qualifying subsidiary for each scheme but also extends it to include assets created by a company that the investee company acquires in a share-for-share exchange at a time when the investee company's shares consist solely of subscriber shares or by a qualifying subsidiary of that acquired company. Paragraph 13 is a commencement provision and para 14 a transitional provision for paras 9–12. Paragraphs 15–17 amend the definition of 'qualifying 90 per cent subsidiary' for the three schemes. Currently, a qualifying trade may be carried on only by the investee company or its direct 90 per cent subsidiary. These amendments provide for a qualifying trade also to be carried on by a 100 per cent subsidiary of the 90 per cent subsidiary or by a 90 per cent subsidiary of the investee company's direct 100 per cent subsidiary. Paragraph 18 is a commencement provision. Paragraph 19 extends with respect to the enterprise investment scheme from six to 12 months the time limit within which at least 90 per cent of the funds raised by an approved investment fund must be invested in qualifying shares. Paragraph 20 inserts new ITA 2007 s 280A relating to the disposal of holdings under the venture capital trust scheme. It provides that a disposal wholly or partly for money of a qualifying holding will be overlooked for a maximum of six months when applying the 70 per cent qualifying holdings test. Finally, para 21 allows for regulations to be made with respect to the venture capital trust scheme to give HMRC discretion not to withdraw approval for a scheme where conditions for approval are breached in specified circumstances. The amendments made by this Schedule generally apply variously from 6 April 2007 or the date of Royal Assent (s 51 and Sch 16).

REITs. Section 52 introduces Sch 17, which makes amendments to the legislation on real estate investment trusts (REITs). They apply generally from 1 January 2007. FA 2006 s 106 is amended so that a company need no longer satisfy the listing condition before it gives notice for the REIT régime to apply to it. The definition of what is a (disqualified) profit-linked loan is relaxed (para 2). The tax-exempt business condition is removed from FA 2006 s 107 and a consequential amendment is made to FA 2006 s 123 (paras 3 and 10). Additional items are to be excluded from the definition of profits in FA 2006 s 108 (para 4). The listing and trading requirement in FA 2006 s 109 is relaxed (para 5). The calculation of the financing-cost ratio in FA 2006 s 115 is amended (para 6). The manner in which the regulatory power under FA 2006 s 116 in relation to minor or inadvertent breaches may be exercised is amended (para 7). On an appeal against a notice under FA 2006 s 117 cancelling a tax advantage, the Special Commissioners may quash, affirm or vary the notice (para 8). Derivative contracts hedging risk may be taken into account when calculating profits under FA 2006 s 120 (para 9). Paragraph 11 inserts new FA 2006 s 126A, dealing with demergers. Where a tax-exempt company disposes of an asset to a 75 per cent subsidiary and then disposes of its interest in the subsidiary to another company, the entry charge and the provisions relating to the effects of entry (FA 2006 ss 111, 112) are not to apply to the group of which the subsidiary is a member if the company to which the subsidiary is transferred gives a notice under FA 2006 s 1090 and other specified conditions are satisfied. Paragraph 12 makes a consequential amendment. Paragraphs 13 and 14 make minor amendments. Paragraph 15 amends the definition in FA 2006 Sch 16 para 3 of owner-occupied property. Paragraph 16 makes amendments to FA 2006 Sch 17 (groups), including the insertion of a new Sch 17 para 34 to apply to demergers, parallel to new s 126A inserted by para 11. Paragraphs 17 and 18 exempt distributions to charities from tax under FA 2006 s 121 (s 52 and Sch 17).

Alternative finance. New FA 2005 ss 48A and 48B are inserted and consequential amendments made to treat Shari'a-compliant investment bonds known as *sukuk*, which are in economic substance similar to debt securities, to have the same tax consequences for issuers and holders as a conventional security (s 53). The definition of a 'profit-share agency' in FA 2005 s 49A is amended to clarify the treatment of the agent under an alternative finance arrangement known as a *wakala* (s 54).

Trusts. With respect to payments made to trustees after 5 April 2006, both TA 1988 s 686A (which applies before 6 April 2007) and ITA 2007 s 482 (which applies from 6 April 2007) are amended to ensure that trustees are charged to the special rates for trustees only on the excess over the subscription price when they receive qualifying distributions on the redemption or repurchase by a company of its own shares (s 55). Where trustees receive amounts in respect of chargeable-event gains on life policies, the notional 20 per cent tax credit is not to be included in the trustees' tax pool (s 56).

Other corporation tax measures. The conditions that an offshore fund must meet to be certified as a distributing fund are amended and other amendments are made to clarify the operation of the offshore-funds legislation (s 57). Provision is made for certain film-production companies to elect not to be subject to the special rules in FA 2006 ss 31–53 and Schs 4 and 5 for the taxation of film-production activities (s 58). FA 2005 s 83 (as amended) provides that old UK GAAP is to apply to securitisation companies for accounting periods ending before 1 January 2008. Provision is made for regulations to extend the 'closing date' for the application of old UK GAAP in specified circumstances (s 59).

Other income tax measures. The limits on the value that individual and corporate donors may derive from their donations under the gift-aid scheme without losing tax relief are increased: the proportionate limit is doubled to 5 per cent and the overriding monetary limit is doubled to £500 (s 60). A trade consisting substantially of the receipt of royalties or licence fees is not for that reason an excluded trade for the enterprise management incentive scheme if substantially the whole of the royalties or fees are attributable to 'relevant intangible assets'. The definition of 'relevant intangible asset' in ITEPA 2003 Sch 5 para 19 is amended to limit it to assets created by the company granting the options or its qualifying subsidiary but also extended to include assets created by a company that the grantor company acquires in a share-for-share exchange at a time when the grantor company's shares consist solely of subscriber shares or by a qualifying subsidiary of that acquired company. This amendment is of a piece with the identical amendments to the same definition relating to venture capital schemes made by Sch 15 paras 9–12 of this Act (s 61). Extra-statutory concession A104, relating to the calculation of whether an employment is lower-paid employment for the purposes of ITEPA 2003, is given statutory effect from 6 April 2007 (s 62). Payments or other benefits provided under the Armed Forces (Pensions and Compensation) Act 2004 are exempted from the charge to tax under ITEPA 2003 Part 6 Chapter 3 (s 63). Operational allowances whenever paid to members of the armed forces in high-risk areas are exempted from income tax (s 64). Income from service charges etc held on trust by private-sector landlords is exempted from the special rate for trusts with effect from 6 April 2007 (s 65). HMRC is given discretion to accept late elections under FA 2004 Sch 15 para 23 for the inheritance tax provisions on gifts with reservation to apply instead of the income tax charge on pre-owned assets (s 66). Amendments are made to ITTOIA 2005 to correct the inadvertent omission of unpaid remuneration and employee-benefit contributions from payments in respect of which an employer liable to income tax may claim a deduction for income tax purposes in the relevant period only if the payments are made within nine months of the period end (s 67).

PART 4
PENSIONS

Sections 68–70 and Schs 18–20 make changes to the pensions legislation of FA 2004 Part 4.

Section 68 introduces Sch 18, which removes tax relief for contributions in relation to personal term-assurance policies. Schedule 18 para 1 is introductory. Paragraph 2 amends FA 2004 s 188(3) to include contributions that are 'life-insurance premium contributions' under new FA 2004 s 195A. Paragraph 3 inserts new s 195A. That section defines life-insurance premium contributions ineligible for relief as contributions paid by an individual who is a member of a registered pension scheme towards a 'non-group life policy'. This is defined in turn as a policy under which the only benefits payable are in respect of the death of the scheme member or one of a group of individuals of which the scheme member is one, or, alternatively, in respect of the death of more than one individual from a group consisting of the scheme member and persons connected with him or her. Paragraph 4 provides that the amendments made by this Schedule apply, with respect to schemes other than occupational pension schemes, to contributions paid after 5 April 2007, and para 5 makes an exception for premiums under a 'protected' policy (as defined). Paragraph 6 provides that the amendments made by this Schedule apply with respect to occupational pension schemes to contributions paid after 31 July 2007, except in respect of premiums under a 'protected policy', as defined in para 7. HMRC is given the power to amend paras 4–7 by regulation (para 8).

Section 69 introduces Sch 19, which makes changes with respect to alternatively secured pensions and transfer lump-sum death benefits. Paragraph 1 is introductory. Paragraph 2 amends FA 2004 s 165(1) ('the pension rules') to remove alternatively secured pensions from the pensions guaranteed under pension rule 2, and amends pension rule 7 to increase the maximum amount of alternatively secured pension payable in each alternatively secured pension year in respect of a money-purchase arrangement from 70 per cent to 90 per cent of the basis amount. Paragraph 3 makes a consequential amendment. Paragraph 4 complements para 2 by amending pension death-benefit rule 6 in FA 2004 s 167(1) to increase the maximum amount of dependant's alternatively secured pension payable in each alternatively secured pension year in respect of a money-purchase arrangement from 70 per cent to 90 per cent of the basis amount. Paragraph 5 amends FA 2004 s 168(1) to omit a transfer lump-sum death benefit from the list of authorised lump-sum death-benefit payments. Paragraphs 6–10 make amendments consequential on para 5. Paragraph 11 amends FA 2004 Sch 28 para 11 so that where a member of an alternatively secured pension fund who has reached the age of 75 is untraceable, the sums and assets held for the purposes of the fund on behalf of that member are not immediately to become held in an alternatively secured fund. FA 2004 s 172B provides that where the death of a member of a registered pension scheme causes a connected member's rights under the scheme to increase, the scheme is to be treated as making an unauthorised payment to the connected member. Paragraph 12 amends s 172B so as to exclude rights under an alternatively secured pension fund or a dependant's alternatively secured pension fund. Paragraph 13 inserts new FA 2004 s 172BA, which provides that where the rights of a deceased member of a registered pension scheme are at any time subsequently reallocated to another member of the scheme, the scheme is to be treated as making an unauthorised payment. Paragraph 14 inserts new FA 2004 s 181A, which provides that the total alternatively secured pension or dependant's alternatively secured pension payable to a member or a dependant as the case may be in each alternatively secured pension year in respect of a money-purchase arrangement must normally be no less than 55 per cent of the basis amount. Where this requirement is not met, the scheme is treated as having made a scheme chargeable payment. Paragraph 15 makes a consequential amendment. Paragraph 16 amends the rules in FA 2004 Sch 29 para 18 for the payment of lump sums to charities on the death of a member or dependant. The occasions on which scheme administrators may apply for a discharge of their liability to a scheme sanction charge is extended (para 17). Para 18 makes amendments in respect of charges applicable to non-UK schemes consequential on para 5 above. It also confers the power on HMRC to make regulations imposing liability to the unauthorised payment charge on transfer members or relieved members of a non-UK scheme.

Paragraphs 19 to 27 are concerned with inheritance tax. Paragraph 19 is introductory. Paragraph 20 amends IHTA 1984 s 151A so that alternatively secured pension funds forming part of a deceased person's estate are to be treated as the top slice of that estate. Furthermore, it now provides that the value of such funds to be taken into account is to be reduced by any charge to income tax in respect of unauthorised payments charges arising after the death. Both s 151A and s 151B are to apply in relation to members who would have had an alternatively secured pension fund immediately before death had they been traceable and the provisions introduced by para 11 above not had effect (paras 20 and 21). Paragraph 22 inserts new IHTA 1984 s 151BA, which provides new rules for computing the rates at which tax is to be charged where s 151B applies. Section 151B applies where a person who was a dependant of a scheme member who died after reaching the age of 75 while holding an alternatively secured pension fund has inherited a dependant's unsecured pension fund or a dependant's alternatively secured pension fund. When that dependant dies in turn, or ceases to be a dependant, there is a charge under s 151B based on the value of those funds. The rule for calculating that charge to tax, previously in s 151B(5) – now repealed – is replaced by the rule in new s 151BA. Paragraph 23 amends IHTA 1984 s 151C. That section also applies where a dependant dies with funds in a dependant's unsecured pension fund but such that s 151B does not apply. It imposes a charge to tax on the value of that fund and contains a rule for computing the amount of the charge. The amendments made by para 23 match those made to s 151A by paras 20 and 21. They provide that the fund is to be treated as if it were the top slice of the deceased's estate and also that the value of such funds to be taken into account is to be reduced by any charge to income tax in respect of unauthorised payments charges arising after the death. Paragraphs 24 to 27 make consequential amendments to other provisions of IHTA 1984.

Paragraph 28 amends ITEPA 2003 s 636A to remove references to transfer lump-sum death benefits as authorised payments not liable to a charge to income tax. Paragraph 29 deals with commencement. Most of the amendments made by the Schedule apply as from 6 April 2007, but some are deemed to have come into force on 6 April 2006 (s 69 and Sch 19).

Section 70 introduces Sch 20, which makes miscellaneous other amendments in relation to pension schemes. Paragraph 1 is introductory. Paragraph 2 amends FA 2004 s 154 to provide that an application to register a pension scheme other than an occupational pension scheme may be made only if the scheme has been established by a person with permission under the Financial Services and Markets Act 2000 to establish a personal pension scheme or a stakeholder pension scheme. Paragraphs 3 and 4 make consequential amendments. Paragraph 5 amends FA 2004 s 160 so that an unauthorised member payment or an unauthorised employer payment is to be increased by any amount withheld by the administrator to cover the scheme sanction charge in respect of the payment. Paragraph 6 amends FA 2004 s 172A to add two further occasions of surrender of rights or benefits to those not considered to give rise to an unauthorised payment. Paragraph 7 amends FA 2004 Sch 28 paras 2 and 2A revising the rule allowing for the reduction of scheme pensions paid before the normal minimum pension age on the grounds of ill health. Paragraph 8 amends the reference periods in FA 2004 Sch 28 paras 10 and 24 for a review of the annual maximum withdrawal from a member's or dependant's unsecured pension fund. Paragraph 9 amends FA 2004 s 166(2)(*a*) to the effect that a person who has taken a lump sum in respect of a pension within six months of death and before becoming entitled to the pension itself is to be treated as having become entitled to the pension commencement lump sum immediately before death. Paragraph 10 amends FA 2004 s 219(7) to provide that the pension commencement lump sum referred to in the amended s 166(2)(*a*) is to be tested against the lifetime allowance before any lump-sum death benefits treated as paid immediately before the death. Paragraph 11 amends FA 2004 Sch 29 paras 1 and 2 to provide, inter alia, that one of the conditions for a lump sum to be treated as a pension commencement lump sum is that the member must become entitled to it before reaching the age of 75, rather than that the lump sum must be paid to the member before he or she reaches 75. Paragraph 12 amends FA 2004 Sch 29 para 10 with the intention of easing the administrative requirements for paying winding-up lump sums. Paragraph 13 also amends FA 2004 Sch 29 to establish an alternative commencement date for the two-year period in which a lump-sum death benefit under a defined-benefits scheme or from uncrystallised funds in a money-purchase arrangement must be paid. FA 2004 Sch 29A para 22 contains the conditions that must be satisfied for an investment-regulated pension scheme having an interest in a UK REIT to be treated as not holding an indirect interest in the taxable property held directly by the REIT. Paragraph 14 amends the condition and makes consequential amendments. Paragraphs 15 to 19 make amendments to the transitional provisions for pre-commencement rights of FA 2004 Sch 36. Paragraph 15 amends Sch 36 para 11D, which provides primary protection from the lifetime-allowance tax charge to certain lump-sum death benefits. Paragraph 16 is an introductory paragraph. Paragraph 17 amends Sch 36 para 12 dealing with the circumstances in which enhanced transitional protection for pre-commencement rights ceases. Paragraph 18 amends Sch 36 para 14, which defines the 'relevant contributions' that, where made to a money-purchase arrangement that is not a cash-balance arrangement, would cause enhanced protection to be lost. Paragraph 19 makes a consequential amendment. Paragraph 20 amends IHTA 1984 s 58 to extend the protection of settled property held for the purposes of a registered pension scheme or TA 1988 s 615(3) scheme from the inheritance tax charge on discretionary trusts from the death of the member to the point at which the lump-sum death benefits are paid. Paragraph 21 provides for a power to make regulations having retroactive effect under ITEPA 2003 s 393B. Paragraphs 22 and 23 make various consequential amendments and para 24 provides for commencement (s 70 and Sch 20).

PART 5
SDLT, STAMP DUTY AND SDRT

SDLT: anti-avoidance provisions. Three new sections – ss 75A–75C – are inserted in FA 2003 to counter avoidance SDLT avoidance schemes disclosed to HMRC. New s 75A, which replaces the current s 75A, applies where one person disposes of a chargeable interest and another person acquires that interest or another chargeable interest deriving from it and a number of transactions are involved in connection with the disposal and acquisition. Where the total SDLT payable as a result of all the transactions is less than the tax that would have been payable on a notional transaction directly between the disponer and the acquirer, the notional transaction is deemed to have taken place for SDLT purposes and such of the transactions that actually take place as are land transactions are to be ignored. Section 75B is supplementary to new s 75A and provides that in calculating the chargeable consideration under the notional transaction referred to in s 75A, any consideration for transactions that are merely incidental to the transfer of the chargeable interest from the disponer to the acquirer is to be ignored. Section 75C makes further supplementary provisions. Subject to transitional provisions, the new sections are to have effect for any disposals made after 5 December 2006 (s 71). Section 72 makes amendments to the complex rules of FA 2003 Sch 15, dealing with transactions by partnerships. The amendments are intended to counter avoidance schemes involving the 'seeding' of partnerships and are made to the provisions of that Schedule before they were varied by the SDLT (Variation of FA 2003) Regulations 2006 (SI 2006 No. 3237) and replace any variations made by those Regulations. The provisions affected are Sch 15 paras 10–12, which provide for the charge on transfers into partnerships; Sch 15 paras 18–20, which provide for the charge on transfers out of partnerships; and Sch 15 para 14, which provides for the charge on transfers of an interest in a property-investment partnership (s 72).

Reliefs in relation to shares etc. Section 73 introduces Sch 21, which amends stamp duty and stamp duty reserve tax exemptions with respect to intermediaries, repurchases, stock lending and recognised investment exchanges. The amendments are made in connection with the coming into force on 1 November 2007 of the EC's Markets in Financial Instruments Directive ('MiFID'), 2004/39/EC.

Paragraph 1 amends FA 1986 s 80A, which provides for exemption from stamp duty for sales to intermediaries. Broadly, the effect is to remove the requirement that an intermediary be a member of an exchange, to provide for relief for transfers of stock to an intermediary or an options intermediary where the stock is regularly traded on a regulated market as defined by MiFID and for sales on a multilateral trading facility or recognised foreign exchange of stock regularly traded there. Paragraph 2 makes consequential amendments to FA 1986 s 80B, which supplements s 80A. Paragraph 3 makes similar amendments to those of para 1 to FA 1986 s 88A, which provides for exemption from stamp duty reserve tax for sales to intermediaries. Paragraph 4 makes consequential amendments to FA 1986 s 88B, which supplements s 88A. Paragraph 5 amends FA 1986 s 80C, which provides for exemption from stamp duty for repurchases and stock lending. Broadly, the section as amended will now exempt repurchase and stock-lending agreements between investment firms with EEA authorisation under MiFID and for such agreements effected on a multilateral trading facility or recognised foreign exchange on which the stock is regularly traded. Paragraph 6 makes parallel amendments to those of para 5 to FA 1986 s 89AA, which provides for exemption from stamp duty reserve tax for repurchases and stock lending. Paragraph 7 makes consequential amendments to FA 1991 s 116, and para 8 repeals F(No. 2)A 2005 s 50 (s 73). FA 1986 s 75 provides relief from stamp duty where a company acquires all or part of the undertaking of another company ('the target'), and FA 1986 s 77 provides stamp duty relief for acquisition by a company of the entire share capital of another company. FA 2003 Sch 7 para 7 is the provision granting relief from stamp duty land tax on a qualifying reconstruction. Amendments are made to both sections and to the equivalent SDLT provision to provide that treasury shares held by the target or the acquirer are regarded as having been cancelled, thus ensuring that they qualify for the relief without actually having to be cancelled. The amendments apply from Royal Assent (s 74).

Other reliefs etc. Where a financial institution has acquired a chargeable interest in an alternative property-finance product within FA 2003 ss 71A, 72 or 72A, any further dealings in that interest or in an interest deriving from it are to be exempt from stamp duty land tax, as provided by new FA 2003 s 73B, inserted by this section, which also makes consequent amendments (s 75). Where an exchange of property takes place between connected persons, the two legs of the transaction are not to be regarded as linked transactions for the purposes of SDLT (s 76). Paragraphs 7–10 are inserted in FA 2003 Sch 9 to extend the relief from SDLT provided by that Schedule to shared-ownership leases also to shared-ownership trusts (s 77). Where a market-value election is made in respect of a shared-ownership lease, the rent payable under the lease is to be disregarded for all purposes of stamp duty land tax (s 78). School Standards and Framework Act 1998 ss 79 and 79A, granting relief from stamp duty and stamp duty land tax for certain transfers of school land are repealed, on grounds of redundancy (s 79).

SDLT: administration. Various provisions in FA 2003 requiring that land transaction returns must be accompanied by payment of the associated stamp duty land tax are replaced by the requirement that the tax be paid within the 30-day time limit for filing the return (s 80). Provision is made for the declaration of completeness and correctness on a self-certificate that must be delivered by a purchaser under FA 2003 Sch 11 para 2 to be made on the purchaser's behalf by an agent or by the Official Solicitor (s 81).

PART 6
INVESTIGATION, ADMINISTRATION ETC

Investigation etc. Police and Criminal Evidence Act 1984 s 114 provides that certain provisions of the Police and Criminal Evidence Act ('PACE') may by regulation be made to apply to criminal investigations by officers of Customs and Excise. The section is amended to substitute references to investigations conducted by officers of Revenue and Customs for the current references to officers of Customs and Excise. The order applying the provisions of PACE is to have effect as if a PACE 1984 s 14B were inserted. This permits an officer of HMRC to invoke certain existing powers to call for documents only where the office thinks that an application under PACE 1984 Sch 1 would not succeed because the material required does not include 'special procedure material'. Orders applying PACE provisions may direct that HMRC officers with search warrants may have the power to search persons as the order specifies (s 82). Parallel provisions are made in respect of criminal investigations in Northern Ireland under article 85 of the Police and Criminal Evidence (Northern Ireland) Order 1989 (s 83). Consequential amendments are made by s 84 and Sch 22. In particular, Sch 22 Part 2 repeals provisions relating to search warrants and powers of arrest with respect to individual direct and indirect taxes (s 84 and Sch 22) and it is provided that the amendments made by ss 82 and 83 are to take effect from a day to be appointed. Similar provisions to those of ss 82 and 83 are made in respect of criminal investigations by HMRC officers in Scotland (s 85 and Sch 23). PACE 1984 s 8 is amended to provide that a warrant issued in England and Wales in connection with an HMRC criminal investigation may be executed in Scotland (s 86). Amendments are made to the Criminal Justice and Public Order Act 1994 so that officers of HMRC may avail themselves of the ability to exercise powers granted in one jurisdiction in the UK in another (s 87).

Filing dates. Personal tax returns under TMA 1970 s 8 will in future need to be filed by 31 October following the end of the tax year concerned where they are in non-electronic format but may continue to be filed no later than 31 January if they are in electronic form. The three-month time limit for filing returns in response to late notices to deliver a return remain in force (s 88). Parallel amendments are made to the filing dates for trustees' returns under TMA 1970 s 8A (s 89), and to the filing dates for partnership returns under TMA 1970 s 12AA (s 90). Consequential amendments are made (s 91), and it is provided that the amendments made by ss 88–91 are first to have effect with respect to returns for the tax year 2007–08 (s 92).

Other administration. The power HMRC has under FA 2002 s 135 to require returns to be made electronically is extended to apply to every tax or duty under the care of HMRC. With respect to VAT, a penalty for failure to comply with a requirement under FA 2002 s 135 may be assessed under VATA 1994 s 76 (s 93). The power HMRC has under FA 2003 s 204 to require large employers to make payments by electronic means is extended to apply to every tax or duty under the care of HMRC (s 94). Where payment of tax is made by cheque, HMRC may make regulations to provide that the payment is made when the cheque clears, as defined in the regulations (s 95). Where a return is made under TMA 1970 s 8 or 8A (personal and trustee returns), TMA 1970 s 12AA (partnership returns) or FA 1998 Sch 18 para 3 (company tax return), on time, the 12-month period during which HMRC may enquire into the return is to commence on the date on which the return is delivered and not from the due date. For income tax, these amendments apply with respect to returns for tax years from 2007–08 onwards; for corporation tax, they apply to returns relating to accounting periods ending after 31 March 2008 (s 96).

Section 97 introduces Sch 24, which contains new provisions imposing penalties on taxpayers who make errors in certain documents sent to HMRC or who unreasonably fail to report errors on HMRC assessments. The new provisions are to apply from a date to be appointed. Schedule 24 para 1 imposes a penalty on the documents specified (e.g. income tax returns, company tax returns, VAT returns) where the documents contain careless or deliberate inaccuracies amounting to or leading to an understatement of the tax due, a false or inflated statement of a loss or a false or inflated claim to a repayment. Paragraph 2 provides for a penalty where an assessment by HMRC understates a person's liability to income tax, capital gains tax, corporation tax or VAT and that person fails within 30 days of the date of the assessment to take reasonable steps to notify HMRC of the error. Paragraph 3 provides when an inaccuracy is to be regarded as 'careless', 'deliberate but not concealed' and 'deliberate and concealed'. Schedule 24 Part 2 (paras 4–12) fix the amount of the penalty imposed by Part 1. The penalty is to be defined by reference to the 'potential lost revenue'. For careless action, it is to be 30 per cent of that revenue; for deliberate but not concealed action, 70 per cent, and for deliberate and concealed action, 100 per cent (para 4). The normal rule for defining potential lost revenue is that it is the tax or additional tax payable as a result of correcting the inaccuracy (para 5). Where there are multiple errors, careless inaccuracies are to be taken as corrected before deliberate inaccuracies and deliberate but not concealed inaccuracies before deliberate and concealed inaccuracies. Other priorities in respect of understatements and overstatements are set (para 6). Paragraph 7 provides how losses are to be taken into account in calculating potential lost revenue. When an inaccuracy has the result that an amount of tax is declared later than it should have been, the potential lost revenue is taken to be 5 per cent of the delayed tax for each year of delay, and a pro rata amount for delays of less than a year (para 8). Paragraph 9 specifies what reductions are to be made for disclosures. The amount of the reduction is to depend on whether the disclosure is prompted or unprompted, and on its quality. Special reductions may be made in special circumstances (para 11). Paragraph 12 provides for the interaction of penalties under Part 1 with other penalty provisions. Schedule 24 Part 3 deals with procedure. Penalties under Part 1 are to be imposed by assessment (para 13). HMRC may suspend all or part of a penalty for a careless inaccuracy by notice in writing (para 14). Appeals against the imposition of a penalty, as to the amount, against a decision not to suspend a penalty or against any conditions for suspension may be brought to the General Commissioners in respect of direct taxes and to a VAT and duties tribunal in respect of VAT (paras 15–17). Paragraph 18 provides for the liability of agents, para 19 with that of company officers and para 20 with that of partnerships. Paragraph 21 provides that a person is not to be liable to a penalty under Part 1 if he has already been convicted of an offence in relation to the default. Paragraphs 22 to 28 are interpretation provisions and paras 29–31 make consequential amendments (s 97 and Sch 24).

PART 7
MISCELLANEOUS

Value added tax and insurance premium tax. HMRC may make regulations amending the joint and several liability provisions of VATA 1994 s 77A to extend or otherwise alter the circumstances in which persons are to be presumed to have reasonable grounds for suspecting that VAT will go unpaid in a supply chain (s 98). The European Court of Justice held in *P Charles & T S Charles Tijmens v Staatssecretaris van Financiën* (Case C-434/03) that Member States may not legislate to limit the effect of the Court's decision in *Lennartz v Finanzamt München III* (Case C-97/90). The decision in *Lennartz* effectively requires input VAT on an asset that is intended only partly for business use to be deductible immediately, with adjustments for non-business use to be made over a specified period (so-called 'Lennartz accounting'). VATA 1994 Sch 4 para 5(4A), which disapplies Lennartz accounting in respect of land and buildings, is hence in breach of Community law and is therefore repealed with effect from 1 September 2007. However, in light of the European Court's judgment in *Hausgemeinschaft Jörg und Stefanie Wollny v*

Finanzamt Landshut (Case C–72/05), HMRC is given power to make regulations to fix the period over which non-business-use adjustments are made, to align it more closely with the recovery period for capital goods (s 99). Amendments are made to the provisions on the transfer of a business as a going concern, in connection with the duty to keep records, and with the disclosure by HMRC to the transferee of information needed by the transferee to comply with his duties. It is also made explicit that the transfer of a going concern includes the transfer of part of a business (s 100). An amendment is made to the definition in FA 1994 s 72 of 'premium' for the purposes of insurance premium tax (s 101).

Petroleum revenue tax. With effect from 1 July 2007, no petroleum revenue tax is to be charged in respect of oil or gas fields that are developed and recommissioned after having been decommissioned (s 102). A field so exempted under s 102 is to be classified for the purposes of Oil Taxation Act 1983 s 6A (tax-exempt tariffing receipts) as if it were a new field (s 103). The winning of oil from an oil field is to be regarded as having permanently ceased only once all the oil wells in the field have been permanently abandoned (s 104).

Other miscellaneous measures. Section 105 introduces Sch 25, which makes amendments consequent on the enactment of the Gambling Act 2005. Paragraphs 1 and 2 preserve the tax exemption for charitable companies and charitable trusts for the profits of certain charitable lotteries. Part 2 (paras 3–12) makes amendments to the Betting and Gaming Duties Act 1981. Part 3 (paras 13–15) makes amendments to the provisions on lottery duty under FA 1993 Part 1 Chapter 2. Part 4 (paras 16–20) makes amendments to the provisions on gaming duty in FA 1997. Part 5 (paras 21 and 22) makes miscellaneous amendments while Part 6 (para 23) provides for commencement (s 105 and Sch 25). Vehicle Excise and Registration Act 1994 s 5 is amended to give the Secretary of State power to make regulations on descriptions of agricultural vehicles that are to be exempt from vehicle excise duty (s 106). In response to the majority decision of the House of Lords in *Deutsche Morgan Grenfell Group v HMRC* [2007] STC 1, the limitation period for recovery of direct tax paid by reason of a mistake of law is to be set at six years from the date of payment. The Lords held that the extended period offered by Limitation Act 1980 s 32(1)(c) applied to actions for recovery in such cases. It is provided that that section is not to apply to actions brought before 8 September 2003, except where the action has been the subject of a judgment of the House of Lords given before 6 December 2006 or where a group litigation order has the effect of making such a judgment binding (s 107). Where there is doubt as to whether a scheme is subject to the disclosure rules of FA 2004 Part 7, new FA 2004 s 306A allows HMRC to apply to the Special Commissioners for an order that the scheme must be disclosed. Similarly, where HMRC believes that a promoter has not provided all the prescribed information under FA 2004 s 308, it may apply under new FA 2004 s 308A to the Special Commissioners for an order requiring the promoter to provide specified information. Under new FA 2004 s 313A, HMRC may also by written notice require a promoter who it suspects is promoting a proposal or arrangements that may need to be disclosed to state whether in the promoter's opinion there is a need to disclose the proposal or arrangements and if not, why not, with sufficient evidence. In the event of a negative answer from the promoter to a notice under s 313A, HMRC may apply under new FA 2004 s 313B to the Special Commissioners for an order requring the promoter to provide specified information or documents. Further, HMRC may, under new FA 2004 s 314A, apply to the Special Commissioners for a disclosure order in respect of a proposal or arrangements. The procedure and practice for hearings before the Special Commissioners under TMA 1970 ss 56B–56D is to apply to applications under FA 2004 Part 7 with any necessary modifications. The penalty provisions of TMA 1970 s 98C are amended to apply also to defaults under the new provisions (s 108). New definitions are provided of the term 'recognised stock exchange' for the purposes of the Tax Acts and TCGA 1992 (s 109 and Sch 26). The Treasury may make regulations concerning the tax consequences of a merger, transfer of a business or part of a business, a share exchange or the residence of a European company (SE) or European cooperative company (SCE) where it is necessary to do so to ensure compliance with the EC Mergers Directive (90/434/EEC) (s 110). 'Small consignment relief' from excise duty on non-commercial imports of excisable goods is repealed (s 111). References in tax legislation to Parliamentary Standing Committees are replaced by references to Public Bill Committees (s 112).

PART 8
FINAL PROVISIONS

Abbreviations of the full titles of Acts used in this Act are explained (s 113). Section 114 introduces Sch 27, which contains repeals, and section 115 is the short title.

FINANCE ACT 2007

(2007 Chapter 11)

CONTENTS

PART 5

SDLT, STAMP DUTY AND SDRT

SDLT: anti-avoidance provisions

Reliefs in relation to shares etc

Other reliefs etc

SDLT: administration

PART 6

INVESTIGATION, ADMINISTRATION ETC

Investigation etc

Filing dates

Other administration

PART 7

MISCELLANEOUS

Value added tax and insurance premium tax

Petroleum revenue tax

Other miscellaneous measures

PART 8

FINAL PROVISIONS

SCHEDULES

An Act to Grant certain duties, to alter other duties, and to amend the law relating to the National Debt and the Public Revenue, and to make further provision in connection with finance.

[19 July 2007]

PART 1

CHARGES, RATES, THRESHOLDS ETC

Income tax

1 Charge and rates for 2007–08

Income tax is charged for the tax year 2007–08; and for that tax year—

(*a*) the starting rate is 10%,
(*b*) the basic rate is 22%, and
(*c*) the higher rate is 40%.

GENERAL NOTE

Income tax rates for 2007–8 are unchanged.

In the Budget speech the Chancellor announced that for 2008–9 the basic rate of tax will be reduced to 20% and that the 10% rate will be abolished other than for savings income and capital gains tax.

Corporation tax

2 Charge and main rates for financial year 2008

(1) Corporation tax is charged for the financial year 2008; and for that year the rate of corporation tax is—

(*a*) 28% on profits of companies other than ring fence profits, and
(*b*) 30% on ring fence profits of companies.

(2) In this section "ring fence profits" has the same meaning as in Chapter 5 of Part 12 of ICTA (see section 502(1) and (1A)).

GENERAL NOTE

The main rate of corporation tax for the financial year beginning 1 April 2008 will be reduced from 30% to 28%. This is except for ring-fenced profits (i.e. profits from oil extraction and oil rights), which will remain taxable at 30%.

3 Small companies' rates and fractions for financial year 2007

(1) For the financial year 2007 the small companies' rate is—

(*a*) 20% on profits of companies other than ring fence profits, and
(*b*) 19% on ring fence profits of companies.

(2) For the financial year 2007 the fraction mentioned in section 13(2) of ICTA is—

(*a*) 1/40th in relation to profits of companies other than ring fence profits ("the standard fraction"), and
(*b*) 11/400ths in relation to ring fence profits of companies ("the ring fence fraction").

(3) If—

(*a*) a company makes a claim under subsection (2) of section 13 of ICTA in respect of any accounting period any part of which falls in the financial year 2007, and

(*b*) its profits for that accounting period consist of both ring fence profits and other profits,

that subsection applies with the following modification.

(4) The corporation tax charged on its basic profits for that period is reduced by the aggregate of—

(*a*) the sum equal to the ring fence fraction of the ring fence amount, and

(*b*) the sum equal to the standard fraction of the remaining amount.

(5) For the purposes of subsection (4)(*a*) "the ring fence amount" is the amount given by the formula—

$$(MR - PR) \times \frac{IR}{PR}$$

where—

MR is the sum equal to the appropriate fraction of the upper relevant maximum amount,

PR is so much of the profits for the accounting period as consist of ring fence profits, and

IR is so much of the basic profits for that period as consist of ring fence profits,

and the appropriate fraction is the fraction of the profits for the accounting period that consist of ring fence profits.

(6) For the purposes of subsection (4)(*b*) "the remaining amount" is the amount given by the formula—

$$(MNR - PNR) \times \frac{INR}{PNR}$$

where—

MNR is the sum equal to the appropriate fraction of the upper relevant maximum amount,

PNR is so much of the profits for the accounting period as do not consist of ring fence profits, and

INR is so much of the basic profits for that period as do not consist of ring fence profits,

and the appropriate fraction is the fraction of the profits for the accounting period that do not consist of ring fence profits.

(7) In this section "ring fence profits" has the same meaning as in Chapter 5 of Part 12 of ICTA (see section 502(1) and (1A)).

GENERAL NOTE

There is an increase in the small companies' rate of corporation tax. Note that this applies for financial year 2007 – i.e. a year earlier than the decrease in the main rate.

For financial year 2007 the small company rate will be 20% (other than for ring-fence profits, where it will be 19%).

The small company relief fraction for financial year 2007 will be 1/40.

A company with profits of £600,000 and no associated companies will therefore pay tax as follows:

£600,000 @ 30%	£180,000
Less relief (£1,500,000 – £600,000) 1/40	£22,500
Tax payable	£157,500

For ring-fenced profits the fraction is 1/1//40%.

There is an apportionment formula where a company has both ring-fenced profits and other profits.

Inheritance tax

4 Rates and rate bands for 2010–11

(1) For the Table in Schedule 1 to IHTA 1984 substitute—

"Table

Portion of value		*Rate of tax*
Lower limit (£)	Upper limit (£)	Per cent
0	350,000	Nil
350,000	—	40"

(2) The amendment made by subsection (1) has effect in relation to chargeable transfers made on or after 6th April 2010.

(3) That amendment does not affect the application of section 8 of IHTA 1984 (indexation) by virtue of the difference between the retail prices index for September 2009, or September in any later year, and that for September in the following year.

(4) But that section does not have effect by virtue of the difference between the retail prices index for September 2008 and that for September 2009.

GENERAL NOTE

One of the features of this year's Budget and the associated Finance Act is that many of the announcements relate to future years.

The nil-rate band for Inheritance Tax for years up to 2009–10 was set in FA 2006. In this year's Act the band for 2011–12 has been set at £350,000.

The rate of Inheritance Tax is unchanged at 40%.

Alcohol and tobacco

5 Rates of duty on alcoholic liquor

(1) The Alcoholic Liquor Duties Act 1979 (c 4) is amended as follows.

(2) In section 36(1AA)(*a*) (standard rate of duty on beer), for "£13.26" substitute "£13.71".

(3) In section 62(1A) (rates of duty on cider)—

(*a*) in paragraph (*a*) (rate of duty per hectolitre in the case of sparkling cider of a strength exceeding 5.5 per cent), for "£166.70" substitute "£172.33",

(*b*) in paragraph (*b*) (rate of duty per hectolitre in the case of cider of a strength exceeding 7.5 per cent which is not sparkling cider), for "£38.43" substitute "£39.73", and

(*c*) in paragraph (*c*) (rate of duty per hectolitre in any other case), for "£25.61" substitute "£26.48".

(4) For Part 1 of the Table in Schedule 1 substitute—

"Part 1
Wine and Made-Wine of a Strength Not Exceeding 22 Per Cent

Description of wine or made-wine	*Rates of duty per hectolitre*
	£
Wine or made-wine of a strength not exceeding 4 per cent	54.85
Wine or made-wine of a strength exceeding 4 per cent but not exceeding 5.5 per cent	75.42
Wine or made-wine of a strength exceeding 5.5 per cent but not exceeding 15 per cent and not sparkling	177.99
Sparkling wine or sparkling made-wine of a strength exceeding 5.5 per cent but less than 8.5 per cent	172.33
Sparkling wine or sparkling made-wine of a strength of 8.5 per cent or of a strength exceeding 8.5 per cent but not exceeding 15 per cent	227.99

Wine or made-wine of a strength exceeding 15 per cent but not exceeding 22 per cent	237.31"

(5) The amendments made by this section are deemed to have come into force on 26th March 2007.

GENERAL NOTE

This section increases the rate of duty charged under the Alcoholic Liquor Duties Act 1979 on beer, cider and wine, in most cases by 3.4 per cent, in line with the increase in the Retail Price Index (RPI). There is no increase in the rate of duty on spirits.

The Treasury points out that the real cost of duty on beer, cider and wine has fallen since 1997 (when the Labour government took power), in the case of cider by no less than 19 per cent.

As a consequence of the rise in beer duty, the duty on small-brewery beer under FA 2002 s 4 and Sch 1 also rises.

The increases had effect from 26 March 2007.

6 Rates of tobacco products duty

(1) For the Table in Schedule 1 to the Tobacco Products Duty Act 1979 (c 7) substitute—

"Table

1. Cigarettes	An amount equal to 22 per cent of the retail price plus £108.65 per thousand cigarettes.
2. Cigars	£158.24 per kilogram.
3. Hand-rolling tobacco	£113.74 per kilogram.
4. Other smoking tobacco and chewing tobacco	£69.57 per kilogram."

(2) The amendment made by subsection (1) is deemed to have come into force at 6pm on 21st March 2007.

GENERAL NOTE

This section increases the rates of excise duty charged under the Tobacco Products Duty Act 1979 on all tobacco products, but by no more than inflation, as measured by the RPI, i.e. by 3.4 per cent.

The *ad valorem* rate of duty on cigarettes remains unchanged at 22 per cent.

The increases, which took effect from 18:00 hrs on 21 March 2007, result in a price increase of approximately 11p for a packet of 20 cigarettes and of 7p on a 25g pack of pipe tobacco.

Gambling

7 Rates of gaming duty

(1) For the Table in section 11(2) of FA 1997 substitute—

"Table

Part of gross gaming yield	*Rate*
The first £1,836,500	15 per cent
The next £1,266,000	20 per cent
The next £2,217,500	30 per cent
The next £4,680,000	40 per cent
The remainder	50 per cent"

(2) In section 11(3) of that Act, for "40 per cent" substitute "50 per cent".

(3) The amendments made by this section have effect in relation to accounting periods beginning on or after 1st April 2007.

GENERAL NOTE

This section makes significant changes to the rates of gaming duty charged under FA 1997 ss 10–15. In addition to a revalorisation for inflation, the Chancellor has chosen to aggregate the first two duty bands and introduce a new top rate of 50 per cent.

Gaming duty is charged on premises in the UK where 'dutiable gaming' takes place. Dutiable gaming includes the playing of such games as blackjack, roulette, baccarat etc. The rates of duty are progressive, and are charged on 'gross gaming yield', broadly the gross profits of the operator from gaming in a given duty accounting period. Accounting periods for gaming duty are six-monthly periods, ending on 31 March and 30 September.

The table below shows the comparison between the previous rates of duty and the new rates, which take effect for accounting periods beginning after 31 March 2007.

Previous rates		*New rates*	
Gross gaming yield	Duty rate	Gross gaming yield	Duty rate
First £546,500	2.5%	First £1,836,500	15%
Next £1,212,500	12.5%	Next £1,266,000	20%
Next £1,212,500	20.0%	Next £2,217,500	30%
Next £2,124,500	30.0%	Next £4,680,000	40%
Balance over £5,095,500	40.0%	Balance over £10,000,000	50%

The rate of duty charged under FA 1997 s 11(3) on unregistered gaming is increased from 40 per cent to 50 per cent.

The Treasury estimates that these changes will yield an extra £175 million of revenue.

8 Remote gaming duty

(1) Schedule 1 contains amendments of and relating to Part 2 of BGDA 1981 (gaming duties) imposing a remote gaming duty.

(2) The amendments made by Schedule 1 have effect in respect of the provision of facilities on or after a date appointed by the Commissioners for Her Majesty's Revenue and Customs by order made by statutory instrument.

GENERAL NOTE

This section introduces Schedule 1, which imposes a new excise duty, to be known as remote gaming duty, to be charged under the Betting and Gaming Duties Act (BGDA) 1981.

It is a response to the phenomenal increase in online gaming. Whereas, hitherto, it has not been illegal for UK citizens to gain access to, and take part in, online gaming (cf the situation in the United States, where it is effectively illegal to take part in online gaming), with a very few exceptions it has been illegal for operators based in the UK to provide online gaming. By the imposition of this duty, the Treasury is seeking to regulate the situation by allowing online and other remote-gaming operators to base themselves in the UK, and of course to raise revenue from this form of gambling.

9 Amusement machine licence duty

(1) Section 23 of BGDA 1981 (amount of duty payable on amusement machine licence) is amended as follows.

(2) In subsection (3), in the definition of "Category C", in paragraph (ii)(*b*) for "£25" substitute "£35".

(3) After subsection (6) insert—

"(7) The Commissioners may by order substitute for a sum for the time being specified in subsection (3) such higher sum as they consider appropriate."

(4) Subsection (2) is deemed to have come into force on 22nd March 2007.

GENERAL NOTE

This section increases the maximum permitted prize from a Category C gaming machine from £25 to £35 from 22 March 2007. It also provides that future changes to the definition of gaming machines subject to amusement machine licence duty and the values of permitted prizes may be made by order.

Environment

10 Fuel duty rates and rebates

(1) The Hydrocarbon Oil Duties Act 1979 (c 5) is amended as follows.

(2) In section 6(1A) (hydrocarbon oil: rates of duty)—

(*a*) in paragraph (*a*) (ultra low sulphur petrol), for "£0.4835" substitute "£0.5035",

(*b*) in paragraph (*aa*) (sulphur-free petrol), for "£0.4835" substitute "£0.5035",

(*c*) in paragraph (*b*) (light oil other than ultra low sulphur petrol and sulphur-free petrol), for "£0.5768" substitute "£0.6007",

(*d*) in paragraph (*c*) (ultra low sulphur diesel), for "£0.4835" substitute "£0.5035",

(*e*) in paragraph (ca) (sulphur-free diesel), for "£0.4835" substitute "£0.5035", and

(*f*) in paragraph (*d*) (heavy oil other than ultra low sulphur diesel and sulphur-free diesel), for "£0.5468" substitute "£0.5694".

(3) In section 6AA(3) (biodiesel), for "£0.2835" substitute "£0.3035".

(4) In section 6AD(3) (bioethanol), for "£0.2835" substitute "£0.3035".

(5) In section 8(3) (road fuel gas)—

(*a*) in paragraph (*a*) (natural road fuel gas), for "£0.1081" substitute "£0.1370", and

(*b*) in paragraph (*b*) (other road fuel gas), for "£0.1221" substitute "£0.1649".

(6) In section 11(1) (rebate on heavy oil)—

(*a*) in paragraph (*a*) (fuel oil), for "£0.0729" substitute"£0.0929",

(*b*) in paragraph (*b*) (gas oil which is not ultra low sulphur diesel), for "£0.0769" substitute "£0.0969", and

(*c*) in paragraph (*ba*) (ultra low sulphur diesel), for "£0.0769" substitute "£0.0969".

(7) In section 13A(1) (rebate on unleaded petrol), for "£0.0617" substitute "£0.0642".

(8) In section 14(1) (rebate on light oil for use as furnace oil), for "£0.0729" substitute "£0.0929".

(9) The amendments made by this section come into force on 1st October 2007.

GENERAL NOTE

This section increases the rates of excise duty on hydrocarbon oils used as main road fuels by 2p per litre (equivalent to an increase of 4.14 per cent). The effective rates of duty (i.e. duty minus rebate) for non-road fuels are also increased by 2p per litre.

Further increases maintain the existing differentials with the duties on main road fuels, with the exception of road fuel gas other than natural gas, where the duty differential is reduced by 1p per litre.

The increases take effect from 1 October 2007.

11 Rates of vehicle excise duty

(1) Schedule 1 to VERA 1994 (annual rates of duty) is amended as follows.

(2) In paragraph 1 (general)—

(*a*) in sub-paragraph (2) (vehicle not covered elsewhere in Schedule otherwise than with engine cylinder capacity not exceeding 1,549cc), for "£175" substitute "£180", and

(*b*) in sub-paragraph (2A) (vehicle not covered elsewhere in Schedule with engine cylinder capacity not exceeding 1,549cc), for "£110" substitute "£115".

(3) Paragraph 1B (graduated rates for light passenger vehicles) is amended as follows.

(4) For the words from "Table A" to "date," substitute "the following table".

(5) For ", or is liable to the standard rate or the premium" substitute "or is liable to the standard".

(6) For Tables A and B substitute—

"Table

CO_2 emissions figure		*Rate*	
(1)	*(2)*	*(3)*	*(4)*
Exceeding	*Not exceeding*	*Reduced rate*	*Standard rate*
g/km	*g/km*	*£*	*£*
100	120	15	35
120	150	95	115
150	165	120	140
165	185	145	165
185	225	190	205
225	—	285	300

The table has effect in relation to vehicles first registered before 23rd March 2006 as if—

(*a*) in column (3), in the last row, "190" were substituted for "285", and

(*b*) in column (4), in the last row, "205" were substituted for "300"."

(7) For paragraphs 1D and 1E substitute—

"The standard rate

1D A vehicle is liable to the standard rate of duty if it does not qualify for the reduced rate of duty."

(8) In paragraph 1J (light goods vehicles)—

(*a*) in sub-paragraph (*a*) (vehicle which is not lower-emission van), for "£170" substitute "£175", and

(*b*) in sub-paragraph (*b*) (lower-emission van), for "£110" substitute "£115".

(9) In paragraph 2(1) (motorcycles)—

(*a*) in paragraph (*b*) (motorbicycle and engine's cylinder capacity more than 150cc but not more than 400cc), for "£31" substitute "£32",

(*b*) in paragraph (*c*) (motorbicycle and engine's cylinder capacity more than 400cc but not more than 600cc), for "£46" substitute "£47", and

(*c*) in paragraph (*d*) (any other case), for "£62" substitute "£64".

(10) The amendments made by this section have effect in relation to licences taken out on or after 22nd March 2007.

GENERAL NOTE

This section makes changes to the rates of vehicle excise duty charged under the Vehicle Excise and Registration Act (VERA) 1994. Rates for the lowest polluting vehicles have been frozen or reduced; rates for other vehicles have been increased, notably for vehicles emitting over 225g/km.

In particular, the premium rate, payable by vehicles using diesel fuel, has been scrapped. so that only two rates remain per emission band – the reduced rate, payable by vehicles using 'alternative' fuels, and the standard rate, now payable by vehicles using petrol or diesel. Vehicles in Band A (emissions of 100 gm/km or less) remain free of duty, and the rate of duty in Band B (emissions in excess of 100 gm/km but no more than 120 gm/km) has been reduced to £35 (standard rate) and £15 (reduced rate). Rates for the other bands have been increased; the increase for the highest band, Band G (emissions over 225 gm/km) have been increased from £200 (reduced) and £210 (standard) to £285 and £300 respectively. Although this represents an increase of 40 per cent or so, it has nevertheless disappointed environmental campaigners. What is more, these higher rates apply to vehicles first registered after 22 March 2006; for vehicles registered before that date, duty in Band G is £190 and £205, which are the rates applicable also to Band F. This reflects the fact that when Band G was introduced in 2006, it was enacted to apply solely to cars first registered after Budget Day.

The new rates apply to all licences taken out after 21 March 2007.

12 Rates of air passenger duty

(1) Section 30 of FA 1994 (rates of air passenger duty) is amended as follows.

(2) In subsection (3A) (destinations in EEA States and qualifying territories etc)—

(*a*) in paragraph (*a*) (standard class travel), for "£5" substitute "£10", and
(*b*) in paragraph (*b*) (any other case), for "£10" substitute "£20".

(3) In subsection (4) (other destinations)—

(*a*) in paragraph (*a*) (standard class travel), for "£20" substitute "£40", and
(*b*) in paragraph (*b*) (any other case), for "£40" substitute "£80".

(4) The amendments made by this section have effect in relation to any carriage of a passenger on an aircraft which begins on or after 1st February 2007.

(5) But if the amount of duty due from any operator in the accounting period ending before 21st March 2007 increased as a result of those amendments, the operator is to pay the amount of that increase as if it became due in the first accounting period ending after that day.

(6) Expressions which are used in subsection (5) and in the Air Passenger Duty Regulations 1994 (SI 1994/1738) have the same meaning in that subsection as in those regulations.

GENERAL NOTE

Air passenger duty (APD) is charged (under FA 1994 Part I Chapter IV) in respect of every passenger carried on a flight beginning in the UK. There are two rates of duty: one for flights to destinations within the EEA and certain other designated territories, and the other for flights to other destinations. The rate of duty also varies depending on the class of travel – the rates for passengers travelling in the lowest class (standard, economy etc) being one-half of those for passengers in other classes (business etc).

This section amends FA 1994 s 30 so as to double the existing rates of duty as follows:

EEA and other qualifying territories:

— standard class – from £5 to £10
— other than standard – from £10 to £20
— other destinations:
— standard class – from £20 to £40
— other than standard – from £40 to £80

The qualifying territories other than EEA states currently consist of Croatia, Switzerland and Turkey. By a separate Treasury order, Albania, Bosnia Herzegovina, Kosovo, Macedonia, Montenegro and Serbia have been added to the list.

The increases had effect from 1 February 2007.

13 Rates of climate change levy

(1) For the Table in paragraph 42(1) of Schedule 6 to FA 2000 substitute—

"Table

Taxable commodity supplied	*Rate at which levy payable if supply is not a reduced-rate supply*
Electricity	£0.00456 per kilowatt hour

Taxable commodity supplied	*Rate at which levy payable if supply is not a reduced-rate supply*
Gas supplied by a gas utility or any gas supplied in a gaseous state that is of a kind supplied by a gas utility	£0.00159 per kilowatt hour
Any petroleum gas, or other gaseous hydrocarbon, supplied in a liquid state	£0.01018 per kilogram
Any other taxable commodity	£0.01242 per kilogram".

(2) The amendment made by subsection (1) has effect in relation to supplies treated as taking place on or after 1st April 2008.

GENERAL NOTE

Climate change levy is charged under FA 2000 s 30 and Schs 6 and 7 on the non-domestic use of energy. The levy came into effect on 1 April 2001, and rates remained frozen until 1 April 2007, when FA 2006 s 171(1) came into effect, to increase them by approximately 2.6 per cent, corresponding to the rate of increase of the RPI at the time of the legislation.

This section makes further increases, which are to have effect from 1 April 2008. As last year, the increases are inflation-linked, and are in the order of 3.3 per cent.

14 Rate of aggregates levy

(1) In section 16(4) of FA 2001 (rate of aggregates levy), for "£1.60" substitute "£1.95".

(2) The amendment made by subsection (1) has effect in relation to aggregate subjected to commercial exploitation on or after 1st April 2008.

GENERAL NOTE

Aggregates levy is charged under FA 2001 Part 2 on aggregate subject to commercial exploitation. The rate of duty is set by FA 2001 s 16(4), and at £1.60 per tonne, has remained unchanged since the inception of the tax on 1 April 2002.

This section increases the rate of duty to £1.95 per tonne (an increase of 2.2 per cent), with effect from 1 April 2008. Registered operators in Northern Ireland in possession of a valid credit certificate enjoy a reduction of 80 per cent. The rate payable by them accordingly increases from 32p per tonne to 39p per tonne.

15 Rates of landfill tax

(1) Section 42 of FA 1996 (amount of landfill tax) is amended as follows.

(2) In—

(*a*) subsection (1)(*a*) (the standard rate), and

(*b*) subsection (2) (reference to the standard rate taken to be £2 in cases of disposals of qualifying material),

for "£21" substitute "£24".

(3) The amendments made by subsection (2) have effect in relation to disposals made (or treated as made) on or after 1st April 2007 (but before 1st April 2008).

(4) In subsection (1)(*a*), for "£24" substitute "£32" and, in subsection (2), for "£24 were to £2" substitute "£32 were to £2.50".

(5) The amendments made by subsection (4) come into force on 1st April 2008 and have effect in relation to disposals made (or treated as made) on or after that date.

GENERAL NOTE

Landfill tax is charged under FA 1996 Part III on the disposal of active and non-active waste in authorised landfill sites, and falls mostly on local authorities. The rates of the tax have been regularly increased over the years as an incentive to reduce the amount of waste committed to landfill.

This section makes further increases to the rate of tax, to be imposed in two stages. The standard rate is increased from £21 per tonne to £24 per tonne (an increase of 14 per cent) on relevant waste disposal made after 31 March 2007 but before 1 April 2008. For disposals made on or after 1 April 2008, the standard rate increases to £32 per tonne (an increase of 33.3 per cent) and the lower rate is increased from £2 per tonne to £2.50 per tonne (an increase of 25 per cent).

It is the Government's announced intention to establish a standard rate of £35 per tonne in the 'medium to long term'.

16 Emissions trading: charges for allocations

(1) The Treasury may impose charges by providing for Community tradeable emissions allowances to be allocated in return for payment.

(2) The Treasury must by regulations make provision for and in connection with allocations of allowances in return for payment.

(3) The regulations must provide for allocations to be overseen by an independent person appointed by the Treasury.

(4) The regulations may make any other provision about allocations which the Treasury consider appropriate, including (in particular)—

(*a*) provision as to the imposition of fees, and as to the making and forfeiting of deposits, in connection with participation in allocations,

(*b*) provision as to the persons by whom allocations are to be conducted,

(*c*) provision for the imposition and recovery of penalties for failure to comply with the terms of a scheme made under subsection (5),

(*d*) provision for and in connection with the recovery of payments due in respect of allowances allocated (including provision as to the imposition and recovery of interest and penalties), and

(*e*) provision conferring rights of appeal against decisions made in allocations, the forfeiting of deposits and the imposition of penalties (including provision specifying the person, court or tribunal to hear and determine appeals).

(5) The Treasury may make schemes about the conduct and terms of allocations (to have effect subject to any regulations under this section); and schemes may in particular include provision about—

(*a*) who may participate in allocations,

(*b*) the allowances to be allocated, and

(*c*) where and when allocations are to take place.

(6) "Community tradeable emissions allowances" are transferable allowances which—

(*a*) relate to the making of emissions of greenhouse gases, and

(*b*) are allocated as part of a system made for the purpose of implementing any Community obligation of the United Kingdom relating to such emissions;

and "greenhouse gases" means carbon dioxide, methane, nitrous oxide, hydrofluorocarbons, perfluorocarbons and sulphur hexafluoride.

(7) Regulations under this section are to be made by statutory instrument.

(8) A statutory instrument containing regulations under this section is subject to annulment in pursuance of a resolution of the House of Commons unless a draft of the regulations has been laid before, and approved by a resolution of, that House.

GENERAL NOTE

The European Union Emissions Trading Scheme (EU ETS) is a Community-wide scheme, which runs from 2008 to 2012, for trading allowances ('Community tradeable emissions') for the emission of specified 'greenhouse gases' – as a means of reducing emissions and meeting the EU's commitments under the Kyoto Protocol.

The UK Government's National Allocation Plan for Phase 2 of EU ETS, submitted to the European Commission in August 2006, sets out the basis for allocation by the Government of emissions allowances to UK companies participating in the Scheme. Whereas most of the allowances will be allocated free of charge, the Government intends to submit 7 per cent of them to auction, thus disposing of them for value.

This section gives the Treasury power to allocate Community tradeable emissions in return for payment and provides the framework for a scheme to do so. The scheme will be overseen by an independent regulator.

Phase 2 covers only carbon dioxide (CO_2) but it is anticipated that Phase 3 will extend to other greenhouse gases. Accordingly, the regulations will apply to greenhouse gases generally and s 16(6) defines those gases to include also methane (CH_4), nitrous oxide (N_2O), hydrofluorocarbons (HFCs, such as hydrofluoroethane), perfluorocarbons (PFCs, such as tetrafluoromethane) and sulphur hexafluoride (SF_6).

PART 2
ENVIRONMENT

Energy-saving: houses

17 Corporation tax deduction for expenditure on energy-saving items

(1) In ICTA, after section 31 insert—

"31ZA Deduction for expenditure on energy-saving items

(1) This section applies if—

(*a*) a company carries on a Schedule A business in relation to land which consists of or includes a dwelling-house,

(*b*) the company incurs expenditure in acquiring and installing an energy-saving item in the dwelling-house or in a building containing the dwelling-house (see subsections (5) to (7)),

(*c*) the expenditure is incurred before 1st April 2015,

(*d*) a deduction for the expenditure is not prohibited by the wholly and exclusively rule but would otherwise be prohibited by the capital prohibition rule (see subsection (8)), and

(*e*) no allowance under the Capital Allowances Act may be claimed in respect of the expenditure.

(2) In calculating the profits of the Schedule A business, a deduction for the expenditure is allowed.

(3) But any deduction is subject to—

(*a*) section 31ZB (restrictions on the relief), and

(*b*) any provision made by regulations under section 31ZC.

(4) If, on a just and reasonable apportionment of any expenditure, part of the expenditure would qualify for the relief (but the remainder would not), a deduction is allowed for that part.

(5) "Energy-saving item" means an item of an energy-saving nature of such description as is for the time being specified in regulations made by the Treasury.

(6) The Treasury may by regulations provide for an item to be an energy-saving item only if it satisfies such conditions as may be—

(*a*) specified in, or

(*b*) determined in accordance with,

the regulations.

(7) The conditions may include conditions imposed by reference to information or documents issued by any body, person or organisation.

(8) In this section—

"the capital prohibition rule" means the rule in section 74(1)(*f*) or (*g*) (capital expenditure), as applied by section 21A, and

"the wholly and exclusively rule" means the rule in section 74(1)(*a*) or (*e*) (expenses not wholly and exclusively for trade and unconnected losses), as applied by section 21A.

31ZB Restrictions on relief

(1) This section restricts deductions that would otherwise be allowable under section 31ZA.

(2) No deduction is allowed if, when the energy-saving item is installed, the dwelling-house—

(*a*) is in the course of construction, or

(*b*) is comprised in land in which the company does not have an interest or is in the course of acquiring an interest or further interest.

(3) No deduction is allowed in respect of expenditure in an accounting period if—

(*a*) the Schedule A business consists of or includes the commercial letting of furnished holiday accommodation for the purposes of section 503, and

(*b*) the dwelling-house constitutes some or all of that accommodation for the accounting period.

(4) No deduction is allowed in respect of expenditure treated by section 401 (as applied by section 21B) as incurred on the date on which the company starts to carry on the Schedule A business unless the expenditure was incurred not more than 6 months before that date.

(5) No deduction is allowed in respect of expenditure incurred in acquiring and installing the energy-saving item in a building containing the dwelling-house in so far as the expenditure is not for the benefit of the dwelling-house.

31ZC Regulations

(1) In relation to any deduction under section 31ZA, the Treasury may make regulations for—

(*a*) restricting or reducing the amount of expenditure for which the deduction is allowable,

(*b*) excluding entitlement to the deduction in such cases as may be specified in, or determined in accordance with, the regulations,

(*c*) determining who is (and is not) entitled to the deduction if different persons have different interests in land that consists of or includes the whole or part of a building containing one or more dwelling-houses,

(*d*) making apportionments if the Schedule A business is carried on by persons in partnership or an interest in land is beneficially owned by persons jointly or in common.

(2) The apportionments that may be made include apportionments to persons within the charge to income tax.

(3) Regulations under this section may—

(*a*) make different provision for different cases, and

(*b*) contain incidental, supplemental, consequential and transitional provision and savings (including provision as to appeals in relation to apportionments mentioned in subsection (1)(*d*))."

(2) The amendment made by subsection (1) has effect in relation to expenditure incurred on or after such day as the Treasury may by order appoint.

GENERAL NOTE

Provisions are introduced that enable landlords who pay corporation tax to deduct the cost of acquiring and installing certain energy-saving items in residential properties that they let in computing the profits of the property business. Similar deductions are already available for landlords who pay income tax. The aim of the deduction is to encourage landlords to install certain energy-saving items in the properties that they let.

The provisions are contained in new TA 1988 ss 31ZA and 31ZB and take effect from the day appointed by the Treasury.

Deduction for expenditure on energy-saving items

New TA 1988 s 31ZA introduces a corporation tax deduction for the costs of installing energy-saving items in residential properties. This essentially provides the landlord with a revenue deduction for capital expenditure. The deduction is available where a company carries on a Sch A business in relation to land which consists of or includes a dwelling house and the company incurs expenditure in acquiring and installing an energy-saving item in the dwelling-house or in a building that contains the dwelling-house. For the deduction to be available, the expenditure must be incurred before 1 April 2015 and the deduction is not prohibited by the wholly and exclusively rule (but in the absence of this provision deduction for the expenditure would be denied by the capital prohibition rules). Where a deduction is given under this provision, capital allowances cannot be claimed in respect of the expenditure (new TA 1988 s 31ZA(1)).

The deduction is subject to any restrictions on the relief imposed by new TA 1988 s 31ZB and the provisions of any regulations made under new TA 1988 s 31ZC (new TA 1988 s 31ZA(2)).

The scope of the deduction extends to items of an energy-saving nature specified in regulations made for this purposes. The regulations may impose conditions that must be met for the item to qualify for the deduction and these conditions can include those imposed by reference to information or documents issued by any body, person or organisation (new TA 1988 s 31ZA(5), (6), (7)).

Regulations are to be introduced following Royal Assent to the FA 2007 which will specify that energy-saving item means loft insulation, cavity wall insulation, solid wall insulation, hot water system insulation or draught proofing. Regulations will also impose a cap on the amount of deduction of £1,500 per property.

Restrictions on relief

Restrictions on the corporation tax deduction for expenditure on energy saving items given by new TA 1988 s 31ZA are imposed by new TA 1988 s 31ZB. A deduction is denied for energy-saving items that are installed in the dwelling house in the course of its construction or which are comprised in land in which the company does not have an interest or in the course of acquiring and interest or further interest (new TA 1988 s 31ZB (2))

The deduction is also denied for expenditure in an accounting period in which the Sch A business consists of or includes the commercial letting for furnished holiday accommodation and the dwelling house is used that purpose (new TA 1988 s 31ZB(3)).

A deduction is not given for expenditure incurred more than six months before the date on which the company started to carry on the Sch A business (new TA 1988 s 31ZB(4)).

No deduction is given for the cost of acquiring and installing an energy-saving item in a building containing the dwelling house to the extent that the expenditure is not applied for the purposes of the dwelling house.

Regulations

The Treasury is given the power to make regulations for the purposes of:

— restricting or reducing the amount of expenditure for which the deduction is given;

— excluding entitlement to the deduction in cases specified in the regulations;

— determining who is and who is not entitled to a deduction where different persons have different interests in land that includes the whole or part of a building that contains one or more dwelling houses; and

— making apportionments if the Sch A business is carried on by person in partnership or if an interest in land is beneficially owned by persons jointly or in common,

by new TA 1988 s 31ZC.

Apportionments may be made to include persons within the charge to income tax (new TA 1988 s 31ZC(2). Provision is made for the regulations to make different provision in different cases (new TA s 31ZC(3)).

18 Extension of income tax deduction for expenditure on energy-saving items

(1) Section 312 of ITTOIA 2005 (deduction for expenditure on energy-saving items) is amended as follows.

(2) In subsection (1)(*b*) (expenditure incurred in acquiring and installing energy-saving item in dwelling-house), for "in the dwelling-house an energy-saving item" substitute "an energy-saving item in the dwelling-house or in a building containing the dwelling-house".

(3) In subsection (1)(*c*) (expenditure incurred before 6th April 2009), for "2009" substitute "2015".

(4) In section 313 of that Act (restrictions on relief), insert at the end—

> "(6) No deduction is allowed in respect of expenditure incurred in acquiring and installing the energy-saving item in a building containing the dwelling-house in so far as the expenditure is not for the benefit of the dwelling-house."

(5) In section 314 of that Act (regulations), insert at the end—

> "(3) Regulations under this section may—
>
> (*a*) make different provision for different cases, and

(*b*) contain incidental, supplemental, consequential and transitional provision and savings (including provision as to appeals in relation to apportionments mentioned in subsection (1)(*d*))."

(6) The amendments made by subsections (2) and (4) have effect in relation to expenditure incurred on or after 6th April 2007.

(7) The amendment made by subsection (5) is deemed always to have had effect.

(8) Regulations under section 314 of ITTOIA 2005 made on or after the day on which this Act is passed but before 31st December 2007 may include provision having effect in relation to expenditure incurred on or after 6th April 2007.

GENERAL NOTE

An income tax deduction is available which allows landlords the deduct the cost of acquiring and installing certain energy-saving items in residential properties that they let when computing the profits of the property business. The deduction, known as the landlord's energy saving allowance, was introduced from 6 April 2004. A number of amendments are made to those provisions.

The availability of the deduction is extended by six years to cover expenditure incurred before 6 April 2015 (ITTOIA 2005 s 312(1)(*c*) as amended by sub-s (3)). The extension was announced in the 2006 pre-Budget report.

Changes are also made to ensure that the income tax deduction remains available where energy saving items are installed elsewhere in a building containing an appropriate dwelling-house, provided that the items benefit the dwelling house (ITTOIA s 312(1)(*b*)). This change has effect in relation to expenditure incurred on or after 6 April 2007.

Mirroring the rules for the new corporation tax deduction introduced by s 17, new ITTOIA s 313(6) (inserted by sub-s (4)) ensures that a deduction is only given for expenditure that benefits the dwelling house (sub-s (4)). This change applies in relation to expenditure incurred on or after 6 April 2007.

Again, bringing the income tax provisions in line with those applying for corporation tax purposes as introduced by s 17, new ITTOIA 2005 s 314(3) is introduced (by sub-s (5)) which provides that regulations may be laid which may different provision for different cases or which contain incidental provisions. This new subsection is deemed always to have had effect. Provision is made (by sub-s (8)) allowing regulations made after the date on which the FA 2007 receives Royal Assent to have effect from 6 April 2007.

As announced in the pre-Budget report, floor insulation has been added to the list of energy-saving items. Further, the deduction is available to a limit of £1,500 per property rather than per building as previously. A statutory instrument has been laid enacting these changes.

19 SDLT relief for new zero-carbon homes

(1) In FA 2003, after section 58A insert—

"58B Relief for new zero-carbon homes

(1) The Treasury may make regulations granting relief on the first acquisition of a dwelling which is a "zero-carbon home".

(2) In subsection (1) "first acquisition of a dwelling" means the acquisition of a building which—

(*a*) has been constructed for use as a single dwelling, and

(*b*) has not previously been occupied.

(3) For the purpose of subsection (2) land occupied or enjoyed with a dwelling as a garden or grounds is part of the dwelling.

(4) The regulations shall define "zero-carbon home" by reference to specified aspects of the energy efficiency of a building; for which purpose "energy efficiency" includes—

(*a*) consumption of energy,

(*b*) conservation of energy, and

(*c*) generation of energy.

(5) The relief may take the form of—

(*a*) exemption from charge, or

(*b*) a reduction in the amount of tax chargeable.

(6) Regulations under this section shall not have effect in relation to acquisitions on or after 1st October 2012.

(7) The Treasury may by order—

(*a*) substitute a later date for the date in subsection (6);

(*b*) make transitional provision, or provide savings, in connection with the effect of subsection (6).

58C Relief for new zero-carbon homes: supplemental

(1) Regulations under section 58B—

(*a*) shall include provision about the method of claiming relief (including documents or information to be provided), and

(*b*) in particular, shall include provision about the evidence to be adduced to show that a building satisfies the definition of "zero-carbon home".

(2) Regulations made by virtue of subsection (1)(*b*) may, in particular—

(*a*) refer to a scheme or process established by or for the purposes of an enactment about building;

(*b*) establish or provide for the establishment of a scheme or process of certification;

(*c*) specify, or provide for the approval of, one or more schemes or processes for certifying energy efficiency.

(3) In defining "zero-carbon home" regulations under section 58B may include requirements which may be satisfied in relation to a building either—

(*a*) by features of the building itself, or

(*b*) by other installations or utilities.

(4) Regulations under section 58B may modify the effect of section 108, or another provision of this Part about linked transactions, in relation to a set of transactions of which at least one is the first acquisition of a dwelling which is a zero-carbon home.

(5) In determining whether section 116(7) applies, and in the application of section 116(7), a transaction shall be disregarded if or in so far as it involves the first acquisition of a dwelling which is a zero-carbon home.

(6) Regulations under section 58B—

(*a*) may provide for relief to be wholly or partly withdrawn if a dwelling ceases to be a zero-carbon home, and

(*b*) may provide for the reduction or withholding of relief where a person acquires more than one zero-carbon home within a specified period.

(7) Regulations under section 58B may include provision for relief to be granted in respect of acquisitions occurring during a specified period before the regulations come into force."

(2) In section 114 of FA 2003 (stamp duty land tax: orders and regulations), insert at the end—

"(5) The first set of regulations under section 58B (new zero-carbon homes) may not be made unless a draft has been laid before and approved by resolution of the House of Commons.

(6) An order or regulations under this Part—

(*a*) may make provision having effect generally or only in specified cases or circumstances,

(*b*) may make different provision for different cases or circumstances, and

(*c*) may include incidental, consequential or transitional provision or savings."

GENERAL NOTE

Provisions are introduced which allow for regulations to be laid introducing a relief from SDLT for new zero-carbon homes at the point of sale. The relief is only available on the first purchase of a new zero-carbon home. Homes that qualify for the relief will receive a certificate confirming that they meet the criteria set for zero-carbon homes. The Government's standard procedure for the energy rating of dwellings (laid out in reg 17A of the Building Regulations 2000 (SI 2000/2531)) will be used to determine whether a home reaches a zero carbon level. The criteria for such homes will be set out in regulations.

The provisions are contained in new FA 2003 ss 58B and 58C.

Relief for new zero-carbon homes

New FA 2003 s 58B provides for regulations to be made granting relief from SDLT on the first acquisition of a dwelling that is a zero carbon home. Regulations made under this section will not have effect in relation to acquisitions on or after 1 October 2012 (new FA 2003 s 58B(6)) However, a later date may be set by regulations (new FA 2003 s 58B(7)).

For these purposes, the first acquisition of a dwelling means the acquisition of a dwelling that has been constructed for use as a single dwelling and which has not been previously occupied (new FA 2003 s 58B(2)). For these purposes, land occupied or enjoyed with the dwelling as garden or grounds is treated as part of the dwelling (FA 2003 s 58C(3)).

Provision is made for regulations to define the homes that will be deemed to be eligible for the relief from SDLT as zero carbon homes. The definition will be by reference to the energy efficiency of the building, including energy consumption, conservation of energy and generation of energy (new FA 2003 s 58B(4)).

The relief from SDLT may be given either in the form of a total exemption from charge or as a reduction in the amount of tax chargeable (new FA 2003 s 58B(5)).

Supplementary provisions

Provisions supplemental to the relief are contained in new FA 2003 s 58C. new FA 2003 s 58C(1) provides that regulations will be made that will set out the method by which SDLT relief can be claimed, including the information and documentation to be provided, and also the evidence that will be needed to shown that a first acquisition of a home will meet the criteria for relief from SDLT as a zero carbon home.

In particular, the regulations may refer to a scheme or process established by or for the purposes of an enactment about a building, establish or provide for the establishment of a scheme or process of certification or specify or provide for the approval or one or more schemes or processes for certifying energy efficiency (new FA 2003 s 58C(2)),

In defining a zero-carbon homes for the purposes of the relief, the regulations may include requirements that may be satisfied in relation to a building either by features of the building itself or by other installations or utilities (new FA 2003 s 58C(3)).

Provision is made (in new FA 2003, s 58B(4)) for regulations to be made that modify the effect of FA 2003 s 108 or other provisions of Pt 4 of that Act relating to linked transactions, in relation to a series of transactions of which at least one is the first acquisition of a dwelling which is a zero-carbon home for SDLT purposes.

For the purposes of determining whether and how FA 2003 s 116(7) applies, the a transaction is disregarded if it is the first acquisition of a zero-carbon home (new FA 2003 s 58B(5)),

By virtue of new FA 2003 s 58B(6), regulations may be made under s 58B to provide that relief may be wholly or partly withdrawn if a dwelling ceases to be a zero-carbon home and that relief may be reduced or withheld if a person acquires more than one zero carbon home within a specified period. Regulations may also provide for relief to be granted din respect of acquisition occurring during a specified period before the regulations came into force (new FA 2003 s 58B(7)).

Stamp duty land tax: order and regulations

A new subsection (sub-s (5)) is inserted in FA 2003 s 114 which provides that orders or regulations made under FA 2003 Pt 4 may make provisions having effect generally or only in specified cases, may make different provision for different cases or circumstances and may include incidental, consequential or transitional provisions or savings.

Domestic microgeneration

20 Income tax exemption for domestic microgeneration

(1) In ITTOIA 2005, after section 782 insert—

"782A Domestic microgeneration

(1) No liability to income tax arises in respect of income arising to an individual from the sale of electricity generated by a microgeneration system if—

(*a*) the system is installed at or near domestic premises occupied by the individual, and

(*b*) the individual intends that the amount of electricity generated by it will not significantly exceed the amount of electricity consumed in those premises.

(2) In subsection (1)—

"domestic premises" means premises used wholly or mainly as a separate private dwelling, and

"microgeneration system" has the same meaning as in section 4 of the Climate Change and Sustainable Energy Act 2006."

(2) The amendment made by subsection (1) has effect for the tax year 2007–08 and subsequent tax years.

GENERAL NOTE

An income tax exemption is introduced for income arising from the sale of electricity generated by certain microgeneration systems. To qualify for the exemption, the system must be installed at or near domestic premises, which must be occupied by the individual receiving the income. Further, the individual must intend to generate electricity mainly for use in those premises and must intend that the amount of electricity generated the microgeneration system will not significantly exceed the amount of electricity consumed on the premises

The exemption, which is contained in new ITTOIA s 782A takes effect for 2007–08 and subsequent tax years.

21 Renewables obligation certificates for domestic microgeneration

(1) In ITTOIA 2005, after section 782A (inserted by section 20) insert—

"782B Renewables obligation certificates for domestic microgeneration

(1) No liability to income tax arises in respect of the receipt by an individual of a renewables obligation certificate if—

(*a*) the individual receives the certificate in connection with the generation of electricity by a microgeneration system,

(*b*) the system is installed at or near domestic premises occupied by the individual, and

(*c*) the individual intends that the amount of electricity generated by it will not significantly exceed the amount of electricity consumed in those premises.

(2) In subsection (1)—

"domestic premises" and "microgeneration system" have the same meaning as in section 782A, and

"renewables obligation certificate" means a certificate issued under section 32B of the Electricity Act 1989 or Article 54 of the Energy (Northern Ireland) Order 2003."

(2) In TCGA 1992, after section 263 insert—

"263AZA Renewables obligation certificates for domestic microgeneration

(1) A gain accruing to an individual on a disposal of a renewables obligation certificate is not a chargeable gain if—

(*a*) the individual acquired the certificate in connection with the generation of electricity by a microgeneration system,

(*b*) the system is installed at or near domestic premises occupied by the individual, and

(*c*) the individual intends that the amount of electricity generated by it will not significantly exceed the amount of electricity consumed in those premises.

(2) In subsection (1)—

"domestic premises" means premises used wholly or mainly as a separate private dwelling,

"microgeneration system" has the same meaning as in section 4 of the Climate Change and Sustainable Energy Act 2006, and

"renewables obligation certificate" means a certificate issued under section 32B of the Electricity Act 1989 or Article 54 of the Energy (Northern Ireland) Order 2003."

(3) The amendment made by subsection (1) has effect for the tax year 2007–08 and subsequent tax years.

(4) The amendment made by subsection (2) has effect in relation to disposals on or after 6th April 2007.

GENERAL NOTE

An income tax exemption is introduced for the income arising from receipts from the receipt of a renewables obligation certificate. A capital gains tax exemption is also introduced for any gains made on the sale the disposal of a renewables obligation certificate. A renewables obligation certificate is a certificate issued under the Electricity Act 1989 s 32B, or Northern Ireland equivalent.

The measures were announced in the 2007 Budget.

Income tax exemption

The income tax exemption is contained in new ITTOIA 2005 s 782B. It provides that no liability to income tax arises in respect of the receipt by an individual of a renewables obligation certificate if the individual receives the certificate in connection with the generation of electricity by a microgeneration system, the system is installed at or near domestic premises occupied by the individual and the individual intends that the amount of electricity generated by it will not significantly exceed the amount of electricity consumed in those premises.

The exemption applies for 2007–08 and subsequent tax years.

Capital gains tax exemption

The capital gains tax exemption is set out in new TCGA 1992 s 263AZA. It provides that a gain accruing to an individual on the disposal of a renewables obligation certificate is not a chargeable gain if the individual acquired the certificate in connection with the generation of electricity by a microgeneration system, the system is installed at or near domestic premises occupied by the individual and the individual intends that the amount of electricity generated by it will not significantly exceed the amount of electricity consumed in those premises.

The exemption applies in relation to disposals made on or after 6 April 2007.

Other measures

22 Aggregates levy: exemption for aggregate removed from railways etc

(1) Section 17(3) of FA 2001 (exempt aggregate) is amended as follows.

(2) Omit "or" at the end of paragraph (*d*).

(3) After that paragraph insert—

"(*da*) it consists wholly of aggregate won by being removed from the ground along the line or proposed line of any railway, tramway or monorail or proposed railway, tramway or monorail and in the course of excavations carried out—

(i) for the purpose of improving or maintaining the railway, tramway or monorail or of constructing the proposed railway, tramway or monorail; and

(ii) not for the purpose of extracting that aggregate;".

(4) Insert "or" at the end of paragraph (*e*).

(5) The amendment made by subsection (3) comes into force on such day as the Treasury may by order made by statutory instrument appoint.

GENERAL NOTE

Aggregates levy was introduced with effect from 1 April 2002. Its aim is to achieve environmental benefits by ensuring that the price of aggregates better reflects their true environmental cost and to encourage the use of recycling and alternative materials.

An exemption from the levy is introduced for aggregate removed from the ground along the line, or proposed line, of any railway, tramway or monorail in the course of maintaining, constructing or improving it, provided that the exemption was not excavated for the purposes of extracting the aggregate. The exemption was introduced after lobbying to ensure consistency with the levy's environmental rationale of providing a commercial advantage for true aggregate by-product over quarried aggregate. The exemption for aggregate from railways, tramways and monorails is in line with the existing aggregate from highways and waterways.

The exemption will take effect from a date appointed by regulations made after FA 2007 receives Royal Assent.

23 Climate change levy: reduced-rate supplies etc

Schedule 2 contains amendments of Schedule 6 to FA 2000 in relation to reduced-rate supplies and other matters.

GENERAL NOTE

Section 23 introduces Schedule Two.

24 Landfill tax: bodies concerned with the environment

(1) In section 53(4) of FA 1996 (credit: bodies concerned with the environment), after paragraph (*c*) insert—

> "(*ca*) provision for an environmental body to be and remain approved only if it complies with conditions imposed from time to time by the regulatory body or for the regulatory body to be and remain approved only if it complies with conditions imposed from time to time by the Commissioners (including provision for the variation or revocation of such conditions);".

(2) The amendment made by subsection (1) is deemed to have come into force on 22nd March 2007.

GENERAL NOTE

The Landfill Communities Fund enables landfill site operators to claim landfill tax credits for contributions made to controlled environmental bodies for spending on approved objects. A regulatory body is approved by HMRC to oversee the fund.

A power is introduced (new FA 1996 s 53(4)(*ca*)) that enables regulations to be made which impose conditions under which the regulatory body for the Landfill Communities Fund is and remains approved and enable the regulatory body to specify the conditions under which environmental bodies are and remain approved. Provision is also made for the regulatory body or HMRC to revoke or vary the conditions.

The power is deemed to have come into force on 22 March 2007.

The regulatory body is appointed under a document known and the terms of approval. Regulations amending the Landfill Tax Regulations 1996 were made under a power in the clause to enable HMRC to attach conditions to the approval. HMRC will be able to enforce the conditions. The amending regulations are effective from 1 April 2007.

PART 3

INCOME TAX, CORPORATION TAX AND CAPITAL GAINS TAX

Anti-avoidance

25 Managed service companies

(1) Schedule 3 contains provision about managed service companies.

(2) That Schedule is deemed to have come into force on 6th April 2007.

GENERAL NOTE

The section introduces Schedule 3 and provides for an early commencement date, deeming the changes to have been made on 6 April 2007.

26 Restrictions on trade loss relief for partners

Schedule 4 contains provision restricting reliefs for losses made by individuals carrying on trades in partnership.

GENERAL NOTE

Section 26 introduces Schedule 4.

27 Extension of restrictions on allowable capital losses

GENERAL NOTE

This is a very short section which nonetheless introduces profound changes to the taxation of capital gains. In FA 2006 a targeted anti-avoidance provision was introduced for corporate capital gains: at that stage it did not apply to individuals. The Government has however been increasingly concerned by the continued proliferation of capital gains tax avoidance schemes being promoted to individuals. On 6 December 2006 therefore it announced that it would introduce a general anti-avoidance rule which would apply to all capital gains tax losses regardless of the nature of the taxpayer.

Section 27(1) introduces the new provisions.

Section 27(2) abolishes the specific anti-avoidance rules which were introduced last year for corporation tax purposes only.

Section 27(3) introduces a new TCGA 1992 s 16A, which imposes a general restriction on capital losses. It applies to all capital losses, whether incurred by individuals, companies or trusts etc.

(1) TCGA 1992 is amended as follows.

(2) In section 8 (company's total profits to include chargeable gains)—

(*a*) in subsection (2), for the words from "does not include—" to the end substitute "does not include a loss accruing to a company in such circumstances that if a gain accrued the company would be exempt from corporation tax in respect of it.", and

(*b*) omit subsections (2A) to (2C).

(3) After section 16 insert—

"16A Restrictions on allowable losses

(1) For the purposes of this Act, "allowable loss" does not include a loss accruing to a person if—

(*a*) it accrues to the person directly or indirectly in consequence of, or otherwise in connection with, any arrangements, and

(*b*) the main purpose, or one of the main purposes, of the arrangements is to secure a tax advantage.

GENERAL NOTE

An allowable loss does not include a loss which accrues to a person directly or indirectly in consequence of, or otherwise in connection with, any arrangements where the main purpose, or one of the main purposes, of the arrangements is to secure a tax advantage.

(2) For the purposes of subsection (1)—

"arrangements" includes any agreement, understanding, scheme, transaction or series of transactions (whether or not legally enforceable), and

"tax advantage" means—

(*a*) relief or increased relief from tax,

(*b*) repayment or increased repayment of tax,

(*c*) the avoidance or reduction of a charge to tax or an assessment to tax, or

(*d*) the avoidance of a possible assessment to tax,

and for the purposes of this definition "tax" means capital gains tax, corporation tax or income tax.

GENERAL NOTE

"Arrangements" includes any agreement, understanding, scheme transaction or series of transactions (whether or not legally enforceable).

"Tax advantage" is widely drawn. It means:

— relief, or increased relief from tax;

— repayment or increased repayment of tax;

— the avoidance or reduction of a charge to tax or an assessment to tax; or

— the avoidance of a possible assessment to tax,

"Tax" means capital gains tax, corporation tax or income tax.

(3) For the purposes of subsection (1) it does not matter—

(*a*) whether the loss accrues at a time when there are no chargeable gains from which it could otherwise have been deducted, or

(*b*) whether the tax advantage is secured for the person to whom the loss accrues or for any other person."

GENERAL NOTE

It does not matter if the loss accrues in circumstances where there are no chargeable gains against which it could be set. In other words, schemes which produce capital losses which can be carried forward against possible future gains are also within the scope of these new provisions.

The new rules also apply whether the tax advantage is secured for the person who incurred the loss or by another person.

(4) In section 288(1) (interpretation), in the definition of "allowable loss", after "16" insert ", 16A".

(5) In section 834(1) of ICTA (interpretation of the Corporation Tax Acts), in the definition of "allowable loss", for the words from "or a loss" to the end substitute "or a loss accruing to a company in the circumstances mentioned in section 16A of the 1992 Act".

GENERAL NOTE

These are consequential amendments of no substantive effect.

(6) The amendments made by this section have effect in relation to losses accruing on disposals made on or after 6th December 2006.

GENERAL NOTE

These new loss restrictions apply to losses accruing on disposals made on or after 6 December 2006.

AFTER NOTE

Inevitably such broad-brush legislation is highly controversial and will be subject of much dispute as to where the boundaries lie between acceptable tax planning and unacceptable tax avoidance. HMRC has introduced draft guidance on the operation of these new rules: the latest version of this was released on 1 May 2007. This guidance has come under much criticism. See for example the comments of the CIOT at http://www.tax.org.uk/attach.pl/5585/5942/CGTandTAAR%20final010607.pdf.

28 Restriction on expenses of management

GENERAL NOTE

This section was not included within the Finance Bill as originally published. It was introduced at a late stage in the Parliamentary process following the issue of an HMRC press release on 20 June 2007.

The purpose of the section is to strengthen the rules denying relief for management expenses which are incurred for tax avoidance arrangements. An allowable purpose test was introduced in 2004, but HMRC has now decided that this does not give sufficient protection in all tax avoidance contexts. In particular the test was only effective against the purpose of the expenditure and not against the quantum of the expense. The new provisions seek to ensure that both purpose and quantum are taken into account in determining whether or not management expenses are subject to an anti-avoidance restriction.

Section 28(1) introduces amendments to TA 1988 s 75.

Section 28(2) introduces a new TA 1988 s 75(2A) to (2C).

(1) Section 75 of ICTA (expenses of management: companies with investment business) is amended as follows.

(2) After subsection (2) insert—

> "(2A) A deduction is not to be allowed under that subsection for any particular expenses of management if any part of those expenses is incurred directly or indirectly in consequence of, or otherwise in connection with, any arrangements the main purpose, or one of the main purposes, of which is to secure the allowance of a deduction (or increased deduction) under that subsection or any other tax advantage.
>
> (2B) Subsection (2A) above does not apply if, as a result of paragraph 7A of Schedule 23A (manufactured payments under arrangements having an unallowable purpose), the company incurring the expenses is not entitled to a relevant tax relief (within the meaning of that paragraph) in respect of, or referable to, the whole or any part of the expenses.
>
> (2C) The reference in subsection (2A) above to expenses of management includes amounts treated by any provision as deductible under this section."

GENERAL NOTE

Sub-sections 75(2A)–(2C) bring in a very wide anti-avoidance test. An expense which would otherwise be deductible is not deductible if any part of the expense is incurred directly or indirectly in consequence of, or otherwise in connection with, any arrangements the main purpose of which is to secure the allowance of a deduction (or an increased deduction) as a management expense, or any other tax advantage. Thus quantum as well as purpose is included. If part of the expense is incurred for tax avoidance purposes the whole of that expense is prevented from being deducted as a management expense.

Where there is also a disallowance of expenses under TA 1988 Sch 23A para 7A (manufactured payments with an unallowable purpose) the denial of relief under para 7A takes priority over the disallowance under s 75(2A).

The new anti avoidance test applies to amounts deemed to be management expenses under the Taxes Acts as well as to actual management expenses.

(3) After subsection (5) insert—

> "(5A) For the purposes of subsection (5)(*a*) above investments are not held for a business or other commercial purpose if they are held directly or indirectly in consequence of, or otherwise in connection with, any arrangements the main purpose, or one of the main purposes, of which is to secure the allowance of a deduction (or increased deduction) under subsection (1) above or any other tax advantage."

GENERAL NOTE

This makes it clear that if assets are held for purposes which include the avoidance of tax that is not a commercial or business purpose. This means that expenses incurred in respect of those assets will not be qualifying management expenses.

(4) After subsection (10) insert—

"(11) In this section—

"arrangements" includes any agreement, understanding, scheme, transaction or series of transactions (whether or not legally enforceable), and

"tax advantage" has the meaning given by section 840ZA."

GENERAL NOTE

This defines arrangements to include any agreement, understanding, and scheme, transaction or series of transactions (whether or not legally enforceable). Tax advantage takes the definition in TA 1988 s 840ZA.

(5) The amendments made by this section have effect in relation to accounting periods beginning on or after 20th June 2007, but have no effect in any case where the particular management expenses in question were paid before that date.

GENERAL NOTE

The amendments have full effect for accounting period beginning or after 20 June 2007, but have no effect where the management expenses were paid before that date.

(6) In the case of an accounting period of a company beginning before, and ending on or after, that date, those amendments have effect as if, for determining the amounts that are deductible for the period under section 75(1) of ICTA, so much of the period as falls before that date, and the rest of it, were separate accounting periods.

GENERAL NOTE

Where an accounting period straddles 20 June 2007 it is divided into two notional accounting periods at 20 June: only expenses attributable to the second notional account period are subject to the new rules.

29 Life policies etc: effect of rebated or reinvested commission

GENERAL NOTE

This is a specific anti-avoidance provision designed to exploit the fact that rebates of commission paid to individuals who are not financial traders in their own right are generally free of income tax. A number of investment products have been devised which are designed to give an investment return which is wholly or partly made up of rebated commission. Because this commission is tax free it gives a much higher equivalent rate of return compared with similar investments which produce taxable income.

The new rules are designed to stop these arrangements. They do not withdraw the exemption completely but put a financial limit on the investments which can attract tax-free commission rebates. This is doubtless to allow "normal" commission arrangements to continue, so that HMRC does not have to spend time dealing with amounts where the tax at risk is small.

EXAMPLE

The following may assist in explaining the background to these changes.

Mary invests £1m into a life insurance policy. The terms are such that commission of 5% is paid to Mary's advisor, who rebates the whole of the commission to Mary. The insurance company therefore only actually invests £950K into the bond. After one year the bond has grown in value from £950K to £1m and Mary gets back £1m.

In total therefore she has received £1m from the bond and £50K from the rebate of commission.

In calculating the gain on the bond Mary was able to deduct the £950K actually invested into the bond plus the £50K commission paid by the insurance company which was rebated to her. She therefore has neither a gain nor a loss on the bond. The £50K which she has received is rebated commission and is tax free in her hands. Therefore she would have made a 5% after-tax return on her investment. Had the insurance company invested the full £1m and not paid commission the bond might have grown to (say) £1,050,000 and she would have then paid income tax on the £50K growth on the bond.

Under the new rules the commission rebated to her would not be deductible in computing the gain on the bond and therefore she would have a taxable gain of £50K (i.e. the £1m she got back less the £950K actually invested into the bond). The commission itself is still tax free. So in total she will invest £1m, get back £1,050,000 and pay tax on £50,000. Her economic return and taxable income are thus back in synchronisation.

Section 29(1) introduces a new TA 1988 s 548A.

(1) In ICTA, after section 548 insert—

"548A Effect of rebated or reinvested commission in certain cases

(1) This section applies if—

(*a*) a relevant chargeable event occurs in respect of a policy or contract,

(*b*) commission in respect of the policy or contract has at any time been rebated or reinvested, and

(*c*) condition A or B is met.

GENERAL NOTE

This sets out the scope of the new provisions. The apply where there is a relevant chargeable event in respect of a policy or contract and commission in respect of the policy or contract has at any time been rebated or reinvested.

If these basic tests are met then there are two circumstances in which the new rules apply. These are set out in new TA 1988 s 548A(3).

(2) For the purposes of performing the calculation under section 541(1)(*b*) or (*c*) or 543(1)(*a*) or (*b*) for the chargeable event, the total amount paid under the policy or contract by way of premiums in any period is to be reduced by the total amount of commission attributable to those premiums that has been rebated or reinvested.

GENERAL NOTE

This is the substantive measure. In computing the gain arising on a chargeable event caught by the new rules no relief is given for the amount of commission which is paid on the policy if it has been rebated or reinvested.

(3) Condition A is that the total amount paid under the policy or contract by way of premiums in a relevant period exceeds £100,000.

GENERAL NOTE

This sets out the first of the two conditions mentioned in TA 1988 s 548A(1). The total premium paid under the policy or contract in the relevant period exceeds £100,000.

(4) Condition B is that—

(*a*) at a time when the policy or contract was the taxable person's, the taxable person's policies and contracts exceeded the relevant threshold as respects a relevant period, and

(*b*) payments under the policy or contract by way of premiums were made in that relevant period.

GENERAL NOTE

The second condition is designed to ensure that the new rule cannot be avoided by holding a number of separate policies, each of which is below the £100K limit. The second condition applies where all of a person's policies and contracts taken together exceed £100,000 AND payments were made under the policy or contract during the relevant period.

(5) In subsection (4)(*a*) "taxable person" means the person whose policy or contract the policy or contract is, immediately before the chargeable event.

GENERAL NOTE

In applying the test in TA 1988 s 548A(4) a taxable person is the person who holds the contract or policy immediately before the chargeable event.

(6) For the purposes of subsection (4)(*a*) a person's policies and contracts "exceed the relevant threshold" as respects a relevant period if the total amount of payments under them by way of premiums in that relevant period exceeds the sum specified in subsection (3).

GENERAL NOTE

This makes it clear that in applying the first of the tests in TA 1988 s 548A(4) you look at the total premiums paid in the relevant period, even if those policies were not at the time the property of the person to whom the chargeable event will arise.

(7) In this section "relevant chargeable event" means a chargeable event within—

(*a*) any of sub-paragraphs (ii) to (iv) of section 540(1)(*a*) (including those sub-paragraphs as they apply in relation to a qualifying policy),
(*b*) section 542(1)(*a*) or (*b*), or
(*c*) section 545(1)(*a*) to (*c*).

GENERAL NOTE

This is a drafting amendment to ensure consistency of definitions across this legislation.

(8) In this section "relevant period" means—

(*a*) the period beginning with the beginning of the year of assessment in which the chargeable event occurs and ending with the chargeable event, or
(*b*) any of the 3 preceding years of assessment.

GENERAL NOTE

The relevant period is the period between the beginning of the year of assessment in which the chargeable event occurs and ending with the chargeable event, or any of the three preceding years of assessment.

(9) References in this section to a premium include, in relation to a contract for a life annuity, lump sum consideration.

GENERAL NOTE

This defines a premium to include, in the case of a life annuity contract, lump sum consideration.

(10) The Treasury may by order—

(*a*) substitute another sum for the time being specified in subsection (3);
(*b*) amend the definition of "relevant period".

GENERAL NOTE

The Treasury is given power to change the £100,000 limit and amend the definition of relevant period.

548B Section 548A: further definitions

(1) This section supplements section 548A.

GENERAL NOTE

This introduces further definitions.

(2) "Commission", in relation to a policy or contract, includes any passing of value to or for the benefit of an intermediary, or a person connected with an intermediary, that can reasonably be taken to represent a reward in respect of the policy or contract.

GENERAL NOTE

This gives a detailed definition of commission.

(3) Commission in respect of a policy or contract is "reinvested" if, as a result of a waiver of an entitlement to it, there is an increase in the total value of a relevant person's policies and contracts.

(4) The amount of commission reinvested is the amount of the increase.

GENERAL NOTE

This defines what is meant by reinvestment of commission.

(5) Commission in respect of a policy or contract is "rebated" if—

(*a*) value passes (directly or indirectly) from an intermediary, or a person connected with an intermediary, to or for the benefit of a relevant person (and the passing of value does not amount to the reinvestment of the commission), and
(*b*) the passing of value can reasonably be taken to be in respect of the commission.

(6) The amount of commission rebated is the amount of value passed.

GENERAL NOTE

This defines what is meant by rebated commission.

(7) A policy or contract is a person's policy or contract if a gain arising in connection with it would be—

(*a*) a gain for which the person, or (if the person is an individual) the person's spouse or civil partner, would be liable to tax under Chapter 9 of Part 4 of ITTOIA 2005, or
(*b*) treated by virtue of section 547(1) above as forming part of the person's income.

GENERAL NOTE

This defines what is a person's policy or contract. It is a policy or contract where a gain arising in connection with it would be taxable on that person or on that person's spouse or civil partner, or it would be treated under TA 1988 s 547(1) as forming part of that person's income.

(8) Any necessary apportionment is to be made (on a just and reasonable basis) as regards—

(*a*) commission which is attributable to two or more premiums, and
(*b*) any part of such commission that has been rebated or reinvested.

(9) Commission which is in respect of one or more policies or contracts (but is not attributable to particular premiums) is to be attributed to such premiums as is just and reasonable.

GENERAL NOTE

These allow for just and reasonable apportionments to be made where premiums or commission are attributable to more than one contract.

(10) In subsections (3) and (5), "relevant person" means—

(*a*) any of the policyholders (including any of the persons who hold the contract),
(*b*) a person who beneficially owns the rights under the policy or contract,
(*c*) if those rights are held on trust, any of the trustees, or
(*d*) a person connected (within the meaning of section 839) with a person within any of paragraphs (*a*) to (*c*).

GENERAL NOTE

This defines relevant person.

(11) In subsections (8) and (9), references to a premium include, in relation to a contract for a life annuity, lump sum consideration."

GENERAL NOTE

This again states that premium includes, in relation to life annuity contracts, lump sum consideration.

(2) In section 552 of that Act (information: duty of insurers), after subsection (12) insert—

"(13) For the purposes of this section, no account is to be taken of the effect of section 548A above or section 541A of ITTOIA 2005."

GENERAL NOTE

This ensures that there are no additional reporting obligations for insurers as a result of these new provisions.

(3) In ITTOIA 2005, after section 541 insert—

"Rebated or reinvested commission

541A Effect of rebated or reinvested commission in certain cases

(1) This section applies if—

(*a*) a chargeable event within section 484(1)(*a*)(i) to (iii), (*c*) or (*e*) occurs in respect of a policy or contract,
(*b*) commission in respect of the policy or contract has at any time been rebated or reinvested, and
(*c*) condition A or B is met.

(2) For the purposes of performing the calculation in section 494 (total allowable deductions) for the chargeable event, the total amount of premiums under the policy or contract paid in the period mentioned in section 494(1) or (2)(*b*) is to be reduced by the total amount of commission attributable to those premiums that has been rebated or reinvested.

(3) Condition A is that the total amount of premiums under the policy or contract paid in a relevant period exceeds £100,000.

(4) Condition B is that—

(*a*) at a time when the policy or contract was the taxable person's, the taxable person's policies and contracts exceeded the relevant threshold as respects a relevant period, and

(*b*) premiums under the policy or contract were paid in that relevant period.

(5) In subsection (4)(*a*) "taxable person" means the person whose policy or contract the policy or contract is, immediately before the chargeable event.

(6) For the purposes of subsection (4)(*a*) a person's policies and contracts "exceed the relevant threshold" as respects a relevant period if the total amount of premiums under them paid in that relevant period exceeds the sum specified in subsection (3).

(7) In this section "relevant period" means—

(*a*) the period beginning with the beginning of the tax year in which the chargeable event occurs and ending with the chargeable event, or

(*b*) any of the 3 preceding tax years.

(8) The Treasury may by order—

(*a*) substitute another sum for the sum for the time being specified in subsection (3);

(*b*) amend the definition of "relevant period".

541B Section 541A: further definitions

(1) This section supplements section 541A.

(2) "Commission", in relation to a policy or contract, includes any passing of value to or for the benefit of an intermediary, or a person connected with an intermediary, that can reasonably be taken to represent a reward in respect of the policy or contract.

(3) Commission in respect of a policy or contract is "reinvested" if, as a result of a waiver of an entitlement to it, there is an increase in the total value of a relevant person's policies and contracts.

(4) The amount of commission reinvested is the amount of the increase.

(5) Commission in respect of a policy or contract is "rebated" if—

(*a*) value passes (directly or indirectly) from an intermediary, or a person connected with an intermediary, to or for the benefit of a relevant person (and the passing of value does not amount to the reinvestment of the commission), and

(*b*) the passing of value can reasonably be taken to be in respect of the commission.

(6) The amount of commission rebated is the amount of value passed.

(7) A policy or contract is a person's policy or contract if a gain arising in connection with it would be—

(*a*) a gain for which the person, or (if the person is an individual) the person's spouse or civil partner, would be liable to tax under this Chapter, or

(*b*) treated by virtue of section 547(1) of ICTA as forming part of the person's income.

(8) Any necessary apportionment is to be made (on a just and reasonable basis) as regards—

(*a*) commission which is attributable to two or more premiums, and

(*b*) any part of such commission that has been rebated or reinvested.

(9) Commission which is in respect of one or more policies or contracts (but is not attributable to particular premiums) is to be attributed to such premiums as is just and reasonable.

(10) In subsections (3) and (5), "relevant person" means—

(*a*) any of the policyholders (including any of the persons who hold the contract),

(*b*) a person who beneficially owns the rights under the policy or contract,

(*c*) if those rights are held on trust, any of the trustees, or

(*d*) a person connected with a person within any of paragraphs (*a*) to (*c*)."

GENERAL NOTE

This is potentially very confusing because it appears to duplicate everything that is in the new TA 1988 s 548B above.

The explanation is that we now have different acts for companies and individuals. Companies are still governed by TA 1988 and hence all of the above changes relate to companies. Individuals are, however, now governed by ITA 2007 and hence it is necessary to insert identical provisions into ITA 2007. So the tax law rewrite project has had the result here of doubling the amount of legislation needed to give effect to this change.

(4) The amendments made by this section have effect in relation to a policy or contract if—

(*a*) it is made on or after 21st March 2007, or

(*b*) on or after that date, any of its terms are varied, or a right under it is exercised, so as to increase the benefits under it.

30 Avoidance involving financial arrangements

Schedule 5 contains provision in relation to tax avoidance involving financial arrangements.

GENERAL NOTE

Section 30 introduces Schedule 5.

31 Companies carrying on business of leasing plant or machinery

Schedule 6 contains provision in relation to companies carrying on a business of leasing plant or machinery.

GENERAL NOTE

Section 31 introduces Schedule 6.

32 Restrictions on companies buying losses or gains: tax avoidance schemes

GENERAL NOTE

This is a highly technical amendment intended to block a loophole in the existing legislation denying relief for purchases and sales of companies which are primarily carried out to take advantage of their exiting capital losses.

The scheme which is blocked involved a group buying a capital loss company which also had a subsidiary company. There was no restriction on the set off of gains and losses on assets which were under common ownership before the change of ownership. So a gain on the disposal of the shares in the subsidiary could be set off against the capital loss in the acquired company. This was the case even if the subsidiary company's gain was in reality attributable to assets which it acquired after the capital loss company had been acquired by the new group.

An example will make this clearer.

EXAMPLE

XYZ Plc wants to acquire a capital loss company.

It identifies ABC as a company with a £10m capital loss.

In normal circumstances it cannot use the loss in ABC to offset gains on assets which it owned before it acquired ABC,

However if ABC has a subsidiary company EFG Ltd the shares of EFG Ltd are an asset of ABC Ltd predating the acquisition by XYZ Ltd. Therefore they are a pre-change assets and any gain that ABC makes on the disposal of the shares of EFG Ltd would not be caught by the anti-avoidance rules and thus could be set off against ABC's losses.

Until these new provisions were introduced there was nothing to stop the XYZ group, after it had acquired the shares of ABC Ltd, transferring some of its own pre-existing assets into EFG Ltd. This would increase the value of EFG Ltd . If ABC Ltd then sold the shares of EFG Ltd it would be able to set the gain made on the shares against the losses of XYZ Ltd, even through the gain was in reality attributable to the value of assets which XYZ Ltd had held before it acquired the shares in ABC Ltd.
The new provisions are intended to stop this by removing the relief for pre-change assets.

(1) TCGA 1992 is amended as follows.

GENERAL NOTE

This introduces amendments to TCGA 1992.

(2) In section 184A(2) (losses accruing on disposals of pre-change assets not deductible from gains unless gains accrue on disposals of pre-change assets), omit "unless the gains accrue to the company on a disposal of a pre-change asset".

GENERAL NOTE

This removes the reference to pre-change assets from TCGA 1992 s 184A(2).

(3) In section 184B(2) (losses not deductible from gains accruing on disposals of pre-change assets unless losses accrue on disposals of pre-change assets), omit "unless the loss accrues to the company on a disposal of a pre-change asset".

GENERAL NOTE

This removes the reference to pre-change assets from the corresponding provisions in TCGA 1992 s 194B restricting gains on pre-change assets being set against existing capital losses.

(4) Section 70 of FA 2006 (which inserted sections 184A to 184F of TCGA 1992) is amended as follows.

GENERAL NOTE

This introduces amendments to FA 2006 s 70.

(5) In subsection (9) (special provision for qualifying changes of ownership and disposals before 5th December 2005)—

(*a*) for "The following subsection applies" substitute "Subsections (10) to (12) apply",
(*b*) in paragraph (*a*), omit "or 184B",
(*c*) in paragraph (*c*), for "at all subsequent times," substitute "immediately afterwards,",
(*d*) after that paragraph insert—

"(ca) no qualifying change of ownership occurs at any time in relation to the principal company of that group for the purposes of section 184A of TCGA 1992 directly or indirectly in consequence of, or otherwise in connection with, any arrangements the main purpose, or one of the main purposes, of which is to secure a tax advantage falling within subsection (1)(*d*) of that section, and",

(*e*) omit paragraph (*d*) (together with the "and" following it), and
(*f*) in paragraph (*e*), omit ", or a qualifying gain for the purposes of section 184B of that Act,".

GENERAL NOTE

This rule simplifies the rules where a change of ownership is ignored for the purpose of the restrictions on capital loss relief. It slightly widens the circumstances in which a change of ownership is ignored.

Essentially it now allows the change of ownership rules to be ignored where there is takeover or merger of the original company or the company whose change of ownership gave rise to the qualifying loss is sold or liquidated.

However this is subject to a restriction which was introduced late in the Parliamentary process (press release 9 May 2007). The new relief will not apply where there is a change in ownership of the parent company and that company is acquired in consequence of arrangements where the main purpose, or one of the main purposes, is to secure a tax advantage which involves the deduction of a qualifying loss from a chargeable gain.

(6) For subsections (10) and (11) substitute—

"(10) Subsection (2) of that section has effect in relation to that qualifying loss subject to the following modifications.

(11) That subsection has effect as if there were inserted at the end of it "unless the gains accrue to the company on a disposal of a pre-change asset".

(12) That subsection (modified as mentioned above) has effect as if the reference to a pre-change asset included an asset held before the relevant time by any company—

(*a*) which, immediately before that time, was a member of the same group of companies as the relevant company, and

(*b*) which, throughout the period beginning with that time and ending immediately after the making of the disposal referred to in that subsection, has remained under the control of the company which was the principal company of that group at the relevant time.

(13) Expressions which are used in subsections (9) to (12) have the same meaning as in sections 184A and 184C of TCGA 1992."

GENERAL NOTE

This inserts new subsections (10)–(13) to FA 2006 s 70.

This is intended to preserve continuity of treatment under FA 2006 s 70 for losses where there is no economic change of ownership or where there is a loss triggered by a degrouping charge. This only applies where the qualifying losses were realised before 5 December 2005 (i.e. before the introduction of the previous anti-avoidance provisions).

(7) The amendment made by subsection (2) has effect in relation to gains accruing on disposals made on or after 21st March 2007.

(8) The amendment made by subsection (3) has effect in relation to losses accruing on disposals made on or after that date.

(9) The amendments made by subsections (5) and (6) have effect in relation to disposals made on or after that date; but the amendment made by subsection (5)(*d*) has no effect in relation to disposals made before 9th May 2007.

GENERAL NOTE

Subsections (7)–(9) set out the commencement rules. The new provisions apply to disposals of pre-change assets on or after 21 March 2007 (with the exception of new s 5(d) which only applies to disposals made on or after 9 May 2007.)

33 Lloyd's corporate members: restriction of group relief

GENERAL NOTE

This is another anti-avoidance measure prompted by disclosures made under Disclosure of Tax Avoidance Scheme rules.

The planning sought to exploit the rules relating to the taxation of corporate members of the Lloyd's insurance market. To simply a complex issue, the final result of Lloyd's syndicates are not known for three years. In other words a loss triggered in year one will only be declared in year four. The tax rules follow this, so that corporation tax relief for the loss will be available in year four. This loss would be available for surrender against the profits of other group companies in that year.

Towards the end of year three it is likely that the final amount of the profits/loss for year one will be known with some degree of certainty. A corporate group could therefore buy a loss making corporate member of Lloyds towards the end of year three, so that in year four, when the loss actually arises for tax purposes, the loss is available for group relief against profits of members of that new corporate group.. A group is not likely to want to take on the risk of buying an open syndicate, so in practice such schemes are only likely to have been carried out in cases where the corporate member had decided to withdraw from the market.

This type of arrangement is blocked by these new provisions.

Section 33(1) introduces a new FA 1994 s 227A.

(1) In FA 1994, after section 227 insert—

"227A Restriction of group relief

(1) Losses of the last active underwriting year of a corporate member are not eligible for surrender by the corporate member as group relief to another company unless the group-relief continuity condition is satisfied.

GENERAL NOTE

This restricts group relief for losses of a corporate member for the last active underwriting year unless what is termed the "group relief continuity condition" is met.

(2) In this section "last active underwriting year", in relation to a corporate member, means—

(*a*) if the corporate member writes insurance business in only one underwriting year, that underwriting year, and

(*b*) otherwise, the last underwriting year in which the corporate member writes insurance business.

GENERAL NOTE

The last active underwriting year is the last underwriting year in which the corporate member writes insurance business, unless the corporate member only wrote business in one year, in which case that year is the last active underwriting year.

(3) Where in an underwriting year—

(*a*) the corporate member writes an amount of insurance business which is insignificant when compared with that written by it in the preceding underwriting year, or

(*b*) the only insurance business written by the corporate member consists of the acceptance of reinsurance to close premiums,

the underwriting year is not to be regarded for the purposes of subsection (2)(*b*) above as an underwriting year in which the corporate member writes insurance business.

GENERAL NOTE

It would be easy to circumvent this rule by arranging for the corporate member to undertake a trivial amount of underwriting in a subsequent year when, to all intents and purposes, it had already ceased its real underwriting business. To prevent this a year in which a member writes an amount of insurance business that is trivial compared to that written in the previous year is not to be regarded as a year in which it is writing insurance business.

Acceptance of reinsurance to a close premiums is not regarded as writing insurance business.

(4) In subsection (3)(*b*) above "reinsurance to close premium" means a premium or other consideration under a contract in pursuance of which, in accordance with the rules or practice of Lloyd's, one underwriting member agrees with another to meet liabilities arising from the latter's underwriting business in an underwriting year so that the accounts of the business for that year may be closed.

GENERAL NOTE

This defines reinsurance to a close.

(5) The group-relief continuity condition is satisfied if the corporate member (as the surrendering company) and the other company (as the claimant company) meet the conditions in section 402(2) or (3) of the Taxes Act 1988 throughout the period—

(*a*) beginning with the last day of the last active underwriting year of the corporate member, and

(*b*) ending with the first day of the first underwriting year in which losses of the last active underwriting year are declared."

GENERAL NOTE

This defines the group-relief continuity condition. The corporate member (which will be the surrendering company for group relief purposes) must meet all of the normal group relief requirements by reference to the claimant company for the whole of the period from the last day of the last active underwriting period to the first day of the first underwriting year in which the losses of the last active underwriting year are declared.

In other words if the company is acquired after the end of the last active underwriting period then the losses cannot be used as group relief against the profits of the acquiring company. As the scheme relied on the corporate member having ceased to be an active underwriting member before it was acquired by the group wishing to use its losses this means that the scheme has effectively been blocked.

(2) The amendment made by subsection (1) has effect in relation to any case where the corporate member (as the surrendering company) and the other company (as the claimant company) first meet the conditions in section 402(2) or (3) of ICTA on or after 21st March 2007.

GENERAL NOTE

The new rules apply where the surrendering company and the claimant company first meet the group relief conditions in TA 1988 s 402(2) or (3) on or after 21 March 2007.

34 Employee benefit contributions

GENERAL NOTE

Employee Benefit Trusts [EBTs] have been a thorn in the side of HMRC for many years. The basic principle underlying all the various EBT schemes is that funds were contributed to an EBT, thus creating a corporation tax deduction, without those funds reaching the hands of employees in taxable form. Many different schemes have been used over the years but they all rely on attempts to create asymmetry between corporation tax and PAYE/NIC.

HMRC had some success in combating EBT schemes through the decision in the *Dextra* case, and modern accountancy practice (particularly UITF 32) has made it less easy for companies to charge EBT contributions through their profit and loss accounts where they still retain effective economic control of the funds. But EBT schemes have proved very durable. ITTOIA 2005 contains rules which prevent companies from obtaining tax relief for employee benefit contributions unless, within 9 months of the end of the accounting period in which the contribution is made, the funds are paid out in a form which attracts PAYE and NIC.

The DOTAS regime disclosures have shown that it has been possible to get round these rules by arranging matters so that a company declares a trust round part of its own funds. In these cases there is no actual contribution to an EBT and as such there is nothing to disallow. The company has still, however, deprived itself of the benefit of those funds in favour of its employees and is thus, it is argued, entitled to a deduction under general principles for the amount of those funds.

These new provision seek to block this device.

(1) Schedule 24 to FA 2003 (restriction on deductions for employee benefit contributions) is amended as follows.

GENERAL NOTE

This introduces amendments to FA 2003 Sch 24.

(2) In paragraph 1 (restriction of deductions), for sub-paragraphs (1) and (2) substitute—

"(1) This Schedule applies if, in calculating for corporation tax purposes the profits of a person ("the employer") for a period, a deduction would otherwise be allowable for the period in respect of employee benefit contributions made or to be made (but see paragraph 8).

GENERAL NOTE

The language is recast. The schedule now refers to Employee Benefit Contributions made or to be made.

An employee benefit contribution arises where, as a result of any act or omission, property is held, or may be used, under an employee benefit scheme, or there is an increase in the total value of property that is so held or may be so used (or a reduction in any liabilities under an EBT scheme).

The effect of this is to move away from looking at the mechanism under which the EBT acquired funds and instead to look at matters from the perspective of the EBT. If there is an increase in the value of property held under an EBT scheme then there is an EBT contribution and that contribution is subject to the normal anti-avoidance rule in FA 2003 Sch 24.

(2) For the purposes of this Schedule, an "employee benefit contribution" is made if, as a result of any act or omission—

(*a*) property is held, or may be used, under an employee benefit scheme, or

(*b*) there is an increase in the total value of property that is so held or may be so used (or a reduction in any liabilities under an employee benefit scheme)."

(3) In paragraph 3, for "the third party" substitute "a scheme manager".

(4) In paragraph 4—

(*a*) in sub-paragraphs (1) and (2), for "the third party" (in both places) substitute "a scheme manager", and

(*b*) in sub-paragraph (3), for "third party" substitute "scheme manager".

(5) In paragraph 5, for "the third party" (in both places) substitute "a scheme manager".

(6) In paragraph 9(1) (interpretation)—

(*a*) after the definition of "relevant migrant member" insert—

""scheme manager" means a person who administers an employee benefit scheme (acting in that capacity);", and

(*b*) omit the definition of "the third party".

GENERAL NOTE

The existing EBT provisions are written in term of contributions to third parties (i.e. the EBT). In schemes where a company declares a trust round its own funds there is no third party. References to third parties are thus replaced by reference to the scheme manager. A scheme manager is a "person who administers an EBT scheme (acting in that capacity)" The words in brackets are to distinguish a person who is acting in his capacity as scheme manager from any other capacity in which is acting (say as company secretary or director).

(7) Part 2 of ITTOIA 2005 (trading income) is amended as follows.

(8) In section 38 (restriction of deductions for employee benefit contributions), for subsection (1) substitute—

"(1) This section applies if, in calculating for income tax purposes the profits of a trade of a person ("the employer") for a period, a deduction would otherwise be allowable for the period in respect of employee benefit contributions made or to be made (but see subsection (4))."

(9) In section 39 (making of "employee benefit contributions), for subsection (1) substitute—

"(1) For the purposes of section 38, an "employee benefit contribution" is made if, as a result of any act or omission—

(*a*) property is held, or may be used, under an employee benefit scheme, or

(*b*) there is an increase in the total value of property that is so held or may be so used (or a reduction in any liabilities under an employee benefit scheme)."

(10) In section 41 (timing and amount of certain benefits), for "the third party" (in both places) substitute "a scheme manager".

(11) In section 42 (provision or payment out of employee benefit contributions)—

(*a*) in subsection (1), for "the third party", in the first place, substitute "a scheme manager" and, in the second place, substitute "the scheme manager",

(*b*) in subsection (3), for "the third party", in the first place, substitute "a scheme manager" and, in the second place, substitute "the scheme manager", and

(*c*) in subsection (5), for "third party" substitute "scheme manager".

(12) In section 44(1) (interpretation), for the definition of "the third party" substitute—

""scheme manager" means a person who administers an employee benefit scheme (acting in that capacity)."

GENERAL NOTE

Again, because the rules for companies and individuals are in different Acts there are identical clauses for income tax purposes. These would apply where a sole trader, or more likely a partnership, establishes an EBT for its employees.

(13) The amendments made by this section have effect in relation to employee benefit contributions made on or after 21st March 2007.

GENERAL NOTE

The new rules apply to EBT contributions (as defined) made on or after 21 March 2007.

35 Schemes etc designed to increase double taxation relief

GENERAL NOTE

TA 1988 s 804ZA contains complex rules to prevent the avoidance of tax through obtaining increased double taxation relief. HMRC has received disclosures under the DOTAS regime which claim to sidestep s 804ZA by arguing that it is in fact UK tax relief rather than foreign tax which is being claimed in a double taxation relief claim. HMRC does not accept this argument but FA 2007 s 35 is designed to put the matter beyond doubt.

(1) Section 804ZA of ICTA (schemes and arrangements designed to increase relief) is amended as follows.

GENERAL NOTE

This introduces amendments to TA 1988 s 804ZA.

(2) In subsection (8)(*c*), omit "resident in a territory outside the United Kingdom".

GENERAL NOTE

This puts beyond doubt that a notice under TA 1988 s 804ZA may specify a UK company as well as a non-UK one.

(3) After subsection (11) insert—

"(11A) In this section "foreign tax" includes any tax which for the purpose of allowing credit under any arrangements against corporation tax is treated by section 801 as if it were tax payable under the law of any territory outside the United Kingdom."

GENERAL NOTE

This is designed to confirm that TA 1988 s 804ZA includes UK tax as well as tax under the laws of any other territory.

(4) The amendments made by this section have effect in relation to a credit for foreign tax which relates to—

(*a*) a payment of foreign tax on or after 6th December 2006, or

(*b*) income received on or after that date in respect of which foreign tax has been deducted at source,

but see also subsections (6) and (7).

GENERAL NOTE

The new rules apply to credits for foreign tax which relate to payments of foreign tax on or after 6 December 2006 or income received on or after that date in respect of which foreign tax has been deducted at source.

(5) In subsection (4)—

(*a*) references to foreign tax are to be construed in accordance with section 804ZA(11A) of ICTA (as inserted by subsection (3) above), and

(*b*) the reference to tax deducted at source is to tax deducted (or treated as deducted) from income or treated as paid in respect of income.

GENERAL NOTE

This is a drafting amendment.

(6) The DTR anti-avoidance provisions have effect in relation to any action (or failure to act) that occurs under any scheme or arrangement on or after 6th December 2006 (as well as in relation to the cases mentioned in section 87(3) of FA 2005 or subsection (4) above).

(7) "The DTR anti-avoidance provisions" means section 804ZA of ICTA (as amended by this section), sections 804ZB and 80ZC of that Act and Schedule 28AB to that Act.

GENERAL NOTE

These ensure that TA 1988 s 804ZA (and the associated legislation) applies to schemes or arrangements where any action under them occurs on or after 6 December 2006.

Capital allowances

36 Industrial and agricultural buildings allowances

(1) No balancing adjustment is to be made under Part 3 of CAA 2001 (industrial buildings allowances) if—

(*a*) the qualifying expenditure in question is not qualifying enterprise zone expenditure for the purposes of that Part, and

(*b*) the balancing event in question is a post-commencement balancing event,

and in paragraph (*b*) "post-commencement balancing event" means any balancing event for the purposes of that Part which occurs on or after 21st March 2007, but does not include an event which occurs before 1st April 2011 in pursuance of a relevant pre-commencement contract (see subsection (7)).

(2) For the purposes of section 311 of that Act (calculation of allowance after sale of relevant interest) the amount of the residue of qualifying expenditure immediately after a post-commencement relevant event is taken to be the amount of the residue of qualifying expenditure immediately before that event.

(3) In subsection (2)—

"qualifying expenditure" does not include any expenditure which is qualifying enterprise zone expenditure for the purposes of that Part, and

"post-commencement relevant event" means any relevant event within the meaning of section 311 of that Act which occurs on or after 21st March 2007, but does not include an event which occurs before 1st April 2011 in pursuance of a relevant pre-commencement contract.

(4) No balancing adjustment is to be made under Part 4 of that Act (agricultural buildings allowances) if the balancing event in question is a post-commencement balancing event.

(5) For the purposes of section 376 of that Act (calculation of allowance after acquisition) the amount of the residue of qualifying expenditure immediately after a post-commencement balancing event is taken to be the amount of the residue of qualifying expenditure immediately before that event.

(6) In subsections (4) and (5) "post-commencement balancing event" means any balancing event under section 381 of that Act (as a result of an election made in accordance with section 382 of that Act) which occurs on or after 21st March 2007, but does not include an event which occurs before 1st April 2011 in pursuance of a relevant pre-commencement contract.

(7) For the purposes of this section a contract is "a relevant pre-commencement contract" if—

(*a*) the contract is a contract in writing made before 21st March 2007,

(*b*) the contract is unconditional or its conditions have been satisfied before that date,

(*c*) no terms remain to be agreed on or after that date, and

(*d*) the contract is not varied in a significant way on or after that date.

GENERAL NOTE

This section withdraws, with immediate effect, balancing adjustments and the recalculation of writing-down allowances for purchasers of second-hand industrial buildings. Though not announced as such, this is in effect a pre-emptive anti-avoidance measure, pending the phasing-out of industrial buildings allowances by April 2011, announced in the Budget.

Presently, when a second-hand industrial building is sold, the vendor is subject to a 'balancing adjustment' (a balancing charge or allowance) which has the general effect of ensuring that the net allowances obtained by the vendor equate to the fall in economic value of the building during his ownership. If a building is sold at a profit, this can mean that all allowances given to the vendor in earlier years are clawed back in the year of disposal.

The purchaser would be able to claim allowances going forward, based on the 'residue after sale' (which in most cases, in an age of rising property prices, equates to the original cost of construction) which is written off equally over the period between his acquisition of the property and (in most cases) the 25th anniversary of the building first being used.

With effect from 21 March 2007, the treatment for both vendor and purchaser changes. Instead, for IBA purposes, the building will effectively be transferred at it tax written-down value, so that no balancing adjustment is made on the vendor, and the purchaser merely 'inherits' the vendor's annual claim.

There are similar provisions for agricultural buildings allowances.

Transitional provisions apply, which mean the old rules and treatment apply to transactions on or after 21 March 2007, in pursuance of a 'pre-commencement contract'. This is defined as a written contract in existence at 21 March 2007, which is unconditional or where all conditions have been met, and which is not varied in any significant way after 21 March 2007.

37 Temporary increase in first-year capital allowances for small enterprises

(1) The amount of a first-year allowance under section 44 of CAA 2001 (expenditure incurred by small or medium-sized enterprises) is to be determined, in the case of expenditure to which this subsection applies, as if the percentage specified in the entry relating to that section in the Table in section 52(3) of that Act were 50%.

(2) Subsection (1) applies to expenditure incurred by a small enterprise (within the meaning of section 44 of that Act) in the period of 12 months beginning with—

(*a*) 1st April 2007, if the small enterprise is within the charge to corporation tax, or

(*b*) 6th April 2007, if the small enterprise is within the charge to income tax.

(3) Accordingly, in section 52(3) of CAA 2001, in the sentence following the Table, insert at the end—

"(*c*) section 37 of the Finance Act 2007 (substitution of 50% in the case of expenditure incurred by a small enterprise in 2007–08 or financial year 2007)."

GENERAL NOTE

Expenditure on plant by small enterprises attracts a first year allowance of 50% of the amount of the expenditure. The allowance has been extended for another year.

The rate of first year allowance for medium-sized enterprises remains unchanged at 40%.

Whether an enterprise is small or medium-sized is determined by applying the criteria set out in the Companies Act 1985 s 247.

Insurance and friendly societies

38 Insurance companies: gross roll-up business etc

(1) Part 1 of Schedule 7 contains provisions relating to gross roll-up business, capital redemption business and miscellaneous minor matters relating to insurance companies.

(2) The amendments made by that Part of that Schedule have effect—

(*a*) for the purposes of corporation tax, for periods of account of insurance companies beginning on or after 1st January 2007, and

(*b*) for the purposes of income tax, for the tax year 2007–08 and subsequent tax years.

(3) Subsection (2) is subject to the transitional provisions in Part 2 of that Schedule.

GENERAL NOTE

Section 38 is the first of four sections introducing Schedules 7 to 10 that make major revisions to the corporation tax provisions applying to life insurance companies. These changes stem from a consultation process announced at the time of the 2006 Budget. Since the publication of a technical consultation document in May 2006 the insurance industry, the Association of British Insurers (as representatives of the industry) and HMRC have been involved in intensive discussions aimed at simplifying the tax code for life insurance companies and making changes to it to deal with issues affecting both the industry and HMRC.

Section 38 introduces Sch 7 which simplifies the tax law relating to the categories of business which are taxed under Schedule D Case VI. These five categories, pension business, overseas life assurance business ("OLAB"), life reinsurance business, ISA business and child trust fund business, share many features in common, in particular that the investment return accruing for the benefit of policy holders rolls up gross of tax and the company is taxed on the profit it makes from writing the business. From 1 January 2007 these categories are amalgamated for tax computation purposes into one category that will be known as gross roll up business. Notwithstanding the amalgamation for computational purposes, the separate categories remain important for tax so their definitions have been retained and, in some cases, amended.

Although Sch 7 contains the necessary statutory provisions to give effect to this change, the greater part of the schedule is given over to the consequential amendments caused by the redefinition.

The initial consultation considered an alternative approach under which permanent health insurance business ("PHI") would also be included in the gross roll up category but this was rejected as unsatisfactory by both the industry and HMRC. The reasons for rejecting this option were based on the fact that PHI is taxed on a Schedule D Case I basis. For the industry the loss of the exemption from corporation tax on dividends provided by TA 1988 s 208 was thought to be too high a cost to bear; while HMRC were faced with the prospect of giving tax relief on deferred acquisition costs that are spread forward in the statutory accounts but which would be written off all at once if the taxation basis for PHI moved to follow the FSA return in the same way as it does for life insurance business. It is possible however that this further amalgamation may be reconsidered in the future.

39 Insurance companies: basis of taxation etc

(1) Part 1 of Schedule 8 contains provision about the basis of taxation of insurance companies and related matters.

(2) The amendments made by that Part of that Schedule have effect for periods of account of insurance companies beginning on or after 1st January 2007.

(3) Subsection (2) is subject to the transitional provisions in Part 2 of that Schedule.

GENERAL NOTE

Section 39 introduces Schedule 8 which is another development arising from the consultation process although the particular subject matter of the schedule, the exercise of the Crown Option, was not one of the four workstreams originally set up under the consultation.

Although life insurance business is a trade, the profits of which may be assessed under Schedule D Case I, it has long been established in case law that HMRC are not obliged to assess profits under Schedule D Case I if there is an alternative head of charge available. HMRC are therefore entitled to forgo the right to assess profits under Schedule D Case I, and instead to assess the investment income of the company plus gains on the realisation of investments calculated according to the capital gains tax rules allowing relief for management expenses, the so-called I-E basis. The exercise of this choice by HMRC is referred to as the Crown Option. The effect is that nearly all life insurance companies, with the exception of pure reinsurers, are taxed on the I-E basis which, despite having been used for over a century, was not defined in statute until it was codified in F(No2)A 1992 s 65(3)(*a*).

The phrase Crown Option does not mean that HMRC must decide on a year by year basis whether to invoke it or not. HMRC are of the view that it is appropriate to change the basis of assessment only if there is a gradual change in the company's activities or there is an isolated but significant change in the company's business, often associated in HMRC's eyes with tax avoidance. In the former case HMRC have in the past looked to give the company as much notice as possible of their intention to change the basis of assessment; in the latter case an immediate change would normally be appropriate. It is this very uncertainty as to when the option might be exercised that has led the industry to ask that the taxation basis for life insurance companies be put on a firm statutory footing. Schedule 8 therefore now puts into statute the existing position based on judicial precedent and past practice.

The measures introduced by s 39 are effective for periods of account beginning on or after 1 January 2007.

40 Insurance companies: transfers etc

Schedule 9 contains provision about transfers by insurance companies and related matters.

GENERAL NOTE

Section 40 is the third section relating to life insurance company taxation coming from the 2006 consultation exercise. It introduces Schedule 9 which makes changes to the rules for taxing the transfer of insurance business from one company to another under the provisions of FSMA 2000 Part VII.

41 Insurance companies: miscellaneous

Schedule 10 contains miscellaneous provisions relating to insurance companies.

GENERAL NOTE

Section 41 introduces Schedule 10 which is the fourth and final output from the consultation process begun last year. Unlike its three predecessors, Sch 10 does not deal with one discrete area of the corporation tax regime for life insurance companies, rather it picks up a number of issues covered in the original consultation document as well as some others that arose during the consultation process. It also tidies up the legislation, repealing a number of obsolete provisions and providing clarification about others.

42 Technical provisions made by general insurers

Schedule 11 contains provision in relation to technical provisions made by general insurers.

GENERAL NOTE

Section 42 introduces Schedule 11 which makes changes to the tax rules about the extent to which reserves established by a general insurer are allowable for tax purposes.

43 Lloyd's: cessation of business by corporate members

(1) In FA 1994, after section 227A (inserted by section 33) insert—

"227B Transfer of underwriting business without change of ownership

(1) This section applies where, in accordance with the rules or practice of Lloyd's, a corporate member ("the successor") has taken up the syndicate capacity of another corporate member ("the predecessor").

(2) Section 343 of the Taxes Act 1988 (company reconstructions without a change of ownership) applies as if—

(*a*) the trade mentioned in that section were the underwriting business of the predecessor,

(*b*) the predecessor ceases to carry it on, and the successor begins to carry it on, at the end of the first underwriting year in which profits or losses of the predecessor's last active underwriting year are declared, and

(*c*) subsections (8) to (10) and (12) were omitted.

(3) For the purposes of subsection (1) above the successor has taken up the predecessor's syndicate capacity if it has taken up the rights to participate in syndicates which were (or otherwise would be) offered to the predecessor.

(4) In subsection (2)(*b*) above "last active underwriting year" has the same meaning as in section 227A above (see subsections (2) to (4) of that section)."

(2) The amendment made by subsection (1) has effect in any case where the first underwriting year in which profits or losses of the predecessor's final underwriting year are declared is 2007 or a later underwriting year.

GENERAL NOTE

TA 1988 s 343 applies where one company ("the predecessor") ceases to carry on a trade or part of a trade and another company ("the successor") begins to carry it on. Provided certain conditions are met, any unused trading losses of the predecessor's trade can be utilised by the successor against future profits of the same trade (or part trade).

Because a year of account at Lloyd's remains open for at least three years, HMRC have always held the view that s 343 could not apply to Lloyd's corporate members.

The primary reason for this view was that there would be a period of overlap where both the predecessor and the successor were trading, and therefore the requirement for one company to cease the trade at a particular point in time and at the same time for another company to begin to carry it on could not be met.

FA 2007 introduces s 227B to FA 1994, which applies s 343 to Lloyd's corporate members as if the trade in question is the underwriting business. It is understood that HMRC intend to look at all of the facts in determining whether a transfer of the underwriting business has occurred. This new provision should allow Lloyd's groups with several corporate members to consolidate their business into one corporate member without losing the benefit of any unused trading losses.

In applying s 343 to Lloyd's, the ownership requirements contained within s 343(1) must be met.

FA 1994 s 227B applies where, under the rules and practices of Lloyd's, one corporate member takes up the capacity of another. The successor is regarded as having taken up the capacity rights of the predecessor where it takes up capacity rights which were offered to the predecessor or which "otherwise would be" offered to the predecessor. Where a Lloyd's group is reducing the number of corporate members through a consolidation, there is no physical transfer of capacity from one member to another. Instead, the predecessor gives up its right to participate on the syndicate and the successor increases its capacity. In this case, the successor should be regarded as having taken up the capacity rights which were offered to the predecessor.

Section 227B can also apply where there has been a merger of syndicates. For example, in 2007 corporate member 1 participates only on syndicate 1 and corporate member 2 participates only on syndicate 2. In the subsequent year, the business of syndicate 2 is transferred to syndicate 1 following a merger of the two syndicates, but corporate member 2 does not take up any right to participate on syndicate 1, instead corporate member 1 increases its capacity. Provided that corporate member 1 can be said to have taken up the rights to participate on syndicate 1 which corporate member 2 would have been offered had it been continuing then corporate member 1 should be regarded as having taken up the syndicate capacity of corporate member 2. HMRC are unlikely to require that the total combined capacity of the group prior to the consolidation/merger be exactly equal to the total combined capacity after, but you might expect the capacity of the successor to increase as a result of the consolidation/merger. Again, HMRC will look at the facts in determining whether there has been a transfer of the underwriting business to corporate member 1 from corporate member 2 for the purposes of TA 1988 s 343.

Section 343 requires there to be no overlap between the predecessor ceasing to carry on the trade and the successor starting to carry it on. Since, a Lloyd's year of account remains open for three years there will always be a period of overlap. FA 2004 s 227B(2)(b) determines that for the purposes of s 343 only the point at which the predecessor is regarded as having ceased to carry on the underwriting business and the successor begins to carry it on, is the last day of the year in which the profits of the predecessor's last active underwriting year are first declared. The final underwriting year is defined in s 227A and is the last underwriting year in which the member writes business. For example, if the predecessor writes on the 2004 year of account but the successor takes up the right to participate on the 2005 year of account, the last active underwriting year of the predecessor would be 2004. The profits of the 2004 year of account are first declared in 2007. Any unused trading losses as at 31 December 2007 would therefore be available for the successor to offset any profits of its trade from 1 January 2008. If the predecessor goes into run off at 31 December 2006, then any unused losses as at 31 December 2007 will not be available to offset future profits of the trade of the predecessor.

TA 1988 s 343(8)–(10) of s 343 do not apply to Lloyd's, and therefore any unused losses of the predecessor's trade are available for offset against all of the profits of the successor's trade, and not limited to the profits arising from the trade transferred from the predecessor.

Section 343 will not apply to Lloyd's if there is only a part transfer of the underwriting business.

44 Transfers of business by friendly societies to insurance companies etc

Schedule 12 contains provisions about transfers of business by friendly societies to insurance companies etc

GENERAL NOTE

Section 44 and Schedule 12 provide for continuing exemption of certain friendly society business transferred to life offices.

45 Tax exempt business of friendly societies

(1) Section 462 of ICTA (conditions for tax exempt business) is amended as follows.

(2) For subsection (1) substitute—

"(1) Subject to subsections (2) to (4) below, section 460 does not afford any exemption from corporation tax in relation to so much of the profits arising to a friendly society or insurance company from any business as is attributable to a policy which—

(*a*) is not a qualifying policy (by virtue of sub-paragraph (2) of paragraph 6 of Schedule 15) and is not an excluded policy, and

(*b*) would not be a qualifying policy (by virtue of that sub-paragraph) if all excluded policies were left out of account.

(1A) For the purposes of subsection (1) above a policy is an excluded policy if—

(*a*) it is a policy held otherwise than with the friendly society or insurance company, or

(*b*) the person who has the contract effecting the policy acquired the rights under it on an assignment (or, in Scotland, assignation) otherwise than for money or money's worth."

(3) In subsection (2), for "under section 460(1) for profits arising from any part of a life or endowment" substitute "in relation to profits arising from any part of a".

(4) In subsection (3), for the words after "section" substitute "460 does not afford any exemption from corporation tax in relation to so much as is attributable to that policy of the profits of the friendly society or insurance company concerned."

(5) In section 462A(8)(*b*) of ICTA (election to tax exempt business), for ""societies"" substitute ""policies"".

(6) The amendments made by this section are deemed to have come into force on 1st January 2007.

GENERAL NOTE

Section 45 provides partial relief for friendly society policies assigned other than for money or monies worth.

Life or Endowment Business (L or E business) is defined in TA 1988 s 466 and is applicable only to business entered into by friendly societies. It includes life assurance business plus some hybrid and miner classes. The funds underlying L or E business are exempt from corporation tax to the extent that the member holds policies under which premiums do not exceed £270 per annum or £25 per month. If the policy meets certain conditions it is a qualifying policy and the member is not normally taxable on benefits received.

Before the Act, the provisions were as follows. TA1988 s 464 sets out the above benefit limits. TA 1988 Sch 15 para 6(2) removes qualifying status from any policy which causes the s 464 limits to be breached. Such a breach might arise when a policy is assigned to a spouse who already holds a policy, the assignment perhaps being under a divorce settlement. Section 462 removes exempt status from a policy which has lost its qualifying status by virtue of Sch 15 para 6(2) above, but only if such status would be lost if all policies with other societies are ignored.

The provision recognises that a society may not know of the existence of policies with other societies. Exemption is only lost if policies with the society in question breach the limits. In testing for loss of exemption, there is a disregard for policies with other societies. FA 2007 s 45 extends this disregard to all policies which have been assigned to a member other than for money or monies worth.

Example. A husband and wife each hold a policy for the maximum exempt limit with the same society. A divorce court orders assignment of the policy from the husband to the wife. The wife then holds two policies which together breach her limit. The policy which caused the breach becomes non-qualifying. Benefits received from it become fully subject to income tax. However, the effect of s 45 is that the policy remains exempt and the underlying funds of the society retain exemption from corporation tax. The result would be the same if the policies were not with same society. Section 45 is deemed to come into force on 1 January 2007, apparently granting exemption from that date, whenever the assignment took place.

Note that neither the pre-existing legislation nor s 45 gives any guidance as to how to determine which policy causes the breach in the circumstances described.

46 Purchased life annuities: self-assessment

(1) In section 437(1C) of ICTA (general annuity business), omit paragraphs (*c*)(i) and (*d*)(i).

(2) In section 656 of that Act (purchased life annuities other than retirement annuities), omit subsections (5) and (6).

(3) In section 658 of that Act (supplementary), omit subsections (1) and (4) to (6).

(4) In section 828(4) of that Act (parliamentary procedure for orders and regulations), omit "658(3)".

(5) In section 717 of ITTOIA 2005 (exemption for part of purchased life annuity payment), omit subsection (3).

(6) Omit section 723 of that Act (officer of Revenue and Customs to determine certain questions).

(7) In section 724 of that Act (regulations)—

(*a*) in subsection (1)(*a*), for "723" substitute "722", and
(*b*) omit subsection (2).

(8) In section 873(3) of that Act (parliamentary procedure for orders and regulations), omit paragraph (*b*).

(9) The amendments made by subsections (1) to (3) and (5) to (7) come into force on such day as the Treasury may by order appoint; and different days may be appointed for different purposes.

GENERAL NOTE

Section 46 deals with procedural matters only, in respect of purchased life annuities.

Since 1956 a purchased life annuity has been regarded partially as a return of capital. The capital element is not subject to tax in the hands of the recipient. Since 1993, the paying life office gets a deduction only for the interest element, being the whole less the capital element.

ITTOIA 2005 s 723 requires HMRC to determine eligibility for, and the amount of, the capital element. This has applied on a case by case basis notwithstanding that both aspects are laid down in detail in statute and regulation.

The cumbersome process of individual certification by HMRC does not sit well with self assessment and is to be discontinued.

Section 46 repeals the relevant procedural provisions from a date to be set out in regulations. Regulations to be drafted after consultation with interested parties will also specify a replacement procedure.

There is no intention to change the amount of tax payable on purchased life annuities. It is a procedural change.

Repos

47 Sale and repurchase of securities

(1) Schedule 13 contains provision for corporation tax purposes about the sale and repurchase of securities.

(2) Schedule 14 contains minor and consequential amendments in relation to the sale and repurchase of securities.

(3) The Treasury may by order make such other amendments (including repeals and revocations) of enactments or instruments as may appear appropriate in consequence of, or otherwise in connection with, those Schedules.

(4) Schedule 13, and the amendments made by Schedule 14, have effect in accordance with provision made by the Treasury by order.

(5) Any order under this section—

(*a*) may make different provision for different purposes, and
(*b*) may contain transitional provision and savings.

GENERAL NOTE

This section introduces Schedule 13 (which sets out the new corporation tax regime for repos, replacing the existing rules in TA 1988 ss 731–738) and Schedule 14 (which makes minor and consequential amendments). The new rules will apply from a day to be appointed by Treasury order.

CFCs

48 Controlled foreign companies

Schedule 15 contains provision in relation to controlled foreign companies.

GENERAL NOTE

This section introduces Schedule 15.

R&D

49 Vaccine research relief: amount of deduction for SMEs

(1) Part 2 of Schedule 13 to FA 2002 (manner of giving effect to vaccine research relief: small and medium-sized companies) is amended as follows.

(2) In paragraph 14 (deduction in computing profits of trade), for sub-paragraph (2) substitute—

"(2) The appropriate deduction is 50% of the qualifying expenditure."

(3) In paragraph 15 (alternative treatment of pre-trading expenditure: deemed trading loss)—

(*a*) in sub-paragraph (2)(*b*), for the words from "not" to the end substitute "non-Schedule 20 expenditure.", and

(*b*) after sub-paragraph (6) insert—

"(7) Qualifying expenditure is "non-Schedule 20 expenditure" if the company is not entitled to relief under Schedule 20 to the Finance Act 2000 in respect of it."

(4) In paragraph 16 (entitlement to tax credit), for sub-paragraph (3) substitute—

"(3) The amount of the surrenderable loss is equal to the lower of A and B where—

A is so much of the trading loss referred to in sub-paragraph (2) as is unrelieved, and

B is—

(*a*) if paragraph 14 applies, the sum of the amount deductible under that paragraph and so much of the qualifying expenditure mentioned in that paragraph as is non-Schedule 20 expenditure;

(*b*) if paragraph 15 applies, the total deemed trading loss under that paragraph."

(5) After sub-paragraph (5) of that paragraph insert—

"(6) Paragraph 15(7) (meaning of "non-Schedule 20 expenditure") applies for the purposes of sub-paragraph (3)."

(6) The amendments made by this section have effect in relation to expenditure incurred on or after 1st April 2007.

GENERAL NOTE

Section 49 corrects a potential problem with the Vaccine Research Relief (VRR) Provisions in FA 2002 Sch 13. This could have resulted in too much relief being given to SMEs in certain situations.

As originally drafted, para 14 (2) of FA 2002 Sch 13 provided that the appropriate deduction in computing the profits of the trade was:

(*a*) 50% of so much of the qualifying expenditure in respect of which the company is also entitled to relief under Sch 20 to the Finance Act 2000 (c17), and

(*b*) 150% of so much of the qualifying expenditure as is not expenditure in respect of which the company is also entitled to relief under that schedule.

The potential problem arose where the SME had expenditure that qualified for VRR but did not, for some reason, qualify for relief under FA 2000 Sch 20. For that expenditure, FA 2002 para 14(2)(*b*) gave a deduction of 150 percent. However, the expenditure might already have been fully deductible as revenue expenditure under s 82A TA 1988, resulting in a total deduction of 250 percent which was unintended.

To correct this, s 49 replaces para 14(2) of FA 2002 Sch 13 with a new sub-para (2) which provides for a deduction of 50% of qualifying expenditure in all cases.

Paragraph 3 of s 49 introduces and defines a new term "non-schedule 20 expenditure". The remaining paragraphs are incidental amendments.

These amendments are effective for expenditure incurred on or after 1 April 2007.

50 Research and development tax relief: definition of SME etc

(1) In Part 1 of Schedule 20 to FA 2000 (entitlement to R&D tax relief), paragraph 2(1) (meaning of "small or medium-sized enterprise") is amended as follows.

(2) Before Qualification 1 insert—

"Qualification A1

In Article 2(1) of the Annex the references to 250 persons, 50 million euros and 43 million euros are to be read as references to 500 persons, 100 million euros and 86 million euros (respectively)."

(3) In Qualification 1—

(*a*) after "micro, small or medium-sized enterprise" insert "(or would be if the Annex were read as set out in Qualification A1)";

(*b*) at the end insert "(read as set out in Qualification A1)".

(4) Part 2 of Schedule 13 to FA 2002 (giving effect to VRR tax relief) is amended as follows.

(5) After paragraph 15 insert—

"Paragraphs 14 and 15: modifications for larger SMEs claiming R&D tax credits

15A— (1) This paragraph applies in relation to a company for an accounting period if—

(*a*) the company is a larger SME in the accounting period, and

(*b*) it claims a tax credit under paragraph 15 of Schedule 20 to the Finance Act 2000 (R&D tax credit) for the accounting period.

(2) The appropriate deduction under paragraph 14 above is 50% of so much of the qualifying expenditure as is non-Schedule 20 expenditure (as defined by paragraph 15(7)).

(3) Paragraph 15 above has effect as if sub-paragraph (2)(*a*) were omitted.

(4) In this paragraph "larger SME" means a company which qualifies as a small or medium-sized enterprise by virtue of Qualification A1 in paragraph 2(1) of Schedule 20 to the Finance Act 2000."

(6) After paragraph 16 insert—

"Entitlement to tax credit: modification for larger SMEs

16A— (1) Paragraph 16(3) has effect in relation to a larger SME as if for the definition of "B" there were substituted—

"B is 150% of so much of the qualifying expenditure mentioned in paragraph 14 or 15 as is non-Schedule 20 expenditure."

(2) "Larger SME" has the same meaning as in paragraph 15A."

(7) The amendments made by this section have effect in relation to expenditure incurred on or after such day as the Treasury may by order appoint.

(8) A day before the day on which this Act is passed may be appointed, but not one before 1st April 2007.

(9) For the purpose of determining, in relation to expenditure incurred on or after the appointed day, whether a company is a small or medium-sized enterprise, the amendments are to be treated as always having had effect.

GENERAL NOTE

Section 50 extends the definition of an SME for R&D purposes and introduces the concept of a "larger SME". The clause amends the employee and financial limits in the definition of a SME for R&D purposes as follows:

Current Limits *New Limits*

Employees	250	500
Turnover	€50m	€100m
Balance Sheet	€43m	€86m

As the definition of a SME is actually a European Commission definition, this change is achieved by creating a new Qualification A1 and then providing that the EC definition is read in accordance with that qualification.

Section 50 then restricts the availability of Vaccines Research Relief (VRR) in the following situations.

(*a*) A larger SME may only claim a VRR repayable credit in respect of appropriate non-schedule 20 expenditure.

(*b*) A larger SME which is also claiming a Sch 20 credit may only get a VRR deduction of 50% of its appropriate non-sch 20 expenditure. This applies for the deduction against trading profits and for the deemed trading loss for pre-trading expenditure.

In both situations, "non-Sch 20 expenditure" means expenditure on which the company is not entitled to relief under FA 2000 Sch 20. That definition was introduced by s 49.

As these amendments affect the SME scheme, which is notified state aid, EU approval is needed. Accordingly, these changes do not have effect until an appointed day. It is considered that this is likely to be 1 April 2007.

Venture capital schemes etc

51 Venture capital schemes etc

Schedule 16 contains provision about venture capital schemes (and provision consequential on such provision).

GENERAL NOTE

The venture capital schemes are:

— the Enterprise Investment Scheme (EIS);

— the Venture Capital Trust scheme (VCT scheme);

— the Corporate Venturing Scheme (CVS);

— relief for capital losses (VC loss relief).

The detail of the changes made by this section are set out in Schedule 16, however in summary the main changes restrict the size of companies which will be able to benefit from the Venture Capital Schemes and also to restrict the amount of capital which can be raised under the Venture Capital Schemes in any twelve month period. As a result of the new provisions, it would be expected that the numbers of companies and investors who utilise the venture capital schemes in future will reduce.

REITs

52 Real Estate Investment Trusts

(1) Schedule 17 contains provisions about Real Estate Investment Trusts.

(2) The amendments made by that Schedule have effect in respect of—

(*a*) an accounting period, of a company to which Part 4 of FA 2006 (REITs) applies, which begins on or after 1st January 2007,

(*b*) an accounting period, of the principal company of a group to which that Part applies, which begins on or after 1st January 2007, and

(*c*) a distribution to which section 121 of FA 2006 applies and which is received on or after 1st January 2007.

GENERAL NOTE

Section 52 gives effect to Schedule 17.

This section and Schedule amend provisions in FA 2006 Part IV, which introduced Real Estate Investment Trusts (REITs), a new regime for the UK taxation of certain companies with qualifying property rental businesses and their shareholders.

The modified provisions are intended to apply to REITs and their shareholders from the date on which the REIT regime came into force, being 1 January 2007. As a result, provision is made for the amendments to apply in respect of accounting periods of single company and group REITs beginning on or after 1 January 2007 and in respect of dividends paid by a REIT on or after 1 January 2007, out of property income earned since entry into the REIT regime.

Alternative finance

53 Alternative finance investment bond

(1) In FA 2005, after section 48 insert—

"48A Alternative finance arrangements: alternative finance investment bond: introduction

(1) Subject to section 52, arrangements fall within this section if—

(*a*) the arrangements provide for one person ("the bond-holder") to pay a sum of money ("the capital") to another ("the bond-issuer"),

(*b*) the arrangements identify assets, or a class of assets, which the bond-issuer will acquire for the purpose of generating income or gains directly or indirectly ("the bond assets"),

(*c*) the arrangements specify a period at the end of which they cease to have effect ("the bond term"),

(*d*) the bond-issuer undertakes under the arrangements—

(i) to dispose at the end of the bond term of any bond assets which are still in the bond-issuer's possession,

(ii) to make a repayment of the capital ("the redemption payment") to the bond-holder during or at the end of the bond-term (whether or not in instalments), and

(iii) to pay to the bond-holder other payments on one or more occasions during or at the end of the bond term ("additional payments"),

(*e*) the amount of the additional payments does not exceed an amount which would be a reasonable commercial return on a loan of the capital,

(*f*) under the arrangements the bond-issuer undertakes to arrange for the management of the bond assets with a view to generating income sufficient to pay the redemption payment and additional payments,

(*g*) the bond-holder is able to transfer the rights under the arrangements to another person (who thereby becomes the bond-holder),

(*h*) the arrangements are a listed security on a recognised stock exchange (within the meaning of section 1005 of ITA 2007), and

(*i*) the arrangements are wholly or partly treated in accordance with international accounting standards as a financial liability of the bond-issuer (or would be if the bond-issuer applied those standards).

(2) For the purposes of subsection (1)—

(*a*) the bond-issuer may acquire bond assets before or after the arrangements take effect,

(*b*) bond assets may be property of any kind, including rights in relation to property owned by someone other than the bond-issuer,

(*c*) the identification of the bond assets mentioned in subsection (1)(*b*) and the undertakings mentioned in subsection (1)(*d*) and (*f*) may (but need not) be described as, or accompanied by a document described as, a declaration of trust,

(*d*) a reference to the management of assets includes a reference to disposal,

(*e*) the bond-holder may (but need not) be entitled under the arrangements to terminate them, or participate in terminating them, before the end of the bond term,

(*f*) the amount of the additional payments may be—

(i) fixed at the beginning of the bond term,

(ii) determined wholly or partly by reference to the value of or income generated by the bond assets, or

(iii) determined in some other way,

(*g*) if the amount of the additional payments is not fixed at the beginning of the bond term, the reference in subsection (1)(*e*) to the amount of the additional payments is a reference to the maximum amount of the additional payments,

(*h*) the amount of the redemption payment may (but need not) be subject to reduction in the event of a fall in the value of the bond assets or in the rate of income generated by them, and

(i) entitlement to the redemption payment may (but need not) be capable of being satisfied (whether or not at the option of the bond-issuer or the bond-holder) by the issue or transfer of shares or other securities.

(3) An order under section 1005 of ITA 2007 (recognised stock exchanges: designation) may designate a stock exchange for the purposes of that section in its application for the purposes of this section only.

48B Alternative finance arrangements: alternative finance investment bond: effects

(1) Additional payments under arrangements falling within section 48A are alternative finance return for the purpose of this Chapter (subject to the provisions in section 51A about the treatment of discount).

(2) For the purposes of an enactment about any tax (and irrespective of the position for other purposes)—

(*a*) a bond-holder shall not be treated as having a legal or beneficial interest in the bond assets,

(*b*) the bond-issuer shall not be treated as a trustee of the bond assets,

(*c*) profits and gains accruing to the bond-issuer in connection with the bond assets are profits and gains of the bond-issuer and not of the bond-holder (and do not arise to the bond-issuer in a fiduciary or representative capacity),

(*d*) payments made by the bond-issuer by way of redemption payment or additional payment are not made in a fiduciary or representative capacity, and

(*e*) a bond-holder shall not be entitled to relief for capital expenditure in connection with bond assets.

(3) Arrangements falling within section 48A are securities for the purposes of an enactment about any tax (including Chapters 1 to 5 of Part 7 of ITEPA 2003); for which purpose—

(*a*) a reference to redemption shall be taken as a reference to making the redemption payment,

(*b*) a reference to interest shall be taken as a reference to alternative finance return, and

(*c*) for the purposes of section 84 the bond issuer shall be treated as being party as debtor to a capital market arrangement.

(4) Arrangements falling within section 48A are a corporate bond, issued on the date on which the arrangements are entered into, for the purposes of section 117 of TCGA 1992 (qualifying corporate bonds) if—

(*a*) the capital is expressed in sterling,

(*b*) the arrangements do not include provision for the redemption payment to be in a currency other than sterling,

(*c*) entitlement to the redemption payment is not capable of conversion (directly or indirectly) into an entitlement to the issue of securities apart from other arrangements falling within section 48A, and

(*d*) the additional payments are not determined wholly or partly by reference to the value of the bond assets;

and section 117(2) shall have effect for the purposes of this subsection as for the purposes of section 117(1).

(5) Arrangements falling within section 48A shall not be treated—

(*a*) as a unit trust scheme for the purposes of TCGA 1992,

(*b*) as a unit trust scheme for the purposes of section 469 of ICTA or section 1007 of ITA 2007 (distributions),

(*c*) as an offshore fund for the purposes of Chapter 5 of Part 17 of ICTA (offshore funds), or

(*d*) as a relevant holding for the purposes of paragraph 4 of Schedule 10 to FA 1996 (loan relationships: collective investment schemes).

(6) A bond-issuer is not a securitisation company for the purposes of section 83 (unless it is one by virtue of arrangements which do not fall within section 48A).

(7) For the purposes of section 417 of ICTA (close companies)—

(*a*) a bond-holder is a loan creditor in respect of the bond-issuer;

(*b*) arrangements falling within section 48A shall be disregarded in the application of section 417(1)(*d*).

(8) For the purposes of Schedule 18 to ICTA (group relief)—

(*a*) a bond-holder is a loan creditor in respect of the bond-issuer;

(*b*) paragraph 1(5)(*b*) shall be disregarded in determining whether a person is an equity holder by virtue of arrangements falling within section 48A."

(2) Chapter 5 of Part 2 of FA 2005 (alternative finance arrangements) is amended as follows.

(3) In section 46 (introduction)—

(*a*) in subsection (1), after "47A," insert "48A,", and

(*b*) in subsection (2), after paragraph (*d*) (before "or" at the end) insert—

"(da) a bond-issuer within the meaning of section 48A below, but only in relation to any bond assets which are rights under arrangements falling within section 47 or 47A,".

(4) In section 50(1) (treatment of alternative finance arrangements: companies), for "or 47A" substitute ", 47A or 48A".

(5) After section 51 insert—

"51A Discount

(1) This section applies where part of the additional payments in respect of arrangements falling within section 48A equates in substance to discount ("the discount element").

(2) The discount element shall not be treated as alternative finance return for the purposes of income tax.

(3) The discount element shall be treated—

(*a*) in accordance with section 381 of ITTOIA 2005, or

(*b*) where the arrangements falling within section 48A are deeply discounted securities for the purpose of Chapter 8 of Part 4 of ITTOIA 2005, in accordance with that Chapter."

(6) In section 52 (provision not at arm's length)—

(*a*) in subsection (1), after "47A," insert "48A,",

(*b*) in subsection (3), after "47A," insert "48A,", and

(*c*) in subsection (4), for "or 47A" substitute ", 47A or 48A".

(7) In section 53 (sale and purchase of asset)—

(*a*) in subsection (1) (and in the heading), for "or 47A" substitute ", 47A or 48A", and

(*b*) in subsection (3), after "47A" insert "or 48A".

(8) In section 54 (return not to be treated as distribution)—

(*a*) the existing provision becomes subsection (1),

(*b*) after that subsection insert—

"(2) Neither additional payments nor any part of the redemption payment under arrangements falling within section 48A are to be treated by virtue of section 209(2)(*e*)(iii) of ICTA as being a distribution for the purposes of the Corporation Tax Acts.", and

(*c*) the heading accordingly becomes "**Return not to be treated as distribution**".

(9) In Schedule 2 (supplementary provision), in paragraph 1(*b*) (definition of "relevant arrangements"), after "section" insert "48A,".

(10) In section 117 of TCGA 1992 (qualifying corporate bonds), after subsection (6C) insert—

"(6D) Section 48B(4) of the Finance Act 2005 (alternative finance arrangements) provides for certain arrangements falling within section 48A to be a corporate bond for the purposes of this section."

(11) In section 127(1)(*ca*) of FA 1995 (persons not treated as UK representatives), for "subsection (5) of section 47" substitute "Chapter 5 of Part 2".

(12) In section 148(5A) of FA 2003 (meaning of "permanent establishment"), for "subsection (5) of section 47" substitute "Chapter 5 of Part 2".

(13) Section 56 of FA 2005 (commencement and transitional) shall have effect in relation to the commencement of this section—

(*a*) as if references to Chapter 5 of Part 2 of that Act were references to this section,

(*b*) as if references to 6th April 2005 were references to—

(i) 1st April 2007 in relation to corporation tax, and

(ii) 6th April 2007 in relation to income tax and capital gains tax, and

(*c*) as if references to section 49 were references to sections 48A and 48B.

(14) But—

(*a*) for the purposes of income tax and capital gains tax in relation to the disposal after 6th April 2007 of arrangements to which new section 48A applies (whenever entered into) that section and new section 48B shall be treated as always having had effect, and (*b*) an order made after the passing of this Act under section 1005 of ITA 2007 (recognised stock exchanges: designation) and by virtue of new section 48A(3) may be expressed—

(i) to have effect as from 1st April 2007 for the purposes of arrangements entered into on or after that date, and

(ii) for the purposes mentioned in paragraph (*a*), as always having had effect.

GENERAL NOTE

Section 53 continues the process begun in FA 2005 of adapting UK tax law to facilitate Islamic finance transactions. The newly inserted FA 2005 s 48A defines a new category of alternative finance arrangement, called an 'alternative finance investment bond' and s 48B sets out the applicable taxation treatment. In recent years, Islamic finance has developed traded instruments, sukuk (a plural noun, singular is "sakk", which is Arabic for certificates) which have similar economic characteristics to corporate bonds. Sections 48A and 48B continue the FA 2005 approach of defining transactions explicitly in UK tax law, without any reference to Islamic law and practice; transactions falling within these definitions will receive the tax treatment specified, irrespective of any intention to comply with Islamic law or otherwise.

Sukuk are most easily understood by considering an example:

Diagram 1

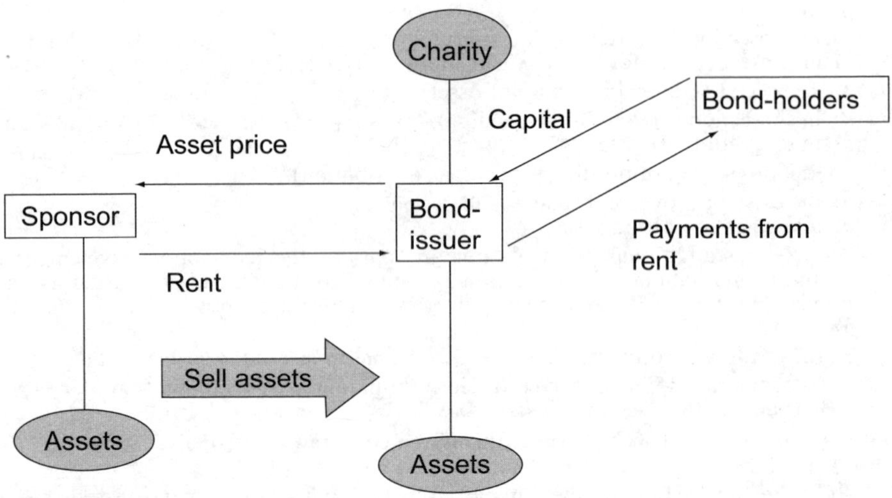

Here the sponsor sells assets to the bond-issuer for cash and rents them back. The rental flows are used to make payments to the holders of the sukuk (the bond-holders) and at the expiry of the arrangements the sponsor will buy back the assets. While sub-s 48A(1) allows the bond assets to be acquired from and disposed to any person, the most common arrangement is for them to be acquired from the sponsor and sold back, to enable a predictable redemption payment to the bond-holders.

Subsection 48A(1) requires alternative finance investment bonds to have similar characteristics to traded debt instruments, including being listed on a recognised stock exchange (which enables the quoted eurobond exemption from withholding tax to apply), being transferable, giving rise to a return no greater than a reasonable commercial return on the capital invested and being accounted for by the issuer as a financial liability.

If the requirements of s 48A are met, then s 48B applies the loan relationships rules to corporate issuers and to corporate investors. For non-corporate taxpayers, alternative finance investment bonds are treated as if they were securities paying interest, with any discount taxed under ITTOIA 2005 s 381 or under the deeply discounted securities rules, as appropriate.

Although in law the bond-issuer will often hold the bond assets on trust for the bond-holders, the effect of sub-s 48B(2) is that for tax purposes the bond-issuer is deemed to own the bond assets beneficially; if there is any relief for capital expenditure it is due to the bond-issuer and not to the bond-holders.

While most sukuk are issued (as illustrated above) by special purpose 'orphan' companies which are not part of the sponsor's group, conventional corporate bonds are often issued by group companies, and sub-ss 48B(7) and (8) were introduced at Committee stage to facilitate this, as illustrated below.

Diagram 2

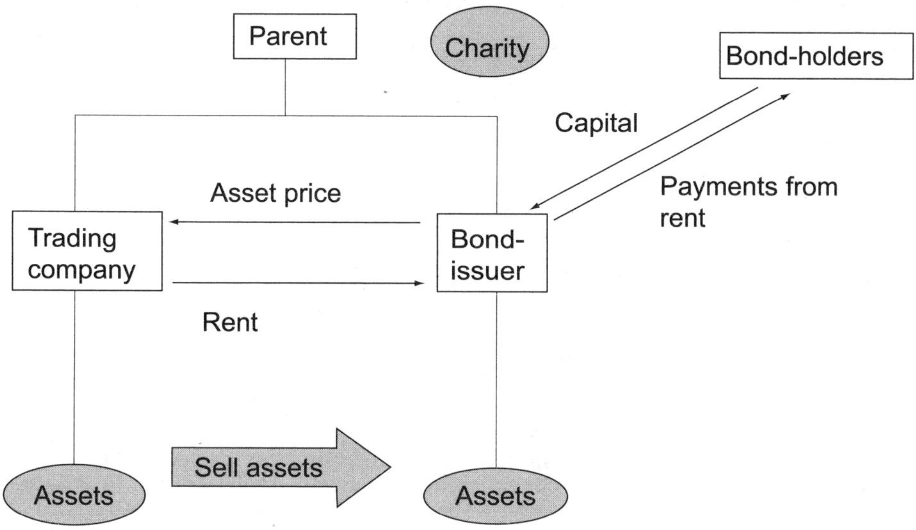

Subsection 48B(7) ensures that the close company rules operate as they would in the case of a conventional debt instrument. More importantly, sub-s 48B(8)(b) means that an alternative finance investment bond is capable of qualifying as a normal commercial loan for group relief purposes. Otherwise if issued by a subsidiary (as illustrated above) it would, in many cases, have the effect of de-grouping the subsidiary for group relief purposes and for chargeable gain purposes due to TCGA 1992 sub-s 170(8) applying the definitions of TA 1988 Sch 18.

FA 2007 sub-s 53(3) provides that a bond-issuer is treated as a financial institution for the alternative finance arrangements provisions, but only in relation to bond assets which fall within FA 2005 s 47 (purchase and resale) and s 47A (diminishing shared ownership). These are the two provisions most commonly used by Islamic banks to grant mortgages, and the new rules should facilitate such banks securitising their mortgage portfolios. However, the narrowness of the extension to the definition of a financial institution means that other transactions could entail taxation costs. For example, if in the first diagram the assets being sold to the bond-issuer comprised UK land then stamp duty land tax would be due. The transaction would not benefit from the relief in FA 2003 s 71A because the bond issuer would not qualify as a financial institution.

54 Profit share agency

In section 49A(3) of FA 2005 (profit share agency: principal not treated as entitled to agent's share of profits), insert at the end "(and the agent is treated as entitled to the profits specified in subsection (1)(*c*) and (*d*))".

GENERAL NOTE

When FA 2006 inserted FA 2005 s 49A (profit share agency) it expressly provided that payments made to the principal by the agent were tax deductible to the agent. However, it did not state that the agent was taxable on the underlying profits produced with the principal's money. Although HMRC did not accept that s 49A was flawed, the amendment made by FA 2007 s 54 puts it beyond doubt that the agent is taxable on all the profits made, before being given a deduction for payments made to the principal.

Trusts

55 Trust income

(1) In section 686A(2)(*a*) of ICTA (receipts to be treated as income subject to special rate of tax: payment by company), after "made" insert "by way of qualifying distribution".

(2) In Type 1(*b*) in section 482 of ITA 2007 (types of amount to be charged at special rates for trustees), after "made" insert "by way of qualifying distribution".

(3) The amendments made by this section have effect in respect of payments made to the trustees of a settlement on or after 6th April 2006.

GENERAL NOTE

When a company purchases its own shares from trustees the receipt in the trustees' hands is capital for trust law purposes. However, since 6 April 1999 the receipt has been liable to income tax. TA 1988 s 686 caught only income which is to be accumulated or is payable at the discretion of the trustees. The old s 686A applied to the consideration given by a company to trustee shareholders when it bought in shares and deemed the qualifying distribution element to be income for the purposes of s 686. The effect of s 686A was that s 686 could apply to an interest in possession trust as well as to an accumulation and maintenance trust as the receipts were not taxed as the income of the life tenant. FA 2006 Sch 13 para 3 inserted a new s 686A into TA 1988 that also gathered together a series of *ad hoc* provisions that deemed other instances of capital receipts to be income for the purposes of s 686. The legislation in FA 2006 contained an omission, the effect of which was that the entirety of the payment was liable to income tax, rather than the part which falls within the definition of "qualifying distribution". The section remedies that omission with effect from 6 April 2006 and reflects the transition from TA 1988 to ITA 2007 that took effect from 6 April 2007. The legislation previously contained in TA s 686A is now ITA 2007 ss 481 and 482. The intention to legislate to rectify the omission was announced in a

Ministerial Written Statement by the Paymaster General on 9 October 2006. During the Committee stage Ed Balls, the then Economic Secretary to the Treasury, said that he estimated that only approximately 20 trusts were affected. Although at present something of a moot point it appears that if the trustees obtain clearance under TA 1988 s 219 capital gains tax treatment may in fact apply. This view is supported by HMRC's Trusts, Settlements and Estates Manual at TSEM3205.

56 Trust gains on contracts for life insurance

(1) Section 498 of ITA 2007 (trustees' tax pool) is amended as follows.

(2) In subsection (1)—

(*a*) in Type 1, for "2 or 3" substitute "2, 3 or 3A", and

(*b*) after Type 3 insert—

"*Type 3A*

The amount of tax at the nominal rate on any amount in respect of which—

(*a*) the trustees are liable to income tax under section 467 of ITTOIA 2005 (gains from contracts for life insurance etc),

(*b*) the trustees are liable to income tax at the trust rate by virtue of section 482 above, and

(*c*) tax at the savings rate is treated as having been paid by virtue of section 530 of ITTOIA 2005 (life insurance)."

(3) After subsection (2) insert—

"(2A) In relation to Type 3A, the reference to the nominal rate is a reference to a rate equal to the difference between the trust rate and the savings rate."

(4) The amendments made by this section have effect in relation to gains arising to the trustees of a settlement on or after 6th April 2007.

GENERAL NOTE

Accumulation and maintenance and discretionary trusts have "tax pools". The tax pool is a statutory mechanism for ensuring that tax credits given to beneficiaries of a discretionary or accumulation trust are covered by the tax paid by the trustees. While tax actually paid goes into the pool, tax covered by non-repayable tax credits or notional tax credits does not. The notional tax credit on dividend income has not gone into the tax pool since 1999. Income tax charges can arise on gains from certain life insurance policies, capital redemption policies and life annuity contracts when a "chargeable event" occurs. UK resident trustees are potentially liable under ITTOIA 2005 s 467 (although a living, UK resident settlor of a non-charitable trust would normally be liable under s 465). There is a notional tax credit of 20% on chargeable event gains from some of these policies which should not enter the "tax pool". However the legislation relating to the tax pool – TA s 687 – was not amended at the time of FA 2006 to ensure that this notional tax credit did not do so. The section reflects the transition from TA 1988 s 687 to ITA 2007 s 498 and adds an additional type of income tax, Type 3A, to s 498 (1). The amendments are effective from 6 April 2007 so some trusts may have benefited from the notional tax credit of 20% going into the tax pool in the period up to that date.

Other corporation tax measures

57 Offshore funds

(1) In section 396 of ICTA (corporation tax: setting off of Case VI losses), in subsection (2) (losses to which subsection (1) does not apply), insert at the end "or on a disposal to which Chapter 5 of Part 17 applies."

(2) In section 756A of ICTA (definition of "offshore fund"), for subsection (3) substitute—

"(3) In this section "collective investment scheme" means any arrangements which are a collective investment scheme for the purposes of Part 17 of the Financial Services and Markets Act 2000 (see section 235 of that Act and orders made under subsection (5) of that section) or would be if the words ", within a period appearing to him to be reasonable," were omitted from section 236(3)(*a*) of that Act.

(4) But the reference to offshore funds in section 760(3)(*a*) does not include any arrangements which are not a collective investment scheme for the purposes of that Part of that Act."

(3) In section 842 of ICTA (investment trusts), after subsection (3) insert—

"(3A) References in this section to income do not include income treated as arising under section 761(1)(*a*)."

(4) In Schedule 27 to ICTA (distributing funds), in sub-paragraph (1)(*c*) of paragraph 6 (investments of offshore fund in other offshore funds which could, apart from that paragraph, be certified as distributing funds not to count towards limit in section 760(3)(*a*)), omit "without regard to the provisions of this paragraph,".

(5) In section 152 of ITA 2007 (losses from miscellaneous transactions), in subsection (8), insert at the end "except that income on which income tax is charged under section 761(1)(*b*)(i) of ICTA is not "section 1016 income" for the purposes of subsection (2)(*a*)".

(6) The amendment made by subsection (1) has effect in relation to disposals on or after 1st April 2007.

(7) The amendment made by subsection (3) has effect in relation to accounting periods beginning on or after the day on which this Act is passed.

(8) The amendment made by subsection (4) has effect in relation to account periods (within the meaning of Chapter 5 of Part 17 of ICTA) beginning on or after 1st January 2007.

(9) The amendment made by subsection (5) has effect in relation to transactions on or after 6th April 2007.

GENERAL NOTE

It was announced in October 2006 that the Government would consult with a view to reforming the offshore fund regime in FA 2007. During the HC Standing Committee proceedings Ed Balls explained that the purpose of the offshore fund regime was to put UK investors in offshore funds on a similar fiscal footing as UK investors in UK funds. The FA 2007 changes were seen by Government as a response to concerns that given the rapid changes in the sector, aspects of the offshore fund regime have begun to act as a barrier to commercial developments. He stated that the consultation process is ongoing. Further changes could, therefore, be made.

This section makes four amendments to the rules with respect to offshore funds.

1. Widening of the TA 1988 s 756A offshore fund definition (but not for the purposes of the TA 1988 s 760(3)(a) test).

TA 1988 s 756A provides the general definition of an offshore fund, so as to require an offshore fund to be a collective investment scheme.

Before the amendment in FA 2007 the definition of collective investment scheme for these purposes, was that of the Financial Services and Markets Act 2000 (FSMA).

FA 2007 s 57(2) modifies TA 1988 s 756A, such that for taxation purposes the FSMA definition is amended slightly. The condition, that an investor should expect to realise the investment within a "reasonable period", is omitted. The FSA definition of a reasonable period was generally for a period of less than 6 months. The change means that for taxation purposes the standard test of an expectation that the underlying asset value could be realised within 7 years, as provided by s 759(2) now applies. As such more funds will come within the collective investment scheme definition. From a tax perspective companies that look to a reasonable investor like an open ended investment company will fall within the definition. A company with fixed capital will still be outside the offshore fund definition unless there are special conditions.

Initially the change was to take effect from 1 January 2007 but following a Government Amendment the new definition applies from the date of Royal Assent. The change to the effective date was made as initially it had been thought by Government that the modification to the definition was a clarification of the definition of reasonable period (that is that the tax definition rather than the FSA definition should be used) and so a retrospective start date would be appropriate. Industry representations made it clear that the modification did effect a change (as the FSA definition of a period less than six months was universally used as the reasonable period definition) and so it was accepted by Government that a retrospective start date was not appropriate.

A serious difficulty with the new definition was also brought to the attention of Government. In order to be certified as a distributor fund (gains thereby being taxable under the capital gains rules rather than the income tax regime) the fund must comply with specified conditions set down in TA 1988 s 760 and Schedule 27 with respect to its income distribution policy and its investments.

To satisfy the investment condition test set down in TA 1988 s 760(3)(*a*) no more than 5% of the underlying value of a fund's assets can be in other offshore funds (after FA 2007 other non qualifying offshore funds).

The widening of the definition of offshore funds meant that certain funds that had hitherto been excluded from the offshore fund definition would come within the definition. Compliant distributor funds which had carefully avoided over investing in offshore funds could, through no action of the fund managers or the investors, find that they had breached the 5% limit through a change in status of their underlying investments. Having been alerted to the problem Government decided that for the purposes of the qualifying offshore funds investment condition test the old definition of an offshore fund (that is a fund that complies with the full FSMA definition of a collective investment scheme) should continue to apply. This means that no existing qualifying distributor funds will find their status has been altered as a result of the change and investors in such funds will not be disadvantaged.

2. Change to the investment trust definition.

TA 1988 s 842 sets down the conditions to be met for a company to gain approval as an investment trust. One of the conditions is that the company's income must be derived wholly or mainly from shares and securities. FA 2007 s 57(3) provides that offshore income gains will not count as income for the purposes of this test. The change is effective for accounting periods beginning on or after Royal Assent. The amendment is purely with respect to the s 842 test and offshore income gains will remain taxable as income in the hands of approved investment trusts

3. Provision that an offshore loss can only be set off against a capital gain.

FA 2007 s 57(1) and (5) provide that a taxpayer (whether an individual, trustee, personal representative or corporate) can only set an offshore income loss against a capital gain. The change with respect to corporates is effective with respect to disposals occurring on or after 1 April 2007 with the change for individuals, trustees and personal representatives being effective from 6 April 2007.

4. Change to the qualifying fund investment criteria test.

The TA 1988 s 760(3)(*a*) investment criteria test has been explained above. It has long been felt by those within the industry that the criteria multi-tiered vehicles had to meet to achieve distributor status, and thus take advantage of Capital Gains Tax taper relief, was too restrictive. FA 2007 s 57(4) modifies the test so as to make it easier for multi-tiered funds to qualify as distributor funds.

Prior to the FA 2007 amendment if the fund held investments in other offshore funds, even with distributor status such holdings would disqualify the investor fund unless they also met the specified test with respect to their underlying investments. The test was that the distributor fund invested in did not, have more than 5% of its assets invested in offshore funds (whether distributor or non-distributor). Multi-tiered funds generally did not meet this test and so did not qualify for distributor status. The amendment widens the exemption such that for accounting periods beginning on or after 1 January 2007 holdings in other distributor funds are ignored for the purposes of the investment test.

EXAMPLE

The Phoenix Fund is an offshore fund with a holding in the Grey Fund equal to 50% of the value of the Phoenix Fund and various smaller investments in UK securities. The Grey Fund is a Distributor Fund with a similar portfolio consisting of a 50% holding in the Jean Fund and the remainder in UK securities. The Jean Fund itself was a qualifying distributor status fund.

Before 1 January 2007 the Phoenix Fund would have been a non qualifying fund as the Grey Fund had more than 5% of its assets invested in offshore funds. From 1 January 2007 the Phoenix Fund is a qualifying fund as the Grey Fund is a distributor fund so the holding of The Phoenix Fund in the Grey Fund is ignored.

58 Election out of special film rules for film production companies

(1) In section 32 of FA 2006 (meaning of "film production company"), insert at the end—

"(7) A company may elect to be regarded as a company which does not meet the description in subsection (3) or (4).

(8) The election—

(*a*) must be made by the company by being included in its company tax return for an accounting period (and may be included in the return originally made or by amendment), and

(*b*) may be withdrawn by the company only by amending its company tax return for that accounting period.

(9) The election has effect in relation to films which commence principal photography in that or any subsequent accounting period.

(10) "Company tax return" has the same meaning as in Schedule 18 to FA 1998 (see paragraph 3(1))."

(2) In paragraph 10 of Schedule 18 to FA 1998 (other claims and elections to be included in company tax return), insert at the end—

"(5) An election under section 32(7) of the Finance Act 2006 (election not to be a film production company) can only be made by being included in a company tax return (see section 32(8)(*a*) of that Act)."

GENERAL NOTE

FA 2006 Part 3 Ch 3 (ss 31–53) introduced a new incentive for qualifying British films in the form of a tax credit. This can provide the producer of such a film with a cash rebate based on enhanced losses of up to 20 per cent of the core budget of films with qualifying expenditure of £20 million or less and up to 16 per cent for more expensive films. The tax credit is only available to companies within the charge to UK corporation tax and is obtained by the company making the appropriate claim in its tax return. The company in question has to be the maker of the film and has to fit the definition of "film production company" set out in FA 2006 s 32(3) and (4).

The film rules introduced by FA 2006 created a new regime for the taxing of films. These rules required each film to be treated as a separate trade by the production company. New loss relief rules were introduced which permitted losses on the individual film trade to be offset against other profits of the company only in the accounting period in which the film is completed and subsequent periods. Terminal loss relief rules also introduced by FA 2006 permitted film production companies to transfer losses from one qualifying film trade to another on the termination of the first trade. However, these terminal loss rules do not apply to non-qualifying films.

The definition of 'film' in FA 2006 includes all films made for release in the commercial cinema and television programmes. However, only qualifying British films made for release in the commercial cinema can enhance their losses and claim the film tax credit. Television companies, in particular, are therefore faced with the extra compliance burden relating to the reporting of separate trades, the delay in their use of losses and no terminal loss relief whilst not being able to access the advantages of the film tax credit. As a consequence, the television industry lobbied HMRC for a change to the FA 2006 rules. Section 58 is the result of this lobbying.

Section 58 allows a company to elect not to be treated as a "film production company" and therefore fall outside the FA 2006 rules. The election must be made in the company's tax return and will affect all films commencing principal photography in that accounting period and any subsequent accounting periods. The election can be withdrawn by the company amending its tax return for that accounting period.

59 Securitisation companies

(1) Section 83 of FA 2005 (continued application of old UK GAAP to securitisation companies during transitional period) is amended as follows.

(2) In subsection (1)(*b*) (old UK GAAP to apply to periods of account ending before 1st January 2008), insert at the beginning "(subject to subsection (7A)(*a*))".

(3) After subsection (7) insert—

"(7A) The Treasury may by regulations—

(*a*) make provision for subsection (1) to apply in relation to periods of account ending on or after 1st January 2008 but before a date specified by the regulations, and

(*b*) make provision modifying any provision of, or made under, the Corporation Tax Acts in relation to the first period of account of securitisation companies in the case of which subsection (1) does not apply (whether by virtue of that subsection itself or regulations under paragraph (*a*)).

(7B) Regulations under subsection (7A)(*a*) may, in particular—

(*a*) specify a date only in relation to specified descriptions of company,
(*b*) specify different dates in relation to different descriptions of company, and
(*c*) include provision for a company to elect that the regulations are to apply to it or provision for a company to elect that they are not to apply to it."

(4) Section 84 of FA 2005 (power to make provision as to application of Corporation Tax Acts in relation to securitisation companies) is amended as follows.

(5) In subsection (3)(*d*), for "to that effect is made," substitute "that they are to apply is made or that the regulations do not apply to a company if an election that they are not to apply is made,".

(6) For subsection (5) substitute—

"(5) The regulations—

(*a*) may make incidental, supplementary, consequential or transitional provision or savings (including provision amending any provision of, or made under, the Taxes Acts (within the meaning of section 118(1) of TMA 1970)), and
(*b*) may include provision having effect (in the case of provision relating to corporation tax) from the beginning of periods of account current when the regulations are made or (in the case of provision relating to income tax or capital gains tax) in relation to times before the regulations are made."

GENERAL NOTE

Finance Act 2005 s 83 allowed securitisation companies to defer adoption of International Accounting Standards in respect of accounting periods ending before 1 January 2007 to allow time to develop a satisfactory corporation tax regime based on IAS accounts for securitisation companies.

This deadline was extended by FA 2006 to accounting periods ending before 1 January 2008, and FA 2007 s 59 now makes provision for the deadline to be extended further by regulation in certain circumstances.

Regulations made under FA 2005 s 84 (The Taxation of Securitisation Companies Regulations 2006), which create a permanent regime, came into force on 12 December 2006 and have effect for periods of account beginning on or after 1 January 2007.

Securitisation companies are typically set up as companies or trusts independent of the enterprise from which they acquire the assets to be securitised. These may be financial assets, such as batches of mortgages, or other debts receivable, made marketable by the issue of bonds by the securitisation company. The cash flows in and out are often finely matched, and the marketability of the bonds depends on credit ratings, for which purpose the bonds may be divided into tranches of seniority. Securitisation is a significant source of business finance, with the UK playing a major role in the European market.

Fears exist that, under IAS, financial assets would have to be valued by fair value accounting, while the corresponding funding liabilities may be valued at amortised cost. The resulting mismatch may generate unpredictable corporation tax liabilities, and adversely affect credit ratings.

Temporary regime – UK GAAP

Finance Act 2005 s 83 defers implementation of IAS, and ensures that assets can be matched to liabilities under UK GAAP for tax purposes, for accounting periods ending before 1 January 2008.

FA 2007 s 59(3) enables the Treasury to make regulations extending this regime to apply to periods of account ending on or after 1 January 2007, up to a date specified in the regulations. Such regulations may also modify the corporation tax rules for companies in respect of the first period of account in which UK GAAP ceases to apply.

The regulations may be limited to particular types of company, or specify different dates for different types of company, and may require companies to elect to come within the regime, or alternatively enable a company to elect that the regulations are not to apply to it.

Permanent regime

FA 2005 s 84 enables the Treasury to make regulations establishing a permanent regime for the taxation of securitisation companies. The Taxation of Securitisation Companies Regulations 2006 establish such a regime for companies involved in the securitisation of financial assets, with effect for periods of account beginning on or after 1 January 2007.

FA 2007 s 59(5) enables the Treasury to provide by regulation that the permanent regime will only apply to a company where that company makes an election to that effect, or alternatively that a company will be able to elect that the regulations are not to apply to it.

Subsection (6) provides that regulations made under FA 2005 s 84 will, in respect of corporation tax, be capable of containing provision effective from the beginning of periods of account which are current when the regulations are made but that, in respect of income tax and capital gains tax, the regulations will be capable of having effect in relation to earlier periods as well.

Other income tax measures

60 Gift aid: limits

(1) In section 418 of ITA 2007 (donations to charity by individuals: limits)—

(*a*) in subsection (2)(*c*), for "2.5%" substitute "5%", and
(*b*) in subsection (3), for "£250" substitute "£500".

(2) In section 339 of ICTA (donations to charity)—

(*a*) in subsection (3B)(*b*), for "£250" substitute "£500", and
(*b*) in subsection (3DA)(*c*), for "2.5 per cent" substitute "5 per cent".

(3) The amendment made by subsection (1) has effect in relation to gifts made on or after 6th April 2007.

(4) The amendment made by subsection (2) has effect in relation to gifts made in an accounting period ending on or after 6th April 2007.

GENERAL NOTE

The limits the value of benefits that can be received by individual and corporate donors in return for making a gift aid donation have been increased. The increased limits provide scope for more donations to qualify for Gift Aid where benefits have been received by the donor. The limits, which were previously unchanged since the introduction of Gift Aid in 1990 allow donors to make a gesture of gratitude to the donors whilst preventing abuse of the tax relief.

Donations by individuals

The restrictions on the benefits associated with a gift aid donation are set out in ITA 2007 s 418. The proportionate limit on gifts over £1,000 (in s 418(2)(*c*)) is increased from 2.5% to 5% and the overall limit on the total value of the benefits from all gifts by the donor in a tax year (in s 418(3)) is increased from £250 to £500. The changes apply in relation to gifts made on or after 6 April 2007.

As a result of these changes, the limits of benefits associated with gifts from individuals are as follows:

— 25% of the amount of the gift, if the amount of the gift is £100 or less;
— £25 if the amount of the gift is more than £100 but not more than £1,000; and
— 5% of the amount of the gift if the amount of the gift is more than £1,000,

subject to an overall limit on benefits to the donor in a tax year of £500.

Corporate donations

The gift aid legislation for companies is contained in TA 1988 s 339.

The limit (in s 339(3B)(*b*)) on the value of benefits that can be increased by corporate donors in an accounting period is increased from £250 to £500.

The proportionate limit on the value of the benefit that can be received in connection with a gift of £1,000 or more is increased from 2.5% to 5% (s 339(DA)(*c*)). The limits for gifts of not more than £100 remains at 25 per cent and that for gifts of more than £100 and less than £1,000 remains at £25.

The changes apply in relation to gifts made in an accounting period ending on or after 6 April 2007.

61 Enterprise management incentives: excluded activities

(1) In Part 3 of Schedule 5 to ITEPA 2003 (enterprise management incentives: qualifying companies), in paragraph 19 (excluded activities: receipt of royalties or licence fees)—

(*a*) in sub-paragraph (4), for paragraphs (*a*) and (*b*) substitute—

"(*a*) by the relevant company, or

(*b*) by a company which was a qualifying subsidiary of the relevant company throughout a period during which it created the whole or greater part (in terms of value) of the intangible asset.", and

(*b*) after sub-paragraph (7) insert—

"(8) If—

(*a*) the relevant company acquired all the shares ("old shares") in another company ("the old company") at a time when the only shares issued in the relevant company were subscriber shares, and

(*b*) the consideration for the old shares consisted wholly of the issue of shares in the relevant company,

references in sub-paragraph (4) to the relevant company include the old company."

(2) The amendments made by subsection (1) have effect in relation to options granted on or after 6th April 2007.

(3) They also have effect in relation to a qualifying option within subsection (4), for the purpose of determining at any time on or after that date whether an activity is an excluded activity.

(4) An option is within this subsection if it was granted before 6th April 2007 and, immediately before that date—

(*a*) it had not been exercised, and

(*b*) no disqualifying event had occurred in relation to it.

(5) Subsection (6) applies in respect of an option within subsection (4) if—

(*a*) immediately before 6th April 2007—

(i) the right to exploit an intangible asset ("the asset") was vested in the relevant company or a subsidiary of it (in either case, alone or jointly with others), and

(ii) the asset was a relevant intangible asset,

(*b*) at any time on or after that date, an activity carried on by the relevant company or a subsidiary of it would be an excluded activity by reason only of the receipt of royalties or licence fees attributable to the exploitation of the asset, and

(*c*) the activity would not be an excluded activity if the amendments made by subsection (1) had not been made.

(6) The activity is to be treated, in relation to the option, as not being an excluded activity at that time.

GENERAL NOTE

Enterprise management incentives are tax and NIC advantages share options aimed at helping smaller higher-risk companies to recruit and retain key workers. To qualify for the tax and NIC advantages under the EMI scheme, the company must meet conditions as to size, independence and trading activities.

Certain trading activities are excluded. These include the receipt of income from licence fees and royalties, except where there are derived from 'relevant intangible assets'. The current definition (in ITEPA 2003 Sch 5 para 19(4)) provides that relevant intangible assets are assets created by the company carrying on the trade, or by a company that was a parent or qualifying subsidiary of that company when the assets were created. This definition is replaced by a new definition such that a relevant intangible asset is an asset created by the company issuing the EMI options or by a company that was a qualifying subsidiary of the company issuing EMI options for the whole period during which it created the asset.

The new definition removes an unintended effect of the former wording and allows assets to be transferred to a subsidiary which was not in the group at the time that the assets were created without a loss of qualifying status.

The new definition applies to EMI options granted on or after 6 April 2007 and also to unexercised options which were qualifying options immediately before 6 April 2007 and which have not lost their qualifying status.

Provision is also made to ensure that options that were qualifying options at 6 April 2007 will not lose their qualifying status simply as a result of the changes made by this clause.

62 Benefits code: whether employment is "lower-paid employment"

(1) In section 219 of ITEPA 2003 (exclusion of lower-paid employments from parts of benefits code: extra amounts to be added in connection with a car), omit subsections (5) and (6).

(2) The repeal made by subsection (1) has effect for the tax year 2007–08 and subsequent tax years.

GENERAL NOTE

Legislative effect is given to ESC A104, which removes an anomaly whereby an employee earning at a rate of less than £8,500 per annum could incur a double tax charge where he or she was provided with car and car fuel benefits via an employer's credit token or non-cash voucher.

This is achieved by repealing ITEPA 2003 s 219(5), (6) with effect for 2007–08 and subsequent tax years.

In calculating whether the £8,500 threshold is breached, ITEPA 2003 s 219 currently requires that where an employee is provided with a car or fuel benefit by means of a non cash voucher or credit token both the amount of the car or fuel benefit and the benefit of the non-cash voucher or credit token must be taken into account. This double counting may result in an employee's earnings exceeding the £8,500 threshold and being taxed on both benefits.

63 Armed forces redundancy schemes

(1) In section 411 of ITEPA 2003 (exception for payments and benefits for forces), the existing provision becomes subsection (1) and after that subsection insert—

> "(2) This Chapter does not apply to a payment or other benefit provided under a scheme established by an order under section 1(1) of the Armed Forces (Pensions and Compensation) Act 2004."

(2) The amendments made by subsection (1) have effect for the tax year 2006–07 and subsequent tax years.

GENERAL NOTE

An exemption from tax (in new ITEPA 2003 s 411(2)) is introduced for payments made under the Armed Forces Redundancy Scheme 2006. The exemption, which applies for 2006–07 and subsequent tax years, ensures that recipients of payments under the new Armed Forces Redundancy Scheme that was operational from 6 April 2006 are in the same tax position as those receiving payments under the Armed Forces Redundancy Scheme 1975.

64 Armed forces: the Operational Allowance

(1) In ITEPA 2003, after section 297 insert—

"297A Armed forces: the Operational Allowance

> (1) No liability to income tax arises in respect of payments to members of the armed forces of the Crown of the Operational Allowance.
>
> (2) The Operational Allowance is an allowance designated as such by the Secretary of State."

(2) The amendment made by subsection (1) has effect in relation to payments whenever made.

GENERAL NOTE

A tax exemption is introduced for the operational allowance payable to members of the armed forces serving in specified areas designated by the Secretary of State for Defence. The exemption, which applies to payments of the allowance whenever made, is contained in new ITEPA 2003 s 297A.

The introduction of the allowance was announced by the Secretary of State for Defence on 10 October 2006 for armed forces serving in specified locations, such as Iraq, Afghanistan and the Balkans, where the operational demands are the greatest.

65 Service charge income

(1) Section 480 of ITA 2007 (meaning of "accumulated or discretionary income") is amended as follows.

(2) In subsection (3)(*c*) (income from service charges held on trust by relevant housing body), for the words after "charges" substitute "which are paid in respect of dwellings in the United Kingdom and are held on trust."

(3) For subsections (5) and (6) substitute—

> "(5) In subsection (3)(*c*) "service charges" has the meaning given by section 18 of the Landlord and Tenant Act 1985 (but as if that section also applied in relation to dwellings in Scotland and Northern Ireland)."

(4) The amendments made by this section have effect for the tax year 2007–08 and subsequent tax years.

GENERAL NOTE

Landlords are generally required to hold service charge and sinking fund payments made by tenants and leaseholders in trust. Trusts can accumulate income, for example from holding the funds in interest-bearing accounts, and for tax purposes this income is charged at the special trust rate of tax of 40 per cent.

Provisions introduced by FA 2006 provided that the first £1,000 of trust income was taxed at 20 per cent rather than at 40 per cent. This was intended to benefits small trusts, including trusts for service charges and sinking funds. In addition, FA 2006 also made provision for all income from service charges and sinking funds held on trust by social landlords to be taxable at 20 per cent instead.

This treatment is extended to private sector landlords for 2007–08 and subsequent tax years. This is achieved by amendments to ITA 2007 s 480. The change has the effect of aligning the tax treatment of the social and private housing sectors.

The relief applies to properties situated in the UK.

66 Charge on benefits received by former owner of property: late elections

(1) In paragraph 23 of Schedule 15 to FA 2004 (charge to income tax on benefits received by former owner of property), for sub-paragraphs (3) and (4) substitute—

> "(3) The election must be made on or before—
>
> (*a*) the relevant filing date, or
>
> (*b*) such later date as an officer of Revenue and Customs may, in a particular case, allow."

(2) The amendment made by subsection (1) is deemed to have come into force on 21st March 2007.

GENERAL NOTE

The pre-owned income tax charge was introduced by FA 2004 Sch 15 to prevent avoidance of inheritance tax. It provides an income tax charge from 6 April 2005 on the benefit that people derive from having free or low-cost enjoyment of assets that they formerly owned or provided funds to purchase.

Instead of the income tax charge, taxpayers can elect for the assets to be treated as forming part of their estate for inheritance tax purposes. The time limit for this election is the same as that for the self-assessment return, i.e. 31 January after the end of the tax year in which the individual is first liable to a pre-owned asset charge. This deadline is extended (substituted FA 2004 Sch 15 para 23(3)) to enable HMRC to accept elections made after that date.

The extended time limit is deemed to have come into effect from 21 March 2007.

67 Unpaid remuneration and employee benefit contributions

(1) Section 31 of ITTOIA 2005 (relationship between rules prohibiting and allowing deductions: trading income) is amended as follows.

(2) In subsection (1) (priority of relevant permissive rules over relevant prohibitive rules), in paragraph (*b*) (sections to which that priority rule is subject), for "sections 48 (car or motor cycle hire) and" substitute "section 36 (unpaid remuneration), section 38 (employee benefit contributions), section 48 (car or motor cycle hire) and section".

(3) In subsection (3) (meaning of "relevant prohibitive rule"), after "sections" insert "36, 38,".

(4) Section 274 of ITTOIA 2005 (provision corresponding to section 31 of that Act in case of property income) is amended as follows.

(5) In subsection (1)(*b*), for "sections 48 (car or motor cycle hire) and" substitute "section 36 (unpaid remuneration), section 38 (employee benefit contributions), section 48 (car or motor cycle hire) and section".

(6) In subsection (3), after "sections" insert "36, 38,".

(7) The amendments made by this section have effect for the tax year 2007–08 and subsequent tax years.

GENERAL NOTE

Technical amendments are made to ITTOIA 2005 ss 31, 274 to ensure that the rules on the treatment of salary costs operate as intended in relation to employee benefit contributions and unpaid remuneration.

By virtue of TA 1988 s 74 an employer can deduct expenses incurred wholly and exclusively for the purposes of the trade, profession or vocation when calculating profits for tax purposes. This rule is subject to the provisions of FA 1989 s 43 and FA 2003 Sch 24, which prevent an employer from making a deduction for remuneration where the costs re not paid within nine months of the end of the relevant accounting period.

In redrafting the provisions for income tax purposes in ITTOIA 2005, the provisions in FA 1989 s 43 and FA 2003 Sch 24 were inadvertently disapplied. The technical amendments correct this error and ensure the legislation applies as intended.

The changes have effect for 2007–08 and subsequent tax years.

PART 4
PENSIONS

GENERAL NOTE

Following widespread consultation by the former Inland Revenue on the simplification of the tax regime for pension schemes the Pensions Tax Simplification legislation was enacted in FA 2004 with effect from 6 April 2006. After further consultation and lobbying the legislation was amended in FAs 2005 and 2006. HMRC also issued a consultation document 'Inheritance Tax (IHT) and Pensions Simplification' on 21 July 2005 concerning the new options under the simplified pensions regime in relation to IHT. Following consultation HMRC's proposals for changes to the legislation regarding IHT appeared in FA 2006 s 161 and Sch 22. In the Pre Budget Report of 6 December 2006 the Chancellor proposed removing an individual's entitlement to tax relief on any pension contributions they pay that are used to fund personal term assurance policies and further changes regarding the treatment of alternatively secured pensions to limit their tax advantages as an IHT shelter. He also identified two areas of tax avoidance involving pension schemes and some other minor changes which are contained in FA 2007.

68 Abolition of contributions relief for life assurance premium contributions

Schedule 18 contains provisions denying relief for contributions made by or on behalf of members in respect of life assurance premiums.

GENERAL NOTE

This section introduces Schedule 18 which contains detailed amendments to FA 2004 regarding premiums paid under personal term assurance policies. The proposals will ensure that individuals no longer obtain tax relief on pension contributions that are used to pay premiums paid under personal term assurance policies.

69 Alternatively secured pensions etc

Schedule 19 contains provisions about alternatively secured pensions and transfer lump sum death benefit etc

GENERAL NOTE

This section introduces Schedule 19 containing detailed amendments to FA 2004, to IHTA 1984 and to ITEPA 2003 regarding the treatment of alternatively secured pensions by limiting their tax advantages as an IHT shelter and by requiring a minimum income to be paid each year from a member's or dependant's alternatively secured pension fund.

70 Miscellaneous

Schedule 20 contains miscellaneous provisions about registered pension schemes and employer-financed retirement benefits schemes.

GENERAL NOTE

Section 70 introduces Schedule 20 containing detailed amendments to FA 2004, to IHTA 1984 and to ITEPA 2003 to give schemes, employers and pension savers additional flexibility, to provide measures dealing with the transition to the pensions tax simplification regime and to prevent abuse of the new rules.

PART 5

SDLT, STAMP DUTY AND SDRT

SDLT: anti-avoidance provisions

71 Anti-avoidance

BACKGROUND NOTE

Since the introduction of SDLT with effect from 1 December 2003 attempts have been made to avoid SDLT and the Inland Revenue (now HMRC) attempted to block avoidance by introducing targeted anti-avoidance provisions and disclosure obligations.

As a result of changes made in FA 2007 to FA 2003 Sch 15 (partnerships) increasingly transactions involving partnerships and sub-sales were being used to minimise SDLT, although some sub-sales were coupled with distributions of assets in specie to take advantage of FA 2003 s 54. On 6 December 2006 HMRC announced as part of the Pre-Budget Report that it would introduce a new s 75A into FA 2003 and tabled the SDLT (Variation of Finance 2003) Regulations 2006, SI 2006/3217, which contained a previous version of s 75A, stated in the accompanying explanatory material as intended to stop such "schemes" and other SDLT minimisation techniques. The version of s 75A contained in section 71 is intended with retrospective effect to replace the 2006 Regulations.

(1) In FA 2003, after section 75 insert (in place of the section inserted by the Stamp Duty Land Tax (Variation of the Finance Act 2003) Regulations 2006 (SI 2006/3237))—

"75A Anti-avoidance

(1) This section applies where—

(*a*) one person (V) disposes of a chargeable interest and another person (P) acquires either it or a chargeable interest deriving from it,

(*b*) a number of transactions (including the disposal and acquisition) are involved in connection with the disposal and acquisition ("the scheme transactions"), and

(*c*) the sum of the amounts of stamp duty land tax payable in respect of the scheme transactions is less than the amount that would be payable on a notional land transaction effecting the acquisition of V's chargeable interest by P on its disposal by V.

(2) In subsection (1) "transaction" includes, in particular—

(*a*) a non-land transaction,

(*b*) an agreement, offer or undertaking not to take specified action,

(*c*) any kind of arrangement whether or not it could otherwise be described as a transaction, and

(*d*) a transaction which takes place after the acquisition by P of the chargeable interest.

(3) The scheme transactions may include, for example—

(*a*) the acquisition by P of a lease deriving from a freehold owned or formerly owned by V;

(*b*) a sub-sale to a third person;

(*c*) the grant of a lease to a third person subject to a right to terminate;

(*d*) the exercise of a right to terminate a lease or to take some other action;

(*e*) an agreement not to exercise a right to terminate a lease or to take some other action;

(*f*) the variation of a right to terminate a lease or to take some other action.

(4) Where this section applies—

(*a*) any of the scheme transactions which is a land transaction shall be disregarded for the purposes of this Part, but

(*b*) there shall be a notional land transaction for the purposes of this Part effecting the acquisition of V's chargeable interest by P on its disposal by V.

(5) The chargeable consideration on the notional transaction mentioned in subsections (1)(*c*) and (4)(*b*) is the largest amount (or aggregate amount)—

(*a*) given by or on behalf of any one person by way of consideration for the scheme transactions, or

(*b*) received by or on behalf of V (or a person connected with V within the meaning of section 839 of the Taxes Act 1988) by way of consideration for the scheme transactions.

(6) The effective date of the notional transaction is—

(*a*) the last date of completion for the scheme transactions, or

(*b*) if earlier, the last date on which a contract in respect of the scheme transactions is substantially performed.

(7) This section does not apply where subsection (1)(*c*) is satisfied only by reason of—

(*a*) sections 71A to 73, or

(*b*) a provision of Schedule 9.

75B Anti-avoidance: incidental transactions

(1) In calculating the chargeable consideration on the notional transaction for the purposes of section 75A(5), consideration for a transaction shall be ignored if or in so far as the transaction is merely incidental to the transfer of the chargeable interest from V to P.

(2) A transaction is not incidental to the transfer of the chargeable interest from V to P—

(*a*) if or in so far as it forms part of a process, or series of transactions, by which the transfer is effected,

(*b*) if the transfer of the chargeable interest is conditional on the completion of the transaction, or

(*c*) if it is of a kind specified in section 75A(3).

(3) A transaction may, in particular, be incidental if or in so far as it is undertaken only for a purpose relating to—

(*a*) the construction of a building on property to which the chargeable interest relates,

(*b*) the sale or supply of anything other than land, or

(*c*) a loan to P secured by a mortgage, or any other provision of finance to enable P, or another person, to pay for part of a process, or series of transactions, by which the chargeable interest transfers from V to P.

(4) In subsection (3)—

(*a*) paragraph (*a*) is subject to subsection (2)(*a*) to (*c*),

(*b*) paragraph (*b*) is subject to subsection (2)(*a*) and (*c*), and

(*c*) paragraph (*c*) is subject to subsection (2)(*a*) to (*c*).

(5) The exclusion required by subsection (1) shall be effected by way of just and reasonable apportionment if necessary.

(6) In this section a reference to the transfer of a chargeable interest from V to P includes a reference to a disposal by V of an interest acquired by P.

75C Anti-avoidance: supplemental

(1) A transfer of shares or securities shall be ignored for the purposes of section 75A if but for this subsection it would be the first of a series of scheme transactions.

(2) The notional transaction under section 75A attracts any relief under this Part which it would attract if it were an actual transaction (subject to the terms and restrictions of the relief).

(3) The notional transaction under section 75A is a land transaction entered into for the purposes of or in connection with the transfer of an undertaking or part for the purposes of paragraphs 7 and 8 of Schedule 7, if any of the scheme transactions is entered into for the purposes of or in connection with the transfer of the undertaking or part.

(4) In the application of section 75A(5) no account shall be taken of any amount paid by way of consideration in respect of a transaction to which any of sections 60, 61, 63, 64, 65, 66, 67, 69, 71, 74 and 75, or a provision of Schedule 6A or 8, applies.

(5) In the application of section 75A(5) an amount given or received partly in respect of the chargeable interest acquired by P and partly in respect of another chargeable interest shall be subjected to just and reasonable apportionment.

(6) Section 53 applies to the notional transaction under section 75A.

(7) Paragraph 5 of Schedule 4 applies to the notional transaction under section 75A.

(8) For the purposes of section 75A—

(*a*) an interest in a property-investment partnership (within the meaning of paragraph 14 of Schedule 15) is a chargeable interest in so far as it concerns land owned by the partnership, and

(*b*) where V or P is a partnership, Part 3 of Schedule 15 applies to the notional transaction as to the transfer of a chargeable interest from or to a partnership.

(9) For the purposes of section 75A a reference to an amount of consideration includes a reference to the value of consideration given as money's worth.

(10) Stamp duty land tax paid in respect of a land transaction which is to be disregarded by virtue of section 75A(4)(*a*) is taken to have been paid in respect of the notional transaction by virtue of section 75A(4)(*b*).

(11) The Treasury may by order provide for section 75A not to apply in specified circumstances.

(12) An order under subsection (11) may include incidental, consequential or transitional provision and may make provision with retrospective effect."

(2) The amendment made by subsection (1) has effect in respect of disposals and acquisitions if the disposal mentioned in new section 75A(1)(*a*) (inserted by that subsection) takes place on or after 6th December 2006.

(3) But—

(*a*) the transitional provisions of sub-paragraphs (2) to (5) of paragraph 1 of the Schedule to the Stamp Duty Land Tax (Variation of the Finance Act 2003) Regulations 2006 (SI 2006/3237) continue to have effect in relation to this section as in relation to that paragraph, and

(*b*) a provision of new section 75C (inserted by subsection (1) above) shall not have effect where the disposal mentioned in new section 75A(1)(*a*) took place before the day on which this Act is passed, if or in so far as the provision would make a person liable for a higher amount of tax than would have been charged in accordance with those regulations.

GENERAL NOTE

Section 75A(1) requires there to be a disposal by one person (V) and an acquisition of a chargeable interest or an interest derived from it by another person (P); a number of transactions to be "involved in connection" with the disposal and acquisition (referred to as "scheme transactions"); and for less SDLT to be payable in respect of the scheme transactions than the SDLT payable on a notional land transaction whereby P acquired the relevant interest direct from V. Note that there is no motive test and the scheme transactions merely have to be connected -in an unspecified manner – with the disposal and acquisition, even in respect of bona fide commercial transactions with no intention to avoid SDLT, before s 75A applies. HMRC are understood to believe that if there is no linkage between V and P: in particular that there has to be more than a series of transactions which, with hindsight, could be regarded as a scheme. "Chargeable interest" is undefined but can be assumed to have the meaning set out in FA 2003 s 48(1).

Section 75A(2) provides an inclusive definition of "transaction" (used in s 75A(1)(*b*)) and s 75A(3) provides examples of "scheme transactions".

Where s 75A applies, ss (4) provides for actual land transactions to be disregarded and for there to be a notional land transaction in respect of which, presumably, V should file a Land Transaction Return ("LTR") by reference to the consideration determined in accordance with s 75A(5). It is not clear (despite s 75C(10)) if LTRs have been filed and SDLT referable to such of the scheme transactions as are land transactions has been paid whether the SDLT is refundable and/or creditable against the SDLT on the notional land transaction where V is not a party to those land transactions. Subsection (6) provides that the effective date of the notional transaction is the earlier of the last completion date for a scheme transaction or when such a contract is substantially performed. The SDLT on the notional land transaction equals the largest amount (or aggregate amounts) given by or on behalf of any one person in respect of a scheme transaction (whether or not that scheme transaction is a land transaction) or received by or on behalf of V or a person connected (within TA 1988 s 839) with V – see s 75A(5).

LIMITATIONS

Given the very wide wording of s 75A(1), the new legislation reduces the possible number of transactions affected by removing certain transactions from its ambit or modifying its impact:

(*a*) where the notional land transaction would attract more SDLT than the actual transaction only because of the reliefs provided for by the alternative finance regime (FA 2003 s 71A–73) or the right to buy legislation (FA 2003 Sch 9), s 75A does not apply – see s 75A(7);

(*b*) where the consideration attributable to incidental transactions (as defined in s 75B) is ignored in computing the SDLT on the notional transaction – see s 75B(1);

(*c*) a transfer of shares or securities can be ignored in determining what are "scheme transactions" if the transfer would be the first such transaction – see s 75C(1);

(*d*) a notional land transactions attracts the same SDLT reliefs it would have obtained had it been an actual transaction – see s 75C(2) – and if any actual scheme transaction would have obtained relief under FA 2003 Sch 7 paras 7 or 8 the notional land transaction has the same purpose – see s 75C(3);

(*e*) consideration referable to an actual land transaction benefiting from certain reliefs is ignored in computing the SDLT on the notional land transaction – see s 75C(4).

INCIDENTAL TRANSACTIONS

Sections 75B(2) and (3) limit the extent to which transactions are incidental and in particular provides that transaction of the type listed in s 75A(3) are not incidental. Section 75B(3) is intended to enable a stand alone building contract; financing transactions; and transactions only having the purpose of supplying assets other than land to be regarded as incidental.

MISCELLANEOUS

Section 75(C)(5) provides for an appropriate apportionment where more than one chargeable interest is involved, perhaps where sub-sales to different persons occur.

Section 75C(6) enables a market value consideration to be imputed if a notional land transaction would otherwise be subject to FA 2003 s 53, but only with effect from Royal Assent: see Section 70(3)(b). Section 75C(7) causes the market value rules in sch 4 para 5 to apply to a notional land transaction involving an exchange.

Section 75C(8) attempts to apply s 75A to transactions involving dealings in partnership interests where and to the extent that the underlying asset is land, and where either P or V is a partnership (and hence not a "person" within s 75A(1)).

Section 75C(9) makes it clear that consideration in moneys worth can be taken into account for the purposes of s 75A(5) and s 75C(10) provides that SDLT paid in respect of an actual transaction that is disregarded is credited against SDLT due on the notional land transaction. Given that HMRC believe they can decide which transactions are to be taken into account on the application of s 75A, this might mean that a party to the notional land transaction receives credit for tax paid by a third part in respect of an actual land transaction.

Section 75C(11) and (12) confer regulation making powers on the Treasury to disapply s 75A in certain circumstances.

COMMENCEMENT

Section 71(2) makes it clear that new s 75A has effect for any disposal occurs on or after 6 December 2003 subject to the same transitional provisions (eg transactions pursuant to certain pre 6 December 2006 contracts) as applied under the 2006 Regulations (see s 71(3)(a) and the restriction (principally referable to s 75C(5)) in s 70(3)(b)).

72 Partnerships

BACKGROUND NOTE

HMRC has struggled to apply SDLT to transactions involving partnerships and so partly for this reason SDLT only applied fully to partnerships with effect from Royal Assent to FA 2004 (see Schedule 15). Considerable legislative and administrative changes have been made to these provisions culminating in changes made by the 2006 Regulations referred to in the commentary on Section 71. Section 72 re-enacts and extends the changes made by those Regulations. Sub-section 72(2) makes clear that the amendments contained in subsequent subsections are to Schedule 15 in its form pre 6 December 2006.

(1) Schedule 15 to FA 2003 (stamp duty land tax: partnerships) is amended as follows.

(2) A reference in this section to a provision of that Schedule is to the provision as it had effect before variation by the Stamp Duty Land Tax (Variation of the Finance Act 2003) Regulations 2006.

(3) In Step Two of paragraph 12(1) (transfer to partnership: how to calculate the "sum of the lower proportions")—

(*a*) in paragraph (*b*), for "or is connected with the relevant owner" substitute "or is an individual connected with the relevant owner", and

(*b*) insert at the end—

"(If there is no relevant owner with a corresponding partner, the sum of the lower proportions is nil.)"

(4) In paragraph 12, after sub-paragraph (2) insert—

"(3) For the purpose of paragraph (*b*) of Step 2 a company is to be treated as an individual connected with the relevant owner in so far as it—

(*a*) holds property as trustee, and

(*b*) is connected with the relevant owner only because of section 839(3) of the Taxes Act 1988."

(5) Omit paragraph 13 (transfer to partnership where all partners are companies).

(6) In paragraph 14 (transfer of interest in property-investment partnership)—

(*a*) omit sub-paragraphs (1)(*b*) and (4), and

(*b*) insert at the end—

"(9) An interest in respect of the transfer of which this paragraph applies shall be treated as a chargeable interest for the purposes of paragraph 3(1) of Schedule 7 to the extent that the relevant partnership property consists of a chargeable interest.",

and in the italic cross-heading before it, omit "*for consideration*".

(7) In Step Two of paragraph 20(1) (transfer from partnership: how to calculate the "sum of the lower proportions")—

(*a*) in paragraph (*b*), for "or was connected with the relevant owner" substitute "or was an individual connected with the relevant owner", and

(*b*) insert at the end—

"(If there is no relevant owner with a corresponding partner, the sum of the lower proportions is nil.)"

(8) In paragraph 20, after sub-paragraph (2) insert—

"(3) For the purpose of paragraph (*b*) of Step 2 a company is to be treated as an individual connected with the relevant owner in so far as it—

(*a*) holds property as trustee, and

(*b*) is connected with the relevant owner only because of section 839(3) of the Taxes Act 1988."

(9) After paragraph 27 insert—

"**27A**— (1) This paragraph applies where in calculating the sum of the lower proportions in relation to a transaction (in accordance with paragraph 12)—

(*a*) a company ("the connected company") would have been a corresponding partner of a relevant owner ("the original owner") but for the fact that paragraph (*b*) of Step Two includes connected persons only if they are individuals, and

(*b*) the connected company and the original owner are members of the same group.

(2) The charge in respect of the transaction shall be reduced to the amount that would have been payable had the connected company been a corresponding partner of the original owner for the purposes of calculating the sum of the lower proportions.

(3) The provisions of Part 1 of Schedule 7 apply to group relief under sub-paragraph (2) above as to group relief under paragraph 1(1) of Schedule 7, but—

(*a*) with the omission of paragraph 2(2)(*a*),

(*b*) with the substitution for "the purchaser" in paragraph 3(1)(*a*) of "a partner who was, at the effective date of the transaction, a partner and a member of the same group as the transferor ("the relevant partner")", and

(*c*) with the other modifications specified in paragraph 27(3) to (6) above."

(10) For paragraph 36 substitute—

"**36** For the purposes of this Part of this Schedule, where a person acquires or increases a partnership share there is a transfer of an interest in the partnership (to that partner and from the other partners)."

(11) In paragraph 39 ("connected persons"), insert at the end—

"(3) As applied by sub-paragraph (1) for the purposes of paragraph 12 or 20, that section has effect with the omission of subsection (3)(*c*) (trustee connected with settlement)."

(12) In Schedule 16 to FA 2003 (trusts and powers)—

(*a*) in paragraph 3(1) (bare trust), after "a chargeable interest" insert "or an interest in a partnership", and

(*b*) in paragraph 4 (trustees of settlement), after "a chargeable interest" insert "or an interest in a partnership".

(13) The amendments made by subsections (1) to (11) have effect in respect of transfers occurring on or after the day on which this Act is passed.

(14) But the amendments made by subsections (6) and (10) do not have effect in respect of anything done in respect of a property-investment partnership established before the day on which this Act is passed if—

(*a*) the partnership does not acquire a chargeable interest on or after that day, and

(*b*) stamp duty land tax was paid in respect of each chargeable interest acquired before that day, by reference to chargeable consideration of not less than the market value.

(15) The amendment made by subsection (12) has effect in respect of acquisitions occurring on or after the day on which this Act is passed.

(16) An amendment made by this section replaces, to the extent provided for by subsections (13) to (15), any variation made by the Stamp Duty Land Tax (Variation of the Finance Act 2003) Regulations 2006 (SI 2006/3237).

(17) Despite subsections (13) to (16), the transitional provisions of sub-paragraphs (8) to (10) of paragraph 2 of the Schedule to the Stamp Duty Land Tax (Variation of the

Finance Act 2003) Regulations 2006 (SI 2006/3237) continue to have effect in relation to the amendments made by this section as in relation to that paragraph.

GENERAL NOTE

Acquisitions by partnerships

(*a*) In calculating the SDLT due on acquisitions of land by partnerships in circumstances where Schedule 15 para 10 applies, very broadly regard is had to the reduction in the interest that the transferor had in the land pre transfer compared with its interest post transfer: this is achieved by the sum of lower proportions formula in para 12. Section 72(3) limits the extent to which the interests of persons connected with a partner are taken into account by providing only that interests of individuals connected with a relevant owner are taken into account in Step Two of para 12. So for example if a company had a 100% interest in property transferred to a partnership and it held a 10% interest (and a company connected with it had an 80% interest) in the land once vested in the partnership, previously the SDLT charge would have been on the 10% interest vested in the unconnected partners. Now the connected company's interest is ignored and so 90% of the reduction in market value of the transferor's interest is potentially chargeable. Section 72(4) enables the interest of a company which is a trustee and connected with an individual only because of TA 1988 s 839(3) (settlements), as amended by s 72(11), to be regarded as held by a (connected) individual for the purposes of Step Two para 12.

(*b*) Section 72(5) repeals Sch 15 para 13 (substitution of market value where the sum of lower proportions is 75 or greater and all partners are bodies corporate), broadly because this is achieved by the modifications made to Step Two of para 12 (in particular ignoring interests held by connected companies), effectively requiring companies in group relationships to claim group relief.

Group relief

Section 72(9) inserts a new para 27A(2) into FA 2003 Sch 15 to provide a limited group relief where, but for the disregard of connected persons who are not individuals, the SDLT charge on a transfer of land into a partnership would have been lower. Para 27A(3) provides for a clawback where the partner with an interest which benefited from relief under para 27A(2) leaves the group within the relevant 3 year period.

Transfers of partnership interests

Section 72(6)(*a*), coupled with the amendment made by s 72(10), extends the circumstances in which transfers of interests in partnerships owning land are liable to SDLT. Section 72(6) removes the requirement (in para 14(1)(*b*)) that consideration is given for a transfer before the charge can arise. Further para 36 in its current form limits when an interest is in a partnership is transferred: in particular if eg 3 partners have one-third interests in land worth £450,000 and a new partner contributes £150,000 in cash so that each partner has £150,000 interest in mixed assets totalling £600,000 no transfer currently would arise under para 36. Section 72(10) amends para 36 to make it clear that an increase in or acquisition of a partnership interest is a transfer even though the value of each partner's interest is unchanged.

Section 72(6)(*b*) clarifies for the purposes of recovery of group relief (under FA 2003 Sch 7 para 3(1)) that an interest in a partnership is a chargeable interest.

Transfers from partnerships

Section 72(7) makes a similar amendment to the calculation of the sum of lower proportions in Sch 15 para 18 as was made to para 10, namely to disregard the interest of persons (other than individuals) connected with a partner in determining the SDLT due on the transfer of land from a partnership. Section 72(8) similarly extends the meaning of individuals to include bodies corporate acting as trustees as was made by s 72(4). There is no equivalent extension of group relief in respect of paragraph 18 as was made for transfers to a partnership under Schedule 15, paragraph 10 by virtue of section 71(9).

MISCELLANEOUS

Section 72(11) amends the definition of connected persons contained in TA 1988 s 839(3) so that companies connected with a trustee are ignored for the purpose of para 12 or 20.

Section 72(12) amends paras 3 and 4 of FA 2003 Schedule 16 (trustees) to provide that the acquisition of an interest in a partnership by a person as bare trustee is to be treated as if acquired by the beneficiaries and that where trustees acquire an interest in a partnership as trustees they are treated as if they had acquired the whole interest beneficially.

COMMENCEMENT

The amendments made by section 72 apply with effect from Royal Assent: to the extent that similar amendments were made under the 2006 Regulations with effect from 6 December 2006 those amendments apply to pre Royal Assent transactions. However to the extent that transitional provisions in the 2006 Regulations protected pre 6 December 2006 transactions, they continue to apply – see s 72 (13)–(17). There is a limited saving in s 72(14) as regards the changed definitions of what is a transfer of a partnership interest where a property investment partnership was established prior to Royal Assent, no further interests in land are acquired on or after Royal Assent and SDLT by reference to market value was paid on each interest acquired prior to Royal Assent.

Reliefs in relation to shares etc

73 Exemptions: intermediaries, repurchases etc

Schedule 21 contains provision in relation to exemptions from stamp duty and stamp duty reserve tax in cases involving intermediaries, repurchases, stock lending or recognised investment exchanges.

Prospective amendment

This section to be repealed by FA 2007 s 114, Sch 27 Pt 4(2) with effect in accordance with the provisions of FA 1990 ss 108, 110.

GENERAL NOTE

The Stamp Duty and SDRT legislation contains reliefs (in respect of these two taxes) from charges that would otherwise arise where intermediaries acquire shares, and in relation to stock lending and repo (sale and repurchase) transactions which are economically not sales but transactions designed to produce fees (stock lending fees) or income (amounts economically equivalent to loans at interest as a result of different sale and repurchase prices). These are currently contained in ss 80A, 80B and 80C for stamp duty and in ss 88A and s 88B, and s 89AA for SDRT. These are to be rewritten in a wholesale manner by Sch 21, effective from 1 November 2007 as a result of implementation of MiFID (EU Directive 2004/39/EC – Markets in Financial Instruments Directive).

74 Acquisition relief: disregard of company holding own shares

(1) In section 75 of FA 1986 (relief on acquisition of undertaking of company in pursuance of scheme for reconstruction of that company), after subsection (5) insert—

> "(5A) If immediately before the acquisition the target company or the acquiring company holds any of its own shares, the shares are to be treated for the purposes of subsections (4) and (5) as having been cancelled before the acquisition (and, accordingly, the company is to be treated as if it were not a shareholder of itself)."

(2) In section 77 of that Act (relief on acquisition of target company's share capital), after subsection (3) insert—

> "(3A) If immediately before the acquisition the target company or the acquiring company holds any of its own shares, the shares are to be treated for the purposes of subsection (3) as having been cancelled before the acquisition (and, accordingly, the company is to be treated as if it were not a shareholder of itself)."

(3) In Part 2 of Schedule 7 to FA 2003 (SDLT: reconstruction and acquisition reliefs), in paragraph 7 (reconstruction relief) after sub-paragraph (5) insert—

"(5A) If immediately before the acquisition the target company or the acquiring company holds any of its own shares, the shares are to be treated for the purposes of sub-paragraphs (2) and (4) as having been cancelled before the acquisition (and, accordingly, the company is to be treated as if it were not a shareholder of itself)."

(4) The amendments made by subsections (1) and (2) have effect in relation to any instrument executed on or after the day on which this Act is passed.

(5) The amendment made by subsection (3) has effect in relation to any land transaction of which the effective date is on or after that day.

GENERAL NOTE

Finance Act 1986 section 75 (in relation to stamp duty) and FA 2003 Schedule 7 para 2 (in relation to stamp duty land tax) provide relief from these to taxes in relation to schemes of reconstruction. FA 1986 s 77 provides a relief from stamp duty where a new company is interposed between a company and its shareholders. All these reliefs require certain conditions to be satisfied.

Section 74(1) introduces a new FA 1986 s 75(5A) which provides that, in deciding whether the conditions in s 75(4)(*a*) and (5)(*b*) and (*c*) are satisfied, shares that the company holds in itself (so called "treasury shares") can be ignored. Section 74(3) makes an equivalent change for the purposes of SDLT, by inserting para 7(5A) into FA 2003 Sch 7, for the purpose of interpreting paras 7(2) and (4).

Section 74(2) introduces a new FA 1986 s 77(5A) for the purpose of deciding if the shareholder conditions in ss 77(3) are satisfied, again enabling treasury shares to be ignored.

COMMENCEMENT

The changes for stamp duty apply to instruments executed on or after Royal Assent and for SDLT purposes to land transactions whose effective date are on or after that date.

Other reliefs etc

75 SDLT: alternative finance arrangements

BACKGROUND NOTE

FA 2003 ss 71–73 contain certain reliefs from SDLT intended to have the effect that so called sharia compliant transactions (although the legislation does not require them to be compliant) do not attract more SDLT than a conventionally structured transaction which involves the payment of interest. These can involve the purchase of an interest by a financial institution and the grant by it of a lease or sub-lease or right to occupy pending a transfer to the lessee/occupier of the interest acquired by the institution. The terms of the transactions give the financial institution a reward similar to interest and could be likened to mortgages, the transfer of which are exempt SDLT (see s 48(2)(a) and (3)(a)).

(1) In FA 2003, after section 73A insert—

"73B Exempt interests

(1) An interest held by a financial institution as a result of the first transaction within the meaning of section 71A(1)(*a*), 72(1)(*a*) or 72A(1)(*a*) is an exempt interest for the purposes of stamp duty land tax.

(2) That interest ceases to be an exempt interest if—

(*a*) the lease or agreement mentioned in section 71A(1)(*c*), 72(1)(*b*) or 72A(1)(*b*) ceases to have effect, or

(*b*) the right under section 71A(1)(*d*), 72(1)(*c*) or 72A(1)(*c*) ceases to have effect or becomes subject to a restriction.

(3) Subsection (1) does not apply if the first transaction is exempt from charge by virtue of Schedule 7.

(4) Subsection (1) does not make an interest exempt in respect of—

(*a*) the first transaction itself, or
(*b*) a further transaction or third transaction within the meaning of section 71A(4), 72(4) or 72A(4)."

(2) In section 48 of that Act (stamp duty land tax: exempt interests), after subsection (3) insert—

"(3A) Section 73B makes additional provision about exempt interests in relation to alternative finance arrangements."

(3) For the text of sections 71A(8), 72(7), 72A(8) and 73(5)(*a*) of that Act (alternative finance arrangements: meaning of "financial institution"), substitute "In this section "financial institution" has the meaning given by section 46 of the Finance Act 2005 (alternative finance arrangements)."

(4) The amendments made by this section—

(*a*) have effect in relation to anything that would, but for the exemption provided by new section 73B inserted by subsection (1) above, be a land transaction with an effective date on or after 22nd March 2007, and
(*b*) apply, in accordance with paragraph (*a*), to interests irrespective of the date of their creation.

GENERAL NOTE

Section 75(1) introduces a new FA 2003 s 73B which provides that if an interest in land has been acquired in circumstances qualifying for relief under s 7lA, 72 or 72A by a financial institution any dealing in that interest constitutes an exempt interest (see FA 2003 s 48) unless the sub-lease or right to occupy granted by the financial institution has come to an end or the right granted to the lessee/occupier by the institution comes to an end or becomes subject to a restriction: see s 73B(2). The effect of the exemption is to make exempt from SDLT dealings in land that are in economic substance equivalent to mortgages by the financial institutions.

The exemption contained in s 73B(1) does not apply if the interest acquired by the financial institution is exempt SDLT as result of group or acquisition relief (within FA 2003 Sch 7): see s 73B(3). The relief does not apply either to:

(*a*) the transaction whereby the institution acquires the interest prior to its entry into a lease or other transaction with the lessee/occupier (unless acquired from the individual in question or other financial institution in circumstances in which it will already be exempt under ss 71A(2), 72(2) or 72A(2)); or
(*b*) to any transaction during or at the end of the financial institution's involvement under which as contemplated by s 71A, 72 or 72A the lessee/occupier obtains the or part of the financial institution's interest in the land: see s 73B(4).

This is consistent with the rationale of the relief, namely that the lessee's or occupier's acquisition of the financial institution's interest in the land is not liable to SDLT but that the preceding acquisition by the institution is liable to SDLT, unless acquired from another institution or the individual concerned in circumstances in which the institution or individual has already paid SDLT.

MISCELLANEOUS

Section 75(2) makes a cross-reference to new s 73B in s 48 (exempt interests) by inserting new s 48(3A). The importance of being an exempt interest is that no land transaction return is required to be submitted.

Section 75(3) replaces the definition of "financial institution" in the SDLT relieving provisions (ss 7lA, 72, 72A and 73) with a cross-reference to the definition contained in FA 2005 s 46, essentially to extend relief to those licensed under consumer credit and overseas legislation.

COMMENCEMENT

Section 75(4)(*a*) provides for any transaction affected by s 73B with an effective date after 21 March 2007 to constitute an exempt interest, irrespective of whether the interests in land so dealt with were acquired by financial institutions before 22 March 2007: see s 75(4)(*b*).

76 SDLT: exchanges

(1) In section 47(1) of FA 2003 (exchanges), insert at the end "(and they are not linked transactions within the meaning of section 108)".

(2) In section 108 of that Act (linked transactions), insert at the end—

"(4) This section is subject to section 47(1)."

(3) The amendments made by this section have effect in relation to a set of land transactions if the effective date of any of them is on or after the day on which this Act is passed.

GENERAL NOTE

Section 76 is a relieving provision. Currently the SDLT legislation (s 47 and Sch 5) generally provides for a transactions between A and B in consideration of a transaction between B and A to take place at market value and to constitute linked transactions. The effect of transactions being linked is to provide for a higher rate of SDLT to be charged if the aggregate consideration exceeds the relevant thresholds: see s 108(2) and (3).

Section 76(1) provides for transactions involved in exchanges not to be linked for the purposes of FA 2003 s 108 and s 75(2) introduces a new s 108(4) which cross-refers to s 47(l) as amended. Given that transactions between connected companies are generally at market value (see FA 2003 s 53, subject to s 54 and other relieving provisions) the change made by s 76 principally benefits individuals connected with one another within TA 1988 s 839.

COMMENCEMENT

Section 76 applies to any set of land transactions provided one transaction has an effective date on or after Royal Assent: see s 76(3).

77 SDLT: shared ownership trusts

BACKGROUND NOTE

FA 2003 Schedule 9 already provides for relief from SDLT for transactions involving shared ownership leases ie leases where the occupier has a right to acquire the reversion from a qualifying landlord (defined in para 5(2) of that Schedule) or under a preserved right to buy. The relief varies dependent on whether an election has been made – broadly to elect to pay SDLT by reference to a market value at the outset (and to ignore rental payments – but see s 78 below) and pay no SDLT on further acquisitions of interest in the property – or not in which case acquisitions taking the tenant's interest over 80% do attract SDLT.

The concept of commonhold (as an alternative to leasehold structures) was introduced by the Commonhold and Leasehold Reform Act 2002. To provide a similar way of occupiers obtaining interests in a commonhold structure the concept of shared ownership trusts were developed under which the purchaser has a beneficial interest in the property under which it has a right to exclusively occupy the property in return for making regular payments (rather like rent).

(1) In Schedule 9 to FA 2003 (right to buy and shared ownership leases), insert at the end—

"Shared ownership trust: introduction

7— (1) In this Schedule "shared ownership trust" means a trust of land, within the meaning of section 1 of the Trusts of Land and Appointment of Trustees Act 1996, which satisfies the following conditions.

(2) Condition 1 is that the trust property is—

(*a*) a dwelling, and
(*b*) in England or Wales.

(3) Condition 2 is that one of the beneficiaries ("the social landlord") is a qualifying body (within the meaning of paragraph 5(2)).

(4) Condition 3 is that the terms of the trust—

(*a*) provide for one or more of the individual beneficiaries ("the purchaser") to have exclusive use of the trust property as the only or main residence of the purchaser,
(*b*) require the purchaser to make an initial payment to the social landlord ("the initial capital"),
(*c*) require the purchaser to make additional payments to the social landlord by way of compensation under section 13(6)(*a*) of the Trusts of Land and Appointment of Trustees Act 1996, ("rent-equivalent payments"),
(*d*) enable the purchaser to make other additional payments to the social landlord ("equity-acquisition payments"),
(*e*) determine the initial beneficial interests of the social landlord and of the purchaser by reference to the initial capital,
(*f*) specify a sum, equating or relating to the market value of the dwelling, by reference to which the initial capital was calculated, and
(*g*) provide for the purchaser's beneficial interest in the trust property to increase, and the social landlord's to diminish (or to be extinguished), as equity-acquisition payments are made.

(5) Section 118 (meaning of "market value") does not apply to this paragraph.

(6) In Condition 1 "dwelling" includes—

(*a*) a building which is being constructed or adapted for use as a dwelling,
(*b*) land which is to be used for the purpose of the construction of a dwelling, and
(*c*) land which is, or is to become, the garden or grounds of a dwelling.

Shared ownership trust: "purchaser"

8 For the purposes of the application of stamp duty land tax in relation to a shared ownership trust, the person (or persons) identified as the purchaser in accordance with paragraph 7, and not the social landlord or any other beneficiary, is (or are) to be treated as the purchaser of the trust property.

Shared ownership trust: election for market value treatment

9— (1) This paragraph applies where—

(*a*) a shared ownership trust is declared, and
(*b*) the purchaser elects for tax to be charged in accordance with this paragraph.

(2) An election must be included in—

(*a*) the land transaction return for the declaration of the shared ownership trust, or
(*b*) an amendment of that return.

(3) An election may not be revoked.

(4) Where this paragraph applies—

(*a*) the chargeable consideration for the declaration of the shared ownership trust shall be taken to be the amount stated in accordance with paragraph 7(4)(*f*), and
(*b*) no account shall be taken for the purposes of stamp duty land tax of rent-equivalent payments.

(5) The transfer to the purchaser of an interest in the trust property upon the termination of the trust is exempt from charge if—

(*a*) an election was made under this paragraph, and
(*b*) any tax chargeable in respect of the declaration of the shared ownership trust has been paid.

Shared ownership trust: treatment of staircasing transaction

10— (1) An equity-acquisition additional payment under a shared ownership trust, and the consequent increase in the purchaser's beneficial interest, shall be exempt from charge if—

(*a*) an election was made under paragraph 9, and
(*b*) any tax chargeable in respect of the declaration of trust has been paid.

(2) An equity-acquisition additional payment under a shared ownership trust, and the consequent increase in the purchaser's beneficial interest, shall also be exempt from charge if following the increase the purchaser's beneficial interest does not exceed 80% of the total beneficial interest in the trust property.

Shared ownership trust: treatment of additional payments where no election made

11 Where no election has been made under paragraph 9 in respect of a shared ownership trust—

(*a*) the initial capital shall be treated for the purposes of stamp duty land tax as chargeable consideration other than rent, and

(*b*) any rent-equivalent additional payment by the purchaser shall be treated for the purposes of stamp duty land tax as a payment of rent."

(2) The amendment made by subsection (1) has effect in relation to land transactions with an effective date on or after the day on which this Act is passed.

GENERAL NOTE

Shared ownership Trusts

Paragraph 7 defines a trust to be a shared ownership trust if it satisfies 3 conditions contained in paras 7(2)–(4), one of which involves (as with shared ownership leases) one of the beneficiaries (in the legislation a so called" social landlord") being a qualifying body as defined in para 5(2) and another that the trust relates to a dwelling. Paragraph 8 makes clear that for the purposes of the SDLT legislation the individual trust beneficiary (as opposed to the social landlord beneficiary) is the "purchaser" i e the person liable to SDLT.

The reliefs

Paragraph 9 enables a "purchaser" (see para 8 above) to elect that SDLT is charged on the initial amount of capital treated as provided (see para 7(4)(*f*)) without regard to "rent equivalent payments" (see para 7(4)(*c*)) that the purchaser is to make and for no SDLT to be chargeable on a transfer to the purchaser when the trust comes to an end. (The equivalent reliefs are in para 2(4) and 4 in relation to shared ownership leases).

Paragraph 10(1) provides for no further SDLT to be due as the purchaser increases its interest in the trust property (so called "staircasing") if an election under para 9 has been made. Para 10(2) provides for a further exemption even where an election has not been made where the purchaser increases its interest in the trust property unless the increase causes the purchaser's interest in the property to exceed 80% (and implicitly the social landlord's to fall below 20%). The equivalent reliefs for shared ownership leases are in paras 4 and 4A. Where no election under para 9 has been made SDLT is calculated as if "rent equivalent payments" were rent – see para 11.

COMMENCEMENT

The changes made by Sch 9 apply to land transactions with an effective date on or after Royal Assent

78 SDLT: shared ownership lease

In paragraph 2 of Schedule 9 to FA 2003 (stamp duty land tax: shared ownership lease), after sub-paragraph (4) insert—

"(4A) Where this paragraph applies no account shall be taken for the purposes of stamp duty land tax of the rent mentioned in sub-paragraph (2)(*d*)."

GENERAL NOTE

Section 78 introduces a new para 2(4A) into FA 2003 Sch 9 to make clear that where an election has been made to pay SDLT by reference to market value at the outset, the SDLT is calculated without reference to rent payable under the lease. The change will be effective from Royal Assent.

79 Certain transfers of school land

(1) In Chapter 7 of Part 2 of the School Standards and Framework Act 1998 (c 31) ("the 1998 Act") (new framework for maintained schools), omit sections 79 and 79A (no stamp duty or SDLT payable in respect of certain transfers).

(2) The repeal of—

(*a*) section 79A of the 1998 Act, and

(*b*) section 79 of that Act as it applies for the purposes of section 79A, has effect in relation to any land transaction of which the effective date is on or after the day on which this Act is passed.

(3) Subject to that, the repeal of section 79 of the 1998 Act has effect in relation to any instrument executed on or after that day.

GENERAL NOTE

Section 79 repeals certain relief from stamp duty (obsolete consequent upon the introduction of SDLT) and SDLT in respect of school land which, once appropriate regulations are made, can instead be given under FA 2003 s 66 (public bodies-relief from SDLT). The change is with effect from Royal Assent.

SDLT: administration

80 Payment of tax

(1) FA 2003 is amended as follows.

(2) In section 76(3) (payment to accompany land transaction return), omit paragraph (*b*).

(3) In section 80(2) (adjustment for change of circumstance: payment to accompany return), for paragraph (*d*) substitute—

"(*d*) the tax or additional tax payable must be paid not later than the filing date for the return."

(4) In section 81 (withdrawal of relief: further return)—

(*a*) in subsection (2), omit paragraph (*b*), and
(*b*) after that subsection insert—

"(2A) Tax payable must be paid not later than the filing date for the return."

(5) In section 81A(1) (later linked transaction: return), for paragraph (*d*) substitute—

"(*d*) the tax or additional tax payable must be paid not later than the filing date for the return."

(6) In section 86 (payment of tax)—

(*a*) in subsection (1), for "at the same time that a land transaction return is made in respect of the transaction." substitute "not later than the filing date for the land transaction return relating to the transaction.", and
(*b*) in subsection (2), for "at the same time that a return is made in respect of the withdrawal" substitute "not later than the filing date for the return relating to the withdrawal".

(7) In paragraph 2 of Schedule 10 (payment to accompany land transaction return), omit sub-paragraph (2)(*b*).

(8) For each of paragraphs 3(3)(*d*), 4(3)(*d*) and 8(3)(*d*) of Schedule 17A (leases) substitute—

"(*d*) the tax or additional tax payable must be paid not later than the filing date for the return."

(9) The amendments made by this section have effect as follows—

(*a*) the amendment made by subsection (2) has effect in relation to land transactions with an effective date on or after the day on which this Act is passed,
(*b*) the amendment made by subsection (3) has effect in relation to returns where the event as a result of which the return is required occurs on or after the day on which this Act is passed,
(*c*) the amendment made by subsection (4) has effect in relation to returns where the disqualifying event occurs on or after the day on which this Act is passed,
(*d*) the amendment made by subsection (5) has effect in relation to returns where the effective date of the later transaction is on or after the day on which this Act is passed,
(*e*) the amendment made by subsection (6) has effect in relation to land transactions with an effective date on or after the day on which this Act is passed,
(*f*) the amendment made by subsection (7) has effect in relation to land transactions with an effective date on or after the day on which this Act is passed, and
(*g*) the amendment made by subsection (8) has effect in respect of requirements to deliver a return or further return which arise on or after the day on which this Act is passed.

GENERAL NOTE

Section 80 makes a change to various provisions in the SDLT legislation which currently require payment of the SDLT to accompany land transaction returns, instead providing for payment to be made by the end of the period (currently 30 days) after the effective date of the transaction within which LTRs are required to be lodged. This facilities electronic lodgement of LTRs and future plans for "e-conveyancing" whereby payment of Land Registry fees can also be combined with SDLT payments.

COMMENCEMENT

The changes are to FA 2003 ss 76(3), 80(2)(d), 81(2), 8IA(1)(d), 86(1), (2), Sch 10 para 2 and Sch 17A, in all cases referable to events on or after Royal Assent: see s 79(9).

81 Self-certificate declarations

(1) Schedule 11 to FA 2003 (self-certificates) is amended as follows.

(2) After paragraph 2 insert—

"Declaration by Agent

2A— (1) The requirement in paragraph 2(1)(*c*) shall be deemed to be met where—

(*a*) the purchaser (or each of them) authorises an agent to complete a self-certificate,

(*b*) the purchaser (or each of them) makes a declaration that, with the exception of the effective date, the information provided in the self-certificate is to the best of the purchaser's knowledge correct and complete, and

(*c*) the self-certificate includes a declaration by the agent that the effective date provided in the self-certificate is to the best of the agent's knowledge correct.

(2) Sub-paragraph (1) applies only where the self-certificate is in a form specified by Her Majesty's Revenue and Customs for the purposes of that sub-paragraph.

(3) Nothing in this paragraph affects the liability of the purchaser (or each of them) under this Part of this Act.

Declaration by the relevant Official Solicitor

2B— (1) The requirement in paragraph 2(1)(*c*) shall be deemed to be met where—

(*a*) the purchaser (or any of them) is a person under a disability,

(*b*) the Official Solicitor is acting for the purchaser (or any of them), and

(*c*) the self-certificate includes a declaration by the Official Solicitor that the self-certificate is correct and complete to the best of the Official Solicitor's knowledge.

(2) Sub-paragraph (1) applies only where the self-certificate is in a form specified by Her Majesty's Revenue and Customs for the purposes of that sub-paragraph.

(3) Nothing in this paragraph affects the liability of the purchaser (or each of them) under this Part of this Act.

(4) In this paragraph "the Official Solicitor" means the Official Solicitor to the Supreme Court of England and Wales or the Official Solicitor to the Supreme Court of Northern Ireland."

(3) In paragraph 3(1), for "person" substitute "purchaser".

(4) The amendments made by this section have effect in relation to transactions with an effective date on or after the day on which this Act is passed.

GENERAL NOTE

Currently the SDLT legislation requires the purchaser, and not his or her solicitor, to complete the LTRs personally. Section 81(2) introduces a change which permits a declaration to be made by the purchaser's agent, rather than the purchaser (except as regards the effective date) where self-certification – rather than completion of an LTR – suffices.

Section 81(2) permits self-certification required by Sch 11 currently to be completed by the purchaser to be treated as satisfied by the Official Solicitor (if the purchaser is subject to a disability and the Official Solicitor is acting for him).

COMMENCEMENT

The changes apply to transactions requiring self-certification where the effective date is on or after Royal Assent.

PART 6

INVESTIGATION, ADMINISTRATION ETC

Investigation etc

82 Criminal investigations: powers of Revenue and Customs

(1) Section 114 of the Police and Criminal Evidence Act 1984 (c 60) (application of Act to customs and excise) is amended as follows.

(2) In paragraph (*a*) of subsection (2)—

(*a*) for "investigations conducted by officers of Customs and Excise of offences which relate to assigned matters, as defined in section 1 of the Customs and Excise Management Act 1979," substitute "investigations conducted by officers of Revenue and Customs", and

(*b*) for "persons detained by officers of Customs and Excise;" substitute "persons detained by officers of Revenue and Customs;".

(3) In the opening words of paragraph (*b*) of that subsection, for "investigations of offences conducted by officers of Customs and Excise" substitute "investigations of offences conducted by officers of Revenue and Customs".

(4) In sub-paragraph (i) of that paragraph, for "section" substitute "sections".

(5) In the section 14A deemed to be inserted by that sub-paragraph—

(*a*) for "and which relates to an assigned matter, as defined in section 1 of the Customs and Excise Management Act 1979," substitute "and which relates to a matter in relation to which Her Majesty's Revenue and Customs have functions," and

(*b*) in the heading, for "**Customs and Excise**" substitute "**Revenue and Customs**".

(6) After that section insert—

"14B Revenue and Customs: restriction on other powers to apply for production of documents

(1) An officer of Revenue and Customs may make an application for the delivery of, or access to, documents under a provision specified in subsection (3) only if the condition in subsection (2) is satisfied.

(2) The condition is that the officer thinks that an application under Schedule 1 would not succeed because the material required does not consist of or include special procedure material.

(3) The provisions are—

(*a*) section 20BA of, and Schedule 1AA to, the Taxes Management Act 1970 (serious tax fraud);
(*b*) paragraph 11 of Schedule 11 to the Value Added Tax Act 1994 (VAT);
(*c*) paragraph 4A of Schedule 7 to the Finance Act 1994 (insurance premium tax);
(*d*) paragraph 7 of Schedule 5 to the Finance Act 1996 (landfill tax);
(*e*) paragraph 131 of Schedule 6 to the Finance Act 2000 (climate change levy);
(*f*) paragraph 8 of Schedule 7 to the Finance Act 2001 (aggregates levy);
(*g*) Part 6 of Schedule 13 to the Finance Act 2003 (stamp duty land tax)."

(7) In paragraph (*c*) of subsection (2)—

(*a*) for "customs detention" substitute "Revenue and Customs detention", and
(*b*) for "an officer of Customs and Excise" substitute "an officer of Revenue and Customs".

(8) After that paragraph (*c*) insert—

"(*d*) that where an officer of Revenue and Customs searches premises in reliance on a warrant under section 8 of, or paragraph 12 of Schedule 1 to, this Act (as applied by an order under this subsection) the officer shall have the power to search persons found on the premises—

(i) in such cases and circumstances as are specified in the order, and
(ii) subject to any conditions specified in the order; and

(*e*) that powers and functions conferred by a provision of this Act (as applied by an order under this subsection) may be exercised only by officers of Revenue and

Customs acting with the authority (which may be general or specific) of the Commissioners for Her Majesty's Revenue and Customs."

(9) After that subsection insert—

"(2A) A certificate of the Commissioners that an officer of Revenue and Customs had authority under subsection (2)(*e*) to exercise a power or function conferred by a provision of this Act shall be conclusive evidence of that fact."

(10) For subsection (3) substitute—

"(3) An order under subsection (2)—

(*a*) may make provision that applies generally or only in specified cases or circumstances,

(*b*) may make different provision for different cases or circumstances,

(*c*) may, in modifying a provision, in particular impose conditions on the exercise of a function, and

(*d*) shall not be taken to limit a power under section 164 of the Customs and Excise Management Act 1979."

(11) The heading of section 114 accordingly becomes "**Application of Act to Revenue and Customs**".

GENERAL NOTE

When HMRC were established in 2005, the existing powers of Customs (including their powers under the Police and Criminal Evidence Act 1984 (PACE)) and the Revenue were preserved and transferred to HMRC. However, the powers were ring-fenced so that they could only be used for their original purpose. In particular the PACE powers relating to search warrants and arrests, which were available to ex-Customs, could not be used in connection with investigations concerned with ex-Revenue matters.

Following consultation, however, as part of the *Modernising Powers Deterrents and Safeguards* programme, it was recommended that changes be made to provide HMRC with consistent powers to be used in criminal investigations, whether they related to ex-Customs or ex-Revenue matters.

The amendments in FA 2007 will increase the powers available to ex-Revenue investigators and some of the powers available to ex-Customs officers will be reduced. HMRC will no longer need to follow different procedures in the same investigation where both direct and indirect tax fraud are suspected.

This section makes the appropriate amendment to PACE 1984 s 114 to allow an order to be made which will extend the powers and safeguards of PACE to investigations into criminal fraud carried out by all authorised HMRC officers, and makes consequential changes to the PACE provisions relating to production orders, search warrants, powers of arrest and search and entry powers in connection with arrests.

With regard to application for production orders and search warrants, some of the notable changes to current powers are—

(a) under PACE there must be reasonable grounds for 'believing' that an offence has been committed, as opposed to the current lower test of 'suspecting';

(b) all applications to the judge will be made *inter partes*. At the moment some can be made *ex parte*;

(c) the judge will only be able to issue an order where he is satisfied that there are reasonable grounds for believing that an offence 'has been' committed and no longer where one 'is being, or is about to be' committed;

(d) unless special procedure material is involved, a search warrant will be issued by a magistrate, not a judge;

(e) application for a search warrant will no longer need authorisation by two Commissioners of HMRC, but will need internal authorisation at a senior level.

A notable change is therefore that HMRC officers will have the PACE powers of search, seizure and arrest in connection with ex-Revenue matters. The document *Criminal Investigation Powers: Publication of Draft Clauses and Explanatory Notes* proposes that the use of this power will be restricted to suitably trained officers authorised by the Commissioners of HMRC. In this way the power will be removed from many VAT officers who never in fact use it.

The amendments will come into force on a date to be appointed by Treasury Order. Budget Note BN78 indicates that this is likely to be before the end of 2007.

Further comment

The existing search warrant powers and procedures under TMA 1970 s 20C will be repealed when the new provisions come into effect.

PACE applies in England and Wales only.

83 Northern Ireland criminal investigations

(1) Article 85 of the Police and Criminal Evidence (Northern Ireland) Order 1989 (SI 1989/1341 (NI 12)) (application of Order to customs and excise) is amended as follows.

(2) In sub-paragraph (*a*) of paragraph (1)—

(*a*) for "investigations conducted by officers of Customs and Excise of offences which relate to assigned matters, as defined in section 1 of the Customs and Excise Management Act 1979," substitute "investigations conducted by officers of Revenue and Customs", and

(*b*) for "persons detained by officers of Customs and Excise;" substitute "persons detained by officers of Revenue and Customs;".

(3) In the opening words of sub-paragraph (*b*) of that paragraph, for "investigations of offences conducted by officers of Customs and Excise" substitute "investigations of offences conducted by officers of Revenue and Customs".

(4) In paragraph (i) of that sub-paragraph, for "Article" substitute "Articles".

(5) In the Article 16A deemed to be inserted by that paragraph—

(*a*) for "and which relates to an assigned matter, as defined in section 1 of the Customs and Excise Management Act 1979," substitute "and which relates to a matter in relation to which Her Majesty's Revenue and Customs have functions," and

(*b*) in the heading, for "**Customs and Excise**" substitute "**Revenue and Customs**".

(6) After that Article insert—

"16B Revenue and Customs: restriction on other powers to apply for production of documents

(1) An officer of Revenue and Customs may make an application for the delivery of, or access to, documents under a provision specified in paragraph (3) only if the condition in paragraph (2) is satisfied.

(2) The condition is that the officer thinks that an application under Schedule 1 would not succeed because the material required does not consist of or include special procedure material.

(3) The provisions are—

(*a*) section 20BA of, and Schedule 1AA to, the Taxes Management Act 1970 (serious tax fraud);
(*b*) paragraph 11 of Schedule 11 to the Value Added Tax Act 1994 (VAT);
(*c*) paragraph 4A of Schedule 7 to the Finance Act 1994 (insurance premium tax);
(*d*) paragraph 7 of Schedule 5 to the Finance Act 1996 (landfill tax);
(*e*) paragraph 131 of Schedule 6 to the Finance Act 2000 (climate change levy);
(*f*) paragraph 8 of Schedule 7 to the Finance Act 2001 (aggregates levy);
(*g*) Part 6 of Schedule 13 to the Finance Act 2003 (stamp duty land tax)."

(7) After sub-paragraph (*b*) of paragraph (1) insert—

"(*c*) that where an officer of Revenue and Customs searches premises in reliance on a warrant under Article 10 of, or paragraph 9 of Schedule 1 to, this Order (as applied by an order under this paragraph) the officer shall have the power to search persons found on the premises—

(i) in such cases and circumstances as are specified in the order, and
(ii) subject to any conditions specified in the order; and

(*d*) that powers and functions conferred by a provision of this Order (as applied by an order under this paragraph) may be exercised only by officers of Revenue and Customs acting with the authority (which may be general or specific) of the Commissioners for Her Majesty's Revenue and Customs."

(8) After that paragraph insert—

"(1A) A certificate of the Commissioners that an officer of Revenue and Customs had authority under paragraph (1)(*d*) to exercise a power or function conferred by a provision of this Order shall be conclusive evidence of that fact."

(9) For paragraph (2) substitute—

"(2) An order under paragraph (1)—

(*a*) may, in modifying a provision, in particular impose conditions on the exercise of a function, and

(*b*) shall not be taken to limit a power under section 164 of the Customs and Excise Management Act 1979."

(10) The heading of Article 85 accordingly becomes "**Application of Order to Revenue and Customs**".

GENERAL NOTE

Comparable provisions to PACE apply in Northern Ireland by virtue of the *Police and Criminal Evidence (Northern Ireland) Order* 1989 SI 1989/1341, but these currently apply to ex-Customs officers only. This section makes changes to that order to parallel, for Northern Ireland, the changes made by s 82 for England and Wales, so that the provisions relating to criminal investigations conducted and persons detained apply consistently to all authorised HMRC officers.

According to the Explanatory Notes which accompanied the Finance Bill, further details will be set out in a draft order which is to be issued 'shortly'.

The amendments will come into force on a date to be appointed by Treasury Order. Budget Note BN78 indicates that this is likely to be before the end of 2007.

84 Sections 82 and 83: supplementary

(1) In Schedule 2 to CRCA 2005 (restrictions on the exercise of functions), omit—

(*a*) paragraph 7 (Police and Criminal Evidence Act 1984 (c 60), and

(*b*) paragraph 9 (Police and Criminal Evidence (Northern Ireland) Order 1989 (SI 1989/1341 (NI 12))).

(2) Nothing in section 6 or 7 of CRCA 2005 (initial functions) restricts the functions in connection with which officers of Revenue and Customs may exercise a power under—

(*a*) the Police and Criminal Evidence Act 1984 by virtue of section 114 of that Act (as amended by section 82 above), or

(*b*) the Police and Criminal Evidence (Northern Ireland) Order 1989 by virtue of Article 85 of that Order (as amended by section 83 above).

(3) But neither an order under section 114 of the Police and Criminal Evidence Act 1984 nor an order under Article 85 of the Police and Criminal Evidence (Northern Ireland) Order 1989 has effect in relation to a matter specified in section 54(4)(*b*) or (*f*) of, or in paragraphs 3, 7, 10, 13 to 15, 19 or 24 to 29 of Schedule 1 to, CRCA 2005 (former Inland Revenue matters).

(4) Schedule 22 contains amendments and repeals consequential on extension of police powers to Revenue and Customs.

(5) Sections 82 and 83 and this section come into force in accordance with provision made by the Treasury by order.

(6) The power to make an order under subsection (5) is exercisable by statutory instrument.

GENERAL NOTE

The amendments made by this section to CRCA 2005 and the further amendments and repeals made by Sch 22 which it introduces, make changes consistent with the changes to HMRC powers in PACE made by ss 82 and 83.

85 Criminal investigations: Scotland

Schedule 23 contains provision for Scotland about the investigation of offences by Her Majesty's Revenue and Customs.

GENERAL NOTE

This section gives effect to Sch 23 which introduces new and consistent criminal investigation powers and accompanying safeguards for HMRC to use in Scotland. These provisions, together with ss 82–84, harmonise HMRC's powers across England, Wales, Northern Ireland and Scotland.

86 Search warrants

In section 8 of the Police and Criminal Evidence Act 1984, after subsection (6) insert—

"(7) Section 4 of the Summary Jurisdiction (Process) Act 1881 (execution of process of English courts in Scotland) shall apply to a warrant issued on the application of an officer of Revenue and Customs under this section by virtue of section 114 below."

GENERAL NOTE

The Summary Jurisdiction (Process) Act 1881 s 4 allows a process (e.g. a search warrant) issued by a court of summary jurisdiction in England, and endorsed by a similar court in Scotland, to be executed in the same way as it would be in England, and vice versa.

This section extends the application of those provisions so that a warrant granted in England and Wales under PACE 1984 s 8, in connection with an HMRC criminal investigation, can be executed in Scotland. This is designed to facilitate investigations involving more than one UK jurisdiction.

87 Cross-border exercise of powers

(1) This section relates to the Criminal Justice and Public Order Act 1994 (c 33).

(2) Sections 136 to 139 (execution of warrants and powers of arrest and search) shall apply to an officer of Revenue and Customs as they apply to a constable; and for that purpose—

(*a*) a reference to a constable (including a reference to a constable of a police force in England and Wales, a constable of a police force in Scotland or a constable of a police force in Northern Ireland) shall be treated as a reference to an officer of Revenue and Customs, and

(*b*) a reference to a police station, or a designated police station, includes a reference to an office of Revenue and Customs or (in England and Wales and Northern Ireland) a designated office of Revenue and Customs.

(3) In the application of section 138 to an officer of Revenue and Customs—

(*a*) in subsection (2)—

(i) the reference to subsections (2) to (8) of section 14 of the Criminal Procedure (Scotland) Act 1995 (c 46) ("the 1995 Procedure Act") shall be treated as a reference to subsections (2) to (7) of section 24 of the Criminal Law (Consolidation) (Scotland) Act 1995 (c 39) ("the 1995 Consolidation Act"), and

(ii) the reference to subsections (1), (2) and (4) to (6) of section 15 of the 1995 Procedure Act shall be treated as a reference to subsections (1) to (4) of section 25 of the 1995 Consolidation Act, and

(*b*) in subsection (6)—

(i) the references to section 14 of the 1995 Procedure Act shall be treated as references to section 24 of the 1995 Consolidation Act,

(ii) the references to section 15 of the 1995 Procedure Act shall be treated as references to section 25 of the 1995 Consolidation Act,

(iii) in paragraph (*a*), sub-paragraph (ii) shall not apply, and

(iv) paragraph (*b*) shall not apply.

(4) An officer of Revenue and Customs may exercise a power under sections 136 to 139 only in the exercise of a function relating to tax (including duties and tax credits).

(5) In subsection (2)—

"office of Revenue and Customs" means premises wholly or partly occupied by Her Majesty's Revenue and Customs, and

"designated office of Revenue and Customs" has the meaning given by an order under section 114 of the Police and Criminal Evidence Act 1984 (c 60) (power to extend provisions to HMRC) or, in Northern Ireland, by an order under Article 85 of the Police and Criminal Evidence (Northern Ireland) Order 1989 (SI 1989/1341 (NI 12)) (power to extend Order to HMRC).

(6) In section 136, after subsection (8) insert—

"(9) Powers under this section and sections 137 to 139 may be exercised by an officer of Revenue and Customs in accordance with section 87 of the Finance Act 2007."

GENERAL NOTE

Provisions of the Criminal Justice and Public Order Act 1994 allow various powers from one country in the UK, concerning the execution of warrants, search and arrest, to be exercised in another country of the UK. Currently these provisions apply only to police constables and police stations

This section sets out the detail of how these provisions are extended to apply to HMRC officers in the exercise of their functions relating to tax, duties or tax credit matters, and to HMRC offices.

Filing dates

GENERAL NOTE

The introduction of legislation providing for different filing dates of paper and online self-assessment tax returns has not been without controversy.

In July 2005, Lord Carter of Coles was commissioned by the Government to carry out a review of HMRC's online services, including online filing, and his report, published in March 2006, recommended acceleration of the filing dates from the current 31 January to 30 September for paper returns, and to 30 November for online returns, to take effect from 2008. At the same time, a comment was published in the Treasury's *Budget 2006* (the Red Book) that the Government accepted the recommendations.

Following significant representations about the impracticality of these recommendations made by all the main taxation and accountancy bodies, Lord Carter changed his recommendations in favour of retaining the existing online filing date of 31 January and advancing the filing date for paper returns to 31 October. The Government subsequently announced that it accepted those revised recommendations, and it is these that are set out in FA 2007.

The new rules are outlined at ss 88–92 below.

Further comment

HMRC have advised that paper substitute returns will no longer be approved or accepted from April 2008 (2007/08 return and subsequent returns), but that for those taxpayers for whom online filing facilities are not yet available, paper returns prepared using HMRC downloaded pdfs incorporated into commercial software will be accepted up to the 31 January deadline.

88 Personal tax returns

(1) Section 8 of TMA 1970 (personal tax return) is amended as follows.

(2) In subsection (1)(*a*), omit ", on or before the day mentioned in subsection (1A) below".

(3) Omit subsection (1A).

(4) After subsection (1C) insert—

"(1D) A return under this section for a year of assessment (Year 1) must be delivered—

(*a*) in the case of a non-electronic return, on or before 31st October in Year 2, and
(*b*) in the case of an electronic return, on or before 31st January in Year 2.

(1E) But subsection (1D) is subject to the following two exceptions.

(1F) Exception 1 is that if a notice in respect of Year 1 is given after 31st July in Year 2 (but on or before 31st October), a return must be delivered—

(*a*) during the period of 3 months beginning with the date of the notice (for a non-electronic return), or
(*b*) on or before 31st January (for an electronic return).

(1G) Exception 2 is that if a notice in respect of Year 1 is given after 31st October in Year 2, a return (whether electronic or not) must be delivered during the period of 3 months beginning with the date of the notice.

(1H) The Commissioners—

(*a*) shall prescribe what constitutes an electronic return, and
(*b*) may make different provision for different cases or circumstances."

GENERAL NOTE

This section sets out the revised filing dates for personal returns issued under TMA 1970 s 8. The new rules will apply to returns issued on or after 6 April 2008 for the year 2007–08 and subsequent years.

Exceptions to the normal filing dates will apply where a return is issued after 31 July following the end of the tax year to which it relates, so that a filing period of a minimum of three months will be allowed. This rule currently applies only to returns issued after 31 October and has been changed to ensure that the three-month rule can apply to paper returns whose filing date is 31 October.

HMRC will have the power to prescribe what constitutes an electronic return. The Explanatory Notes accompanying the Finance Bill set out that broadly, this will mean a return that is capable of passing through HMRC's electronic gateway. All other returns will be classed as non-electronic returns which will need filing by the earlier filing date of 31 October.

89 Trustee's tax return

(1) Section 8A of TMA 1970 (trustee's tax return) is amended as follows.

(2) In subsection (1)(*a*), omit ", on or before the day mentioned in subsection (1A) below".

(3) Omit subsection (1A).

(4) After subsection (1AA) insert—

"(1B) A return under this section for a year of assessment (Year 1) must be delivered—

(*a*) in the case of a non-electronic return, on or before 31st October in Year 2, and
(*b*) in the case of an electronic return, on or before 31st January in Year 2.

(1C) But subsection (1B) is subject to the following two exceptions.

(1D) Exception 1 is that if a notice in respect of Year 1 is given after 31st July in Year 2 (but on or before 31st October), a return must be delivered—

(*a*) during the period of 3 months beginning with the date of the notice (for a non-electronic return), or

(*b*) on or before 31st January (for an electronic return).

(1E) Exception 2 is that if a notice in respect of Year 1 is given after 31st October in Year 2, a return (whether electronic or not) must be delivered during the period of 3 months beginning with the date of the notice.

(1F) The Commissioners—

(*a*) shall prescribe what constitutes an electronic return, and
(*b*) may make different provision for different cases or circumstances."

GENERAL NOTE

This section sets out the revised filing dates for trustees' returns issued under TMA 1970 s 8A. The new rules will apply to returns issued on or after 6 April 2008 for the year 2007–08 and subsequent years. Where a return is issued after 31 July following the end of the tax year to which it relates, a filing period of a minimum of three months will be allowed. This rule currently applies only to returns issued after 31 October.

HMRC will have the power to prescribe what constitutes an electronic return. The Explanatory Notes accompanying the Finance Bill set out that broadly, this will mean a return that is capable of passing through HMRC's electronic gateway. All other returns will be classed as non-electronic returns which will need filing by the earlier filing date of 31 October.

90 Partnership tax returns

(1) In section 12AA of TMA 1970, for subsection (4) (partnership return: filing date) substitute—

"(4) In the case of a partnership which includes one or more individuals, a notice under subsection (2) or (3) above may specify different days depending on whether a return in respect of a year of assessment (Year 1) is electronic or non-electronic.

(4A) The day specified for a non-electronic return must not be earlier than 31st October of Year 2.

(4B) The day specified for an electronic return must not be earlier than 31st January of Year 2.

(4C) But subsections (4A) and (4B) are subject to the following two exceptions.

(4D) Exception 1 is that if the notice is given after 31st July in Year 2 (but on or before 31st October)—

(*a*) the day specified for a non-electronic return must be after the end of the period of three months beginning with the date of the notice, and

(*b*) the day specified for an electronic return must not be earlier than 31st January.

(4E) Exception 2 is that if the notice is given after 31st October in Year 2, the day specified for a return (whether or not electronic) must be after the end of the period of three months beginning with the date of the notice."

(2) For subsection (5) of that section (partnership return where a company is a partner: filing date) substitute—

"(5) In the case of a partnership which includes one or more companies, a notice may specify different dates depending on whether a notice in respect of a relevant period is electronic or non-electronic.

(5A) The day specified for a non-electronic return must not be earlier than the end of the period of nine months beginning at the end of the relevant period.

(5B) The day specified for an electronic return must not be earlier than the first anniversary of the end of the relevant period.

(5C) But where the notice is given more than nine months after the end of the relevant period, the day specified for a return (whether or not electronic) must be after the end of the period of three months beginning with the date of the notice.

(5D) For the purposes of this section "relevant period" means the period in respect of which the return is required.

(5E) The Commissioners—

(*a*) shall prescribe what constitutes an electronic return for the purposes of this section, and

(*b*) may make different provision for different cases or circumstances."

GENERAL NOTE

This section sets out the revised filing dates for returns issued under—

(*a*) TMA 1970 s 12AA(4) to partnerships that include one or more individuals; or

(*b*) TMA 1970 s 12AA(5) to partnerships that include one or more companies.

The new rules will apply, in the case of (a) above, to returns issued on or after 6 April 2008 for the year 2007–08 and subsequent years. In the case of (b) above, the changes will apply where the period covered by the return begins on or after 6 April 2007

Exceptions to the normal filing dates are prescribed where a return is issued late (i.e. in the case of partnerships including individuals, after 31 July following the end of the tax year to which the return relates and in the partnerships with corporate partners, returns issued more than nine months after the end of the period for which the return is required) to allow a filing period of a minimum of three months.

HMRC will have the power to prescribe what constitutes an 'electronic return'. The Explanatory Notes set out that broadly, this will mean a return that is capable of passing through HMRC's electronic gateway. All other returns will be classed as non-electronic returns which will need filing by the earlier filing date of 31 October, or the nine-month filing date, as appropriate.

91 Consequential amendments

(1) In section 9(2) of TMA 1970 (returns to include self-assessment)—

(*a*) in paragraph (*a*), for "30th September" substitute "31st October", and

(*b*) in paragraph (*b*), for "31st July" substitute "31st August".

(2) In section 9ZA of TMA 1970 (amendment of personal or trustee return), for subsection (3) substitute—

"(3) In this section "the filing date", in respect of a return for a year of assessment (Year 1), means—

(*a*) 31st January of Year 2, or

(*b*) if the notice under section 8 or 8A is given after 31st October of Year 2, the last day of the period of three months beginning with the date of the notice."

(3) In section 9A(6) of TMA 1970 (notice of enquiry: "the filing date"), for the words from "means" to the end substitute "means, in relation to a return, the last day for delivering it in accordance with section 8 or 8A."

(4) In section 12ABA of TMA 1970 (amendment of partnership return by taxpayer), for subsection (4) substitute—

"(4) In this section "the filing date" means—

(*a*) in the case of a partnership which includes one or more individuals, in respect of a return for a year of assessment (Year 1)—

(i) 31st January of Year 2, or

(ii) if the notice under section 12AA is given after 31st October of Year 2, the last day of the period of three months beginning with the date of the notice, and

(*b*) in the case of a partnership which includes one or more companies, the end of the period specified in section 12AA(5B) or (5C)."

(5) In section 28C of TMA 1970 (determination of tax where no return delivered), for subsection (6) substitute—

"(6) In this section "the filing date" in respect of a return for a year of assessment (Year 1) means either—

(*a*) 31st January of Year 2, or

(*b*) if the notice under section 8 or 8A was given after 31st October of Year 2, the last day of the period of three months beginning with the day on which the notice is given."

(6) In section 33A of TMA 1970 (error in partnership return)—

(*a*) in subsection (1), insert at the end "for a year of assessment (Year 1), or for a relevant period which ends in Year 1",

(*b*) in subsection (2), for "five years after the filing date" substitute "31st January of Year 6",

(*c*) in subsection (9), omit the definition of "filing date", and

(*d*) in that subsection, after the definition of "relevant partner" insert—

""relevant period" means a period in respect of which a return is required."

(7) In section 93(10) of TMA 1970 (penalty for failure to make individual or trustee return), for the definition of "filing date" substitute—

""the filing date" in respect of a return for a year of assessment (Year 1) means—

(*a*) 31st January of Year 2, or

(*b*) if the notice under section 8 or 8A was given after 31st October of Year 2, the last day of the period of three months beginning with the day on which the notice is given."

(8) In section 93A of TMA 1970 (failure to make partnership return), after subsection (7) insert—

"(7A) For the purposes of this section the filing date for a year of assessment (Year 1) in the case of a partnership which includes one or more individuals is—

(*a*) 31st January of Year 2, or

(*b*) if the notice under section 12AA was given after 31st October of Year 2, the last day of the period of three months beginning with the date of the notice.

(7B) For the purposes of this section the filing date for a year of assessment (Year 1) in the case of a partnership which includes one or more companies is—

(*a*) the first anniversary of the period for which the return is required, or

(*b*) where the notice is given more than nine months after the end of the period for which the return is required, the last day of the period of three months beginning with the date of the notice."

(9) In subsection (8) of section 93A, omit the definition of "the filing date".

(10) In paragraph 4 of Schedule 15 to FA 2006 (accountancy change: spreading of adjustment)—

(*a*) in sub-paragraph (1), after "a tax year" insert "(Year 1)", and

(*b*) in sub-paragraph (2), for "normal self-assessment filing date for the tax year." substitute "31st January of Year 2."

GENERAL NOTE

This section provides for a number of consequential amendments to be made to existing statutory provisions that have time limits linked to the current income tax self-assessment return filing dates which are amended by ss 88–90 and the definition of 'filing date' is clarified. These amendments ensure that existing filing dates are retained, despite the introduction of earlier filing dates for paper returns.

In addition, changes are made to the following—

(*a*) currently, HMRC will calculate the liability of a taxpayer who files a paper return where it is submitted—

(i) by 30 September following the end of the tax year (TMA 1970 s 9(2)(*a*)). This date will be extended to 31 October to align with the new paper return filing date; and

(ii) within two months of the date of issue, where HMRC issue the return after the 31 July following the end of the tax year (TMA 1970 s 9(2)(*b*)). This cut off date will be extended to 31 August.

(*b*) the 12-month period during which a taxpayer may amend a return is specified to commence from 31 January filing date for all returns, both paper and electronic (or the last day of the three-month filing period in the case of returns issued late).

92 Commencement

(1) Sections 88 to 91 have effect—

(*a*) in relation to a return under section 8 or 8A of TMA 1970, or a return under section 12AA of that Act for a partnership which includes one or more individuals, in respect of a return for a year of assessment beginning on or after 6th April 2007, and

(*b*) in relation to a return under section 12AA of that Act for a partnership which includes one or more companies, in respect of a return for a relevant period beginning on or after 6th April 2007.

(2) In subsection (1)(*b*) "relevant period" means a period in respect of which a return is required.

GENERAL NOTE

This section provides the commencement date for the operation of the differential filing dates for electronic and paper returns introduced by ss 88–91. For returns required by notices to partnerships with corporate partners, the changes will apply to relevant periods that begin on or after 6 April 2007. For all other personal, trustee and partnership returns, the changes apply to notices issued after 6 April 2008 and relating to the year beginning 6 April 2007 or to any subsequent years.

Other administration

93 Mandatory electronic filing of returns

(1) Section 135 of FA 2002 (mandatory electronic filing) is amended as follows.

(2) In subsection (7), after paragraph (*b*) insert—

"(*ba*) to specify other consequences of contravention of, or failure to comply with, the regulations (which may include disregarding a return delivered otherwise than by the use of electronic communications);".

(3) In subsection (10), for the definition of "taxation matter" substitute—

""taxation matter" means any matter relating to a tax (or duty) for which the Commissioners are responsible."

(4) Section 76 of VATA 1994 (assessment) is amended as follows.

(5) In subsection (1), after paragraph (*c*) insert—

"or

(*d*) a penalty under regulations made under section 135 of the Finance Act 2002 (mandatory electronic filing of returns) in connection with VAT,".

(6) In that subsection, before "may have ceased" insert "or the regulations".

(7) In subsection (3), insert at the end—

"; and

(*f*) in the case of a penalty under regulations made under section 135 of the Finance Act 2002, the relevant period is the prescribed accounting period in respect of which the contravention of, or failure to comply with, the regulations occurred."

(8) In section 83 of VATA 1994 (appeals), after paragraph (*zb*) insert—

"(*zc*) a decision of the Commissioners about the application of regulations under section 135 of the Finance Act 2002 (mandatory electronic filing of returns) in connection with VAT (including, in particular, a decision as to whether a requirement of the regulations applies and a decision to impose a penalty);".

(9) In section 84 of VATA 1994 (appeals), after subsection (6A) insert—

"(6B) Nothing in section 83(*zc*) shall be taken to confer on a tribunal any power to vary an amount assessed by way of penalty except in so far as it is necessary to reduce it to the amount which is appropriate under regulations made under section 135 of the Finance Act 2002."

GENERAL NOTE

In July 2005, the Government asked Lord Carter to undertake a review of HMRC's online services and in his report in March 2006, Lord Carter recommended that HMRC should phase in requirements to submit company tax returns, VAT returns and in-year PAYE forms electronically.

Section 135 of FA 2002 and VATA 1994 Sch 11 currently provide for regulations to require electronic filing. This section extends those provisions to apply to all the taxes and duties for which HMRC are responsible and thus provides the framework for implementing Lord Carter's recommendations.

Draft regulations covering the requirements for large and medium-sized companies (i.e. those with more than 50 employees) to submit in-year PAYE forms electronically with effect from 6 April 2009 were published on 29 March 2007. Budget Note BN80 indicates that these are expected to be laid, subject to consultation, in September 2007.

Further comment

HMRC have set out on their website (at www.hmrc.gov.uk/budget2007/carter.htm) their proposed timetable for the implementation of electronic filing and payment (see also s 94 below), as follows—

Service	*Implementation date*
PAYE	Large and medium sized employers (those with 50 or more employees) required to file in-year forms online from April 2009. Small employers (with fewer than 50 employees) required to file in-year forms online from April 2011.
VAT	Large, medium sized and most small traders (those with turnover > £100K) and all newly registered VAT traders required to file online and pay electronically from April 2010 at the earliest.
CT	Online filing and electronic payment for all CT returns using XBRL standard mandated from April 2011. Joint filing facility with Companies House by 2011. The CT enquiry window will still change in 2008 for most companies for accounting periods after 31/3/2008.

94 Mandatory electronic payment

(1) Section 204 of FA 2003 (mandatory electronic payment by large employers) is amended as follows.

(2) For subsections (1) and (2) substitute—

"(1) The Commissioners for Her Majesty's Revenue and Customs may make regulations requiring a person to use electronic means in making specified payments under legislation relating to a tax (or duty) for which the Commissioners are responsible.

(2) The regulations may provide for exceptions."

(3) In subsection (5)(*b*), for "the Inland Revenue" substitute "Her Majesty's Revenue and Customs".

(4) In subsection (6)(*a*), for "the Inland Revenue" substitute "Her Majesty's Revenue and Customs".

(5) In subsection (8)—

(*a*) in paragraph (*a*), for "a contravention of, or any failure to comply with," substitute "a contravention by a large employer of, or any failure by a large employer to comply with,", and

(*b*) in paragraph (*b*), for "taxation matter within the care and management of the Commissioners" substitute "matter relating to a tax (or duty) for which the Commissioners are responsible".

(6) In subsection (12)—

(*a*) for the definition of "the Inland Revenue" substitute—

""Her Majesty's Revenue and Customs" includes a person acting under the authority of the Commissioners in relation to payment by electronic means;", and

(*b*) after that definition insert—

""large employer" means a person paying PAYE income to 250 or more recipients (and regulations under this section may make provision as to the date or period by reference to which this is to be determined and the circumstances in which a person is to be treated as paying PAYE income to a recipient);".

(7) The heading accordingly becomes "**Mandatory electronic payment**".

(8) In section 205(1) of FA 2003 (application of section 204 for other purposes)—

(*a*) after "taxation" insert "(or duty)", and

(*b*) for "the Commissioners of Inland Revenue" substitute "the Commissioners for Her Majesty's Revenue and Customs".

GENERAL NOTE

Following his review of HMRC's online services, Lord Carter, in his report in March 2006, recommended that HMRC should require businesses to pay corporation tax and VAT electronically.

HMRC currently have the power to make regulations to require large employers (i e those with 250 or more employees) to make payments by electronic means and to impose a surcharge on an employer that fails to comply. Large employers have been required to make electronic payments since April 2004 (FA 2003, ss 204, 205 and the Income Tax (Pay As You Earn) Regulations 2003 SI 2003/2682).

This section extends those provisions so that they apply to all the taxes and duties for which HMRC are responsible, thus providing the framework for implementing Lord Carter's recommendations.

95 Payment by cheque

(1) The Commissioners may make regulations providing for a payment to HMRC made by cheque to be treated as made when the cheque clears, as defined in the regulations.

(2) Section 70A of TMA 1970 (payment by cheque treated as made on receipt by HMRC) is subject to regulations under subsection (1).

(3) Regulations under subsection (1)—

(*a*) may make provision generally or only for specified purposes,

(*b*) may make different provision for different purposes, and

(*c*) may include incidental, consequential or transitional provision.

(4) Regulations under subsection (1)—

(*a*) shall be made by statutory instrument, and

(*b*) shall be subject to annulment in pursuance of a resolution of the House of Commons.

(5) In this section—

(*a*) "the Commissioners" means the Commissioners for Her Majesty's Revenue and Customs, and

(*b*) "HMRC" means Her Majesty's Revenue and Customs.

(6) In section 204 of FA 2003 (electronic payment), insert at the end—

"(13) Regulations under section 95(1) of the Finance Act 2007 (payment by cheque) may, in particular, provide for a payment which is made by cheque in contravention of regulations under this section to be treated as made when the cheque clears, as defined in the regulations under that section."

(7) In section 70A of TMA 1970 (payments by cheque), insert at the end—

"(3) This section is subject to regulations under section 95(1) of the Finance Act 2007 (payment by cheque)."

(8) In VATA 1994, after section 58A insert—

"58B Payment by cheque

Regulations under section 95(1) of the Finance Act 2007 (payment by cheque) may, in particular, provide for a payment which is made by cheque in contravention of regulations under section 25(1) above to be treated as made when the cheque clears, as defined in the regulations under section 95(1) of that Act."

GENERAL NOTE

One of the recommendations by Lord Carter in his report in March 2006 following his review of HMRC's online services, was that HMRC should require businesses to pay corporation tax and VAT electronically.

Currently, where payment of tax or VAT is made by cheque and the cheque clears on first presentation, payment is treated as made on the day the cheque is received by HMRC (TMA 1970 s 70A; VATA 1994 s 25(1) and the VAT Regulations 1995 reg 40 (SI 1995/2518)).

This section gives HMRC the power to make regulations, by statutory instrument, to treat payment by cheque for tax and VAT purposes as made only once the funds have cleared into HMRC's account. This will remove any cash flow advantage obtained by making payment by cheque.

Budget Note BN80 indicates that HMRC expect to make regulations that will apply this rule to all payments of VAT and corporation tax from the time that requirements to pay electronically start to be phased in.

96 Enquiry into returns

(1) In section 9A(2)(*a*) of TMA 1970 (period during which HMRC can open enquiry into return), for "after the filing date;" substitute "after the day on which the return was delivered;".

(2) In section 12AC(2)(*a*) of TMA 1970 (period during which HMRC can open enquiry into partnership return), for "after the filing date;" substitute "after the day on which the return was delivered;".

(3) In paragraph 24(2) of Schedule 18 to FA 1998 (period during which HMRC can open enquiry into company tax return), for "from the filing date." substitute "from the day on which the return was delivered (subject to sub-paragraph (6))."

(4) In paragraph 24 of that Schedule, insert at the end—

"(6) In the case of a company which is a member of a group other than a small group, the 12-month period in sub-paragraph (2) shall start not from the day on which the return was delivered but from the filing date.

(7) In sub-paragraph (6) "group" and "small group" have the same meaning as in sections 383(2) and 474(1) of the Companies Act 2006 (or, until their commencement, as in the provisions that they replicate)."

(5) The amendments made by subsections (1) and (2) apply to returns which relate to the tax year 2007–08 or a later tax year.

(6) The amendments made by subsections (3) and (4) apply to returns which relate to accounting periods ending after 31st March 2008.

GENERAL NOTE

Section 96 introduces a significant change in the operation of HMRC's self-assessment enquiry procedure. The 'enquiry window', the period of time that HMRC have to open an enquiry into a return has historically been linked to the fixed filing date of 31 January (for returns filed on time), and over the years, there have been many suggestions that this should be changed to run from 12 months the tax return is submitted.

Many advisers have considered that the risk of an enquiry was increased by early filing, although HMRC have always refuted this. In addition, the issue of enquiry notices have been spread unevenly throughout the year, with a significant peak being issued close to the expiry of the enquiry window, creating administrative difficulties. At the same time, HMRC are known to be concerned about the number of taxpayers filing their returns late.

These issues came together during Lord Carter's review of online filing, when he found that the enquiry window rules acted as a disincentive to early filing. One of the recommendations in his report is therefore that—

> 'the rules relating to the timing of queries about a return should be designed with the aim of encouraging early filing, by linking the date at which the taxpayer has certainty and knows that the return will not be queried, to the date on which the return is submitted.'

This section introduces the legislation implementing that recommendation. The change is likely to have the benefit of encouraging a more even flow of work for advisers and HMRC alike.

The new rule applies to the following returns—

(*a*) income tax self-assessment returns for 2007–08 and subsequent years;

(*b*) most company tax returns for accounting periods ending after 31 March 2008,

provided they are received on or before the statutory deadline. There is no change to the enquiry window for large groups of companies, or to the deadline for enquiries into returns issued late.

97 Penalties for errors

(1) Schedule 24 contains provisions imposing penalties on taxpayers who—

(*a*) make errors in certain documents sent to HMRC, or
(*b*) unreasonably fail to report errors in assessments by HMRC.

(2) That Schedule comes into force in accordance with provision made by the Treasury by order.

(3) An order—

(*a*) may commence a provision generally or only for specified purposes,
(*b*) may make different provision for different purposes, and
(*c*) may include incidental, consequential or transitional provision.

(4) The power to make an order is exercisable by statutory instrument.

GENERAL NOTE

The section introduces Schedule 24 which amends the rules relating to the imposition of penalties for incorrect returns and for unreasonable failure to report errors in assessments made by HMRC.

PART 7

MISCELLANEOUS

Value added tax and insurance premium tax

98 VAT: joint and several liability of traders in supply chain where tax unpaid

(1) In section 77A of VATA 1994 (joint and several liability of traders in supply chain where tax unpaid), for subsection (9) substitute—

"(9) The Treasury may by order amend subsection (1) above.

(9A) The Treasury may by order amend this section in order to extend or otherwise alter the circumstances in which a person shall be presumed to have reasonable grounds for suspecting matters to be as mentioned in subsection (2)(*b*) above.

(9B) Any order under this section may make such incidental, supplemental, consequential or transitional provision as the Treasury think fit."

(2) In section 97(4) of that Act (orders ceasing to have effect unless approved by House of Commons), after paragraph (*ea*) insert—

"(*eb*) an order under section 77A(9) or (9A);".

GENERAL NOTE

VATA 1994 s 77A applies to taxable persons purchasing goods listed in s 77A(1) as amended by VAT (Amendment of s 77A of the Value Added Tax Act 1994) Order 2007 (SI 2007/939) art 2. In broad terms, the goods comprise telephones, computers, electronic equipment for leisure, amusement or entertainment use by individuals, and related parts and accessories.

The Commissioners can serve a notice on a taxable person who, at the time of purchase, knew – or had reasonable grounds to suspect – that some or all of the VAT payable by his supplier, his customer, or any earlier or later supplier would go unpaid (VATA 1994 s 77A(2)). The effect of the notice is that the taxable person and his supplier are jointly and severally liable for the VAT payable by the supplier (VATA 1994 s 77A(3)).

The purchaser is presumed to have reasonable grounds for suspicion if the purchase price was less than their lowest open market value or less than the price for an earlier purchase. The onus lies on the purchaser to demonstrate that the low purchase price was unconnected with a failure to pay VAT (VATA 1994 s 77A(6), (7)).

This presumption was considered by the Court of Justice in *Customs and Excise Comrs and another v Federation of Technological Industries and others* [2006] ECR I–4191, [2006] STC 1483, ECJ. The Court made a number of observations (see paras 29–34 of the judgment). First, member states must comply with the general principles of Community law when exercising powers under EU directives. Secondly, while it is legitimate for measures adopted on the basis of Directive 77/388/EEC art 21(3), now Directive 2006/112/EC art 205, to seek to preserve the rights of the public exchequer as effectively as possible, such measures must not go further than is necessary for that purpose. Thirdly, while art 21(3) (now art 205) allows member states to make a person jointly and severally liable for payment of VAT if the factual situation in VATA 1994 s 77A(2) is met, and rely on presumptions in that regard, those presumptions must not be formulated in such a way as to make it practically impossible, or excessively difficult, for the taxable person to rebut them with evidence to the contrary. Fourthly, traders who take every precaution which could reasonably be required of them to ensure that their transactions do not form part of a chain which includes a transaction vitiated by VAT fraud must be able to rely on the legality of those transactions without risk of being made jointly and severally liable to pay the VAT due from another person. Fifthly, it is for the national court to determine whether the national legislation complies with the general principles of Community law.

It follows from the fifth observation that the vires of the presumption in s 77A(6) and the defence in s 77A(7) will be decided when the case returns to the Court of Appeal. Subsection (1) allows HMRC to respond to any adverse judgment by amending s 77A by order. It does so by repealing s 77A(9) and substituting a new s 77A(9)–(9B).

In detail:

(*a*) The new s 77A(9) re-enacts the existing power to make orders varying the descriptions of goods to which this section applies.

(*b*) The new s 77A(9A) enables the Treasury to make orders varying, or otherwise altering, the circumstances in which the purchaser is presumed to have reasonable grounds for suspicion.

(*c*) The new s 77A(9B) re-enacts the existing power to make incidental, supplemental, consequential or transitional provisions in such an order.

Subsection (2) inserts a new VATA 1994 s 97(4)(*eb*). This provides that an order made under the new s 77A(9) or (9A) must be approved by the House of Commons within 28 days of being made and that it ceases to have effect unless this condition is met.

99 VAT: non-business use etc of business goods

(1) Schedule 4 to VATA 1994 (matters to be treated as supply of goods or services) is amended as follows.

(2) In paragraph 5 (non-business use etc of business goods), omit sub-paragraph (4A) (exception to rule in case of interests in land and buildings etc that non-business use of business assets treated as supply of services).

(3) In paragraph 9 (application of paragraphs 5 to 8 where land forms part of assets of business), insert at the end—

> "(4) In this paragraph "grant" includes surrender."

(4) Paragraph 7 of Schedule 6 to VATA 1994 (valuation of supply of services otherwise than for consideration by virtue of paragraph 5(4) of Schedule 4 etc) is amended as follows.

(5) The existing provision becomes sub-paragraph (1) and after that sub-paragraph insert—

> "(2) Regulations may, in relation to a supply of services by virtue of paragraph 5(4) of Schedule 4 (but otherwise than for a consideration), make provision for determining how the full cost to the taxable person of providing the services is to be calculated.
>
> (3) The regulations may, in particular, make provision for the calculation to be made by reference to any prescribed period.
>
> (4) The regulations may make—
>
> (*a*) different provision for different circumstances;
>
> (*b*) such incidental, supplementary, consequential or transitional provision as the Commissioners think fit."

(6) The amendment made by subsection (2) comes into force on 1st September 2007.

(7) The amendment made by subsection (3) has effect in relation to surrenders on or after 21st March 2007.

GENERAL NOTE

Under EU law, the tax treatment of goods purchased partly for business purposes and partly for other purposes ("mixed use goods") is derived from a long line of cases starting in 1991 with *Lennartz v Finanzamt München III* (case C-97/90) [1991] ECR I–3795, [1995] STC 514, ECJ. In brief, taxable persons can opt for full input tax deduction in respect of mixed used goods with a corresponding charge to tax on their private or non-business use. This is referred to by the Commissioners as "the Lennartz approach".

In 2003, the Government took the view that the Lennartz approach "works less well for assets like land and buildings that depreciate very slowly" and "provides an opportunity to delay or avoid payment of VAT" (see Explanatory Notes to cl 22 of the Finance Bill 2003; Budget Notice 18/03, 9 April 2003, para 2). FA 2003 s 22 and VAT (Supply of Services) (Amendment) Order 2003 (SI 2003 No 1055) were accordingly enacted to in order to withdraw the Lennartz approach in relation to land, buildings, civil engineering works and goods incorporated in buildings and civil engineering works ("land"). The broad effect of these provisions is as follows:

(*a*) the private or non-business use of land does not amount to a supply of services for the purpose of determining whether a taxable person is entitled to input tax deduction when the land is acquired (VAT (Supply of Services) Order 1993 (SI 1993 No 1507) arts 3, 3A as amended or inserted by the 2003 Order);

(*b*) in consequence, land gives rise to full input tax deduction if it is used or to be used for wholly for business purposes ("business land"), no deduction if the land is used or to be used wholly for private or non-business purposes ("non-business land"), or partial deduction if the land is used or to be used for both purposes ("mixed use land") (VATA 1994 s 24(1) (5));

(*c*) any subsequent use of business land or mixed use land for private or non-business purposes without consideration is treated as a supply of services and charged to tax accordingly (arts 3, 3B, 6 of the 1993 Order as amended or inserted by the 2003 Order);

(*d*) this charge to tax does no more than claw back all or part of the input tax previously deduced (art 7 of the 1993 Order).

The Commissioners considered that these changes "fall squarely" within the derogation conferred by Directive 77/388/EEC art 6(2), now Directive 2006/112/EC art 26 (see Business Brief 22/03, 19 November 2003). However, this view has since been decisively rejected in *Charles and another v Staatssecretaris van Financiën* (case C-434/03) [2005] ECR I–7037, [2006] STC 1429, ECJ. In Business Brief 15/05, 9 August 2005, the Commissioners accordingly conceded that the 2003 legislation is ultra vires and that, in consequence:

> "... where businesses incur VAT on certain construction services or on purchasing land, buildings and civil engineering works for mixed business and non-business use, they can now rely on the direct effect of the Sixth Directive to treat all VAT incurred as input tax and, subject to the normal rules, recover all the tax up front. They must then account for output tax on the non-business use over the economic lifetime of the asset.

The services concerned are those which result in, or will result in, the construction of a new building or civil engineering work, or a major refurbishment or extension of an existing building."

This section makes three changes.

First, sub-ss (1), (2), (6) repeal VATA 1994 Sch 4 para 5(4A) with effect from 1 September 2007. The 2003 Order will presumably be revoked in due course. The consequence of these changes is that the private or non-business use of land, buildings, civil engineering works and goods incorporated in buildings and civil engineering works revert to being chargeable under Sch 4 para 5(4) (as interpreted in accordance with Sch 4 para 9) in the same manner as for goods generally.

Secondly, sub-ss (1), (3), (7) insert a new Sch 4 para 9(4) in relation to surrenders made after 20 March 2005. This provision effectively provides that the references to a "grant or assignment" in Sch 4 para 9(2), (3) are construed as references to a "grant, assignment or surrender". The purpose of this change is to close a potential loophole (see Explanatory Notes to Clause 98, paras 3, 8). It has three consequences in relation to land transactions:

(*a*) The terms "transfer", "disposition" or "sale" in Sch 4 paras 5–8 are construed as references to the grant, assignment or surrender of any interest in, right over or licence to occupy land.

(*b*) For the purposes of Sch 4 para 5(1), this grant, assignment or surrender gives rise to a supply of goods (if it made without consideration or relates to a major interest in land) and a supply of services in other circumstances.

(*c*) The charge to tax under Sch 4 para 5(4) in respect of grants and assignments is extended to include surrenders.

Thirdly, sub-ss (4), (5) amend VATA 1994 Sch 6 para 7. They provide that the existing provision becomes para 7(1) and insert new para 7(2)–(4). What is now para 7(1) deals, inter alia, with the valuation of the supply of services made when business goods are used for private or non-business purposes without consideration. In principle, it provides that the value of the supply is full cost to the taxable person of providing the services. The new para 7(2)–(4) enables the Commissioners to make regulations determining how "full cost" is to be calculated. In particular, the regulations may provide that calculations are made by reference to a prescribed accounting period. This change enables the UK to implement the basis of calculation set out in *Hausgemeinschaft Jörg und Stefanie Wollny v Finanzamt Landshut* (case C-72/05) [2006] ECR I–8297 (see *Simon's Weekly Tax Intelligence* 2006, p 2205).

100 VAT: transfers of going concerns

(1) Section 49 of VATA 1994 (transfers of going concern) is amended as follows.

(2) In subsection (1) (transferor's supplies treated as transferee's supplies for purposes of registration and transferor's records to be kept by transferee after transfer)—

(*a*) after "Where a business" insert ", or part of a business,",

(*b*) after "on the business" insert "or part of the business", and

(*c*) omit paragraph (*b*) (together with the "and" before it).

(3) In subsection (2) (regulations for securing continuity of Act in case of transfers of going concerns), after "a business" insert ", or part of a business,".

(4) After that subsection insert—

"(2A) Regulations under subsection (2) above may, in particular, provide for the duties under this Act of the transferor to preserve records relating to the business or part of the business for any period after the transfer to become duties of the transferee unless the Commissioners, at the request of the transferor, otherwise direct."

(5) In subsection (3) (provision which may be made by regulations), in paragraph (*a*), after "the transferor" insert "(other than the duties mentioned in subsection (2A) above)".

(6) After that subsection insert—

"(4) Subsection (5) below applies where—

(*a*) a business, or part of a business, carried on by a taxable person is transferred to another person as a going concern, and

(*b*) the transferor continues to be required under this Act to preserve for any period after the transfer any records relating to the business or part of the business.

(5) So far as is necessary for the purpose of complying with the transferee's duties under this Act, the transferee ("E") may require the transferor—

(*a*) to give to E, within such time and in such form as E may reasonably require, such information contained in the records as E may reasonably specify,

(*b*) to give to E, within such time and in such form as E may reasonably require, such copies of documents forming part of the records as E may reasonably specify, and

(*c*) to make the records available for E's inspection at such time and place as E may reasonably require (and permit E to take copies of, or make extracts from, them).

(6) Where a business, or part of a business, carried on by a taxable person is transferred to another person as a going concern, the Commissioners may disclose to the transferee any information relating to the business when it was carried on by the transferor for the purpose of enabling the transferee to comply with the transferee's duties under this Act."

(7) In section 94(6) of VATA 1994 (meaning of "business" etc)—

(*a*) after "a business" insert ", or part of a business,", and

(*b*) for "its assets or liabilities" substitute "the assets or liabilities of the business or part of the business".

(8) In paragraph 1(2) of Schedule 1 to that Act (registration in respect of taxable supplies), after "Where a business" insert ", or part of a business,".

(9) In paragraph 8(2)(*b*) of Schedule 4 to that Act (matters to be treated as supply of goods or services), after "a business" insert ", or part of a business,".

(10) The amendments made by this section have effect in relation to transfers pursuant to contracts entered into on or after 1st September 2007.

GENERAL NOTE

VATA 1994 ss 49(1), 49(2), 94(6), Sch 1 para 1(2) and Sch 4 para 8(2)(*b*) make provision for the transfer of "a business" as a going concern. VAT (Special Provisions) Order 1995 (SI 1995/1268) art 5(1)(a) and (b), on the other hand, makes separate provision for transfers of "a business" and "part of a business". This section corrects this anomaly by amending the 1994 Act to replace the references to "a business" with references to "a business or part of a business" (sub-ss (1), (2)(*a*), (2)(*b*), (3) and (7)–(9)).

When a business is transferred as a going concern, VATA 1994 s 49(1)(b) provides that the vendor's business records must be preserved by the purchaser of the business. This creates problems for the vendor as he needs to retain his records, at least temporarily, in order to prepare his final VAT return and cessation accounts, and may later need the records if, for example, his tax affairs are subject to an investigation. The vendor can avoid these problems by requesting the Commissioners to make a direction making him responsible for preserving the records after the transfer. However, a direction creates problems for the purchaser if essential information has been omitted from the completion statement prepared in respect of the transfer: the purchaser must rely on the vendor's co-operation in order to fill any gaps.

This section amends VATA 1994 s 49 (sub-ss (1), (2)(*c*) and (4)–(6)) in order to alleviate the practical problems experienced by both vendors and purchasers. These amendments have effect in relation to transfers under a contract entered into after 31 August 2007 (sub-s (10)).

Person liable to retain the vendor's business records

Subsection (2)(*c*) repeals VATA 1994 s 49(1)(*b*). This results in a general rule that the vendor is liable for the preservation his records following the transfer of all or part of his business as a going concern. However, subsections (4) and (5) make provision for an exception in relation to transfers which also involve a transfer of the vendor's VAT registration number to the purchaser.

Subsections (4) and (5) insert a new VATA 1994 s 49(2A) and make a consequential amendment to s 49(3). The new s 49(2A) extends the Commissioners' power to make regulations under s 49(2). These regulations may now provide that, following transfer of the business (or part) and VAT registration number, the vendor's business records must be preserved by the purchaser unless the Commissioners direct otherwise. Thus, regulations may provide that the vendor's records are retained by the vendor (if a direction is made) and by the purchaser (in other cases), thereby restoring the effect of the repealed VATA 1994 s 49(1)(*b*).

Provision of information to the purchaser

Subsection (6) inserts a new VATA 1994 s 49(4)–(6) designed to ameliorate the difficulties experienced by purchasers when the vendor retains his records following a transfer. Two reliefs are introduced.

First, the new s 49(5) provides that the purchaser may require the vendor to:

(*a*) provide him with information contained in the records;

(*b*) provide him with copies of specified documents forming part of the records;

(*c*) make the records available for inspection by him, and;

(*d*) permit him to take copies of the documents inspected or make extracts from them.

Secondly, the new VATA 1994 s 49(6) authorises the Commissioners to disclose information to the purchaser regarding the vendor's business so as to enable the purchaser to comply with his statutory duties in relation to VAT.

101 IPT: meaning of "premium"

(1) In section 72 of FA 1994 (interpretation: "premium"), after subsection (1A) insert—

"(1B) Where—

(*a*) an amount is charged (to the insured or any other person) in respect of the acquisition of a right (whether of the insured or any other person) to require the insurer to provide, or offer to provide, any of the cover included in a taxable insurance contract, and

(*b*) any payment in respect of that amount is not regarded as a payment received under that contract by the insurer by virtue of subsection (1A) above,

the payment is to be regarded as a payment received under that contract by the insurer unless it is chargeable to tax at the higher rate by virtue of section 52A above."

(2) The amendment made by subsection (1) has effect in relation to amounts charged on or after 22nd March 2007.

GENERAL NOTE

This section extends the definition of 'premium' for the purposes of insurance premium tax (IPT). Section 101 now ensures that 'premium' will include any payments received in respect of a right to require an insurer to provide, or offer to provide, cover under a taxable insurance contract. This extension was deemed necessary to close a gap in the current definition of 'premium' which could have been exploited for tax avoidance purposes. The extended definition of 'premium' has effect to amounts charged on or after 22 March 2007.

Petroleum revenue tax

102 Abolition of PRT for fields recommissioned after earlier decommissioning

(1) Section 185 of FA 1993 (abolition of PRT for oil fields with development consents on or after 16th March 1993) is amended as follows.

(2) In subsection (1) (meaning of "non-taxable field" and "taxable field"), after paragraph (*b*) insert "or an oil field which does not meet the conditions in paragraphs (*a*) and (*b*) above but which does meet the conditions in subsection (1A) below".

(3) After that subsection insert—

"(1A) An oil field meets the conditions in this subsection if—

(*a*) the Secretary of State has at any time approved one or more abandonment programmes under Part 4 of the Petroleum Act 1998 (or Part 1 of the Petroleum Act 1987) in relation to all assets of the field which are relevant assets;

(*b*) those programmes have been carried out to the satisfaction of the Secretary of State;

(*c*) a development decision is made in relation to the field; and

(*d*) that decision is made on or after 16th March 1993 and after those programmes have been so carried out.

(1B) For the purposes of subsection (1A)(*a*) above, an asset is a relevant asset of an oil field if—

(*a*) it has at any time been a qualifying asset (within the meaning of the 1983 Act) in relation to any participator in the field; and (*b*) it has at any time been used for the purpose of winning oil from the field.

(1C) For the purposes of subsection (1A)(*c*) and (*d*) above, a development decision is made in relation to an oil field when—

(*a*) consent for development is granted to a licensee by the Secretary of State in respect of the whole or part of the field; or

(*b*) a programme of development is served on a licensee or approved by the Secretary of State for the whole or part of the field."

(4) In subsection (7) (meaning of "development" etc), for "subsections (1) and (2)" substitute "this section".

(5) An oil field which meets the conditions in subsection (1A) of section 185 of FA 1993 (as inserted by subsection (3) above) becomes a non-taxable field for the purposes of any enactment relating to petroleum revenue tax—

(*a*) in any case where the development decision is made before 1st July 2007, on that date, and

(*b*) in any other case, on the date on which the development decision is made.

GENERAL NOTE

Petroleum Revenue Tax (PRT) is a field based tax on income generated from extracting oil and gas in the UK or on the UK Continental Shelf. PRT is no longer applicable to any field which was awarded development consent by the Secretary of State for the Department of Trade and Industry (DTI) after 16 March 1993. Section 102 extends those fields outside of the scope to PRT to include oil or gas fields which have been decommissioned and are subsequently recommissioned. This extension was necessary due to the field based nature of PRT as previously even when completely decommissioned a field would remain within the charge to PRT if further production took place. However, unlike new fields, for recommissioned fields most of the reliefs and allowances available to offset PRT may have already been used such that PRT would become due at a much earlier stage in production. Ministers believed that this difference in treatment could distort investment decisions and reduce the overall recovery of oil and gas from the UKCS. This section seeks to prevent this distortion by treating recommissioned fields in the same way as new fields and outside the scope of PRT.

To qualify as a recommissioned field under this section it is necessary that all qualifying assets of a field previously used for the purposes of winning oil must have been decommissioned in accordance with a DTI approved abandonment programme, that the DTI have agreed that this programme has been satisfactorily completed and that subsequent to the completion of the decommissioning further consent for redevelopment has be given. All fields which meet the new qualifying criteria will cease to be chargeable to PRT as at 1 July 2007 or at the date consent for redevelopment is given by the DTI if later.

103 Tax-exempt tariffing receipts

(1) Section 6A of the Oil Taxation Act 1983 (c 56) (tax-exempt tariffing receipts) is amended as follows.

(2) In subsection (4), insert at the end "or

(*c*) use in relation to a UK recommissioned field (see subsection (5) below) or oil won from such a field."

(3) In subsection (5), insert at the end—

""UK recommissioned field" means any oil field which is not a new field or qualifying existing field but as respects which the conditions in section 185(1A) of the Finance Act 1993 are satisfied (fields recommissioned after earlier decommissioning)."

(4) The amendments made by this section are deemed to have come into force on 1st July 2007.

GENERAL NOTE

This section makes further adjustments with respect to recommissioned oil and gas fields (see s 102).

Prior to 16 March 1993 Petroleum Revenue Tax (PRT) was due not only on income generated from extracting oil and gas in the UK or on the UK Continental Shelf but also on tariffs or rents paid by companies to the owners of North Sea pipelines for transporting their oil. PRT is no longer applicable to oil and gas fields that received development consent after 16 March 1993 and likewise tariffs for the use of new infrastructure commissioned to serve these new fields are outside of the scope of PRT. This situation has led to a distortion in tax treatment between pipelines based purely on the age of the infrastructure or the field that it was built to serve. Changes in FA 2004 included an exemption from PRT for new tariffing business given development consent after 9 April 2003 and for fields that use PRT liable infrastructure for the first time, that is new contracts entered into on or after 9 April 2003. This section extends these measures to ensure that recommissioned fields are added to the list of tariffing businesses that qualify for PRT-exempt tariffing receipts.

104 Allowance of unrelievable loss from abandoned field

(1) In section 6 of the Oil Taxation Act 1975 (c 22) (allowance of unrelievable loss from abandoned field), after subsection (4) insert—

> "(4A) For the purposes of this section and Schedule 8 to this Act, the winning of oil from an oil field shall not be regarded as having permanently ceased until all the oil wells in the field have been permanently abandoned."

(2) The amendment made by subsection (1) is deemed to have come into force on 1st July 2007.

GENERAL NOTE

This section amends the Petroleum Revenue Tax (PRT) rules regarding losses arising within a PRT field by providing clarity on the meaning of certain key terms. Currently any losses arising in a PRT field may be carried back against profits generated for the entire life of the field. When abandoned or decommissioned in accordance with an approved decommissioning programme any unrelieved costs may be carried back in that field as losses. Where there are more losses available than profits with which to offset them an unrelievable field loss is created. An unrelievable field loss may then be used to offset profits in another PRT field. Importantly an unrelievable field loss can only be created when it has been agreed that the winning of oil from that field has 'permanently ceased'. Due to changes in both technology and oil price, production from fields which was once viewed as uneconomic may now once more be regarded as profitable. As such in recent years there has been an increasing tension between HMRC and taxpayers as to when permanent cessation of production can actually be said to have occurred.

Section 104 introduces additional clarification on what is meant by 'permanent cessation' in the context of the winning of oil. Permanent cessation is deemed to occur only when all the oil wells in a field have been permanently abandoned.

Other miscellaneous measures

105 Amendments connected with Gambling Act 2005

Schedule 25 contains amendments that are consequential on, or otherwise connected with, the Gambling Act 2005 (c 19).

GENERAL NOTE

This section merely introduces Schedule 25.

106 VED: exempt vehicles

(1) In section 5 of VERA 1994 (exempt vehicles), after subsection (2) insert—

> "(3) The Secretary of State may by order amend Schedule 2 in order to make provision about the descriptions of—
>
> (*a*) tractors, and
>
> (*b*) vehicles used for purposes relating to agriculture, horticulture or forestry,
>
> that are to be exempt vehicles.
>
> (4) An order under subsection (3) may in particular repeal any of paragraphs 20A to 20D of Schedule 2."

(2) In section 60(3) of that Act (orders subject to affirmative procedure), after "under" insert "section 5(3) or".

GENERAL NOTE

This section gives the Secretary of State a new power to make orders which amend the descriptions of tractors and vehicles used for purposes relating to agriculture, horticulture or forestry that are exempt from vehicle excise duty. The new power will allow the descriptions of agricultural vehicles to be changed in line with technological developments. The new power is necessary as the current descriptions are no longer sufficiently precise to distinguish between those vehicles intended to benefit and those not intended to benefit from the exemption.

107 Limitation period in old actions for mistake of law relating to direct tax

(1) Section 32(1)(*c*) of the Limitation Act 1980 (c 58) (extended period for bringing action in case of mistake) does not apply in relation to any action brought before 8th September 2003 for relief from the consequences of a mistake of law relating to a taxation matter under the care and management of the Commissioners of Inland Revenue.

(2) Subsection (1) has effect regardless of how the grounds on which the action was brought were expressed and of whether it was also brought otherwise than for such relief.

(3) But subsection (1) does not have effect in relation to an action, or so much of an action as relates to a cause of action, if—

(*a*) the action, or cause of action, has been the subject of a judgment of the House of Lords given before 6th December 2006 as to the application of section 32(1)(*c*) in relation to such relief, or

(*b*) the parties to the action are, in accordance with a group litigation order, bound in relation to the action, or cause of action, by a judgment of the House of Lords in another action given before that date as to the application of section 32(1)(*c*) in relation to such relief.

(4) If the judgment of any court was given on or after 6th December 2006 but before the day on which this Act is passed, the judgment is to be taken to have been what it would have been had subsections (1) to (3) been in force at all times since the action was brought (and any defence of limitation which would have been available had been raised).

(5) And any payment made to satisfy a liability under the judgment which (in consequence of subsection (4)) is to be taken not to have been imposed is repayable (with interest from the date of the payment).

(6) In this section—

"group litigation order" means an order of a court providing for the case management of actions which give rise to common or related issues of fact or law, and

"judgment" includes order (and "given" includes made).

GENERAL NOTE

In July 2003 Park J gave judgement in *Deutsche Morgan Grenfell v IRC*, in which he held that the common law remedy of restitution for a payment made under a mistake of law applies to payments made to HMRC (as well as to payments made to others).

The main importance of that was in the context of limitation periods. Generally speaking, a claim made to recover overpaid tax had to be made within six years (or less) of the date upon which the tax was paid. But if that claim could be expressed to be a claim for restitution for tax paid under a mistake of law, the six year limitation period ran from the date upon which the mistake was discovered (or could with reasonable diligence have been discovered) – Limitation Act 1980 s 32(1)(*c*).

That meant that, potentially, taxpayers could make claims to recover tax paid many years earlier, on the basis that they had only recently discovered that the tax was paid under a mistake of law. To protect itself against that, the Government announced on 8 September 2003 the legislation that became FA 2004 s 320.

That section had the effect that the extended limitation period for which Limitation Act 1980 s 32(1)(*c*) provided was not to apply "in relation to a mistake of law relating to a taxation matter under the care and management of the Commissioners of Inland Revenue" with effect from 8 September 2003 (the date of the Government's announced intention to legislate).

Views were expressed at the time that because it lacked any transitional period, s 320 would be contrary to the EC Treaty insofar as it affected claims based on European Community rights; and it is understood that the validity of s 320 is likely to be challenged on those grounds.

In the meantime, HMRC appealed against the decision of Park J to the Court of Appeal which (at least, on this aspect of the case) allowed their appeal; but Deutsche Morgan Grenfell then appealed to the House of Lords which, on 25 October 2006, held that Park J had been right.

In the light of that decision, the Government decided that FA 2004 s 320 did not afford it sufficient protection, and announced on 6 December 2006 that legislation would be introduced in the 2007 Finance Act to disapply Limitation Act 1980 s 32(1)(*c*) in all direct tax measures (whenever the relevant claim was made). The effect of that legislation (s 107) is that Limitation Act 1980 s 32(1)(c) no longer applies to rights of action that had accrued before 8 September 2003, subject to a very limited exception where the action was covered by a judgement of the House of Lords given before 6 December 2006 (the date of the Government's latest announcement).

The section also provides that any judgement given after this new legislation had been announced but before the enactment of the Finance Act 2007 is taken to be what it would have been had s 107 already been in force (see sub-s (4)) and that any payment made to satisfy a liability under any such judgement is to be repayable (see sub-s (5)).

The Law Society is not alone in having pointed out that the section is clearly contrary to the principle against retrospective legislation.

108 Disclosure of tax avoidance schemes

(1) Part 7 of FA 2004 (disclosure of tax avoidance schemes) is amended as follows.

(2) After section 306 insert—

"306A Doubt as to notifiability

(1) HMRC may apply to the Special Commissioners for an order that—

(*a*) a proposal is to be treated as notifiable, or
(*b*) arrangements are to be treated as notifiable.

(2) An application must specify—

(*a*) the proposal or arrangements in respect of which the order is sought, and
(*b*) the promoter.

(3) On an application the Special Commissioners may make the order only if satisfied that HMRC—

(*a*) have taken all reasonable steps to establish whether the proposal or arrangements are notifiable, and
(*b*) have reasonable grounds for suspecting that the proposal or arrangements may be notifiable.

(4) Reasonable steps under subsection (3)(*a*) may (but need not) include taking action under section 313A or 313B.

(5) Grounds for suspicion under subsection (3)(*b*) may include—

(*a*) the fact that the relevant arrangements fall within a description prescribed under section 306(1)(*a*);
(*b*) an attempt by the promoter to avoid or delay providing information or documents about the proposal or arrangements under or by virtue of section 313A or 313B;
(*c*) the promoter's failure to comply with a requirement under or by virtue of section 313A or 313B in relation to another proposal or other arrangements.

(6) Where an order is made under this section in respect of a proposal or arrangements, the prescribed period for the purposes of section 308(1) or (3) in so far as it applies by virtue of the order—

(*a*) shall begin after a date prescribed for the purpose, and
(*b*) may be of a different length than the prescribed period for the purpose of other applications of section 308(1) or (3).

(7) An order under this section in relation to a proposal or arrangements is without prejudice to the possible application of section 308, other than by virtue of this section, to the proposal or arrangements."

(3) In section 307 ("promoter"), insert at the end—

"(6) In the application of this Part to a proposal or arrangements which are not notifiable, a reference to a promoter is a reference to a person who would be a promoter under subsections (1) to (5) if the proposal or arrangements were notifiable."

(4) After section 308 insert—

"308A Supplemental information

(1) This section applies where—

(*a*) a promoter (P) has provided information in purported compliance with section 308(1) or (3), but

(*b*) HMRC believe that P has not provided all the prescribed information.

(2) HMRC may apply to the Special Commissioners for an order requiring P to provide specified information about, or documents relating to, the notifiable proposal or arrangements.

(3) The Special Commissioners may make an order under subsection (2) in respect of information or documents only if satisfied that HMRC have reasonable grounds for suspecting that the information or documents—

(*a*) form part of the prescribed information, or

(*b*) will support or explain the prescribed information.

(4) A requirement by virtue of subsection (2) shall be treated as part of P's duty under section 308(1) or (3).

(5) In so far as P's duty under section 308(1) or (3) arises out of a requirement by virtue of subsection (2) above, the prescribed period shall begin after a date prescribed for the purpose.

(6) In so far as P's duty under section 308(1) or (3) arises out of a requirement by virtue of subsection (2) above, the prescribed period—

(*a*) may be of a different length than the prescribed period for the purpose of other applications of section 308(1) or (3), and

(*b*) may be extended by HMRC by direction."

(5) After section 313 insert—

"313A Pre-disclosure enquiry

(1) Where HMRC suspect that a person (P) is the promoter of a proposal or arrangements which may be notifiable, they may by written notice require P to state—

(*a*) whether in P's opinion the proposal or arrangements are notifiable by P, and

(*b*) if not, the reasons for P's opinion.

(2) A notice must specify the proposal or arrangements to which it relates.

(3) For the purpose of subsection (1)(*b*)—

(*a*) it is not sufficient to refer to the fact that a lawyer or other professional has given an opinion,

(*b*) the reasons must show, by reference to this Part and regulations under it, why P thinks the proposal or arrangements are not notifiable by P, and

(*c*) in particular, if P asserts that the arrangements do not fall within any description prescribed under section 306(1)(*a*), the reasons must provide sufficient information to enable HMRC to confirm the assertion.

(4) P must comply with a requirement under or by virtue of subsection (1) within—

(*a*) the prescribed period, or

(*b*) such longer period as HMRC may direct.

313B Reasons for non-disclosure: supporting information

(1) Where HMRC receive from a person (P) a statement of reasons why a proposal or arrangements are not notifiable by P, HMRC may apply to the Special Commissioners for an order requiring P to provide specified information or documents in support of the reasons.

(2) P must comply with a requirement under or by virtue of subsection (1) within—

(*a*) the prescribed period, or

(*b*) such longer period as HMRC may direct.

(3) The power under subsection (1)—

(*a*) may be exercised more than once, and
(*b*) applies whether or not the statement of reasons was received under section 313A(1)(*b*)."

(6) After section 314 insert—

"314A Order to disclose

(1) HMRC may apply to the Special Commissioners for an order that—
(*a*) a proposal is notifiable, or
(*b*) arrangements are notifiable.

(2) An application must specify—
(*a*) the proposal or arrangements in respect of which the order is sought, and
(*b*) the promoter.

(3) On an application the Special Commissioners may make the order only if satisfied that section 306(1)(*a*) to (*c*) applies to the relevant arrangements."

(7) After section 317 insert—

"317A Special Commissioners: procedure

Sections 56B to 56D of the Taxes Management Act 1970 (procedure) shall apply (with any necessary modifications) to applications under this Part as to appeals."

(8) In section 318(1) (interpretation)—
(*a*) after the definition of "corporation tax" insert—
""HMRC" means the Commissioners for Her Majesty's Revenue and Customs;" and
(*b*) after the definition of "reference number" insert—
""the Special Commissioners" has the meaning given by section 4 of the Taxes Management Act 1970;".

(9) In section 98C of TMA 1970 (notifications under Part 7 of FA 2004)—
(*a*) in subsection (2), at the end insert—
", and
(*e*) sections 313A and 313B (duty of promoter to respond to inquiry).", and
(*b*) after that subsection insert—

"(2A) Where a failure to comply with a provision mentioned in subsection (2) concerns a proposal or arrangements in respect of which an order has been made under section 306A of the Finance Act 2004 (doubt as to notifiability), the amount specified in subsection (1)(*b*) above shall be increased to the prescribed sum.

(2B) Where a failure to comply with a provision mentioned in subsection (2) concerns a proposal or arrangements in respect of which an order has been made under section 314A of the Finance Act 2004 (order to disclose), the amount specified in subsection (1)(*b*) above shall be increased to the prescribed sum in relation to days falling after the prescribed period.

(2C) In subsection (2A) and (2B)—
(*a*) "the prescribed sum" means a sum prescribed by the Treasury by regulations, and
(*b*) "the prescribed period" means a period beginning with the date of the order under section 314A and prescribed by the Commissioners by regulations.

(2D) The making of an order under section 314A of that Act does not of itself mean that, for the purposes of section 118(2) of this Act, a person either did or did not have a reasonable excuse for non-compliance before the order was made.

(2E) Where an order is made under section 314A of that Act then for the purposes of section 118(2) of this Act—
(*a*) the person identified in the order as the promoter of the proposal or arrangements cannot, in respect of any time after the end of the period mentioned in subsection (2B), rely on doubt as to notifiability as an excuse for failure to comply with section 308 of that Act, and
(*b*) any delay in compliance with that section after the end of that period is unreasonable unless attributable to something other than doubt as to notifiability.

(2F) Regulations under subsection (2C)—
(*a*) may include incidental or transitional provision,
(*b*) shall be made by statutory instrument,
(*c*) in the case of regulations under subsection (2C)(*a*), shall not be made unless a draft has been laid before and approved by resolution of the House of Commons, and

(*d*) in the case of regulations under subsection (2C)(*b*), shall be subject to annulment in pursuance of a resolution of the House of Commons."

(10) The amendments made by this section come into force on the passing of this Act; and—

(*a*) regulations made under section 56B of TMA 1970 (Special Commissioners: procedure) before the passing of this Act apply (with any necessary modifications) to applications under Part 7 of FA 2004 as amended by this section as they apply to appeals (but subject to any regulations made after the passing of this Act), and

(*b*) a power under Part 7 of FA 2004 as amended by this section may be exercised in relation to, or by virtue of, matters arising wholly or partly before the passing of this Act.

GENERAL NOTE

When the present disclosure of tax avoidance scheme rules were introduced in FA 2004 they contained a simple penalty regime for a failure to make a disclosure or to notify a client of the allocated reference number for a notified scheme. The rules did not contain any powers enabling HMRC to investigate cases of suspected non-compliance and nearly three years into the disclosure regime HMRC believe that there is a sufficient problem with non-compliant promoters of tax schemes to justify the taking of new powers. These powers will allow HMRC enquire into reasons why a scheme has not been notified; obtain an order from the Special Commissioners that a scheme is notifiable or should be treated as a notifiable scheme; and, obtain specified information where a notification is incomplete.

Section 108(2) inserts new s 306A into Part 7 of FA 2004. This allows HMRC to apply to the Special Commissioners for an order that a scheme be treated as notifiable. The Special Commissioners must be satisfied that HMRC have taken all reasonable steps to establish whether the scheme is notifiable and have reasonable grounds for their suspicion before an order can be granted.

Section 108(3) inserts a new sub-s 6 to section 307 FA 2004 which provides that in the case of a non-notifiable scheme, a reference in the rules to a promoter is to be taken as a reference to a person who would be a promoter if the scheme was notifiable. This promotes linguistic tidiness although it could be taken to pre-judge the issue somewhat.

Section 108(4) inserts new s 308A into Part 7 of FA 2004. This allows HMRC to apply to the Special Commissioners for an order requiring the promoter to provide specified information including documents relating to a scheme, where HMRC believe that not all the prescribed information has been provided. This power is of course subject to the exemption from disclosure of legally privileged information in FA 2004 s 314 which can include clients' names and addresses.

Section 108(5) inserts new s 313A into Part 7 of FA 2004. This allows HMRC to require someone whom they suspect of being a promoter of a scheme to state whether the scheme is notifiable and if not, the reasons why. It is not sufficient for a promoter to refer to the fact that he has an opinion that the scheme is not notifiable and the reasons given must provide sufficient information to enable HMRC to confirm the promoter's assertion. The section also inserts new s 313B. This allows HMRC to apply to the Special Commissioners for an order requiring a promoter who has supplied reasons why a scheme is not notifiable, to supply HMRC with specified information and documents in support of the reasons given.

Section 108(6) inserts new s 314A into Part 7 of FA 2004. This allows HMRC to apply to the Special Commissioners for an order that a scheme is notifiable. If such an order is granted the promoter will then be obliged to notify the scheme under FA 2004 s 308.

Section 108(7) inserts new s 317A into Part 7 of FA 2004. This section applies ss 56B–56D of the TMA 1970 (tax appeals procedures) to applications to the Special Commissioners under the above new rules.

Section 108(8) adds definitions of 'HMRC' and 'the Special Commissioners' to the definitions in section 318(1) FA 2004.

Section 108(9) amends s 98C of the TMA 1970 which provides for penalties for failure to comply with the requirements of Part 7 of FA 2004. There is an initial penalty of up to £5,000 and a daily penalty of up to £600 if the failure continues after the initial penalty is imposed. The amendment adds new ss 313A and 313B (promoter to supply reasons and specified information where HMRC challenge a scheme as notifiable) to the list of provisions which carry these penalties for failure to comply.

Power has also been taken to increase the amounts of the penalties to such a sum as is prescribed by the Treasury in regulations. Where a scheme is subject to an order making it notifiable under FA 2004 s 314A nothing is to turn on this should the promoter argue that he had a reasonable excuse for not previously notifying the scheme in order to avoid a penalty under TMA 1970 s 118(2). A failure to comply with an order under s 314A attracts an increased penalty as prescribed after a period to be prescribed by regulations. After the expiry of the time allowed before the increased penalty applies, any doubt as to notifiability cannot amount to a reasonable excuse under TMA 1970 s 118(2).

The new rules come into force at Royal Assent but will apply to things that occurred before then. This means that HMRC may use their new powers in relation to schemes made available at any time since the start of the tax scheme disclosure rules in 2004.

109 Meaning of "recognised stock exchange" etc

Schedule 26 contains—

(*a*) new definitions of "recognised stock exchange" for the purposes of the Tax Acts and TCGA 1992,

(*b*) provision for the valuation for the purposes of TCGA 1992 of certain shares or securities listed on recognised stock exchanges,

(*c*) provision for the valuation for the purposes of Chapter 8 of Part 4 of ITTOIA 2005 of strips and securities exchanged for strips, and

(*d*) minor and consequential amendments in relation to stock exchanges.

GENERAL NOTE

Section 109 introduces Schedule 26.

110 Mergers Directive: regulations

(1) The Treasury may by regulations make provision about—

(*a*) the tax consequences of a merger to form an SE or SCE,

(*b*) the tax consequences of a merger where—

(i) each party to the merger is resident in a member State, and

(ii) the parties are not all resident in the same member State,

(*c*) the tax consequences of a transfer between companies of a business or part of a business, where—

(i) each party to the transfer is resident in a member State, and

(ii) the parties are not all resident in the same member State,

(*d*) the tax consequences of a share exchange to which section 135 of TCGA 1992 (exchange of securities) applies where companies A and B are resident in different member States,

(*e*) the residence of an SE or SCE.

(2) Regulations may, in particular, make provision—

(*a*) about the taxation of chargeable gains (including conferring relief from taxation in relation to transfers or mergers which satisfy specified conditions),

(*b*) conferring relief from taxation on a distribution of a company which satisfies specified conditions,

(*c*) about the treatment of securities issued on a transfer or merger,

(*d*) about the treatment of loan relationships,

(*e*) about the treatment of derivative contracts,

(*f*) about the treatment of intangible fixed assets, and

(*g*) about capital allowances.

(3) Regulations may make provision only if the Treasury think it necessary or expedient for the purposes of complying with the United Kingdom's obligations under the Mergers Directive.

(4) In this section—

"the Mergers Directive" means Council Directive 90/434/EEC,

"SCE" means an SCE formed in accordance with Council Regulation (EC) 1435/2003 on the Statute for a European Cooperative Society, and

"SE" means an SE formed in accordance with Council Regulation (EC) 2157/2001 on the Statute for a European Company.

(5) Regulations under this section may—

(*a*) amend the Taxes Acts,
(*b*) make incidental or consequential amendments of enactments other than the Taxes Acts,
(*c*) make provision having retrospective effect,
(*d*) make provision generally or only for specified cases or circumstances,
(*e*) make different provision for different cases or circumstances,
(*f*) make incidental, consequential or transitional provision.

(6) In this section "the Taxes Acts" has the meaning given by section 118(1) of TMA 1970.

GENERAL NOTE

This section provides the Treasury with powers to update tax legislation by regulations to ensure that United Kingdom tax provisions are compliant with the UK's obligations under the European Directive on the common system of taxation applicable to mergers, divisions, transfer of assets and exchanges of shares concerning companies of different Member States (90/434/EEC) ("the Mergers Directive").

The scope of the regulations

Per sub-s (1), the regulations may cover the following:

— the tax consequences of a merger to form a Société Européenne (SE) or a Société Co-opérative Européenne (SCE);
— the tax consequences of a merger where—
— each party to the merger is resident in a member State; but
— the parties are not all resident in the same member State;
— the tax consequences of a transfer between companies of a business or part of a business, where—
— each party to the transfer is resident in a member State; but
— the parties are not all resident in the same member State;
— the tax consequences of a share exchange to which TCGA 1992, s 135 (exchange of securities) applies where the two companies are resident in different member States;
— the residence of an SE or SCE.

However, regulations are permitted only to the extent that the Treasury think it necessary or expedient for the purposes of complying with the UK's obligations under the Mergers Directive (s 110(3)).

Specific areas covered by the potential amendments

Section 110(2) provides that the regulations may, in particular, deal with:

— the taxation of chargeable gains (including conferring relief in relation to transfers or mergers which satisfy specified conditions);
— relief from taxation on a distribution of a company which satisfies specified conditions;
— the treatment of securities issued on a transfer or merger;
— the treatment of loan relationships;
— the treatment of derivative contracts;
— the treatment of intangible fixed assets; and
— capital allowances.

Administration

Per sub-ss (5)(a) and (b) and (6), the regulations may:

— amend any of the Taxes Acts (as defined by TMA 1970, s 118(1)); and also
— make incidental or consequential amendments of other Acts.

To ensure the regulations have flexibility, the powers provide that they may make:

— provision generally or only for specified cases or circumstances;
— different provision for different cases or circumstances; and
— incidental, consequential or transitional provision (s 110(5)(d)–(f)).

Expected commencement

The regulations may also have retrospective effect (s 110(5)(c)). According to the consultation papers detailing the proposed amendments, it is expected that the amendments will generally have effect from 1 January 2007. However, those amendments that relate to mergers to form an SE or SCE are expected to be backdated to 18 August 2006.

Definitions

Subsection (4) defines the Mergers Directive, SE and SCE for the purposes of the section.

111 Excise duties: small consignment relief

(1) The Excise Duties (Small Non-Commercial Consignments) Relief Regulations 1986 (SI 1986/938) are revoked.

(2) The revocation made by subsection (1) does not apply in relation to goods consigned before the day on which this Act is passed.

GENERAL NOTE

This section revokes the Excise Duties (Small Non-Commercial Consignments) Relief Order, SI 1986/938. The Order exempted consignments of excisable goods, such as tobacco, alcoholic beverages, perfumes etc, of a small quantitative value (e.g. 50 cigarettes, 1 litre of spirits) from excise duty on their importation into the UK. The Order did not apply to accompanied goods (such as those carried in passengers' luggage on their arrival from abroad at ports, airports etc). There is a parallel VAT exemption order (The Value Added Tax (Small Non-Commercial Consignments) Relief Order, SI 1986/939), which applies to goods imported from outside the EU. This is not being revoked.

The reason for the revocation is the recent decision by the European Court of Justice in *Staatssecretaris van Financiën v B F Joustra* (Case C-5/05), which confirmed that excisable goods moving between different EU Member States were subject to excise duty in the Member State of destination, unless transported personally by a private individual. Although the judgment does not affect goods imported into the UK from outside the EU, the Government has decided that it will not take steps to reintroduce the exemption for such third-country imports.

112 Updating references to Standing Committees

(1) In section 1(4)(*b*) of the Provisional Collection of Taxes Act 1968 (c 2) (circumstances in which a resolution affecting income tax etc ceases to have effect), for "Standing Committee" substitute "Public Bill Committee".

(2) In section 50(2)(*a*) of FA 1973 (corresponding provision for stamp duty), for "Standing Committee" substitute "Public Bill Committee".

GENERAL NOTE

This provision, which merely updates references to Standing Committees, was added to the Finance Bill at Report Stage on 25 June (see Hansard, 25 June 2007, Cols 43–44).

PART 8

FINAL PROVISIONS

113 Interpretation

(1) In this Act—

"BGDA 1981" means the Betting and Gaming Duties Act 1981 (c 63),

"CAA 2001" means the Capital Allowances Act 2001 (c 2),

"CEMA 1979" means the Customs and Excise Management Act 1979 (c 2),

"CRCA 2005" means the Commissioners for Revenue and Customs Act 2005 (c 11),

"ICTA" means the Income and Corporation Taxes Act 1988 (c 1),

"IHTA 1984" means the Inheritance Tax Act 1984 (c 51),
"ITA 2007" means the Income Tax Act 2007 (c 3),
"ITEPA 2003" means the Income Tax (Earnings and Pensions) Act 2003 (c 1),
"ITTOIA 2005" means the Income Tax (Trading and Other Income) Act 2005 (c 5),
"TCGA 1992" means the Taxation of Chargeable Gains Act 1992 (c 12),
"TMA 1970" means the Taxes Management Act 1970 (c 9),
"VATA 1994" means the Value Added Tax Act 1994 (c 23), and
"VERA 1994" means the Vehicle Excise and Registration Act 1994 (c 22).

(2) In this Act—

"FA", followed by a year, means the Finance Act of that year, and
"F(No 2)A", followed by a year, means the Finance (No 2) Act of that year.

114 Repeals

Schedule 27 contains repeals.

115 Short title

This Act may be cited as the Finance Act 2007.

SCHEDULES

SCHEDULE 1
REMOTE GAMING DUTY

Section 8

PART 1
IMPOSITION OF DUTY

1 The sections set out below are to be inserted in Part 2 of BGDA 1981 (gaming duties) before section 26A (which is renumbered 26N).

2 Those sections are—

"Remote gaming duty

26A Interpretation

(1) For the purposes of remote gaming duty "remote gaming" means gaming in which persons participate by the use of—

(*a*) the internet,
(*b*) telephone,
(*c*) television,
(*d*) radio, or
(*e*) any other kind of electronic or other technology for facilitating communication.

(2) For the purposes of remote gaming duty the expressions listed below shall be construed (for the whole of the United Kingdom) in accordance with the Gambling Act 2005.

Expression	*Defining provision of Gambling Act 2005*
Provision of facilities	Section 5(1) to (3)
Remote gambling equipment	Section 36(4) and (5)
Remote operating licence	Section 67

(3) In relation to remote gaming duty "P" means a person who provides facilities for remote gaming.

(4) The Treasury may by order amend the definition of "remote gaming" in subsection (1) (and an order may include incidental, consequential or transitional provision).

26B The duty

A duty of excise to be known as remote gaming duty shall be charged on the provision of facilities for remote gaming if—

(*a*) the facilities are provided in reliance on a remote operating licence, or
(*b*) at least one piece of remote gambling equipment used in the provision of the facilities is situated in the United Kingdom (whether or not the facilities are provided for use wholly or partly in the United Kingdom).

26C The rate

(1) Remote gaming duty is chargeable at the rate of 15% of P's remote gaming profits for an accounting period.

(2) P's remote gaming profits for an accounting period are—

(*a*) the amount of P's remote gaming receipts for the period (calculated in accordance with section 26E), minus
(*b*) the amount of P's expenditure for the period on remote gaming winnings (calculated in accordance with section 26F).

26D Accounting periods

(1) The following are accounting periods for the purposes of remote gaming duty—

(*a*) the period of three months beginning with 1st January,
(*b*) the period of three months beginning with 1st April,
(*c*) the period of three months beginning with 1st July, and

(*d*) the period of three months beginning with 1st October.

(2) The Commissioners may agree with P for specified periods to be treated as accounting periods, instead of those described in subsection (1), for purposes of remote gaming duty relating to P.

(3) The Commissioners may by direction make transitional arrangements for the periods to be treated as accounting periods where—

(*a*) P becomes registered, or ceases to be registered, under section 26J, or
(*b*) an agreement under subsection (2) begins or ends.

26E Remote gaming receipts

(1) The amount of P's remote gaming receipts for an accounting period is the aggregate of—

(*a*) amounts falling due to P in that period in respect of entitlement to use facilities for remote gaming provided by P, and

(*b*) amounts staked, or falling due to be paid, in that period by a user of facilities for remote gaming provided by P, if or in so far as responsibility for paying any amount won by the user falls on P (or a person with whom P is connected or has made arrangements).

(2) Amounts in respect of VAT shall be ignored for the purposes of subsection (1).

(3) The Treasury may by order provide that where a person who uses facilities (U) relies on an offer which waives payment or permits payment of less than the amount which would have been required to be paid without the offer, U is to be treated for the purposes of this section as having paid that amount.

26F Remote gaming winnings

(1) The amount of P's expenditure on remote gaming winnings for an accounting period is the aggregate of the value of prizes provided by P in that period which have been won (at any time) by persons using facilities for remote gaming provided by P.

(2) Prizes provided by P to one user on behalf of another are not to be treated as prizes provided by P.

(3) A reference to providing a prize to a user (U) includes a reference to crediting money in respect of gaming winnings by U to an account if U is notified that—

(*a*) the money is being held in the account, and
(*b*) U is entitled to withdraw it on demand.

(4) The return of a stake is to be treated as the provision of a prize.

(5) Where P participates in arrangements under which a number of persons who provide facilities for remote gaming contribute towards a fund which is wholly used to provide prizes in connection with the use of those facilities (sometimes described as arrangements for "linked progressive jackpot games")—

(*a*) the making by P of a contribution which relates to the provision by P of facilities for remote gaming shall be treated as the provision of a prize, and

(*b*) the award of a prize from the fund shall not be treated as the provision of a prize by P.

(6) Where P credits the account of a user of facilities provided by P (otherwise than as described in subsection (3)), the credit shall be treated as the provision of a prize; but the Commissioners may direct that this subsection shall not apply in a specified case or class of cases.

(7) Subsections (2) to (6) of section 20 shall apply (with any necessary modifications) for the purpose of remote gaming duty as for the purpose of bingo duty.

26G Losses

Where the calculation of P's remote gaming profits for an accounting period produces a negative amount, it may be carried forward in reduction of the profits of one or more later accounting periods.

26H Exemptions

(1) Remote gaming duty shall not be charged in respect of the provision of facilities for remote gaming if and in so far as—

(*a*) the provision is charged with another gambling tax, or
(*b*) the use of the facilities is charged with another gambling tax.

(2) Remote gaming duty shall not be charged in respect of the provision of facilities for remote gaming if and in so far as—

(*a*) the provision would be charged with another gambling tax but for an express exception, or

(*b*) the use of the facilities would be charged with another gambling tax but for an express exception.

(3) In this section "gambling tax" means—

(*a*) amusement machine licence duty,
(*b*) bingo duty,
(*c*) gaming duty,
(*d*) general betting duty,
(*e*) lottery duty, and
(*f*) pool betting duty.

(4) The Treasury may by order—

(*a*) confer an exemption from remote gaming duty, or

(*b*) remove or vary (whether or not by textual amendment) an exemption under this section.

(5) In calculating P's remote gaming profits for an accounting period, no account shall be taken of amounts or prizes if, or in so far as, they relate to the provision of facilities to which an exemption applies under or by virtue of this section.

26I Liability to pay

(1) P is liable for any remote gaming duty charged on P's remote gaming profits for an accounting period.

(2) If P is a body corporate, P and P's directors are jointly and severally liable for any remote gaming duty charged on P's remote gaming profits for an accounting period.

(3) The Commissioners may make regulations about payment of remote gaming duty; and the regulations may, in particular, make provision about—

(*a*) timing;
(*b*) instalments;
(*c*) methods of payment;
(*d*) when payment is to be treated as made;
(*e*) the process and effect of assessments by the Commissioners of amounts due.

(4) Subject to regulations under subsection (3), section 12 of the Finance Act 1994 (assessment) shall apply in relation to liability to pay remote gaming duty.

26J Registration

(1) The Commissioners shall maintain a register of persons who provide facilities for remote gaming in respect of which remote gaming duty may be chargeable.

(2) A person may not provide facilities for remote gaming in respect of which remote gaming duty may be chargeable without being registered.

(3) The Commissioners may make regulations about registration; in particular, the regulations may include provision (which may include provision conferring a discretion on the Commissioners) about—

(*a*) the procedure for applying for registration;
(*b*) the timing of applications;
(*c*) the information to be provided;
(*d*) notification of changes;
(*e*) de-registration;
(*f*) re-registration after a person ceases to be registered.

(4) The regulations may require a registered person to give notice to the Commissioners before applying for a remote operating licence.

(5) The regulations may permit the Commissioners to make registration, or continued registration, of a foreign person conditional; and the regulations may, in particular, permit the Commissioners to require—

(*a*) the provision of security for payment of remote gaming duty;

(*b*) the appointment of a United Kingdom representative with responsibility for discharging liability to remote gaming duty.

(6) In subsection (5) "foreign person" means a person who—

(*a*) in the case of an individual, is not usually resident in the United Kingdom,

(*b*) in the case of a body corporate, does not have an established place of business in the United Kingdom, and

(*c*) in any other case, does not include an individual who is usually resident in the United Kingdom.

(7) The regulations may include provision for the registration of groups of persons; and may provide for the modification of the provisions of this Part about remote gaming duty in their application to groups.

(8) The regulations—

(*a*) may make provision which applies generally or only for specified purposes, and
(*b*) may make different provision for different purposes.

26K Returns

(1) The Commissioners may make regulations requiring persons who provide facilities for remote gaming in respect of which remote gaming duty may be chargeable to make returns to the Commissioners in respect of their activities.

(2) The regulations may, in particular, make provision about—

(*a*) liability to make a return;
(*b*) timing;
(*c*) form;
(*d*) content;
(*e*) method of making;
(*f*) declarations;
(*g*) authentication;
(*h*) when a return is to be treated as made.

(3) The regulations—

(*a*) may make provision which applies generally or only for specified purposes, and
(*b*) may make different provision for different purposes.

26L Enforcement

(1) Contravention of a provision made by or by virtue of sections 26I to 26K—

(*a*) is conduct to which section 9 of the Finance Act 1994 applies (penalties), and
(*b*) attracts daily penalties under that section.

(2) A person who is knowingly concerned in, or in taking steps with a view to, the fraudulent evasion of remote gaming duty commits an offence.

(3) A person guilty of an offence under subsection (2) shall be liable on summary conviction to—

(*a*) a penalty of—
  (i) the statutory maximum, or
  (ii) if greater, three times the duty which is unpaid or the payment of which is sought to be avoided,
(*b*) imprisonment for a term not exceeding six months, or
(*c*) both.

(4) A person guilty of an offence under subsection (2) shall be liable on conviction on indictment to—

(*a*) a penalty of any amount,
(*b*) imprisonment for a term not exceeding seven years, or
(*c*) both.

26M Review and appeal

(1) Sections 14 to 16 of the Finance Act 1994 (review and appeal) shall apply in relation to liability to pay remote gaming duty.

(2) Sections 14 to 16 of that Act shall also apply to the decisions listed in subsection (3) below.

(3) Those decisions are—

(*a*) a decision to refuse a request for an agreement under section 26D(2),
(*b*) a decision to give a direction under section 26D(3),
(*c*) a decision not to give a direction under section 26D(3),
(*d*) a decision to direct that section 26F(6) shall not apply in a specified case,
(*e*) a decision under regulations by virtue of section 26J(3), and
(*f*) a decision about security by virtue of section 26J(5)(*a*).

(4) A decision of a kind specified in subsection (3) shall be treated as an ancillary matter for the purposes of sections 14 to 16 of the Finance Act 1994."

PART 2
CONSEQUENTIAL AMENDMENTS

3 In BGDA 1981, before section 26N (non-sterling amounts) (as renumbered by paragraph 1 above) insert the italic cross-heading "*General*".

4 In section 31 of that Act (protection of officers), after "bingo duty" insert ", remote gaming duty".

5 In section 32 of that Act (subordinate legislation), after subsection (2) insert—

"(3) But in the case of an order under section 26H(4) which has the effect of adding to the class of activities in respect of which remote gaming duty is chargeable—

(*a*) subsection (2) above shall not apply, and

(*b*) the order may not be made unless a draft has been laid before and approved by resolution of the House of Commons."

6 In section 33(2) of that Act (no legalising effect), after "bingo duty" insert ", remote gaming duty".

GENERAL NOTE

Schedule 1 makes amendments to BGDA 1981 Part 2.

Part 1 of the Schedule introduces new BGDA 1981 ss 26A–26M. The existing s 26A is renumbered s 26N.

Section 26A is an interpretation section. In particular, it defines 'remote gaming' as gaming in which participation is via the internet, telephone, television, radio or "any other kind of electronic or other technology for facilitating communication". A person who provides facilities for remote gaming is referred to in the new legislation by the abbreviation 'P', but will be referred to in these notes as 'the operator'.

Section 26B is the charging section. Remote gaming duty, which is to be a duty of excise, is to be charged on the provision of facilities for remote gaming where either:

(*a*) those facilities are provided under a 'remote operating licence'; or

(*b*) at least one piece of 'remote gambling equipment' used in providing those facilities is situated in the UK.

The terms 'remote operating licence', 'remote gambling equipment' and 'provision of facilities' are defined by direct reference to the Gambling Act 2005.

Section 26C sets the rate for remote gaming duty (RGD). RGD is to be charged at a single flat rate of 15% of the operator's 'remote gaming profits' for an accounting period. 'Remote gaming profits' are computed by deducting the operator's expenditure for the period on 'remote gaming winnings' (as defined in s 26F) from the operator's 'remote gaming receipts' (as defined in s 26E) for that period.

Section 26D defines accounting periods for RGD purposes. These are to be three-monthly periods, ending on 31 March, 30 June, 30 September and 31 December respectively. However, HMRC may agree different accounting periods with the operator. Transitional arrangements, to have effect when an operator becomes, or ceases to be, registered may be specified by direction.

Section 26E defines 'remote gaming receipts'. These are essentially the aggregate of the operator's receipts from making the facilities available to users (access fees, subscriptions etc) and stake monies paid or payable by users of those facilities (to the extent that the operator or a person with whom the operator is connected or has made the relevant arrangements is responsible for paying amounts won by users). All these amounts are to be taken into account exclusive of VAT. Where users are able to make use of facilities that waive payment or provide for reduced access fees, the user is regarded as having paid the full amount (and hence the full amount is included in the operator's receipts).

Section 26F defines what is expenditure on remote gaming winnings. That expenditure is essentially the aggregate value of prizes provided by the operator in the relevant accounting period and won (at any time, not just in that period) by users of the facilities provided by the operator. A prize is regarded as provided also where a sum of money in respect of gaming winnings is credited to an account on which the user can draw on demand. The return of a stake is treated as provision of a prize, but prizes provided to a user on behalf of another are not (to avoid double counting). In cases of 'linked progressive jackpot games' and other arrangements under which operators join together to contribute to a common fund used exclusively to provide prizes, contributions made by the operator to the fund relating to the facilities provided by the operator are regarded as the provision of a prize, but awards of prizes from the fund are not so regarded.

Non-cash prizes are to be valued as they are under BGDA 1981 s 20 for bingo games.

Section 26G provides for the treatment of losses. Where for any accounting period, expenditure on remote gaming winnings exceeds remote gaming receipts, the excess (the loss) may be carried forward to reduce the profits of subsequent accounting periods.

Section 26H provides for exemptions. RGD is not due where either the provision or use of the facilities for remote gaming is already charged with another gambling tax, namely amusement machine licence duty, bingo duty, gaming duty, general betting duty, lottery duty or pool betting duty. Where an exemption applies under s 26H, no prizes relating to the provision of those facilities are to be taken into account in computing the operator's remote gaming profits.

Section 26I provides for the liability to pay RGD. It is the operator who is primarily liable for payment of RGD in respect of the facilities the operator provides. Where the operator is a body corporate, its directors are jointly and severally liable with the operator. Details of timing, instalments, payment methods etc are to be determined by regulation.

Section 26J deals with registration. A register of all persons who provide remote gaming facilities is to be maintained by HMRC and persons are not allowed to provide dutiable facilities unless they are registered. The detailed procedure for registration and deregistration is to be determined by regulation. Where 'foreign persons' intend to provide such facilities, registration may require the provision of security and the appointment of a UK representative. A 'foreign person' for this purpose is either:

(*a*) a body corporate without an established place of business in the UK; or

(*b*) an individual not usually resident in the UK.

Section 26K provides that regulations may be made to determine matters in respect of RGD returns.

Enforcement is dealt with in s 26L. Contravention of any requirements set by the regulations to be made under ss 26I–26K is made liable to the penalty regime for all gambling duties under FA 1994 s 9. Fraudulent evasion of RGD is made an offence, in respect of which a person may on summary conviction become liable to a penalty that is the greater of the statutory maximum (£5000) and three times the unpaid or evaded duty, or to imprisonment of up to six months, or to both.

Section 26M makes the RGD provisions subject to the review and appeal procedures in FA 1994 ss 14–16.

Part 2 (paras 2–6) makes consequential amendments.

EFFECTIVE DATE

The provisions concerning RGD are to come into effect from a date still to be appointed.

SCHEDULE 2

CLIMATE CHANGE LEVY: REDUCED-RATE SUPPLIES ETC

Section 23

Introductory

1 Schedule 6 to FA 2000 (climate change levy) is amended as follows.

Reduced-rate supplies

2 In paragraph 4(2)(*b*) (taxable supplies: introduction), after "paragraph 24" insert "or 45A".

3 In paragraph 5(3) (supplies of electricity), for "or 24" substitute ", 24 or 45A".

4 In paragraph 6(2A) (supplies of gas), after "24" insert "or 45A".

5— (1) Paragraph 34 (other commodities: deemed supplies) is amended as follows.

(2) In sub-paragraph (1)(*b*), for "or 24" substitute ", 24 or 45A".

(3) After sub-paragraph (3) insert—

"(4) A supply that is deemed to be made under paragraph 45A is treated as taking place upon the later determination."

6 In paragraph 39(1)(*c*) (regulations as to time of supply), for "or 24" substitute ", 24 or 45A".

7 For paragraph 44 substitute—

"44— (1) For the purposes of this Schedule, a taxable supply is a reduced-rate supply if—

(*a*) the taxable commodity is supplied to a facility specified in a certificate given by the Secretary of State to the Commissioners as a facility which is to be taken as being covered by a climate change agreement for a period specified in the certificate, and

(*b*) the supply is made at a time falling in that period.

(2) Sub-paragraph (1) has effect subject to paragraph 45.

(3) The Commissioners may by regulations make provision for giving effect to sub-paragraph (1).

(4) Regulations under this paragraph may, in particular, include provision for determining whether any taxable commodity is supplied to a facility.

(5) The provision that may be made by virtue of sub-paragraph (4) includes, in particular, provision for a taxable commodity of any description specified in the regulations to be taken as supplied to a facility only if the commodity is delivered to the facility."

8— (1) Paragraph 45 (reduced-rate supplies: variation of notices under paragraph 44) is amended as follows.

(2) Omit sub-paragraphs (2) to (4).

(3) In sub-paragraph (5)—

(*a*) in paragraph (*b*), for "the variation notice is published" substitute "the variation certificate is given", and

(*b*) for the words following that paragraph substitute "the original certificate has effect as if the facility had never been specified in it".

(4) In sub-paragraph (6)—

(*a*) in paragraph (*b*), for "the variation notice is published" substitute "the variation certificate is given", and

(*b*) for the words following that paragraph substitute "the original certificate has effect as if the last day of the period specified for the facility in the original certificate were the day on which the variation certificate is given".

(5) In sub-paragraph (7), for the words from "the original notice" to the end substitute "the original certificate has effect as if the last day of the period specified for the facility in the original certificate were the later of—

(*a*) the day on which the variation certificate is given, and

(*b*) the day specified in the variation certificate."

(6) The italic heading before that paragraph accordingly becomes "*Reduced-rate supplies: variation of certificates under paragraph 44*".

9 After that paragraph insert—

"Reduced-rate supplies: deemed supply

45A— (1) This paragraph applies where—

(*a*) a taxable supply has been made to any person ("the recipient"),

(*b*) the supply was made on the basis that it was a reduced-rate supply, and

(*c*) it is later determined that the supply was not a reduced-rate supply.

(2) For the purposes of this Schedule—

(*a*) the recipient is deemed to make a taxable supply to itself of the taxable commodity, and

(*b*) the amount payable by way of levy on that deemed supply is 80 per cent. of the amount that would be payable if the supply were not a reduced-rate supply."

10 In paragraph 147 (interpretation), in the definition of "reduced-rate supply"—

(*a*) for "44(3)" substitute "44(1)", and

(*b*) for "44(4)" substitute "44(2)".

Notifications and certificates

11— (1) Paragraph 11 (exemption: supply not for burning in UK) is amended as follows.

(2) In sub-paragraph (1)—

(*a*) omit "has, before the supply is made, notified the supplier", and
(*b*) omit "that he" (in both places).

(3) In sub-paragraph (3)—

(*a*) omit "has, before the supply is made, notified the supplier that", and
(*b*) omit "he".

12— (1) Paragraph 101 (civil penalties: incorrect notifications etc) is amended as follows.

(2) Omit sub-paragraph (1).

(3) In sub-paragraph (2)—

(*a*) after "paragraphs" insert "11," and
(*b*) after "the certificate is" insert "(or becomes)".

(4) In sub-paragraph (3)—

(*a*) for "sub-paragraph (1) or (2)" substitute "this paragraph", and
(*b*) omit "notification or".

(5) In sub-paragraph (4)—

(*a*) for "notification or certificate" substitute "certificate (or not revoking or varying it)",
(*b*) for "the person who gave it" substitute "the person concerned", and
(*c*) for the words from "there is" to the end substitute "the person has a reasonable excuse".

(6) In sub-paragraph (5)—

(*a*) for "notification or certificate" substitute "certificate (or not revoking or varying it)", and
(*b*) for "the giving of the notification or certificate" substitute "that".

(7) The italic heading before paragraph 101 accordingly becomes "*Civil penalties: incorrect certificates*".

Commencement

13— (1) Paragraphs 2 to 10 come into force on such day as the Treasury may by order made by statutory instrument appoint.

(2) But any power to make regulations under any provision inserted or amended by any of those paragraphs may be exercised at any time after this Act is passed.

(3) The power to make an order under sub-paragraph (1)—

(*a*) may be exercised so as to bring a provision into force only in such cases as may be described in the order,
(*b*) may be exercised so as to make different provision for different cases or descriptions of case,
(*c*) includes power to make incidental, consequential, supplemental or transitional provision or savings.

GENERAL NOTE

Climate change levy provides a number of exemptions and reliefs. These are contained in FA 2000 Sch 6.

For the majority of the reliefs, the Climate Change Levy (General) Regulations 2001 provide a statutory responsibility on the recipients of energy who are entitled to relief to submit a certificate of entitlement to their energy supplier in order for the relief to be given effect.

The certificate is used by the claimant to notify the extent of relief entitlement in terms of a percentage of total consumption. To ensure the relief claimed is accurate, claimants must review the correctness of certificates annually.

In the event that relief has been overclaimed, the excess should be accounted to HMRC. In the event of an under claim, the claimant can apply for payment of a tax credit.

The statutory certification regime does not apply to supplies made at the reduced rate of 20 per cent of the full levy, which is available to eligible facilities that are covered by and comply with the terms of a climate change agreement negotiated with the Department for Environment, Food and Rural Affairs. However, for practical purposes, energy suppliers and reduced rate recipients have adopted the use of certificates of entitlement in applying

Provisions are introduced by Sch 2 that align reduced rate supplies with the procedures that are in place for other CCL reliefs. Related changes are also made to exported and onward supplies. The civil penalty provisions in respect of incorrect certification are extended.

The changes in respect of reduced rate supplies take effect from a date to be appointed by Treasury order. The changes made in respect or exports and onward supplies and to the penalty provisions take effect from the date of Royal Assent to the 2007 Finance Bill.

Reduced rate supplies

Changes are made to the reduced rate supplies provisions in Sch 2 which simplify the administration of reduced-rate CCL by removing the requirement for HMRC to publish details of facilities that are taken to be covered by a climate change agreement and aligning the procedures for reduced-rate supplies with those in place for other CCL reliefs.

Provision is also made for a deemed self-supply to arise where a taxable supply is made on the basis that it was a reduced rate supply and it is later determined not to be a reduced-rate supply (new FA 2000 Sch 6 para 45A). The levy them payable by the recipient is 80 per cent of the amount that would be payable if the supply was not a reduced-rate supply.

Regulations will bring reduced-rate supplies fully within the CCL certification regime, reflecting the practices adopted by energy suppliers and reduced-rate recipients.

Exported and onward supplies

A supply of a taxable commodity is exempt from CCL where the person to whom the supply is made has given the supplier specific and prior notification that the commodity is to be used in making supplies of it to another person or it is to be exported permanently from the UK. This notification requirement is removed. Instead, the exemption will be permitted only on the basis of certificates of entitlement, which are used as the basis for the application of the majority of reliefs.

Penalty provisions

Penalty provisions are contained within FA 2000 Sch 6 para 101. Penalties are charged where a relief recipient incorrectly certifies in circumstances that cause the supplier to receive a supply of CCL. The penalty is 105 per cent of the CCL at stake. This effectively recovers the shortfall and charges a five per cent penalty.

Under the existing rules, no penalty is charged if the information on the certificate was correct when it was first given, but subsequently becomes incorrect. Changes made to para 101 (by Sch 2 para 12) extend the penalty provisions to include cases where a certificate becomes incorrect after its initial submission to an energy supplier.

SCHEDULE 3

MANAGED SERVICE COMPANIES

Section 25

PART 1

AMENDMENTS OF ITEPA 2003

1 ITEPA 2003 is amended as follows.

2 In section 7(5) (meaning of "employment income" etc), for paragraph (*a*) substitute—

> "(*a*) Chapters 7 to 9 of this Part (agency workers, workers under arrangements made by intermediaries, and workers providing services through managed service companies),".

3 In section 48(2) (workers under arrangements made by intermediaries: scope of Chapter) for "or" at the end of paragraph (*a*) substitute—

> "(*aa*) applies to services provided by a managed service company (within the meaning of Chapter 9 of this Part), or".

4 After section 61 insert—

"CHAPTER 9

MANAGED SERVICE COMPANIES

Application of this Chapter

61A Scope of this Chapter

(1) This Chapter has effect with respect to the provision of services by a managed service company.

(2) Nothing in this Chapter—

(*a*) affects the operation of Chapter 7 of this Part (agency workers), or

(*b*) applies to payments or transfers to which section 966(3) or (4) of ITA 2007 applies (visiting performers: duty to deduct and account for sums representing income tax).

61B Meaning of "managed service company"

(1) A company is a "managed service company" if—

(*a*) its business consists wholly or mainly of providing (directly or indirectly) the services of an individual to other persons,

(*b*) payments are made (directly or indirectly) to the individual (or associates of the individual) of an amount equal to the greater part or all of the consideration for the provision of the services,

(*c*) the way in which those payments are made would result in the individual (or associates) receiving payments of an amount (net of tax and national insurance) exceeding that which would be received (net of tax and national insurance) if every payment in respect of the services were employment income of the individual, and

(*d*) a person who carries on a business of promoting or facilitating the use of companies to provide the services of individuals ("an MSC provider") is involved with the company.

(2) An MSC provider is "involved with the company" if the MSC provider or an associate of the MSC provider—

(*a*) benefits financially on an ongoing basis from the provision of the services of the individual,

(*b*) influences or controls the provision of those services,

(*c*) influences or controls the way in which payments to the individual (or associates of the individual) are made,

(*d*) influences or controls the company's finances or any of its activities, or

(*e*) gives or promotes an undertaking to make good any tax loss.

(3) A person does not fall within subsection (1)(*d*) merely by virtue of providing legal or accountancy services in a professional capacity.

(4) A person does not fall within subsection (1)(*d*) merely by virtue of carrying on a business consisting only of placing individuals with persons who wish to obtain their services (including by contracting with companies which provide their services).

(5) Subsection (4) does not apply if the person or an associate of the person—

(*a*) does anything within subsection (2)(*c*) or (*e*), or

(*b*) does anything within subsection (2)(*d*) other than influencing the company's finances or activities by doing anything within subsection (2)(*b*).

61C Section 61B: supplementary

(1) The Treasury may by order provide that persons of a prescribed description do not fall within section 61B(1)(*d*).

(2) An order under subsection (1) may be made so as to have effect in relation to the whole of the tax year in which it is made.

(3) In section 61B and this section, "company" means a body corporate or partnership.

(4) References in section 61B to an associate of a person ("P") include a person who, for the purpose of securing that the individual's services are provided by a company, acts in concert with P (or with P and other persons).

(5) In section 61B(2)(*e*), "undertaking to make good any tax loss" means an undertaking (in any terms) to make good (in whole or in part, and by any means) any cost to the individual or an associate of the individual resulting from a relevant provision, or a particular kind of relevant provision, applying in relation to payments made to the individual or associate.

(6) In subsection (5) "relevant provision" means—

(*a*) a provision of the Tax Acts,
(*b*) an enactment relating to national insurance, or
(*c*) a provision of subordinate legislation made under any such provision or enactment.

The deemed employment payment

61D Worker treated as receiving earnings from employment

(1) This section applies if—

(*a*) the services of an individual ("the worker") are provided (directly or indirectly) by a managed service company ("the MSC"),
(*b*) the worker, or an associate of the worker, receives (from any person) a payment or benefit which can reasonably be taken to be in respect of the services, and
(*c*) the payment or benefit is not earnings (within Chapter 1 of Part 3) received by the worker directly from the MSC.

(2) The MSC is treated as making to the worker, and the worker is treated as receiving, a payment which is to be treated as earnings from an employment ("the deemed employment payment").

(3) The deemed employment payment is treated as made at the time the payment or benefit mentioned in subsection (1)(*b*) is received.

(4) In this Chapter—

"the worker" has the meaning given by subsection (1),
"the relevant services" means the services mentioned in that subsection, and
"the client" means the person to whom the relevant services are provided.

(5) Section 61F supplements this section.

61E Calculation of deemed employment payment

(1) The amount of the deemed employment payment is the amount resulting from the following steps—

Step 1 Find (applying section 61F) the amount of the payment or benefit mentioned in section 61D(1)(*b*).

Step 2 Deduct (applying Chapters 1 to 5 of Part 5) the amount of any expenses met by the worker that would have been deductible from the taxable earnings from the employment if—

(*a*) the worker had been employed by the client to provide the relevant services, and
(*b*) the expenses had been met by the worker out of those earnings.

If the result at this point is nil or a negative amount, there is no deemed employment payment.

Step 3 Assume that the result of step 2 represents an amount together with employer's national insurance contributions on it, and deduct what (on that assumption) would be the amount of those contributions.

The result is the deemed employment payment.

(2) In step 2 of subsection (1), the reference to expenses met by the worker includes, where the MSC is a partnership and the worker is a member of the partnership, expenses met by the worker for and on behalf of the partnership.

(3) In step 2 of subsection (1), the expenses deductible include the amount of any mileage allowance relief which the worker would have been entitled to in respect of the use of a vehicle falling within subsection (4) if—

(*a*) the worker had been employed by the client to provide the relevant services, and
(*b*) the vehicle had not been a company vehicle (within the meaning of Chapter 2 of Part 4).

(4) A vehicle falls within this subsection if—

(*a*) it is provided by the MSC for the worker, or
(*b*) where the MSC is a partnership and the worker is a member of the partnership, it is provided by the worker for the purposes of the business of the partnership.

(5) For the purposes of subsection (1) any necessary apportionment of payments or benefits that are referable partly to the provision of the relevant services and partly to other matters is to be made on a just and reasonable basis.

61F Sections 61D and 61E: application of rules relating to earnings from employment

(1) The following provisions apply for the purposes of sections 61D and 61E.

(2) A "payment or benefit" means anything that, if received by an employee for performing the duties of an employment, would be general earnings from the employment.

(3) The amount of a payment or benefit is taken to be—

(*a*) in the case of a payment or cash benefit, the amount received, and
(*b*) in the case of a non-cash benefit, the cash equivalent of the benefit.

(4) The cash equivalent of a non-cash benefit is taken to be—

(*a*) the amount that would be general earnings if the benefit were general earnings from an employment, or
(*b*) in the case of living accommodation, whichever is the greater of that amount and the cash equivalent determined in accordance with section 398(2).

(5) A payment or benefit is treated as received—

(*a*) in the case of a payment or cash benefit, when payment is made of or on account of the payment or benefit;
(*b*) in the case of a non-cash benefit, when it would have been treated as received for the purposes of Chapter 4 or 5 of this Part (see section 19 or 32) if—

(i) the worker had been an employee, and
(ii) the benefit had been provided by reason of the employment.

61G Application of Income Tax Acts in relation to deemed employment

(1) The Income Tax Acts (in particular, the PAYE provisions) apply in relation to the deemed employment payment as follows.

(2) They apply as if—

(*a*) the worker were employed by the MSC to provide the relevant services, and
(*b*) the deemed employment payment were a payment by the MSC of earnings from that employment;

but this is subject to subsection (3).

(3) No deduction under Part 5 (deductions allowed from employment income) or section 232 (mileage allowance relief) may be made from the deemed employment payment.

(4) The worker is not chargeable to tax in respect of the deemed employment payment if, or to the extent that, by reason of any combination of the factors mentioned in subsection (5), the worker would not be chargeable to tax if—

(*a*) the worker were employed by the client to perform the relevant services, and
(*b*) the deemed employment payment were a payment by the client of earnings from that employment.

(5) The factors are—

(*a*) the worker being resident, ordinarily resident or domiciled outside the United Kingdom,
(*b*) the client being resident or ordinarily resident outside the United Kingdom, and
(*c*) the relevant services being provided outside the United Kingdom.

(6) Where the MSC is a partnership and the worker is a member of the partnership, the deemed employment payment is treated as received by the worker in the worker's personal capacity and not as income of the partnership.

(7) Where—

(*a*) the worker is resident in the United Kingdom, and
(*b*) the relevant services are provided in the United Kingdom,

the MSC is treated as having a place of business in the United Kingdom, whether or not it in fact does so.

Supplementary provisions

61H Relief in case of distributions by managed service company

(1) A claim for relief may be made under this section where the MSC—

(*a*) is a body corporate,
(*b*) is treated as making a deemed employment payment in any tax year, and
(*c*) either in that tax year (whether before or after that payment is treated as made), or in a subsequent tax year, makes a distribution (a "relevant distribution").

(2) A claim for relief under this section must be made—

(*a*) by the MSC by notice to an officer of Revenue and Customs, and (*b*) within 5 years after 31st January following the tax year in which the distribution is made.

(3) If on a claim being made an officer of Revenue and Customs is satisfied that relief should be given in order to avoid a double charge to tax, the officer must direct the giving of such relief by way of amending any assessment, by discharge or repayment of tax, or otherwise, as appears to the officer appropriate.

(4) Relief under this section is given by setting the amount of the deemed employment payment against the relevant distribution so as to reduce the distribution.

(5) In the case of more than one relevant distribution, an officer of Revenue and Customs must exercise the power conferred by this section so as to secure that so far as practicable relief is given by setting the amount of a deemed employment payment—

(*a*) against relevant distributions of the same tax year before those of other years,

(*b*) against relevant distributions received by the worker before those received by another person, and

(*c*) against relevant distributions of earlier years before those of later years.

(6) Where the amount of a relevant distribution is reduced under this section, the amount of any associated tax credit is reduced accordingly.

61I Meaning of "associate"

(1) Subsections (2) to (4) apply for the purposes of this Chapter.

(2) "Associate", in relation to an individual, means—

(*a*) a member of the individual's family or household,

(*b*) a relative of the individual,

(*c*) a partner of the individual, or

(*d*) the trustee of any settlement in relation to which the individual, or a relative of the individual or member of the individual's family (living or dead), is or was a settlor.

(3) "Associate", in relation to a company, means a person connected with the company.

(4) "Associate", in relation to a partnership, means any associate of a member of the partnership.

(5) If—

(*a*) a managed service company ("the MSC") is a partnership, and

(*b*) a person is an associate of another person by virtue only of being a member of the partnership,

the person is to be treated, for the purposes of this Chapter as it applies in relation to the MSC, as if the person were not an associate of that other person.

(6) In subsection (2), "relative" means ancestor, lineal descendant, brother or sister.

(7) For the purposes of subsection (2)—

(*a*) a man and woman living together as husband and wife are treated as if they were married to each other, and

(*b*) two persons of the same sex living together as if they were civil partners of each other are treated as if they were civil partners of each other.

61J Interpretation of Chapter

(1) In this Chapter—

"associate" has the meaning given by section 61I,

"business" means any trade, profession or vocation,

"the client" has the meaning given by section 61D(4),

"employer's national insurance contributions" means secondary Class 1 or Class 1A national insurance contributions,

"managed service company" has the meaning given by section 61B,

"national insurance contributions" means contributions under Part 1 of SSCBA 1992 or Part 1 of SSCB(NI)A 1992,

"PAYE provisions" means the provisions of Part 11 or PAYE regulations,

"the relevant services" has the meaning given by section 61D(4), and

"the worker" has the meaning given by section 61D(4).

(2) Nothing in section 995 of ITA 2007 (meaning of control) applies for the purposes of this Chapter."

5 In section 218(1) (exclusion of lower-paid employments from parts of benefits code: calculation of earnings rate), in Step 1, at the end of paragraph (*d*) insert "and (*e*) in the case of an employment within section 61G(2) (deemed employment payment by managed service company), the total amount of deemed employment payments for the year."

6 After section 688 insert—

"688A Managed service companies: recovery from other persons

(1) PAYE regulations may make provision authorising the recovery from a person within subsection (2) of any amount that an officer of Revenue and Customs considers should have been deducted by a managed service company ("the MSC") from a payment of, or on account of, PAYE income of an individual.

(2) The persons are—

(*a*) a director or other office-holder, or an associate, of the MSC,

(*b*) an MSC provider,

(*c*) a person who (directly or indirectly) has encouraged or been actively involved in the provision by the MSC of the services of the individual, and

(*d*) a director or other office-holder, or an associate, of a person (other than an individual) who is within paragraph (*b*) or (*c*).

(3) A person does not fall within subsection (2)(*c*) merely by virtue of—

(*a*) providing legal or accountancy advice in a professional capacity, or

(*b*) placing the individual with persons who wish to obtain the services of the individual (including by contracting with the MSC for the provision of those services).

(4) The supplementary provision that may be made by the regulations includes provision as to the liability of one person within subsection (2) to another such person.

(5) In this section—

"associate" has the meaning given by section 61I,

"director" has the meaning given by section 67,

"managed service company" has the meaning given by section 61B, and

"MSC provider" means an MSC provider who is involved with the MSC (within the meaning of section 61B).

(6) Section 61C(4) (extended meaning of "associate") applies for the purposes of subsection (2)(*d*).

(7) The Treasury may by order amend this section (but not this subsection or subsection (8)).

(8) The Treasury must not make an order under subsection (7) unless a draft of it has been laid before and approved by a resolution of the House of Commons."

7 In section 717(4) (orders and regulations not subject to negative procedure), insert at the end "or section 688A(7) (PAYE regulations: managed service companies)".

8 In Part 2 of Schedule 1 (index of defined expressions), insert at the appropriate places—

"associate (in Chapter 9 of Part 2)	section 61I (but see section 61C(4))"
"business (in Chapter 9 of Part 2)	section 61J"
"the client (in Chapter 9 of Part 2)	section 61D(4)"
"employer's national insurance contributions (in Chapter 9 of Part 2)	section 61J"
"managed service company (in Chapter 9 of Part 2)	section 61B"
"national insurance contributions (in Chapter 9 of Part 2)	section 61J"
"PAYE provisions (in Chapter 9 of Part 2)	section 61J"
"the relevant services (in Chapter 9 of Part 2)	section 61D(4)"
"the worker (in Chapter 9 of Part 2)	section 61D(4)".

PART 2
CALCULATION OF PROFITS OF MSCS: DEDUCTION FOR DEEMED EMPLOYMENT PAYMENTS

Deduction for deemed employment payments for income tax purposes

9 In ITTOIA 2005, after section 164 insert—

"Managed service companies

164A Deduction for deemed employment payments

(1) This section applies for the purpose of calculating the profits of a trade, profession or vocation carried on by a managed service company ("the MSC") which is treated as making a deemed employment payment in connection with the trade, profession or vocation.

(2) A deduction is allowed for—

(*a*) the amount of the deemed employment payment, and

(*b*) the amount of any employer's national insurance contributions paid by the MSC in respect of it.

(3) The deduction is allowed for the period of account in which the deemed employment payment is treated as made.

(4) The amount of the deduction allowed under subsection (2) is limited to the amount that reduces the profits of the firm for the tax year to nil.

(5) No deduction in respect of—

(*a*) the deemed employment payment, or

(*b*) any employer's national insurance contributions paid by the MSC in respect of it,

may be made except in accordance with this section.

(6) In this section "deemed employment payment", "employer's national insurance contributions" and "managed service company" have the same meaning as in Chapter 9 of Part 2 of ITEPA 2003."

Deduction for deemed employment payments for corporation tax purposes

10— (1) This paragraph applies for the purpose of calculating for corporation tax purposes the profits of a business carried on by a managed service company ("the MSC") which is treated as making a deemed employment payment in connection with the business.

(2) A deduction is allowed for—

(*a*) the amount of the deemed employment payment, and

(*b*) the amount of any employer's national insurance contributions paid by the MSC in respect of it.

(3) The deduction is allowed for the period of account in which the deemed employment payment is treated as made.

(4) If the MSC is a partnership, the amount of the deduction allowed under sub-paragraph (2) is limited to the amount that reduces the profits of the partnership for the period of account to nil.

(5) No deduction in respect of—

(*a*) the deemed employment payment, or

(*b*) any employer's national insurance contributions paid by the MSC in respect of it,

may be made except in accordance with this paragraph.

(6) In this paragraph "business", "deemed employment payment", "employer's national insurance contributions" and "managed service company" have the same meanings as in Chapter 9 of Part 2 of ITEPA 2003.

GENERAL NOTE

The Schedule introduces a new Chapter 9 into Part 2 of ITEPA 2003, following Chapter 8, which deals with the taxation of services provided through intermediaries, otherwise known as IR35.

Chapter 9 creates a tax charge on income now regarded as deriving from an employment by virtue of para 2, which adds amounts treated as earnings of workers provided by managed service companies to the definition of employment income in ITEPA 2003 s 7(5).

Paragraph 3 excludes managed service company workers from Chapter 8, so workers taxed under the MSC legislation are statutorily excluded from IR35. Thus the MSC legislation replaces IR35 for income of affected workers. This is significant in two respects: the calculation on the deemed employment payment differs, and the debt transfer provisions which apply to tax due under MSC rules only.

Paragraph 4 of the schedule contains new Chapter 9 of Part 2 of ITEPA 2003 which runs from new ss 61A to 61J as follows:

Section 61A sets the scope of the Chapter as applying to the provision of services by managed service companies, but excludes the Chapter from applying to agency workers or foreign visiting performers taxed under existing s 966(3) and (4) of ITA 2007.

Section 61B defines managed service companies in two stages:

Subsection 1 sets out the main criteria of a managed service company, in four elements. The company (including, by virtue of s 61C(3) any body corporate or partnership) provides the service of individuals who are paid the income arising from their services more or less intact, in such a way as the tax and NIC burden is less than that which would apply to employment income. Finally "a person who carries on a business of promoting or facilitating the use of companies to provide the service of individuals" (a scheme provider) is involved with the company. The term "involved with" is further defined. One key aspect of this legislation is that many service companies, whether potentially caught by IR35 or not, would satisfy the first three criteria, and it is the involvement of the MSC scheme provider that brings the company within the scope of the legislation.

The definition of a scheme provider is therefore regarded as crucial, and the definition here excludes persons who merely provide legal or accountancy services in a professional capacity, and businesses which are pure employment and recruitment agencies; the exemption for the latter is somewhat convoluted to permit agencies some small influence over companies they place. It is anticipated that these exclusions will be sufficient to target the legislation only at the known scheme providers, and not cause any unwanted effects on firms of accountants, tax advisers and lawyers. In any event, the term "involved with" which is defined in new s 61B(2) should ensure that professional firms are not affected in spite of concerns about the definition. There are powers to specify further descriptions of persons deemed not to fall within the definition of scheme provider by order in s 61C(1).

A scheme provider is involved with an MSC if the provider or an associate of the provider:

— benefits financially on an ongoing basis from the provision of services of the individual, or

— influences or controls the provision of services, the way in which payments are made to the individual or his associate, or the company's finances or activities, or

— Gives or promotes an undertaking to make good any tax loss.

Section 61C extends the concept of associate for these purposes to anyone who acts in concert with the scheme provider and others to ensure that the service of an individual are provided through a company, and provides an explanation of the term "undertaking to make good any tax loss" which thus extends to situations where the MSC provider insures some or all of any tax loss suffered.

This level of control or influence is likely to go beyond the advice and services provided by the average professional firm, even where it might be regarded that the level of support goes beyond the normal level of "accountancy services" provided to these businesses. It is important to recognise that the test of involvement only applies when it has already been established that there is a scheme provider present.

The amendments proposed in Committee sought to clarify the exclusions for accountants, tax advisers, company secretarial service providers and similar still further, but the Government was not willing to modify the legislation in this respect. The Minister indicated that the amendments sought would not make progress towards clarification, and could introduce confusion. He was also concerned that the amendments would also provide scope for the real targets of this legislation to avoid its impact. The clarification offered by the Minister (HC Finance Bill Public Bill Committee (15 May 2007 pm) cols175) made it clear that even where there was concern that firms of accountants might fall foul of the definition of MSC provider the concept of influence would go much further than the mere providing of advice, which permits the client to make a choice between appropriate courses of action. It would only be when the client is offered a standard solution or product which he accepts that the involvement would extend to influence. He then went further to state quite categorically that even where the specific exclusion for accountants does not apply, the purpose of the legislation is not to include within the definition of MSC provider accountants, tax advisers, lawyers and company secretaries who provide advice or other professional services to companies in general. Those persons are not in the business of promoting or facilitating the use of companies to provide the services of individuals, nor are they regarded as involved with the company in the way in which the legislation envisages. (HC Finance Bill Public Bill Committee (15 May pm) cols 175, 176).

Section 61D deems amounts paid to the worker – the person performing the services through the MSC – to the extent not already charged to tax as employment income to be earnings from an employment at the time of receipt. The amount so deemed includes any payment or benefit made to the worker or his associates by any person which can reasonably be taken to be in respect of the services provided, which are now referred to as “the relevant services”.

Section 61E provides the computation of the deemed employment payment, which differs in detail from that performed under the intermediaries legislation. Starting with the amount of the payment or benefit which is the subject of the deeming provision, there are first deducted amounts met by the worker which relate to expenses deductible by employees, construing the relationship between the worker and the end user client as one of employment. The remainder (if any) is treated as an amount including employer’s national insurance contributions, and thus the deemed employment payment can now be arrived at. Sub-ss (2) to (5) provide various other qualifications regarding the deductible expenses, allowing partnership expenses met by the worker to be deducted if the MSC is a partnership, and providing a deduction for mileage allowance relief for a car provided by the MSC or the partnership for the worker. The legislation seeks to put the worker in precisely the same tax position as if he had been employed by the client, but of course he will ultimately bear the employer national insurance contributions on the sums paid to him through his MSC.

Section 61F continues the analogy with the position of an employee, by defining payments and benefits for this purpose as any amount that if received by an employee for performing the duties of an employment, would be general earnings from the employment. The section provides valuation and timing rules for benefits which mirror the normal benefit code and timing rules in ITEPA 2003.

Section 61G explains how the deemed employment payment is treated for income tax. In particular it brings the deemed payment within the scope of PAYE provisions, and excludes any deduction from the deemed payment in respect of mileage allowance relief or other expenses – relief having already been given in the computation of the deemed payment.

The deemed payment is excluded from tax on the worker when his circumstances match those of an employee of the client who would not be taxable on earnings from the employment. The deemed payment is not treated as income of a partnership of which the worker is a member, and finally under sub-s (7) the MSC is treated as having a place of business in the UK when the worker is resident here and the services are performed here, thus keeping the MSC within the PAYE responsibilities applying to UK businesses.

There are no other provisions in Part 9 which relate to the application of PAYE to the deemed payment, as having triggered the normal PAYE rules, no further separate legislation is needed.

Section 61H provides relief from income tax, on a claim by an individual, for distributions made by companies within the MSC legislation which have been treated as making deemed payments. The imitates the relief available in similar circumstances under the intermediaries legislation, and reduces the taxable amount of the distribution (and the related tax credit) when matched with deemed employment payments.

Sections 61I and 61J provide interpretative background and definitions; of particular importance is the definition of an associate in s 61I which includes as associates of as partnership, associates of members of the firm (s 61I(4)).

Debt transfer provisions

The debt transfer provisions are perhaps the most controversial aspect of this legislation. Paragraph 6 of Sch 3 inserts new s 688A into ITEPA 2003 to provide the statutory machinery for the debt transfer provisions. These provisions will allow HMRC to collect PAYE and NIC due under the MSC provisions from third parties if the MSC fails to pay the liabilities. Essentially, the new section is enabling legislation allowing the detail to be prescribed by secondary legislation, amending the PAYE Regulations (the principal Regulations). These amending Regulations will not be laid until after Royal Assent.

Section 688A(1) allows amendment of the principal Regulations to authorise recovery from specified persons of any amount that an officer of HMRC considers should have been deducted by an MSC in respect of PAYE.

The persons specified for this purpose are given by s 688A(2). They include directors, office holders and associates of the MSC, MSC providers and a person who has encouraged or been actively involved in the provision by the MSC of the services of the individual. Finally, the provisions are extended to directors, office holders and associates of the last two categories. Although not within the body of the legislation, this aspect of the law will commence on 5 August for the first two categories of third party – directors, office holders and MSC providers, and from 5 January 2008 for the remainder. The debt transfer provisions apply only to PAYE debts arising from the commencement dates, not prior liabilities. It is anticipated that mirroring Regulations will apply to the National Insurance liabilities relating to the MSC legislation.

Subsection (3) provides an exclusion from these provisions for persons providing legal or accountancy advice (not services) and for employment agencies concerned solely with placing the services of the workers. This limited exclusion is narrower than that applying to the definition of an MSC provider, but it was considered that the requirement for the third party to have either encouraged or been actively involved in the provision of services through MSC's would sufficiently limit the application of these provisions. For example, it is unlikely that in most situations the client (end user of the services) would be a specified person; however this might arise where a client actively promotes a scheme by transferring existing staff to MSC arrangements. (HC Finance Bill Public Bill Committee (15 May pm) col 190)

Part 2 of the Schedule provides exclusively for a deduction for the deemed employment payment in computing the taxable profits of the MSC. There are parallel provisions relating to MSC's tax under income tax rules, inserting s 164A into ITTOIA 2005, and similar provisions for MSC's liable to corporation tax on their profits. The corporation tax provisions stand alone, probably in view of the tax law rewrite project currently under way, rewriting the corporation tax code.

A deduction is provided in both cases for the amount of the deemed employment payment together with the employer's national insurance contributions paid by the MSC in respect of that deemed payment. In a similar way to the matching rules in the existing intermediaries legislation, the deduction is given in the period in which the deemed payment is treated as made. For income tax the deduction is restricted to an amount which would reduce the profits to nil, which is mirrored in the corporation tax provisions to the extent they apply to an MSC which is a partnership.

SCHEDULE 4

RESTRICTIONS ON TRADE LOSS RELIEF FOR PARTNERS

Section 26

GENERAL NOTE

Where an individual or a partner makes a trading loss he may set that loss against other income and gains for the year of loss or of the previous year. This has always been known colloquially as "sideways relief" and this term is given statutory effect in ITA 2007. Avoidance schemes have been structured in such as way as to enable an individual to become a partner in a partnership which generates a trading loss in circumstances where there is no underlying economic loss, or where the partner personally does not suffer an economic loss. Schemes have been devised, for example, to exploit the rules relating to the exploitation of intangibles, or the ability under TA 1988 s 574 to turn a capital loss on certain unquoted shares into an income tax loss. As a result of the changes to the disclosure regime in 2006 HMRC has become more aware of the extent to which such schemes have been promoted. Section 26 and Schedule Four have therefore been introduced to block such schemes .

There are two main features to the new rules.

In the first place relief is excluded where a capital contribution is made by a non-active partner if the main purpose of the investment is for the partner to obtain a tax advantage. In the second place, there is an annual restriction to £25,500 of the amount of sideways loss relief which can be obtained by a non-active partner. This latter applies regardless of whether or not there is a tax avoidance motive.

Limit on amount of sideways relief and capital gains relief available in any tax year

1— (1) In ITA 2007, before section 104 (and the italic cross-heading before it) insert—

"Limit on amount of sideways relief and capital gains relief

103C Limit on reliefs in any tax year not to exceed cap for tax year

(1) This section applies if an individual carries on one or more trades—

(*a*) as a non-active partner in a firm during a tax year, or

(*b*) as a limited partner in a firm at a time in that tax year,

and the individual makes a loss in any of those trades (an "affected loss") in that tax year.

GENERAL NOTE

Paragraph 1(1) introduces a new s 103C to ITA 2007.

1 This states that the section is to apply where an individual carries on one or more trades as a non-active partner or as a limited partner. (These terms are explained at para 8 below).

2 This introduces the concept of restriction to sideways relief and capital gains tax relief.

3 This states that the amount of sideways relief for all of the affected losses must not exceed the cap for the year.

4 The cap is set at £25,000.

5 There is power for the Treasury to amend the cap.

6 The restriction does not apply for losses on qualifying film expenditure (this is deal with separately below).

7 The restriction only applies to sideways relief and relief against capital gains. There is no restriction on the amount of loss which can be carried forward and set against future profits of the same trade.

The section does not apply to Lloyds losses.

(2) There is a restriction on the amount of sideways relief and capital gains relief which (after applying the restrictions under the other provisions of this Chapter) may be given to the individual for any affected loss (but see subsections (6) and (7)).

GENERAL NOTE

Paragraph 2 sets out the basic commencement provisions. The new loss restrictions apply for losses made in 2007–8 and subsequent years.

(3) The restriction is that the total amount of the sideways relief and capital gains relief given to the individual for all the affected losses must not exceed the cap for that tax year.

GENERAL NOTE

These are transitional provisions.

The announcement to legislate in this area was announced by the Paymaster General on 2 March 2007. The restriction to loss relief applies from this date and therefore there are provisions to apportion losses incurred after that date but before 6 April 2007.

(4) The cap for any tax year is £25,000.

(5) The Treasury may by order amend the sum for the time being specified in subsection (4).

(6) The restriction under this section does not apply to so much of any affected loss as derives from qualifying film expenditure (see section 103D).

(7) The restriction under this section does not affect the giving of sideways relief for a loss made in a trade against the profits of that trade.

(8) In this section "trade" does not include a trade which consists of the underwriting business of a member of Lloyd's (within the meaning of section 184 of FA 1993)."

(2) The amendment made by sub-paragraph (1) has effect in relation to any loss made by an individual in a trade in the tax year 2007–08 or any subsequent tax year.

(3) But, in the case of a loss made by an individual in a trade in a tax year the basis period for which begins before 2nd March 2007 (a "straddling basis period"), the amount of that loss for the purposes of section 103C of ITA 2007 is—

(*a*) the amount of sideways relief and capital gains relief which (after applying the restrictions under the other provisions of Chapter 3 of Part 4 of that Act) may be given to the individual for that loss, less

(*b*) the amount (if any) of the pre-announcement loss.

(4) "The pre-announcement loss" is determined as follows.

(5) Calculate the profits or losses of the straddling basis period, but without regard to capital allowances and qualifying film expenditure (within the meaning of section 103D of ITA 2007).

(6) If that calculation produces a loss and the individual has made a contribution of an amount as capital to the firm or LLP in question—

(*a*) on or before the start of the straddling basis period, or

(*b*) after the start of that period but before 2nd March 2007,

apportion the loss produced by that calculation to the part of the straddling basis period which begins with the relevant date and falls before 2nd March 2007 in proportion to the number of days in that part.

(7) Calculate so much of the loss of the straddling basis period as derives from relevant pre-announcement capital expenditure.

(8) The pre-announcement loss is the sum of—

(*a*) the amount of the loss apportioned under sub-paragraph (6) (if any), and

(*b*) so much of the loss of the straddling basis period (if any) as derives from relevant pre-announcement capital expenditure.

(9) In sub-paragraph (6) "the relevant date" means—

(*a*) in any case where a contribution was made on or before the start of the straddling basis period, the start of that period, and

(*b*) in any other case, the date on which the contribution was made or, if more than one contribution was made, the date on which the first contribution was made.

(10) For the purposes of this paragraph the amount of the loss of the straddling basis period that derives from relevant pre-announcement capital expenditure is determined on a just and reasonable basis.

(11) In this paragraph "relevant pre-announcement capital expenditure" means—

(*a*) any capital allowance in respect of expenditure paid before 2nd March 2007, and

(*b*) any capital allowance in respect of expenditure paid on or after that date pursuant to an unconditional obligation in a contract made before that date,

and for this purpose "an unconditional obligation" means an obligation which may not be varied or extinguished by the exercise of any right conferred on the firm or LLP in question (whether or not under the contract).

(12) For the purposes of this paragraph—

(*a*) an amount of money is not to be taken as contributed as capital to a firm or LLP until the money is paid to the firm or LLP, and

(*b*) a right or other asset is not to be taken as contributed as capital to a firm or LLP until it is transferred to the firm or LLP.

GENERAL NOTE

The order of paras 4–12 does not, in the view of the writer, set out the calculation process very logically. This commentary is therefore in a slightly different order. Cross references to the relevant paragraphs of the legislation are included in brackets.

The legislation approaches the transitional period by requiring a calculation of the loss of the period for which the basis year straddles 2 March 2007. It is then necessary to compute how much of this loss is a "pre-announcement" loss. The total loss less the "pre-announcement" loss is subject to the new restrictions.

The first step is to calculate the profits or losses of the straddling period, but without taking account of capital allowances or qualifying film expenditure. (para 5)

If that calculation produces a loss the next step is to determine whether the individual has made a contribution to the capital of the firm or LLP on or before the start of the straddling basis period or after the start of the basis period but before 2 March 2007. If there was such a contribution then the loss is to be apportioned, on a strict daily basis, by reference to the period from the relevant date to 2 March 2007. (para 6)

The definition of the relevant date depends on whether or not the capital contribution was made before or after the beginning of the straddling accounting period. (para 9)

For this purpose a capital contribution is not treated as being contributed until it is actually paid. (para 12)

Where the contribution was made before the beginning of the straddling accounting period the relevant date is the first day of that accounting period. In other cases the relevant date is the date on which the contribution was made. If there was more than one contribution the date of the earliest contribution is taken. (para 9)

It is then necessary to do a separate calculation of the amount of the loss which derives from relevant pre-announcement capital expenditure. (para 7)

Pre-announcement capital expenditure is capital expenditure paid before 2 March 2006 or paid on or after that date but which is pursuant to an unconditional obligation under a contract made before that date. An unconditional obligation is an obligation which may not be varied or extinguished by the exercise of any right incurred on the firm or the LLP. (para 11)

The loss of the straddling basis period deriving from relevant pre-announcement capital expenditure is determined on a just and reasonable basis. (para 10)

Having computed the two separate losses (i.e. the loss ignoring capital expenditure and qualifying film expenditure, and the loss attributable to capital expenditure) the two figures are added together. This gives the total "pre-announcement" loss. (para 8)

The amount of the total loss for the straddling basis period less the "pre-announcement loss" is the loss which is subject to the new restrictions in s 103C. (para 3)

(13) Section 62 of ITA 2007 (partners: losses of a tax year etc) applies for the purposes of this paragraph as it applies for the purposes of Chapter 3 of Part 4 of that Act.

GENERAL NOTE

The normal rules in ITA 2007 regarding partnership trading losses also apply to these loss restrictions.

Disregard of contributions made for purpose of accessing sideways relief and capital gains relief

2— (1) In ITA 2007, before section 114 insert—

"Exclusion of amounts in calculating contribution to the firm or LLP

113A Exclusion of amounts contributed to access relief

(1) An amount which an individual contributes to a firm as capital is to be excluded in calculating the individual's contribution to the firm for the purposes of section 104 or 110 if the contribution was made for a prohibited purpose (but see subsection (4)).

(2) If—

(*a*) an individual carries on a trade as a member of an LLP at a time in a tax year,
(*b*) the individual does not devote a significant amount of time to the trade in the relevant period for that year, and
(*c*) the individual contributes an amount to the LLP as capital at any time in that year,

that amount is to be excluded in calculating the individual's contribution to the LLP for the purposes of section 107 if the contribution was made for a prohibited purpose (but see subsection (4)).

(3) For the purposes of this section a contribution is made for a prohibited purpose if the main purpose, or one of the main purposes, of making the contribution is the obtaining of a reduction in tax liability by means of sideways relief or capital gains relief.

(4) This section has no effect in relation to the application of any restriction under section 104, 107 or 110 to any loss that derives wholly from qualifying film expenditure."

GENERAL NOTE

Paragraph two introduces a new ITA 2007 s 113A, to expand the existing rules which govern loss relief for limited partners or non-active partners in partnerships and LLPs.

Currently ITA 2007 s 104 restricts loss relief for limited partners to the amount of capital which the partner has contributed. Section 110 similar restricts relief for members of LLPs and non-active partners. Section 113A introduces a further restriction. Any capital contribution which is made for a "prohibited purpose" is to be ignored in determining the amount of capital contributed. (s 113A(1))

Where a member of an LLP does not devote a significant amount of time to the trade during the relevant period for the year but contributes an amount to the LLP, that amount is excluded in computing his contribution for the purposes of sideways loss relief if it is made for a "prohibited purpose". (s 113A(2))

A contribution is made for a prohibited purpose if the main purpose, or one of the main purposes, of making the contribution is the obtaining a reduction in tax liability by sideways relief or capital gains tax relief. (s 113A(3))

As in the new s 103C, these restrictions do not apply to relief deriving from qualifying film expenditure. (s 113A(4))

(2) The amendment made by sub-paragraph (1) has effect in relation to any amount contributed to a firm or LLP as capital on or after 2nd March 2007 (but see sub-para (4)).

GENERAL NOTE

The new provisions apply to contributions made on or after 2 March 2007.

(3) For this purpose—

(*a*) an amount of money is not to be taken as contributed as capital to a firm or LLP until the money is paid to the firm or LLP, and

(*b*) a right or other asset is not to be taken as contributed as capital to a firm or LLP until it is transferred to the firm or LLP.

GENERAL NOTE

An amount of money is not treated as contributed to the capital of a firm or an LLP until the money is actually paid. A similar rule applies to rights or other assets contributed to a firm or LLP.

(4) The amendment made by sub-paragraph (1) has no effect in relation to any amount contributed by an individual on or after 2nd March 2007 if—

(*a*) the amount is contributed pursuant to an obligation in a contract made before that date, and

(*b*) the obligation may not be varied or extinguished by the exercise of any right conferred on the individual (whether or not under the contract).

GENERAL NOTE

The new restrictions do not apply to any amount contributed by an individual on or after 2 March 2007 if the amount is contributed pursuant to an obligation in a contract made before that date where the obligation may not be varied or extinguished by the exercise of any right conferred on the individual.

Provision corresponding to paragraphs 1 and 2 for tax year 2006–07

3— (1) ICTA has effect, in relation to any loss made by an individual in a trade in the tax year 2006–07 the basis period for which ends on or after 2nd March 2007, as if provision corresponding to section 103C of ITA 2007 were included in Chapter 7 of Part 4 of ICTA.

(2) Sub-paragraphs (3) to (13) of paragraph 1 apply for the purposes of sub-paragraph (1) above.

(3) ICTA has effect for the tax year 2006–07 as if provision corresponding to section 113A of ITA 2007 were included in that Chapter.

(4) Sub-paragraphs (2) to (4) of paragraph 2 apply for the purposes of sub-paragraph (3) above.

(5) The provisions which are treated by this paragraph as included in Chapter 7 of Part 4 of ICTA have effect as if—

(*a*) any reference in section 103C of ITA 2007 to sideways relief were to relief under section 380 or 381 of ICTA,

(*b*) any reference in section 103C of ITA 2007 to capital gains relief in relation to a loss were to the treatment of the loss as an allowable loss by virtue of section 72 of FA 1991,

(*c*) any reference in section 103C or 113A of ITA 2007 to any provision of Chapter 3 of Part 4 of ITA 2007 were to the corresponding provision of Chapter 7 of Part 4 of ICTA, and

(*d*) any reference in section 113A of ITA 2007 to a contribution to a firm or an LLP were to a contribution to a trade carried on by the firm or LLP,

and references in paragraphs 1(3) to (13) and 2(2) to (4) to any of those expressions are to be read accordingly.

GENERAL NOTE

This is a consequence of the introduction of the new Income Tax Act 2007 from 6 April 2007. These new provisions apply from 2 March 2007, and technically, in respect of the period from 2 March to 5 April 2007, they should have been introduced as amendments to the old legislation in TA 1988. This would have resulted in a huge amount of redrafting for a period of only one month, so the draftsman has taken the sensible approach of deeming these amendments to have been made to ITA 2007 with effect from 2 March, even though ITA 2007 was not actually in force at that time.

Consequential amendments

4 ITA 2007 is amended as follows.

5 In section 32 (liability not dealt with in the calculation), for "section 112(5)" substitute "section 103B(5)".

6 In section 82(*a*) (exploitation of films), for "sections 115 and 116" substitute "section 115".

7— (1) Section 102 (overview of Chapter 3 of Part 4) is amended as follows.

(2) In subsection (1)—

(*a*) in paragraph (*a*), for "104 to 106 and section 114)" substitute "103A, 103C to 105, 113A and 114)",

(*b*) in paragraph (*b*), for "107 to 109 and section 114)" substitute "103C, 103D, 107 to 109, 113A and 114)", and

(*c*) in paragraph (*c*), for "in an early tax year (see sections 110 to 114)" substitute "(see sections 103B to 103D and 110 to 114)".

(3) In subsection (2), for "sections 115 and 116" substitute "section 115".

GENERAL NOTE

Paragraphs four to seven are consequential amendments with no substantive effect.

8 After section 103 insert—

"103A Meaning of "limited partner"

(1) In this Chapter "limited partner" means an individual who carries on a trade—

(*a*) as a limited partner in a limited partnership registered under the Limited Partnerships Act 1907,

(*b*) as a partner in a firm who in substance acts as a limited partner in relation to the trade (see subsection (2)), or

(*c*) while the condition mentioned in subsection (3) is met in relation to the individual.

(2) An individual in substance acts as a limited partner in relation to a trade if the individual—

(*a*) is not entitled to take part in the management of the trade, and
(*b*) is entitled to have any liabilities (or those beyond a certain limit) for debts or obligations incurred for the purposes of the trade met or reimbursed by some other person.

(3) The condition referred to in subsection (1)(*c*) is that—

(*a*) the individual carries on the trade jointly with other persons,
(*b*) under the law of a territory outside the United Kingdom, the individual is not entitled to take part in the management of the trade, and
(*c*) under that law, the individual is not liable beyond a certain limit for debts or obligations incurred for the purposes of the trade.

(4) In the case of an individual who is a limited partner as a result of subsection (1)(*c*), references in this Chapter to the individual's firm are to be read as references to the relationship between the individual and the other persons mentioned in subsection (3)(*a*).

103B Meaning of "non-active partner" etc

(1) For the purposes of this Chapter an individual carries on a trade as a non-active partner during a tax year if the individual—

(*a*) carries on the trade as a partner in a firm at a time during the year,
(*b*) does not carry on the trade as a limited partner at any time during the year, and
(*c*) does not devote a significant amount of time to the trade in the relevant period for the year.

(2) For the purposes of this Chapter an individual devotes a significant amount of time to a trade in the relevant period for a tax year if, in that period, the individual spends an average of at least 10 hours a week personally engaged in activities carried on for the purposes of the trade.

(3) For this purpose "the relevant period" means the basis period for the tax year (unless the basis period is shorter than 6 months).

(4) If the basis period for the tax year is shorter than 6 months, "the relevant period" means—

(*a*) the period of 6 months beginning with the date on which the individual first started to carry on the trade (if the basis period begins with that date), or
(*b*) the period of 6 months ending with the date on which the individual permanently ceased to carry on the trade (if the basis period ends with that date).

(5) If—

(*a*) any relief is given on the assumption that the individual devoted or will devote a significant amount of time to the trade in the relevant period for a tax year, but
(*b*) the individual in fact failed or fails to do so,

the relief is withdrawn by the making of an assessment to income tax under this section."

GENERAL NOTE

Paragraph 8 defines a limited partner and a non-active partner

A limited partner is somebody who carries on a trade as a limited partner in a partnership registered under the Limited Partnership Act 1907; a person who in substance acts as a limited partner; or a person who meets a specified condition in relation to overseas partnerships.

A person acts in substance as a limited partner if he is not entitled to take part in the management of the trade and is entitled to have any liabilities for trade debts or obligations met or reimbursed by some other person.

The specified condition is that the individual carried on a trade jointly with other persons; is not, under the law of a territory outside the UK, entitled to take part in the management of the trade; and, under that law, is not liable beyond a certain limit for debts and obligations incurred for the purposes of the trade.

This rule is clearly introduced to ensure that individuals do not circumvent the new rules by setting up structures which are not technically limited partnerships but which none-the-less have many of the same characteristics.

A non-active partner is somebody who carried on a trade as a partner during the year (other than as a limited partner) and does not devote a significant amount of time to the trade in the relevant period.

A person devotes a significant amount of time to the trade in the relevant period if he spends an average of at least ten hours a week personally engaged in activities carried on for the purpose of the trade.

The relevant period is the basis period for the tax year unless the basis period is shorter than six months. But there is a specific rule for basis periods of less than six months. Where the (short) basis period begins with the date of commencement to trade the relevant period is six months from commencement. Where the (short) basis period ends with the cessation of trade the relevant period is the six months to the date of cessation.

This rule prevents structures being set up which have a very short life. For example some loss schemes only operated for few weeks and therefore it might have been possible to contrive situations where an individual could in fact devote only very small amount of time to the trade and still get the benefit of the loss.

Where relief is given on the assumption that an individual will devote a significant amount of time to the trade but in fact fails to do so, any relief which has been given can be withdrawn by the making of an assessment.

9 After section 103C (as inserted by paragraph 1(1) above) insert—

"103D Meaning of "qualifying film expenditure"

(1) For the purposes of this Chapter expenditure is qualifying film expenditure if—

(*a*) it is deducted under a relevant film provision for the purposes of the calculation required by section 849 of ITTOIA 2005 (calculation of firm's profits or losses), or

(*b*) it is incidental expenditure which (although not deducted under a relevant film provision) is incurred in connection with the production of a film, or the acquisition of the original master version of a film, in relation to which expenditure is so deducted.

(2) Expenditure is incidental if it is on management, administration or obtaining finance.

(3) The extent to which expenditure is within subsection (1)(*b*) is determined on a just and reasonable basis.

(4) For the purposes of this Chapter the amount of any loss that derives from qualifying film expenditure is determined on a just and reasonable basis.

(5) In this section—

"the acquisition of the original master version of a film" has the same meaning as in Chapter 9 of Part 2 of ITTOIA 2005 (see sections 130 and 132 of that Act),

"film" is to be read in accordance with paragraph 1 of Schedule 1 to the Films Act 1985, and

"a relevant film provision" means any one of sections 137 to 140 of ITTOIA 2005 (relief for certified master versions of films)."

GENERAL NOTE

Paragraph 9 defines qualifying film expenditure. This is either expenditure under ITTOIA 2005 s 849, or incidental expenditure otherwise incurred in connection with the production of a film or the acquisition of the original master version of a film

Expenditure is incidental if it is incurred on management, administration or obtaining finance.

A just and reasonable method of apportionment applies where it is necessary to determine the extent to which expenditure is or is not qualifying film expenditure.

10 In—

(*a*) section 104(5) (restriction on reliefs for limited partners),

(*b*) section 107(2) (restriction on reliefs for members of LLPs),

(*c*) section 110(1)(*a*) (restriction on reliefs for non-active partners in early tax years), and

(*d*) section 115(1)(*d*) (restrictions on relief for firms exploiting films),

omit "(see section 112)".

11 In—

(*a*) section 105(11) (meaning of "contribution to the firm" for purposes of section 104),
(*b*) section 108(9) (meaning of "contribution to the LLP" for purposes of section 107), and
(*c*) section 111(12) (meaning of "contribution to the firm" for purposes of section 110),

for the words from "any regulations" to "excluded" substitute "section 113A and any regulations made under section 114 (exclusion of amounts".

12 Omit section 106 (meaning of "limited partner").

13 In section 112 (meaning of "non-active partner" and "early tax year" etc)—
(*a*) omit subsections (1) to (5), and
(*b*) the heading accordingly becomes "**Meaning of "early tax year"**".

14 Omit the italic-cross heading before section 114 (regulations: exclusion of amounts in calculating contribution to the firm or LLP) and for the heading of that section substitute "**Power to exclude other amounts**".

15 In section 115 (restrictions on reliefs for firms exploiting films), for subsection (4) substitute—

"(4) The restrictions under this section do not apply to so much of the loss (if any) as derives from qualifying film expenditure."

16 Omit section 116 (exclusion from restrictions under section 115: certain film expenditure).

17 In section 792 (partners claiming excess sideways or capital gains relief)—
(*a*) in subsection (7), for "106" substitute "103A", and
(*b*) in subsection (8), for "106(3)(*a*)" substitute "103A(3)(*a*)".

18 In section 809 (individuals in partnership claiming relief for licence-related trading losses: other definitions)—
(*a*) in subsection (1), for "112" substitute "103B", and
(*b*) in subsection (2), for "112(1)(*b*)" substitute "103B(1)(*b*)".

19 In paragraph 148(3)(*b*) of Schedule 2 (transitionals and savings: tax avoidance)—
(*a*) for "106" substitute "103A", and
(*b*) for "112" substitute "103B".

20 In Schedule 4 (index of defined expressions)—
(*a*) in the definition of "limited partner", for "106" substitute "103A",
(*b*) in the definition of "non-active partner", for "112" substitute "103B", and
(*c*) after the definition of "qualifying donation (in Chapter 2 of Part 8)" insert—

"qualifying film expenditure (in Chapter 3 of Part 4)	section 103D"

GENERAL NOTE

Paragraphs 10–20 are consequential amendments of no substantive effect.

21 The amendments made by paragraphs 5 to 20 are deemed always to have had effect.

GENERAL NOTE

The amendments in paras 5–20 are deemed always to have had effect. Again, this is a consequence of the introduction of ITA 2007. It means that there is no need to make all of the consequential amendments to the previous legislation which would otherwise strictly be due.

SCHEDULE 5

AVOIDANCE INVOLVING FINANCIAL ARRANGEMENTS

Section 30

Amounts not forming part of a company's income

1— (1) ICTA is amended as follows.

(2) In section 347A(1) (annual payments: general rule), as it had effect before ITA 2007, omit paragraph (*b*) together with the "and" before it (payment to which section applies not income of any company for corporation tax purposes).

(3) The amendment made by sub-paragraph (2) has effect in relation to payments made on or after 6th December 2006 but before 6th April 2007.

(4) Omit section 347A (as amended by ITA 2007).

(5) The amendment made by sub-paragraph (4) has effect in relation to payments made on or after 6th April 2007.

2— (1) In section 660C of ICTA, omit subsection (4) (income which is income of settlor alone for income tax purposes by virtue of section 624 or 629 of ITTOIA 2005 not income of any company for corporation tax purposes).

(2) The amendment made by sub-paragraph (1) has effect in relation to accounting periods ending on or after 6th March 2007.

(3) But income which arises in an accounting period beginning before that date is to be chargeable to corporation tax as a result of that amendment only if it arises on or after that date.

Structured finance arrangements

3— (1) Section 774B of ICTA (disregard of intended effects of arrangement involving disposals of assets) is amended as follows.

(2) For subsection (1) substitute—

"(1) This section applies if an arrangement is a structured finance arrangement in relation to a person ("the borrower").

(1A) If the arrangement would (disregarding this section) have had the relevant effect (see subsections (2) and (3)), the arrangement is not to have that effect.

(1B) If the arrangement would (disregarding this section) not have had that effect, the payments mentioned in section 774A(2)(*d*) are to be treated for tax purposes as income of the borrower payable in respect of the security (whether or not those payments are also the income of anyone else for tax purposes)."

(3) In subsection (4)(*a*) (income tax relief for finance charge in respect of advance), for the words from the beginning to "is a person" substitute "a person in relation to whom this section applies is".

(4) In subsection (5) (corporation tax relief for finance charge in respect of advance), for the words from the beginning to "is a company" substitute "If a person in relation to whom this section applies is".

4 In section 774D of ICTA (disregard of intended effects of arrangement involving change in relation to a partnership), after subsection (2) insert—

"(2A) In determining whether the condition in subsection (1)(*b*) is met it is to be assumed that amounts of income equal to the payments mentioned in section 774C(2)(*f*) or (4)(*e*) were payable to the borrower partnership before the time at which the relevant change in relation to its membership involving the lender or a person connected with the lender occurs."

5 In section 774E of ICTA (exceptions), in subsection (7)(*a*) (meaning of "relevant person" where section 774B applies), for the words from "a person" to "of that section)" substitute "the borrower under the structured finance arrangement, a person connected with that borrower or (if that borrower is a partnership) a member of the partnership".

6— (1) Section 774G of ICTA (minor definitions etc for purposes of sections 774A to 774D) is amended as follows.

(2) In paragraph (*a*) of subsection (3) (meaning of receiving asset)—

(*a*) for "include the person's" substitute "include—

(i) the person's", and

(*b*) after "it" insert ", and

(ii) the discharge (in whole or in part) of any liability of the person,".

(3) In paragraph (*c*) of that subsection (meaning of payments in respect of asset), for "include obtaining" substitute "include—

(i) payments in respect of any other asset substituted for it under the arrangement, and

(ii) obtaining".

(4) After subsection (5) insert—

"(5A) In determining for the purposes of sections 774A to 774D whether an amount is recorded as a financial liability in respect of the advance it is to be assumed that the period of account in which the advance is received ended immediately after the receipt of the advance."

7— (1) The amendments made by paragraphs 3 to 5 and 6(2) and (3) have effect in relation to any arrangements whenever made.

(2) But, in relation to arrangements made before 6th March 2007, amounts are as a result of any of those amendments—

(*a*) to be charged to tax, or

(*b*) to be brought into account in calculating any income for tax purposes or deducted from any income for tax purposes,

only if the amounts arise on or after that date.

(3) In any case where, in relation to arrangements made before that date, a person is treated as a result of any of those amendments as being a party to any loan relationship—

(*a*) a period of account is to be treated for the purposes of Chapter 2 of Part 4 of FA 1996 as beginning on that date, and

(*b*) the loan relationship is to be treated for those purposes as being entered into by the person for a consideration equal to the notional carrying value of the liability representing the relationship.

(4) For this purpose the notional carrying value is the amount that would have been the carrying value of the liability in the accounts of the person if a period of account had ended immediately before that date.

(5) "Carrying value" has the same meaning here as it has for the purposes of paragraph 19A of Schedule 19 to FA 1996.

(6) The amendment made by paragraph 6(4) comes into force on the day on which this Act is passed.

8— (1) Section 263E of TCGA 1992 (structured finance arrangements) is amended as follows.

(2) In subsection (2) (condition A: person making disposal of asset subsequently acquires it), for the words from "subsequently" to the end substitute "(and no-one else) has the right or obligation under the arrangement to acquire the asset disposed of by that disposal at any subsequent time (whether or not the right or obligation is subject to any conditions)."

(3) In subsection (3) (condition B: asset ceases to exist)—

(*a*) in paragraph (*a*), for "subsequently ceases" substitute "will subsequently cease", and

(*b*) in paragraph (*b*), for "that asset was held" substitute "it is intended that that asset will be held".

(4) After subsection (4) insert—

"(4A) If, at any time after that disposal, it becomes apparent that—

(*a*) the person making the disposal will not subsequently acquire under the arrangement the asset disposed of by that disposal, or

(*b*) that asset will not be held as mentioned in subsection (3)(*b*),

that person is to be treated for the purposes of this Act as disposing of that asset at that time for a consideration equal to its market value at that time."

(5) In subsection (5) (disregard of subsequent acquisitions), for "Any" substitute "Except in a case falling within subsection (4A), any".

(6) The amendments made by this paragraph have effect in relation to disposals made on or after 6th March 2007.

(7) The amendments made by this paragraph also have effect in relation to any disposal made by a person before that date if the person makes a claim to that effect under this sub-paragraph.

Manufactured payments under arrangements having an unallowable purpose

9— (1) In paragraph 7A(10) of Schedule 23A to ICTA (manufactured payments under arrangements having an unallowable purpose), in the definition of "manufactured payment", after paragraph (*c*) insert—

"(*d*) any payment which by virtue of paragraph 7(1) constitutes a fee;".

(2) The amendment made by sub-paragraph (1) has effect in relation to payments made (or treated as made) on or after 6th December 2006.

(3) But, in the case of any payment made (or treated as made) by a company in pursuance of old arrangements, that amendment has no effect in relation to so much of the payment as (on such just and reasonable apportionments as may be necessary) represents any old taxable income or gains arising or accruing to the company as a result of those arrangements.

(4) For this purpose—

"old arrangements" means arrangements in pursuance of which (or of any part of which) a transaction has taken place before 6th December 2006, and

"old taxable income or gains arising or accruing" means income or gains within the charge to corporation tax arising or accruing (or treated as arising or accruing) before that date.

Options and groups of companies

10— (1) In section 171(2) of TCGA 1992 (exceptions to rule that disposals within the same group of companies produce neither a gain nor a loss), after paragraph (da) insert "or

(db) a disposal by company A in fulfilment of its obligations under an option granted to company B at a time when those companies were not members of the same group;".

(2) The amendment made by sub-paragraph (1) has effect in relation to cases where the option is exercised on or after 6th March 2007 (whenever the option was granted).

Loan relationships: amounts not fully recognised for accounting purposes

11— (1) Section 85C of FA 1996 (amounts not fully recognised for accounting purposes) is amended as follows.

(2) In subsection (1)—

(*a*) in paragraph (*c*), for the words from "has at any time" to "liability")" substitute "an amount (a "relevant capital contribution") has at any time been contributed to the company which forms part of its capital (whether share or other capital)", and

(*b*) in paragraphs (*d*) and (*e*), for "relevant accounting liability" substitute "relevant capital contribution".

(3) In subsection (2)—

(*a*) for "or relevant accounting liability of the company" substitute "of the company or any relevant capital contribution made to the company", and

(*b*) for "or liability" (in both places) substitute "or contribution".

(4) The amendments made by this paragraph have effect in relation to periods of account ending on or after 9th May 2007.

(5) But, in relation to periods of account beginning before that date, amounts are to be brought into account for the purposes of Chapter 2 of Part 4 of FA 1996 as a result of those amendments only if the amounts relate to any time on or after that date.

Shares treated as loan relationships

12— (1) Section 91A of FA 1996 (shares subject to outstanding third party obligations) is amended as follows.

(2) In subsection (4) (debits in respect of certain transactions to be ignored), for "No debits are to be brought into account" substitute "In determining those debits and credits there are to be left out of account amounts".

(3) Insert at the end—

"(11) In this section "share" does not include a share in a building society."

(4) The amendment made by sub-paragraph (2) has effect in relation to accounting periods ending on or after 6th March 2007.

(5) But, in relation to accounting periods beginning before that date, amounts are to be left out of account as a result of that amendment only if they relate to any time on or after that date.

(6) The amendment made by sub-paragraph (3) has effect in relation to shares held on or after 6th March 2007.

13— (1) Section 91B of FA 1996 (non-qualifying shares) is amended as follows.

(2) In subsection (4) (debits in respect of certain transactions to be ignored), for "no debits are to be brought into account" substitute "in determining those debits and credits there are to be left out of account amounts".

(3) Insert at the end—

"(8) In this section "share" does not include a share in a building society."

(4) The amendment made by sub-paragraph (2) has effect in relation to accounting periods ending on or after 6th March 2007.

(5) But, in relation to accounting periods beginning before that date, amounts are to be left out of account as a result of that amendment only if they relate to any time on or after that date.

(6) The amendment made by sub-paragraph (3) has effect in relation to shares held on or after 6th March 2007.

14— (1) In section 103(1) of FA 1996 (interpretation of Chapter 2 of Part 4), in the definition of "share", before ", in relation to a company," insert "(except in sections 91A to 91G)".

(2) The amendment made by sub-paragraph (1) has effect in relation to shares held on or after 6th March 2007.

Exchange gains and losses where loan not on arm's length terms

15— (1) In paragraph 11A of Schedule 9 to FA 1996 (exchange gains and losses where loan not on arm's length terms), insert at the end—

"(7) Where—

(*a*) a company would be treated as having a debtor relationship in any accounting period if a claim were made under paragraph 6D(2) of Schedule 28AA to the Taxes Act 1988 in relation to that period, and

(*b*) for that period there is a connection between that company and the company which would have the corresponding creditor relationship,

it shall be assumed that such a claim is made for the purpose of determining the debits or credits to be brought into account for the purposes of this Chapter in respect of any exchange gains or losses arising in that period in respect of the liability representing that debtor relationship.

(8) Section 87(3) and (4) (connection between a company and another person) apply for the purposes of sub-paragraph (7)(*b*) above as they apply for the purposes of section 87.

(9) Where, by virtue of any claim made (or assumed by virtue of sub-paragraph (7) above to be made) under paragraph 6D(2) of Schedule 28AA to the Taxes Act 1988, more than one company is treated for any purpose as having a debtor relationship represented by the same liability—

(*a*) the total debtor exchange gains must not exceed the total creditor exchange losses, and

(*b*) the total debtor exchange losses must not exceed the total creditor exchange gains.

(10) For the purposes of sub-paragraph (9) above—

(*a*) any reference to the total debtor exchange gains is to the total amount of the credits brought into account for the purposes of this Chapter in respect of exchange gains from those debtor relationships,

(*b*) any reference to the total debtor exchange losses is to the total amount of the debits brought into account for those purposes in respect of exchange losses from those debtor relationships,

(*c*) any reference to the total creditor exchange gains is to the total amount of the credits brought into account for those purposes in respect of exchange gains from the corresponding creditor relationship, and

(*d*) any reference to the total creditor exchange losses is to the total amount of the debits brought into account for those purposes in respect of exchange losses from that relationship."

(2) The amendment made by sub-paragraph (1) has effect in relation to loan relationships of any company in accounting periods ending on or after 6th December 2006.

(3) But, in relation to an accounting period of any company beginning before that date, that amendment has no effect if the company ceases to be a party to the loan relationship before that date.

Loan relationships and collective investment schemes

16— (1) Paragraph 4 of Schedule 10 to FA 1996 (company holdings in unit trusts and offshore funds) is amended as follows.

(2) In sub-paragraph (2) (relevant holding treated as rights under creditor relationship), for "and (4)" substitute "to (5)".

(3) After sub-paragraph (4) insert—

"(5) In determining the debits and credits under sub-paragraph (3) there shall be left out of account amounts relating to any investment or liability of the scheme or fund where—

(*a*) the investment was made, or the liability was incurred, with the relevant avoidance intention, or

(*b*) any transaction (or series of transactions) was entered into in relation to the investment or liability with that intention.

(6) The relevant avoidance intention is the intention of—

(*a*) eliminating or reducing the credits to be brought into account for the purposes of this Chapter as respects the company's relevant holdings, or

(*b*) creating or increasing the debits to be so brought into account."

(4) In the case of amounts relating to investments, the amendments made by this paragraph have effect in relation to accounting periods ending on or after 6th March 2007.

(5) But in that case, in relation to accounting periods beginning before that date, amounts are to be left out of account as a result of those amendments only if they relate to any time on or after that date.

(6) In the case of amounts relating to liabilities, those amendments have effect in relation to accounting periods ending on or after 9th May 2007.

(7) But in that case, in relation to accounting periods beginning before that date, amounts are to be left out of account as a result of those amendments only if they relate to any time on or after that date.

Plant or machinery subject to a lease and finance leaseback

17— (1) Chapter 17 of Part 2 of CAA 2001 (plant and machinery allowances: anti-avoidance) is amended as follows.

(2) In section 228A(2) (application of sections 228B to 228D in case of a lease and finance leaseback), for "Sections 228B to 228D" substitute "Sections 228B and 228C".

(3) In section 228F (lease and finance leaseback)—

(*a*) in subsection (1), for "Sections 228B, 228C and 228D" substitute "Sections 228B and 228C",

(*b*) omit subsection (4), and

(*c*) in subsection (8), for "sections 228B to 228D" substitute "sections 228B and 228C" and omit paragraph (*b*) (together with the "and" before it).

(4) In section 774E(5)(*b*) of ICTA (structured finance arrangements: exceptions), for "sections 228B to 228D" substitute "sections 228B and 228C".

(5) The amendments made by this paragraph have effect in relation to post-commencement rentals that fall to be taken into account in calculating for tax purposes the income or profits for any post-commencement period of account.

(6) In this paragraph—

"post-commencement period of account" means any period of account ending on or after 6th December 2006, and

"post-commencement rental" means—

(*a*) any amount receivable on or after 6th December 2006 in respect of any period beginning on or after that date, or

(*b*) the appropriate fraction of any amount receivable on or after that date in respect of any period beginning before, and ending on or after, that date,

but does not include any amount received before that date.

(7) For this purpose the "appropriate fraction", in relation to any amount received in respect of any period, means the fraction—

$$\frac{PCP}{WP}$$

where—

"PCP" means the number of days in the part of the period falling on or after 6th December 2006, and

"WP" means the number of days in the whole of the period.

(8) Sub-paragraph (9) applies if the amounts that, in accordance with section 228D of CAA 2001 as applied by section 228F of that Act, fall to be taken into account in calculating for tax purposes the income or profits for any post-commencement period of account comprise both post-commencement rentals and other amounts.

(9) For the purposes of section 228D of CAA 2001 as applied by section 228F of that Act, the amount of the gross earnings is taken to be so much of the gross earnings as, on a just and reasonable basis, relates to those other amounts. "Gross earnings" has the meaning given by section 228D(5) of CAA 2001.

Derivative contracts: contracts treated for accounting purposes as financial asset or liability

18— (1) In paragraph 17A of Schedule 26 to FA 2002 (computation in accordance with generally accepted accounting practice), after sub-paragraph (1) insert—

"(1A) But, in the case of a contract which is a derivative contract for the purposes of this Schedule by virtue of paragraph 3(1)(*b*) (contracts treated for accounting purposes as financial asset or liability), the amounts to be so brought into account as respects the contract must be determined on the basis of fair value accounting."

(2) The amendment made by sub-paragraph (1) has effect in relation to periods of account ending on or after 6th March 2007.

(3) But, in relation to a period of account beginning before that date, the fair value of the derivative contract at the beginning of that period is to be taken to be the carrying value of the contract recognised for accounting purposes at the beginning of that period.

(4) For this purpose "carrying value" has the same meaning as it has for the purposes of paragraph 50A of Schedule 26 to FA 2002.

Derivative contracts: transfers of value to connected companies

19— (1) Paragraph 26 of Schedule 26 to FA 2002 (transfers of value to connected companies) is amended as follows.

(2) In sub-paragraph (1)(*a*) (transfer of value between connected companies as a result of expiry of option), for "the expiry of an option of a company which, until its expiry," substitute "the failure to exercise in full all the rights under an option of a company which, until that failure,".

(3) In sub-paragraph (2) (rules for determining whether there is a transfer of value)—

(*a*) in paragraph (*a*), for "the option would not have expired" substitute "all the rights under the option would have been exercised in full", and

(*b*) in paragraph (*b*), for "it would have been exercised on the date on which it expired" substitute "all those rights would have been exercised in full on the latest date on which they were exercisable".

(4) In sub-paragraph (3) (transferor to bring into account amount in respect of the option), for "the expiry of the option" substitute "an option".

(5) In sub-paragraph (4) (period in which amount is to be brought into account and the amount to be brought into account)—

(*a*) in paragraph (*a*), after "the option expired" insert "or would have expired if none of the rights under it had been exercised", and

(*b*) for paragraph (*b*) substitute—

"(*b*) the appropriate amount—

(i) if the option expired, is the amount (if any) paid by the transferor to the transferee for the grant of the option by the transferee, and

(ii) if any rights under the option were exercised (in whole or in part), is the amount (if any) so paid less so much of it as is referrable, on a just and reasonable basis, to the rights which have been so exercised."

(6) The amendments made by this paragraph have effect in relation to any failure on or after 6th March 2007 to exercise in full all the rights under an option.

GENERAL NOTE

Amounts not forming part of a company's income (paras 1 and 2)

Paragraph 1 abolishes s 347A with regard to payments made on or after 6 April 2007. Section 347A had the effect of excluding certain payments made by individuals from being treated as "charges" so that they were no longer deductible in determining income. Any payments covered by this legislation were not to be treated as income for the purposes of corporation tax. HMRC have stated that the abolition of this section is designed to counter certain schemes whereby the rights to such income were purchased by financial traders. Such traders would claim that the purchase price was a deduction in calculating the profits of their trade but would then claim that the income was exempt as specified by this section.

There is an interim provision, which applies to payments made in the period beginning 6 December 2006 and ending on 5 April 2007. During this period s 347A continues to apply but with the omission of subsection (1)(*b*). This has the effect of denying deductibility to payers whilst removing the exemption from corporate recipients.

Paragraph 2 removes TA 1988 s 660C(4). The legislation previously found in s 660A–G was broadly designed to prevent higher rate taxpayers from avoiding tax by transferring income into a settlement. In recent years this legislation has been rewritten into ITTOIA 2005. Section 660C(4) provides that income which is treated as the income of the settler alone by virtue of ITTOIA 2005 ss 624 or 629 will not be the income of any company for the purposes of corporation tax.

HMRC have stated that the abolition is intended to frustrate moves by companies to exploit this provision by entering into arrangements that would fall to be treated as a settlement.

Structured Finance arrangements (paras 3 to 8)

These paragraphs cover "structured finance arrangements" ("SFA") and amend ss 774A to 774G TA 1988 and s 263E TCGA 1992. The underlying legislation deals with the factoring of income receipts. These provisions have the intention of countering what is known as "the relevant effect". In broad terms this arises when the tax effect of a transaction is not even-handed i e income is not charged to tax or an income deduction is generated. There are also special rules for partnerships.

The Finance Bill provisions introduce further anti-avoidance measures in this area. They cover the following situations:

- Where existing liabilities are refinanced using an SFA then the new arrangements will fall within the SFA rules notwithstanding that the borrower does not physically receive any additional funds or assets.
- Where the assets transferred as part of an SFA are not income producing at the time of the transfer it could be argued that there has been no alienation of income as at that time. Such arrangements will be brought within the SFA rules.
- Where there is a substitution of the assets used as collateral in an SFA the SFA rules will apply to the income from the new assets.

To this end the legislation introduces new sub-ss 774B(1A) and (1B). Subsection 1A merely reproduces the current s 774B(1) but the new 1B applies where there is no relevant effect as no income has been alienated. In such circumstances any payments which the lender receives in respect of the asset disposed of by the borrower, and which are applied in reducing the liability reflected in the borrower's accounts, are to be treated as the borrower's income.

Sub-paragraphs 3 and 4 amend s 774B(4)(*a*) and (5) respectively so that they apply in any case where 1A and 1B apply and not just where there is a relevant effect.

Paragraph 4 introduces similar rules for the complex partnership provisions of the SFA rules.

Paragraph 5 is a consequential amendment that extends the meaning of "relevant person".

Paragraph 6 amends 774G(3) as follows:

- 774G(3)(*a*) is extended so that a person is treated as receiving an asset if there is a discharge in whole or part of any liability or there is an actual receipt of an asset. Thus ensuring that the conditions required in sections 774A (2)(*a*), 774C (2)(*c*) and (4)(*b*) are met in such cases.
- 774G(3)(*c*) is extended to include cases where payments are received in respect of any security that is substituted for the original security.
- Sub-paragraph (4) of 774G states that for the purposes of the SFA rules in determining whether an amount is to be recorded as a financial liability in respect of any asset it must be assumed that the period of account in which the asset is received ended immediately after the receipt of the asset.

Commencement

The commencement rules are covered in para 7. The paragraph states that the new rules apply to "any arrangements whenever made" but then goes on to limit their application with regard to arrangements made before 6 March 2007 to amounts arising on or after that date. The paragraph also provides that for the purposes of Chapter 2 of Part 4 of FA 1996 a new period of account is deemed to begin on

6 March 2007 with a value being equal to the notional carrying value of the liability, carrying value having the same meaning as for the purposes of para 19A of sch 19 FA 1996.

Paragraph 8 deals with the TCGA 1992 implications by amending s 263E of that Act. Under this section if an SFA is caught by the anti avoidance rules it is ignored for TCGA 1992 purposes if one of two conditions is met:

— Condition A is that the person making the disposal subsequently reacquires the same asset under the arrangement.

— Condition B is that the asset subsequently ceases to exist and until that time the asset was held by the lender (or a person connected to the lender).

Condition A is amended so that it refers to the person making the disposal as having "the right or obligation to acquire the asset disposed of (whether or not this is subject to conditions)."

Condition B is amended so that the condition is that the asset will cease to exist without having been reacquired (but in circumstances that it is intended to be held by the lender or person connected with the lender from the time of the disposal until that time).

In both cases the emphasis shifts from a review of the facts to consideration of the terms of arrangement.

Paragraph 4 introduces a new s 263E(4) that is intended to ensure that it is not necessary to wait until the end of the arrangements before the consequences of a failure of the arrangements is felt. It does this by providing that if at any time it becomes apparent that the person making the disposal will not reacquire the asset or that the asset will not be held by a connected person until it ceases to exist, then the borrower will be treated as having made a disposal of the asset at market value at that time.

These provisions have effect in respect of disposals on or after 6 March 2007 but may also be applied earlier than that if a claim to that effect is made.

Manufactured payments (para 9)

Schedule 23A TA 1988 restricts the deduction in respect of manufactured payments where the manufactured payment is considered to have been made for an unallowable purpose (broadly for the purposes of tax avoidance). This rule only applies to manufactured payments and by virtue of para 7(1) Sch 23A certain payments which are deemed to be fees (e g where the amount paid exceeds the amount of underlying dividend to which it relates) do not fall within these provisions. This legislation seeks to prevent schemes which exploit this feature by including such fees within the ambit of the unallowable purpose test. This is achieved by inserting a new para 7A(10)(*d*) which specifically includes the payments referred to in para 7(1).

Commencement

The provisions apply in relation to payments made or treated as made on or after 6 December 2006. However this is subject to the rules regarding "old arrangements" and "old taxable income or gains arising or accruing". These relate to arrangements made before 6 December 2006 and provide that taxable income and gains accruing or arising before that date do not fall within the new rules.

Options and Groups (para 10)

The provisions introduced by para 10 are further anti avoidance measures designed to counter exploitation of the interaction of the rules regarding options and those relating to intra-group disposals. This is done by introducing a new exception to the standard rule that intra-group disposals produce neither a chargeable gain nor an allowable loss. A new para (*db*) is introduced to s 171(2) TCGA 1992. This excludes disposals between group companies of options which were entered into when the companies involved were not members of the same group.

Commencement

The amendment has effect in relation to cases where the option is exercised on or after 6 March 2007 (whenever the option was granted).

Loan relationships: amounts not fully recognised for accounting purposes (para 11)

FA 1996 s 85C operates to ensure that where a company is a party to a loan relationship under which GAAP requires or permits matching as a result of which income is not recognised such matching does not apply for tax purposes. Included within the circumstances that might lead to the operation of this section is that the company has issued share capital "which falls to be treated for accounting purposes as a liability". The proposed amendment substitutes an extended concept namely "a relevant capital contribution" which can include share capital but is not restricted to it and which also dispenses with the references to a liability.

Commencement

These amendments apply in relation to periods of account ending on or after 9 May 2007 but where an accounting period begins before that date then the amounts to be brought into account are those which relate to any time on or after that date.

Shares treated as loan relationships – amendments to s 91A FA 1996 (para 12)

FA 1996 s 91A was introduced by F(No2)A 2005 as an anti-avoidance measure. Its intention was to draw into the loan relationship regime certain shares that generated an interest like return. This section dealt particularly with shares that were subject to an outstanding third party obligation.

The proposed amendments clarify the wording of s 91A(4) by making it clear that this subsection covers both debits and credits and not just debits. Section 91A(4) is intended to ensure that transactions which would have the effect of causing the value of the shares not to move in an interest like way are ignored for the purposes of this legislation.

This measure also includes a clause specifically excluding building society shares from being included in the definition of shares. This is a consequential amendment which flows from the

changes to the definition of shares in s 103(1) made by para 13 (see comments below).

Commencement

The amendment has effect in relation to accounting periods ended on or after 6 March 2007, but only amounts relating to any time on or after that date are to be brought into account.

Shares treated as loan relationships – amendments to s 91B FA 1996 (para 13)

The changes in para 13 are parallel to the changes in para 12. Section 91B FA 1996 was designed to counter arrangements which generated an interest like return from shares but covered different arrangements to those dealt with in s 91A FA 1996. The proposed amendments clarify the wording of s 91B(4) by making it clear that this sub-section covers both debits and credits and not just debits. Section 91B(4) is intended to ensure that transactions which would have the effect of causing the value of the shares not to move in an interest like way are ignored for the purposes of this legislation.

Commencement

The amendment has effect in relation to accounting periods ended on or after 6 March 2007, but only amounts relating to any time on or after that date are to be brought into account.

Shares treated as loan relationships – meaning of shares (para 14)

This paragraph excludes the definition of shares found in s 103(1) FA 1996 from applying in the context of FA 1996 ss 91A–G .

HMRC have stated that the changes to the definition of shares in the context of ss 91A to 91G were anti avoidance in nature. It was deemed necessary to remove ss 91A to 91G from the ambit of s 103(1) because that section defined shares in the following terms "any share in the company under which an entitlement to receive distributions may arise". Taken together with the definition of distribution found in TA 1988 s 209 this meant that certain shares, issued on terms that no distribution could be paid except on winding up, were excluded from the operation of s 91A to 91G.

These changes to the wording of FA 1996 s 103 have led to consequential amendments to FA 1996 s 91A and 91B under which Building Society Shares are excluded from the definition of shares for the purposes of these sections.

Commencement

The changes have effect in respect of shares held on or after 6th March 2007.

Exchange gains and losses where loan not at arms length (para 15)

This paragraph introduces a new subsection to FA 1996 Sch 9 para 11A. This is an anti avoidance section designed to counter abuse of the treatment of exchange differences and in particular claims available under paragraph 6D.

The scheme referred to in the HMRC notes involves a series of currency denominated loans which whilst originating externally includes an intra group loan which is also subject to an intra group guarantee. The operation of 6D before these amendments meant that it was possible to claim a deduction in respect of the guarantee when there was a loss but to leave gains out of account by simply failing to make a claim.

To counter this form of scheme a new sub-para 7 is introduced to para 11A. This deems a claim under paragraph 6D to have been made. The definition of "connection" for these purposes will be that found in s 87(3) and (4) FA 1996.

The proposed new measures also introduce, in new paras 9 and 10, provisions to ensure that in cases where there is more than one guarantor that the amount of debtor exchange gains or losses claimed cannot exceed the total creditor gains or losses in the respect of the underlying loan.

Commencement

The new measures take effect in relation to loan relationships of any company in accounting periods ending on or after 6 December 2006. There does not appear to be any provision that limits the application to debtor or creditor accruals arising after that date, so to that extent this measure has a retrospective impact. However no adjustment is required if the company ceases to be a party to the loan relationship before 6th December 2006.

Loan relationships and collective investments schemes (para 16)

These provisions introduce an amendment to FA 1996 Sch 10 para 4. Paragraph 4 covers investments in collective investment schemes and lays down rules whereby such investments will fall to be treated as loan relationships. The rules relate to the investments of the underlying collective investment scheme and broadly imposed a 60% limit in respect of interest bearing and similar securities ("qualifying investments" as defined by para 8). Thus if the market value of these investments exceeded 60% of the scheme's total investments then the company's investment in that scheme was to be treated as falling within the loan relationship regime.

The new measures are designed to counter efforts to manipulate the calculation of the percentage holding of "qualifying investments". The rules stipulate that an investment or liability will be left out of account where the investment was made or the liability incurred with the "relevant avoidance intention" or there are transactions in respect of the investment that have that intention. The "relevant avoidance intention" is defined in terms of "eliminating or reducing the credits" or "creating or increasing the debits" brought into account for the purposes of that chapter.

Commencement

It should be noted that due to the introduction of a late amendment to FA 2007 the commencement dates vary between the treatment of investments and liabilities. The amendments in respect of investments apply in relation to accounting periods ending on or after 6 March 2007 but only apply in respect of movements on or after that date. The amendments that relate to liabilities have effect in respect of accounting periods ending on or after 9 May 2007 and similarly only apply in respect of movements after that date.

Plant or machinery subject to a lease and finance lease back (para 17)

This paragraph introduces anti avoidance provisions which have the effect that CAA 2001 s 228D no longer apply to lease and finance leaseback transactions. It is intended that these measures will discourage use of schemes involving pre payments of rent and exploitation of the restriction on the taxable amount of gross earnings under the sub-lease.

Commencement

The provision includes detailed commencement rules which have the effect of ensuring that the amendments only apply to "post commencement rentals" which impact on income or profits of a "post commencement period of account". For these purposes the "post commencement rentals" are those which are receivable in respect of periods beginning on or after 6 December 2006. Where there is a straddle period then it is the appropriate proportion. A post commencement period of account is any period of account ending on or after 6 December 2006. Post commencement rentals do not include any amount received before 6 December 2006.

Derivative contracts: contracts treated for accounting purposes as a financial asset or liability (para 18)

This provision introduces a new sub-paragraph (1A) to FA 2002 Sch 26 para 17A. The change deals with the application of fair value accounting to derivatives and is designed to ensure that fair value accounting will apply to futures contracts even where there is a large pre-payment element (Such contracts are accounted for as "financial assets" because of the pre-payment element). This is achieved by stating that the amounts to be brought into account in respect of contracts falling within the description found in para 3(1)(b) of Sch 26 must be determined on the basis of fair value accounting.

Commencement

The changes come into effect in relation to periods of account ending on or after 6 March 2007. For accounting periods beginning before that date the fair value of the derivative contract at the beginning of the period is to be taken as the "carrying value" of the contract, as defined in Sch 26 para 50A, recognised for accounting purposes at the beginning of that period.

Derivatives contracts: transfers of value to connected parties (para 19)

This anti avoidance measure introduces amendments designed to tighten up the application of FA 2002 Sch 26 para 26. Paragraph 26 deals with the situation where an option between two connected parties is allowed to expire. The original provisions were intended to ensure that where there is a transfer of value between connected parties that a corresponding credit is brought into account to counteract the debit arising as a result of the expiry.

The new measures are designed to ensure that the rules apply even where there has been a partial exercise of rights so that arguably the option cannot be said to have expired. Thus where the option has only been partially exercised para 26 will still apply to the extent that the option has not been exercised.

Commencement

These amendments have effect in relation to any failure to exercise in full the rights under an option occurring on or after 6 March 2007.

SCHEDULE 6

COMPANIES CARRYING ON BUSINESS OF LEASING PLANT OR MACHINERY

Section 31

Company reconstructions without change of ownership

1— (1) In section 343 of ICTA (company reconstructions without change of ownership), in subsection (2) (continuity of treatment for capital allowances), insert at the end "and are subject to section 343A (company reconstructions involving business of leasing plant or machinery)".

(2) After that section insert—

"343A Company reconstructions involving business of leasing plant or machinery

(1) This section applies if the trade is or forms part of a business of leasing plant or machinery which the predecessor or the successor carries on on the day of cessation.

(2) If, on the day of cessation, both the predecessor and the successor carry on the trade otherwise than in partnership, section 343(2) does not apply unless—

(*a*) the principal company or companies of the predecessor immediately before the cessation are the same as the principal company or companies of the successor immediately afterwards, and

(*b*) if any such principal company is a consortium principal company, the relevant fraction in relation to the predecessor immediately before the cessation is the same as the relevant fraction in relation to the successor immediately afterwards (irrespective of whether the members of each consortium are the same).

(3) If, on the day of cessation, the predecessor or the successor carries on the trade in partnership, section 343(2) does not apply unless—

(*a*) the predecessor ceases to carry on the whole of its trade, and

(*b*) that trade is a business of leasing plant or machinery which the predecessor carries on in partnership on the day of cessation.

(4) In any case where section 343(2) does not apply as a result of this section, the plant or machinery belonging to the trade shall be treated for the purposes of the Corporation Tax Acts as sold by the predecessor to the successor on the day of the cessation for an amount equal to its market value as at that day.

(5) In this section—

"business of leasing plant or machinery"—

(*a*) has the same meaning as in Part 2 of Schedule 10 to the Finance Act 2006 (sale etc of lessor companies etc) (if the business is carried on otherwise than in partnership), and

(*b*) has the same meaning as in Part 3 of that Schedule (if the business is carried on in partnership),

"consortium principal company" means a company which is a principal company as a result of paragraph 12 of that Schedule,

"market value", in relation to plant or machinery, is to be construed in accordance with paragraph 41(8) of that Schedule,

"plant or machinery" has the same meaning as in Part 2 of the Capital Allowances Act,

"principal company" is to be construed in accordance with paragraph 11 or (as the case may be) 12 of Schedule 10 to the Finance Act 2006, and

"relevant fraction" has the same meaning as in paragraph 12 of that Schedule."

(3) Subsection (2) of section 343A of ICTA (as inserted by sub-paragraph (2) above) has effect in relation to cessations occurring on or after 22nd November 2006.

(4) But, if the cessation occurs before 21st March 2007, that subsection has effect as if for paragraphs (*a*) and (*b*) there were substituted "on that day each company which is a principal company of the predecessor is also a principal company of the successor".

(5) Subsection (3) of section 343A of ICTA has effect in relation to cessations occurring on or after that date.

Sale etc of lessor companies etc

2— (1) Schedule 10 to FA 2006 (sale etc of lessor companies etc) is amended as follows.

(2) In paragraph 1(4) (contents of Schedule), for "an anti-avoidance provision" substitute "anti-avoidance provisions".

(3) In—

(*a*) paragraph 7(3)(*b*) (provision for the purposes of condition A in paragraph 6), and

(*b*) paragraph 17(2)(*b*) (meaning of "PM" in paragraph 16),

for "it transfers" substitute "is transferred".

(4) After paragraph 38 insert—

"38A— (1) This paragraph applies if—

(*a*) a question arises as to the application of this Schedule,

(*b*) for the purpose of determining that question regard must be had to amounts (if any) which fall (or would fall) to be shown in any balance sheet of any company in respect of plant or machinery, (*c*) there would (but for this paragraph) be a reduction or increase in any such amount,

(*d*) the reduction or increase arises directly or indirectly in consequence of, or otherwise in connection with, any arrangements, and

(*e*) the main purpose, or one of the main purposes, of the arrangements is to secure that there is a relevant tax advantage.

(2) There is a relevant tax advantage if (but for this paragraph)—

(*a*) any company would not be regarded for the purposes of any provision of this Schedule as carrying on a business of leasing plant or machinery (whether alone or in partnership),

(*b*) the amount of any income which any company is treated as receiving under any provision of this Schedule would be reduced, or

(*c*) the amount of any expense which any company is treated as incurring under any provision of this Schedule would be increased.

(3) For the purpose of determining any question which arises as to the application of this Schedule, the reduction or increase in the amount which falls (or would fall) to be shown in the balance sheet in respect of plant or machinery is to be ignored.

(4) For the purposes of this paragraph and paragraph 38B a question arises as to the application of this Schedule if a question arises—

(*a*) as to whether any company carries on a business of leasing plant or machinery (whether alone or in partnership) for the purposes of any provision of this Schedule, or

(*b*) as to the amount (if any) of any income or expense which any company is treated as receiving or incurring under any provision of this Schedule.

(5) In this paragraph—

"arrangements" includes any agreement, understanding, scheme, transaction or series of transactions—

(*a*) whether or not legally enforceable, and

(*b*) whether or not the company for which the relevant tax advantage is intended to be secured is a party to the arrangements,

"increase" includes an increase from nil, and

"reduction" includes a reduction to nil.

38B— (1) This paragraph applies if—

(*a*) a company owns any plant or machinery at any time on any day ("the relevant day"),

(*b*) a question arises as to the application of this Schedule,

(*c*) for the purpose of determining that question regard must be had to the amount (if any) which falls (or would fall) to be shown in any balance sheet of the company in respect of the plant or machinery, and

(*d*) condition A or B is met.

(2) Condition A is met if there would (but for this paragraph) be no amount which would fall to be shown in the balance sheet of the company in respect of the plant or machinery.

(3) Condition B is met if the amount which (but for this paragraph) would fall to be shown in the balance sheet of the company in respect of the plant or machinery is less than the amount which, on the relevant assumption, would fall to be so shown.

(4) For the purpose of determining any question which arises as to the application of this Schedule, the amount which falls (or would fall) to be shown in any balance sheet of the company in respect of the plant or machinery is to be determined on the relevant assumption (as well as on the other assumptions applicable under other provisions of this Schedule).

(5) The relevant assumption is that the company has no liabilities of any kind at any time on that day.

(6) For this purpose "liabilities" includes any share capital issued by the company which falls to be treated for accounting purposes as a liability."

(5) For the purposes of Schedule 10 to FA 2006 the amendments made by sub-paragraphs (3) and (4) have effect in relation to—

(*a*) any qualifying change of ownership in relation to a company which occurs on or after 22nd November 2006, and

(*b*) any qualifying change in a company's interest in a business which occurs on or after that date.

(6) For all other purposes those amendments have effect for the purpose of determining whether a company carries on a business of leasing plant or machinery (whether alone or in partnership) on or after that date.

GENERAL NOTE

Schedule 6 contains anti-avoidance provisions which apply to companies carrying on a business of leasing plant or machinery. In particular, it seeks to prevent the undermining of legislation introduced in FA 2006 aimed at countering tax avoidance involving the sale of companies that lease out assets.

Prior to that legislation, it had been possible for a leasing company to be used to generate what was seen as an unacceptable permanent deferral of tax. This most commonly took the form of a leasing company using capital allowances to generate loses in its early years (those losses being group relieved), before being sold to a loss-making group just as the reduced level of capital allowances meant that it was becoming profitable. Those later profits were then covered by losses surrendered by the new group.

Despite the provisions of FA 2006, it was perceived that tax was being avoided by schemes that sought to exploit a mismatch between different concepts of control in order to transfer assets without tax effect, and also by schemes which manipulated the accounting value of leased assets.

Company reconstruction without a change in ownership

Paragraphs 3 to 9 amend TA 1988 s 343(2) where a leasing company is involved. TA 1988 s 343(2) provides that, upon a company reconstruction not involving a change in ownership, the transfer of any assets between companies will be regarded for capital allowances purposes as a transfer at tax written-down value. There is therefore no exposure to a balancing charge, or the possibility of a balancing allowance.

Sub-paragraph (2) inserts a new TA 1988 s 343A, to be applied in cases involving the leasing of machinery or plant. In such cases, rather than the plant being deemed to be transferred at written-down value, it is in effect deemed to be sold (and reacquired) at its market value on the day of transfer. This addresses schemes which sought to exploit a difference in the definition of control between TA 1988 s 343 and FA 2006 Schedule 10. Henceforth a company cannot enjoy the tax neutrality afforded by TA 1988 s 343 if it transfers assets to another company outside the group defined by FA 2006 Schedule 10.

The effect in such circumstances is therefore that a balancing charge may arise equal to the difference between market value and tax written-value, effectively clawing back any capital allowances given in excess of the actual fall (if any) in economic value.

Sale of lessor companies

Paragraphs 10 to 28 amend TA 1988 s 343 to disregard adjustments to the balance sheet values of plant or machinery where the adjustments arise from entering into arrangements that affect the application of FA 2006 Sch 10.

This prevents groups from artificially reducing income or increasing expenditure computed under Schedule 10, or from avoiding Sch 10 altogether by manipulating the outcome of the test which establishes whether a company is carrying on a business of leasing plant or machinery.

SCHEDULE 7

INSURANCE BUSINESS: GROSS ROLL-UP BUSINESS ETC

Section 38

PART 1

AMENDMENTS

Taxes Management Act 1970 (c 9)

1 In section 98 of TMA 1970 (special returns etc), in the Table, omit the entries relating to section 333B of ICTA.

Income and Corporation Taxes Act 1988 (c 1)

2 ICTA is amended as follows.

3— (1) Section 76 (expenses of insurance companies) is amended as follows.

(2) In subsection (1), omit the second sentence.

(3) In subsection (7), in Step 5—

(*a*) for "sum ("amount S") of the amounts" substitute "amount ("amount S")", and
(*b*) for "436 or 439B" substitute "436A".

(4) Omit subsection (14).

(5) In subsection (15), omit the definition of "capital redemption business".

4 Omit section 333B (involvement of insurance companies with plans and accounts).

5 In section 403E (relief for overseas losses of UK resident companies), omit subsection (3).

GENERAL NOTE

Many of the amendments introduced by Sch 7 are to make the existing provisions of the life tax code fit the new gross roll up regime. Paras 1–5 and 7 make consequential amendments to various parts of the legislation to reflect the new single tax category.

6— (1) Section 431 (interpretative provisions relating to insurance companies) is amended as follows.

(2) In subsection (2), insert at the appropriate places—

""child trust fund business" has the meaning given by section 431BA;",

""foreign currency assets", in relation to an insurance company and any time during a period of account, means assets, other than assets linked to gross roll-up business, which—

(*a*) are at that time managed under the control of a person whose normal place of work is at a permanent establishment outside the United Kingdom at or through which the company carries on gross roll-up business; or

(*b*) are denominated in a foreign currency and specified in a certificate given by a director of the company no later than three months after the end of the period of account as being all of the assets of the company's long-term insurance fund which are held at that time during the period of account to enable the company to meet liabilities of its gross roll-up business which are denominated in that currency;",

""gross roll-up business" has the meaning given by section 431EA;",

""immediate needs annuities business" means business which consists of the effecting or carrying out of immediate needs annuities (within the meaning of section 725 of ITTOIA 2005);",

""individual savings account business" has the meaning given by section 431BB;", and

""PHI business" means long-term business other than life assurance business (including the reinsurance of such long-term business);".

(3) In subsection (2), omit the definitions of—

(*a*) "annuity business", and
(*b*) "overseas life assurance fund".

(4) In subsection (2), for the definition of "life assurance business" substitute—

""life assurance business" means business which—

(*a*) consists of the effecting or carrying out of contracts of insurance which fall within paragraph I, II, III or VII(*b*) of Schedule 1 to the Financial Services and Markets Act 2000 (Regulated Activities) Order 2001, or

(*b*) is capital redemption business,

other than immediate needs annuities business;".

(5) In subsection (2), for the definition of "reinsurance business" substitute—

""reinsurance" includes retrocession;".

(6) After subsection (2ZE) insert—

"(2ZF) In this Chapter "capital redemption business" means any business of a company carrying on insurance business in so far as it consists of the effecting on the basis of actuarial calculations, and the carrying out, of contracts under which, in return for one or more fixed payments, a sum or series of sums of a specified amount become payable at a future time or over a period."

GENERAL NOTE

Paragraph 6 adds definitions to the statutory library of definitions in TA 1988 s 431(2). One of the benefits of the legislative changes coming from the consultation process has been a general tidying up of the legislation and a centralising of definitions and key concepts (see Sch 10 below). Paragraph 6 also amends some existing definitions to tie them in with the new regime.

One key change in the definitions is to that of life assurance itself which previously had been unclear. It is now defined in terms of the classes of business set out in FSA regulations together with capital redemption business but specifically excludes immediate needs annuities which remain taxed as PHI. This change ought to remove such doubt as previously existed and may be viewed as part of the ongoing closer linking of the tax regime to the regulatory environment. Although this is generally welcome, it does introduce uncertainties of its own because the FSA does on occasion use tax definitions to drive its own regulations. There is therefore the potential for some circularity.

Foreign currency assets are a new concept and are intended to replace the overseas life assurance fund ("OLAF") that is abolished now that OLAB is taxed as part of the amalgamated gross roll up category. Agreeing on the precise the mechanism for replacing the OLAF was one of the more difficult parts of the consultation exercise on amalgamating the categories and the final wording was not agreed until late in the day. The first part of the definition in sub-para (a) shares much in common with the previous concept but the second part is new and it is still not clear that it works as intended. In particular the relationship between the point in time for which the certificate is given and the actual period during which the assets need to be held to meet gross roll up liabilities is unclear. The three month deadline is stretching and may give rise to compliance difficulties. In broad terms however the effect of the legislation is that foreign currency assets are treated as though they were linked assets so that the income and gains arising on them are apportioned wholly to gross roll up business as discussed under para 13 below.

A statutory definition of PHI is now included to cover all categories of long-term business that are not life insurance business. In practice this will cover all of the remaining categories that a UK company is allowed to write.

Finally it is now made clear that capital redemption business is included in the statutory definition of life insurance business notwithstanding the fact that because it is not dependent on human mortality, it does not meet the accepted definition of life insurance business and is not so classified by the FSA.

7 In section 431A(3)(*a*) (power to amend), omit "and Schedule 19AA".

8 After section 431B insert—

"431BA Meaning of "child trust fund business"

(1) In this Chapter "child trust fund business" means so much of a company's life assurance business as is referable to child trust fund policies (but not including the reinsurance of such business).

(2) In this section "child trust fund policy" means a policy of life insurance which is an investment under a child trust fund (within the meaning of the Child Trust Funds Act 2004).

431BB Meaning of "individual savings account business"

(1) In this Chapter "individual savings account business" means so much of a company's life assurance business as is referable to individual savings account policies (but not including the reinsurance of such business).

(2) In this section "individual savings account policy" means a policy of life insurance which is an investment of a kind specified in regulations made by virtue of section 695(1) of ITTOIA 2005."

GENERAL NOTE

Paragraph 8 introduces two new sections defining child trust fund business and ISA business. Previously these two tax categories (they are not recognised by the FSA as regulator as separate classes of business) were defined in regulations which will no longer apply. In both cases, reinsurance of this business is treated as life reinsurance business which is different to the previous treatment under which reinsurance was generally treated as belonging to the same category as the business reinsured.

9— (1) Section 431D (meaning of "overseas life assurance business") is amended as follows.

(2) For subsection (1) substitute—

"(1) In this Chapter "overseas life assurance business" means so much of a company's relevant life assurance business as is with a policy holder or annuitant not residing in the United Kingdom (but not including the reinsurance of such business).

(1A) In subsection (1) above "relevant life assurance business" means life assurance business other than—

(*a*) pension business
(*b*) individual savings account business,
(*c*) child trust fund business, and
(*d*) business of any description prescribed by regulations made by the Commissioners for Her Majesty's Revenue and Customs."

(3) In subsections (2) and (4), for "(1)" substitute "(1A)".

(4) In subsection (4), insert at the end "(including provision amending any enactment or any instrument made under an enactment)".

GENERAL NOTE

Paragraph 9 amends the definition of overseas life assurance business. It remains defined by exclusion but the doubt over whether reinsured overseas business is itself overseas life assurance business is now resolved by making it clear that the category does not include reinsurance of overseas business. Previously it was possible to elect certain overseas business out of life reinsurance business, this will no longer be possible. The OLAB compliance regulations will be amended accordingly. It is also proposed to repeal TA 1988 s 441B which deems UK land linked to overseas business to be BLAGAB. The effect of that section will be maintained by amending the excluded business regulations (SI 2000/2089) to take such business outside the definition of OLAB.

10 After section 431E insert—

"431EA Meaning of "gross roll-up business"

In this Chapter "gross roll-up business" means business of any of the following kinds—

(*a*) pension business;
(*b*) child trust fund business;
(*c*) individual savings account business;
(*d*) life reinsurance business; and
(*e*) overseas life assurance business."

GENERAL NOTE

Paragraph 10 introduces the definition of gross roll up business and defines it by reference to the five categories previously taxed on similar but separate bases: pension business, overseas life assurance business, life reinsurance business, ISA business and child trust fund business.

11 In section 431F (meaning of "basic life assurance and general annuity business"), for the words from "(including" to the end substitute "other than gross roll-up business".

12 In section 432ZA(7) (linked assets), for "long-term business other than life assurance" (in both places) substitute "PHI".

GENERAL NOTE

Paragraphs 11 and 12 make further consequential amendments to accommodate the change of basis. In particular BLAGAB is now any business that is not gross roll up business, including any reinsured BLAGAB which is excluded from being life reinsurance business by regulations.

13— (1) Section 432A (apportionment of income and gains) is amended as follows.

(2) In subsection (1A), for "shall be" substitute "is".

(3) In subsection (2), for paragraphs (*a*) to (*f*) substitute—

"(*a*) basic life assurance and general annuity business,
(*b*) gross roll-up business, and
(*c*) PHI business."

(4) In subsection (3), for "(apart from overseas life assurance business) shall be" substitute "is".

(5) Omit subsection (4).

(6) Before subsection (5) insert—

"(4A) Income arising from, and gains or losses accruing on the disposal of, foreign currency assets is referable to gross roll-up business."

(7) In subsection (5)—

(*a*) for "shall be" substitute "is", and
(*b*) omit "(apart from overseas life assurance business)".

(8) For subsections (6) to (6AA) substitute—

"(6) For the purposes of subsection (5) above "the relevant fraction", in relation to basic life assurance and general annuity business, is—

$$\frac{A}{A + B + C}$$

where—

A is the aggregate of—

(*a*) the mean of the opening and closing liabilities of the basic life assurance and general annuity business (but taking that mean to be nil if it would otherwise be below nil), reduced (but not below nil) by the mean of the opening and closing net values of any assets directly referable to that category of business,
(*b*) if there has been a relevant reattribution, the mean of the opening and closing amounts of the shareholders' excess assets, and
(*c*) the mean of the appropriate parts (that is, the parts relating to that category) of the opening and closing amounts of the free assets amounts;

B is the aggregate of—

(*a*) the mean of the opening and closing liabilities of the gross roll-up business (but taking that mean to be nil if it would otherwise be below nil), reduced (but not below nil) by the mean of the opening and closing net values of any assets directly referable to that category of business, and
(*b*) the mean of the appropriate parts (that is, the parts relating to that category) of the opening and closing amounts of the free assets amounts; and

C is the aggregate of—

(*a*) the mean of the opening and closing liabilities of the PHI business (but taking that mean to be nil if it would otherwise be below nil), reduced (but not below nil) by the mean of the opening and closing net values of any assets directly referable to that category of business, and
(*b*) the mean of the appropriate parts (that is, the parts relating to that category) of the opening and closing amounts of the free assets amounts.

(6A) For the purposes of subsection (5) above "the relevant fraction", in relation to gross roll-up business, is—

$$\frac{B}{A + B + C}$$

where A, B and C have the same meaning as in subsection (6) above.

(6B) For the purposes of subsection (5) above "the relevant fraction", in relation to PHI business, is—

$$\frac{C}{A + B + C}$$

where A, B and C have the same meaning as in subsection (6) above.

(6C) But if the denominator found in accordance with subsection (6), (6A) or (6B) above is nil, the relevant fraction for the purposes of subsection (5) above in relation to the category of business in question is such fraction as is just and reasonable."

(9) In subsection (7)—

(*a*) for "and (6A)" substitute ", (6A) and (6B)",
(*b*) in paragraph (*a*), for "(4)" substitute "(4A)",
(*c*) in paragraph (*b*), after "(3)" insert "or (4A)", and
(*d*) in paragraph (*c*), omit "438B,".

(10) In subsection (8), for "subsections (6) and (6A)" substitute "subsection (6)".

(11) In subsection (8ZA), for "subsections (6) and (6A)" substitute "paragraph (*c*) of the definition of A and paragraph (*b*) of the definitions of B and C in subsection (6)".

(12) Omit subsection (9).

GENERAL NOTE

Paragraph 13 makes the necessary changes to TA 1988 s 432A to deal with the reduction in the number of categories of business. It was always to be expected that the apportionment rules would require considerable change but the result is actually a simplification on what went before, the use of fractions in the legislation being particularly helpful in providing clarity. It is important to note that the underlying principles of apportionment have not changed, merely some of the terminology. The amalgamation has also allowed the repeal of redundant material eg that relating to income and gains from the OLAF. Instead income and gains from foreign currency assets (the replacement for the OLAF) are now apportioned directly to the gross roll up category.

14— (1) Section 432AA (Schedule A business or overseas property business) is amended as follows.

(2) Omit subsection (3).

(3) In subsection (4), for paragraphs (*a*) to (*d*) substitute—

"(*a*) basic life assurance and general annuity business;
(*b*) gross roll-up business; and
(*c*) PHI business."

(4) In subsection (5), omit "(3) or".

15 In section 432AB (losses from Schedule A business or overseas property business), omit subsection (6).

GENERAL NOTE

Paragraphs 14 and 15 respectively make consequential amendments and repeal a redundant provision to accommodate the change of basis.

16— (1) Section 432B (apportionment of receipts brought into account) is amended as follows.

(2) In subsection (1)—

(*a*) for "432F" substitute "432G", and
(*b*) for "any category of life assurance business" substitute "gross roll-up business".

(3) In subsection (2), for "432F" substitute "432G".

(4) In subsection (3)—

(*a*) for "Sections 432C and 432D apply" substitute "Section 432C applies", and
(*b*) insert at the end "(and section 432G applies in either case)".

(5) In subsection (4)—

(*a*) for "sections 432C and 432D" substitute "section 432C",
(*b*) in paragraph (*a*), for "apply" substitute "applies", and
(*c*) omit paragraph (*b*) and the word "and" before it.

(6) In subsection (5)—

(*a*) for the words from "any category" to the end of paragraph (*b*) substitute "gross roll-up business", and (*b*) omit "the relevant fraction of".

(7) In subsection (6), for the words from "432D" to "annuity business" substitute "432C to gross roll-up business".

(8) In subsection (7), omit "the relevant fraction of" (in both places).

(9) In subsection (8A), omit "the relevant fraction of".

(10) In subsection (8C), omit "the relevant fraction of".

(11) In subsection (9), omit the definitions of—

(*a*) "the relevant fraction", and
(*b*) "the section 83 net amount".

(12) In subsection (10)—

(*a*) in paragraphs (*a*) and (*b*), for "paragraph (*a*)(ii)" substitute "the definition of A, in paragraph (*b*)", and
(*b*) for paragraph (*c*) substitute—

"(*c*) the substitution for the definitions of B and C of—

"B is the amount that would be given by A if A applied in relation to gross roll-up business; and
C is the amount that would be given by A if A applied in relation to PHI business." ".

GENERAL NOTE

Paragraph 16 performs a similar function to para 13, applying instead to TA 1988 s 432B, modifying the rules for apportioning income and gains to the Case VI computation of profits on gross roll up business. Again the paragraph does not change the principle (with one important exception); rather it amends the law as it currently stands to make it work in the new regime.

The key difference with what has gone before is that TA 1988 s 432D has been repealed (see para 18 below) so references to that section and concepts associated with it are also repealed.

17 For section 432C substitute—

"432C Section 432B apportionment: non-participating funds

(1) This section specifies the extent to which the net amount is referable to life assurance business or to gross roll-up business.

(2) In this section "the net amount" means the aggregate of the amounts brought into account—

(*a*) as investment income,
(*b*) as an increase in the value of assets, or
(*c*) as other income,

less the aggregate of the amounts brought into account as a decrease in the value of assets.

(3) To the extent that the net amount is attributable to—

(*a*) assets linked to life assurance business, or
(*b*) foreign currency assets,

it is referable to life assurance business.

(4) There is also referable to life assurance business the appropriate fraction of so much of the net amount as is not attributable to linked assets or foreign currency assets.

(5) For the purposes of subsection (4) above "the appropriate fraction" is—

$$\frac{A}{A + B}$$

where—

A is the mean of the opening and closing liabilities of the relevant business so far as referable to life assurance business (but taking that mean to be nil if it would otherwise be below nil), reduced (but not below nil) by the aggregate of the mean of the opening and closing net values of assets linked to the relevant business so far as so referable and foreign currency assets; and

B is the mean of the opening and closing liabilities of the relevant business so far as referable to PHI business, reduced (but not below nil) by the mean of the opening and closing net values of any assets linked to PHI business.

(6) But if the denominator found in accordance with subsection (5) above is nil, the appropriate fraction for the purposes of subsection (4) above is such fraction as is just and reasonable.

(7) To the extent that the net amount is attributable to—

(*a*) assets linked to gross roll-up business, or
(*b*) foreign currency assets,

it is referable to gross roll-up business.

(8) There is also referable to gross roll-up business the relevant fraction of so much of the net amount as is not attributable to linked assets or foreign currency assets.

(9) For the purposes of subsection (8) above "the relevant fraction" is—

$$\frac{C}{C + D}$$

where—

C is the mean of the opening and closing liabilities of the relevant business so far as referable to gross roll-up business (but taking that mean to be nil if it would otherwise be below nil), reduced (but not below nil) by the aggregate of the mean of the opening and closing net values of any assets linked to gross roll-up business and foreign currency assets; and

D is the mean of the opening and closing liabilities of the relevant business so far as referable to basic life assurance and general annuity business or PHI business (but taking that mean to be nil if it would otherwise be below nil), reduced (but not below nil) by the mean of the opening and closing net values of any assets linked to either of those categories of business.

(10) But if the denominator found in accordance with subsection (9) above is nil, the relevant fraction for the purposes of subsection (8) above is such fraction as is just and reasonable.

(11) For the purposes of this section, so much of the net amount—

(*a*) as is brought into account as other income in an internal linked fund of the company, and
(*b*) as is not attributable to assets of that fund,

is to be treated as linked to a category of business to the same extent as income attributable to an asset of the fund would, by virtue of section 432ZA, be referable to that category of business."

GENERAL NOTE

Paragraph 17 replaces TA 1988 s 432C in its entirety and provides new rules for apportioning income and gains although the broad principle remains the same as before. New TA 1988 s 432C prescribes a two step process for apportioning the company's income and gains, firstly between its life assurance business and its PHI business (for Case I purposes) and secondly between gross roll up business and other categories of business (for Case VI purposes). As in the previous version of the rules, apportionment fractions are based on the mean of liabilities reduced by the mean of linked assets.

As normal in an apportionment calculation, linked amounts are not apportioned but are taken straight to the relevant category as are amounts arising on foreign currency assets which go straight to gross roll up business given their quasi-linked status.

The new TA 1988 s 432C also provides rules for situations in which the calculation of the apportionment fractions gives rise to negative denominators. This was always a theoretical possibility before but following changes to the reserving rules introduced by the FSA in 2006 it is now possible to have negative liabilities (i.e. assets) on some classes of business so the situation may become more commonplace going forward. In such a situation, the apportionment will be made on a just and reasonable basis.

18 Omit section 432D (section 432B apportionment: value of non-participating funds).

GENERAL NOTE

Paragraph 18 repeals TA 1988 s 432D in its entirety. That section was previously required because of the OLAF. While income on OLAF assets could be included in the general apportionment rules in old TA 1988 s 432C, the special computational provisions applying to assets moving into the out of the OLAF did not allow a simple apportionment of asset value movements shown in the regulatory revenue account. Hence TA 1988 s 432D provided rules for apportioning those amounts. The abolition of the OLAF means that there is no longer any need to have separate computational rules.

19— (1) Section 432E (section 432B apportionment: participating funds) is amended as follows.

(2) For subsection (1) substitute—

"(1) The part of the net amount which is referable to life assurance business or to gross roll-up business is—

(*a*) the amount determined in accordance with subsections (2) and (2A) below, or

(*b*) if greater, the amount determined in accordance with subsection (3) below.

(1A) In this section "the net amount" means the aggregate of the amounts brought into account—

(*a*) as investment income,

(*b*) as an increase in the value of assets, or

(*c*) as other income,

less the aggregate of the amounts brought into account as a decrease in the value of assets."

(3) In subsection (2)—

(*a*) in the definition of CAS, for "the category of business concerned" substitute "life assurance business or of gross roll-up business", and

(*b*) in the definition of CS, for "business of the category concerned" substitute "life assurance business or to gross roll-up business".

(4) In subsection (3)—

(*a*) in paragraph (*a*), after "that category of business" insert "and foreign currency assets", and

(*b*) in paragraph (*b*)—

(i) omit "mentioned in subsection (1) above", and

(ii) insert at the end "and foreign currency assets".

(5) In subsection (4), for the words following "case," substitute "is—

$$\frac{A}{B} \times 100$$

where—

A is so much of the net amount as is brought into account in respect of the relevant business less such part of it as is attributable to linked assets and foreign currency assets; and

B is the mean of the opening and closing liabilities of the relevant business reduced by the mean of the opening and closing values of any assets of the relevant business which are linked assets and foreign currency assets."

(6) In subsection (4A), after "linked assets" insert "or foreign currency assets".

(7) Omit subsections (5) and (6).

20 In section 432F(2) (section 432B apportionment: supplementary provisions)—

(*a*) omit "For each category of business in relation to which section 432E falls to be applied", and

(*b*) omit ", after making any reduction required by section 432E(5),".

GENERAL NOTE

Paragraphs 19 and 20 make the necessary changes to TA 1988 ss 432E and 432F to deal with the reduction in the number of categories of business and to make the wording of the former consistent with the revised wording of TA 1988 s 432C.

21 For section 432G substitute—

"432G Section 432B apportionment: business transfers-in

(1) There is referable to the life assurance business of the transferee the appropriate fraction of the amount brought into account as a business transfer-in and of any amount taken into account as profits under section 444ABD(1).

(2) For the purposes of subsection (1) above "the appropriate fraction" is—

$$\frac{LABL}{TL}$$

where—

LABL is the amount of the liabilities transferred that are referable to the life assurance business (but is nil if it would otherwise be below nil); and

TL is the whole of the liabilities transferred.

(3) But if the amount of the liabilities transferred is nil, the appropriate fraction for the purposes of subsection (1) above is such fraction as is just and reasonable.

(4) There is referable to the gross roll-up business of the transferee the relevant fraction of the amount brought into account as a business transfer-in and of any amount taken into account as profits under section 444ABD(1).

(5) For the purposes of subsection (4) above "the relevant fraction" is—

$$\frac{GRBL}{TL}$$

where—

GRBL is the amount of the liabilities transferred that are referable to the gross roll-up business (but is nil if it would otherwise be below nil); and

TL has the same meaning as in subsection (2) above.

(6) But if the amount of the liabilities transferred is nil, the relevant fraction for the purposes of subsection (4) above is such fraction as is just and reasonable."

GENERAL NOTE

Paragraph 21 replaces TA 1988 s 432G in its entirety and provides new rules for apportioning amounts received by the transferee under an insurance business transfer scheme. Like new TA 1988 s 432C, it follows a two step process for apportioning the amount shown as a business transfer in. The first step apportions the amount between life assurance business and other business in the ratio that the transferred liabilities of the former bear to the totality of liabilities transferred. The second step calculates what proportion of the amount transferred in relates to gross roll up business again using a simple ratio of liabilities, this time the fraction that gross roll up liabilities bear to total liabilities transferred. In both cases if the amount of liabilities is less than zero, the apportionment is to be performed on a just and reasonable basis although it is not clear what method might produce such a result.

22— (1) Section 434 (franked investment income etc) is amended as follows.

(2) For subsections (1) and (1B) substitute—

"(1) Where an insurance company makes a payment representative of a distribution made by a company resident in the United Kingdom in respect of an asset of its long-term insurance fund, the payment is to be taken into account in computing its profits in accordance with the provisions applicable to Case I of Schedule D unless the amount taken into account in accordance with section 83(2)(*a*) of the Finance Act 1989 includes the amount of the payment."

(3) Omit subsection (6A)(*b*).

GENERAL NOTE

Paragraph 22 amends TA 1988 s 434(1). In practice the subsection has been redundant since the enactment of FA 1989 s 83. Now the subsection is replaced by a new version that allows a life insurance company to claim a deduction for any manufactured dividend that it pays unless that payment has already been relieved by netting it off against the actual dividend received.

23— (1) Section 434A (computation of losses and limitation on relief) is amended as follows.

(2) In subsection (2)(*a*)—

(*a*) omit "the aggregate of", and

(*b*) omit sub-paragraph (iii).

(3) In subsection (2)(*b*), for the words following sub-paragraph (ii) substitute—

"any loss for that period under section 436A shall be reduced (but not below nil) by the total of the amounts set off as mentioned in sub-paragraphs (i) and (ii) above."

24 Omit section 436 (pension business: separate charge on profits).

GENERAL NOTE

Paragraphs 23 and 24 respectively make consequential amendments and repeal a redundant provision to accommodate the change of basis.

25 Before section 437 insert—

"436A Gross roll-up business: separate charge on profits

(1) Profits arising to an insurance company from gross roll-up business—

(*a*) are to be treated as income within Schedule D, and

(*b*) are chargeable under Case VI of that Schedule.

(2) For that purpose—

(*a*) the gross roll-up business is to be treated separately, and

(*b*) the profits from it are to be computed in accordance with the provisions of this Act applicable to Case I of Schedule D.

(3) In making that computation, sections 82 and 82B to 83AB of the Finance Act 1989 apply with the necessary modifications.

(4) If in any accounting period an insurance company incurs a loss, to be computed on the same basis as the profits, arising from its gross roll-up business—

(*a*) the loss must be set off against the amount of any profits chargeable under this section for any subsequent accounting period, and

(*b*) accordingly, the amount of the company's profits so charged in any such accounting period is to be treated as reduced by the amount of the loss or so much of that amount as cannot be relieved under this section against profits of an earlier accounting period.

(5) Section 396 does not apply to a loss incurred by an insurance company on its gross roll-up business.

(6) No loss to which section 396 applies may be set off under subsection (4) above against the amount of any profits chargeable under this section.

(7) This section does not apply in relation to an insurance company for an accounting period if the profits of its long-term business for the accounting period are charged to tax under Case I of Schedule D.

436B Gains referable to gross roll-up business not to be chargeable gains

(1) Gains referable to gross roll-up business are not chargeable gains.

(2) For the purposes of this section "gains referable to gross roll-up business" means gains which—

(*a*) accrue to an insurance company on the disposal by it of assets of its long-term insurance fund, and

(*b*) are referable (in accordance with section 432A) to gross roll-up business."

GENERAL NOTE

Paragraph 25 introduces TA 1988 s 436A, the charging section for the gross roll up category. Although this is a completely new section, its language is the same as that used by those sections that previously governed the charge to tax and computation of profits for the previous categories of pension business, life reinsurance business and overseas life assurance business. As such it remains familiar in concept and introduces no new issues to practitioners.

Paragraph 26 also inserts new TA 1988 s 436B which makes it clear that gains (and hence also losses) referable to gross roll up business by the action of TA 1988 s 432A are not chargeable gains (nor allowable losses). Again this new section does no more than repeat what was previously already explicit in statute.

26— (1) Section 438 (pension business: exemption from tax) is amended as follows.

(2) In subsection (1), for the words after "income" substitute "from assets solely linked to pension business."

(3) Omit subsections (2) and (4).

GENERAL NOTE

Paragraph 26 amends TA 1988 s 438 which previously gave the general exemption from tax for pension business. The original intention was to repeal this section in full but it was pointed out during the consultation process that companies used the explicit exemption from tax in making claims under various double taxation treaties, particularly that with the USA, for income to be paid gross of withholding taxes. HMRC therefore accepted that it was reasonable for the exemption to remain for companies writing linked pension business (which in practice were the only companies able to benefit from the treaty claims).

27 Omit section 438B (income or gains arising from property investment LLP).

28 Omit section 438C (determination of policy holders' share for purposes of s 438B).

GENERAL NOTE

Paragraphs 27 and 28 remove the previous statutory fiction that income and gains referable to pension business arising from investments in property LLPs were automatically referable to BLAGAB and could not benefit from the lower policy holders' rate of tax. This provision no longer applies to the amalgamated category of business in which pension business has no separate existence for corporation tax purposes.

29 Omit section 439 (restricted government securities).

30 Omit section 439B (life reinsurance business: separate charge on profits).

31— (1) Section 440 (transfers of assets etc) is amended as follows.

(2) In subsection (3), for "(*a*) to (*e*)" substitute "(*a*), (*d*) and (*e*)".

(3) In subsection (4), for paragraphs (*a*) to (*c*) substitute—

> "(*a*) assets which are linked solely to gross roll-up business or are foreign currency assets;",

and, in paragraph (*e*), for "any" substitute "either".

32 In section 440A(2) (securities)—

(*a*) in paragraph (*a*), for sub-paragraphs (i) to (iii) substitute—

> "(i) basic life assurance and general annuity business, or
> (ii) gross roll-up business,",

(*b*) omit paragraph (*c*), and

(*c*) in paragraph (*d*)—

(i) for "any of the preceding paragraphs" substitute "paragraph (*a*)", and

(ii) for "any of the descriptions mentioned in those paragraphs" substitute "the description mentioned in that paragraph".

33 In section 440B(4) (modifications where tax charged under Case I of Schedule D)—

(*a*) for "(*a*) to (*e*)" substitute "(*a*), (*d*) and (*e*)", and

(*b*) for the notionally substituted paragraph (*a*) substitute—

> "(*a*) so many of the securities as are included in the company's long-term insurance fund shall be treated for the purposes of corporation tax as a separate holding which is an asset of that fund, and".

34 Omit section 441 (overseas life assurance business).

35 In section 444A(3) (transfers of business)—

(*a*) for "436(3)(*c*) or 439B(3)(*c*)" substitute "436A(4)",

(*b*) omit paragraph (*b*) and the word "or" before it, and

(*c*) for "the same category of business as that in which it arose)" substitute "gross roll-up business)".

36— (1) Section 444AC (transfers of business: excess of assets or liabilities) is amended as follows.

(2) In subsection (2B)—

(*a*) for "each category of its life assurance business" substitute "its gross roll-up business",

(*b*) for "a category of the transferee's life assurance business" substitute "the transferee's gross roll-up business", and

(*c*) for "that category" substitute "gross roll-up business".

(3) In subsection (2D), for "a category of its life assurance business" substitute "its gross roll-up business".

(4) In subsection (10), in the definition of "the transferor's business", for paragraph (*b*) substitute—

"(*b*) its gross roll-up business."

37— (1) Section 444AF (demutualisation surplus: life assurance business) is amended as follows.

(2) In subsection (4)(*b*), for "sections 432C and 432D apply" substitute "section 432C applies".

(3) In subsection (5)(*b*), for "the profits of any category of the company's life assurance business chargeable to tax under Case VI of Schedule D" substitute "profits of the company chargeable under Case VI of Schedule D under section 436A (gross roll-up business)".

38— (1) Section 444AK (mutual surplus: Case VI categories of life assurance business) is amended as follows.

(2) In subsection (1), for paragraph (*b*) substitute—

"(*b*) the company carries on gross roll-up business."

(3) In subsection (3), for "any category of the company's life assurance business chargeable to tax under Case VI of Schedule D" substitute "the company's gross roll-up business".

(4) In subsection (5)(*b*), for "sections 432C and 432D apply" substitute "section 432C applies".

(5) The heading accordingly becomes "**Mutual surplus: gross roll-up business**".

GENERAL NOTE

Many of the amendments introduced by Schedule 7 are to make the existing provisions of the life tax code fit the new gross roll up regime. This has required all existing references to categories of business other than BLAGAB to be replaced with references to the new gross roll up category. Paragraphs 29 to 38 make the necessary changes to a wide range of legislative provisions, including the repeal of a number of now redundant provisions. Although there are many such changes, none ought to have any impact other than facilitating the preparation of the single tax computation required for the new category of business.

39 Omit sections 458 and 458A (capital redemption business).

GENERAL NOTE

Paragraph 39 removes the definition of capital redemption business as a separate category of business. The definition is now moved into the statutory library in TA 1988 s 431(2). The regulation making power in TA 1988 s 458A is no longer required now that capital redemption business is brought within the scope of the primary legislation and so it is repealed.

40 In section 460(2) (registered friendly societies: exemption from tax in respect of life or endowment business)—

(*a*) for "pension business" substitute "gross roll-up business",
(*b*) at the end of paragraph (*ca*), insert "and", and
(*c*) omit paragraph (*cb*).

41 In section 461 (registered friendly societies: other business), omit subsection (3A).

42 In section 461B (incorporated friendly societies), omit subsection (2A).

43— (1) Section 466 (interpretation of Chapter 2 of Part 12) is amended as follows.

(2) For subsection (1) substitute—

"(1) In this Chapter "life or endowment business" means, subject to subsections (1A) and (1B) below—

(*a*) any life assurance business, and
(*b*) any PHI business."

(3) In subsection (2)—

(*a*) omit the definition of "life assurance business", and
(*b*) insert the following definition at the appropriate place—
""gross roll-up business" shall be construed in accordance with section 431;".

(4) Omit subsections (2ZA), (2A) and (2B).

GENERAL NOTE

Paragraphs 40–43 make such consequential amendments as are necessary to the tax rules for friendly societies to accommodate the move to gross roll up business.

44 In section 502H(2)(*a*)(ii) and (4)(*b*) (insurance company as lessor), for "long-term business which is not life assurance" substitute "PHI".

45 In section 539(3) (life policies, life annuities and capital redemption policies), in the definition of "capital redemption policy", for "as defined in section 458(3)" substitute ", within the meaning of Chapter 1 of Part 12".

46— (1) Section 553B (overseas life assurance business: capital redemption policies) is amended as follows.

(2) In subsection (2), in the definition of "overseas policy", for "431D(1)(*a*)" substitute "431D(1)".

(3) In subsection (3), for the words from "after" to the end substitute "on or after 23rd March 1999".

47— (1) Section 755A (treatment of chargeable profits and creditable tax apportioned to company carrying on life assurance business) is amended as follows.

(2) In subsection (4), for the words after "referable to" substitute "gross roll-up business carried on by the UK company".

(3) In subsection (6)(*c*), for "a category of business specified in paragraphs (*a*) to (*c*) of subsection (4) above" substitute "gross roll-up business".

(4) In subsection (13), for paragraphs (*a*) to (*d*) substitute—

"(*a*) basic life assurance and general annuity business, or
(*ba*) gross roll-up business,".

48 In section 804A(1) (life assurance companies with overseas branches etc: restriction of credit), for "any category of life assurance business" substitute "gross roll-up business".

49— (1) Section 804B (insurance companies carrying on more than one category of business: restriction of credit) is amended as follows.

(2) In subsection (1)(*a*), after "category of" insert "long-term".

(3) In subsection (2), omit "or section 438B".

(4) For subsection (3) substitute—

"(3) Where the relevant income arises from an asset which is linked solely to a category of business, the whole of the foreign tax is attributable to that category of business, unless the case is one where subsection (7) below applies.

(3A) Where the relevant income arises from foreign currency assets, the whole of the foreign tax is attributable to gross roll-up business, unless the case is one where subsection (7) below applies."

(5) In subsection (4)—

(*a*) for "long-term business which is not life assurance" substitute "PHI", and
(*b*) omit "or 438B".

(6) In subsection (5), for the words following "is" substitute "gross roll-up business."

(7) In subsection (6)—

(*a*) omit "or 432D" (in both places), and

(*b*) for "the category of business in question" and "that category" substitute "gross roll-up business".

(8) In subsection (7), for—

(*a*) "the category of business in question", and

(*b*) "that category",

substitute "gross roll-up business".

(9) For subsection (9) substitute—

"(9) Where for the purposes of this section an amount of foreign tax is attributable to gross roll-up business, credit in respect of the foreign tax so attributable shall be allowed only against corporation tax in respect of profits chargeable under section 436A."

50 In section 804C(14) (insurance companies: allocation of expenses etc in computations under Case I of Schedule D), for—

(*a*) "a category of life assurance business", and

(*b*) "any category of life assurance business",

substitute "gross roll-up business".

51— (1) Section 804D (interpretation of section 804C in relation to life assurance business etc) is amended as follows.

(2) In subsection (1), for "a category of life assurance business" substitute "gross roll-up business".

(3) In subsection (3), for "432F" substitute "432G".

52 In section 804E (interpretation of section 804C in relation to other insurance business), for "any category of life assurance business" substitute "gross roll-up business".

53 In section 806L(5) (carry forward or carry back of unrelieved foreign tax), for paragraph (*b*) substitute—

"(*b*) included in the profits of gross roll-up business chargeable under Case VI of Schedule D by virtue of section 436A."

54 In section 808 (restriction on deduction of interest or dividends from trading income), for "436" substitute "436A".

55 Omit Schedule 19AA (overseas life assurance fund).

56 In paragraph 2(1A)(*a*) of Schedule 25 (cases where section 747(3) does not apply), for "436, 439B or 441" substitute "436A".

Finance Act 1989 (*c 26*)

57 FA 1989 is amended as follows.

58 In section 88(3A) (corporation tax: policy holders' fraction of profits), for paragraph (*b*) substitute—

"(*b*) profits of the company chargeable under Case VI of Schedule D under section 436A of the Taxes Act 1988 (gross roll-up business)."

59 In section 89(1A) (policy holders' share of profits), for paragraph (*a*) substitute—

"(*a*) deducting from any profits of the company for the period chargeable under Case VI of Schedule D under section 436A of the Taxes Act 1988 so much of the Case I profits of the company for the period in respect of its life assurance business as does not exceed the amount of any profits of the company for the period so chargeable, and".

Taxation of Chargeable Gains Act 1992 (*c 12*)

60 TCGA 1992 is amended as follows.

61 In section 204(10) (policies of insurance and non-deferred annuities)—

(*a*) for "as defined in section 458(3)" substitute "within the meaning of Chapter 1 of Part 12", and

(*b*) omit "other".

62 In section 210B—

(*a*) omit paragraph (*b*) of subsection (6) and the word "or" before it, and

(*b*) in subsection (8) (disposal and acquisition of section 440A securities), in the definition of "chargeable section 440A holding", for "(2)(*a*)(iii)" substitute "(2)(*a*)(i)".

63 In section 212(2) (annual deemed disposal of holdings of certain assets), for the words from "pension business" to the end substitute "gross roll-up business".

64 In section 213(1A) (spreading of gains and losses under section 212), omit the words following "general annuity business".

Finance Act 1996 (*c 8*)

65 FA 1996 is amended as follows.

66 In paragraph 12(3) of Schedule 9 (loan relationships: special computational provisions), for "440(4)(*a*) to (*e*)" substitute "440(4)(*a*), (*d*) and (*e*)".

67— (1) Schedule 11 (loan relationships: special provisions for insurers) is amended as follows.

(2) In paragraph 2, for sub-paragraph (1) substitute—

"(1) Where an insurance company carries on basic life assurance and general annuity business, a separate computation, using only the non-trading credits and non-trading debits referable to that business, shall be made for the purposes of this Chapter in relation to that business."

(3) In paragraph 3A(5)—

(*a*) after "(6A)" insert ", (6B)",
(*b*) for "subsections (6)(*a*) and (6A)(*a*)" substitute "subsection (6)", and
(*c*) omit paragraph (*c*) and the word "and" before it.

(4) In paragraph 4—

(*a*) in sub-paragraph (1), omit paragraph (*b*) and the word "or" before it,
(*b*) in sub-paragraph (2)(*a*), for "the relevant category of business" substitute "basic life assurance and general annuity business",
(*c*) in sub-paragraph (7), for "the relevant category of business" substitute "its basic life assurance and general annuity business",
(*d*) in sub-paragraph (10), for "the relevant category of business" (in both places) substitute "basic life assurance and general annuity business", and
(*e*) omit sub-paragraph (16).

Capital Allowances Act 2001 (*c 2*)

68 CAA 2001 is amended as follows.

69— (1) Section 255 (apportionment of allowances and charges) is amended as follows.

(2) For subsections (1) and (1A) substitute—

"(1) Except where subsection (3) applies, any allowance to which the company is entitled, and any charge to which it is liable, for a chargeable period in respect of a management asset must be apportioned between basic life assurance and general annuity business, gross roll-up business and PHI business in accordance with subsections (1A) and (1B).

(1A) The allowance or charge is to be apportioned to a category of business using the formula—

$$A \times \frac{B}{C}$$

where—

A is the amount of the allowance or charge,
B is the mean of the opening and closing liabilities of that category of business, and
C is the mean of the opening and closing liabilities of all the categories of business mentioned in subsection (1) which are carried on by the company.

(1B) If C is nil or below nil, the allowance or charge to be apportioned to a category of business is such as is just and reasonable."

(3) Omit subsection (2).

(4) In subsection (3)—

(*a*) in paragraph (*a*), for "section 441 of ICTA in respect of its overseas life assurance business" substitute "section 436A of ICTA (gross roll-up business)", and
(*b*) in paragraph (*b*), for "provided outside the United Kingdom for use for the management of that business" substitute "held for the purposes of a permanent establishment outside the United Kingdom at or through which the company carries on gross roll-up business".

70— (1) Section 256 (different giving effect rules for different categories of business) is amended as follows.

(2) In subsection (3), for paragraphs (*a*) to (*c*) substitute "section 436A of ICTA (gross roll-up business)".

(3) In subsection (4)—

(*a*) for "profit" substitute "profits",

(*b*) in paragraph (*a*), for "any particular category of business" substitute "gross roll-up business" and for "that category of business" substitute "its gross roll-up business", and

(*c*) in paragraph (*b*), for "any particular category of business" substitute "gross roll-up business" and for "that category of business" substitute "its gross roll-up business".

71— (1) Section 545 (investment assets) is amended as follows.

(2) In subsection (3), in the second sentence, for "sections 432ZA to 432E, or section 438B," substitute "section 432A".

(3) In subsection (5)—

(*a*) for the words from "under—" to "no allowance" substitute "under section 436A of ICTA (gross roll-up business), no allowance", and

(*b*) for "the category of life assurance business in question" substitute "gross roll-up business".

Finance Act 2001 (*c 9*)

72 In paragraph 20 of Schedule 22 to FA 2001 (remediation of contaminated land), for the words from the beginning to "Schedule D," substitute "In computing in accordance with the provisions of the Taxes Act 1988 applicable to Case I of Schedule D the profits for any accounting period arising to an insurance company from its life assurance business, or from its gross roll-up business,".

Finance Act 2002 (*c 23*)

73 FA 2002 is amended as follows.

74— (1) Schedule 12 (tax relief for expenditure on research and development) is amended as follows.

(2) In paragraph 13, for sub-paragraph (3) substitute—

"(3) Part 3 of this Schedule has effect in relation to any gross roll-up business of the company as if the references to the trade carried on by the company were references to that business (and sub-paragraph (2) does not apply in relation to that business)."

(3) In paragraph 15(3)—

(*a*) for "(profits of life assurance business chargeable to tax under Case VI of Schedule D)" substitute "(gross roll-up business)" and for "a part of the life assurance business" substitute "the gross roll-up business", and

(*b*) for "that part" substitute "the gross roll-up business".

75— (1) Schedule 26 (derivative contracts) is amended as follows.

(2) In paragraph 12(2), for "section 458" substitute "Chapter 1 of Part 12".

(3) In paragraph 29(1), for "440(4)(*a*) to (*e*)" substitute "440(4)(*a*), (*d*) and (*e*)".

Income Tax (*Trading and Other Income*) *Act 2005* (*c 5*)

76 ITTOIA 2005 is amended as follows.

77 In section 473(2) (policies and contracts to which Chapter 9 applies), in the definition of "capital redemption policy", for "as defined in section 458(3)" substitute "within the meaning of Chapter 1 of Part 12".

78 In section 476(3) (special rules: foreign policies), in the definition of "foreign capital redemption policy", for "431D(1)(*a*)" substitute "431D(1)".

79 In Schedule 2 (transitionals and savings etc), in paragraph 118(2), for "from "other than" onwards in the definition of "annuity business"" substitute "following paragraph (*b*) in the definition of "life assurance business"".

GENERAL NOTE

As noted above, many of the amendments introduced by Sch 7 are to make the existing provisions of the life tax code fit the new gross roll up regime. This has required all existing references to categories of business other than BLAGAB to be replaced with references to the new gross roll up category. Paragraphs 44–79 make the necessary changes to a wide range of legislative provisions. Although there are many such changes, none ought to have any impact other than facilitating the preparation of the single tax computation required for the new category of business.

PART 2

TRANSITIONAL PROVISIONS

Introduction

80— (1) A loss incurred by an insurance company in a pre-commencement period may not be set off against profits of the company chargeable under section 436A of ICTA in a post-commencement period, except in accordance with this Part.

(2) In this Part of this Schedule—

"the commencement period", in relation to an insurance company, means the first period of account of the company to begin on or after 1st January 2007,

"pre-commencement period", in relation to an insurance company, means a period of account of the company beginning before 1st January 2007, and

"post-commencement period", in relation to an insurance company, means a period of account of the company beginning on or after 1st January 2007.

(3) Expressions which are—

(*a*) used in this Part of this Schedule in relation to a period of account, and

(*b*) used in Chapter 1 of Part 12 of ICTA,

have the same meaning in this Part of this Schedule in relation to that accounting period as they have in that Chapter (as that Chapter has effect in relation to that period of account).

GENERAL NOTE

The transition to the new gross roll up category required a mechanism to deal with unrelieved losses brought forward from the five previous categories. In order to do this the legislation looks at losses sustained in each of three separate periods and prescribes the order of set off of those losses. The three periods are the first period of account beginning on or after 1 January 2007, i e the period in which the company first came within the new regime (the commencement period); a period of account beginning before 1 January 2007, i.e. the last period of the old regime (the pre-commencement period); and a period of account beginning on or after 1 January 2007 that is not the commencement period (a post-commencement period).

Carry forward of unused pension business losses

81— (1) An unused pension business loss of an insurance company (see sub-paragraph (4)) is to be treated as if it were a loss incurred by the company on its gross roll-up business in the period of account immediately preceding the commencement period.

(2) Subsections (4) and (5) of section 436A of ICTA accordingly apply to the loss, but subject to sub-paragraph (3) (and to subsection (7) of that section).

(3) The amount by which the company's profits charged under that section in a period of account is to be treated as reduced under subsection (4)(*b*) of that section by virtue of this paragraph must not exceed—

$$\mathrm{CP} \times \frac{\mathrm{PBL}}{\mathrm{GRBL}}$$

where—

"CP" is the amount of the company's profits chargeable under that section in the period of account,

"PBL" is the mean of the opening and closing liabilities of the company's pension business for the period of account, and

"GRBL" is the mean of the opening and closing liabilities of the company's gross roll-up business for the period of account.

(4) In this paragraph "unused pension business loss", in relation to an insurance company, means so much of any losses incurred by the company on its pension business in any pre-commencement period as were not set off under section 436(3)(*c*) of ICTA against profits in any such period.

GENERAL NOTE

The industry had hoped that losses arising on the Case VI categories would be fully fungible following amalgamation but the Government was concerned that the amount of unrelieved pension business losses that might be offset against the combined profits of the new category would impose an unacceptable cost on the Exchequer.

This was despite statistics provided by the industry that showed that the bulk of these unrelieved losses were stranded in companies that otherwise wrote no gross roll up business and that the Exchequer cost was small.

Paragraph 81 therefore provides a simple streaming mechanism for unrelieved pension business losses brought forward on the transition to the new regime. The amount of the company's gross roll up profits against which those losses can be set is the proportion that the mean of its opening and closing pension business liabilities bear to the mean of its opening and closing liabilities for all categories of gross roll up business.

Carry forward of unused non-pension business losses

82— (1) An unused non-pension business loss of an insurance company (see paragraph 83) is to be treated as if it were a loss incurred by the company on its gross roll-up business in the period of account immediately preceding the commencement period.

(2) Subsections (4) and (5) of section 436A of ICTA accordingly apply to the loss, but subject to sub-paragraph (3) (and to subsection (7) of that section).

(3) The amount by which an insurance company's profits charged under that section in a period of account are to be treated as reduced under subsection (4)(*b*) of that section is to be determined—

(*a*) first by giving effect to subsection (4)(*b*) in respect of a loss treated as incurred by the company on its gross roll-up business by virtue of paragraph 81, and

(*b*) then by giving effect to subsection (4)(*b*) in respect of a loss treated as incurred by the company on its gross roll-up business by virtue of this paragraph,

(before giving effect to subsection (4)(*b*) in respect of losses incurred by the company on its gross roll-up business in post-commencement periods).

GENERAL NOTE

Unrelieved losses arising on categories other than pension business are brought forward into the new regime as one indivisible sum but the order of offset of such losses is set out in the statute. The first amount to be offset is the appropriate proportion of unrelieved pension business losses capped at the level given by the formula in para 81. The second amount to be offset is any unrelieved losses of the pre-commencement period arising on non-pension business. Only after these offsets are made will any relief be given for losses sustained on the new amalgamated category. This rule can give some anomalous results under which a company might be denied relief which it might have legitimately expected to obtain.

As an example, consider a company with unrelieved pension business losses of 60 that writes both pension and overseas business, the mean liabilities of which are 200 and 100 respectively. In the first post-commencement period it makes a gross roll up business profit of 75 of which 50 relates to pension business and 25 to overseas business (in practice it would not need to calculate these amounts, they are for example only). In the absence of the streaming rules it would be able to cover the whole of the pension business profit with losses brought forward, leaving just the overseas business profit of 25 in charge. Now it will have to apportion the brought forward losses in the ratio of mean liabilities, resulting in relief for just 40, leaving a profit of 35 in charge. However the converse situation, in which the company obtains accelerated relief for non-pension business losses, is far less likely to apply because of the fact that unrelieved pre-commencement losses are overwhelmingly in respect of pension business although there may be some companies that could benefit.

83— (1) In paragraph 82 "unused non-pension business loss", in relation to an insurance company, means the aggregate of the following amounts—

(*a*) any unexhausted individual savings account business loss (see sub-paragraph (2)),

(*b*) any unexhausted child trust fund business loss (see sub-paragraph (3)),

(*c*) any unexhausted life reinsurance business loss (see sub-paragraph (4)), and

(*d*) any unexhausted overseas life assurance business loss (see sub-paragraph (5)).

(2) In this paragraph "unexhausted individual savings account business loss", in relation to an insurance company, means so much of any losses incurred by the company on its individual savings account business in any pre-commencement period as were not set off by virtue of a relevant provision (see sub-paragraph (6)) against profits in any such period.

(3) In this paragraph "unexhausted child trust fund business loss", in relation to an insurance company, means so much of any losses incurred by the company on its child trust fund business in any pre-commencement period as were not set off by virtue of a relevant provision against profits in any such period.

(4) In this paragraph "unexhausted life reinsurance business loss", in relation to an insurance company, means so much of any losses incurred by the company on its life reinsurance business in any pre-commencement period as were not set off under section 439B(3)(*c*) of ICTA against profits in any such period.

(5) In this paragraph "unexhausted overseas life assurance business loss", in relation to an insurance company, means so much of any losses incurred by the company on its overseas life assurance business in any pre-commencement period as were not set off under section 441(4)(*b*) of ICTA against profits in any such period.

(6) In this paragraph "relevant provision" means—

(*a*) regulation 13 of the Individual Savings Account (Insurance Companies) Regulations 1998 (SI 1998/1871), or

(*b*) regulation 11 of the Child Trust Funds (Insurance Companies) Regulations 2004 (SI 2004/2680).

"Section 432F(2) excesses"

GENERAL NOTE

Paragraph 83 simply defines what constitutes a non-pension business loss. Unsurprisingly it is a loss that was incurred on a Case VI category of business other than pension business.

84 Where there is a subsection (2) excess (within the meaning of section 432F of ICTA) for any category of business of an insurance company in the period of account immediately preceding the commencement period it shall be taken to be, or form part of, the subsection (2) excess falling to be carried forward under subsection (3) of that section (as amended by this Schedule) and used in a post-commencement period.

GENERAL NOTE

Paragraph 84 amalgamates any excess needs basis income within the meaning of TA 1988 s 432F for a company's with-profits business. These amounts go forward into the new regime as one indivisible sum for offset against future amounts arising under the "floor" in TA 1988 s 432E.

SCHEDULE 8

INSURANCE COMPANIES: BASIS OF TAXATION ETC

Section 39

PART 1

AMENDMENTS

Income and Corporation Taxes Act 1988 (c 1)

1 ICTA is amended as follows.

2— (1) Section 76 (expenses of insurance companies) is amended as follows.

(2) In subsection (1)(*b*), for "not charged to tax in respect of that business under Case I of Schedule D" substitute "charged to tax in respect of that business under the I minus E basis".

(3) In subsection (7)—

(*a*) in Step 8, for "basic" substitute "expenses", and

(*b*) omit Steps 9 and 10.

(4) Omit subsections (10) and (11).

(5) In subsection (12)—

(*a*) for "Step 10" substitute "Step 8", and

(*b*) after "next accounting period" insert "for which the company is charged to tax in respect of its life assurance business under the I minus E basis".

(6) For subsection (13) substitute—

"(13) Where for any accounting period excess adjusted Case I profits are charged to tax under section 85A of the Finance Act 1989, an amount equal to the profits is to be carried forward to the next accounting period for which the company is charged to tax in respect of its life assurance business under the I minus E basis and brought into account for that period in accordance with Step 7."

GENERAL NOTE

Paragraphs 1 and 2 amend the existing statutory provisions to accommodate the new formal basis of taxing life insurance companies. As with other changes brought about by the consultation process, the changes have allowed the repeal of a number of redundant pieces of legislation.

Subparagraph 3 repeals the previous minimum profits test under which profits taxed on an I-E basis were compared with the company's notional Case I (trading) profit and if the former were smaller, management expenses were restricted to bring the two into equilibrium. This test has now been replaced by a potential charge under new FA 1989 s 85A (see para 14 below).

Subparagraph 5 contains an important relief. Previously one of the reasons why a failure by HMRC to exercise the Crown Option was so expensive was that reliefs such as excess management expenses were lost following a change of basis to Schedule D Case I. Now any unrelieved management expenses on the occasion of a move onto a Case I basis are retained and will be available for relief if the company is taxed on an I-E basis again.

Subparagraph 6 provides a relieving mechanism should the company incur a charge under new FA 1989 s 85A. In those circumstances an amount equal to the charge under that section is carried forward to the next accounting period in which the company is charged on the I-E basis and is brought into the calculation of management expenses for that period. To a certain extent this parallels the restriction of management expenses and their carry forward under the current regime.

3 In section 431(2) (interpretative provisions relating to insurance companies), insert at the appropriate place—

""the I minus E basis" means the basis under which a company carrying on life assurance business is charged to tax on the relevant profits (within the meaning of section 88(3) of the Finance Act 1989) of that business otherwise than under Case I of Schedule D;".

GENERAL NOTE

Paragraph 3 takes the definition of the I-E basis from F(No2)A 1992 s 65(3)(*a*), expands it slightly and writes it into the statutory library of terms affecting the corporate taxation of life insurance companies in TA 1988 s 431(2). The expansion makes it clear that the I-E basis includes the charge under Schedule D Case VI on the profits of the company's gross roll up business.

4 For section 432 (and the italic cross-heading before it) substitute—

"Basis of taxation etc

431G Company carrying on life assurance business

(1) This section applies in relation to an insurance company which carries on life assurance business (whether or not it also carries on insurance business of any other kind).

(2) Subject as follows, the profits of the life assurance business for any accounting period shall be charged to tax under the I minus E basis.

(3) Where in the case of an insurance company for an accounting period either—

(*a*) all of its life assurance business is reinsurance business and none of that business is of a type excluded from this subsection by regulations made by the Board, or (*b*) all, or substantially all, of its life assurance business is gross roll-up business,

the profits of that business for the accounting period shall be charged to tax in accordance with Case I of Schedule D and not otherwise.

(4) Where—

(*a*) the profits of the life assurance business of an insurance company for any accounting period are charged to tax under the I minus E basis, and

(*b*) had those profits been charged to tax in accordance with Case I of Schedule D, a loss would have arisen to the company from that business for the period,

the loss (after being reduced in accordance with section 434A(2)(*a*)) may be set-off under section 393A or section 403(1).

(5) The application, in relation to the life assurance business of an insurance company, of any provision of Case I of Schedule D is not to be taken—

(*a*) to prevent the application of the I minus E basis in relation to that business of the company for any accounting period, or

(*b*) to affect the operation of the I minus E basis in relation to the that business of the company for any accounting period except as specifically provided by the Corporation Tax Acts.

431H Company carrying on life assurance business and other insurance business

(1) This section applies in relation to an insurance company which carries on life assurance business and insurance business of any other kind.

(2) For the purposes of the Corporation Tax Acts—

(*a*) the life assurance business, and

(*b*) the other insurance business,

are to be treated as separate businesses.

(3) The profits of the other insurance business shall be charged to tax under Case I of Schedule D as the profits of a separate trade.

(4) But subsection (3) above does not apply where that business is mutual business.

(5) As to the profits of the life assurance business, see section 431G."

GENERAL NOTE

Paragraph 4 introduces two new sections to TA 1988, the first providing the basis of taxation for all companies that carry on life insurance business, whether in conjunction with other types of insurance business or not; the second maintaining the statutory separate business fiction that life insurance is always taxed as if it were carried on in a separate company.

The first new section, TA 1988 s 431G, applies to all companies writing life insurance business and makes the I-E basis of assessment mandatory; there is no longer any Crown Option available to HMRC, nor may the alternative Case I basis of assessment be invoked. However if the company in question is a pure reinsurer or writes all, or substantially all, gross roll up business (as defined by the legislation introduced by Sch 7, see above), it is instead taxed on a Schedule D Case I basis and in no other way. This parallels the existing treatment for reinsurers in the now repealed TA 1988 s 439A and what ought to have been the case for companies writing business that fell exclusively into the gross roll up category. In practice although companies in the latter category were said to be assessed on an I-E basis, the effect of the Case VI computational rules which applied a Case I treatment was to tax them as quasi-trading companies. There is no definition of what constitutes substantially all of a company's business and HMRC are keen to emphasise that there is no absolute test. In practice 5% of a company's business has been used as a benchmark in similar situations in the past and the same is likely to be true here. In practice companies that may move across this threshold, perhaps due to being in a start up situation or because they have moved into run off, should discuss the situation with their inspectors at the earliest opportunity.

New TA 1988 s 431G also preserves the existing rules under which the I-E basis of assessment does not of itself preclude the calculation of a loss on trading principles and its offset or surrender as group relief. Similarly it retains the existing rules that the calculation of a Case I loss, whether relieved or not, does not prevent the application of the I-E basis.

Finally the fact that a company has been assessed on a Case I basis does not preclude a subsequent return to the I-E basis.

The second new section, TA 1988 s 431H, ensures that the profits from a company's life insurance business are taxed separately from the profits of any other insurance business which would typically be permanent health insurance but which, in the case of the few remaining composite insurers, may also include general insurance business. It is also made clear that with the exception of mutual companies for which a Case I charge is inappropriate, all other such insurance business is taxed under Schedule D Case I.

5 In section 432A(7)(*c*)(ii) (apportionment of income and gains), for "85(2C)(*c*)" substitute "85(2C) or 85A".

GENERAL NOTE

Paragraph 5 ensures that any charge under FA 1989 s 85A (see para 14 below) is always referable to BLAGAB without apportionment and hence it will form part of the company's relevant profits. The mechanics of the legislation mean that this charge will always effectively bear tax at the shareholders' rather than the policy holders' rate.

6 In section 437(1A) (annuities), for ", otherwise than in accordance with the provisions applicable to Case I of Schedule D," substitute "under the I minus E basis".

GENERAL NOTE

Paragraph 6 makes a consequential amendment to accommodate the change of basis.

7 Omit section 439A (taxation of pure reinsurance business).

GENERAL NOTE

Paragraph 7 repeals TA 1988 s 439A which dealt with the taxation basis of pure reinsurers. Those companies are now covered by new TA 1988 s 431G(3), replicating the previous regime under which such companies were taxed on a Case I basis and never on the I-E basis.

8— (1) Section 440B (modifications where tax charged under Case I of Schedule D) is amended as follows.

(2) In subsection (1), insert at the end "in accordance with section 431G(3)".

(3) In subsection (3), for "Section 440(1) and (2) apply" substitute "Subsection (1) of section 440 applies".

(4) After subsection (4) insert—

> "(4A) Section 440(2) does not apply if either the transferor or the company by which the asset is acquired is a company whose profits are charged to tax in accordance with Case I of Schedule D (or if they both are).
> (4B) Section 211 of the 1992 Act does not apply if the transferor is a company whose profits are charged to tax in accordance with Case I of Schedule D."

(5) Omit subsection (5).

GENERAL NOTE

Paragraph 8 makes a number of consequential changes, the most important of which are to ensure parity of treatment to the parties in an insurance business transfer scheme if the transferor is a company taxed under Schedule D Case I on its life insurance business.

9 After that section insert—

"440C Modifications for change of tax basis

(1) Subsection (2) makes provision for a case where—

(*a*) subsection (4) of section 431G applies in relation to the profits of the life assurance business of an insurance company for any accounting period, but

(*b*) the profits of that business for a succeeding accounting period fall to be charged to tax in accordance with Case I of Schedule D by virtue of subsection (3) of that section.

(2) The loss referred to in section 431G(4)(*b*) (less any loss for the same accounting period set off under section 436A for any intervening accounting period and any amount deducted for any such period in respect of the loss by virtue of section 85A(3)(*b*) of the Finance Act 1989) may be set off under section 393 against profits of that succeeding accounting period (without being reduced in accordance with section 434A(2)(*a*)).

(3) In determining whether any loss has been set off under section 436A for any intervening accounting period, or whether any amount has been deducted for any such period in respect of the loss by virtue of section 85A(3)(*b*) of the Finance Act 1989, losses of earlier accounting periods are to be assumed to be set off before those of later accounting periods.

(4) Subsection (5) makes provision for a case where—

(*a*) a loss arises to an insurance company for an accounting period for which the profits of its life assurance business fall to be charged to tax in accordance with Case I of Schedule D by virtue of section 431G(3)(*b*),

(*b*) the profits of that business for a subsequent accounting period are charged to tax under the I minus E basis, and

(*c*) had those profits (instead) been charged to tax in accordance with Case I of Schedule D, any of that loss would have been available to be set off against them under section 393.

(5) The loss is to be treated for the purposes of the operation of section 436A in relation to the subsequent accounting period as if it were a loss arising from its gross roll-up business in the accounting period in which it arose.

(6) Subsections (7) and (8) make provision for a case where—

(*a*) the profits of the life assurance business of an insurance company for an accounting period are charged to tax under the I minus E basis,

(*b*) the profits of that business for its next accounting period fall to be charged to tax in accordance with Case I of Schedule D by virtue of section 431G(3), and

(*c*) that prevents the giving of relief in accordance with section 86(8) of the Finance Act 1989 (acquisition expenses relieved in fractions under section 76).

(7) Any relief which would have been so given in—

(*a*) the next accounting period, or

(*b*) any subsequent accounting period for which the profits of the company's life assurance business continue to be charged to tax in accordance with Case I of Schedule D,

may be given by set-off against any gains treated as accruing under section 213(1) of the 1992 Act at the end of the accounting period.

(8) But if the profits of the company's life assurance business for a subsequent accounting period are charged to tax under the I minus E basis, any relief not previously given under subsection (7) is to be treated for the purposes of the operation of section 76 in relation to the first subsequent accounting period for which profits are so charged as if it were an amount which is to be relieved under that section by virtue of section 86(8) and (9) of the Finance Act 1989."

GENERAL NOTE

Paragraph 9 introduces new TA 1988 s 440C which caters for losses brought forward to a period in which a company changes from an I-E basis to a Case I basis or *vice versa*. These rules are perhaps the most complex part of Sch 8 and caused some difficulty in drafting to the satisfaction of the parties to the consultation although their impact is likely to be relatively limited in day to day tax practice.

In the former case any loss arising in the earlier I-E basis period of account which is not set off elsewhere in the company (including a notional set off against amounts chargeable by virtue of new FA 1989 s 85A) is treated as a trading loss brought forward and may be set against the Case I profits of a subsequent accounting period

in accordance with TA 1988 s 393. If there are losses bought forward from multiple periods, losses of earlier periods are deemed to be offset sideways, leaving losses of later periods available for carry forward.
In the latter case a Case I loss may be carried forward for relief against profits on the company's gross roll up business in a subsequent period in which it is taxed on the I-E basis.
Finally if a company moves on to a Case I basis but has unrelieved spread acquisition expenses under FA 1989 s 86, those expenses may be relieved against spread forward deemed gains on collective investment schemes. This allows a limited matching of I-E items which are both spread forward and remain taxable in the Case I period.

10 In section 755A(2) and (6)(*a*) (controlled foreign companies: apportionments to companies carrying on life assurance business), for "not charged to tax under Case I of Schedule D in respect of its profits from" substitute "charged to tax under the I minus E basis in respect of".

Finance Act 1989 (*c 26*)

11 FA 1989 is amended as follows.

12 In section 83(6)(*c*) (receipts to be taken into account), for the words from "the reinsurer" to the end substitute "section 431G(3)(*a*) of the Taxes Act 1988 (pure reinsurance) applies to the reinsurer under the contract for the accounting period of the reinsurer during which the transfer of business occurs".

13 In subsection (1) of section 85 (charge of certain receipts of BLAGAB)—

(*a*) for "the profits of an insurance company in respect of its life assurance business are not charged under Case I of Schedule D" substitute "an insurance company is charged to tax under the I minus E basis in respect of its life assurance business", and
(*b*) for "those profits" substitute "the profits of the life assurance business".

GENERAL NOTE

Paragraphs 10–13 make consequential amendments to accommodate the change of basis and the new legislation introduced to give effect to it.

14 After that section insert—

"85A Excess adjusted Case I profits

(1) Where for any accounting period an insurance company is charged to tax under the I minus E basis in respect of its life assurance business, the company shall be chargeable on any excess adjusted Case I profits under Case VI of that Schedule.

(2) "Excess adjusted Case I profits" means any amount by which—

(*a*) the adjusted Case I profits (see subsection (3)), exceeds
(*b*) the relevant amount (see subsection (5)).

(3) "The adjusted Case I profits" means the amount that would be the profits of the company's life assurance business for the accounting period if—

(*a*) computed in accordance with the provisions applicable to Case I of Schedule D, and
(*b*) adjusted in respect of losses (see subsection (4)).

(4) The adjustment in respect of losses is a deduction of the amount which, disregarding section 434A(2)(*a*) of the Taxes Act 1988, would fall to be set off under section 393 of that Act against the company's income for the accounting period if the company had always been charged to tax under Case I of Schedule D.

(5) The relevant amount (which may be a negative amount) is found by—

(*a*) taking the relevant income (see subsection (6)), and
(*b*) deducting from it the relevant aggregate (see subsection (8)).

(6) "The relevant income" means—

(*a*) any income (including distributions received from companies resident in the United Kingdom) referable (in accordance with section 432A of the Taxes Act 1988) to the company's basic life assurance and general annuity business for the accounting period, (*b*) any chargeable gains referable (in accordance with section 432A of that Act) to the company's basic life assurance and general annuity business for the accounting period (see subsection (7)), and

(*c*) any profits of the company chargeable for the accounting period under Case VI of Schedule D under section 436A of that Act.

(7) "Chargeable gains referable (in accordance with section 432A of the Taxes Act 1988) to the company's basic life assurance and general annuity business" has the same meaning as in subsection (3A)(*a*) of section 88 below (see subsection (3B) of that section).

(8) "The relevant aggregate" means the sum of—

(*a*) the expenses deduction (see Step 8 in section 76(7) of the Taxes Act 1988) in the case of the company for the accounting period,

(*b*) any non-trading deficit on the company's loan relationships which is produced for the accounting period in relation to the company's basic life assurance and general annuity business by a separate computation under paragraph 2(1) of Schedule 11 to the Finance Act 1996, and

(*c*) any amount which in pursuance of a claim under paragraph 4(3) of that Schedule is carried back to the accounting period and (in accordance with paragraph 4(5) of that Schedule) applied in reducing profits of the company for the accounting period.

(9) The Treasury may by regulations provide—

(*a*) that, in circumstances prescribed by the regulations, the charge imposed by this section for an accounting period may be reduced or eliminated, and

(*b*) that the amount by which the charge is reduced, or (where the charge is eliminated) the amount of the charge, is instead imposed for a subsequent accounting period (or part of the amount is instead imposed for more than one subsequent accounting period).

(10) Regulations under subsection (9) may include provision having effect in relation to times before they are made."

GENERAL NOTE

Paragraph 14 introduces FA 1989 s 85A which replaces the previous test under which a company's profits on an I-E basis were compared with its notional Case I profits and if the latter exceeded the former, management expenses were restricted to bring the two into equilibrium. This test was the cause of some of the uncertainty in the previous regime because if management expenses could not be restricted by enough to increase the measure of I-E profits to that of the notional Case I profit, in theory the company ought to have been assessed on an actual Case I basis.

The notional Case I test no longer exists and is replaced by an automatic measure designed to ensure that the taxable profits of a company assessed on the I-E basis can never be less than its Case I profit. Companies will now be taxed under Schedule D Case VI on the amount of the excess of their Case I profits, reduced by losses brought forward under TA 1988 s 393, over the aggregate of the income (including distributions) and capital gains referable to BLAGAB plus any profits on gross roll up business chargeable to tax by virtue of TA 1988 s 436A less management expenses due for the period and non-trading deficits on loan relationships both of the period and brought back from later periods. Effectively the comparison is between the Case I profit and the I-E profit plus the BLAGAB share of any distributions. The latter are included because distributions are included in the measure of Case I profits and to exclude them would mean the test did not compare like with like.

Paragraph 14 also includes a regulation making power under which the Treasury may reduce or eliminate any charge under FA 1989 s 85A or cause it to be spread forward to later accounting periods. This regulation making power is designed to allow flexibility in reacting to changes in the regulatory regime which might otherwise cause an increase in Case I profits and an unwarranted charge under FA 1989 s 85A. The most recent example of this was the FSA's introduction of Policy Statement 06/14 under which companies were able to make significant releases of reserves. In those circumstances, regulations were laid allowing companies to spread the profit created by those releases over three years and HMRC gave written assurances that companies would not be moved on to an actual Case I basis of assessment solely as a result of those releases.

15— (1) Section 88 (policy holders' fraction of profits) is amended as follows.

(2) Omit subsection (2).

(3) In subsection (3)(*a*), for "basic" substitute "expenses".

16— (1) Section 89 (policy holders' share of profits) is amended as follows.

(2) In subsection (1B)(*b*), for "basic" substitute "expenses".

(3) In subsection (7), for the words after "Schedule D" substitute "; but for the purposes of subsections (1), (1A) and (2) they are to be adjusted in respect of losses in accordance with section 85A(4)."

Finance Act 1991 (*c 31*)

17 In paragraph 16(1) of Schedule 7 to FA 1991 (transitional relief for old general annuity contracts), for ", otherwise than in accordance with the provisions applicable to Case I of Schedule D," substitute "under the I minus E basis".

Taxation of Chargeable Gains Act 1992 (*c 12*)

18 In section 212 of TCGA 1992 (annual deemed disposal of holdings of unit trusts etc), omit subsection (7A) (which applies section 440B(5) of ICTA).

Finance (*No 2*) *Act 1992* (*c 48*)

19 In F(No 2)A 1992, omit section 65 (life assurance business: I minus E basis).

Finance Act 1996 (*c 8*)

20 In paragraph 4 of Schedule 11 to FA 1996 (loan relationships: special provisions for insurers: treatment of deficit), omit sub-paragraphs (12) to (14).

Finance Act 1998 (*c 36*)

21 In paragraph 84 of Schedule 18 to FA 1998 (company tax returns, assessments and related matters), for sub-paragraphs (1) to (3) substitute—

> "(1) This paragraph applies where amounts may be brought into charge to tax either—
>
> (*a*) in computing profits chargeable to tax under Case I of Schedule D, or
>
> (*b*) as amounts within Case III or V of that Schedule.";

and the italic heading before that paragraph accordingly becomes "*Choice between Case I and Case III or V of Schedule D*".

Capital Allowances Act 2001 (*c 2*)

22 CAA 2001 is amended as follows.

23 In section 256(1), for paragraph (*b*) substitute—

> "(*b*) is charged to tax under the I minus E basis in respect of its life assurance business."

24 In section 257(2) (life assurance: supplementary), for paragraphs (*a*) and (*b*) substitute—

> "(*a*) section 85A(3) of the Finance Act 1989 (excess adjusted Case I profits), or
>
> (*b*) section 89 of that Act (policy holders' share of profits)."

Finance Act 2002 (*c 23*)

25 FA 2002 is amended as follows.

26 In paragraph 13(1) of Schedule 12 (tax relief on R&D: special provisions for insurance companies), for "the profits arising to a company from its life assurance business are not charged to corporation tax under Case I of Schedule D" substitute "an insurance company is charged to tax under the I minus E basis in respect of its life assurance business".

27 In Schedule 29 (gains and losses of a company from intangible fixed assets), omit paragraph 36(6) (meaning of I minus E basis).

GENERAL NOTE

Paragraphs 15–27 make further consequential amendments to accommodate the change of basis.

PART 2

TRANSITIONAL PROVISIONS

Unused pre-commencement section 76(12) etc excesses

28 Step 7 in subsection (7) of section 76 of ICTA applies in relation to an insurance company for the first accounting period beginning on or after 1st January 2007 for which the profits of the life assurance business are charged to tax under the I minus E basis as if the amounts carried forward to the accounting period under subsection (12) of that section included—

(*a*) any excess such as is mentioned in that subsection relating to the company for an accounting period beginning on or after 1st April 2004 but not later than 1st January 2007 which was not brought into account for the next accounting period in accordance with Step 7 in subsection (7) of that section, and

(*b*) any excess such as was mentioned in subsection (3) of section 75 of ICTA relating to the company for an accounting period beginning before 1st April 2004 which was not deducted for the succeeding accounting period in accordance with that section (as applied by section 76 of that Act).

GENERAL NOTE

Paragraph 28 provides a measure of relief by bringing unrelieved management expenses forward to the first period of account in which the company is charged to tax on an I-E basis under the new regime. For most companies this will happen automatically in their first accounting period but it means that companies that were previously assessed on an I-E basis but which moved to an actual Case I basis under the old regime will not be denied relief for excess management expenses which would now be available to them on a change of basis. Paragraph 28 is drafted in a way that permits it to apply whether those otherwise stranded expenses were calculated under the rules for management expenses applying before or after 1 April 2004.

Shifts in basis of taxation at first post-commencement accounting period

29— (1) This paragraph applies where—

(*a*) the profits of the life assurance business of an insurance company for the first accounting period of the company beginning on or after 1st January 2007 ("the first accounting period") are charged to tax in accordance with Case I of Schedule D by virtue of subsection (3)(*b*) of section 431G of ICTA, but

(*b*) the profits of the life assurance business of the company for the preceding accounting period were charged to tax under the I minus E basis.

(2) The amount of the losses available to be set off under section 393 of ICTA against the profits of the first accounting period is the amount of any loss under section 436, 439B or 441 of ICTA carried forward to that period by virtue of Part 2 of Schedule 7 to this Act.

GENERAL NOTE

Paragraph 29 provides a similar measure of transitional relief for companies with unrelieved losses moving from an I-E basis to a Case I basis. In those circumstances any unrelieved losses on the company's gross roll up business will be available for set off under TA 1988 s 393 in calculating the Case I profit in the first period of account. This has the effect of converting a Case VI loss into a Case I loss with the greater potential for relief that implies.

SCHEDULE 9

INSURANCE COMPANIES: TRANSFERS ETC

Section 40

GENERAL NOTE

Schedule 9 makes extensive changes to the tax regime dealing with transfers of insurance business under FSMA 2000 Part VII. It is acknowledged by both the industry and HMRC that the existing rules have become cumbersome in operation and subject to the law of unintended consequences as the tax legislation has struggled to keep abreast of developments in the commercial environment. The new rules are designed to streamline the process as well as to protect HMRC by the introduction of a targeted anti-avoidance rule. Schedule 9 must however be viewed as work in progress because the consultation process remains ongoing on a number of points and therefore much of the new legislation will not take effect until a day to be appointed by Treasury order (see para 17 below). The legislation as drafted will be changed and will certainly be added to by regulations to be introduced following further discussions between the industry and HMRC, probably later in the summer of 2007.

Definition of "insurance business transfer scheme"

1— (1) In section 431(2) of ICTA (interpretative provisions for purposes of Corporation Tax Acts), for the definition of "insurance business transfer scheme" substitute—

""insurance business transfer scheme" means—

(*a*) a scheme falling within section 105 of the Financial Services and Markets Act 2000, including an excluded scheme falling within Case 2, 3 or 4 of subsection (3) of that section, or

(*b*) a scheme which would fall within that section but for subsection (1)(*b*) of that section;".

(2) In consequence of sub-paragraph (1), omit—

(*a*) the definition of "insurance business transfer scheme" in section 12(7B) of ICTA,

(*b*) section 444AB(11) of that Act (as originally enacted),

(*c*) in section 444AC(11) of that Act (as originally enacted), the definition of "insurance business transfer scheme",

(*d*) section 460(10B) of that Act,

(*e*) the definition of "insurance business transfer scheme" in paragraph 12(9) of Schedule 9 to FA 1996,

(*f*) section 560(5)(*b*) of CAA 2001,

(*g*) paragraph 28(5) of Schedule 26 to FA 2002, and

(*h*) the definition of "insurance business transfer scheme" in paragraph 89(3) of Schedule 29 to that Act.

(3) In section 431 of ICTA, insert at the end—

"(2ZG) The Treasury may by order amend the definition of "insurance business transfer scheme" given by subsection (2) above where it is expedient to do so in consequence of any amendment of section 105 of the Financial Services and Markets Act 2000.

(2ZH) The power conferred by subsection (2ZG) above includes power to make incidental, supplementary, consequential or transitional provisions and savings (including provision amending any provision of the Corporation Tax Acts relating to insurance companies)."

(4) In section 66 of FA 2002 (election to continue postponement of mark to market)—

(*a*) in subsection (4)(*a*), for "a transfer" substitute "an insurance business transfer",

(*b*) in subsection (5), omit the definition of "transfer scheme", and

(*c*) omit subsections (6) and (7).

(5) In paragraph 10 of Schedule 22 to that Act—

(*a*) in sub-paragraph (1)(*a*), for "a transfer" substitute "an insurance business transfer",

(*b*) in sub-paragraph (4), omit the definition of "transfer scheme", and

(*c*) omit sub-paragraphs (5) and (6).

Transfer schemes: expenses, losses etc

GENERAL NOTE

Paragraph 1 amends the current definition of an insurance business transfer scheme. Although it remains couched in terms of Part VII FSMA 2000, it is extended by sub-para (*b*) to include such schemes where the transferee carries on its business outside the EEA. A number of past schemes have involved such transfers and there is no over-riding policy reason why they should not be subject to the same rules as transfers within the EEA.

Paragraph 1 also removes redundant references to an insurance business transfer scheme from other parts of the legislation.

Finally para 1 contains a regulation making power allowing the Treasury to amend the definition of an insurance business transfer scheme if there is a change to the relevant Part of FSMA 2000 thereby providing flexibility in adapting the tax regime for changes in the regulatory environment.

2— (1) Section 444A of ICTA (transfers of business: expenses, losses and section 432F(2) excesses) is amended as follows.

(2) In subsection (1), omit "Subject to subsection (7) below,".

(3) Omit—

(*a*) subsection (7) (section not to apply if transfer is not for bona fide commercial reasons or forms part of avoidance scheme), and

(*b*) subsection (8) (clearance procedure as to non-application of subsection (7)).

GENERAL NOTE

Paragraph 2 repeals the clearance process previously in TA 1988 sub-ss 444A(7) and (8) that was available to ensure the transfer of tax attributes such as unrelieved management expenses, Case VI losses and excess amounts under TA 1988 s 432F. This clearance process was based on concepts in TCGA 1992 ss 138 and 139 which did not sit naturally with the life tax regime and a number of refinements had to be introduced to marry the two regimes, not always successfully. The decoupling of the clearance process from that in TCGA 1992 s 139 is welcome because it will in future allow consideration to be paid for a transfer of business. The protection previously offered to HMRC by the clearance process is now replaced by the targeted anti-avoidance rule.

There is however a gap between the repeal of the old clearance regime for periods of account beginning on or after 1 January 2007 and the introduction of the targeted anti-avoidance rule, probably in the spring of 2008. Companies with calendar year accounting periods contemplating an insurance business transfer scheme in late 2007 or early 2008 therefore find themselves in a state of uncertainty which is unwelcome.

Transfer schemes: deemed periodical returns

3— (1) In ICTA, for section 444AA substitute—

"444AA Transfers of business: deemed periodical return

(1) This section applies where the whole, or substantially the whole, of the long-term business of a person ("the transferor") is transferred from that person—

(*a*) by one insurance business transfer scheme, or

(*b*) by two or more insurance business transfer schemes which are associated.

(2) For the purposes of subsection (1) above two or more insurance business transfer schemes are associated if they form part of an arrangement for the transfer of the whole, or substantially the whole, of the transferor's long-term business.

(3) Where (apart from this subsection) there would not be a periodical return of the transferor covering a period ending immediately before a relevant transfer date, there is to be deemed for the purposes of corporation tax to be a periodical return of the transferor covering the period—

(*a*) beginning immediately after the last period ending before the relevant transfer date which is covered by a periodical return of the transferor, and

(*b*) ending immediately before the relevant transfer date,

containing such entries as would be included in an actual periodical return of the transferor covering that period (and so making that period a period of account of the transferor).

(4) There is to be deemed for the purposes of corporation tax to be a periodical return of the transferor—

(*a*) covering a relevant transfer date, and

(*b*) containing such entries as would be included in an actual periodical return covering the relevant transfer date,

(and so making the relevant transfer date a period of account of the transferor).

(5) Any actual periodical return covering a period which includes a relevant transfer date is to be ignored for the purposes of corporation tax.

(6) Where the transferor continues to carry on long-term business after a relevant transfer date, there is to be deemed for the purposes of corporation tax to be a periodical return of the transferor covering the immediate post-RTD period containing such entries as would be included in an actual periodical return covering that period (and so making that period a period of account of the transferor).

(7) In this section "relevant transfer date" means—

(*a*) in relation to a case within paragraph (*a*) of subsection (1) above, the date that is the transfer date in relation to the insurance business transfer scheme, and

(*b*) in relation to a case within paragraph (*b*) of that subsection—

(i) the earliest date that is the transfer date in relation to any of the insurance business transfer schemes, other than one that is a preliminary non-EEA transfer scheme, and

(ii) (where there are two or more insurance business transfer schemes that are not preliminary non-EEA transfer schemes) the latest date that is the transfer date in relation to any of them.

(8) In subsection (6) above "the immediate post-RTD period" means the period beginning immediately after the relevant transfer date mentioned in that subsection and (subject to subsection (9) below) ending with—

(*a*) the end of the period covered by the periodical return covering a period which includes a relevant transfer date (if there is one), or

(*b*) (if there is not) the period covered by the accounts of the company prepared in accordance with generally accepted accounting practice which includes the relevant transfer date.

(9) If the case is within subsection (1)(*b*) above and two or more of the insurance business transfer schemes are not preliminary non-EEA transfer schemes, the period ends with the latest date that is the transfer date in relation to any of them if that is before the end of the period mentioned in paragraph (*a*) or (*b*) of subsection (8) above.

(10) In this section and sections 444AB to 444AEC "the transfer date", in relation to an insurance business transfer scheme, means the date on which it takes effect.

(11) For the purposes of this section an insurance business transfer scheme is a preliminary non-EEA transfer scheme if—

(*a*) it is an insurance business transfer scheme by virtue of paragraph (*b*) of the definition of "insurance business transfer scheme" in section 431(2), and

(*b*) the transfer date in relation to it is earlier than the transfer date in relation to an associated insurance business transfer scheme which is an insurance business transfer scheme by virtue of paragraph (*a*) of that definition."

(2) In section 12 of ICTA (accounting periods), for subsection (7C) substitute—

"(7C) Where section 444AA applies, an accounting period of the transferor (within the meaning of that section) shall end for the purposes of corporation tax with the end of any period covered by a periodical return deemed by that section."

(3) In—

(*a*) section 432YA(2A) of ICTA, and

(*b*) section 82D(2A) of FA 1989,

for "444AA(3)" substitute "444AA(4)".

(4) In section 213(10) of TCGA 1992, for "before the transfer" substitute "before the relevant transfer date (within the meaning of that section)".

GENERAL NOTE

Paragraph 3 replaces the existing TA 1988 s 444AA that deals with deemed regulatory returns on a transfer of business. This legislation was originally introduced because some companies that transferred the whole of their long-term business were not required by the FSA to file a regulatory return for the period including the transfer so there was no return on which to base the tax computation. Even if a return was made, it would show values of "nil" for closing assets and liabilities with the same result . The new rules, while appearing complex, deal with some of the complaints that were voiced about the previous regime during the consultation process. In particular, new TA 1988 s 444AC applies when the whole or substantially the whole of the transferor's business is transferred and that transfer is achieved by either one or two or more associated insurance business transfer schemes. The former is important because it is not unusual for whole business transfers to actually leave behind some policies and matching assets which cannot be transferred as a matter of law and which are often reinsured to the transferee as part of the scheme of transfer. The latter ensures that the legislation applies to transfers to multiple parties, either simultaneously or in succession, or in different jurisdictions when the transfers are connected.

As before the new TA 1988 s 444A(3) requires a deemed regulatory return to be prepared for the period leading up to immediately before the transfer if a "real" return is not prepared, thereby giving HMRC a taxing basis for the truncated period. New sub-s (4) replicates the existing provision that there is a deemed return for the date of the transfer and therefore a period of account for the same period. There is however an extension to the rules for the deemed regulatory return for the transfer date itself. Previously that return was effective only for the purposes of FA 1989 s 83(2B) in determining whether and to what extent an insurance business transfer had been brought into account. Now the deemed return is effective for all corporation tax purposes so if, for example, it shows a loss, the company's ability to offset that loss by way of group relief will be curtailed by the one day accounting period.

Much of the rest of new TA 1988 s 444AA deals with multiple transfers in the same period, provisions that were lacking in its previous version and these introductions are responsible for much of the complexity. A number of drafting points remain which will be addressed during the ongoing consultation process because the rules remain unwieldy and can still give rise to anomalous results in certain, albeit limited, circumstances. In practice the number of companies likely to be affected is small and those to which the rules will apply ought to be able to plan appropriately to manage any risk.

Transfer schemes: taxing the transferor

4— (1) In ICTA, for sections 444AB and 444ABA substitute—

"444AB Transfer schemes transferring whole of business: transferor

(1) This section applies where an insurance business transfer scheme has effect to transfer the whole, or substantially the whole, of the long-term business of a person ("the transferor") to another person ("the transferee") and either or both of conditions A and B are met.

(2) Condition A is met if any of the assets of the transferor's long-term insurance fund which are transferred from the transferor to the transferee by the insurance business transfer scheme are not, immediately after their transfer—

(*a*) if the transferee is an insurance company, assets of the transferee's long-term insurance fund, or

(*b*) if the transferee is not an insurance company, assets of a with-profits fund of the transferee,

("relevant non-transferred assets").

(3) Condition B is met if, immediately after the transfer date, the transferor—

(*a*) does not carry on long-term business, but

(*b*) holds any assets which, immediately before the transfer date, were assets of its long-term insurance fund ("retained assets").

(4) If there are relevant non-transferred assets or retained assets (or both) the relevant amount in relation to them (see subsection (5) below) is to be taken into account under section 83(2) of the Finance Act 1989 as an increase in value of the assets of the long-term insurance fund of the transferor for the relevant period of account (see subsection (6) below).

(5) Section 444ABA makes provision for the calculation of the relevant amount in relation to relevant non-transferred assets; and section 444ABB makes provision for its calculation in relation to retained assets.

(6) In this section and sections 444ABA to 444AC "the relevant period of account" means the period of account of the transferor ending (or treated by section 444AA as ending) immediately before the transfer date.

(7) See section 444AA for the meaning of "the transfer date" in this section.

444ABA Relevant non-transferred assets

(1) For the purposes of section 444AB the relevant amount in relation to assets that are relevant non-transferred assets is—

$$FVA - RVA$$

where—

FVA is the fair value of the assets on the transfer date, and

RVA is the recognised value of the assets.

(2) For the purposes of this section and section 444ABB—

(*a*) the recognised value of any assets which, immediately before the transfer date, are held by the transferor in a non-profit fund which is not a Form 14 line 51 fund is the relevant Form 13 value of those assets, and

(*b*) the recognised value of any other assets is the appropriate fraction of the relevant Form 13 value of those assets.

(3) For the purposes of subsection (2) above a non-profit fund is a Form 14 line 51 fund if an amount in respect of the fund is shown (or treated as shown) in line 51 of Form 14 in the periodical return of the transferor covering the relevant period of account.

(4) For the purposes of subsection (2) above the relevant Form 13 value of any assets is the value which is shown (or treated as shown) in respect of the assets in Form 13 in the periodical return of the transferor covering the relevant period of account (ignoring lines 91 to 99 of that Form).

(5) For the purposes of subsection (2)(*b*) above the appropriate fraction is—

$$1 - \frac{A}{B}$$

where—

A is the amount shown (or treated as shown) in line 51 of Form 14 in the periodical return of the transferor covering the relevant period of account in respect of the fund in which, immediately before the transfer date, the assets are held by the transferor, increased or reduced as mentioned in subsection (6) below, and

B is the amount shown (or treated as shown) in line 89 of Form 13 in that periodical return in respect of that fund.

(6) The increase or reduction referred to in the definition of A in subsection (5) above is any increase or decrease deemed to be brought into account by section 83YA(3) or (4) of the Finance Act 1989 in respect of the fund for the relevant period of account.

(7) See section 444AA for the meaning of "the transfer date", and section 444AB for the meaning of "the relevant period of account", in this section.

444ABB Retained assets

(1) For the purposes of section 444AB the relevant amount in relation to assets that are retained assets is the lesser of FVA and UTA, where—

(*a*) FVA is the fair value of the assets on the transfer date, and

(*b*) UTA is the amount by which the fair value of the assets of the long-term insurance fund of the transferor immediately before the transfer date exceeds the amount shown (or treated as shown) in line 32 of Form 40 in the periodical return of the transferor covering the transfer date.

(2) See section 444AA for the meaning of "the transfer date" in this section.

444ABC Transfer scheme transferring part of business: transferor

(1) This section applies where an insurance business transfer scheme has effect to transfer part (but not the whole or substantially the whole) of the long-term business of a person ("the transferor") to another person ("the transferee") and the condition in subsection (2) below is met.

(2) That condition is that any of the assets of the transferor's long-term insurance fund which are transferred from the transferor to the transferee by the insurance business transfer scheme are not, immediately after their transfer—

(*a*) if the transferee is an insurance company, assets of the transferee's long-term insurance fund, or

(*b*) if the transferee is not an insurance company, assets of a with-profits fund of the transferee,

("relevant non-transferred assets").

(3) The relevant amount in relation to the relevant non-transferred assets (see subsection (4) below) is to be taken into account under section 83(2) of the Finance Act 1989 as an increase in value of the assets of the long-term insurance fund of the transferor for the period of account covering the transfer date.

(4) The relevant amount in relation to the relevant non-transferred assets is—

$$FVA - BTO$$

where

FVA is the fair value of the assets on the transfer date, and

BTO is any amount brought into account in respect of the assets as a business transfer-out.

(5) See section 444AA for the meaning of "the transfer date" in this section."

(2) In section 432E(2A) of ICTA (apportionments: participating funds)—

(*a*) before "444AF(2)" insert "444AB, 444ABC,", and

(*b*) after paragraph (*a*) insert—

"(*aa*) section 444AB or 444ABC of this Act;".

GENERAL NOTE

Paragraph 4 provides the rules for taxing the transfer in the transferor. Sub-paragraph 1 introduces four new sections to TA 1988 to deal with various combinations of circumstances. Much of the material in those new sections is already in place in the current rules although some new concepts are introduced. Of more concern however is that some reliefs currently present have not, as yet, made the transition to the new regime. This will be a key feature of the consultation process going forward.

In broad terms the new legislation looks to ensure that assets transferred from one long-term insurance fund to another move on a tax neutral basis. In contrast, assets that break the ring-fence around the long-term fund, either by moving to the transferee's shareholders' fund or by remaining in a company that no longer writes long-term business, come within the charge to tax.

New TA 1988 s 444AB covers transfers of the whole, or substantially the whole, of the transferor's business when one of two conditions is met.

The first condition is that transferred assets end up other than in the long-term fund of the transferee in which case it taxes an amount in respect of those "relevant non-transferred assets" calculated in accordance with new TA 1988 s 444ABA (see below). The seemingly strange reference in sub-para 2(*b*) to the with-profits fund of a company that is not an insurance company aims to allow relief if the assets are transferred to a non-EEA insurance company that operates business in a manner analogous to UK with-profits business and so needs assets in excess of liabilities to meet future policy holder bonuses. The aim of the first part of the sub-paragraph is met because the statutory definition of an insurance company relies on an FSA definition which deals with UK and EEA companies, so an insurance company based outside the EEA is not an insurance company for tax purposes. A view has been expressed that the aim of the legislation is defeated however because the statutory definition of a with-profits fund also relies on FSA definitions which when taken back to first principles can apply only to a UK or EEA company. The same considerations apply to new TA 1988 s 444ABC which deals with part transfers of insurance business. HMRC have said that a purposive interpretation of the new rules together with use of the phrase "unless the context requires otherwise" in the preamble to TA 1988 s 431(2) taken together mean that the legislation will work, and be interpreted, as intended.

The second condition, which replicates existing TA 1988 s 444AB, is that after the transfer the transferor no longer writes insurance business. There is however no replication of the existing relief for assets retained to meet liabilities that were not transferred, nor of the exemption for assets retained on trust for the transferee because, for example, they are prohibited by law from being transferred. HMRC have since stated that this relief will be reinstated.

New TA 1988 s 444ABA calculates the taxable amount if any assets are not transferred (relevant non-transferred assets). Unfortunately the drafting is defective in a number of places so for example the reference to a periodical return in TA 1988 s 444ABA(5) is not consistent with that in TA 1988 s 444AB(6). Although these issues can be picked up as part of the ongoing discussions between the industry and HMRC, it is unfortunate that the legislation was not correct from day one because simplification and removal of anomalies were two of the main drivers for change. Similarly the increase or reduction by reference to amounts brought into account by FA 1989 s 83YA should be for all such amounts, not just those of the period in question. Nor do the adjustments in sub-s (6) to the formula in sub-s (5) work as intended, resulting in the reverse of what is required. Likewise there may be other non-taxable elements that should be excluded from the charge to tax for example the exclusion in the current regime for assets referable to PHI business which has disappeared from the current version.

New TA 1988 s 444ABC deals with part transfers but uses a different method for calculating the amount brought into account compared with whole transfers. It is not clear why this different approach has been taken when consistency between transfers ought to have been the guiding principle.

Finally para 4(2) ensures that any taxable amounts are added to the amount of investment return apportioned to with-profits business, otherwise the needs basis would simply over-write the adjustments, making them ineffective in a with-profits fund.

Transferor's period of account including transfer

5 In ICTA, after section 444ABC (inserted by paragraph 4) insert—

"444ABD Transferor's period of account including transfer

(1) Any profits representing the amount by which—

(*a*) the value of the liabilities transferred by an insurance business transfer scheme, exceeds

(*b*) the value of the assets transferred by the insurance business transfer scheme shown (or treated as shown) in line 32 of the periodical return of the transferor for the period of account of the transferor including the transfer date,

are to be taken into account as profits of that period of account.

(2) See section 444AA for the meaning of "the transfer date" in this section."

GENERAL NOTE

Paragraph 5 introduces new TA 1988 s 444ABD which is designed to be purely clarificatory in scope. On a transfer of insurance business the transfer of liabilities will broadly be matched by a near equal transfer of assets. While there is little doubt that the release or assumption of liabilities is on trading account, the position for assets is less clear. This is true even though the assets of a life insurance company may be viewed as akin to trading stock within TA 1988 s 100. The purpose of new TA 1988 s 444ABD is to put beyond doubt that a profit that accrues to the transferor due to the transfer of an excess of liabilities is on revenue account. Unfortunately the wording used is less clear than it might be, for example it does not specify in whose hands the profits are taxed or how they are actually brought into the charge to tax. This may be due to the essentially clarificatory nature of the new section which can be construed purposively given its obvious intent.

FA 2007 was to have contained a similar clarification for losses sustained on a transfer. This was removed during the Act's progress through Parliament because HMRC became aware that it could be over-generous in providing relief from tax. It is unfortunate that the provision was removed rather than amended and it is to be hoped that a similar but less Exchequer costly replacement will be enacted.

Transfer schemes: taxing the transferee

6— (1) In ICTA, for section 444AC substitute—

"444AC Transfer schemes transferring whole of business: reduction in income of transferee

(1) This section applies where an insurance business transfer scheme has effect to transfer the whole, or substantially the whole, of the long-term business of a person ("the transferor") to another person ("the transferee") and conditions A and B are met.

(2) Condition A is that the transferor did not carry on life assurance business that is mutual business during the relevant period of account.

(3) Condition B is that an amount is shown (or treated as shown) in line 13 of Form 14 in the periodical return of the transferor covering the relevant period of account.

(4) The amount which (apart from this section) would be regarded as other income of the transferee for the purposes of section 83(2)(*e*) of the Finance Act 1989 for the period of account of the transferee which includes the transfer date is to be reduced by an amount equal to the transferred surplus.

(5) In subsection (4) above "the transferred surplus" means the amount shown (or treated as shown) in line 13 of Form 14 in the periodical return of the transferor covering the relevant period of account.

(6) See section 444AA for the meaning of "the transfer date", and section 444AB for the meaning of "the relevant period of account", in this section.

444ACZA Transfer schemes transferring part of business: reduction in income of transferee

(1) This section applies where an insurance business transfer scheme has effect to transfer part (but not the whole or substantially the whole) of the long-term business of a person ("the transferor") to another person ("the transferee") and the condition in subsection (2) below is met.

(2) The condition is that the transferor did not carry on life assurance business that is mutual business during the period of account of the transferor covering the transfer date.

(3) The amount which (apart from this section) would be regarded as other income of the transferee for the purposes of section 83(2)(*e*) of the Finance Act 1989 for the period of account of the transferee which includes the transfer date is to be reduced by an amount equal to the transferred surplus.

(4) In subsection (4) above "the transferred surplus" means such part of the amount shown (or treated as shown) in line 13 of Form 14 in the periodical return of the transferor covering the last period of account of the transferor ending before the transfer date as it is just and reasonable to regard as being attributable to the transfer.

(5) See section 444AA for the meaning of "the transfer date" in this section."

(2) In section 83(2A) of FA 1989 (receipts not to be taken into account), omit paragraph (*b*).

GENERAL NOTE

Paragraph 6 introduces two new sections to TA 1988 whose purpose is to provide relief in the transferee for surplus previously taxed in the transferor, so preventing a double charge to tax. New TA 1988 s 444AC applies when the whole or substantially the whole of the transferor's business is transferred. The latter is important because it is not unusual for whole business transfers to actually leave behind some policies and matching assets which cannot be transferred as a matter of law and which are often reinsured to the transferee as part of the scheme of transfer. HMRC accepted during the consultation process that to deny relief in such circumstances was inequitable. New TA 1988 s 444ACZA deals with part transfers in a similar way.

Although these relieving provisions are welcome, a number of issues remain which the ongoing consultation process will look to eliminate. Firstly both new sections rely on entries on Form 14 of the regulatory return which may not be available if the transfer takes place part way through an accounting period, particularly if it is a part transfer. Secondly Condition A in new TA 1988 s 444AC(2) overlooks that mutual companies bear tax on surplus and that there is legislation in TA 1988 ss 444AF to 444AL which deals with planning to avoid tax on previously declared mutual surplus. Thirdly the part transfer provisions require an apportionment of previously taxed surplus on a just and reasonable basis which introduces an element of uncertainty although in practice the commercial negotiations leading up to the scheme may well have identified what amount of previously taxed surplus, if any, is to be transferred.

Repeal of section 444AD

7— (1) In ICTA, omit section 444AD (transfers of business: modification of section 83(2B) of FA 1989).

(2) In section 83YA(7) of FA 1989 (changes in value of assets brought into account: transfer-in amount), for the words after "if" substitute "a transfer takes place in the following period of account; and the amount of the transfer-in amount for the previous period of account is any amount by which—

(*a*) the fair value of such of the assets of the long-term insurance fund of the company immediately after the transfer as were assets of the transferor's long-term insurance fund immediately before the transfer, exceeds

(*b*) the amount of any business transfer-in brought into account in accordance with section 83(2)(*e*) in relation to the transfer."

GENERAL NOTE

Paragraph 7 repeals TA 1988 s 444AD which previously allowed the parties to a transfer to jointly elect that assets transferred from the investment reserve of one to the investment reserve of the other should be outside the charge to tax imposed by FA 1989 s 83(2B). Because that sub-section no longer governs the calculation of taxable amounts on a transfer of business, its role having been taken by new TA 1988 ss 444AB to 444ACZA, the election is no longer required. As a consequence FA 1989 s 83YA, which refers to TA 1988 s 444AD, is amended by para 7(2) by writing the relevant parts of the latter section into the former in place of the current cross-reference. This ensures that companies to which FA 1989 s 83YA applies may continue to benefit from the relief for amounts they receive from the transferor's investment reserve.

Transfer schemes: anti-avoidance

8— (1) In ICTA, before section 444AF (and the italic cross-heading before it) insert—

"444AEA Transfer schemes: anti-avoidance rule

(1) This section applies where—

(*a*) as a result of the whole or any part of transfer scheme arrangements involving the transfer of long-term business from one person ("the transferor") to another ("the transferee") a Case I advantage is obtained by the transferor or the transferee (or by both), and

(*b*) the sole or main purpose, or one of the main purposes, of the whole or any part of the transfer scheme arrangements is the obtaining of that Case I advantage.

(2) In subsection (1) above "transfer scheme arrangements" means an insurance business transfer scheme ("the relevant transfer scheme") together with any relevant associated operations.

(3) If a Case I advantage is obtained by the transferor (see subsection (1) of section 444AEB), the amount of the transferor's Case I advantage (see subsection (2) of that section) is to be taken into account as an increase in value of the assets of the long-term insurance fund of the transferor for the period of account of the transferor covering the transfer date.

(4) If a Case I advantage is obtained by the transferee (see subsection (1) of section 444AEC), the amount of the transferee's Case I advantage (see subsection (2) of that section) is to be taken into account as an increase in value of the assets of the long-term insurance fund of the transferee for the first period of account of the transferee ending after the transfer date.

(5) In this section and sections 444AEB and 444AEC "relevant associated operations", in relation to the relevant transfer scheme, means—

(*a*) any other insurance business transfer scheme,

(*b*) any contract of reinsurance,

(*c*) any reconstruction or amalgamation involving the transferor, a dependant of the transferor which is an insurance undertaking or the transferee, or

(*d*) any surplus-increasing transfer of assets,

which is effected in connection with the relevant transfer scheme.

(6) In subsection (5) above—

"dependant" and "insurance undertaking" have the same meaning as in the Insurance Prudential Sourcebook, and

"surplus-increasing transfer of assets" means a transfer of assets of the transferor's long-term insurance fund to the transferee which is not brought into account for any period of account of the transferee but increases the amount of total surplus shown in line 39 of Form 58 in any periodical return of the transferee.

(7) See section 444AA for the meaning of "the transfer date" in this section.

444AEB Case I advantage: transferor

(1) A Case I advantage is obtained by the transferor if—

(*a*) Case I profits of its life assurance business for a period of account to which this section applies are less than they would be but for the transfer scheme arrangements or any part of the transfer scheme arrangements, or

(*b*) Case I losses of its life assurance business for such a period of account are greater than they would be but for the transfer scheme arrangements or any part of the transfer scheme arrangements.

(2) If a Case I advantage is obtained by the transferor, the amount of the Case I advantage is the aggregate of—

(*a*) the amounts (if any) by which Case I profits for each period of account to which this section applies are less than they would be but for the transfer scheme arrangements or part, and

(*b*) the amounts (if any) by which Case I losses for each such period of account are greater than they would be but for the transfer scheme arrangements or part.

(3) This section applies to a period of account if it is—

(*a*) the period of account of the transferor covering the transfer date,
(*b*) any earlier period of account of the transferor, or
(*c*) where any relevant associated operations are effected in any later period of account, that period of account.

(4) In this section and section 444AEC "Case I profits" and "Case I losses" means profits and losses computed in accordance with the provisions of Case I of Schedule D.

(5) See section 444AA for the meaning of "the transfer date", and section 444AEA for the meaning of "relevant associated operations", in this section.

444AEC Case I advantage: transferee

(1) A Case I advantage is obtained by the transferee if—

(*a*) Case I profits of its life assurance business for a period of account to which this section applies are less than they would be but for the transfer scheme arrangements or any part of the transfer scheme arrangements, or
(*b*) Case I losses of its life assurance business for such a period of account are greater than they would be but for the transfer scheme arrangements or any part of the transfer scheme arrangements.

(2) If a Case I advantage is obtained by the transferee, the amount of the Case I advantage is—

(*a*) the amount by which Case I profits for each period of account to which this section applies are less than they would be but for the transfer scheme arrangements or part, or
(*b*) the amount by which Case I losses for each such period of account are greater than they would be but for the transfer scheme arrangements or part.

(3) This section applies to a period of account if it is—

(*a*) the first period of account of the transferee ending after the transfer date or after the effecting of the first of any relevant associated operations (if that occurs before the transfer date),
(*b*) the second period of account of the transferee ending after the transfer date or after the effecting of the last of any relevant associated operations (if that occurs after the transfer date), or
(*c*) any intervening period of account.

(4) See section 444AA for the meaning of "the transfer date", section 444AEA for the meaning of "relevant associated operations" and section 444AEB for the meaning of "Case I profits" and "Case I losses", in this section.

444AED Clearance: no avoidance or group advantage

(1) Section 444AEA does not apply in relation to the transferor or the transferee if, on an application under this section, the Commissioners for Her Majesty's Revenue and Customs ("the HMRC Commissioners") have given a notice under subsection (2) below.

(2) A notice under this subsection is a notice stating that the HMRC Commissioners are satisfied—

(*a*) that the obtaining of a Case I advantage by the applicant is not the sole or main purpose of the whole or any part of the transfer scheme arrangements, or
(*b*) that the transferor and the transferee are members of the same group of companies and that there is no advantage to the group arising from any Case I advantage obtained by the transferor or by the transferee.

(3) For the purposes of this section there is no advantage to a group arising from any Case I advantage obtained by the transferor or by the transferee if—

(*a*) as a result of transfer scheme arrangements, there is an increase in the liability to corporation tax of one or more companies which are members of the group of companies, and
(*b*) the amount (or aggregate amount) of that increase is not less than the reduction in the liability to corporation tax of the transferor or the transferee (or both) arising from the obtaining of the Case I advantage.

(4) An application under this section must be in writing and contain particulars of the transfer scheme arrangements.

(5) The HMRC Commissioners may by notice require the applicant to provide further particulars in order to enable them to determine the application.

(6) A requirement may be imposed under subsection (5) above within 30 days of the receipt of the application or of any further particulars required under that subsection.

(7) If a notice under subsection (5) above is not complied with within 30 days or such longer period as the HMRC Commissioners may allow, they need not proceed further on the application.

(8) The HMRC Commissioners must give notice of their decision on an application under this section to the applicant within 30 days of receiving the application or, if they give a notice under subsection (5) above, within 30 days of that notice being complied with.

(9) If the HMRC Commissioners—

(*a*) give notice to the applicant under subsection (8) above that they are not satisfied as mentioned in subsection (2) above, or

(*b*) do not comply with subsection (8) above,

the applicant may require them to transmit the application to the Special Commissioners.

(10) A requirement under subsection (9) above must be imposed within 30 days of the giving of the notice or the failure to comply and must be accompanied by any notice given under subsection (5) above and further particulars provided pursuant to any such notice.

(11) Any notice given by the Special Commissioners has effect for the purposes of subsection (1) above as if it were given by the HMRC Commissioners.

(12) If any particulars provided under this section do not fully and accurately disclose all facts and considerations material for the decision of the HMRC Commissioners or the Special Commissioners, any resulting notice that they are satisfied as mentioned in subsection (2) above is void.

(13) For the purposes of this section two companies are members of the same group of companies if they are for the purposes of Chapter 4 of Part 10."

(2) In section 432E(2A) of ICTA (as amended by paragraph 4(2)), after "444ABC," insert "444AEA," and after paragraph (*aa*) insert—

"(*ab*) section 444AEA of this Act;".

GENERAL NOTE

Paragraph 8 introduces a targeted anti-avoidance rule ("TAAR") in TA 1988 s 444AEA to protect the Exchequer from tax planning involving transfers of insurance business. The introduction of the TAAR reflects the fact that many of the changes to this part of the legislation have been caused by transactions that HMRC have seen as abusive.

The TAAR applies when an insurance business transfer scheme gives rise to a Case I advantage (see below) and the sole or main purpose, or one of the main purposes, of the whole or any part of the scheme was to secure that Case I advantage for either the transferor or the transferee, or both. There is room for debate about the extent to which HMRC can dissect the scheme in ascertaining whether this test is met and the extent to which it should apply. For example a normal, non-abusive transfer scheme might give rise to a genuine Case I loss (a Case I advantage) but when looked at in isolation, parts of that scheme might be said to have as their sole purpose the obtaining of a Case I advantage so the TAAR could apply. HMRC have said that the TAAR will be interpreted in a restrictive way so that it applies only to those parts of the transaction that have the securing of a Case I advantage as their sole or main purpose. It is hoped that HMRC's interpretation will become clearer as the consultation process continues and that there will be adequate guidance as to the circumstances in which the TAAR might apply.

The TAAR also extends to cover a Case I advantage that is derived from "relevant associated operations" entered into in connection with the scheme. Relevant associated operations are defined as any other insurance business transfer scheme; any reinsurance contract; any reconstruction or amalgamation involving the transferor, an insurance dependent of the transferor or the transferee; or a transfer of assets from the transferor's long-term fund to the transferee which is not brought into account for any period by the transferee but which increases its total surplus, having by extension avoided a charge to tax. The extension of the TAAR to encompass associated operations is designed to prevent exploitation of the rules by companies structuring transactions so that those parts at which HMRC would take offence are fragmented from the main scheme itself.

A Case I advantage accrues to the transferor if its profits (losses) computed on Case I basis are less (greater) than they would have been in the absence of the scheme. This will therefore include computations of gross roll up business profits or losses which follow Case I principles. The comparison is made for the period of account covering the transfer; any earlier period of account; or a later period if transactions took place in that period that are associated with the transfer itself. This means that there is a considerable period of time potentially affected and companies will need to keep such records as are necessary to demonstrate that no Case I advantage accrues.

Similar provisions apply to the measure of a Case I advantage in the transferee except that the periods potentially covered are the period ending after the transfer date, unless there were associated operations before that date in which case it is the period ending after the first of those operations takes place; the second period of account ending after the transfer date, unless there were associated operations after the transfer date in which case it is the period ending after the last of those operations takes place; and any intervening periods. Again this means that there will be a considerable record keeping requirement on companies who will need to run parallel tax computations to demonstrate the extent of any Case I advantage, if any. HMRC have stated that the period to which the TAAR applies will be monitored and attempts to manipulate it, presumably by causing the Case I advantage to manifest outside it, may result in its extension.

In neither case does the legislation appear to recognise that a Case I advantage within the meaning of the definition can arise from perfectly proper commercial transactions arising under the scheme.

If a Case I advantage does arise to either party, the amount of that advantage is taken into account as an increase in the value of assets brought into account so that it will flow directly into the calculation of Case VI and Case I profits. If the advantage accrues to the transferor, it is taken into account in the period of account covering the transfer; if it accrues to the transferee it is taken into account in its first period of account ending after the transfer date. Since the Case I advantage is measured over a number of periods of account, this introduces an element of front end loading and also might require refiling of returns as the advantage is measured in subsequent periods.

There is a clearance procedure to allow companies to achieve certainty that any particular transaction will not fall foul of the anti-avoidance provisions. Unlike the previous clearance process (see the note on para 2 above), the new clearance is not a joint approach to HMRC. Instead each party to the transfer may apply on its own behalf. It is too early to say yet whether a requirement for a party to seek clearance will become a standard clause in scheme documents in the future.

A company may apply for clearance on two grounds: firstly that the obtaining of a Case I advantage was not the sole or main purpose of the whole or any part of the scheme; or secondly that the parties to the transfer are members of the same group of companies and that overall the group derives no advantage from any Case I advantage accruing to one of the parties. The first-mentioned clearance is well understood and follows similar mechanisms used elsewhere in the legislation. The second is a novel concept, reflecting the fact that a large number of insurance business transfers take place within the same group following acquisitions and mergers. Unfortunately the test as currently drafted tilts the playing field in HMRC's favour. The industry had sought a group advantage test in which any Case I advantage arising from the scheme could be "franked" by an increase in the tax liability elsewhere leaving just the net amount of the Case I advantage, if any, in charge. However the relief is available only if the tax disadvantage is greater than the Case I advantage, meaning that a "cliff edge" develops as the potential tax increase tends towards the Case I advantage. As an example, suppose that the transferor A would realise a Case I advantage on the scheme of £50 while the transferee B would suffer an additional corporation tax charge of £30. All other things being equal, overall the group has gained a net tax advantage of £20; however because the increase in B's tax charge is not less than the £50 Case I advantage obtained by A, the group will not be able to seek clearance that the TAAR should not apply to the transaction and the full £50 Case I advantage would be taxable.

It is also difficult to see how a group would be able to seek clearance on the second ground at the same time as it looks to obtain clearance on the first, so in practice there may be multiple applications under both parts of this section for a single scheme. This is unsatisfactory because it would involve unnecessary work in demonstrating that the second test was satisfied which would be redundant if the first were met. Conversely, applying on the second ground following a failure to obtain clearance under the first would add additional delay to what is often a tight time scale.

New TA 1988 s 444AED also provides a formal process for the making of a clearance application including requirements for the provision of information and deadlines for reply.

Finally para 8(2) ensures that any Case I advantage is added to the amount of investment return apportioned to with-profits business, otherwise the needs basis would simply over-write the adjustment making it ineffective in a with-profits fund.

Repeal of FA s 82C

9 In FA 1989, omit section 82C (relevant financial reinsurance contracts).

GENERAL NOTE

Paragraph 9 repeals FA 1989 s 82C from the appointed day. The precise application of this legislative provision was always obscure but regardless its purported role in dealing with shortfalls of assets on an insurance business transfer scheme made good by financial reinsurance is now subsumed into the new rules in Sch 9 so it will no longer be required.

Transfers: receipts to be taken into account

10— (1) Section 83 of FA 1989 (receipts to be taken into account) is amended as follows.

(2) In the first sentence of subsection (2B), for the words from "but the transfer" to "the time of the transfer" substitute "the fair value of the assets at the time of the transfer, reduced by any amount brought into account in respect of them (for the period of account in which the transfer takes place or any earlier period of account) as part of total expenditure or as a business transfer-out,".

(3) In that sentence (as amended by sub-paragraph (2))—

(*a*) for "as a business transfer out" substitute "by being netted off against incomings in lines 11 to 15 of a revenue account", and

(*b*) for the words after "value of the assets of that fund" substitute "except to the extent that any of the exclusions in subsections (2C) to (2E) below apply."

(4) Omit the second sentence of subsection (2B).

(5) For subsection (2E) substitute—

"(2E) Assets transferred by an insurance business transfer scheme are excluded from subsection (2B) above."

GENERAL NOTE

Paragraph 10 makes two amendments to FA 1989 s 83(2B). The amendment in sub-para 2 ensures that any transfer of assets out of a company's long-term insurance fund is always brought into account at fair value. This amendment deals with HMRC concerns that companies could exploit the mismatch between admissible and fair values, the former often being lower than the latter for reasons of regulatory valuation, resulting in a lower measure of taxable income. HMRC have publicly stated that they do not accept that the previous legislation was defective in this way, so the amendment may be viewed as a precautionary clarification of their previous view of the law; however that view was not generally shared by others in the industry. In order to prevent fore-stalling and because this amendment may be viewed as at least in part as anti-avoidance law, it takes effect for transfers of assets on or after 6 December 2006, the date of its announcement. Although introduced as part of the schedule dealing with insurance business transfer schemes, its application is not restricted just to assets transferred under such schemes and will potentially apply to all transfers of assets from a company's long-term insurance fund.

The second amendment to FA 1989 s 83(2B) introduced by paragraph 10 ensures that assets transferred under an insurance business transfer scheme are not taxed under that sub-section because the principal charging sections for insurance business transfers are new TA 1988 ss 444AB to 444ACZA. As this change is merely a consequence of the wider changes to the rules for insurance business transfer schemes, it will take effect from the same appointed day as those rules.

Finally the clarificatory tail-piece to FA 1989 s 83(2B) regarding expenses netted off against investment income recorded on line 12 of the regulatory revenue account is expanded to deal with expenses netted off against all other categories of income in that account..

Transfers and demutualisations: losses where assets added to long-term insurance fund

11— (1) FA 1989 is amended as follows.

(2) Omit—

(*a*) in section 83, subsections (3) to (7) and, in subsection (8), the definitions of "add", "demutualisation" and "total reinsurance" (which relate to losses where assets added to long-term insurance fund),

(*b*) section 83AA (amounts added to long-term insurance fund in excess of loss), and

(*c*) section 83AB (treatment of surplus where there is subsequent transfer from company etc).

(3) In section 83B(3) (changes in recognised accounts: attribution of amounts carried forward), for "83AB" substitute "83ZA".

GENERAL NOTE

Paragraph 11 repeals legislation introduced in the mid 1990s to restrict the extent to which a life insurance company could claim a tax allowable loss when there had been an addition of capital to its long-term fund. Those rules potentially applied in circumstances that were always considerably more extensive in scope than the mischief that HMRC were seeking to prevent and in particular could extend across multiple transfers of business from one unconnected company to another. This latter extension caused considerable commercial difficulties as the parties to the transfer sought to protect themselves from unexpected tax charges caused by previous actions over which they had no control. The repeal of these rules, whose policing effect will be replaced by the TAAR, is welcome to the industry as it removes a degree of uncertainty.

The repeals in para 11 will generally be effective from an appointed day, likely to be in 2008 (see para 17 below), but are also effective for transfers of business that took place before 21 March 2007 in a period of account beginning on or after 1 January 2007. The reason for this staggered introduction is to protect companies that undertook insurance business transfers in the period referred to which had relied on commencement dates suggested when the legislation was first exposed for comment at the time of the pre-Budget report.

12 In section 436A(3) of ICTA (gross roll-up business), for "83AB" substitute "83ZA".

GENERAL NOTE

Paragraph 12 makes a minor consequential amendment to a statutory cross reference in the new rules for taxing gross roll up business to cater for the repeals made by para 11. Although it may seem odd that the Finance Bill should contain an amendment to provisions contained elsewhere in the same Bill, the reason relates to the differing commencement provisions for the two pieces of legislation; the gross roll up rules take effect from 1 January 2007 while, as noted above, the repeals in para 11 will not take place until an appointed day.

Transfer schemes: old annuity contracts

13— (1) Paragraph 16 of Schedule 7 to FA 1991 (transitional relief for old general annuity contracts) is amended as follows.

(2) In sub-paragraph (7), in the definition of "old annuity contract", insert at the end "(including one forming part of the business transferred to another insurance company by an insurance business transfer scheme)".

(3) After that sub-paragraph insert—

"(8) Where—

(*a*) business is transferred to an insurance company by an insurance business transfer scheme during an accounting period of the company, and

(*b*) the business transferred consists of or includes old annuity contracts ("the transferred contracts"), the reference in the definition of R1 in sub-paragraph (2) above to the company's opening liabilities for the accounting period is, in relation to the transferred contracts, a reference to the company's liabilities in respect of the transferred contracts immediately after the transfer."

GENERAL NOTE

Paragraph 13 makes it clear that the rules in FA 1991 Sch 7 para 16 for determining what amount of any payment in respect of an "old" general annuity contract (a life annuity issued before 1 January 1992) is to be treated as a management expense continue across an insurance business transfer. In practice the parties to such a transaction used to seek confirmation from HMRC that this was so, such confirmation always being given. However now that the relief operates of a matter of law, it removes one of a number of non-statutory confirmations that used to be sought and gives legislative certainty. Paragraph 13 applies for periods of account beginning on or after 1 January 2007.

Transfer schemes: no gain/no loss

14— (1) TCGA 1992 is amended as follows.

(2) In section 211 (application of section 139), for subsections (2) and (2A) substitute—

"(2) Where this section applies the transferor and the transferee are treated for the purposes of corporation tax on chargeable gains as if any assets included in the transfer which—

(*a*) immediately before they are acquired by the transferee, were assets of the transferor's long-term insurance fund, and

(*b*) immediately after they are so acquired are assets of the transferee's long-term insurance fund,

were acquired for a consideration of such amount as would secure that neither a gain nor a loss would accrue to the transferor on the disposal.

(3) Subsection (2) above is subject to section 212."

(3) In section 35(3)(*d*) (re-basing: exceptions), after "171," insert "211,".

GENERAL NOTE

Paragraph 14 amends TCGA 1992 s 211 for periods of account beginning on or after 1 January 2007 and removes the link to TCGA 1992 s 139 that previously was present and which did not sit naturally with transfers of insurance business which would not normally be schemes of reconstruction as required by that section. Henceforth there will be neither a gain nor a loss on any assets subject to the CGT regime (but not structural assets, see sch 10 para 2 below) that transfer from the long-term insurance fund of one party to that of the other unless they are within TCGA 1992 s 212 which takes priority.

This change has however brought a restriction in the scope of relief available on a transfer of business because previously all transferring assets, whether held in the long-term fund or outside it, could benefit from the relief. This stems from the fact that the previous general application of TCGA 1992 s 139 to all businesses meant that it did not sit easily with the distinction in a life insurance company between assets of its long-term insurance fund and its shareholders' fund. Now that TCGA 1992 s 211 has been amended, the distinction between the two has been made explicit. HMRC has been asked to reconsider this restriction in relief available on a transfer of insurance business, although in a group situation the relief provided by TCGA 1992 s 171 will be available.

Transfer schemes: old reinsurance business

15 In paragraph 57 of Schedule 8 to FA 1995 (application of provisions made by that Schedule), after sub-paragraph (2) (which disapplies section 442A of ICTA in relation to the reinsurance of policies and contracts made and reinsured before 29th November 1994) insert—

"(3) Where business consisting of or including an arrangement for the reinsurance of a policy or contract made before 29th November 1994 which was effected before that date has been transferred by an insurance business transfer scheme sub-paragraph (2) has effect in relation to the transferee."

GENERAL NOTE

Paragraph 15 performs a similar function to para 13 above instead in this instance the relief is for reinsurance contracts that predate the introduction of TA 1988 s 442A in 1995. The latter was an anti-avoidance measure that applied to contracts of reinsurance entered into on or after 29 November 1994. There has previously been some doubt about the extent to which a reinsurance contract transferred by Court Order is the same as the original contract or whether it is novated and re-instated. If the latter were the case, the protection it enjoyed from the effect of the TA 1988 s 442A changes would be lost. Case law and a Treasury consultation exercise have suggested that the former is true and it is now put beyond doubt for tax too. Paragraph 15 applies for periods of account beginning on or after 1 January 2007.

Power to amend transfer provisions

16— (1) The Treasury may by order make provision in relation to insurance business transfer schemes.

(2) The power conferred by sub-paragraph (1) includes power to amend or repeal any provision of the Corporation Tax Acts relating to insurance business transfer schemes and otherwise to amend the Corporation Tax Acts.

(3) The power conferred by sub-paragraph (1) includes power to make—

(*a*) different provision for different cases or otherwise for different purposes, and
(*b*) incidental, supplementary, consequential or transitional provisions and savings.

(4) Provision made by an order under this paragraph may be made so as to have effect in relation to periods of account current when it is made.

(5) No order may be made under this paragraph unless a draft of the statutory instrument containing it has been laid before the House of Commons before 1st April 2008 and has been approved by a resolution of that House.

GENERAL NOTE

Paragraph 16 gives the Treasury regulation making powers to amend the existing legislation or to introduce new provisions. This power was included in the Finance Bill because the transfers of business legislation is not yet in its final form and discussions continue between the industry, its representatives and HMRC. Any regulations made under para 16 may have effect for the period of account in which they are made. At the request of the industry, the regulation making power includes a "sunset" clause causing it to lapse on 1 April 2008. Regulations made under para 16 will also require positive affirmation by the House of Commons. This protection was included at the industry's request because it was believed inappropriate to make fundamental changes to legislation of this importance by simply laying regulations to take effect unless objected to.

Commencement

17— (1) The amendments made by paragraphs 1 to 3 and 13 to 15 have effect in relation to periods of account beginning on or after 1st January 2007.

(2) The amendments made by paragraphs 4, 6 to 9, 10(3) to (5), 11 and 12 have effect in accordance with provision made by an order made by the Treasury.

(3) But the amendments made by paragraphs 11 and 12 also have effect in relation to periods of account beginning on or after 1st January 2007 where the transfer of business or demutualisation concerned took place before 21st March 2007.

(4) The amendment made by paragraph 5 has effect in relation to transfers of business with a transfer date after 21st March 2007.

(5) The amendment made by paragraph 10(2) has effect in relation to transfers taking place on or after 6th December 2006.

GENERAL NOTE

Paragraph 17 sets out the various commencement provisions which are discussed where relevant above. It is likely that the appointed day envisaged by para 17(2) will be in the spring next year, possibly 31 March or 1 April. The reason that there is to be such a long lead time between the hoped for finalisation of the legislation in the summer of 2007 and its introduction next year is because insurance business transfer schemes take a considerable length of time to put in place and it was agreed that the parties to such a transaction needed certainty as to which regime was to apply in their particular circumstances.

SCHEDULE 10
INSURANCE COMPANIES: MISCELLANEOUS

Section 41

Contingent loans

1 In section 83ZA(4) of FA 1989 (contingent loans), for "the end of the" substitute "any time during a".

GENERAL NOTE

Paragraph 1 amends FA 1989 s 83ZA to correct a flaw under which a company could obtain a deduction for the total repayment of a contingent loan. The purpose of the legislation in FA 1989 s 83ZA was that contingent loans recorded in a company's regulatory revenue account should be tax neutral. This was achieved by making a fiscal adjustment to unwind the effect of any entries in that account. For example in a period in which a company received a contingent loan of £100, which would be taken into account for Case I purposes by FA 1989 s 83(2), a deduction would be allowed in the tax computation to reverse the taxable amount of £100. Similarly if the company repaid the £100, the repayment would be relieved as a deduction but an increase in income of £100 would be made in the tax computation to negate that deduction. The wording of the legislation however was defective in the latter situation if the company had no outstanding contingent loan liabilities at the end of the period in which it fully repaid a contingent loan. In those circumstances FA 1989 s 83ZA(13) did not require the adjustment to income so the company would obtain a tax deduction for the amount of any repayment. This flaw is now corrected with effect from 10 May 2007 although it remains to be seen to what extent HMRC will challenge previous deductions under the law ass originally drafted.

"Structural" assets

2— (1) In FA 1989, after section 83 insert—

"83XA Structural assets

(1) Section 83(2) does not require to be taken into account as receipts or expenses of a period of account income from, or an increase or a decrease in the value of, structural assets held by an insurance company in a non-profit fund.

(2) For the purposes of subsection (1) above—

(*a*) an increase in the value of structural assets includes any amount by which their fair value when they cease to be structural assets, or come to be held otherwise than in any of the company's non-profit funds, exceeds their admissible value at the end of the preceding period of account, and

(*b*) a decrease in the value of structural assets includes any amount by which the admissible value of the assets at the end of the period of account in which they become structural

assets, or come to be held in any of the company's non-profit funds, is less than their historic cost.

(3) In this section "structural assets" means—

(*a*) shares, debts and loans the value of which is required to be entered in lines 21 to 24 of Form 13 in the periodical return (UK insurance dependants and other insurance dependants), and

(*b*) assets of such other descriptions as are specified by regulations made by the Treasury.

(4) Where a structural asset held by an insurance company in a non-profit fund ceases to be a structural asset or comes to be held otherwise than in any of the company's non-profit funds and, immediately before it came to be a structural asset held in any of the company's non-profit funds it (or any part of it) was an asset of the company's long-term insurance fund, the relevant value difference is to be taken into account under section 83(2)—

(*a*) as a receipt (if it is a positive amount), or

(*b*) as an expense (if it is a negative amount),

of the relevant period of account.

(5) For the purposes of subsection (4) above "the relevant value difference", in relation to an asset, is—

$$HC - AV$$

where—

HC is its historic cost, and

AV is its admissible value at the relevant time.

(6) In subsection (4) above "the relevant period of account" means—

(*a*) in a case within paragraph (*a*) of that subsection, the period of account in which the asset ceases to be a structural asset or comes to be held otherwise than in any of the company's non-profit funds, and

(*b*) in a case within paragraph (*b*) of that subsection, the period of account in which the asset first comes to be held otherwise than by the company or (where the company is a member of a group) otherwise than by a company which is a member of the group;

and section 170 of the Taxation of Chargeable Gains Act 1992 (meaning of "group" etc) has effect for the interpretation of this subsection.

(7) In subsection (5) above "the relevant time" means—

(*a*) in a case where assets become structural assets held in any of the company's non-profit funds by virtue of the commencement of this section, the end of the last period of account of the company beginning before 1st January 2007, and

(*b*) otherwise, the time when the assets become structural assets held in any of the company's non-profit funds.

(8) In this section "historic cost", in relation to an asset which is or has been held in any of the company's non-profit funds, means—

(*a*) where the asset came to be held in any of the company's non-profit funds on acquisition from another person, the consideration given by the company for the acquisition of the asset, and

(*b*) otherwise, its fair value when it came to be held in any of the company's non-profit funds.

(9) In this section "admissible value", in relation to an asset and a time, means the value of the asset as shown in column 1 of Form 13 of the periodical return for the period ending with that time (or as would be so shown if there were a periodical return covering a period ending with that time).

(10) Regulations made by the Treasury may make provision for computing for the purposes of the Taxation of Chargeable Gains Act 1992 any gain or loss arising on a disposal by an insurance company of a structural asset held in a non-profit fund in any case where the condition in subsection (11) is met.

(11) The condition in this subsection is met if, in any period of account of the company in which the asset was held by it—

(*a*) income arising from the asset was (or, had there been any, would have been) referable to any category of long-term business the profits of which fell for that period of account to be computed in accordance with the provisions applicable to Case I of Schedule D, or

(*b*) the company was charged to tax on the profits of its life assurance business under Case I of Schedule D.

(12) Structural assets held by an insurance company in a non-profit fund are to be treated as being within paragraph (*f*) of subsection (4) of section 440 of the Taxes Act 1988; but no disposal or re-acquisition is to be deemed to occur by virtue of an asset ceasing to be within any other paragraph of that subsection and coming within that paragraph on becoming such a structural asset.

(13) Structural assets held by an insurance company in a non-profit fund are to be treated as being "remaining" securities within section 440A(2)(*e*) of the Taxes Act 1988.

(14) Section 432A of the Taxes Act 1988 does not have effect in relation to income arising from, or gains and losses accruing on the disposal of, structural assets held by an insurance company in a non-profit fund.

(15) Regulations under subsection (3) or (10) above may be made so as to have effect in relation to periods of account current when they are made (as well as periods of account beginning later)."

(2) In ICTA, omit section 444ACA (transfers of business).

(3) In section 432E(2A) of that Act, omit "444ACA(2)," and paragraph (*b*).

(4) In section 211 of TCGA 1992 (transfers of business: application of section 139 of that Act), as amended by paragraph 14 of Schedule 9 to this Act, after subsection (2) insert—

"(2A) The reference in subsection (2) above to assets included in the transfer does not include structural assets within the meaning of section 83XA of the Finance Act 1989."

(5) In paragraph 17 of Schedule 7AC to TCGA 1992 (substantial shareholdings exemption: special rules for assets of insurance company's long-term insurance fund), after sub-paragraph (4) insert—

"(4A) The reference in sub-paragraph (2) to an asset of the investing company's long-term insurance fund, and the references in sub-paragraphs (3) and (4) to shares or an interest in shares held as assets of its long-term insurance fund, do not include a structural asset, or structural assets, within the meaning of section 83XA of the Finance Act 1989."

GENERAL NOTE

Paragraph 2 introduces new FA 1989 s 83XA , a measure that treats structural investments in insurance subsidiaries held in an insurance company's non-profit fund in a way that parallels the treatment afforded to subsidiaries of non-insurance companies. In the case of a non-insurance company, dividends received from a subsidiary benefit from the exemption from corporation tax in TA 1988 s 208 and movements in the capital value of the subsidiary are ignored except to the extent that they contribute to the calculation of any chargeable gain or allowable loss on their eventual disposal, that gain or loss probably benefiting from the substantial shareholdings exemption. In contrast dividends from a subsidiary of a long-term fund would be taxable by virtue of being included on the fund's Form 40 while capital movements in value would also be taken into account in the same way. Finally from HMRC's perspective those subsidiaries would likely be carried at an admissible value considerably lower than their market value and the corresponding write down would have been allowable for tax. Both the industry and HMRC therefore had grounds for wanting this situation to be changed to their mutual benefit.

The new legislation applies only to non-profit funds because companies can manage the emergence of taxable surplus in a with-profits fund by use of the book value election in r 9(10)(*c*) of IPRU(INS). The industry has asked HMRC to reconsider this particular point although measuring the previous impact of r 9(10)(*c*) on the value of assets that would be within the new rules is likely to make this difficult.

The new section applies for accounting periods beginning on or after 1 January 2007 to "structural assets" which are defined in sub-s (3) by reference to those parts of the FSA return on which investments in insurance subsidiaries are held. Typically such assets will be shares in, or loans to, those subsidiaries. There is however provision for regulations to be laid extending the scope of the definition and discussions on this point continue between HMRC and the industry. Income from, and movements in value of, such a structural asset held in a non-profit fund are not required to be included as receipts of a period. Movements in value are explicitly stated in para 2 to include write ups from admissible value to fair value on disposal and write downs from historic cost to admissible value on acquisition. If such an asset ceases to be a structural asset because, for example, it is sold or otherwise leaves the fund, sub-ss 4 and 5 bring into account the difference between the asset's historic cost (ie the value paid for it by the seller or otherwise its fair value when it moved into the non-profit fund) and its admissible value in the company's FSA return at either 1 January 2007 (if it became a structural asset as a result of the enactment of these rules) or the time when then asset became a structural asset. This adjustment effectively reverses any previous regulatory write down. Sub-sections 6 to 9 provide definitions of the terms used in performing the calculation. The new regime originally deemed an asset to come into the capital gains tax regime at its historic cost at the beginning of the first period of account in which it became a structural asset Following industry representations that this appeared to deny companies the benefit of indexation relief and rebasing to March 1982, a regulation making power has been included in paras 10 and 11 to deal with the transition to the capital gains tax regime. An asset that has always been referable to BLAGAB will be subject to the normal CGT rules including indexation and rebasing. The regulations will apply only when income from the asset was previously included in a computation of profit prepared in accordance with Case I principles (ie other than in a BLAGAB I-E computation) or the company was taxed on a Case I basis. The precise form of the regulations remains under discussion between the industry and HMRC although because most structural assets will benefit from the substantial shareholdings exemption, resolution of the issue is not an immediate concern.

A number of minor consequential changes are made to other parts of the legislation. Subsections 12 and 13 deem all structural assets to be in the shareholders' fund "box" in TA 1988 s 440 and the "remaining category in TA 1988 s 440A. Thus such assets are treated in the same way as assets of the company's shareholders' fund, further paralleling the regime applying to companies generally. However the deemed move to the shareholders' fund box does not trigger the normal deemed disposal and reacquisition under TA 1988 s 440. Similarly, the exclusion of the income and capital movements from the Case I/Case VI computations is carried across to the BLAGAB I-E computation by para 14 by removing these amounts from the sums to be apportioned under TA 1988 s 432A. This has the effect of removing these amounts from relevant profits, part of which may benefit from the lower policy holders' rate of tax, providing a further analogy to the rules for subsidiaries of non-insurance companies. HMRC have confirmed that the disapplication of TA 1988 s 432A is also sufficient to remove structural assets from the shareholders' excess assets regime and this point will be confirmed in guidance.

Because structural assets are treated in a manner analogous to assets of the shareholders' fund, they will not be able to benefit from the no gain/no loss provisions for assets of the long-term fund on an insurance business transfer in the amended TCGA 1992 s 211. As a corollary, the company will not need to reach the 30% threshold for the substantial shareholdings exemption to apply to these assets, although it is unclear how a holding of 10% would allow the asset in question to qualify as a structural asset.

Finally the new regime allows the repeal of TA 1988 s 444ACA which was enacted to counter losses created by transferring business from an insurance subsidiary to its parent and then claiming a loss on the write down in the regulatory value of the shares of that subsidiary. As movements in value from structural assets are no longer taxable or relievable, TA 1988 s 444ACA is no longer required to block this planning technique.

The structural assets rules are generally welcome as removing an anomaly between the life tax regime and the general corporate tax code. The insurance industry would however have preferred that the exemption was extended to all subsidiaries and other structural holdings, not just insurance companies.

Losses on disposal of authorised investment fund assets to connected manager

3 In TCGA 1992, after section 210B insert—

"210C Losses on disposal of authorised investment fund assets to connected manager

(1) Section 18(3) does not apply in relation to a loss accruing on the disposal by an insurance company of authorised investment fund assets to the manager of the authorised investment fund.

(2) In this section—

"authorised investment fund assets" means assets of the company's long-term insurance fund consisting of rights under an authorised unit trust or shares in an open-ended investment company,

"the manager of the authorised investment fund" means—

(*a*) in the case of an authorised unit trust, the person who is the manager of the unit trust scheme for the purposes of Chapter 3 of Part 17 of the Financial Services and Markets Act 2000, and

(*b*) in the case of an open-ended investment company, a director or other person having responsibility for the management of its scheme property, and

"open-ended investment company" means a company incorporated in the United Kingdom to which section 236 of the Financial Services and Markets Act 2000 applies."

GENERAL NOTE

Paragraph 3 introduces a welcome relaxation in the rules on "clogged" losses, that is to say allowable losses that arise on disposals to connected parties. Many financial services groups include a unit trust or other collective investment scheme manager. Previously if a life insurer in the same group disposed of assets to that manager any gain would be chargeable but an allowable loss would be relievable only against gains on subsequent disposals to the same manager, which might not occur for a considerable period, if at all. HMRC have now accepted that the annual deemed disposal charge imposed by TCGA 1992 s 212 on such assets makes the clogged losses rules particularly inappropriate in these circumstances. Therefore allowable losses on disposals of interests in an authorised unit trust or OEIC held by an insurance company as assets of its long-term fund to a connected manager will be taken outside the restriction imposed by TCGA 1992 s 18(3). This provision applies to losses accruing in periods of account beginning on or after 1 January 2007. The fate of unrelieved clogged losses arising in earlier periods remains under consideration.

Priority of section 83(2) of FA 1989 etc

4— (1) Section 83 of FA 1989 (receipts to be taken into account) is amended as follows.

(2) After subsection (2) insert—

"(2ZA) Amounts brought into account as mentioned in subsection (2) above are not to be taken into account in any other way; and this subsection applies in spite of—

(*a*) section 80(5) of the Finance Act 1996 (taxation of loan relationships),

(*b*) paragraph 1(2) of Schedule 26 to the Finance Act 2002 (taxation of profits from derivative contracts), and

(*c*) paragraph 1(3) of Schedule 29 to that Act (gains and losses in respect of intangible fixed assets)."

(3) In subsection (2A), after paragraph (*aa*) insert—

"(*ab*) comprises a business transfer-in that is not brought into account in a revenue account prepared for the purposes of Chapter 9 of the Prudential Sourcebook (Insurers) in respect of the whole of the company's long-term business,".

(4) Omit—

(*a*) in section 502H of ICTA, in subsection (2), paragraph (*b*) and the word "and" before it and subsections (8) to (10),

(*b*) paragraph 2(2) and (3) to (5) of Schedule 11 to FA 1996,

(*c*) paragraph 19(1) to (3) of Schedule 12 to FA 1997, and

(*d*) paragraph 36(4) and (5) of Schedule 29 to FA 2002.

GENERAL NOTE

Paragraph 4 makes a number of changes to FA 1989 s 83 which is the principal section governing what amounts are to be taken into account in computing taxable income under Case VI and Case I. It has always been the case that FA 1989 s 83 has had primacy over other sections of the Taxes Acts and until changes made by FA 2003 Sch 33 this was clear in its wording. A number of provisions elsewhere in the tax code make explicit that they take priority as charging sections unless otherwise stated, so FA 1989 s 83 is amended to make it clear that it takes precedence over, amongst others, the regimes for taxing loan relationships, derivatives and intangible fixed assets. Sub-paragraph 4 does the reverse by removing now redundant statements about the primacy of FA 1989 s 83 from other parts of the legislation.

Finally sub-para 3 ensures that transfers of business between different funds of the same company are tax neutral provided they do not feature on the summary revenue account for the whole company. Unlike much of the rest of Sch 10 this provision has a commencement date of 1 January 2005 in order to relieve companies from an unintended tax charge.

Tidying up of TCGA 1992

5— (1) TCGA 1992 is amended as follows.

(2) In section 210B(6)(*a*) (disposal and acquisition of section 440A securities), for the words after "are" substitute "assets within section 212(1).".

(3) Omit—

(*a*) section 212(2A) (disapplication of section 212(1) to assets treated as representing rights under a creditor relationship),

(*b*) section 214 (rights under authorised unit trusts etc: transitional provisions), and

(*c*) section 214A (further transitional provisions).

GENERAL NOTE

Advantage has been taken of the substantial changes made to the life tax regime as a result of the consultation process to tidy up and clarify various provisions. Paragraph 5 makes a number of changes to TCGA 1992 as well as repealing some transitional rules from the introduction of the regime for deemed disposals of unit trusts etc that are now obsolete.

Tidying up of Chapter 2 of Part 4 of FA 1996

6— (1) Chapter 2 of Part 4 of FA 1996 (loan relationships) is amended as follows.

(2) In section 103(3) (loan relationships: interpretation), omit "or" at the end of paragraph (*a*) and after paragraph (*b*) insert "or

(*c*) any basic life assurance and general annuity business,".

(3) In sub-paragraph (1) of paragraph 1A of Schedule 9 (life assurance policies), for the words after "relating to" substitute "liabilities of an insurance company within paragraph (*a*) of the definition of "liabilities" in section 431(2) of the Taxes Act 1988."; and the italic heading before that paragraph accordingly becomes "*Insurance company liabilities*".

(4) In Schedule 11, omit paragraph 1(1A) to (1C).

GENERAL NOTE

Paragraph 6 makes a number of changes to the loan relationship regime as it applies to life insurers, consolidating various provisions that were scattered through the legislation and as a consequence repealing a number of provisions which have in the past sometimes caused difficulties of interpretation.

Correction of erroneous repeal

7 The repeals made by Schedule 3 to ITA 2007 in paragraph 11 of Schedule 6 to FA 1990 are deemed never to have had effect; but Schedule 3 to ITA 2007 is deemed to have included the repeal of the words before the paragraphs in sub-paragraph (1) of that paragraph.

GENERAL NOTE

Paragraph 7 is an interesting comment on the law of unintended consequences. The introduction of ITA 2007 required the repeal of those parts of TA 1988 dealing with the accrued income scheme, such repeals duly being made. Unfortunately FA 1990 Sch 6 para 11 which gave the commencement dates for those rules (and which correctly needed repeal) also gave the commencement rules for the principal parts of the life tax code in FA 1989 ss 82–89 (which did not). If the repeal had not been rescinded the whole basis of calculating a life insurer's profits on a Case I and Case VI basis would have fallen away.

Non-profit companies, non-profit funds and with-profits funds

8— (1) In section 431(2) of ICTA (interpretative provisions relating to insurance companies) insert at the appropriate place—

" "non-profit company", in relation to a period of account, means a company carrying on long-term business where, at the end of the period—

(*a*) none of the liabilities of that business, or

(*b*) none but an insignificant proportion of those liabilities,

are with-profits liabilities;",

" "non-profit fund" means a fund that is not a with-profits fund;", and

" "with-profits fund" has the meaning given by the Prudential Sourcebook (Insurers);".

(2) Omit—

(*a*) in section 432YA(5) of ICTA, the definitions of "non-profit company" and "non-profit fund",

(*b*) section 82D(5) of FA 1989,

(*c*) in section 83YA of that Act, subsection (8) and, in subsection (11), the definition of "with-profits fund", and

(*d*) in section 83A of that Act, in subsections (2)(*b*) and (3D)(*b*) "(see subsection (6))" and subsection (6).

Internal linked funds and net value

9— (1) In section 431(2) of ICTA (interpretative provisions relating to insurance companies) insert at the appropriate place—

" "internal linked fund", in relation to an insurance company, means an account—

(*a*) to which linked assets are appropriated by the company, and

(*b*) which may be divided into units the value of which is determined by the company by reference to the value of those assets;", and

" "net value", in relation to any assets, means the excess of the value of the assets over the value of money debts (within the meaning of Chapter 2 of Part 4 of the Finance Act 1996) attributable to an internal linked fund which are not owed in respect of liabilities;".

(2) Omit—

(*a*) in section 432ZA(6) of ICTA, the definition of "internal linked fund",

(*b*) section 432A(9A) of that Act,

(*c*) the definition of "internal linked fund" in section 210B(8) of TCGA 1992, and

(*d*) paragraph 3A(6) of Schedule 11 to FA 1996.

Fair value

10— (1) In section 431(2) of ICTA (interpretative provisions relating to insurance companies) insert at the appropriate place—

""fair value", in relation to assets, means the amount which would be obtained from an independent person purchasing them or, if the assets are money, its amount;".

(2) In section 440 of ICTA (transfer of assets etc)—

(*a*) in subsections (1) and (2), for "market" substitute "fair", and

(*b*) omit subsection (5).

(3) Omit—

(*a*) section 444AB(6) of ICTA (as originally enacted),

(*b*) in section 444AC(11) of that Act (as originally enacted), the words from the beginning to the end of the definition of "fair value",

(*c*) section 444AD(5) of that Act,

(*d*) in section 83(8) of FA 1989, in the definition of "fair value", paragraph (*a*), and

(*e*) section 83YB(5) of that Act.

Generalisation of definitions

11— (1) Section 431 of ICTA (interpretative provisions relating to insurance companies) is amended as follows.

(2) For subsection (1) substitute—

"(1) This section has effect for the interpretation of the life assurance provisions of the Corporation Tax Acts."

(3) In subsection (2), insert at the appropriate place—

""the life assurance provisions of the Corporation Tax Acts" means—

(*a*) the provisions of this Chapter so far as relating to life assurance business, companies carrying on such business and friendly societies, and

(*b*) any other provisions of the Corporation Tax Acts making separate provision by reference to whether or not the business of a company is or includes life assurance business or any category of business that includes life assurance business;".

GENERAL NOTE

As part of the same general tidying up mentioned under para 5 above, Sch 10 includes a number of provisions to move definitions relevant to the taxation of life insurance companies into one statutory library in TA 1988 s 431(2) thus obviating the need to repeat the same wording through multiple pieces of legislation. Paragraph 8 does this for the definition of a non-profit company, non-profit fund and a with-profits fund and as a consequence those definitions are removed from a number of different places in the legislation. In a similar vein, paras 9 and 10 do the same for the definition of internal linked fund, net value and fair value by consolidating their definitions and repealing redundant references to them throughout other parts of the legislation. Paragraph 11 then provides the operative section for the use of TA 1988 s 431(2) as the library and gives its definitions priority in interpreting those parts of the Corporation Tax Acts relating to life insurance companies.

12— (1) Section 431A (power to amend) is amended as follows.

(2) In subsection (1), for "insurance company taxation provision" substitute "of the life assurance provisions of the Corporation Tax Acts".

(3) Omit subsection (7).

13 In section 83A(1) of FA 1989 ("brought into account")—

(*a*) omit "In sections 82A to 83B", and
(*b*) for "those sections" substitute "sections 82A to 83ZA".

14— (1) Omit the following provisions.

(2) In ICTA—

(*a*) in section 12(7B), the words from the beginning to the end of the definition of "contracts of long-term insurance",
(*b*) in section 76(15), "and other expressions have the same meaning as in Chapter 1 of Part 12",
(*c*) in section 587B(9), ""life assurance business" and related expressions have the same meaning as Chapter 1 of Part 12;",
(*d*) in section 755A(12), the definition of "long-term insurance fund",
(*e*) section 804F, and
(*f*) in paragraph 14(1) of Schedule 28AA, the definition of "insurance company".

(3) In FA 1989—

(*a*) in section 85(2A), the second sentence,
(*b*) in section 89(6), the words from the beginning to "; and", and
(*c*) section 90A.

(4) In paragraph 16(7) of Schedule 7 to FA 1991, the words from "and, subject to that," to the end.

(5) In TCGA 1992—

(*a*) section 214BA, and
(*b*) paragraph 17(5) of Schedule 7AC.

(6) In FA 1996—

(*a*) in section 87A(2), ", within the meaning of Chapter 1 of Part 12 of the Taxes Act 1988," and "(see section 431(2) of that Act)",
(*b*) section 88(7),
(*c*) in paragraph 12(9) of Schedule 9, the definitions of "contracts of long-term insurance" and "overseas life insurance company",
(*d*) in paragraph 20(3)(*b*) of that Schedule, ", within the meaning of Chapter 1 of Part 12 of the Taxes Act 1988," and "(see section 431(2) of that Act)", and
(*e*) in Schedule 11, paragraph 6.

(7) In paragraph 13(3) of Schedule 18 to FA 1998, the words after "1988".

(8) In CAA 2001—

(*a*) section 257(3),
(*b*) section 544(5), and
(*c*) section 560(5)(*a*) and (*c*).

(9) In paragraph 31(1) of Schedule 22 to FA 2001, the definitions of "insurance company" and "life assurance business".

(10) In FA 2002—

(*a*) in section 66(5), the words from the beginning to the end of the definition of "long-term insurance fund",
(*b*) in paragraph 19(1) of Schedule 12, the definition of "life assurance business",
(*c*) in paragraph 10(4) of Schedule 22, the words before the definition of "transfer scheme",
(*d*) in Schedule 26—

(i) in sub-paragraph (1) of paragraph 12, the references to the expressions "Integrated Prudential Sourcebook" and "long-term insurance fund",
(ii) sub-paragraphs (15) and (16) of that paragraph, and
(iii) in paragraph 54(1), the definitions of "insurance company", "life assurance business", "long-term insurance business" and "contract of long-term insurance", and

(*e*) in Schedule 29, in paragraph 89(3), the definition of "contracts of long-term insurance" and paragraph 138(1).

(11) In Schedule 23 to FA 2003—

(*a*) in paragraph 30, the definitions of "insurance company" and "life assurance business", and

(*b*) in paragraph 31, the entries relating to those definitions.

(12) Section 134(4)(*c*) of FA 2006.

Minor changes

15— (1) In section 432ZA(5) of ICTA (linked assets), for "432F" substitute "432E".

(2) In section 434A(2A) of that Act (computation of losses and limitation on relief), for "paragraph 2" substitute "paragraph 2(1)".

(3) In the heading of section 88 of FA 1989, for "**fraction**" substitute "**share**".

(4) In paragraph 17 of Schedule 7 to FA 1991 (transitional provisions for chargeable gains and unrelieved general annuity business)—

(*a*) in sub-paragraph (4), for the words after "in an accounting period" substitute "is so much of the chargeable gains arising to the company in the accounting period as are referable to its basic life assurance and general annuity business.", and

(*b*) omit sub-paragraphs (4A) and (5).

GENERAL NOTE

Paragraphs 12, 13 and 15 make minor amendments, some as a consequence of other changes, as part of the general tidying up of the regime. The most important to note is in para 15(4) which removes the restriction on the offset of old general annuity business losses against a fraction of BLAGAB chargeable gains, allowing the full offset of any unrelieved GAB losses. This measure which reduces the compliance requirements on the small number of companies that still have such unrelieved losses is welcome although the monetary effect is likely to be small.

Obsolete etc provisions

16— (1) Omit the following provisions (which are obsolete or of limited value).

(2) In the Table in section 98 of TMA 1970, the words "or 441A(3)" in both columns.

(3) In ICTA—

(*a*) in section 76(7), in Step 3, the entries relating to section 587B(8)(*b*)(i) of ICTA and paragraph 23(2) of Schedule 13 to FA 2002,

(*b*) section 440(2A) and (2B) (transfer of assets: loan relationships and derivative contracts),

(*c*) section 442(4) (special rule for insurance companies ceasing to be resident in United Kingdom),

(*d*) section 443 (life policies carrying rights not in money),

(*e*) section 444 (life policies issued before 5th August 1965),

(*f*) section 587B(8) (gifts to charities etc: modifications for insurance companies), and

(*g*) in section 807A (disposals and acquisitions of company loan relationships with or without interest), subsections (4) and (5)(*b*) and, in subsection (6)(*a*), "or an insurance credit".

(4) In FA 1989—

(*a*) section 84(2), (3), (5) and (6) (transitional provisions etc),

(*b*) in section 85(3) (commencement of provisions for charge of certain BLAGAB receipts), "(including the 1990 component period)",

(*c*) in section 86 (spreading of relief for acquisition expenses), subsections (3) and (3A) and, in subsection (10), "(including the 1990 component period)", and

(*d*) section 87 (management expenses).

(5) In FA 1996—

(*a*) paragraph 1(1) and (2) of Schedule 11 (loan relationships: I minus E basis),

(*b*) paragraph 4(6) of that Schedule (non-trading deficits: transitional provision),

(*c*) paragraph 5 of that Schedule (elections for accrual basis), and

(*d*) paragraph 1(3) of Schedule 15 (apportionment of loan relationship credits and debits: transitional provision).

(6) Paragraph 18 of Schedule 12 to FA 1997 (leasing arrangements: meaning of "accounting purposes" for insurance companies).

(7) Paragraph 86 of Schedule 18 to FA 1998 (non-annual actuarial investigations).

(8) Paragraph 4 of Schedule 6 to FA 1999 (reverse premiums etc).

(9) Section 87(3) and (4) of FA 2001 (tax credits etc).

(10) In Schedule 13 to FA 2002 (vaccine research), paragraphs 22, 23 and 25(3), and, in paragraph 27, the definition of "life assurance business".

GENERAL NOTE

Finally paragraphs 14 and 16 repeal a number of provisions that are no longer required following the changes referred to above or which are obsolete, in particular legislation which covered the transition to what was then the new regime in 1990.

Commencement

17— (1) The amendment made by paragraph 1 has effect on and after 10th May 2007.

(2) The amendments made by paragraphs 2, 4(2) and (4), 5, 6 and 8 to 15 have effect in relation to periods of account beginning on or after 1st January 2007.

(3) But the amendment made by paragraph 2(4) does not apply where the transfer of business concerned took place before 10th May 2007.

(4) The amendment made by paragraph 3 has effect in relation to losses accruing in a period of account beginning on or after 1st January 2007.

(5) The amendment made by paragraph 4(3) has effect in relation to periods of account beginning on or after 1st January 2005.

GENERAL NOTE

The provisions introduced by Sch 10 generally have a commencement date of 1 January 2007 although the correction in para 1 applies on or after 10 May 2007, para 2(4) does not apply to transfers of business taking place before 10 May 2007 and the relief provided by para 4(3) is fully retrospective to 1 January 2005.

SCHEDULE 11

TECHNICAL PROVISIONS MADE BY GENERAL INSURERS

Section 42

GENERAL NOTE

HMRC have historically been concerned that the reserves for future claims payments established by some general insurance companies have been excessive, resulting in a deferral of taxable profit. To counter this FA 2000 s 107 was enacted to allow for the use of hindsight to compare the actual out-turn of claims with the level of reserves previously established. In broad terms a notional tax charge (deduction) was calculated on any excessive (deficient) reserves and interest was charged on that amount to make good to the Exchequer the time value of the tax underpaid. The rules contained a provision that allowed companies to disclaim part or all of their technical reserves, which was enacted to give companies more flexibility in managing the impact of the regime on them. Companies quickly became aware however that this flexibility allowed them a great deal of control over the timing of the emergence of taxable profits or losses allowing offsets by way of group relief that otherwise might have been unavailable. Because this was never the policy reason behind the legislation and facing a loss of tax, the Government has acted to remove the whole regime including the disclaiming mechanism.

Restriction on amount of technical provisions made by general insurers

1— (1) This paragraph applies if a general insurer makes any technical provisions for a period of account.

(2) The amount of the technical provisions stated in the accounts for that period is to be taken into account in the calculation for tax purposes of the profits of the general insurer's trade for that period unless an officer of Revenue and Customs considers that that amount exceeds the appropriate amount.

(3) In that case—

(*a*) the excess is not to be taken into account in that calculation, and

(*b*) the profits of the general insurer's trade for the next period of account are to be adjusted accordingly for tax purposes.

(4) "The appropriate amount" means such amount as is determined in accordance with regulations made by the Commissioners for Her Majesty's Revenue and Customs to be the appropriate amount to be taken into account in that calculation.

(5) Any such determination must be made by reference to the time at which the technical provisions are made.

GENERAL NOTE

Paragraph 1 now states that the technical provisions in a general insurance company's accounts are to be taken into account in measuring its profit or loss unless an officer of HMRC determines that they are excessive. The measure of what constitutes an excess will be determined in due course by regulations which are still the subject of consultation between the industry and HMRC. If there is such an excess, it will be disallowed and the opening value of the reserves in the next period of account adjusted accordingly. It is hoped that final details of the new regime will be available in time for the pre-Budget Report at the end of 2007.

Enforcement

2— (1) This paragraph applies if an officer of Revenue and Customs gives a notice of enquiry under paragraph 24(1) of Schedule 18 to FA 1998 to a general insurer.

(2) The officer may by notice require the general insurer (at the general insurer's own expense) to provide the officer with a report as to whether (and, if so, the extent to which) the amount of any technical provisions stated in the accounts for any period covered by the company tax return into which the enquiry is made exceeds the appropriate amount.

(3) The report must cover such matters, and be in such form, as the officer may reasonably require for the purposes of the enquiry.

(4) The report must be made by a person who is appointed by the general insurer unless the officer requires the report to be made instead by another person.

(5) As soon as the general insurer appoints a person to make the report, the general insurer must give a notice to the officer specifying that person.

(6) A notice under sub-paragraph (2) must specify the time (which must not be less than 30 days) within which the general insurer is to comply with it.

(7) The following provisions of Schedule 18 to FA 1998—

(*a*) paragraph 28 (appeal against requirements imposed by notice under paragraph 27), and

(*b*) paragraph 29 (penalty for failure to comply with such a notice),

apply in relation to any notice under sub-paragraph (2) as they apply in relation to a notice under paragraph 27 of that Schedule.

(8) But the references in paragraph 28 of that Schedule to the provision of information are to be construed as references to the provision of a report under this paragraph.

GENERAL NOTE

Paragraph 2 sets out the detailed mechanics of how HMRC will enforce the new rules. They follow in many respects the method used by the FSA in its role as regulator of all insurance companies, namely that the company must appoint at its own expense an independent expert to report on the level and appropriateness of the technical provisions it has established. The company will have at least 30 days to commission and provide this report to HMRC, which may prove to be a challenging deadline in all but the simplest cases.

HMRC have stated that they do not intend to routinely ask all insurers to have such reports prepared. Rather inspectors will focus their intention through internal risk assessment processes on a small minority of companies that routinely over-reserve. In particular HMRC officials will not use subjective judgement in selecting companies which need to prepare a report, acknowledging that reserving processes are correctly the province of trained actuaries.

Supplementary

3— (1) In paragraph 1 "general insurer" means—

(*a*) a company within the charge to corporation tax which carries on general business,

(*b*) a controlled foreign company (within the meaning of Chapter 4 of Part 17 of ICTA) which carries on general business, or (*c*) members of a Lloyd's syndicate who carry on general business.

(2) In paragraph 2 "general insurer" means—

(*a*) a company within the charge to corporation tax which carries on general business, or

(*b*) a company which for the purposes of Chapter 4 of Part 17 of ICTA has an interest in a controlled foreign company (within the meaning of that Chapter) which carries on general business.

(3) For the purposes of sub-paragraphs (1) and (2) "general business" means business which consists of the effecting or carrying out of contracts that fall within Part 1 of Schedule 1 to the Financial Services and Markets Act 2000 (Regulated Activities) Order 2001 (SI 2001/544).

(4) In the case of members of a Lloyd's syndicate, references in paragraph 1 to any accounts for a period are to the return of the syndicate's profits or loss for that period under regulation 4 of the Lloyd's Underwriters (Tax) Regulations 2005 (SI 2005/3338).

(5) In paragraph 1 "period of account"—

(*a*) except in the case of members of a Lloyd's syndicate, means a period of account for which an account is made up, and

(*b*) in the case of members of a Lloyd's syndicate, means an underwriting year in which profits or losses are declared for an earlier underwriting year.

(6) In paragraphs 1 and 2 "technical provisions", except in the case of members of a Lloyd's syndicate, means any of the following—

(*a*) provisions for claims outstanding,
(*b*) provisions for unearned premiums, and
(*c*) provisions for unexpired risks.

(7) In paragraphs 1 and 2 "technical provisions", in the case of members of a Lloyd's syndicate ("the syndicate"), means—

(*a*) so much of the reinsurance to close amounts of the members, and

(*b*) so much of the provisions made by an open Lloyd's syndicate of which any member of the syndicate is a member for claims outstanding, unearned premiums and unexpired risks,

as may be determined by or under regulations made by the Commissioners for Her Majesty's Revenue and Customs.

(8) For this purpose—

(*a*) the reference to reinsurance to close amounts of any member of a Lloyd's syndicate is to any consideration which, in accordance with the rules or practice of Lloyd's, is given (or any amount which, in accordance with those rules or practice, is treated as consideration given) by the member in respect of the liabilities arising from the member's underwriting business in an underwriting year for the purpose of closing the accounts of the business for that year, and

(*b*) a Lloyd's syndicate is an "open" Lloyd's syndicate at any time after the end of its closing year if, at that time, the accounts of its business for the underwriting year for which it was formed have not been closed,

and in paragraph (*b*) "closing year" has the same meaning as in Chapter 3 of Part 2 of FA 1993 or Chapter 5 of Part 4 of FA 1994.

(9) In this paragraph—

"Lloyd's syndicate" means a syndicate of underwriting members of Lloyd's formed for an underwriting year, and
"underwriting year" means the calendar year.

(10) In this paragraph references to provisions for claims outstanding, unearned premiums and unexpired risks have the same meaning as in Schedule 9A to the Companies Act 1985 (c 6).

(11) The Commissioners for Her Majesty's Revenue and Customs may by regulations—

(*a*) provide in prescribed circumstances for paragraph 1 not to apply in relation to any member of a Lloyd's syndicate, or

(*b*) provide in prescribed circumstances for a reduction in relation to any member of a Lloyd's syndicate of the amount which (as a result of that paragraph) is not to be taken into account in the calculation mentioned in sub-paragraph (2) of that paragraph.

(12) The Treasury may by regulations amend sub-paragraphs (1) to (3) (definition of "general insurer").

(13) In the event of any changes in the rules or practice of Lloyd's, the Commissioners for Her Majesty's Revenue and Customs may by regulations make such amendments of paragraph 1 and this paragraph as appear to the Commissioners to be expedient having regard to those changes.

(14) Regulations under section 182(1)(*a*) of FA 1993 or section 229(1)(*a*) of FA 1994 (assessment and collection of tax charged in case of Lloyd's underwriters) may, in particular, include provision applying paragraph 2 with modifications in the case of members of a Lloyd's syndicate.

(15) Regulations under paragraph 1 or this paragraph may—

(*a*) make different provision for different purposes, and

(*b*) make supplementary, incidental, consequential and transitional provision.

GENERAL NOTE

Paragraph 3 provides detailed descriptions supplementing the new rules including a definition of which companies are within the scope of the new rules (which extend to captive insurers that are controlled foreign companies and Lloyd's syndicates) and the necessary extensions for the regime to apply to Lloyd's syndicates as well as providing a library of terms used, many of which draw on definitions from the regulatory regime. Finally the Treasury may extend the scope of the rules by regulation by amending the definition of precisely what sort of company is a general insurer.

Repeal of section 107 of FA 2000

4 In FA 2000, omit section 107 (general insurance reserves).

GENERAL NOTE

Paragraph 4 repeals the bulk of the existing rules in FA 2000 s 107 with effect for periods of account ending on or after Royal Assent. However the ability to disclaim technical provisions remains in effect for accounting periods beginning before Royal Assent. The result is that a company with a calendar year end will not be within the old regime for the year ended 31 December 2007 so it will not have to look back at its reserves for prior periods but it will still be able to disclaim part of its technical provisions in that period of account. This is subject to the proviso that any such disclaim may be for no more than 10% of the amount of its technical provisions. This staggered transition to the new regime was agreed between the industry and HMRC as the best way of dealing with both parties' immediate concerns giving companies a measure of transition into the new regime while protecting the Exchequer's position.

Commencement

5— (1) Paragraphs 1 to 3 have effect in relation to periods of account ending on or after the day on which this Act is passed.

(2) The repeal of section 107 of FA 2000 made by paragraph 4 has effect as follows.

(3) The repeal of—

(*a*) subsections (1) to (3) of that section (technical provisions made by a general insurer proving to be excessive or insufficient),

(*b*) subsections (5) to (8) and (10) of that section so far as relating to those subsections, and

(*c*) subsections (9) and (12)(*a*) of that section (which relate to those subsections),

has effect in relation to any amount that would otherwise have been treated as a receipt or an expense of a trade in computing for tax purposes the profits of the trade for any period of account ending on or after the day on which this Act is passed.

(4) The repeal of—

(*a*) subsection (4) of that section (election for any part of technical provisions not to be taken into account in a period of account),

(*b*) subsections (5) to (8) and (10) of that section so far as relating to that subsection, and

(*c*) subsection (12)(*b*) of that section (which relates to that subsection),

has effect so that no election may be made under that subsection in respect of technical provisions made by a general insurer for any period of account which begins on or after that day.

(5) There is a restriction in relation to any election made by a general insurer under that subsection in respect of technical provisions made by the general insurer for the final election period.

(6) The restriction is that the amount of the part of those provisions which the general insurer elects not to be taken into account in computing for tax purposes the profits of the general insurer's trade for that period must not exceed 10% of the total amount of those provisions.

(7) In sub-paragraph (5) "the final election period", in relation to any general insurer, means the general insurer's first period of account ending on or after the day on which this Act is passed.

SCHEDULE 12

FRIENDLY SOCIETIES: TRANSFERS TO INSURANCE COMPANIES ETC

Section 44

Exempt life or endowment business

1— (1) Section 460 of ICTA (exemption from tax in respect of life or endowment business) is amended as follows.

(2) In subsection (10A), after "the transfer" insert ", other than any to which subsection (11) or (12) below applied immediately before the transfer had effect,".

(3) In subsection (11), for "thereafter continue to be tax exempt life or endowment business for the purposes of this Chapter." substitute "continue to be exempt from corporation tax (whether on income or chargeable gains) on profits arising from it."

(4) For subsection (12) substitute—

"(12) Where at any time an insurance company acquires by way of transfer of engagements from a friendly society any life or endowment business consisting of business which—

(*a*) relates to contracts made before that time; and

(*b*) immediately before that time was tax exempt life or endowment business,

that business shall continue to be exempt from corporation tax (whether on income or chargeable gains) on profits arising from it.

(13) But if any contracts constituting or forming part of the business of a company covered by subsection (11) or (12) above are varied during an accounting period of the company so as to increase the premiums payable under them, the business relating to those contracts is not exempt from corporation tax for that or any subsequent accounting period.

(14) For the purposes of the Corporation Tax Acts any part of a company's business which is exempt from corporation tax by virtue of subsection (11) or (12) above shall be treated as a separate business from any other business carried on by the company."

(5) Insert at the end—

"(15) The Treasury may by regulations provide that, where any part of the business of a company is exempt from corporation tax by virtue of subsection (11) or (12) above, the Corporation Tax Acts have effect subject to such modifications (or exceptions) as the Treasury consider appropriate.

(16) Regulations under subsection (15) above—

(*a*) may make different provision for different cases,

(*b*) may include any incidental, supplementary, consequential or transitional provisions which the Treasury consider appropriate, and

(*c*) may include retrospective provision."

2— (1) Section 464 of ICTA (maximum benefits payable to members) is amended as follows.

(2) For the first sentence of subsection (1) substitute—

"(1) Subject to subsections (2) and (3) below, a person is not entitled to have at any time outstanding contracts with any one or more friendly societies, registered branches or insurance companies which (taking them all together) are for the assurance of—

(*a*) more than £750 by way of gross sum under business which is afforded exemption from corporation tax by section 460, or

(*b*) more than £156 by way of annuity under such business."

(3) In subsection (3), for the words preceding the paragraphs substitute "With respect to contracts for the assurance of gross sums under business which is afforded exemption from corporation tax by section 460, a person is not entitled to have outstanding at any time with any one or more friendly societies, registered branches or insurance companies—".

(4) In subsection (4A), for "tax exempt life or endowment business" substitute "business which is afforded exemption from corporation tax by section 460 if they are".

(5) In subsection (6), for "member has outstanding with one or more society or branch" substitute "person has outstanding with one or more societies, branches or companies".

(6) In subsection (7)—

(*a*) for "or registered branch" substitute ", registered branch or insurance company",

(*b*) for "member" (in both places) substitute "person", and

(*c*) for "or registered branches (taking together all such societies or branches throughout the United Kingdom)" substitute ", registered branches or insurance companies (taken together)".

3 In section 466(2) of ICTA, in the definition of "tax exempt life or endowment business", for "(11)" substitute "(10A)".

Other exempt business

4— (1) Section 461 of ICTA (exemption of registered friendly societies from tax in respect of business which is not life or endowment business) is amended as follows.

(2) After subsection (4) insert—

"(4A) Where—

(*a*) at any time an insurance company acquires by way of transfer of engagements from a registered friendly society any business other than life or endowment business, and

(*b*) immediately before that time the society was exempt from corporation tax on profits arising from that business,

the insurance company shall be exempt from corporation tax on its profits arising from any part of that business which relates to contracts made before that time.

(4B) But if during an accounting period of the insurance company there is an increase in the scale of benefits which it undertakes to provide in the course of carrying on any such part of that business, the company shall not be exempt from corporation tax by virtue of subsection (4A) above for that or any subsequent accounting period."

(3) In subsection (5), after "(4)" insert "or (4A)".

(4) Insert at the end—

"(12) The Treasury may by regulations provide that, where any part of the business of a company is exempt from corporation tax by virtue of subsection (4) or (4A) above, the Corporation Tax Acts have effect subject to such modifications (or exceptions) as the Treasury consider appropriate.

(13) Regulations under subsection (12) above—

(*a*) may make different provision for different cases,

(*b*) may include any incidental, supplementary, consequential or transitional provisions which the Treasury consider appropriate, and

(*c*) may include retrospective provision."

5— (1) Section 461B of ICTA (exemption of incorporated friendly societies from tax in respect of business which is not life or endowment business) is amended as follows.

(2) For subsection (6) substitute—

"(6) But if during an accounting period of the company there is an increase in the scale of benefits which it undertakes to provide in the course of carrying on any such part of its business, the company shall not be exempt from corporation tax by virtue of subsection (5) above for that or any subsequent accounting period.

(6A) Where—

(*a*) at any time an insurance company acquires by way of transfer of engagements from a qualifying society any business other than life or endowment business, and

(*b*) immediately before that time the society was exempt from corporation tax on profits arising from that business,

the insurance company shall be exempt from corporation tax on its profits arising from any part of that business which relates to contracts made before that time.

(6B) But if during an accounting period of the insurance company there is an increase in the scale of benefits which it undertakes to provide in the course of carrying on any such part of that business, the company shall not be exempt from corporation tax by virtue of subsection (6A) above for that or any subsequent accounting period."

(3) In subsection (7), after "(5)" insert "or (6A)".

(4) Insert at the end—

"(8) The Treasury may by regulations provide that, where any part of the business of a company is exempt from corporation tax by virtue of subsection (5) or (6A) above, the Corporation Tax Acts have effect subject to such modifications (or exceptions) as the Treasury consider appropriate.

(9) Regulations under subsection (8) above—

(*a*) may make different provision for different cases,

(*b*) may include any incidental, supplementary, consequential or transitional provisions which the Treasury consider appropriate, and

(*c*) may include retrospective provision."

Commencement

6— (1) The amendment made by sub-paragraph (2) of paragraph 1, so far as relating to section 460(11) of ICTA, and the amendments made by sub-paragraph (3) of that paragraph and paragraph 3 are deemed always to have had effect.

(2) The amendments made by paragraph 2 have effect in relation to contracts made after the passing of this Act.

(3) The amendment made by sub-paragraph (2) of paragraph 1, so far as relating to section 460(12) of ICTA, and the amendments made by sub-paragraph (4) of that paragraph and paragraphs 4(2) and (3) and 5(2) and (3) have effect in relation to transfers of engagements and conversions taking place on or after the day on which this Act is passed.

GENERAL NOTE

Schedule 12 paras 1–3 deal with Life or Endowment Business (L or E business). This is defined in TA 1988 s 466 and is applicable only to business entered into by friendly societies. It includes life assurance business plus some hybrid and miner classes. The funds underlying L or E business are exempt from corporation tax to the extent that the member holds policies under which premiums do not exceed £270 per annum or £25 per month.

A friendly society may convert itself to a life office. There has long been statutory provision (in TA 1988 s 460) for the L or E exemption to continue in respect of business existing at date of conversion subject to there being no increase in premiums. Para 1(3) improves the wording of the exemption and is deemed always to have had effect.

Paras 1–3 provide for similar continuing exemption where exempt L or E business of a friendly society is transferred to a life office. It is effective for transfers of business taking place after passing of this Act. The exempt business transferred is to constitute a separate business.

Despite the previous existence of life offices containing exempt business (having converted from a friendly society), there has been no statutory guidance on the method of allocation between taxable and exempt of the investment return, expenses or capital allowance. Provision is made for the Treasury to make statutory regulations.

Schedule 12 paras 4–5 provides similar relief for transfers of Other Exempt Business.

Business other than L or E business is exempt from corporation tax if written by a society which existed before 1 June 1973. There is provision for "old" status to be retained on amalgamation or incorporation. There already existed provision for retention of exemption on conversion of an incorporated society into a life office. The schedule provides similar treatment for transfers of Other Exempt Business from a friendly society (whether incorporated or not) to a life office. The exempt business transferred is to constitute a separate business. Exemption is lost if the life office increases the scale of the benefits which it provides in respect of the transferred business. Regulation making powers are included. The relief is effective for transfers of business taking place after passing of this Act.

It should be noted that there remains no provision to retain exemption on the transfer of Other Exempt Business from an old society to a society which is not old. Furthermore, a transfer of such business from one old society to another old society will lose exemption if the Board deems the recipient to have change its business in scale or character and that a Direction is expedient for the protection of the revenue.

Such Direction making powers, contained in TA 1988 s 461(6) and s 461C(3), effectively deem an old society to be a new society. Perhaps curiously the provisions mean that life offices are better placed to receive transfers of Exempt Other Business from friendly societies than are other friendly societies.

SCHEDULE 13

SALE AND REPURCHASE OF SECURITIES

Section 47

Purpose of Schedule

1— (1) The purpose of this Schedule is to secure that in the case of an arrangement—

(*a*) which involves the sale of securities and the subsequent purchase of securities, and

(*b*) which equates, in substance, to a transaction for the lending of money at interest from or to a company (with the securities which were sold as collateral for the loan),

the charge to corporation tax in that case reflects the fact that the arrangement equates, in substance, to such a transaction.

(2) But this is not to be read as preventing the rules in this Schedule about corporation tax in respect of chargeable gains from having no effect in relation to debtor quasi-repos and creditor quasi-repos.

Meaning of debtor repo

2— (1) For the purposes of this Schedule a company ("the borrower") has a debtor repo if conditions A to E are met.

(2) Condition A is that under an arrangement the borrower receives from another person ("the lender") any money or other asset ("the advance").

(3) Condition B is that, in accordance with generally accepted accounting practice, the accounts of the borrower for the period in which the advance is received record a financial liability in respect of the advance.

(4) Condition C is that under the arrangement the borrower sells any securities at any time to the lender.

(5) Condition D is that the arrangement makes provision conferring a right or imposing an obligation on the borrower to buy those or similar securities at any subsequent time.

(6) Condition E is that, in accordance with generally accepted accounting practice, the subsequent buying of those or similar securities would extinguish the financial liability in respect of the advance recorded in the accounts of the borrower.

(7) For the purposes of conditions A to E references to the borrower include a partnership of which the borrower is a member.

Meaning of debtor quasi-repo

3— (1) For the purposes of this Schedule a company ("the borrower") has a debtor quasi-repo in any case if—

(*a*) the borrower does not have a debtor repo in that case, and

(*b*) conditions A to E are met in that case.

(2) Condition A is that under an arrangement the borrower receives any money or other asset ("the advance").

(3) Condition B is that, in accordance with generally accepted accounting practice, the accounts of the borrower for the period in which the advance is received record a financial liability in respect of the advance.

(4) Condition C is that under that or any other arrangement the borrower or any other person sells any securities at any time.

(5) Condition D is that the arrangement or other arrangement—

(*a*) makes provision conferring a right or imposing an obligation on the borrower to buy the securities or any other securities at any subsequent time, or

(*b*) makes provision conferring such a right or imposing such an obligation on any other person and makes other relevant provision.

(6) For this purpose any arrangement makes "other relevant provision" if it makes provision—

(*a*) for the receipt of any money or other asset from the borrower under that arrangement for the purpose of enabling the other person to make that subsequent purchase, or (*b*) for the discharge of any liability to the borrower under that arrangement for that purpose (whether by way of set off or otherwise).

(7) Condition E is that, in accordance with generally accepted accounting practice—

(*a*) the subsequent buying of the securities or the other securities by the borrower, or

(*b*) the receipt of the asset from the borrower, or the discharge of the liability to the borrower, under the arrangement or other arrangement,

would extinguish the financial liability in respect of the advance recorded in the accounts of the borrower.

(8) For the purposes of conditions A to E references to the borrower include a partnership of which the borrower is a member.

Ignoring effect on borrower of sale of securities: debtor repos, debtor quasi-repos and other arrangements

4— (1) This paragraph applies if a company ("the borrower")—

(*a*) has a debtor repo or a debtor quasi-repo, or

(*b*) has a liability which is discharged under a relevant arrangement.

(2) A relevant arrangement is one in relation to which conditions C and D in paragraph 3 are met and the main purpose, or one of the main purposes, of which is the obtaining of a tax advantage.

(3) For the purposes of the charge to corporation tax in respect of income of the borrower arising while the arrangement is in force, the Corporation Tax Acts have effect as if—

(*a*) the borrower held the securities that are initially sold for any period for which the arrangement is in force, and

(*b*) the borrower did not receive in that period amounts representative of income payable in respect of those securities.

(4) But—

(*a*) no amount is to be charged to corporation tax as a result of sub-paragraph (3)(*a*) unless it is, in accordance with generally accepted accounting practice, recognised in determining the borrower's profit or loss for that or any other period or taken into account in calculating the amounts which are so recognised, and

(*b*) there is the following exception to sub-paragraph (3) if the securities that are initially sold are overseas securities.

(5) In the case of any overseas dividend payable in respect of those securities, the entitlement of the borrower to double taxation relief in respect of that dividend is determined as if—

(*a*) sub-paragraph (3) were omitted,

(*b*) the borrower received a payment of an amount which is representative of that dividend,

(*c*) the payment were made under a requirement of the arrangement, and

(*d*) the payment were made on the date on which that dividend is payable.

(6) For the purposes of this paragraph "double taxation relief" means any relief given under or as a result of Part 18 of ICTA.

Relief for borrower for finance charges in respect of the advance: debtor repos and debtor quasi-repos

5— (1) This paragraph applies if a company ("the borrower") has a debtor repo or a debtor quasi-repo.

(2) The advance under the debtor repo or debtor quasi-repo is, in the case of the borrower, to be treated for the purposes of the loan relationship rules as a money debt which—

(*a*) is owed by the borrower or, if the borrower is a member of a partnership which receives the advance, by the partnership, and

(*b*) is owed to the person to whom the securities are initially sold.

(3) The arrangement is, in the case of the borrower, to be treated for the purposes of those rules as a transaction for the lending of money from which that debt is treated as arising for those purposes.

(4) Any amount which, in accordance with generally accepted accounting practice, is recorded in—

(*a*) the accounts of the borrower, or

(*b*) if the borrower is a member of a partnership which receives the advance, the accounts of the partnership, as a finance charge in respect of the advance is to be treated for the purposes of the loan relationship rules and Part 15 of ITA 2007 (deduction of income tax at source) as interest payable under that debt.

(5) That interest is to be treated for those purposes as paid at the earlier of—

(*a*) the time when the relevant repurchase takes place, and
(*b*) the time when it becomes apparent that that repurchase will not take place.

(6) For this purpose "the relevant repurchase" means—

(*a*) if the borrower has a debtor repo, the subsequent buying of the securities or similar securities, and
(*b*) if the borrower has a debtor quasi-repo, the subsequent buying of the securities or other securities by the borrower, the receipt of the asset from the borrower or (as the case may be) the discharge of the liability to the borrower.

Ignoring sale and subsequent purchase for purposes of chargeable gains: debtor repos

6— (1) This paragraph applies if—

(*a*) a company ("the borrower") has a debtor repo, and
(*b*) the borrower (having sold the securities under the arrangement to the lender) is the only person with the right or obligation under the arrangement to buy those or similar securities at any subsequent time.

(2) The sale of the securities, and the subsequent purchase of those or similar securities, by the borrower under the arrangement are to be ignored for the purposes of corporation tax in respect of chargeable gains (but see sub-paragraph (5)).

(3) If at any time after the initial sale of the securities—

(*a*) it becomes apparent that the borrower will not subsequently buy those or similar securities under the arrangement, or
(*b*) the accounting condition ceases to be met,

the borrower is to be treated for the purposes of corporation tax in respect of chargeable gains as disposing of the securities at that time for a consideration equal to their market value at that time.

(4) The accounting condition ceases to be met if, in accordance with generally accepted accounting practice, the accounts of the borrower for any period after the one in which the advance is received do not record a financial liability in respect of the advance (except as a result of the subsequent purchase of the securities or similar securities).

(5) If sub-paragraph (3) applies because the accounting condition ceases to be met, any subsequent purchase of those or similar securities by the borrower under the arrangement is not to be ignored for the purposes of corporation tax in respect of chargeable gains as a result of this paragraph.

(6) For the purposes of this paragraph references to the borrower include a partnership of which the borrower is a member.

Meaning of creditor repo

7— (1) For the purposes of this Schedule a company ("the lender") has a creditor repo if conditions A to E are met.

(2) Condition A is that under an arrangement another person ("the borrower") receives from the lender any money or other asset ("the advance").

(3) Condition B is that, in accordance with generally accepted accounting practice, the accounts of the lender for the period in which the advance is made record a financial asset in respect of the advance.

(4) Condition C is that under the arrangement the borrower sells any securities at any time to the lender.

(5) Condition D is that the arrangement makes provision conferring a right or imposing an obligation on the lender to sell those or similar securities at any subsequent time.

(6) Condition E is that, in accordance with generally accepted accounting practice, the subsequent sale of those or similar securities would extinguish the financial asset in respect of the advance recorded in the accounts of the lender.

(7) For the purposes of conditions A to E references to the lender include a partnership of which the lender is a member.

Meaning of creditor quasi-repo

8— (1) For the purposes of this Schedule a company ("the lender") has a creditor quasi-repo in any case if—

(*a*) the lender does not have a creditor repo in that case, and (*b*) conditions A to E are met in that case.

(2) Condition A is that under an arrangement another person receives from the lender any money or other asset ("the advance").

(3) Condition B is that, in accordance with generally accepted accounting practice, the accounts of the lender for the period in which the advance is made record a financial asset in respect of the advance.

(4) Condition C is that under that or any other arrangement a person sells any securities at any time to the lender or any other person.

(5) Condition D is that the arrangement or other arrangement—

(*a*) makes provision conferring a right or imposing an obligation on the lender to sell the securities or any other securities at any subsequent time, or

(*b*) makes provision conferring such a right or imposing such an obligation on any other person and makes other relevant provision.

(6) For this purpose any arrangement makes "other relevant provision" if it makes provision—

(*a*) for the receipt of any money, securities or other asset from the lender under that arrangement for the purpose of enabling the other person to make that subsequent sale, or

(*b*) for the discharge of any liability to the lender under that arrangement for that purpose (whether by way of set off or otherwise).

(7) Condition E is that, in accordance with generally accepted accounting practice—

(*a*) the subsequent sale of the securities or the other securities by the lender, or

(*b*) the receipt of the asset from the lender, or the discharge of the liability to the lender, under the arrangement or other arrangement,

would extinguish the financial asset in respect of the advance recorded in the accounts of the lender.

(8) For the purposes of conditions A to E references to the lender include a partnership of which the lender is a member.

Ignoring effect on lender of sale of securities: creditor repos and creditor quasi-repos

9— (1) This paragraph applies if a company ("the lender") has a creditor repo or a creditor quasi-repo.

(2) For the purposes of the charge to corporation tax in respect of income of the lender arising while the arrangement is in force, the Corporation Tax Acts have effect as if—

(*a*) the lender did not hold the securities that are initially sold for any period for which the arrangement is in force, and

(*b*) the lender did not make in that period any payment representative of income payable in respect of those securities.

(3) But—

(*a*) an amount is not to be ignored for the purposes of that charge as a result of sub-paragraph (2)(*a*) if it is, in accordance with generally accepted accounting practice, recognised in determining the lender's profit or loss for that or any other period or taken into account in calculating the amounts which are so recognised, and

(*b*) a payment is not to be ignored for those purposes as a result of sub-paragraph (2)(*b*) if the payment is, in accordance with that practice, so recognised.

(4) Nothing in sub-paragraph (3)(*b*) affects the question whether (apart from that provision) the payment (or any part of it) may be deducted in calculating any income for corporation tax purposes or against total profits.

Charge on lender for finance return in respect of the advance: creditor repos and creditor quasi-repos

10— (1) This paragraph applies if a company ("the lender") has a creditor repo or a creditor quasi-repo.

(2) The advance under the creditor repo or creditor quasi-repo is, in the case of the lender, to be treated for the purposes of the loan relationship rules as a money debt which—

(*a*) is owed to the lender or, if the lender is a member of a partnership which makes the advance, to the partnership, and

(*b*) is owed by the person who initially sold the securities.

(3) The arrangement is, in the case of the lender, to be treated for the purposes of those rules as a transaction for the lending of money from which that debt is treated as arising for those purposes.

(4) Any amount which, in accordance with generally accepted accounting practice, is recorded in—

(*a*) the accounts of the lender, or

(*b*) if the lender is a member of a partnership which makes the advance, the accounts of the partnership,

as a finance return in respect of the advance is to be treated for those purposes as interest receivable under that debt.

(5) That interest is to be treated for those purposes as received at the earlier of—

(*a*) the time when the relevant repurchase takes place, and

(*b*) the time when it becomes apparent that that repurchase will not take place.

(6) For this purpose "the relevant repurchase" means—

(*a*) if the lender has a creditor repo, the subsequent sale of the securities or similar securities, and

(*b*) if the lender has a creditor quasi-repo, the subsequent sale of the securities or other securities by the lender, the receipt of the asset from the lender or (as the case may be) the discharge of the liability to the lender.

Ignoring purchase and subsequent sale for purposes of chargeable gains: creditor repos

11— (1) This paragraph applies if—

(*a*) a company ("the lender") has a creditor repo, and

(*b*) the lender (having bought the securities under the arrangement from the borrower) is the only person with the right or obligation under the arrangement to sell those or similar securities at any subsequent time.

(2) The purchase of the securities, and the subsequent sale of those or similar securities, by the lender under the arrangement are to be ignored for the purposes of corporation tax in respect of chargeable gains (but see sub-paragraph (5)).

(3) If at any time after the initial purchase of the securities—

(*a*) it becomes apparent that the lender will not subsequently sell those or similar securities under the arrangement, or

(*b*) the accounting condition ceases to be met,

the lender is to be treated for the purposes of corporation tax in respect of chargeable gains as acquiring the securities at that time for a consideration equal to their market value at that time.

(4) The accounting condition ceases to be met if, in accordance with generally accepted accounting practice, the accounts of the lender for any period after the one in which the advance is made do not record a financial asset in respect of the advance (except as a result of the subsequent sale of the securities or similar securities).

(5) If sub-paragraph (3) applies because the accounting condition ceases to be met, any subsequent sale of those or similar securities by the lender under the arrangement is not to be ignored for the purposes of corporation tax in respect of chargeable gains as a result of this paragraph.

(6) For the purposes of this paragraph references to the lender include a partnership of which the lender is a member.

Repo under arrangement designed to produce quasi-interest: anti-avoidance

12— (1) This paragraph applies if—

(*a*) under an arrangement a person receives any money or other asset ("the advance") from a company (or a partnership of which the company is a member),

(*b*) the company does not have a creditor repo or creditor quasi-repo by reference to the arrangement but would have one on the applicable accounting assumption (reading condition E in paragraphs 7 and 8 in the light of that assumption),

(*c*) the arrangement is designed to produce a return ("the quasi-interest") to the company (or partnership of which it is a member) which equates, in substance, to the return on an investment of money at interest, and

(*d*) the main purpose, or one of the main purposes, of the arrangement is the obtaining of a tax advantage.

(2) Paragraph 10 is to have effect as if—

(*a*) the company had a creditor repo by reference to the arrangement, and

(*b*) the quasi-interest were an amount recorded as mentioned in sub-paragraph (4) of that paragraph.

(3) In this paragraph "the applicable accounting assumption" is the assumption that, in accordance with generally accepted accounting practice, the accounts of the company (or

the partnership of which it is a member) for the period in which the advance is made record a financial asset in respect of the advance.

Requirements to deduct tax from manufactured payments: creditor repos and debtor repos

13— (1) If a company has a creditor repo, Chapter 9 of Part 15 of ITA 2007 (deduction of income tax at source: manufactured payments) has effect in relation to the lender while the arrangement is in force as if—

(*a*) the lender paid the borrower amounts which are representative of the income payable on the securities that are initially sold,
(*b*) the payments were made under requirements of the arrangement, and
(*c*) the payments were made on the dates on which the income is payable.

(2) If a company has a debtor repo, the reverse charge provisions of Chapter 9 of Part 15 of ITA 2007 have effect in relation to the borrower while the arrangement is in force as if—

(*a*) the lender paid the borrower amounts which are representative of the income payable on the securities that are initially sold,
(*b*) the payments were made under requirements of the arrangements, and
(*c*) the payments were made on the dates on which the income is payable.

(3) If sub-paragraph (1) or (2) applies, any payment actually made under an arrangement which is representative of any income payable on any securities is to be treated for the purposes of Chapter 9 of Part 15 of ITA 2007 as if it had not been made.

(4) In this paragraph "the reverse charge provisions of Chapter 9 of Part 15 of ITA 2007" means—

(*a*) regulations under section 918(4) of ITA 2007 (manufactured dividends on UK shares (Real Estate Investment Trusts): the reverse charge),
(*b*) section 920 of that Act (foreign payers of manufactured interest: the reverse charge), and
(*c*) section 923 of that Act (foreign payers of manufactured overseas dividends: the reverse charge).

Interpretation etc

14— (1) In this Schedule—

"arrangement" includes any agreement or understanding (whether or not legally enforceable),
"creditor quasi-repo" has the meaning given by paragraph 8,
"creditor repo" has the meaning given by paragraph 7,
"debtor quasi-repo" has the meaning given by paragraph 3,
"debtor repo" has the meaning given by paragraph 2,
"discharge", in relation to a liability, means the discharge of the liability in whole or in part (and "discharged" is to be read accordingly),
"the loan relationship rules" means the provisions of Chapter 2 of Part 4 of FA 1996,
"market value" has the same meaning as in TCGA 1992,
"overseas dividend", in relation to overseas securities, means any interest, dividend or other annual payment payable in respect of the securities,
"overseas securities" means shares, stock or other securities issued by—

(*a*) a government or public or local authority of a territory outside the United Kingdom, or
(*b*) any other body of persons not resident in the United Kingdom,

"securities" (except in the definition of "overseas securities") means shares, stock or other securities issued by—

(*a*) the government of the United Kingdom,
(*b*) any public or local authority in the United Kingdom, or
(*c*) any company or other body resident in the United Kingdom,

or overseas securities, and

"tax advantage" has the meaning given by section 840ZA of ICTA.

(2) For the purposes of this Schedule references to a person's receiving any asset include the person's obtaining directly or indirectly the value of any asset or otherwise deriving directly or indirectly any benefit from it.

(3) For the purposes of this Schedule—

(*a*) in any case where a person buys securities (or has a right or obligation to buy securities) but the securities are (or are to be) held for another person's benefit, that other person is treated as buying (or having the right or obligation to buy) the securities, and (*b*) in any case where a person sells securities but the proceeds of the sale are held for another person's benefit, that other person is treated as selling the securities.

(4) For the purposes of this Schedule securities are similar if they entitle their holders to—

(*a*) the same rights against the same persons as to capital, interest and dividends, and
(*b*) the same remedies for the enforcement of those rights,

in spite of any difference in the total nominal amounts of the respective securities or in the form in which they are held or the manner in which they can be transferred.

(5) For the purposes of this Schedule it does not matter whether or not provision of any arrangement conferring a right or imposing an obligation on any person to buy any securities is subject to any conditions.

(6) For the purposes of this Schedule an arrangement is in force from the time when the securities are initially sold until the earlier of—

(*a*) the time when the relevant repurchase takes place, and
(*b*) the time when it becomes apparent that that repurchase will not take place.

(7) For this purpose "the relevant repurchase" means—

(*a*) in the case of a debtor repo, the subsequent buying of the securities or similar securities,
(*b*) in the case of a debtor quasi-repo, the subsequent buying of the securities or other securities by the borrower, the receipt of the asset from the borrower or (as the case may be) the discharge of the liability to the borrower,
(*c*) in the case of a creditor repo, the subsequent sale of the securities or similar securities, and
(*d*) in the case of a creditor quasi-repo, the subsequent sale of the securities or other securities by the lender, the receipt of the asset from the lender or (as the case may be) the discharge of the liability to the lender.

(8) Any reference in this Schedule to an amount being recognised in determining a company's profit or loss for a period is to an amount being recognised for accounting purposes—

(*a*) in the company's profit and loss account or income statement,
(*b*) in the company's statement of recognised gains and losses or statement of changes in equity, or
(*c*) in any other statement of items brought into account in calculating the company's profits and losses for that period.

(9) In determining for the purposes of this Schedule whether an amount is recorded as a financial asset or liability in respect of the advance it is to be assumed that the period of account in which the advance is received or made ended immediately after the receipt or making of the advance.

(10) For the purposes of paragraphs 6(4) and 11(4)—

(*a*) any period of account in which the advance is received or made is treated as if it ended immediately after the receipt or making of the advance, and
(*b*) a new period of account is treated as beginning immediately after the end of that period.

(11) If any person does not draw up accounts in accordance with generally accepted accounting practice, this Schedule applies as if the accounts had been drawn up by the person in accordance with that practice.

Power to modify Schedule

15— (1) The Treasury may by regulations provide for all or any of the provisions of this Schedule to apply with modifications in relation to either or both of the following cases—

(*a*) non-standard repo cases (see sub-paragraphs (2) to (5)), and
(*b*) cases involving redemption arrangements (see sub-paragraph (6)).

(2) A case is a non-standard repo case if—

(*a*) a company has a repo,
(*b*) there has been a sale of the securities under the arrangement or arrangements by reference to which the company has the repo, and
(*c*) any of conditions A to C are met in relation to the repo.

(3) Condition A is that those securities, or similar or other securities, are not subsequently bought under the arrangement or arrangements.

(4) Condition B is that provision is made by or under an arrangement for different or additional securities to be treated as, or as included with, securities which, for the purposes of the subsequent purchase, are to represent those initially sold.

(5) Condition C is that provision is made by or under an arrangement for securities to be treated as not so included.

(6) A case involves redemption arrangements if—

(*a*) arrangements, corresponding to those made in cases where a company has a repo, are made in relation to securities that are to be redeemed in the period after their sale, and

(*b*) the arrangements are such that a person (instead of having the right or obligation to buy those securities, or similar or other securities, at any subsequent time) has a right or obligation in respect of the benefits that will result from the redemption.

(7) The regulations may—

(*a*) make different provision for different cases, and

(*b*) contain incidental, supplemental, consequential and transitional provision and savings.

(8) Regulations about paragraph 6 or 11 may, in particular, include modifications of TCGA 1992 in relation to cases where, as a result of the regulations, any acquisition or disposal is excluded from those which are to be ignored for the purposes of corporation tax in respect of chargeable gains.

(9) In this paragraph—

"modifications" include exceptions and omissions, and

"repo" means—

(*a*) a debtor repo or debtor quasi-repo, or

(*b*) a creditor repo or creditor quasi-repo (including anything treated, as a result of paragraph 12, as a creditor repo for the purposes of paragraph 10).

GENERAL NOTE

Purpose of Schedule

Schedule 13 is introduced by FA 2007 s 47 and sets out a new regime for the taxation of repo arrangements for the purposes of corporation tax. The new rules will apply from a day to be appointed by HM Treasury and will replace the existing legislation in TA 1988 ss 731–738. In economic terms a repo is effectively a loan arrangement, whereby a borrower sells securities to a lender for a fixed price and buys those or similar securities back at a future date. HMRC appear to regard the existing provisions as too mechanistic in their approach, and the new rules contained in Sch 13 seek to align the tax consequences of repos and similar transactions with their economic substance and treatment under generally accepted accounting practice.

Meaning of debtor repo (para 1)

A borrowing company, or a partnership of which the borrowing company is a member, has a debtor repo if it receives an advance (whether in cash or other assets) from a lender under an arrangement (Condition A), a financial liability is required to be recognised in the borrower's accounts under GAAP (Condition B), the borrower sells securities to the lender under the terms of the arrangement (Condition C), the borrower is required to repurchase those or similar securities at a subsequent time (Condition D), and the repurchase extinguishes the financial liability recorded in the borrower's accounts under GAAP (Condition E). This definition encompasses regular repos executed under standard market documentation, but also applies to situations where the borrower does not actually repurchase securities. "Securities" includes UK and overseas securities. GAAP means either UK GAAP or IAS, see FA 2004 s 50(1). It does not matter whether the arrangement for the repurchase of the securities from the lender is conditional or unconditional.

Meaning of debtor quasi-repo (para 2)

A borrowing company, or a partnership of which the borrowing company is a member, has a debtor quasi-repo if the conditions in para 2 are not met (and hence there is no debtor repo), but the arrangements are economically equivalent. A quasi-repo exists where the borrower receives an advance under an arrangement (Condition A), a financial liability is required to be recognised in the borrower's accounts under GAAP (Condition B), the borrower or any other person is required to sell securities under that or any other arrangement at any time (Condition C), an arrangement either confers a right or imposes an obligation on the borrower requiring the repurchase of those or any other securities, or makes provision ("a relevant provision") for another person to repurchase the securities for (Condition D), and the financial liability of the borrower is extinguished, either through the subsequent repurchase of the securities, or the receipt of an asset or discharge of the liability to the borrower under that or any other arrangement (Condition E).

As for a debtor repo, the advance received under Condition A may be in money or other assets and conditional and unconditional arrangements fall within the provisions.

These provisions are intended to apply to arrangements where, for example, the borrower does not sell the securities, but has retained the rights and obligations of the repo agreement transferred to the person making the sale of securities; or the arrangement provides only for a person other than the borrower to repurchase the securities and there is a separate arrangement between the borrower and that other person whereby the borrower is paid to assume the other person's obligations under the repo.

Ignoring effect on borrower of sale of securities: debtor repos, debtor quasi-repos and other arrangements (para 3)

Where a borrowing company has a repo or quasi-repo arrangement, or has a liability discharged under a "relevant arrangement", the arrangements are effectively ignored for corporation tax purposes and the borrower is treated as continuing to hold the securities. Provided income is recognised under GAAP in determining the borrower's profit and loss for the period, the borrower will be taxed on the income arising from the securities while they are subject to the repo (or quasi-repo) arrangement. Any manufactured payments received by the lender are similarly ignored in order to prevent double taxation. A "relevant arrangement" is one which meets the conditions of C and D in para 3 above, and the main purpose or one of the main purposes of which is the obtaining of a tax advantage. This provision is based upon the deemed manufactured payment provisions for stock-lending and repo arrangements currently contained within TA 1988 ss 736B and 737A.

Relief for borrower for finance charges in respect of the advance: debtor repos and debtor quasi-repos (para 4)

An advance received by a borrower under a repo or quasi-repo arrangement is treated as a money debt for the purposes of the loan relationship rules, and finance charges incurred in the borrower's accounts are treated as interest paid.

Ignoring sale and subsequent purchase for purposes of chargeable gains: debtor repos (para 5)

The disposal and subsequent repurchase of securities under a debtor repo arrangement is ignored for the purposes of corporation tax on chargeable gains. If there is a disposal under the repo arrangement but it becomes apparent there will be no subsequent repurchase, or a financial liability ceases to be recognised in the borrower's accounts under GAAP, the borrower is treated as having disposed of the securities for their market value at that time.

Meaning of creditor repo (para 6)

A lending company, or a partnership of which the lending company is a member, has a creditor repo if money or any other asset is advanced to a borrower under an arrangement (Condition A), a financial asset is required under GAAP to be recognised in the lender's accounts (Condition B), the borrower sells securities to the lender under the arrangement (Condition C), the arrangement gives a right or imposes an obligation for the lender to sell those or similar securities at a later time (Condition D), and under GAAP the sale of the securities would extinguish the financial asset recorded in the lender's accounts.

Meaning of creditor quasi-repo (para 7)

A lending company, or a partnership of which the lending company is a member, has a creditor quasi-repo if the conditions in para 2 are not met (and hence there is no creditor repo), but the lender makes an advance under an arrangement (Condition A), a financial asset is required to be recognised in the lender's accounts under GAAP (Condition B), a person sells securities to the lender under that or any other arrangement at any time (Condition C), an arrangement confers a right or imposes an obligation on the lender or another person to sell those or any other securities (Condition D), and the financial asset of the lender is extinguished, either through the subsequent sale of the securities, or the receipt of an asset or discharge of the liability to the lender under that or any other arrangement (Condition E).

As for a creditor repo, the advance made under Condition A may be in money or other assets.

Ignoring the effect on lender of sale of securities: creditor repos and creditor quasi-repos (para 8)

The lender under a repo or quasi-repo arrangement is not subject to corporation tax in respect of income received in respect of the securities, and is similarly not entitled to relief in respect of manufactured payments made to the seller, except to the extent that such income and payments are in accordance with GAAP in determining the lender's profits or loss for a period

Charge on lender for finance return in respect of the advance: creditor repos and creditor quasi-repos (para 9)

The lender's advance under a creditor repo or creditor quasi-repo arrangement is treated as a money debt under the loan relationship rules, and finance returns recognised in the lender's accounts under GAAP are taxed as interest receipts in respect of that debt.

Ignoring purchase and subsequent sale for purposes of chargeable gains: creditor repos (para 10)

The acquisition and subsequent disposal of securities under a creditor repo arrangement are ignored for the purposes of corporation tax on chargeable gains. If there is an acquisition under the repo arrangement but it becomes apparent there will be no subsequent sale, or a financial asset ceases to be recognised in the lender's accounts under GAAP, the lender is treated as having acquired of the securities for their market value at that time.

Repo under arrangement designed to produce quasi-interest: anti-avoidance (para 11)

Where a company makes an advance to another person under an arrangement falling outside the definition of a creditor repo or creditor quasi-repo in paras 7 and 8 above, and is required under GAAP to record a financial asset in respect of the advance, the company is treated as if it had a creditor repo by reference to the arrangement. This rule applies only where the arrangement is designed to produce a quasi-interest return to the lender, and the main purpose of the arrangement is the obtaining of a tax advantage. "Tax advantage" is defined in TA 1988 s 840ZA and means a relief from tax or increased relief from tax, a repayment of tax or increased repayment of tax, the avoidance or reduction of a charge to tax or an assessment to tax, or the avoidance of a possible assessment to tax.

Requirements to deduct tax from manufactured payments: creditor repos and debtor repos (para 12)

The tax deduction provisions of ITA 2007 Part 15 Ch 9 apply to a lender under a creditor repo arrangement as if the lender had paid a manufactured payment to the borrower, representing any income arising on the securities sold. The manufactured payment is treated as made on the same date income is payable.

Similarly, the reverse charge rules in ITA 2007 Part 15 Ch 9 apply to a company with a debtor repo. The effect of the rules is to treat the borrower as receiving a manufactured payment from the lender, representing income arising on the securities sold.

Interpretation etc (para 13)

Various important terms are defined. It is provided that were securities are bought or sold by a person for the benefit of another, it is the beneficial owner who is treated as buying or selling the securities for the purposes of the repo provisions.

Securities are "similar" within the meaning of Sch 13 if they entitle the holder to the same rights to capital interest and dividends and the same remedies for the enforcement of those rights.

Where a company does not prepare accounts in accordance with GAAP, Sch 13 applies as if the company's accounts had been so prepared.

Power to modify Schedule (para 14)

The Treasury has the power to make regulations modifying the application of the Schedule with regard to non-standard repos or cases involving redemption arrangements.

SCHEDULE 14

SALE AND REPURCHASE OF SECURITIES: MINOR AND CONSEQUENTIAL AMENDMENTS

Section 47

Income and Corporation Taxes Act 1988 (*c 1*)

1 ICTA is amended as follows.

GENERAL NOTE

This paragraph provides for ICTA 1988 to be amended in accordance with the following paragraphs.

2— (1) Section 231AA (no tax credit for borrower under stock lending arrangement or interim holder under repurchase agreement) is amended as follows.

(2) In subsection (1)—

(*a*) for "the interim holder under a repurchase agreement" substitute "the lender under a creditor repo or creditor quasi-repo", and

(*b*) for "or agreement" (in both places) substitute "or repo in question".

(3) For subsection (3) substitute—

"(3) In this section "creditor repo" and "creditor quasi-repo" have the meaning given by Schedule 13 to the Finance Act 2007."

(4) In subsection (4), omit "or 737A(5)".

(5) After that subsection insert—

"(5) For the purposes of this section a person is taken to have paid a manufactured dividend representative of a distribution in respect of securities to which a creditor repo relates if (as a result of paragraph 13(1) of Schedule 13 to the Finance Act 2007) the person is treated for the purposes of Chapter 9 of Part 15 of ITA 2007 as making a payment which is representative of the income payable on the securities."

3— (1) Section 231AB (no tax credit for original owner under repurchase agreement in respect of certain manufactured dividends) is amended as follows.

(2) In subsection (1), for paragraphs (*a*) to (*c*) substitute—

"(*a*) the person is the borrower under a debtor repo or debtor quasi-repo;

(*b*) the qualifying distribution is a manufactured dividend paid to the borrower in consequence of that repo; and

(*c*) the arrangement or arrangements in relation to that repo are not such that the actual dividend which the manufactured dividend represents is receivable otherwise than by the borrower under that repo."

(3) For subsection (2) substitute—

"(2) In this section "debtor repo" and "debtor quasi-repo" have the meaning given by Schedule 13 to the Finance Act 2007."

4 Omit sections 730A and 730B (treatment of price differential on sale and repurchase of securities).

5 Omit section 730BB (exchange gains and losses on sale and repurchase of securities).

GENERAL NOTE

Paragraphs 2–5 amend TA 1988 s 231AA to reflect the "creditor repo" and "quasi-creditor repo" terminology adopted in Sch 13 and to ensure that those terms have the meanings given by that Schedule. A new sub-s 5 provides that a person is treated as having paid a manufactured dividend representative of income on securities for the purposes of s 231AA where that person is so treated under para 15 of Sch 13.

6— (1) Section 731 (purchase and sale of securities: application and interpretation of sections 732 to 734) is amended as follows.

(2) In subsection (2A)—

(*a*) omit "section 737A(5) below or", and

(*b*) after "2007" insert "or paragraph 13(1) of Schedule 13 to the Finance Act 2007".

(3) For subsection (2F) substitute—

"(2F) For the purposes of subsections (2B) to (2E) above—

(*a*) agreements are related if they are entered into in pursuance of the same arrangement (regardless of the date on which either agreement is entered into); and

(*b*) references to buying back securities include buying similar securities even if the securities bought have not previously been held by the purchaser (and references in those subsections to repurchase are to be construed accordingly).

(2G) For the purposes of subsection (2F) above securities are similar if they entitle their holders to—

(*a*) the same rights against the same persons as to capital, interest and dividends, and

(*b*) the same remedies for the enforcement of those rights,

in spite of any difference in the total nominal amounts of the respective securities or in the form in which they are held or the manner in which they can be transferred."

7 Omit sections 737A to 737C (sale and repurchase of securities: deemed manufactured payments).

8 Omit section 737E (power to modify sections 730A, 730BB and 737A to 737C).

9 In section 774E(4) (exceptions to sections 774B and 774D), for paragraph (*b*) (together with the "or" at the end of it) substitute—

"(*b*) Schedule 13 to the Finance Act 2007 (sale and repurchase of securities) applies, or".

GENERAL NOTE

Paragraphs 6–9 amend TA 1988 s 231AB to reflect the "debtor repo" and "quasi-debtor repo" terms used in Sch 13 and to ensure that those terms have the meanings given by that Schedule. New sub-ss 2F and 2G provide further details of when agreements are to be treated as related and when securities are to be regarded as being "similar".

10 In section 807A (disposals and acquisitions of company loan relationships with or without interest), for subsection (6A) substitute—

"(6A) In this section "repo or stock-lending arrangements" means—

(*a*) a debtor repo within the meaning of paragraph 2 of Schedule 13 to the Finance Act 2007, or

(*b*) a stock lending arrangement within the meaning of section 263B of the 1992 Act.

(6B) In any case where a debtor repo within the meaning of that paragraph constitutes the repo or stock-lending arrangements—

(*a*) a reference in this section, in relation to those arrangements, to the initial transfer is to the sale mentioned in condition C of that paragraph; and

(*b*) a reference in this section, in relation to those arrangements, to the period for which they have effect is to the period from the making of the initial transfer until the earlier of the time when the subsequent purchase mentioned in condition D of that paragraph takes place and the time when it becomes apparent that that subsequent purchase will not take place.

(6C) In any case where a stock lending arrangement within the meaning of section 263B of the 1992 Act constitutes the repo or stock-lending arrangements—

(*a*) a reference in this section, in relation to those arrangements, to the initial transfer is to the transfer mentioned in subsection (1)(*a*) of that section; and

(*b*) a reference in this section, in relation to those arrangements, to the period for which they have effect is to the period from the making of the initial transfer until the earlier of the time when the transfer mentioned in subsection (1)(*b*) of that section takes place and the time when it becomes apparent that that transfer will not take place."

GENERAL NOTE

TA 1988 s 807A is amended to signpost the definition of "repo or stock-lending arrangements" in para 2 to Sch 13, and . The period to which the arrangements are to have effect is defined in relation to both repo and stock-lending arrangements.

Taxation of Chargeable Gains Act 1992 (*c 12*)

11 TCGA 1992 is amended as follows.

GENERAL NOTE

TCGA 1992 is amended in accordance with the following paragraphs.

12— (1) Section 263A (agreements for sale and repurchase of securities) is amended as follows.

(2) In subsection (1), for the words from the beginning to "were different" substitute "Subject to subsections (3) and (4) below, in any case falling within section 607(1) of ITA 2007 (treatment of price differences under repos)".

(3) After that subsection insert—

"(1A) If, at any time after the acquisition mentioned in subsection (1)(*a*) above, it becomes apparent that the interim holder will not dispose of the securities to the repurchaser, the interim holder shall be treated for the purposes of capital gains tax as acquiring them at that time for a consideration equal to their market value at that time.

(1B) If, at any time after the disposal mentioned in subsection (1)(*b*) above, it becomes apparent that the original owner will not acquire the securities as the repurchaser, the original owner shall be treated for the purposes of capital gains tax as disposing of them at that time for a consideration equal to their market value at that time."

(4) Omit subsection (2).

(5) For subsections (5) and (6) substitute—

"(5) Expressions used in this section and section 607 of ITA 2007 have the same meaning in this section as in that section.

(6) This section does not apply for the purposes of corporation tax in respect of chargeable gains."

(6) The heading accordingly becomes "**Agreements for sale and repurchase of securities: capital gains tax**".

GENERAL NOTE

Provision is made for TCGA 1992 s 263A to cease to apply for the purposes of corporation tax on chargeable gains when Sch 13 comes into effect. It will continue to apply to borrowers and lenders under repo arrangements between non-corporates.

13— (1) For paragraph 12 of Schedule 7AC substitute—

"**12**— (1) This paragraph applies where—

(*a*) a company ("the borrower") which holds shares in another company sells the shares under an arrangement by reference to which the borrower has a debtor repo, and

(*b*) by virtue of paragraph 6 of Schedule 13 to the Finance Act 2007 (sale and repurchase of securities) the sale is ignored for the purposes of corporation tax in respect of chargeable gains.

(2) For the period for which the arrangement is in force—

(*a*) the borrower shall be treated for the purposes of this Part as continuing to hold the shares and accordingly as retaining its entitlement to any rights attaching to them, and (*b*) the lender shall be treated for those purposes as not holding the shares and as not becoming entitled to any such rights.

This is subject to the following qualification.

(3) If at any time before the end of that period the borrower, or another member of the same group as the borrower, becomes the holder—

(*a*) of any of the shares, or

(*b*) of any shares directly or indirectly representing any of them,

sub-paragraph (2) does not apply after that time in relation to those shares or, as the case may be, the shares represented by them.

(4) Expressions used in this paragraph and in Schedule 13 to the Finance Act 2007 have the same meaning in this paragraph as in that Schedule."

GENERAL NOTE

This paragraph sets out a new para 12 to Sch 7AC. The substantial shareholdings exemption continues to be unaffected by any repo arrangements. References to TCGA 1992 s 263A are replaced by references to the new provisions of para 6 of Sch 13.

Finance Act 1996 (c 8)

14 Chapter 2 of Part 4 of FA 1996 (loan relationships) is amended as follows.

GENERAL NOTE

FA 1996 is amended in accordance with the following paragraphs.

15 In section 91C(3) (shares treated as loan relationships: condition 1 for section 91B(6)(*b*)), for paragraph (*f*) substitute—

"(*f*) rights under a creditor repo within the meaning of paragraph 7 of Schedule 13 to the Finance Act 2007;".

16— (1) Section 97 (manufactured interest) is amended as follows.

(2) In subsection (4), for "sections 736B(2) and 737A(5) of the Taxes Act 1988 for cases" substitute "section 736B(2) of the Taxes Act 1988 for a case".

(3) After subsection (4A) insert—

"(4B) This section is subject to Schedule 13 to the Finance Act 2007 (sale and repurchase of securities)."

17 In section 100 (money debts etc not arising from the lending of money), omit subsection (2A).

GENERAL NOTE

By virtue of paras 15–17 signposts are provided to the definition of "creditor repo" under the Schedule.

18 For paragraph 15 of Schedule 9 (and the italic cross-heading before it) substitute—

"Repo and stock-lending transactions and other transactions where a company ceases to be party to a loan relationship

15— (1) This paragraph applies if—

(*a*) a company ceases to be a party to a loan relationship in any period (whether as a result of the disposal of the rights or liabilities under the relationship under a repo or stock lending arrangement or otherwise), but

(*b*) amounts in respect of the relationship are, in accordance with generally accepted accounting practice, nonetheless recognised in determining the company's profit or loss for that period or any subsequent period.

(2) Despite ceasing to be a party to the relationship—

(*a*) the company is to bring into account amounts in respect of the relationship for those periods for the purposes of this Chapter, and (*b*) those amounts are to be those which are so recognised in respect of the relationship (subject to the provisions of this Chapter (including, in particular, section 84(1))).

(3) In relation to any time after the company ceases to be a party to a loan relationship, any question—

(*a*) whether the company is to any extent a party to the relationship for the purposes of a trade carried on by it or for any other particular purpose or purposes, or

(*b*) whether the relationship is to any extent referrable to a particular business, or a particular class, category or description of business, carried on by it,

is to be determined by reference to the circumstances immediately before the company ceased to be a party to the relationship.

(4) This paragraph does not apply in relation to any amount in respect of a loan relationship which is brought into account for the purposes of this Chapter as a result of section 103(6) of this Act or paragraph 4 of Schedule 13 to the Finance Act 2007 (sale and repurchase of securities)."

GENERAL NOTE

A new para 15 of Sch 9 FA 1996 is introduced. The new provisions apply if a company ceases to be party to a loan relationship but amounts continue to be recognised in the company's accounts in respect of that relationship in accordance with GAAP. In that case, the loan relationship rules will continue to apply to amounts recognised in the company's accounts and trading/non-trading credits and/or debits will be brought into account. To ensure that this provision does not result in a double charge under the repo rules, new para 15 does not apply in relation to any amount brought into account under FA 2007 s 103(6) or Sch 13 para 4.

Finance Act 1994 (*c 9*)

19 In section 229(1)(*ca*) of FA 1994 (Lloyd's corporate members: regulations), for sub-paragraph (ii) substitute—

"(ii) arrangements involving repos (within the meaning of paragraph 15 of Schedule 13 to the Finance Act 2007) or redemption arrangements (within the meaning of that paragraph);".

Finance Act 2006 (*c 25*)

20 In section 139 of FA 2006 (Real Estate Investment Trusts: manufactured dividends), omit subsection (5).

GENERAL NOTE

Paragraphs 19–20 make a number of minor consequential amendments in relation to corporate members of Lloyd's and the manufactured payment provisions as they relate to UK REITs.

Income Tax Act 2007 (*c 3*)

21 ITA 2007 is amended as follows.

GENERAL NOTE

ITA 2007 is amended in accordance with the following paragraphs.

22 In section 602(1)(*b*) (deemed manufactured payments: repos), for "the repurchase price of the securities became due" substitute "the distribution was payable".

23 In section 607 (treatment of price differences under repos), after subsection (7) insert—

"(7A) A company within the charge to corporation tax is not to be treated as a result of this section as making any payment of interest for income tax purposes."

24 In section 886(2) (interest paid by recognised clearing houses etc), after "repos)" insert ", or paragraph 5 of Schedule 13 to FA 2007 (relief for borrower for finance charges in case of debtor repos and debtor quasi-repos),".

GENERAL NOTE

The deemed manufactured payment rules in ITA 2007 are amended by paras 22–24 to align the date a manufactured payment is treated as made with the new provisions of Sch 13. A company within the charge to corporation tax which is treated as making a manufactured payment is not regarded under ITA 2007 s 607 as having made a payment of interest for income tax purposes. There is no obligation to deduct income tax in respect of interest falling within para 5 of Sch 13.

SCHEDULE 15

CONTROLLED FOREIGN COMPANIES

Section 48

Imputation of chargeable profits and creditable tax of controlled foreign companies

1— (1) Section 747 of ICTA (imputation of chargeable profits and creditable tax of controlled foreign companies) is amended as follows.

(2) After subsection (3) insert—

"(3A) In the case of an apportionment to a company resident in the United Kingdom which has made an application under section 751A which has been granted, subsection (3) above has effect subject to that section."

(3) After subsection (5) insert—

"(5A) Where the resident company has made an application under section 751A which has been granted, it shall be assumed for the purposes of subsection (5) above that—

(*a*) each of the persons who are connected or associated with the resident company has made an application under that section to the same effect, and

(*b*) all the applications have been granted."

Residence

2 In section 749 of ICTA (residence), insert at the end—

"(10) For the purposes of subsection (8) and (9) above, the effect of any application under section 751A shall be disregarded."

Elections and designations under section 749: supplementary provisions

3 In section 749A of ICTA (elections and designations under section 749: supplementary provisions), insert at the end—

"(9) For the purposes of this section the effect of any application under section 751A shall be disregarded."

Territories with a lower level of taxation

4 In section 750(3) of ICTA (territories with a lower level of taxation), after the "and" at the end of paragraph (*a*) insert—

"(*ab*) there shall be disregarded the effect of any application under section 751A; and".

Reduction in chargeable profits for certain activities of EEA business establishments

5 In ICTA, after section 751 insert—

"751A Reduction in chargeable profits for certain activities of EEA business establishments

(1) This section applies if—

(*a*) an apportionment under section 747(3) falls to be made as regards an accounting period ("the relevant accounting period") of a controlled foreign company,

(*b*) throughout that period the controlled foreign company has a business establishment in an EEA territory,

(*c*) throughout that period there are individuals who work for the controlled foreign company in that territory, and

(*d*) a company resident in the United Kingdom ("the UK resident company") has a relevant interest in the controlled foreign company in that period.

(2) The UK resident company may make an application to the Commissioners for Her Majesty's Revenue and Customs for the chargeable profits of the controlled

foreign company for the relevant accounting period to be reduced by an amount ("the specified amount") specified in the application (including to nil).

(3) If the Commissioners grant the application—

(*a*) those chargeable profits are treated as reduced by the specified amount, and
(*b*) the controlled foreign company's creditable tax (if any) for that period is treated as reduced by so much of that tax as, on a just and reasonable basis, relates to the reduction in those chargeable profits,

for the purpose of applying section 747(3) to (5) for determining the sum (if any) chargeable on the UK resident company under section 747(4)(*a*) (but for no other purpose).

(4) The Commissioners may grant the application only if they are satisfied that the specified amount does not exceed the amount (if any) equal to so much of those chargeable profits as can reasonably be regarded as representing the net economic value which—

(*a*) arises to the appropriate body of persons (taken as a whole), and
(*b*) is created directly by qualifying work.

(5) For the purposes of subsection (4) "net economic value" does not include any value which derives directly or indirectly from the reduction or elimination of any liability of any person to any tax or duty imposed under the law of any territory.

(6) For the purposes of subsection (4) "the appropriate body of persons" means—

(*a*) if the controlled foreign company is not a member of a group of companies, the controlled foreign company and the persons who have an interest in it at any time in the relevant accounting period, and
(*b*) if the controlled foreign company is a member of a group of companies, all the persons falling within paragraph (*a*) and any other person who is a member of that group of companies,

and for the purposes of this subsection "group of companies" means a company and any other companies of which it has control.

(7) For the purposes of subsection (4) "qualifying work" means work which—

(*a*) is done in any EEA territory in which the controlled foreign company has a business establishment throughout the relevant accounting period, and
(*b*) is done in that territory by individuals working for the controlled foreign company there.

(8) Any reference in this section to a business establishment of a controlled foreign company in an EEA territory is to be construed in accordance with paragraph 7 of Schedule 25 (but as if the reference in that paragraph to the territory in which the company is resident were to the EEA territory).

(9) For the purposes of this section individuals are not to be regarded as working for a company in any territory unless—

(*a*) they are employed by the company in the territory, or
(*b*) they are otherwise directed by the company to perform duties on its behalf in the territory.

751B Section 751A: supplementary

(1) An application by a company under section 751A—

(*a*) must be made in such form as the HMRC Commissioners may determine,
(*b*) must be accompanied by such documents (or copies of documents) in the company's possession or power as those Commissioners may reasonably require for the purpose of determining whether to grant the application, and
(*c*) must contain such information as those Commissioners may reasonably require for that purpose.

(2) An application by a company under section 751A—

(*a*) may be made at any time on or before the filing date (within the meaning of Schedule 18 to the Finance Act 1998) for the relevant company tax return of the company, and
(*b*) may be amended or withdrawn at any time before the application is determined by those Commissioners.

(3) If an application by a company under section 751A is granted after the company has delivered its relevant company tax return, it has 30 days beginning with the day on which the application is granted in which to amend that return to give effect to section 751A.

(4) The time limits otherwise applicable to an amendment of a company tax return do not prevent an amendment being made under subsection (3).

(5) If the HMRC Commissioners refuse an application by a company under section 751A, the company may appeal to the Special Commissioners against the refusal.

(6) Notice of an appeal must be given in writing to the HMRC Commissioners within 30 days after the application is refused.

(7) On an appeal—

(*a*) if the Special Commissioners are satisfied that the relevant amount is a different amount from the amount specified in the application, they must direct the HMRC Commissioners to grant the application as if the amount specified in it were that different amount,
(*b*) if the Special Commissioners are satisfied that the relevant amount is the amount specified in the application, they must direct the HMRC Commissioners to grant the application, and
(*c*) in any other case, the Special Commissioners must confirm the refusal.

(8) For the purposes of subsection (7) "the relevant amount" means the amount (if any) equal to so much of the chargeable profits mentioned in subsection (4) of section 751A as can reasonably be regarded as representing the value mentioned in that subsection.

(9) Part 5 of the Management Act (appeals against assessments to tax), apart from section 50, applies in relation to an appeal under this section as it applies in relation to an appeal against an assessment to tax.

(10) In this section "relevant company tax return", in relation to a company, means the return for the accounting period for which—

(*a*) any sum is chargeable on the company under section 747(4)(*a*), or
(*b*) any sum would be so chargeable but for section 751A,

in respect of the chargeable profits of the controlled foreign company for the accounting period mentioned in section 751A(1).

(11) In this section "the HMRC Commissioners" means the Commissioners for Her Majesty's Revenue and Customs."

Interpretation

6 In section 756 of ICTA (interpretation and construction of Chapter 4 of Part 17), after subsection (1) insert—

"(1A) In this Chapter "EEA territory", in relation to any time, means a territory which is an EEA state at that time other than the United Kingdom.

(1B) But a territory is not to be regarded for the purposes of subsection (1A) above as an EEA state at any time if—

(*a*) it is not a member State at that time, and
(*b*) there are no arrangements made in relation to the territory having effect by virtue of section 173 of the Finance Act 2006 (international tax enforcement arrangements) at that time."

GENERAL NOTE

These paragraphs represent the UK Government's response to the decision of the European Court of Justice (ECJ) in *Cadbury Schweppes plc and Cadbury Schweppes Overseas Ltd v Commissioners of Inland Revenue* (Case C-196/04). The ECJ ruled in that case that the UK's controlled foreign companies (CFC) legislation must not be applied where a CFC is actually established in another EU member state and carries on genuine economic activities there. Such a finding must be based on objective factors with regard, in particular, to the extent to which the CFC physically exists in terms of premises, staff and equipment.

Paragraph 5 inserts TA 1988 ss 751A and 751B which allow a UK resident company to make an application to HMRC to reduce the chargeable profits (and any creditable tax) of a CFC for a particular accounting period that would otherwise be apportioned to the UK resident company where, throughout that period, the CFC has a business establishment in an EEA territory and individuals working for it in that territory. Such an application can only be made where the CFC in question cannot satisfy one of the exemptions set out in TA 1988 s 748 for the relevant period.

An "EEA territory" means the EU member states, other than the UK, and those EEA states with which the UK has international tax enforcement arrangements (having effect by virtue of FA 2006 s 173); which currently includes Iceland and Norway, but not Liechtenstein.

Individuals are not treated as working for a CFC in any territory unless they are employed by the company in the territory or they are otherwise directed by the company to perform duties on its behalf in the territory. The draft HMRC guidance that has been published says that this includes people working in essentially the same role as an employee of the CFC (e.g. employees of another group company seconded, or staff provided by an employment agency, to work for the CFC in that territory), but not self-employed individuals or employees of a contractor contracted to provide services for or deliver services on behalf of the CFC.

The term "business establishment" is to be construed in accordance with TA 1988 Sch 25 para 7, so that it means premises (eg an office, shop or factory) which are, or are intended to be, occupied and used with a reasonable degree of permanence from which the company's business in the relevant EEA territory is wholly or mainly carried on.

The amount by which the chargeable profits of a CFC may be reduced under the new relief ("the specified amount") is equal to the net economic value arising to the appropriate body of persons (taken as a whole) that is created directly by work done by individuals working for the CFC in any EEA territory in which the CFC has a business establishment throughout that period. The "appropriate body of persons" means the CFC and all those persons who have an interest in the CFC at any time in the relevant accounting period and, additionally, where the CFC is a member of a group of companies, any other person who is a member of that group. The net economic value does not include any tax reduction achieved by the CFC.

The focus is, therefore, on profits generated by labour itself. The draft HMRC guidance says that, as a guide, the net economic value should equate to what the group would be prepared to pay to a third party to undertake the work done by staff working for the CFC in the relevant EEA territory, over and above the full economic costs of undertaking that work. The guidance also says that this does not include profits arising from activities which are entirely intra-group and which of themselves add no value to the group (such as intra-group lending) as these do not constitute profits from genuine economic activities; nor does it include profits arising from capital or assets (such as intellectual property) placed or retained in the CFC as these do not constitute net economic value to the group created directly by the work of staff in the CFC. This suggests that it will not be possible to exclude much, if any, of the chargeable profits of a CFC which, for example, licenses intellectual property or makes intra-group loans from an apportionment under the new relief.

If HMRC grant the application, the chargeable profits are reduced by the specified amount and any creditable tax is treated as reduced by so much of that tax as on a just and reasonable basis relates to the reduction in the chargeable profits.

The application by the UK resident company must be made on or before the filing date for its relevant corporation tax return. Accordingly, the application will normally need to be made within 12 months of the end of the UK resident company's accounting period in which the relevant accounting period of the CFC ends. HMRC may specify the form of the application and, within reason, the documents and information to be included therein (this is set out in para 39 and Annex 2 of the draft HMRC guidance). The application may be amended or withdrawn at any time before the application is determined by HMRC. If an application is granted after the relevant corporation tax return has been filed, the UK resident company has 30 days from when the application is granted to amend its return (regardless of time limits otherwise applicable to the amendment of a corporation tax return).

It can be seen that, unlike the rest of the CFC legislation, the new relief is not a self-assessment provision. However, if HMRC refuse an application, the UK resident company has the right of appeal to the Special Commissioners, although notice of an appeal must be given to HMRC in writing within 30 days from when the application is refused.

HMRC seem to have applied a very narrow interpretation of the ECJ ruling in *Cadbury Schweppes* in drafting the new relief given that the ECJ made no distinction between "capital" and "labour" profits and did not suggest that intra-group activities could not represent genuine economic activities. Accordingly, there must be a question as to whether the new relief satisfactorily resolves the issue as to whether the CFC rules are EU compliant.

On 21 June 2007, HM Treasury and HMRC published *Taxation of the foreign profits of companies: a discussion document* which marks the beginning of a consultation process with business on some key areas of the UK's corporate tax regime, including the taxation of foreign dividends and the CFC rules. The document proposes the replacement of the current CFC rules with a new controlled companies (CC) regime taxing passive income of foreign and UK CCs and active "mobile" income of foreign CCs on UK companies with an interest of 10% or more. If such a regime is introduced, the legislation is most likely to be included in FA 2009, with a possible start date of 1 April 2009, and it seems likely that the new EEA relief discussed above would be repealed as part of any such a change.

Exempt activities test

7— (1) Part 2 of Schedule 25 to ICTA (supplementary provision in relation to cases where apportionment under section 747(3) does not apply: exempt activities) is amended as follows.

(2) In paragraph 5, after sub-paragraph (1) insert—

"(1A) Except as provided in paragraph 8 below, the provisions of this Part of this Schedule apply in relation to a company which is resident in an EEA territory in the same way as they apply in relation to a company which is resident elsewhere."

(3) In paragraph 8, in sub-paragraph (1), after "fulfilled" insert "in relation to a company which is not resident in an EEA territory".

(4) Insert at the end of that paragraph—

"(5) The condition in paragraph 6(1)(*b*) above shall not be regarded as fulfilled in relation to a company which is resident in an EEA territory unless there are sufficient individuals working for the company in the territory who have the competence and authority to undertake all, or substantially all, of the company's business.

(6) For the purposes of sub-paragraph (5) above, individuals are not to be regarded as working for a company in any territory unless—

(*a*) they are employed by the company in the territory, or

(*b*) they are otherwise directed by the company to perform duties on its behalf in the territory."

GENERAL NOTE

This paragraph amends the "effectively managed" condition in the exempt activities test, but only in relation to CFCs resident in an EEA territory (as defined above). The effectively managed condition in TA 1988 Sch 25 para 6(1)(*b*) requires that, throughout the relevant accounting period, the company's business affairs in its territory of residence must be effectively managed there.

For CFCs resident in an EEA territory, the effectively managed condition will now only be regarded as satisfied if there are sufficient individuals working for the company in its territory of residence who have the competence and authority to undertake all, or substantially all, of the company's business. Individuals are not treated as working for a CFC in any territory unless they are employed by the company in the territory or they are otherwise directed by the company to perform duties on its behalf in the territory.

It is understood that this amendment is being made to align the exempt activities test with the new EEA relief (which is discussed above).

Abolition of public quotation exemption

8— (1) In section 748(1) of ICTA (cases where apportionment under section 747(3) does not apply), omit paragraph (*c*) (together with the "or" at the end of it).

(2) In Schedule 25 to ICTA (supplementary provision in relation to cases where apportionment under section 747(3) does not apply), omit Part 3 (the public quotation condition).

GENERAL NOTE

The public quotation condition is being abolished because HMRC say that disclosed avoidance schemes have shown that this kind of exemption is vulnerable to abuse (it is understood that the schemes in question typically involved listing preference shares in a CFC on a recognised stock exchange carrying the requisite voting rights, but with very limited rights to profits, etc). Genuinely listed CFCs will in future need to satisfy one of the remaining exemptions in TA 1988 s 748 to avoid a CFC apportionment.

Discovery assessments

9 In paragraph 44(3) of Schedule 18 to FA 1998 (discovery assessment: situation not disclosed by return or related documents etc), in the definition of "relevant claim", insert at the end "or an application under section 751A of the Taxes Act 1988 made by or on behalf of the company which affects the company's tax return for the period in question".

Commencement

10— (1) The amendments made by this Schedule have effect in relation to accounting periods of controlled foreign companies beginning on or after 6th December 2006.

(2) In the case of an accounting period (a "straddling period") of a controlled foreign company—

(*a*) beginning before 6th December 2006, and
(*b*) ending on or after that date,

the amendments made by this Schedule have effect as if, for the purposes of Chapter 4 of Part 17 of ICTA, so much of the straddling period as falls before that date, and so much of the straddling period as falls on or after that date, were separate accounting periods.

(3) The company's chargeable profits for the straddling period, and its creditable tax (if any) for that period, are to be apportioned to the two separate accounting periods on a just and reasonable basis.

(4) Each of the following expressions—

"accounting period",
"chargeable profits",
"controlled foreign company", and
"creditable tax",

has the same meaning in this paragraph as in Chapter 4 of Part 17 of ICTA.

GENERAL NOTE

All of the CFC changes will apply to accounting periods of CFCs beginning on or after 6 December 2006. Where a CFC has an accounting period which straddles that date, it will be treated as having two separate periods with the changes applying to the second period deemed to start on 6 December 2006.

SCHEDULE 16

VENTURE CAPITAL SCHEMES ETC

Section 51

BACKGROUND

The venture capital schemes are:

(1) the Enterprise Investment Scheme (EIS);
(2) the Venture Capital Trust scheme (VCT scheme);
(3) the Corporate Venturing Scheme (CVS);
(4) relief for capital losses (VC loss relief).

The purpose of the venture capital schemes is to provide certain tax reliefs to investors who subscribe for shares in smaller, unquoted, high risk, companies. "Unquoted" companies in the context of the venture capital schemes can include those companies who are listed on the Alternative Investment Market.

The EIS aims to attract investment from individuals (and, in the case of deferral relief under the scheme, from certain trustees), while the CVS aims to promote investment by companies and thereby to encourage corporate venturing relationships.

The VCT scheme encourages indirect investment by individuals, through the medium of a corporate vehicle similar to an investment trust.

The venture capital schemes include restrictions on the types of companies which can issue shares which qualify for relief under the venture capital schemes. The restrictions are based, inter alia, on the issuing company's activities, independence and also the issuing company's gross assets (both before and after the qualifying shares are issued).

The changes in the Finance Bill introduce additional limitations on the venture capital schemes which will restrict the companies able to issue shares which qualify for relief under the venture capital schemes. The new restrictions are based upon the number of employees the issuing company (or its group if it is a parent) can have and also the amount of qualifying shares which can be issued in a certain time period.

PART 1

LIMIT ON NUMBER OF EMPLOYEES OF COMPANY IN WHICH INVESTMENT IS MADE

Corporate venturing scheme

1— (1) Part 3 of Schedule 15 to FA 2000 (requirements as to issuing company) is amended as follows.

(2) In paragraph 15 (introduction to Part) after paragraph (*f*) insert—

"(*fa*) number of employees (see paragraph 22A); and".

(3) After paragraph 22 insert—

"The number of employees requirement

22A— (1) If the issuing company is a single company, the full-time equivalent employee number for it must be less than 50 when the relevant shares are issued.

(2) If the issuing company is a parent company, the sum of—

(*a*) the full-time equivalent employee number for it, and

(*b*) the full-time equivalent employee numbers for each of its qualifying subsidiaries,

must be less than 50 when the relevant shares are issued.

(3) The full-time equivalent employee number for a company is calculated as follows—

Step 1 Find the number of full-time employees of the company.

Step 2 Add, for each employee of the company who is not a full-time employee, such fraction as is just and reasonable.

The result is the full-time equivalent employee number.

(4) In this paragraph references to an employee—

(*a*) include a director, but

(*b*) do not include—

(i) an employee on maternity or paternity leave, or

(ii) a student on vocational training."

(4) The amendments made by this paragraph do not have effect in relation to shares issued before the day on which this Act is passed.

GENERAL COMMENT

The companies which can issue shares which qualify for relief under the venture capital schemes are restricted by the provisions of the schemes. The detailed provisions of the CVS are set out in Schedule 15 FA 2000. The changes in this paragraph take effect for CVS from the date of enactment of FA 2007.

From the date of enactment of FA 2007, a company seeking to raise funds from an issue of share capital which qualifies for the Corporate Venturing Scheme relief must have less than 50 full time employees (or the equivalent if the appropriate proportion of part time employees are included).

Where the company issuing the shares is a parent company of a group, the group must have a combined total of less than 50 full time employees (or the equivalent if the appropriate proportion of part time employees are included).

For the purposes of CVS, the date when shares are issued is to be ascertained in accordance with company law (see *National Westminster Bank plc v IRC*). Shares are issued to a person when that person's title to them has become complete. When that happens will depend on the circumstances of the particular case, but normally it will be when the shareholding is entered in the company's Register of Members.

Enterprise investment scheme

2— (1) Chapter 4 of Part 5 of ITA 2007 (the issuing company) is amended as follows.

(2) In section 180 (overview of Chapter 4), after paragraph (*e*) insert—"(ea) number of employees (see section 186A),".

(3) After section 186 insert—

"186A The number of employees requirement

(1) If the issuing company is a single company, the full-time equivalent employee number for it must be less than 50 when the relevant shares are issued.

(2) If the issuing company is a parent company, the sum of—

(*a*) the full-time equivalent employee number for it, and

(*b*) the full-time equivalent employee numbers for each of its qualifying subsidiaries,

must be less than 50 when the relevant shares are issued.

(3) The full-time equivalent employee number for a company is calculated as follows—

Step 1

Find the number of full-time employees of the company.

Step 2

Add, for each employee of the company who is not a full-time employee, such fraction as is just and reasonable.

The result is the full-time equivalent employee number.

(4) In this section references to an employee—

(*a*) include a director, but

(*b*) do not include—

(i) an employee on maternity or paternity leave, or

(ii) a student on vocational training."

(4) The amendments made by this paragraph do not have effect in relation to—

(*a*) shares issued before the day on which this Act is passed, or

(*b*) shares issued to the managers of an approved fund which closed before that day.

(5) For the purposes of sub-paragraph (4)(*b*)—

(*a*) "the managers of an approved fund" has the same meaning as in section 251 of ITA 2007, and

(*b*) the reference to shares issued to the managers of an approved fund is to shares issued to those managers as nominee for an individual who has invested in the fund.

GENERAL COMMENT

The companies which can issue shares which qualify for relief under the venture capital schemes are restricted by the provisions of the schemes. The detailed provisions of the EIS are set out in Part 5 of ITA 2007. With the exception of shares issued to an approved investment fund, the changes in this paragraph take effect for EIS from the date of enactment of FA 2007.

From the date of enactment of the FA 2007, a company seeking to raise funds from an issue of share capital which qualifies for EIS relief must have less than 50 full time employees (or the equivalent if the appropriate proportion of part time employees are included).

Where the company issuing the shares is a parent company of a group, the group must have a combined total of less than 50 full time employees (or the equivalent if the appropriate proportion of part time employees are included).

A situation could arise whereby an investment fund has raised monies from investors prior to the date of enactment but those monies have not been fully utilised at the date of enactment. As a transitional provision, if funds have been raised by an approved investment fund which closed prior to the date of the enactment of FA 2007, shares issued to that fund by a company which would otherwise be qualifying company, will continue to qualify even if the shares are in fact issued after the date of enactment of the legislation.

For the purposes of EIS, the date when shares are issued is to be ascertained in accordance with company law (see *National Westminster Bank plc v IRC*). Shares are issued to a person when that person's title to them has become complete. When that happens will depend on the circumstances of the particular case, but normally it will be when the shareholding is entered in the company's Register of Members.

Venture capital trusts

3— (1) Part 6 of ITA 2007 is amended as follows.

(2) In section 286(3) (qualifying holdings: introduction) after paragraph (j) insert—

"(ja) number of employees (see section 297A),".

(3) After section 297 insert—

"297A The number of employees requirement

(1) If the relevant company is a single company, the full-time equivalent employee number for it must be less than 50 when the relevant holding is issued.

(2) If the relevant company is a parent company, the sum of—

(*a*) the full-time equivalent employee number for it, and

(*b*) the full-time equivalent employee numbers for each of its qualifying subsidiaries,

must be less than 50 when the relevant holding is issued.

(3) The full-time equivalent employee number for a company is calculated as follows—

Step 1

Find the number of full-time employees of the company.

Step 2

Add, for each employee of the company who is not a full-time employee, such fraction as is just and reasonable.

The result is the full-time equivalent employee number.

(4) In this section references to an employee—

(*a*) include a director, but

(*b*) do not include—

(i) an employee on maternity or paternity leave, or

(ii) a student on vocational training."

(4) In section 327 (certain requirements of Chapter 4 to be treated as met)—

(*a*) in subsection (1), at the end insert ", and

section 297A (the number of employees requirement).";

(*b*) in subsection (4)(*b*) for "and 297" substitute ", 297 and 297A".

(5) This paragraph is deemed to have come into force on 6th April 2007.

(6) The amendments made by this paragraph do not have effect in relation to—

(*a*) a relevant holding issued before that date, or

(*b*) a relevant holding acquired by a company ("the investing company") by means of the investment of protected money.

(7) For the purposes of sub-paragraph (6)(*b*), "protected money" is—

(*a*) money raised by the issue before 6th April 2007 of shares in or securities of the investing company, or

(*b*) money derived from the investment of such money.

GENERAL COMMENT

The companies which can issue shares which qualify for relief under the venture capital schemes are restricted by the provisions of the schemes. The detailed provisions of VCT scheme relief are set out in Part 6 of ITA 2007. With the exception of shares issued to a VCT which is employing "protected monies", the changes in this paragraph take effect for VCT from 6 April 2007.

From 6 April 2007, a company seeking to raise funds from an issue of share capital which qualifies as a "qualifying holding" for the purposes of VCT scheme relief must have less than 50 full time employees (or the equivalent if the appropriate proportion of part time employees are included).

Where the company issuing the shares is a parent company of a group, the group must have a combined total of less than 50 full time employees (or the equivalent if the appropriate proportion of part time employees are included).

A situation could arise whereby a VCT has raised monies from investors through the issue of shares or securities prior to 6 April 2007 but those monies have not been fully utilised (eg in the form of acquiring "qualifying holdings") by 6 April 2007.

As a transitional provision, if funds have been raised by a VCT before 6 April 2007, those funds will be deemed to be "protected monies". Shares issued by a company whose shares would, but for the new limit on employees, be considered to be a qualifying holding to that VCT and which are subscribed for using either protected monies, or funds derived from investment of protected monies, will continue to qualify even if the shares are in fact issued after 6 April 2007.

For the purposes of VCT, the date when shares are issued is to be ascertained in accordance with company law (see *National Westminster Bank plc v IRC*). Shares are issued to a person when that person's title to them has become complete. When that happens will depend on the circumstances of the particular case, but normally it will be when the shareholding is entered in the company's Register of Members.

PART 2

LIMIT ON AMOUNT RAISED ANNUALLY BY COMPANY THROUGH RISK CAPITAL SCHEMES

Corporate venturing scheme

4— (1) Schedule 15 to FA 2000 is amended as follows.

(2) In paragraph 34 (introduction to Part) after sub-paragraph (*a*) insert—

"(*aa*) the maximum amount raised annually through risk capital schemes (see paragraph 35A);".

(3) After paragraph 35 insert—

"*Requirement as to maximum amount raised annually through risk capital schemes*

35A— (1) The total amount of relevant investments made in the issuing company in the year ending with the date the relevant shares are issued must not exceed £2 million.

(2) In sub-paragraph (1), the reference to relevant investments made in the issuing company includes relevant investments made in any company that is, or has at any time in the year mentioned there been, a subsidiary of the issuing company (whether or not it was such a subsidiary when the investment was made).

(3) A "relevant investment" is made in a company if—

(*a*) an investment (of any kind) in the company is made by a VCT, or

(*b*) the company issues shares (money having been subscribed for them), and (at any time) the company provides—

(i) a compliance statement under paragraph 42, or

(ii) a compliance statement under section 205 of ITA 2007 (enterprise investment scheme),

in respect of the shares.

(4) An investment within sub-paragraph (3)(*b*) is regarded as made when the shares are issued."

(4) In paragraph 63(1)(*a*) (withdrawal of relief: interest), after sub-paragraph (i) insert—

"(ia) paragraph 35A (maximum amount raised annually through risk capital schemes);".

GENERAL COMMENT

This provision limits the amount of funds which a company can raise from the issue of new shares which could potentially qualify for relief under the CVS to a maximum of £2 million in any twelve month period.

The restriction operates by limiting the amount of qualifying investments under all of the VCT, EIS or CVS made in the issuing company, in the twelve months up to and including the date the latest qualifying shares are issued, to a total of £2 million.

The calculation of the £2 million limit must take into account both the company which is now issuing the shares and also any subsidiary which is now owned by that company. Therefore, any issue of shares within the last twelve months which qualified for EIS, CVS or VCT scheme relief by a company which is now a subsidiary of the parent company now seeking to utilise the venture capital schemes, will reduce the capacity of the parent company to issue shares which qualify under the venture capital schemes.

Before this alteration, the major limiting factor in the amount a company could raise under the venture capital schemes was the gross assets test. For the purposes of the CVS, paragraph 22 of Schedule 15 of FA 2000 established that the 'gross assets' of the issuing company must not exceed £7,000,000 immediately before the issue of the shares or £8,000,000 immediately after the issue. In the case of a company with a subsidiary, these limits apply to the aggregated gross assets of all the companies in the group (excluding shares in, and loans to, the subsidiaries). For shares issued before 6 April 2006 these limits were £15,000,000 and £16,000,000 respectively.

The amount a company can raise using the venture capital schemes will now be limited by both the gross assets test and also the new £2 million limit.

Enterprise investment scheme

5— (1) Part 5 of ITA 2007 is amended as follows.

(2) In section 172 (overview of Chapter), after paragraph (*a*) insert—

"(*aa*) the maximum amount raised annually through risk capital schemes (see section 173A),".

(3) After section 173 insert—

"173A The maximum amount raised annually through risk capital schemes requirement

(1) The total amount of relevant investments made in the issuing company in the year ending with the date the relevant shares are issued must not exceed £2 million.

(2) In subsection (1), the reference to relevant investments made in the issuing company includes relevant investments made in any company that is, or has at any time in the year mentioned there been, a subsidiary of the issuing company (whether or not it was such a subsidiary when the investment was made).

(3) A "relevant investment" is made in a company if—

(*a*) an investment (of any kind) in the company is made by a VCT, or

(*b*) the company issues shares (money having been subscribed for them), and (at any time) the company provides—

(i) a compliance statement under section 205, or

(ii) a compliance statement under paragraph 42 of Schedule 15 to FA 2000 (corporate venturing scheme),

in respect of the shares.

(4) An investment within subsection (3)(*b*) is regarded as made when the shares are issued."

(4) In section 239(1) (withdrawal etc of relief: date from which interest is chargeable), in column 1 of the Table, after "163," insert "173A".

(5) The amendments made by this paragraph do not have effect in relation to shares issued to the managers of an approved fund which closed before the day on which this Act is passed.

(6) Paragraph 2(5) (meaning of "the managers of an approved fund" etc) applies for the purposes of sub-paragraph (5).

GENERAL COMMENT

This provision limits the amount of funds which a company can raise from the issue of new shares which could potentially qualify for relief under EIS to a maximum of £2 million in any twelve month period.

The restriction operates by limiting the amount of qualifying investments under the entire VCT scheme, EIS or CVS made in the issuing company, in the twelve months up to and including the date the latest qualifying shares are issued, to a total of £2 million.

The calculation of the £2 million limit must take into account both the company which is now issuing the shares and also any subsidiary which is now owned by that company. Therefore, any issue of shares within the last twelve months which qualified for EIS, CVS or VCT scheme relief by a company which is now a subsidiary of the parent company now seeking to utilise the venture capital schemes, will reduce the capacity of the parent company to issue shares which qualify under the venture capital schemes.

A situation could arise whereby an investment fund has raised monies from investors prior to the date of enactment but those monies have not been fully utilised at the date of enactment. As a transitional provision, if funds have been raised by an approved investment fund which closed prior to the date of the enactment of Finance Act 2007, shares issued to managers of that fund (ie because monies from the fund have been used to subscribe for new shares in a company which otherwise qualifies for relief) will not be affected by this provision even if the shares are in fact issued after the date the legislation is enacted.

Prior to this alteration, the major limiting factor in the amount a company could raise under the venture capital schemes was the gross assets test. For the purposes of the EIS, para 185 of Part 5 of ITA 2007 established that the gross assets of the issuing company must not exceed £7,000,000 immediately before the issue of the shares or £8,000,000 immediately after the issue. In the case of a company with a subsidiary, these limits apply to the aggregated gross assets of all the companies in the group (excluding shares in, and loans to, the subsidiaries). For shares issued before 6 April 2006 these limits were £15,000,000 and £16,000,000 respectively.

The amount a company can raise using the venture capital schemes will now be limited by both the gross assets test and also the new £2 million limit.

Venture capital trusts

6— (1) Chapter 4 of Part 6 of ITA 2007 (qualifying holdings) is amended as follows.

(2) In section 286(3) (introduction) after paragraph (*e*) insert—

"(*ea*) the maximum amount raised annually through risk capital schemes (see section 292A),".

(3) After section 292 insert—

"292A The maximum amount raised annually through risk capital schemes requirement

(1) The total amount of relevant investments made in the relevant company in the year ending with the date the relevant holding is issued must not exceed £2 million.

(2) In subsection (1), the reference to relevant investments made in the relevant company includes relevant investments made in any company that is, or has at any time in the year mentioned there been, a subsidiary of the relevant company (whether or not it was such a subsidiary when the investment was made).

(3) A "relevant investment" is made in a company if—

(*a*) an investment (of any kind) in the company is made by a VCT, or

(*b*) the company issues shares (money having been subscribed for them), and (at any time) the company provides—

(i) a compliance statement under section 205 (enterprise investment scheme), or

(ii) a compliance statement under paragraph 42 of Schedule 15 to FA 2000 (corporate venturing scheme),

in respect of the shares.

(4) For the purposes of subsections (1) and (2), an investment within subsection (3)(*b*) is regarded as made when the shares are issued.

(5) Subsection (6) applies if, by virtue of the provision of a compliance statement under section 205 above or paragraph 42 of Schedule 15 to FA 2000, the requirement of this section is not met.

(6) The requirement is to be treated as having been met throughout the period—

(*a*) beginning with the time the relevant holding was issued, and

(*b*) ending with the time the compliance statement was provided."

(4) This paragraph is deemed to have come into force on 6th April 2007.

(5) The amendments made by this paragraph do not have effect in relation to an investment made by a VCT of protected money.

(6) "Protected money" means—

(*a*) money raised by the issue on or before 5th April 2007 of shares in or securities of the VCT, and

(*b*) money derived from the investment of such money.

GENERAL COMMENT

This provision limits the amount of funds which a company can raise from the issue of new shares which could potentially qualify for relief under the VCT scheme to a maximum of £2 million in any twelve month period. This provision applies from 6 April 2007.

The restriction operates by limiting the amount of qualifying investments under the entire VCT scheme, EIS or CVS made in the issuing company, in the twelve months up to and including the date the latest qualifying shares are issued, to a total of £2 million.

The calculation of the £2 million limit must take into account both the company which is now issuing the shares and also any subsidiary which is now owned by that company. Therefore, any issue of shares within the last twelve months which qualified for EIS, CVS or VCT scheme relief by a company which is now a subsidiary of the parent company now seeking to utilise the venture capital schemes, will reduce the capacity of the parent company to issue shares which qualify under the venture capital schemes.

A situation could arise whereby a VCT has raised monies from investors through the issue of shares or securities before 6 April 2007 but those monies have not been fully utilised (eg in the form of acquiring "qualifying holdings") at 6 April 2007.

As a transitional provision, if funds have been raised by a VCT prior to 6 April 2007, those funds will be deemed to be "protected monies". Shares issued by a company whose shares would, but for the new annual limit on amounts raised from risk capital, be considered to be a qualifying holding to that VCT and which are subscribed for using either protected monies, or funds derived from investment of protected monies, will continue to qualify even if the shares are in fact issued after 6 April 2007.

Prior to this alteration, the major limiting factor in the amount a company could raise under the venture capital schemes was the gross assets test. For the purposes of the VCT scheme, paragraph 297 of Part 6 of ITA 2007 established that the 'gross assets' of the issuing company must not exceed £7,000,000 immediately before the issue of the shares or £8,000,000 immediately after the issue. In the case of a company with a subsidiary, these limits apply to the aggregated gross assets of all the companies in the group (excluding shares in, and loans to, the subsidiaries). For shares issued before 6 April 2006 these limits were £15,000,000 and £16,000,000 respectively.

The amount a company can raise using the venture capital schemes will now be limited by both the gross assets test and also the new £2 million limit.

Enterprise investment scheme: reinvestment

7— (1) Schedule 5B to TCGA 1992 is amended as follows.

(2) In paragraph 1 (application of Schedule)—

(*a*) in sub-paragraph (2), after paragraph (*d*) insert—

"(*da*) the total amount of relevant investments made in the company in the year ending with the date the shares are issued does not exceed £2 million,", and

(*b*) after sub-paragraph (5) insert—

"(6) Section 173A(3) and (4) of ITA 2007 (meaning of "relevant investment") apply for the purposes of sub-paragraph (2)(*da*).

(7) In sub-paragraph (2)(*da*), the reference to relevant investments made in the company includes relevant investments made in a company that is, or has at any time in the year mentioned there been, a subsidiary of the company (whether or not it was such a subsidiary when the investment was made)."

(3) In paragraph 1A(1) (failure of conditions of application), after "(2)(*b*)" insert "or (2)(*da*)".

GENERAL COMMENT

This provision limits the amount of funds which a company can raise from the issue of new shares which could potentially qualify for relief under the EIS deferral relief provisions (as set our in Schedule 5B of TCGA 1992) to £2 million in any twelve month period.

The restriction operates by limiting the amount of qualifying investments under the entire VCT scheme, EIS or CVS made in the issuing company, in the twelve months up to and including the date the latest qualifying shares are issued, to a total of £2 million.

The calculation of the £2 million limit must take into account both the company which is now issuing the shares and also any subsidiary which is now owned by that company. Therefore, any issue of shares within the last twelve months which qualified for EIS, CVS or VCT scheme relief by a company which is now a subsidiary of the parent company now seeking to utilise the venture capital schemes, will reduce the capacity of the parent company to issue shares which qualify under the venture capital schemes.

Prior to this alteration, the major limiting factor in the amount a company could raise under the venture capital schemes was the "gross assets" test which is determined in accordance with the provisions for EIS income tax relief. For the purposes of EIS, para 185 of Part 5 of ITA 2007 establishes that the gross assets of the issuing company must not exceed £7,000,000 immediately before the issue of the shares or £8,000,000 immediately after the issue. In the case of a company with a subsidiary, these limits apply to the aggregated gross assets of all the companies in the group (excluding shares in, and loans to, the subsidiaries). For shares issued before 6 April 2006 these limits were £15,000,000 and £16,000,000 respectively.

The amount a company can raise using the venture capital schemes will now be limited by both the gross assets test and also the new £2 million limit.

The EIS deferral relief provides a valuable relief for serial entrepreneurs who could roll over gains on the sale of shares of companies which they sold into share capital of other qualifying companies. The amount of share capital which can be issued by any single company in a twelve month period to defer gains will now be limited by this provision and so the application of this relief will be reduced.

Transitional provision

8— (1) This paragraph applies for the purposes of—

(*a*) paragraph 35A of Schedule 15 to FA 2000,

(*b*) section 173A of ITA 2007 (including that section as applied by paragraph 1(6) of Schedule 5B to TCGA 1992), and

(*c*) section 292A of ITA 2007.

(2) References to investments made by a VCT do not include—

(*a*) investments made on or before 5th April 2007,

(*b*) investments of protected money (as defined by paragraph 6(6)).

(3) References to shares in respect of which compliance statements are provided do not include—

(*a*) shares issued before the day on which this Act is passed, or

(*b*) shares issued to the managers of an approved fund which closed before that day.

(4) Paragraph 2(5) (meaning of "the managers of an approved fund" etc) applies for the purposes of sub-paragraph (3)(*b*) above.

PART 3

EXCLUDED ACTIVITIES: RECEIPT OF ROYALTIES AND LICENCE FEES

Corporate venturing scheme

9— (1) Paragraph 29 of Schedule 15 to FA 2000 is amended as follows.

(2) In sub-paragraph (3), for paragraphs (*a*) and (*b*) substitute—

"(*a*) by the issuing company, or

(*b*) by a company which was a qualifying subsidiary of the issuing company throughout a period during which it created the whole or greater part (in terms of value) of the intangible asset."

(3) After sub-paragraph (6) insert—

"(7) If—

(*a*) the issuing company acquired all the shares ("old shares") in another company ("the old company") at a time when the only shares issued in the issuing company were subscriber shares, and

(*b*) the consideration for the old shares consisted wholly of the issue of shares in the issuing company,

references in sub-paragraph (3) to the issuing company include the old company."

10 In paragraph 86(2) (substitution of new shares for old shares), after "Schedule", in the first place it occurs, insert "(except paragraph 29(7))".

Enterprise investment scheme

11— (1) In section 297 of ICTA (qualifying trades)—

(*a*) in subsection (5), for paragraphs (*a*) and (*b*) substitute—

"(*a*) by the company mentioned in section 293(1), or

(*b*) by a company which was a subsidiary of that company throughout a period during which it created the whole or greater part (in terms of value) of the intangible asset.",

(*b*) in subsection (5A), omit paragraphs (*b*) and (*c*) and the words after paragraph (*c*), and

(*c*) after subsection (5C) insert—

"(5D) If—

(*a*) the company mentioned in section 293(1) ("the issuing company") acquired all the shares ("old shares") in another company ("the old company") at a time when the only shares issued in the issuing company were subscriber shares, and

(*b*) the consideration for the old shares consisted wholly of the issue of shares in the issuing company,

references in subsection (5) above to the company mentioned in section 293(1) include the old company."

(2) In section 304A of that Act (acquisition of share capital by new company)—

(*a*) in subsection (3), after "Chapter" insert "(except section 297(5D))", and

(*b*) in subsection (4), after "Chapter" insert "(except section 297(5D))".

(3) In section 576B of that Act (share loss relief: the trading requirement), after subsection (8) insert—

"(9) In section 195 of ITA 2007 as applied by subsection (7) for the purposes mentioned in subsection (8), references to the issuing company are to be read as references to the company mentioned in subsection (1)."

(4) In section 576K of that Act (share loss relief: substitution of new shares for old), after subsection (3) insert—

"(4) Nothing in subsection (2) applies in relation to section 195(7) of ITA 2007 as applied by section 576B(7) above for the purposes mentioned in section 576B(8)."

(5) In section 137 of ITA 2007 (share loss relief: trading requirement for shares to which EIS relief not attributable), after subsection (8) insert—

"(9) In section 195 as applied by subsection (7) for the purposes mentioned in subsection (8), references to the issuing company are to be read as references to the company mentioned in subsection (1)."

(6) In section 146 of that Act (share loss relief: substitution of new shares for old), after subsection (2) insert—

"(3) Nothing in subsection (2) applies in relation to section 195(7) as applied by section 137(7) for the purposes mentioned in section 137(8)."

(7) In section 195 of ITA 2007 (EIS: excluded activities: receipt of royalties and licence fees)—

(*a*) in subsection (4), for paragraphs (*a*) and (*b*) substitute—

"(*a*) by the issuing company, or

(*b*) by a company which was a qualifying subsidiary of the issuing company throughout a period during which it created the whole or greater part (in terms of value) of the intangible asset.",

(*b*) in subsection (6), omit the definition of "holding company", and

(*c*) after that subsection insert—

"(7) If—

(*a*) the issuing company acquired all the shares ("old shares") in another company ("the old company") at a time when the only shares issued in the issuing company were subscriber shares, and

(*b*) the consideration for the old shares consisted wholly of the issue of shares in the issuing company,

references in subsection (4) to the issuing company include the old company."

(8) In section 249 of that Act (substitution of new shares for old shares)—

(*a*) in subsection (2), after "Part" insert "(except section 195(7))", and

(*b*) in subsection (4), after "Part" insert "(except section 195(7))".

Venture capital trusts

12— (1) Section 306 of ITA 2007 (qualifying holdings) is amended as follows.

(2) In subsection (4), for paragraphs (*a*) and (*b*) substitute—

"(*a*) by the relevant company, or

(*b*) by a company which was a qualifying subsidiary of the relevant company throughout a period during which it created the whole or greater part (in terms of value) of the intangible asset."

(3) In subsection (6), omit the definition of "holding company".

(4) After that subsection insert—

"(7) If—

(*a*) the relevant company acquired all the shares ("old shares") in another company ("the old company") at a time when the only shares issued in the relevant company were subscriber shares, and

(*b*) the consideration for the old shares consisted wholly of the issue of shares in the relevant company,

references in subsection (4) to the relevant company include the old company."

Commencement

13 This Part of this Schedule is deemed to have come into force on 6th April 2007.

Transitional provision

14— (1) This paragraph applies if—

(*a*) shares in or securities of a company ("the company") were issued before 6th April 2007,

(*b*) immediately before that date—

(i) the right to exploit an intangible asset ("the asset") was vested in the company or a subsidiary of it (in either case, whether alone or jointly with others), and

(ii) the asset was a relevant intangible asset,

(*c*) at any time on or after that date, an activity carried on by the company or a subsidiary of it would be an excluded activity by reason only of the receipt of royalties or licence fees attributable to the exploitation of the asset, and

(*d*) the activity would not be an excluded activity if the amendments made by this Part of this Schedule had not been made.

(2) The activity is to be treated, in relation to those shares or securities, as not being an excluded activity at that time.

(3) In sub-paragraphs (1) and (2), references to an excluded activity are to be read—

(*a*) for the purposes of Chapter 3 of Part 7 of ICTA (including any provision of that Chapter as applied by any other provision), as references to—

(i) an activity within section 293(3B)(*a*) of ICTA, or

(ii) an activity within subsection (2) of section 297 of ICTA which causes a trade to fail to comply with that section,

(*b*) for the purposes of Schedule 15 to FA 2000, as references to an excluded activity other than the receiving of royalties or licence fees within paragraph 29 of that Schedule in circumstances where the requirements of sub-paragraph (2) of that paragraph are met.

GENERAL COMMENT

The rules governing the venture capital schemes as they existed before 6 April 2007 restrict the transfer of a qualifying trade of exploiting relevant intangible assets around a group of companies.

The new rules will align the rules relating to the transfer of that trade with those currently relating to other qualifying trades so that relevant intangible assets can be moved around within groups without investors losing tax relief.

The rules operate by extending the definition of a relevant intangible asset to include intangible assets where the whole or greater part of its value has been created by the share-issuing company or by a company which was a qualifying subsidiary of the issuing company at all times during which it created the asset.

PART 4

MEANING OF "QUALIFYING 90% SUBSIDIARY"

Corporate venturing scheme

15— (1) Schedule 15 to FA 2000 is amended as follows.

(2) In paragraph 23 (trading activities requirement), omit sub-paragraphs (10) and (11).

(3) After that paragraph insert—

"Meaning of "qualifying 90% subsidiary"

23A— (1) For the purposes of this Schedule, a company ("the subsidiary") is a qualifying 90% subsidiary of the issuing company if the following conditions are met—

(*a*) the issuing company possesses not less than 90% of the issued share capital of, and not less than 90% of the voting power in, the subsidiary;

(*b*) the issuing company would—

(i) in the event of a winding up of the subsidiary, or

(ii) in any other circumstances,

be beneficially entitled to receive not less than 90% of the assets of the subsidiary which would then be available for distribution to the shareholders of the subsidiary;

(*c*) the issuing company is beneficially entitled to not less than 90% of any profits of the subsidiary which are available for distribution to the shareholders of the subsidiary;

(*d*) no person other than the issuing company has control of the subsidiary within the meaning of section 840 of the Taxes Act 1988;

(*e*) no arrangements are in existence by virtue of which any of the conditions in paragraphs (*a*) to (*d*) would cease to be met.

(2) Paragraph 21(3) and (4) (effect of receivership etc) apply in relation to the conditions in sub-paragraph (1) as they apply in relation to the conditions in paragraph 21(2).

(3) If—

(*a*) arrangements are in existence for the disposal by the issuing company of all its interest in the subsidiary, and

(*b*) the disposal is to be for commercial reasons and is not to be part of a scheme or arrangement the main purpose of which, or one of the main purposes of which, is the avoidance of tax,

the subsidiary is not to be regarded as having ceased on that account to be a qualifying 90% subsidiary of the issuing company.

(4) For the purposes of this Schedule, a company ("company A") which is a subsidiary of a company that is not the issuing company ("company B") is a qualifying 90% subsidiary of the issuing company if—

(*a*) company A would be a qualifying 90% subsidiary of company B (if company B were the issuing company), and company B is a qualifying 100% subsidiary of the issuing company; or

(*b*) company A is a qualifying 100% subsidiary of company B, and company B is a qualifying 90% subsidiary of the issuing company.

(5) For the purposes of sub-paragraph (4), no account is to be taken of any control the issuing company may have of company A.

(6) For those purposes, a company ("company X") is a qualifying 100% subsidiary of another company ("company Y") at any time when the conditions in sub-paragraph (1) would be met if—

(*a*) company X were the subsidiary;

(*b*) company Y were the issuing company; and

(*c*) in sub-paragraph (1) for "not less than 90%" in each place there were substituted "100%"."

(4) In paragraph 103 (index of defined expressions), in the entry relating to the definition of "qualifying 90% subsidiary", for "paragraph 23(10) and (11)" substitute "paragraph 23A".

GENERAL COMMENT

This change provides some relaxation to the current rules surrounding CVS, where currently the trade must be carried on by a direct 90% subsidiary of the company invested in. This condition has previously required investee companies to adopt a structure which has not contained intermediate holding companies between the investee company and the trading subsidiary.

The new rules will allow the trade to be carried on by indirectly held subsidiaries that fulfil certain criteria.

The changes provide that, for the purposes of the CVS, a company which is a 90% subsidiary of a 100% subsidiary of the issuing company, or is a 100% subsidiary of a 90% subsidiary of the issuing company, is, for the purposes of Schedule 15 to FA 2000, a qualifying 90% subsidiary of the issuing company.

Enterprise investment scheme etc

16— (1) In Chapter 3 of Part 7 of ICTA—

(*a*) in section 289 (eligibility for relief), for subsections (9) to (13) substitute—

"(9) Section 190 of ITA 2007 (meaning of "qualifying 90% subsidiary") applies for the purposes of this Chapter.";

(*b*) in section 312(1) (interpretation of Chapter), in the definition of "qualifying 90% subsidiary", omit "to (13)".

(2) In section 190 of ITA 2007 (EIS: meaning of "qualifying 90% subsidiary"), after subsection (1) insert—

"(1A) For the purposes of this Part, a company ("company A") which is a subsidiary of another company ("company B") is a qualifying 90% subsidiary of a third company ("company C") if—

(*a*) company A is a qualifying 90% subsidiary of company B, and company B is a qualifying 100% subsidiary of company C, or

(*b*) company A is a qualifying 100% subsidiary of company B, and company B is a qualifying 90% subsidiary of company C.

(1B) For the purposes of subsection (1A), no account is to be taken of any control company C may have of company A.

(1C) For those purposes, a company ("company X") is a qualifying 100% subsidiary of another company ("company Y") at any time when the conditions in subsection (1)(*a*) to (*e*) would be met if—

(*a*) company X were the subsidiary,

(*b*) company Y were the relevant company, and

(*c*) in subsection (1) for "at least 90%" in each place there were substituted "100%"."

GENERAL COMMENT

This change provides some relaxation to the current rules surrounding EIS, where currently the trade must be carried on by a direct 90% subsidiary of the company invested in. This condition has previously required investee companies to adopt a structure which has not contained intermediate holding companies between the investee company and the trading subsidiary.

The new rules will allow the trade to be carried on by indirectly held subsidiaries that fulfil certain criteria.

Paragraph 15(1) amends the existing definition of "qualifying 90% subsidiary" for the purpose of the EIS insofar as it relates to shares issued before 6 April 2007. It omits subsections (9) to (13) of section 289 of TA 1988 and replaces them with a reference to s 190 of ITA 2007. It also amends s 312(1) of ICTA to omit the references to subsections 289(9) to (13) in the definition of "qualifying 90% subsidiary".

Paragraph 15(2) amends the existing definition of "qualifying 90 per cent subsidiary" for the purposes of the EIS insofar as it relates to shares issued on or after 6 April 2007. It inserts new subsections (1A) to (1C) after s 190 (1) of ITA 2007 which provide that, for the purposes of the EIS, a company which is a 90% subsidiary of a 100% subsidiary of another company, or a 100% subsidiary of a 90% subsidiary of another company is, for the purposes of Part 5 of ITA 2007, a qualifying 90% subsidiary of that other company.

Venture capital trusts

17 In section 301 of ITA 2007, after subsection (1) insert—

"(1A) For the purposes of this Chapter, a company ("company A") which is a subsidiary of a company that is not the relevant company ("company B") is a qualifying 90% subsidiary of the relevant company if—

(*a*) company A would be a qualifying 90% subsidiary of company B (if company B were the relevant company), and company B is a qualifying 100% subsidiary of the relevant company, or

(*b*) company A is a qualifying 100% subsidiary of company B, and company B is a qualifying 90% subsidiary of the relevant company.

(1B) For the purposes of subsection (1A), no account is to be taken of any control the relevant company may have of company A.

(1C) For those purposes, a company ("company X") is a qualifying 100% subsidiary of another company ("company Y") at any time when the conditions in subsection (1)(*a*) to (*e*) would be met if—

(*a*) company X were the subsidiary,

(*b*) company Y were the relevant company, and

(*c*) in subsection (1) for "at least 90%" in each place there were substituted "100%"."

GENERAL COMMENT

This change provides some relaxation to the current rules surrounding VCT, where currently the trade must be carried on by a direct 90% subsidiary of the company invested in. The new rules will allow the trade to be carried on by indirectly held subsidiaries that fulfil certain criteria.

Paragraph 17 amends the existing definition of a qualifying 90% subsidiary for the purpose of the VCT scheme. It inserts, after s 301(1) of ITA 2007, new subsections (1A) to (1C), which provide that, for the purposes of the VCT scheme, a company which is a 90% subsidiary of a 100 per cent subsidiary of the relevant company, or a 100% subsidiary of a 90% subsidiary of the relevant company, is, for the purposes of Part 6 of 1TA 2007, a qualifying 90% subsidiary of the relevant company.

Commencement

18 This Part of this Schedule is deemed to have come into force on 6th April 2007.

PART 5

OTHER AMENDMENTS

EIS: approved investment funds

19— (1) In Part 5 of ITA 2007 (enterprise investment scheme), in section 251(1)(*c*) (approved investment fund as nominee), for "6" substitute "12".

(2) The amendment made by this paragraph has effect in relation to approved funds which closed or close on or after 7 October 2006.

GENERAL COMMENT

This provision changes the effective date of investment where individuals invest into an Approved EIS Fund. The date of investment will be the date that the Fund closes, as long as the funds are invested within 12 months of closing.

Paragraph 18(1) amends the existing section 251(1) of ITA 2007, extending the time that managers of an approved EIS fund have to invest 90% of the funds raised.

If a fund investing in EIS companies is approved under section 251 investors can claim EIS income tax relief on the subscription from the date of the fund closure, providing that 90% of the funds are invested within a certain period. Under current rules funds must be 90% invested within 6 months of the date of the closure of the fund. This period is extended to 12 months. The extended time limit will apply to approved funds with a closure date on or after 7 October 2006.

VCTs: disposal of holding

20— (1) Chapter 3 of Part 6 of ITA 2007 (VCT approvals) is amended as follows.

(2) In section 274(3) (requirements for the giving of approval), at the end of paragraph (*d*) insert ", and

(*e*) the 70% qualifying holdings condition by section 280A".

(3) After section 280 insert—

"280A The 70% qualifying holdings condition: disposal of holding

(1) This section applies if—

(*a*) a company which is a VCT disposes of shares or securities ("the holding"),

(*b*) the consideration for the disposal does not consist wholly of new qualifying holdings, and

(*c*) the holding was comprised in the company's qualifying holdings throughout the 6 months ending immediately before the disposal.

(2) For the purpose of determining whether the 70% qualifying holdings condition is, has been or will be met—

(*a*) the company is to be treated as if it continued to hold the holding for the period of 6 months beginning with the disposal (but see subsection (4)), and (*b*) the value of the company's investments in that period is to be treated as reduced by the amount of any monetary consideration for the disposal.

(3) The value of the holding in the period mentioned in subsection (2)(*a*) is to be treated as equal to its value (determined in accordance with this Chapter) immediately before the disposal.

(4) If the consideration for the disposal includes new qualifying holdings, subsection (2)(*a*) has effect as if the reference to the holding were to the appropriate proportion of the holding (the value of which is that proportion of the value of the holding, determined in accordance with subsection (3)).

(5) The appropriate proportion is—

$$\frac{TC - NQH}{TC}$$

where—

TC is the market value (at the time of the disposal) of the total consideration for the disposal, and

NQH is the market value (at that time) of the new qualifying holdings.

(6) If at any time the value of the company's investments would by virtue of subsection (2)(*b*) be reduced to an amount less than the value of its qualifying holdings, the value of its investments at that time is to be treated as equal to the value of its qualifying holdings.

(7) "New qualifying holdings" means shares or securities which (on transfer to the company) are comprised in the company's qualifying holdings.

(8) If (and to the extent that) the holding was acquired with money the use of which is at any time ignored by virtue of section 280(2), subsections (2) to (6) do not apply in relation to that time.

(9) Nothing in this section applies in relation to disposals between companies that are merging (within the meaning of section 323)."

(4) This paragraph is deemed to have come into force on 6th April 2007.

(5) The amendments made by this paragraph have effect in relation to disposals made on or after that date.

GENERAL COMMENT

This change represents a relaxation to the requirement for the VCT Fund to retain 70% by value of its investments in qualifying holdings. The change will allow this rule to be breached for up to 6 months following the disposal of an investment by the VCT, i.e. the VCT will have up to 6 months to reinvest or distribute the proceeds.

The new subsection 280A(2) states that for the six months after the disposal, for the purpose of determining whether the 70 per cent qualifying holding condition is met, the company is treated as continuing to hold the holding disposed of, and the value of the company's investments is treated as reduced by the amount of the sale proceeds.

The changes have effect in relation to disposals made on or after 6 April 2007.

VCTs: power to make regulations as to breaches of conditions

21— (1) In section 284 of ITA 2007 (power to make regulations as to procedure), in the existing provision (which becomes subsection (1))—

(*a*) after paragraph (*a*) insert—

"(*aa*) for and in connection with the making by a company of an application to the Commissioners for Her Majesty's Revenue and Customs ("the Commissioners") for relief in respect of a breach (including a future breach) of the conditions for its VCT approval to continue in force,",

(*b*) in paragraph (*c*), for the words from "that the conditions" to the end substitute—

"(i) that the conditions for its VCT approval to continue in force are no longer met, or

(ii) that it is likely that those conditions will cease to be met,", and

(*c*) in paragraph (*d*) omit "for Her Majesty's Revenue and Customs".

(2) After subsection (1) insert—

"(2) In subsection (1)(*aa*), the reference to relief in respect of a breach of the conditions mentioned there is to a determination by the Commissioners that they will not exercise their power to withdraw the company's VCT approval by reason of the breach for such period as they may determine (and subject to such conditions as they may determine).

(3) The provision that may be made by virtue of subsection (1)(*aa*) includes—

(*a*) provision as to the procedure to be followed in relation to applications and determinations,

(*b*) provision as to the grounds on which applications may be made or determined, and

(*c*) provision conferring a discretion to be exercised by the Commissioners."

GENERAL COMMENT

This change provides a new power to make regulations for and in connection with the making by a company of an application to the Commissioners for HM Revenue & Customs for relief in respect of a breach of the conditions relating to its approval as a VCT.

The changes alter the existing power to make regulations in connection with the obligation of a company if it appears that the conditions for approval are no longer met. The power to make regulations is extended to cases where it is likely that the conditions will cease to be met.

The relief in respect of a breach of the conditions means a determination by the Commissioners that they will not exercise their power to withdraw the company's VCT approval because of the breach. It also provides that the Commissioners may determine the period over which such relief should extend and that the relief may be subject to such conditions as the Commissioners may determine.

SCHEDULE 17

REAL ESTATE INVESTMENT TRUSTS

Section 52

1 Part 4 of FA 2006 (REITs) is amended as follows.

GENERAL NOTE

Schedule 17 details a number of amendments to the provisions in FA 2006 Part IV, which introduced the Real Estate Investment Trust (REIT) regime, a new regime for the UK taxation of certain companies with qualifying property rental businesses and their shareholders.

The majority of the amendments are minor changes clarifying some of the definitions and powers in the existing legislation although in addition a number of the provisions originally enacted are relaxed by virtue of this schedule so as to make it simpler for newly established REITs to meet the requirements of the regime.

2 In section 106 (conditions for company)—

(*a*) in subsection (1), for "1 to 3" substitute "1 and 2", and

(*b*) after subsection (8) insert—

"(9) For the purpose of Condition 6 a loan shall not be treated as dependent on the results of the company's business by reason only that the terms of the loan provide—

(*a*) for the interest to be reduced in the event of the results improving, or

(*b*) for the interest to be increased in the event of the results deteriorating."

GENERAL NOTE

Paragraph 2 amends FA 2006 s 106, the provision which sets out the conditions that need to be met by a REIT in order to give notice to join the REIT regime and the conditions that must be met throughout each accounting period in order for the REIT to remain within the regime.

As enacted in s 106(1), in order to give notice the company had to meet conditions 1 to 3 of the company conditions being:

(1) it must be a company that is resident for tax purposes only in the UK, either by

virtue of incorporation, or as a result of being managed and controlled in the UK where residence is attributed only to the UK by virtue of a tie-breaker clause in a double tax treaty;

(2) It cannot be an open-ended investment company, as defined in FSMA 2000 s 236; and

(3) Its shares must be listed on a recognised stock exchange, as defined in TA 1988 s 841. The Alternative Investment Market is not a recognised stock exchange.

The amendment in this paragraph deletes the requirement to meet condition 3 above before notice of entry into the regime is given. As a result, companies will no longer need to be listed on a recognised stock exchange before they give notice to join the regime but will be able to join the regime on the first day on which they are listed. To be within the regime, the REIT will need to be listed throughout each accounting period thereafter. This is likely to be common in practice for newly established REITs as unlisted property investment vehicles will want to give notice of entry into the REIT regime before listing.

Paragraph 2(*b*) introduces a new subsection (sub-s 9) to FA 2006 s 106. This subsection relaxes condition 6, being the condition which restricts the types of loans to which a REIT can be a party. Such loans include those with terms that entitle the lender to a share of profits. However, the new provision confirms that a REIT can be party to a ratchet loan, where the interest rate reduces where profits increase and vice versa, without failing condition 6.

3 In section 107 (conditions for tax-exempt business)—

(*a*) in subsections (1)(*a*) and (2)(*a*), for "1 to 3" substitute "1 and 2",
(*b*) in subsections (1)(*b*) and (2)(*b*), for "Condition 4" substitute "Condition 3",
(*c*) omit subsection (5),
(*d*) in subsection (6), for "1 to 3" substitute "1 and 2",
(*e*) omit subsections (7) and (7A), and
(*f*) in subsections (8) and (9), for "Condition 4" substitute "Condition 3".

GENERAL NOTE

Paragraph 3 amends section 107, which sets out the conditions that the property rental business of the REIT is required to meet in order to be within the regime.

FA 2006 s 107 provided that:

(1). The business must comprise at least three single rental properties. For these purposes, a property is a single property if it is designed or equipped for rental as a unit separate from other units (sub-s 6). As such, a shopping centre would comprise multiple properties.

(2) No one property can represent more than 40 per cent of the total fair value of the rental property portfolio at any time; and

(3) None of the properties can be owner-occupied by the company or another company whose shares are stapled to the shares of the company.

Paragraph 3 deletes condition 3 above. The deletion clarifies the treatment of owner occupied property by limiting provisions regarding such property to those included in FA 2006 Sch 16. By including condition 3, it was unclear whether a company with owner occupied property could be prevented from being a REIT, which was not intended to be the case. The deletion does not result in a relaxation of the legislation as owner occupied property is included within the definition of excluded business in accordance with FA 2006 Sch 16 para 3. By virtue of this provision, any income derived from owner-occupied property is income of the residual business. The definition of owner-occupied is taken from International Accounting Standard 40. The clarification previously provided in s 107(7)(*a*), which ensures that in certain cases where a property would be treated as owner-occupied for accounting purposes despite being let to unconnected third party tenants (eg where a company provides significant services to the occupier of a property) the property is not treated as owner-occupied for the purposes of this legislation, has been deleted from s 107 but has been inserted in Sch 16 (para 15).

No amendments are made to the distribution condition (FA 2006 s 107(8)), other than that this condition becomes Condition 3, rather than Condition 4.

4 In section 108(2) (profit condition), for paragraph (*b*) substitute—

"(*b*) "profits" means profits before deduction of tax, calculated in accordance with international accounting standards and excluding—

(i) realised and unrealised gains and losses on the disposal of property,

(ii) changes in the fair value of hedging derivative contracts (within the meaning of section 120(4)), and

(iii) items which are outside the ordinary course of the company's business (irrespective of their treatment in the company's accounts), having regard to that company's past transactions."

GENERAL NOTE

Paragraph 4 amends the definition of "profit" for the purposes of the profit balance of business test in FA 2006 s 108(2). The purpose of this test is to ensure that the business of companies within the REIT regime is predominantly property investment and as such, 75% of profits earned by the REIT are required to be profits derived from property rental business. As originally enacted, profits for these purposes were accounting profits calculated under International Accounting Standards, with certain adjustments to disregard realised and unrealised gains on the disposal of property. However, further to consultation with the property industry, HMRC accepted that other items, which are outside the normal course of the REIT's business, could result in the profit test being breached without a shift in the business undertaken by the REIT. This paragraph therefore extends the list of items which should be excluded in calculating profits for the purpose of this test. As such, all items that are outside the ordinary course of business of the REIT are to be excluded, irrespective of their treatment in the accounts, as are changes in the fair value of hedging derivative contracts, which are recognised in the profit and loss account.

The above amendments put into primary legislation provision for adjustment to be made to "profits" for the purposes of the balance of business tests. Provision for certain adjustments to be made had previously been included in the Real Estate Investment Trusts (Financial Statements of Group Real Estate Investment Trusts) Regulations 2006, SI 2006/2865. reg 7, but these only applied to group REITs. Indeed, further to the proposed amendment in s 108(2), which applies for single company REITs, unless the above regulation is amended there will continue to not be parity of treatment of single company REITs and group REITs, since the definition of profits in the regulations differs from that proposed above. Group REITs do not take into account the definition of profits in s 108(2) as a result of FA 2006 Sch 17 para 7, which requires that profits for the purposes of the balance of business test for Group REITs are profits as included in the financial statements prepared by the Group REIT in accordance with FA 2006 Sch 17 para 31.

5 In section 109 (notice), after subsection (2) insert—

"(3) Subsection (4) applies where a company—

(*a*) does not expect to satisfy Condition 4 of section 106 on the first day of an accounting period, by reason only that its shares have not been listed and dealt with on a recognised stock exchange within the preceding 12 months, but

(*b*) reasonably expects to satisfy that Condition throughout the rest of the accounting period in reliance on section 415(1)(*b*) of ICTA.

(4) Where this subsection applies—

(*a*) subsection (2)(*c*) does not apply, but

(*b*) the notice under subsection (1) must be accompanied by a statement by the company containing the assertions specified in subsection (5).

(5) Those assertions are—

(*a*) that Conditions 1, 2, 5 and 6 of section 106 are reasonably expected to be satisfied in respect of the company throughout the specified accounting period,

(*b*) that Condition 3 of section 106 is reasonably expected to be satisfied in respect of the company for at least a part of the first day of the specified accounting period, and throughout the remainder of that period, and

(*c*) that Condition 4 of section 106 is reasonably expected to be satisfied in respect of the company throughout all of the specified accounting period apart from the first day."

GENERAL NOTE

Paragraph 5 inserts three new subsections into FA 2006 s 109 (Notice requirements). The intention of the amendment is to enable newly formed companies to join the REIT regime, by relaxing the requirement for a company's shares to have been listed and traded on a recognised stock exchange within the preceding twelve months.

The insertions therefore enable companies to join the REIT regime even if they cannot meet the close company condition on the first day on which they enter the regime, provided that the only reason they cannot meet the close company condition is that the shares in the company have not been listed and dealt with on a recognised stock exchange within the preceding 12 months. Where this is the case, the company is not required to provide with the notice of entry a declaration stating that it expects to meet all of the company conditions (FA 2006 s 106) throughout the accounting period in which the company joins the regime. Instead, the company is required to submit with the notice of entry a statement that the company reasonably expects to meet:

— Conditions 1 (company only resident in the UK), 2 (company not an open-ended investment company), 5 (only one class of ordinary shares) and 6 (company not a party to certain prohibited loans) throughout the specified accounting period.

— Condition 3 (shares are listed on a recognised stock exchange) for at least part of the first day and throughout the remainder of the specified accounting period.

— Condition 4 throughout the specified accounting period, with the exception of the first day.

The application of this relaxation is limited as it does not apply where the company will fail the close company condition for another reason, or where a widely-held company is intending to list on the day it joins the REIT regime. At the time of writing, it is presumed that the Real Estate Investment Trusts (Breach of Conditions) Regulations 2006, SI 2006/2864, reg 4, will be amended so as to ensure that where this relaxation does apply, and Company Conditions 3 and 4 are met soon after joining the regime, reg 4 does not apply. Without an amendment, the regulation would apply to expel the company from the REIT regime. Therefore, it is expected that reg 4 will be amended so that it does not apply in the case of a "Day 1" breach of these conditions.

6 In section 115 (profit: financing cost ratio)—

(*a*) in the formula in subsection (2), omit "+ Financing Costs", and

(*b*) in paragraph (*a*) of that subsection, after "allowances" insert ", of losses from a previous accounting period and of amounts taken into account under section 120(3)".

GENERAL NOTE

Paragraph 6 introduces an amendment to rectify an inconsistency in the profit:financing cost ratio for single company REITs. A further amendment confirms that this test is based only on current year results.

The formula by which the ratio is determined previously compared profit, as calculated for tax purposes but before deduction of capital allowances, plus financing costs, to financing costs. However, there was an inconsistency in the formula because the financing costs required to be added to taxable profit were not equal to the financing costs that had been deducted in determining taxable profits. This is because the definition of financing costs for the purposes of calculating taxable profit (s 120(3)) is more narrowly defined than the definition of financing costs for the purposes of determining the profit: financing cost ratio.

In addition, as previously drafted it was not clear whether a company was required to use taxable profits as reduced by brought forward losses, which would reduce the interest capacity of the company in future years.

Paragraph 6 therefore rectifies this inconsistency and clarifies the definition of profits for these purposes by adjusting how the numerator is calculated. As revised, instead of the numerator being equal to taxable profit plus financing costs, it is simply "profits". Section 115(2)(*a*) has been revised to clarify that these "profits" are equal to profits of the tax-exempt business, as calculated for tax purposes, but before the deduction of capital allowances, brought forward losses and financing costs required to be deducted under FA 2006 s 120(3).

7 In section 116 (minor or inadvertent breach)—

(*a*) in subsection (3), after paragraph (*c*) insert—

"(*ca*) make provision under paragraph (*c*) either by specifying a sum that arises in relation to a company or by providing for a sum to be treated as arising in relation to a company;" and

(*b*) after that subsection insert—

"(3A) The regulations may make provision about, or by reference to, anything done by or in relation to a company or any sum arising or treated as arising—

(*a*) after the commencement of the regulations, or

(*b*) in the calendar year during which the regulations are made."

GENERAL NOTE

Paragraph 7 adds two further provisions to FA 2006 s 116 (minor or inadvertent breach). These provisions clarify that regulations made in accordance with this section may specify sums to be charged to tax by deeming sums to be treated as arising to the company, and also that the regulations may make provision for sums arising after the commencement of the regulations or in the calendar year in which regulations are made.

One of the purposes of these amendments is to enable regulations to be laid which will make it easier for newly established or newly listed REITs to join the REIT regime as the regulations, currently in draft, allow for a Day 1 breach of the asset balance of business test (FA 2006 s 108(3)) in order to give the REIT time to acquire rental properties whilst within the REIT regime. This is likely to be beneficial for companies that list in connection with entering the REIT regime and offer a subscription for shares, such that on entry to the regime they have large cash amounts that they will use to acquire properties.

Where the asset test is breached at the beginning of the first accounting period in which the company joins the REIT regime, the regulations (currently in draft form) provide for an additional entry charge to be levied at the end of the first accounting period of the REIT. The charge is based on the market value of properties held by the REIT at the end of the accounting period, with credit available for the entry charge already paid.

The effect of this charge, as currently drafted, is that not only is the REIT liable for the entry charge in respect of assets it acquires during its first period as a REIT, but it is also liable in respect of the increase in value of assets during the period between the later of entry into the regime or acquisition, and the end of the period. A breach of the asset balance of business condition on Day 1 will not count as a breach for the purposes of determining how many breaches have been made by the REIT.

If the company still fails the asset balance of business test at the beginning of the following accounting period, the company is treated as never having been within the regime. REITs that take advantage of this relaxation will therefore need to ensure that they are able to acquire sufficient property during the first accounting period in order to meet the asset balance of business test by the end of it.

8 In section 117 (cancellation of tax advantage), insert at the end—

"(8) On an appeal under subsection (7) the Special Commissioners may—

(*a*) quash the notice,

(*b*) affirm the notice, or

(*c*) vary the notice."

GENERAL NOTE

Paragraph 8 inserts a new subsection at the end of FA 2006 s 117 (cancellation of tax advantage). This section gives HM Revenue & Customs broad powers to assess the REIT to tax or otherwise, by notice, so as to counteract a tax advantage obtained by the REIT or another person.

The new subsection provides for the actions that the Special Commissioners can take in the event that a company appeals under FA 2006 s 117(7) against a notice given under this section.

9 In section 120 (calculation of profits)—

(*a*) in paragraph (*a*) of subsection (4), for "an asset," substitute "an asset by the exploitation of which tax-exempt business is conducted,"

(*b*) after that paragraph insert—

"(*aa*) a derivative contract is hedging in relation to a company if or in so far as it is acquired as a hedge of risk in relation to a liability incurred in connection with tax-exempt business," and

(*c*) after that subsection insert—

"(4A) In subsection (4)(*a*) the reference to an asset includes a reference to—

(*a*) the value of an asset, and

(*b*) profits attributable to it."

GENERAL NOTE

Paragraph 9 introduces an extension to the definition of the derivative contracts in respect of which the profits and losses fall to be taken into account in determining the taxable profit or loss of the tax-exempt business under FA 2006 s 120. The amendments confirm that contracts that hedge not only the properties themselves but also cash flows deriving from those assets are hedging derivative contracts for REIT purposes. In addition, contracts that hedge risk in relation to liabilities of the property rental business, as well as assets, are now included.

10 In section 123(*a*) (attribution of distributions), for "Condition 4" substitute "Condition 3".

GENERAL NOTE

The amendment in para 10 is a consequential amendment to FA 2006 s 123 (attribution of distributions), required to be made as a result of the deletion of the owner-occupied condition (previously Condition 3 of the tax-exempt business conditions, FA 2006 s 107) by virtue of Sch 17 para 3.

11 After section 126 (movement of assets into ring fence) insert—

"126A Demergers

(1) This section applies if—

(*a*) C (tax-exempt) disposes of an asset to a 75% subsidiary ("S") of C (residual),

(*b*) C (residual) disposes of its interest in S to another company ("P"),

(*c*) on the date when it acquires the interest in S, P gives a notice under section 109 (as modified by paragraph 8 of Schedule 17) which specifies an accounting period which begins within the period of six months beginning with the date of the disposal of the asset, and

(*d*) this Part begins to apply to the group of which S is a member from the beginning of the specified accounting period.

(2) P may give a notice under section 109 (as modified by paragraph 8 of Schedule 17) in accordance with subsection (1)(*c*) even if it does not expect to satisfy Conditions 3 to 6 of section 106 throughout the accounting period specified in the notice.

(3) Where this section applies—

(*a*) sections 111 and 112 shall not apply to the group of which S is a member in relation to the asset disposed of by C (tax-exempt) or in relation to business conducted by the exploitation of that asset, and

(*b*) section 125 shall not apply to the disposal of the asset by C (tax-exempt).

(4) But if, at the end of the period of six months mentioned in subsection (1)(*c*), Conditions 3 to 6 of section 106 are not satisfied in relation to P, subsection (3) shall be treated as not having had effect."

GENERAL NOTE

Paragraph 11 inserts a new section (FA 2006 s 126A) to ensure that where as a result of a demerger of a single company REIT, the following steps take place:

(*a*) a property is disposed of by C(tax-exempt) to a subsidiary of C(residual) (S), (*b*) the shares in S are then sold to another company (P)

(*c*) on the date that P acquires the shares in S, it gives notice to join the REIT regime with effect from a date within six months of the date of disposal of the asset to S,

then the asset is not treated as leaving and rejoining the REIT regime. The tax consequences of the transaction are therefore similar to those that apply where one REIT is taken over by another (FA 2006 Sch 17 para 33).

The provisions confirm that where this section applies, P and S are treated as joining the REIT regime on the date specified in the notice made by P. On joining the REIT regime, there is no deemed acquisition and disposal under s 111 FA 2006 of the asset that had previously been within the REIT regime. In addition, no entry charge under FA 2006 s 112 is payable in relation to that asset. FA 2006 s 125 (transfers across the ring-fence) also does not apply in connection with the disposal of the asset to S by C(tax-exempt).

By virtue of s 126A(1)(*e*), the company is given time to satisfy the conditions for entry to the REIT regime as P is permitted to give notice to join the REIT regime even if, at the time it does so, it does not expect to satisfy conditions 3 (shares listed on a recognised stock exchange), 4 (not a close company), 5 (only one class of ordinary share capital) or 6 (not a party to certain prohibited loans) of the company conditions in FA 2006 s 106 throughout the first accounting period in which it is within the regime. However, if company conditions 3 to 6 are not met by the date six months after the disposal of the asset by C(tax-exempt) to S, then the relieving provisions set out above do not apply and the property is deemed to have transferred to the residual business on the date of the disposal to S.

Similar provisions are to be included in respect of demergers from group REITs, by virtue of Sch 17 para 16.

12 In section 127 (interpretation), for "126" substitute "126A".

GENERAL NOTE

Paragraph 12 is a consequential amendment to FA 2006 s 127 (Interpretation), required as a result of the insertion of a new section, s 126A (Sch 17 para 11).

13 In section 133 (early exit), insert at the end—

"(6) On an appeal under subsection (5) the Special Commissioners may—

(*a*) quash the direction,

(*b*) affirm the direction, or

(*c*) vary the direction."

GENERAL NOTE

Paragraph 13 inserts a new subsection at the end of FA 2006 s 133 (Early exit), a section which gives HMRC broad powers to modify the application of the regime or the application of general corporation tax provisions to a company where that company was within the REIT regime for a continuous period of less than 10 years and was required to leave the regime either as a result of being given notice of termination by HMRC (FA 2006 s 129) or as a result of breaching one or more of certain of the company conditions in FA 2006 s 106 (FA 2006 s 130)

The new subsection provides for the actions that the Special Commissioners can take in the event that a company appeals under FA 2006 s 133(5) against a direction given under this section.

14 In section 138 (joint ventures), after subsection (3) insert—

"(4) Regulations may make provision having retrospective effect in respect of the calendar year in which they are made."

GENERAL NOTE

Paragraph 14 introduces a new subsection into FA 2006 s 138 (Joint ventures). This provision allows regulations regarding joint ventures that are made under this section to have retrospective effect from the beginning of the calendar year in which they are laid. The reason for the new provision is that the joint venture regulations laid in 2006 (the Real Estate Investment Trusts (Joint Ventures) Regulations 2006, SI 2006/2466) only applied to single company joint ventures, not group joint ventures. Regulations setting out how the current joint venture regulations (currently in draft form) are to be amended for joint venture groups are currently in draft form but, once laid they will, by virtue of this provision, be effective from 1 January 2007.

In normal circumstances, a look-through notice in respect of a joint venture must be given by the REIT and joint venture before the start of the REIT's relevant accounting period. However, given that the provisions under which joint venture groups are required to give notice were not published before 1 January 2007, it is understood that the regulations will allow companies a certain period of time from the date on which the provisions come into force to give joint venture notices for accounting periods beginning on or after 1 January 2007.

15 In paragraph 3 of Schedule 16 (excluded income: owner-occupied property), after sub-paragraph (3) insert—

"(3A) For the purpose of Condition 2, no account shall be taken of the fact that a property may fall to be described as owner-occupied by reason only of the provision by the company of services to an occupant who—

(*a*) is in exclusive occupation of the property, and

(*b*) is not connected with a member of the group (within the meaning given by section 839 of ICTA)."

GENERAL NOTE

Paragraph 15 introduces a new provision into FA 2006 Sch 16. The amendment has been made as a result of the deletion of the owner-occupied condition from FA 2006 s 107 (Conditions for tax-exempt business). The new provision amends the definition in Sch 16 that sets out the kinds of property business that are excluded from the ring fence, by including a provision previously within FA 2006 s 107. The definition of owner-occupied is taken from International Accounting Standard 40, however, this provision confirms that in certain cases where a property would be treated as owner-occupied for accounting purposes despite being let to unconnected third party tenants (e.g. where a company provides significant services to the occupier of a property) the property is not treated as owner-occupied for the purposes of this legislation. As this provision was previously included within FA 2006 s 107, the purpose of this amendment is merely to place all provisions regarding owner occupied property in one paragraph, rather than to amend the purpose of the legislation.

16— (1) Schedule 17 (modifications for groups) is amended as follows.

(2) In paragraph 2(*b*), for "Conditions 1 to 3" substitute "Conditions 1 and 2".

(3) Omit paragraph 6(2) and (3).

(4) In paragraph 6(4) and (5), for "Condition 4" substitute "Condition 3".

(5) In paragraph 14, in the substituted subsection (2)—

(*a*) in the formula in the opening words, omit "+ Financing Costs (all)",

(*b*) in paragraph (*a*), after "allowances" insert ", of losses from a previous accounting period and of amounts taken into account under section 120(3)", and

(*c*) omit paragraph (*b*).

(6) after paragraph 33 insert—

"*Demergers*

34— (1) This paragraph applies in relation to a company if—

(*a*) the company ceases to be a member of a group ("Group 1") to which Part 4 applies,

(*b*) at the time immediately after it ceases to be a member of Group 1, either—

(i) it satisfies Conditions 1 and 2 of section 106 and the conditions specified in sections 107 and 108, or

(ii) it is a member of another group ("Group 2") which satisfies those conditions as modified by the provisions of paragraphs 5 to 7 above, (*c*) the company (or the principal company of Group 2) gives a notice under section 109 (or that section as modified by paragraph 8 above) no later than the date on which it ceases to be a member of Group 1, and

(*d*) the notice specifies an accounting period which begins on the day on which the company ceases to be a member of Group 1.

(2) A company may give a notice under section 109 (or that section as modified by paragraph 8 above) in accordance with sub-paragraph (1)(*c*) even if it does not expect to satisfy Conditions 3 to 6 of section 106 throughout the accounting period specified in the notice.

(3) Where this paragraph applies, the company shall be treated as a company to which Part 4 applies (or as a member of a group to which Part 4 applies) during the period of six months beginning with the time when it ceases to be a member of Group 1.

(4) Where this paragraph applies, the following provisions of Part 4 shall not have effect—

(*a*) section 111 (or that section as modified by paragraphs 9 and 10 above),

(*b*) section 112 (or that section as modified by paragraph 11 above), and

(*c*) section 131 (as modified by paragraphs 25 and 26 above).

(5) But if, at the end of the period of six months mentioned in sub-paragraph (3), Conditions 3 to 6 of section 106 are not satisfied in relation to the company, this paragraph shall not have effect and the company shall be treated as having ceased to be a company to which Part 4 applies (or a member of a group to which Part 4 applies) on the date on which it ceased to be a member of Group 1."

GENERAL NOTE

Paragraph 16 makes amendments to FA 2006 Sch 17, which contains the modifications required to FA 2006 ss 103–145 to apply the single company REIT provisions to groups of companies.

Owner occupied property

Consequential amendments are made to FA 2006 Sch 17 paras 2 and 6 as a result of the removal of the owner-occupied condition from FA 2006 s 107 (see Sch 17 para 3).

Profit: financing cost ratio

Amendments are made to FA 2006 Sch 17 para 14, the paragraph that sets out the formula for determining the profit: financing cost ratio for group REITs, so that the formula for group REITs is brought broadly into line with for single company REITs (Sch 17 para 6). The remaining difference between the single company and group REIT formulas is that for REIT groups, the formula compares the aggregate property rental profits of each company in the group (as calculated for tax purposes under FA 2006 s 120 and set out in the financial statements at FA 2006 Sch 17 para 31(2)(*b*)), but as adjusted for capital allowances, brought forward losses and financing costs, to the external financing costs incurred by the group, as calculated for accounting purposes under International Accounting Standards and ignoring any financing costs paid between group companies. The intention of this is to reduce the impact of differing capital structures by requiring the group to consider the ultimate use of the borrowings.

Demergers

In addition, a new para is introduced in FA 2006 Sch 17, which provides for a relaxation of the REIT cessation rules where a REIT group demerges part of its qualifying property rental business. Where, as a result of a demerger of a company from a group REIT, the following steps take place:

(*a*) a company ceases to be a member of a REIT group ("Group 1");

(*b*) immediately after that time the company either:

(i) meets the tests to become a single company REIT (i.e. it satisfies Conditions 1 and 2 of the company conditions (resident only in the UK and not an open ended investment company), the tax exempt business conditions in FA 2006 s 107 and balance of business tests in FA 2006 s 108), or

(ii) becomes the member of another group ("Group 2") which satisfies those conditions (as modified by FA 2006 Sch 17 paras 5–7);

(*c*) the company, or principal company of Group 2 gives notice to join the REIT regime on or before the date it leaves Group 1, and

(*d*) the date of entry into the REIT regime is specified to be the date on which the company leaves Group 1

then the company is not treated as leaving and rejoining the REIT regime. The tax consequences of the transaction are therefore similar to those that apply where one REIT is taken over by another (FA 2006 Sch 17 para 33).

The provisions confirm that where this paragraph applies, the company is not treated for tax purposes as leaving and rejoining the REIT regime. As a result, there is no deemed acquisition and disposal under FA 2006 s 111 of the assets held by the company; no entry charge under FA 2006 s 112 is payable in relation to those assets and FA 2006 s 131 (effects of cessation) does not apply.

By virtue of para 34(2), the company (or principal company of Group 2) is permitted to give notice of and to join the REIT regime with effect from that date even if, at the time it gives notice and joins the regime it does not expect to satisfy conditions 3 (shares listed on a recognised stock exchange), 4 (not a close company), 5 (only one class of ordinary share capital) or 6 (not a party to certain prohibited loans) of the company conditions in FA 2006 s 106 throughout the first accounting period in which it is within the regime. However, if company conditions 3 to 6 are not met by the date six months after the company leaves Group 1, then the relieving provisions set out above do not apply and the company is deemed to have left the REIT regime on the date it left Group 1.

Similar provisions are included in respect of demergers of assets from single REITs, by virtue of Sch 17 para 11.

17 In section 505(1) of ICTA (charities: exemptions), after paragraph (*a*) insert—

"(*aa*) exemption from tax under Schedules A and D, or under Parts 2 and 3 of ITTOIA 2005, in respect of distributions to which section 121 of the Finance Act 2006 (Real Estate Investment Trusts: distributions) applies to the extent that the distributions—

(i) arise in respect of shares vested in a person for charitable purposes; and

(ii) are applied to charitable purposes only;".

GENERAL NOTE

Paragraph 17 inserts a new subsection into TA 1988 s 505(1). The effect of this amendment is to ensure that property income distributions paid by a REIT to a charity in accordance with FA 2006 s 121 are exempt from tax in the hands of the charity, provided that the distributions arise in respect of shares vested in a person for charitable purposes and are applied to charitable purposes only.

18 In section 531 of ITA 2007 (charities: exemptions)—

(*a*) after subsection (2) insert—

"(2A) Distributions to which section 121 of FA 2006 (Real Estate Investment Trusts: distributions) applies and which are chargeable to income tax under Part 2 or Part 3 of ITTOIA 2005 are not taken into account in calculating total income so far as they arise in respect of shares vested in a person in trust for a charitable trust or for charitable purposes.", and

(*b*) in subsection (3), for "and (2)" substitute "to (2A)".

GENERAL NOTE

Paragraph 18 inserts a new subsection into ITA 2007 s 531. The effect of this amendment is to ensure that property income distributions paid by a REIT to a charity in accordance with FA 2006 s 121, which are chargeable to income tax under ITTOIA 2005 Parts 2 or 3, are not included in the calculation of total income, provided the distributions are in respect of shares vested in a person in trust for a charitable trust or for charitable purposes.

SCHEDULE 18

PENSIONS SCHEMES: ABOLITION OF RELIEF FOR LIFE ASSURANCE PREMIUM CONTRIBUTIONS ETC

Section 68

GENERAL NOTE

The schedule incorporates amendments to FA 2004 announced in the Pre-Budget Report of 6 December 2006 that abolish tax relief on premiums paid on personal fixed term life insurance policies provided via personal or occupational pension schemes where the only benefit payable is a lump sum on death or critical illness. The tax relief available for contributions paid by employers is not affected. The changes affect single life and most joint life term assurance policies where all the insured members belong to the same family.

As part of the pensions tax simplification regime which commenced on 6 April 2006 a term assurance policy could be sold with tax relief provided it terminated before the insured's 75th birthday. The insured person received tax relief on contributions under the scheme that were used to pay for the term assurance policy. However, in 2006 there was a substantial switch in the insurance market from mortgage-related term assurance to term assurance that qualified for pension tax relief, but which was often not marketed as such because it had no pension income. The changes ensure that where there is no pension income in relation to a term assurance policy there is no pension tax relief.

For registered occupational pension schemes the legislation applies to personal contributions in respect of term policies made on or after 1 August 2007 unless the insurer received the application for the policy before 29 March 2007 and the policy was taken out as part of the pension scheme before 1 August 2007. For other registered pension schemes, the legislation applies to personal contributions relating to personal term policies made on or after 6 April 2007 unless the insurer received the application for the policy before 14 December 2006 and the policy was taken out as part of the pension scheme before 6 April 2007 provided the sum assured under the policy is no greater and the term no longer than that applied for. Insurers had until 31 July 2007 to process such business so that appropriate medical evidence could be checked and an appropriate commencement date for cover settled.

HM Revenue and Customs has clarified the position of term assurance applications received after 13 December 2006 that had been sold as part of a personal pension scheme where the insured is also obliged by the terms of the pension scheme to have pension benefits under that scheme. HM Revenue and Customs confirmed that tax relief will continue whether the pension was in place on or before 13 December 2006, or the application for the pension alongside the term assurance was received after 13 December 2006, provided the application was fully completed and submitted to the insurance company and receipt recorded by that insurance company before 13 April 2007. This is provided that the sum assured under the policy is no greater and the term no longer than that applied for. Similarly, insurers had until 31 July 2007 to process such business so that appropriate medical evidence could be checked and an appropriate commencement date for cover settled.

Where relief remains available for contributions paid on or after 1 August 2007 (occupational schemes) or on or after 6 April 2007 (other schemes), the individual will cease to be entitled to tax relief if the policy to which the contribution relates is varied outside its original terms so as to increase the sum assured or lengthen the term. If there is an option under the policy which is then exercised, this will not affect the tax relief due.

Introduction

1 Part 4 of FA 2004 (pension schemes etc) is amended as follows.

GENERAL NOTE

Paragraph 1 makes provision for FA 2004 to be amended by paragraphs 2 and 3.

Life assurance premium contributions not to be relievable pension contributions

2 In section 188(3) (relief for members' contributions: contributions which are not relievable pension contributions), after paragraph (*a*) insert—

"(*aa*) any contributions which are life assurance premium contributions (see section 195A),".

GENERAL NOTE

FA 2004 s 188(3) sets out the criteria where tax relief is not available for members' contributions to pension schemes. Paragraph 2 amends FA 2004 s 188(3) by including any contributions which are life assurance premium contributions as defined by FA 2004 s 195A inserted by paragraph 3 below, so ensuring they do not obtain tax relief.

Life assurance premium contributions

3 After section 195 insert—

"195A Life assurance premium contributions

(1) Contributions paid by or on behalf of an individual under a registered pension scheme are life assurance premium contributions for the purposes of section 188(3)(*aa*) if—

(*a*) rights under a non-group life policy (see subsection (2)) are (or later become) held for the purposes of the pension scheme, and

(*b*) the contributions are treated by this section as paid in respect of premiums under the non-group life policy (see subsections (3) to (5)).

(2) For the purposes of this section a "non-group life policy" is a policy of insurance under which the only benefits which may become payable are benefits payable in consequence, or in anticipation, of—

(*a*) the death of the individual or one of a group of individuals which includes the individual, or

(*b*) the deaths of more than one of a group of individuals—

(i) which includes the individual, and

(ii) the other members of which are connected with the individual.

(3) Contributions paid by or on behalf of the individual under the pension scheme are treated as paid in respect of premiums under the non-group life policy if—

(*a*) the payment of the contributions constitutes the payment of premiums under the policy, or

(*b*) the person by whom the contributions are paid intends the contributions (or an amount equivalent to them) to be applied towards paying premiums under the policy.

(4) Where the amount of the premiums under the policy in a tax year exceeds the amount of any contributions treated as paid in respect of the premiums by subsection (3), other contributions paid by or on behalf of the individual under the pension scheme in the tax year are treated as paid in respect of premiums under the policy to the extent that their amount does not exceed the difference between the amount of the premiums and the amount of any contributions treated as paid in respect of the premiums by subsection (3).

(5) But where—

(*a*) the benefits under the policy relate to the death of one or more of a group of individuals, and

(*b*) contributions are also paid under the pension scheme in the tax year by or on behalf of another member or other members of the group,

the amount of the contributions paid by or on behalf of the individual which are treated as paid in respect of premiums under the policy by subsection (4) does not exceed what is just and reasonable having regard to the operation of section 188(3)(*aa*) in relation to the contributions paid by or on behalf of another member or other members of the group.

(6) The Commissioners for Her Majesty's Revenue and Customs may by regulations amend subsections (2) to (5).

(7) Regulations under subsection (6) which limit—

(*a*) the policies of insurance which are non-group life assurance policies for the purposes of this section, or

(*b*) the contributions which are treated by this section as paid in respect of premiums under such policies,

may be made so as to have effect in relation to times before they are made.

(8) For the purposes of this section an individual ("A") is connected with another individual ("B") if—

(*a*) A is B's spouse or civil partner,
(*b*) A is a relative of B,
(*c*) A is the spouse or civil partner of a relative of B,
(*d*) A is a relative of B's spouse or civil partner, or
(*e*) A is the spouse or civil partner of a relative of B's spouse or civil partner;

and for the purposes of this subsection "relative" means brother, sister, ancestor or lineal descendant."

GENERAL NOTE

This paragraph amends FA 2004 s 195 by inserting s 195A defining life assurance premium contributions paid by or on behalf of an individual under a registered pension scheme that will not qualify for tax relief. These are contributions treated as paid in respect of premiums under a non-group life policy which in turn is defined in s 195A(2) as a policy under which the only benefits payable are those payable in consequence of the death of an individual or one of a group of individuals which includes the individual or other members of a group who are connected with the individual.

Section 195A(3) to (5) explains the circumstances under which contributions paid by an individual to a pension scheme are treated as paid in respect of premiums under a non-group life policy and how much is treated as so paid.

HMRC is given powers under s 195A(6) and (7) to make regulations amending s 195A(2) to (5) and limiting policies of insurance which are non-group life assurance policies or the contributions payable thereunder. The regulations may have retrospective effect provided they are wholly relieving in nature.

Section 195A(8) sets out the circumstances where an individual is connected with another individual for the purposes of s 195A, e.g. there is a family connection, as the definition of non-group life policies includes policies which only pay benefits on the death of more than one individual where all the members of the group insured under the policy are connected with the individual who pays the contribution.

Commencement: schemes other than occupational pension schemes

4— (1) In relation to contributions under any pension scheme that is not an occupational pension scheme, the amendments made by this Schedule have effect in relation to contributions paid on or after 6th April 2007.

(2) But they do not have effect in relation to such contributions paid at any time if the contributions are treated as paid in respect of premiums under a policy of insurance which at that time is a protected policy (see paragraph 5).

GENERAL NOTE

This paragraph provides that, for pension schemes which are not occupational pension schemes, the amendments made at para 2 above only apply to contributions paid on or after 6 April 2007. Paragraph 4 also provides that the amendments made at para 2 do not affect tax relief due for contributions treated as paid as premiums under a protected policy

5— (1) This paragraph specifies when a policy of insurance is a protected policy in a case where the rights under it are held for the purposes of a pension scheme that is not an occupational pension scheme.

(2) A policy of insurance within sub-paragraph (3) or (4) is a protected policy but only until a relevant event occurs (see sub-paragraphs (5) and (6)).

(3) A policy of insurance is within this sub-paragraph if—

(*a*) it is issued in respect of insurances made before 6th December 2006,
(*b*) the pension scheme became a registered pension scheme before that date, and
(*c*) rights under the policy became held for the purposes of the pension scheme before that date.

(4) A policy of insurance is within this sub-paragraph if—

(*a*) it is issued in respect of insurances made before 1st August 2007,
(*b*) the pension scheme became a registered pension scheme before that date,

(*c*) rights under the policy became held for the purposes of the pension scheme before that date,

(*d*) the policy was issued in pursuance of a proposal made in writing (by whatever means) and received by or on behalf of the insurer before the appropriate date,

(*e*) the amount of the benefits payable under the policy (at the latest of the time when the insurances were made, the pension scheme was registered or rights under the policy became held for the purposes of the pension scheme) is no more than the amount applied for in the proposal,

(*f*) the period for which benefits are so payable (at the latest of those times) is no longer than the period specified in the proposal, and

(*g*) the policy is not a protected policy by virtue of sub-paragraph (3).

(5) In sub-paragraph (4)(*d*) "the appropriate date" means—

(*a*) 13th April 2007, in any case where, on the day of the making of the insurances in respect of which the policy of insurance was issued, the rights of the individual under the pension scheme included an actual or prospective entitlement to a pension, and

(*b*) 14th December 2006, in any other case.

(6) For the purposes of sub-paragraph (2) a "relevant event" occurs if, after the relevant time, the terms of the policy are varied so as to—

(*a*) increase the benefits payable under the policy, or

(*b*) extend the period during which benefits are so payable.

(7) But where, on the day of the variation, the rights of the individual under the pension scheme included an actual or prospective entitlement to a pension, a relevant event does not occur by virtue of the variation if it was made in pursuance of a proposal made in writing (by whatever means) and received by or on behalf of the insurer before 13th April 2007.

(8) "The relevant time"—

(*a*) in the case of a policy of insurance within sub-paragraph (3) which is issued in respect of insurances made before 6th April 2006, is 20th March 2007,

(*b*) in the case of any other policy of insurance within sub-paragraph (3), is 5th December 2006, and

(*c*) in the case of a policy of insurance within sub-paragraph (4), is the time when it became a protected policy.

GENERAL NOTE

This paragraph defines when a policy is a protected policy for the purpose of a pension scheme, which is not an occupational pension scheme. Thus it is a protected policy if it falls within para 5(3) to (5) until a relevant event defined in para 5(6) and (8) occurs. Paragraph 5(3) sets out the requirements that must be met for insurances made before 6 December 2006 (the date of the Pre Budget Report) to be a protected policy. Paragraph 5(4) sets out the requirements that must be met for insurances made on or after 6 December 2006 and before 1 August 2007 to be a protected policy. Paragraph 5(5) sets out the requirements that must be met in relation to an insurance proposal received on or before 13 April 2007 to ensure the issued policy is a protected policy.

The measures in para 5(3) to (6) are intended to clarify the position where applications for policies were received by the insurer on or before 6 December 2006, but where the policy was not issued until later due to delays in processing and where applications for policies were received by the insurer after 13 December 2006 but the pension scheme was in place before that date.

Paragraph 5(5) specifies when the relevant time occurs, depending on when the insurance was made. The relevant events that cause protected policy status to be lost are defined in para5(6) as varying the policy so as to increase the benefits or extending the period during which the benefits are payable where the variation occurs after the relevant time. It should be noted that the exercise of a contractual option does not vary the policy and so is not a relevant event.

Commencement: occupational pension schemes

6— (1) In relation to contributions under any occupational pension scheme, the amendments made by this Schedule have effect in relation to contributions paid on or after 1st August 2007.

(2) But they do not have effect in relation to such contributions paid at any time if the contributions are treated as paid in respect of premiums under a policy of insurance which at that time is a protected policy (see paragraph 7).

GENERAL NOTE

This paragraph provides that, for pension schemes which are occupational pension schemes, the amendments made in para 2 above only apply to contributions paid on or after 1 August 2007. Paragraph 6 also provides that the amendments made at para 2 do not affect tax relief due for contributions paid as premiums under a protected policy.

7— (1) This paragraph specifies when a policy of insurance is a protected policy in a case where the rights under it are held for the purposes of an occupational pension scheme.

(2) A policy of insurance within sub-paragraph (3) or (4) is a protected policy but only until a relevant event occurs (see sub-paragraphs (5) to (7)).

(3) A policy of insurance is within this sub-paragraph if—

(*a*) it is issued in respect of insurances made before 21st March 2007,

(*b*) the pension scheme became a registered pension scheme before that date, and

(*c*) rights under the policy became held for the purposes of the pension scheme before that date.

(4) A policy of insurance is within this sub-paragraph if—

(*a*) it is issued in respect of insurances made before 1st August 2007,

(*b*) the pension scheme became a registered pension scheme before that date,

(*c*) rights under the policy became held for the purposes of the pension scheme before that date,

(*d*) the policy was issued in pursuance of a proposal made in writing (by whatever means) and received by or on behalf of the insurer before 29th March 2007,

(*e*) the amount of the benefits payable under the policy (at the latest of the time when the insurances were made, the pension scheme was registered or rights under the policy became held for the purposes of the pension scheme) is no more than the amount applied for in the proposal,

(*f*) the period for which benefits are so payable (at the latest of those times) is no longer than the period specified in the proposal, and

(*g*) the policy is not a protected policy by virtue of sub-paragraph (3).

(5) For the purposes of sub-paragraph (2) a "relevant event" occurs if, after the relevant time, the terms of the policy are varied so as to—

(*a*) increase the benefits payable under the policy, or

(*b*) extend the period during which benefits are so payable.

(6) "The relevant time"—

(*a*) in the case of a policy of insurance within sub-paragraph (3), is 20th March 2007, and

(*b*) in the case of a policy of insurance within sub-paragraph (4), is the time when it became a protected policy.

(7) A variation of the terms of a policy made in order to comply with the Employment Equality (Age) Regulations 2006 (SI 2006/1031) or Employment Equality (Age) Regulations (Northern Ireland) 2006 (S.R. 2006/261) (or any regulations amending or replacing them) is to be ignored for the purposes of sub-paragraph (5).

GENERAL NOTE

This paragraph defines when a policy is a protected policy for the purpose of an occupational pension scheme. Thus it is a protected policy if it falls within para 7(3) and (4) until a relevant event defined in para 7(5) to (7) occurs. Paragraph 7(3) sets out the requirements that must be met for insurances made before 21 March 2007 (Budget Day) to be a protected policy. Paragraph 7(4) sets out the requirements that must be met for insurances made between 21 March 2007 and 1 August 2007 (the final date set for processing such insurances) to be a protected policy.

The relevant events that cause protected policy status to be lost are defined in para 7(5) as varying the policy so as to increase the benefits or extending the period during which the benefits are payable where the variation occurs after the relevant time. It should again be noted that the exercise of a contractual option does not vary the policy and so is not a relevant event. Paragraph 7(6) specifies when the relevant time occurs, depending on when the insurance was made.

The measures in para 7(3) to (6) are intended to clarify the position where applications for policies were received by the insurer on or before 13 December 2006, but where the policy was not issued until later due to delays in processing and where applications for policies were received by the insurer after 13 December 2006 but the pension scheme was in place before that date.

Paragraph 7(7) allows the terms of a policy to be varied to comply with Employment Regulations, or any regulations amending or replacing them, without causing protected policy status to be lost.

Power to amend commencement provisions

8— (1) The Commissioners for Her Majesty's Revenue and Customs may by regulations amend paragraphs 4 to 7.

(2) Regulations under sub-paragraph (1) having the effect of limiting the contributions which are life assurance premium contributions may be made so as to have effect in relation to times before they are made.

GENERAL NOTE

HMRC is given power in para 8 to amend paras 4 to 7 above by regulations and for the regulations to have retrospective effect provided they are relieving in nature.

SCHEDULE 19

ALTERNATIVELY SECURED PENSIONS AND TRANSFER LUMP SUM DEATH BENEFIT ETC

Section 69

GENERAL NOTE

The schedule incorporates amendments to FA 2004, to IHTA 1984 and to ITEPA 2003 announced in the Pre-Budget Report of 6 December 2006 regarding the treatment of alternatively secured pensions, the intention being to limit their tax advantages as an IHT shelter. The amendments will in the main come into effect from 6 April 2007.

Under the new pensions tax regime from 6 April 2006 there has been a facility allowing members of money purchase pension schemes on reaching age 75 to draw down income and avoid having to buy an annuity. Any remaining funds on death could be used to provide a dependant's pension under a transfer lump sum death benefit option. The funds could be paid to a charity if there were no dependants or transferred to the pension funds of other members of the pension scheme. There was an IHT charge on alternatively secured pension funds not paid as pension benefits to a dependant or charity. The Government had been increasingly concerned that alternatively secured pension funds were being used to accumulate tax relieved capital that could be passed down on death to family members instead of providing an income in retirement as intended. So amendments have been made to the original legislation to abolish the transfer lump sum death benefit option and increase the level of draw down income.

Some pension schemes have been unable to trace members who have attained age 75 to pay their benefits. So FA 2004 is amended to include a provision that if a pension scheme has taken reasonable steps to trace a member, the funds will, on the missing member's 75th birthday, become held in suspense and will not automatically become alternatively secured pension funds.

The rules relating to the interaction of the recovery and the IHT charges in respect of alternatively secured pensions have been clarified as previously both could apply and in either order. For deaths on or after 6 April 2007 IHT is to be calculated on the basis that the IHT nil-rate band is set in priority against the estate of the member excluding alternatively secured pension funds.

The Government remains concerned that products are still being designed to enable inheritance of tax-relieved capital in circumstances where alternatively secured pensions are not in point and plans to introduce further measures to prevent such products from being used to pass down tax-relieved pension savings. It published a consultation document, "Tax relief for pensions: Rules to prevent inheriting tax-relieved pension savings", on 21 March 2007 in this connection. Following consultation it intends to introduce measures that will impose pension tax and IHT charges on such arrangements to reflect closely those that will apply to alternatively secured pension funds that remain on the death of a member.

Introduction

1 Part 4 of FA 2004 (pension schemes etc) is amended as follows.

GENERAL NOTE

Paragraph 1 makes provision for FA 2004 to be amended by paragraphs 2 to 18.

Alternatively secured pension: guaranteed pension and maximum

2— (1) In section 165(1) (pension rules) is amended as follows.

(2) In pension rule 2 (guaranteed pensions)—

(*a*) for ", an annuity or alternatively secured pension" substitute "or an annuity", and
(*b*) for ", annuity or alternatively secured pension" substitute "or annuity".

(3) In pension rule 7 (maximum alternatively secured pension), for "70%" substitute "90%".

GENERAL NOTE

FA 2004 s 165(1) sets out the rules for the payment of pensions by a registered pension scheme. Paragraph 2 amends FA 2004 s 165(1) by removing the facility to guarantee a pension for period of up to 10 years after a member's death thus ensuring that a pension from an alternatively secured pension fund can no longer be paid as an authorised payment after a member's death. This does not prevent the remaining funds being used to provide a dependant's pension for one or more dependants of the deceased member. Paragraph 2 further amends FA 2004 s 165(1) by increasing the maximum pension that may be drawn from an alternatively secured pension fund from 70 to 90 per cent of the annual amount of a comparable annuity for a 75 year old.

3 In paragraph 12 of Schedule 28 (pension rules: alternatively secured pension year), omit sub-paragraphs (3) and (4) (guaranteed pensions).

GENERAL NOTE

Paragraph 3 amends FA 2004 Sch 28 para 12 by removing the provisions that apply to alternatively secured pensions being paid after the member has died under a guarantee (see paragraph 2 above).

Maximum dependants' alternatively secured pension

4 In section 167(1) (pension death benefit rules), in pension death benefit rule 6 (maximum dependants' alternatively secured pension), for "70%" substitute "90%".

GENERAL NOTE

Paragraph 4 amends FA 2004 s 165(1) by increasing the maximum pension that may be drawn from a dependant's alternatively secured pension fund from 70 to 90 per cent of the annual amount of a comparable annuity.

Abolition of transfer lump sum death benefit

5 In section 168(1) (lump sum death benefit rule), omit paragraph (*g*) (transfer lump sum death benefit).

GENERAL NOTE

This paragraph deletes from FA 2004 s 168(1) a transfer lump sum death benefit from the list of authorised lump sum death payments. From 6 April 2007 it is not permitted, where a member or dependant dies with alternatively secured pension funds remaining and there are no remaining dependants, for the remaining funds to be passed to other members of the same pension scheme. If such a transfer does take place it is treated as an unauthorised payment and liable to tax of up to 70 per cent.

6 Omit section 172B(5)(*a*) (reduction for transfer lump sum death benefit).

GENERAL NOTE

Paragraph 6 repeals FA 2004 s 172B(5)(*a*) as the provision is no longer required because reallocations of alternatively secured pension funds have been removed from the operation of FA 2004 s 172B and separate provision made for them in FA 2004 s 172BA inserted by para 13 below.

7 In section 188(5) (amounts not to be treated as contributions), omit paragraph (*b*) and the word "and" before it.

GENERAL NOTE

FA 2004 s 188(5) is amended by para 7 by removing the reference to transfer lump sum death benefits.

8 In section 280(2) (index), omit the entry relating to transfer lump sum death benefit.

GENERAL NOTE

Paragraph 8 amends FA 2004 s 280(2) by removing transfer lump sum death benefits from the index of defined expressions.

9 In Schedule 29, omit paragraph 19 (transfer lump sum death benefit).

GENERAL NOTE

Paragraph 9 amends FA 2004 Sch 29 by deleting para 19 and all the provisions relating to transfer lump sum death benefits therein.

10 In paragraph 17A of Schedule 36 ("enhanced protection")—

(*a*) in sub-paragraph (1), insert "or" after paragraph (*a*) and omit paragraph (*c*) and the word "or" before it, and

(*b*) in sub-paragraph (2), omit ", or to a transfer lump sum death benefit being paid,".

GENERAL NOTE

Paragraph 10 amends FA 2004 Sch 36 para 17A by removing the references to transfer lump sum death benefits.

Untraceable members

11 In paragraph 11 of Schedule 28 (member's alternatively secured pension fund), insert at the end—

"(6) Sub-paragraph (7) applies if—

(*a*) at the time when the member reaches the age of 75, the scheme administrator has been unable to ascertain the member's whereabouts after having taken all reasonable steps to do so, and

(*b*) paragraph 8(2) applies in relation to the member and the arrangement and none of the sums or assets held for the purposes of the arrangement are member-designated funds immediately before it applies.

(7) In that case the references in sub-paragraphs (2) and (3) to the time when the member reached the age of 75 are to be read as referring to the end of the period of six months beginning with any later date on which the member's whereabouts are subsequently ascertained by the scheme administrator."

GENERAL NOTE

Paragraph 11 inserts new provisions into FA 2004 Sch 28 para 11 in relation to members of registered pension schemes who cannot be traced after their 75th birthday. The amendments cover the conditions that apply for sums and assets to become held in an alternatively secured pension fund on the member's 75th birthday. Funds held in an unsecured pension fund immediately before a member's 75th birthday are to be treated as held in an alternatively secured pension fund when the member reaches age 75. This measure means that, for members who the scheme administrator cannot trace by their 75th birthday, their funds will not automatically be treated as becoming held in an alternatively secured pension fund at that time. It is a condition that where funds become held under the separate provisions for untraceable members that the scheme administrator has taken reasonable steps to trace a member and has been unable to find them. Another condition is that no part of the funds in the arrangement were treated as member-designated funds under FA 2004 Sch 28 para 8(2), i.e. uncrystallised funds available for unsecured pensions.

A further amendment in paragraph 11 provides that funds which have previously been designated into unsecured pension under FA 2004 Sch 28 para 8(2), are effectively to remain in suspense unless the member is subsequently traced. Whilst funds remain in suspense any payments from the fund are treated as unauthorised as they are not one of the forms of benefits in FA 2004 s 165(1). If a member who was untraceable at age 75 is subsequently traced, and their funds have not within six months been used to purchase or provide a scheme pension or annuity, their funds will then be treated as becoming held as an alternatively secured pension fund. The alternatively secured pension provisions will then commence including the minimum income requirement (see para 14 below).

Increase in rights on death

12— (1) Section 172B (increase in rights of connected person on death) is amended as follows.

(2) In subsection (2)(*b*), for ", alternatively secured pension fund, dependant's unsecured pension fund or dependant's alternatively secured" substitute "or dependant's unsecured".

(3) In subsection (4), for "(6)" substitute "(5)".

(4) In subsection (7)(*a*), after "there" insert "are".

(5) After subsection (8) insert—

> "(8A) Nothing in this section applies in relation to the rights representing the member's unsecured pension fund if those rights would represent the member's alternatively secured pension fund but for paragraph 11(6) and (7) of Schedule 28."

GENERAL NOTE

Paragraph 12 amends FA 2004 s 172B so that it does not apply to the reallocation of rights from an alternatively secured pension fund or a dependant's alternatively secured pension fund and further ensures it does not apply to any reallocation of rights out of funds held in suspense for untraceable members under the new provisions in para 11. Paragraph 12 also corrects some minor errors in FA 2004 s 172B.

13 After that section insert—

"172BA Increase in rights on death arising from alternatively secured pension fund etc

> (1) This section applies if, at any time ("the relevant time") after the death of a member of a registered pension scheme, another member of the pension scheme becomes entitled to alternatively secured rights.
>
> (2) "Alternatively secured rights" are rights representing the whole or part of the dead member's alternatively secured pension fund, or dependant's alternatively secured pension fund, in respect of an arrangement under the pension scheme.
>
> (3) The pension scheme is to be treated as making an unauthorised payment to the other member (or to the other member's personal representatives).
>
> (4) Subject to subsection (5), the amount of the unauthorised payment is the amount by which—

(*a*) the consideration which might be expected to be received in respect of an assignment (or assignation) of the benefits to which the other member is actually or prospectively entitled under the pension scheme immediately after the relevant time, exceeds

(*b*) the consideration which might be expected to be received in respect of such an assignment (or assignation) immediately before the relevant time.

(5) But that amount is to be reduced by so much (if any) of the excess as arises from the other member becoming entitled to pension death benefits or lump sum death benefits in respect of the dead member.

(6) This section does not apply if the other member's entitlement to the alternatively secured rights is brought about by an assignment (or agreement to assign) within section 172.

(7) Rights representing the member's unsecured pension fund are alternatively secured rights for the purposes of this section if they would be rights representing the member's alternatively secured pension fund but for paragraph 11(6) and (7) of Schedule 28."

GENERAL NOTE

This paragraph inserts new section 172BA into FA 2004 the provisions of which treat a registered pension scheme as making an unauthorised payment where the whole or part of alternatively secured pension funds remaining on the death of a member or dependant are reallocated to another member of the pension scheme.

The amount of the unauthorised payment is determined under s 172BA(4). This is the amount by which the amount for which the member could assign their benefit rights immediately after they became entitled to the alternatively secured pension rights exceeds the amount they could have received for assigning their rights immediately beforehand. The amount of the unauthorised payment may be reduced by any excess that arises from the other member becoming entitled to pension death benefits or lump sum death benefits in respect of the deceased member. Such circumstances might be where the whole or part of the remaining funds are used to provide a dependant of the member with an authorised form of pension benefit, eg a dependant's pension or annuity.

The provisions of s 172BA do not apply if an unauthorised payments charge has already been imposed on an assignment of benefits by virtue of FA 2004 s 172. Funds effectively held in suspense because the member could not be traced by their 75th birthday, also on the death of a member come within the unauthorised payment charge if there is a reallocation thereof that increases the benefit rights of another member of the pension scheme.

Minimum alternatively secured pension and dependants' alternatively secured pension

14 After section 181 insert—

"Alternatively secured pensions

"181A Minimum level of payment

(1) The total amount of alternatively secured pension paid to a member of a registered pension scheme in each alternatively secured pension year in respect of a money purchase arrangement under the pension scheme must be at least 55% of the basis amount for the alternatively secured pension year (but subject to subsection (5)).

(2) The total amount of dependants' alternatively secured pension paid to a dependant of a member of a registered pension scheme in each alternatively secured pension year in respect of a money purchase arrangement under the pension scheme must be at least 55% of the basis amount for the alternatively secured pension year (but subject to subsection (5)).

(3) If subsection (1) or (2) is not complied with in an alternatively secured pension year in the case of any arrangement under a registered pension scheme, the pension scheme is to be treated as having made a scheme chargeable payment when the alternatively secured pension year ends.

(4) The amount of the scheme chargeable payment is the difference between—

(*a*) the total amount of alternatively secured pension paid to the member, or of the dependants' alternatively secured pension paid to the dependant, in respect of the arrangement in the alternatively secured pension year, and

(*b*) 55% of the basis amount for the alternatively secured pension year, (or, if nothing is so paid, 55% of the basis amount for the alternatively secured pension year).

(5) Subsection (1) or (2) does not apply in relation to an alternatively secured pension year if—

(*a*) it is the alternatively secured pension year ending immediately before the death of the member or dependant, or

(*b*) in the alternatively secured pension year the member's alternatively secured pension fund, or the dependant's alternatively secured pension fund, in respect of the arrangement is applied on pension or annuity provision (see subsection (6)).

(6) The member's alternatively secured pension fund, or the dependant's alternatively secured pension fund, in respect of the arrangement is applied on pension or annuity provision if all of the sums and assets representing it are applied in one or more of the following ways—

(*a*) towards the provision of a scheme pension or dependants' scheme pension;
(*b*) to purchase a scheme pension or dependants' scheme pension;
(*c*) to purchase a lifetime annuity or dependants' annuity.

(7) Part 1 of Schedule 28 gives the meaning of expressions used in this section so far as it relates to alternatively secured pension; and Part 2 of that Schedule gives the meaning of expressions used in this section so far as it relates to dependants' alternatively secured pension."

GENERAL NOTE

This paragraph inserts new section 181A into FA 2004 imposing a minimum income requirement on a member's or dependant's alternatively secured pension funds. The minimum income requirement must be at least 55 per cent of the annual amount of a comparable annuity. If the minimum level of alternatively secured pension is not paid in the year, then the difference between the amount of pension paid from the alternatively secured pension fund and the minimum income requirement in respect of that fund is treated as a scheme chargeable payment on which the scheme administrator is liable to the scheme sanction charge under FA 2004 s 239.

The minimum level of payment does not apply for an alternatively secured pension year in which all of the sums and assets in the member's or dependant's alternatively secured pension fund are applied in that year towards the provision or purchase of a scheme pension, dependant's scheme pension, lifetime annuity or dependant's annuity.

The expressions used in section 181A are given the same meanings as set out in FA 2004 Sch 28.

15 In section 241(1) (scheme chargeable payment), after paragraph (*a*) insert—

"(*aa*) a scheme chargeable payment which the pension scheme is to be treated as having made by section 181A (minimum alternatively secured pension etc), and".

GENERAL NOTE

Paragraph 15 amends FA 2004 s 241(1) by inserting therein the scheme chargeable payment introduced by s 181A.

Charity lump sum death benefit

16— (1) Paragraph 18 of Schedule 29 (charity lump sum death benefit) is amended as follows.

(2) In sub-paragraph (1)(*c*), for "income withdrawal to which the member was entitled" substitute "the member's alternatively secured pension fund (or what would be the member's alternatively secured pension fund but for paragraph 11(6) and (7) of Schedule 28)".

(3) In sub-paragraph (1)(*d*), insert at the end "(or, if the member made no nomination, selected by the scheme administrator)."

(4) In sub-paragraph (2)(*d*), for "dependants' income withdrawal to which the member was entitled" substitute "the dependant's alternatively secured pension fund".

(5) In sub-paragraph (2)(*e*), for "(or, if the member made no nomination, by the dependant)." substitute "or, if the member made no nomination, by the dependant (or, if neither the member nor the dependant made a nomination, selected by the scheme administrator)."

(6) In sub-paragraph (4), after "representing" insert "what is (or but for paragraph 11(6) and (7) of Schedule 28 would be)".

GENERAL NOTE

Paragraph 16 amends FA 2004 Sch 29 para 18 in respect of the rules for the payment of lump sums to charities on the death of a member or dependant. The legislation is clarified so that payments to charities can be made out of sums and assets held in an alternatively secured pension fund. Provision is made for charity lump sum death benefits to be paid out of funds held in suspense, i.e. where the member could not be traced by age 75 (see para 11 above).

Amendments are made allowing a scheme administrator to select a charity to which a charity lump sum death benefit may be paid in the absence of a member or dependant nomination from a member's or dependant's alternatively secured pension fund.

Another amendment allows a charity lump sum death benefit to be paid out of funds that are effectively held in suspense where the member could not be traced by age 75.

Discharge of liability to scheme chargeable payment

17 In section 268(6) (unauthorised payments surcharge and scheme chargeable payments), for "(assignment)" substitute ", 172A, 172B, 172BA, 172C or 172D or arises under section 181A".

GENERAL NOTE

Paragraph 17 amends FA 2004 s 268(6) allowing a scheme administrator to apply for the discharge of their liability to the scheme sanction charge where it would not be just and reasonable to apply it if it arises under all the provisions relating to the scheme sanction charge including the new sections 172BA and 181A (see paras 13 and 14 above respectively).

Non-UK schemes

18— (1) Schedule 34 (non-UK schemes application of certain charges) is amended as follows.

(2) In paragraph 1(6), omit the words from "but also" to the end.

(3) In paragraph 4(3), omit the words from "but also" to the end.

(4) After paragraph 7 insert—

> "*Unauthorised payment charge: alternatively secured pension etc*
>
> **7ZA** The Commissions for Her Majesty's Revenue and Customs may by regulations make provision for—
>
> (*a*) a relieved member of a relevant non-UK scheme, or
>
> (*b*) a transfer member of such a scheme,
>
> to be liable to the unauthorised payment charge in circumstances which are the same as or similar to those in which the scheme administrator of such a scheme is liable to the scheme sanction charge by virtue of section 181A (minimum alternatively and dependants' alternatively secured pension)."

GENERAL NOTE

This paragraph makes amendments to FA 2004 Sch 34 in relation to alternatively secured pensions payable by non-UK pension schemes which come into charge because UK tax relief has been given in respect of sums or assets held for the purposes of the scheme.

The amendments remove the references to transfer lump sum death benefits from the definition of a relevant transfer and to relevant transferred sums and assets. These changes are consequent on the removal of transfer lump sum death benefits from FA 2004 s 168(1) (see para 5 above).

The amendments also enable HMRC to make regulations making relieved members or transfer members of a relevant non-UK scheme liable to the unauthorised payment tax charge in circumstances similar to those in which the scheme administrator of a registered pension scheme would be liable to the scheme sanction charge, eg where the minimum level of payment has not been paid from a member's or dependant's alternatively secured pension fund.

Inheritance tax

19 IHTA 1984 is amended as follows.

GENERAL NOTE

Paragraph 19 makes provision for IHTA 1984 to be amended by paras 20 to 27.

20— (1) Section 151A (person dying with alternatively secured pension fund) is amended as follows.

(2) For subsection (2) substitute—

"(2) Tax shall be charged on the relevant amount as if it were part of the value transferred by the transfer of value made on the member's death at the rate or rates at which it would be charged if it formed the highest part of that value."

(3) In subsection (3)(*a*), after "death" insert "but reduced by the amount of any previously charged income tax".

(4) After subsection (4) insert—

"(4A) In subsection (3)(*a*) above "the amount of any previously charged income tax" means the amount of any liability to income tax which (after the member's death but before the time when tax is charged on the transfer of value treated as made by the member on death) has arisen by virtue of the making of an unauthorised member payment under Part 4 of the Finance Act 2004 relating to the member's alternatively secured pension fund.

(4B) Subsection (4C) below applies where the maximum that could be transferred by the chargeable transfer made (under section 4 above) on the member's death if it were to be wholly chargeable to tax at the rate of nil per cent. exceeds—

(*a*) the value actually transferred by that chargeable transfer (or nil if there is no such chargeable transfer), less

(*b*) any previously untaxed alternatively secured pension fund amount.

(4C) Where this subsection applies, tax is to be charged on the previously untaxed alternatively secured pension fund amount as if the nil rate band maximum were—

$$\frac{\text{UNRB} \times 100}{100 - \text{MUPR}}$$

where—

UNRB is the unused nil-rate band, that is the excess mentioned in subsection (4B) above, and

MUPR is the maximum unauthorised payment rate, that is the maximum aggregate rate at which tax is chargeable under Part 4 of the Finance Act 2004 in respect of an unauthorised member payment."

(5) In subsection (5), at the end of the definition of "dependants' unsecured pension" (but before "and") insert—

"previously untaxed alternatively secured pension fund amount" means so much of the aggregate mentioned in subsection (3)(*a*) above as has not given rise to any liability to tax by virtue of Part 4 of the Finance Act 2004 before tax is charged on the transfer treated as made by the member on death."

(6) After that subsection insert—

"(6) This section applies in relation to a member who would have an alternatively secured pension fund immediately before death but for sub-paragraphs (6) and (7) of paragraph 11 of Schedule 28 to the Finance Act 2004 as if those sub-paragraphs were omitted (but subject as follows).

(7) In the case of such a member the references in subsection (3)(*a*) and (*b*) to the member's death are to the date on which the scheme administrator becomes aware of the member's death."

GENERAL NOTE

This paragraph provides for IHTA s 151A to be amended to take account of the unauthorised payments pension charges on alternatively secured pension funds arising on deaths on or after 6 April 2007. IHTA 1984 s 151A(2) is replaced with a rule providing that alternatively secured pension funds are to be treated as the top slice of the deceased member's estate instead of being treated the same as other assets making up the member's estate. The value of an alternatively secured pension taken into account for IHT is reduced by any income tax arising from an unauthorised payments tax charge that has been charged on it. The income tax to be taken into account is that which arose after the member's death, but before IHT was charged in respect of unauthorised member payments relating to the alternatively secured pension. These circumstances arise where there is an alternatively secured pension that has not previously given rise to a tax charge, and the value of the estate left by the person who has died net of the alternatively secured pension is less than the amount of IHT nil-rate band available to set against the value of their estate. The legislation includes a formula for calculating the amount of the unused nil-rate band IHT available to set against the alternatively secured pension. This grosses up the unused nil-rate band by reference to the maximum rate of tax that can apply to an unauthorised payments charge before IHT arises on the alternatively secured pension.

A definition is provided of a previously untaxed alternatively secured pension fund amount as that part of a person's alternatively secured pension that has not given rise to an unauthorised payments charge before IHT arises on the alternatively secured pension.

It should be noted that there is no change to the timing of the IHT charges whether this involves a deceased member or their dependant (see para 22 below). The amount of the alternatively secured pension funds charged to IHT differs depending on whether or not the unauthorised payment charges have arisen before or after the IHT due date. Where the unauthorised payment charges have been deducted before IHT is due, then IHT is calculated by reference to the net value of the alternatively secured pension funds. Conversely, where IHT is due before the unauthorised payment charges are made, IHT is calculated by reference to the gross value of the alternatively secured pension funds with an adjustment to the unused nil-rate band to set against the alternatively secured pension funds. Examples 1 and 2 below show respectively how IHT is calculated where IHT is due before the unauthorised payment charge is made and where the unauthorised payment charge is deducted before IHT is due.

A further amendment provides, that where a scheme member died with funds in a pension scheme which would have been an alternatively secured pension had the scheme administrator been able to trace them by the time they reached age 75, those funds are brought within the scope of IHTA s 151A. Another amendment provides that the date when the scheme administrator becomes aware of the scheme member's death is substituted for the dates in IHTA s 151A(3)(*a*) and (*b*).

21— (1) Section 151B (relevant dependant with pension fund inherited from member over 75) is amended as follows.

(2) In subsection (1)(*b*), after "before his death" insert "(or would have but for paragraph 11(6) and (7) of Schedule 28 to the Finance Act 2004)".

(3) Omit subsection (5).

GENERAL NOTE

Paragraph 21 amends IHTA s 151B to include people who did not have an alternatively secured pension on attaining age 75 because the scheme administrator could not trace them at the time. It also deletes the rules covering the rates at which IHT was to be charged where a dependant inherited a pension fund from a member aged over 75.

22 After that section insert—

"151BA Rate or rates of charge under section 151B

(1) Tax charged under section 151B above shall be charged at the rate or rates at which it would be charged on the death of the member if the amount mentioned in subsection (3) of that section (as reduced under subsection (4) of that section) ("the taxable amount") had been included in the aggregate mentioned in section 151A(3)(*a*) above (but subject as follows).

(2) The rate or rates at which tax is charged on the taxable amount shall be determined as if the taxable amount had formed the very highest part of the value of the member's estate immediately before the member's death (above any amount which is part of that value apart from this section).

(3) The rate or rates at which tax is charged on the taxable amount shall be determined on the assumptions that—

(*a*) subsection (3)(*b*) of section 151A above were omitted, and

(*b*) the references in subsections (4A) and (5) of that section to the time when tax is charged on the transfer treated as made by the member on death were to the time when tax is charged under this section.

(4) Subsection (5) below applies where, before the time when the dependant dies or ceases to be a relevant dependant, there have been one or more reductions of tax by virtue of the coming into force of a substitution of a new Table in Schedule 1 to this Act since the member's death.

(5) The rate or rates at which tax is charged under section 151B above is to be determined as if the new Table effecting the reduction of tax (or the most recent reduction of tax) had been in force at the time of the member's death."

GENERAL NOTE

This paragraph inserts section 151BA into IHTA 1984 setting out how IHT charged where a dependant inherits a pension fund from a member over age 75 is to be calculated. It is calculated in the same way as the IHT charge is calculated under IHTA 1984 s 151A where a person dies with an alternatively secured pension fund subject to particular modifications. The alternatively secured pension funds to which the charge relates are to be treated as the very top slice of the estate of the original scheme member. Where the rates of IHT have been reduced since the original member died, IHT on the alternatively secured pension is calculated on the basis that the rates of IHT that apply are those that were in force at the date of the later event.

23— (1) Section 151C (dependant dying with other pension fund) is amended as follows.

(2) For subsection (2) substitute—

"(2) Tax shall be charged on the relevant amount as if it were part of the value transferred by the transfer of value made on the dependant's death at the rate or rates at which it would be charged if it formed the highest part of that value."

(3) In subsection (3)(*a*), after "death" insert "but reduced by the amount of any previously charged income tax".

(4) After that subsection insert—

"(3A) In subsection (3)(*a*) above "the amount of any previously charged income tax" means the amount of any liability to income tax which (after the dependant's death but before the time when tax is charged on the transfer of value treated as made by the dependant on death) has arisen by virtue of the making of an unauthorised member payment under Part 4 of the Finance Act 2004 relating to the dependant's alternatively secured pension fund.

(3B) Subsection (3C) below applies where the maximum that could be transferred by the chargeable transfer made (under section 4 above) on death if it were to be wholly chargeable to tax at the rate of nil per cent. exceeds—

(*a*) the value actually transferred by that chargeable transfer, less

(*b*) any previously untaxed dependant's alternatively secured pension fund amount.

(3C) Where this subsection applies, tax is to be charged on the previously untaxed dependant's alternatively secured pension fund amount as if the nil rate band maximum were—

$$\frac{\text{UNRB} \times 100}{100 - \text{MUPR}}$$

where—

UNRB is the unused nil rate band, that is the excess mentioned in subsection (3B) above; and

MUPR is the maximum unauthorised payment rate, that is the maximum aggregate rate at which tax is chargeable under Part 4 of the Finance Act 2004 in respect of an unauthorised member payment.

(3D) The relevant amount is to be reduced by the aggregate of so much of the sums and the value of the assets of the dependant's alternatively secured pension fund as arises, or (directly or indirectly) derives, from sums or assets forming part of an alternatively secured pension fund of the member which were designated as available for the payment of—

(*a*) dependants' unsecured pension, or

(*b*) dependants' alternatively secured pension,

to the dependant under the arrangement."

(5) In subsection (4), omit "and" at the end of the definition of "dependant" and insert at the end—

""previously untaxed dependant's alternatively secured pension fund amount" means so much of the aggregate mentioned in subsection (3)(*a*) above as has not given rise to any liability to tax by virtue of Part 4 of the Finance Act 2004 before tax is charged on the transfer treated as made by the dependant on death."

GENERAL NOTE

Paragraph 23 amends IHTA 1984 s 151C where a dependant dies with other pension funds. Alternatively secured pension funds are to be treated as the top slice of the deceased member's estate instead of such funds being treated the same as other assets making up the member's estate when they die. The value of an alternatively secured pension taken into account for IHT is reduced by any income tax arising from an unauthorised payments tax charge that has been charged on it. The income tax that is to be taken into account is that which arose after the dependant's death, but before IHT was charged in respect of unauthorised member payments relating to the alternatively secured pension. These circumstances arise where there is an alternatively secured pension that has not previously given rise to a tax charge, and the value of the estate left by the person who has died net of the alternatively secured pension is less than the amount of the IHT nil-rate band available to set against the value of their estate. The legislation includes a formula for calculating the amount of the unused nil-rate band IHT available to set against the alternatively secured pension. This grosses up the unused nil-rate band by reference to the maximum rate of tax that can apply to an unauthorised payments charge before IHT arises on the alternatively secured pension. Examples 3 and 4 below show how IHT is calculated where IHT is due before the unauthorised payment charge is made on the cessation of a relevant dependant's benefits. Example 5 below shows how the IHT charge is calculated where the unauthorised payment charge is deducted before IHT is due.

A definition is provided of a previously untaxed alternatively secured pension fund amount as that part of a person's alternatively secured pension that has not given rise to an unauthorised payments charge before IHT arises on the alternatively secured pension.

24 In section 216(6)(*ac*) (delivery of account)—

(*a*) after "occurs" insert ", the scheme administrator becomes aware of the death", and

(*b*) insert at the end "(depending on which occasions the charge)".

GENERAL NOTE

Paragraph 24 amends IHTA 1984 s 216(6)(*ac*) regarding the administration and collection rules in respect of IHT. The amendment allows the 12 month period for delivery of an account to run from the date on which the scheme administrator became aware of the death of a scheme member who was untraceable at the time they reached age 75.

25 In section 226(4) (payment), after "Act" insert ", or under section 151A above by virtue of subsection (6) of that section,".

GENERAL NOTE

Paragraph 25 amends IHTA 1984 s 226(4) to bring the tax charge under s 151A(6) within the time limit allowed by IHTA 1984 s 226(4) for payment of the tax due.

26 In section 233(1)(*c*) (interest on unpaid tax), after "Act" insert ", or under section 151A above by virtue of subsection (6) of that section,".

GENERAL NOTE

This paragraph amends IHTA 1984 s 233(1)(c) to bring the tax charge under s 151A(6) within the interest charging provision for late payment of tax in IHTA 1984 s 233(1)(c).

27 In Schedule 2 (provisions applying on reduction of tax), omit paragraph 6A.

GENERAL NOTE

Paragraph 27 deletes IHTA 1984 Sch 2 para 6A as the rule providing for a charge thereunder has been replaced.

Consequential amendment

28— (1) Section 636A of ITEPA 2003 (exemption for certain lump sums under registered pension schemes) is amended as follows.

(2) In subsection (1)—

(*a*) insert "or" at the end of paragraph (*d*), and

(*b*) omit paragraph (*f*) and the word "or" before it.

(3) In subsection (7), omit ""transfer lump sum death benefit",".

GENERAL NOTE

Paragraph 28 amends ITEPA 2003 s 636A by removing references to transfer lump sum death benefits which were included therein as authorised payments to ensure they were not liable to an income tax charge which they now will be.

Commencement

29— (1) The amendments made by paragraphs 2(2) and 3 have effect in relation to deaths of members of registered pension schemes occurring on or after 6th April 2007.

(2) The amendments made by paragraphs 2(3), 4, 14 and 15 have effect for alternatively secured pension years beginning on or after 6th April 2007.

(3) The amendments made by paragraphs 5 to 10, 18(2) and (3) and 28 have effect in relation to lump sum death benefits paid in respect of members of schemes whose deaths occur on or after 6th April 2007.

(4) The amendments made by paragraphs 11, 12(5) and 16(2), (4) and (6) are deemed to have come into force on 6th April 2006.

(5) The amendments made by paragraphs 12(2) and 13 have effect in relation to members of registered pension schemes becoming entitled to alternatively secured rights on or after 6th April 2007 in respect of members whose deaths occur on or after that date.

(6) The amendments made by paragraph 16(3) and (5) have effect in relation to charity lump sum death benefits paid on or after 6th April 2007.

(7) The amendment made by paragraph 17 is deemed to have come into force on 6th April 2007.

(8) The amendments made by paragraphs 19 to 27 have effect in relation to deaths, cases where scheme administrators become aware of deaths and cessations of dependency occurring on or after 6th April 2007.

GENERAL NOTE

This paragraph sets out when the provisions of Sch 19 will be effective.

The amendments made by paras 2(2) and 3 that remove the guarantee facility on alternatively secured pensions apply from 6 April 2007.

The amendments made by paras 2(3), 4, 14 and 15 that provide the increased maximum and the minimum level of payment from an alternatively secured pension fund apply to the first alternatively secured pension year starting on or after 6 April 2007.

The amendments made by paras 5 to 10, 18(2) and (3) and 28 that remove transfer lump sum death benefits from the authorised payments rules together with consequential changes apply to such benefits paid in respect of members of schemes whose deaths occur on or after 6 April 2007. Where a member died before 6 April 2007 with sums and assets in an alternatively secured pension fund or in a dependant's alternatively secured pension fund, the new provisions do not apply to reallocations out of the remaining alternatively secured pension or dependant's alternatively secured pension funds.

The amendments made by paras 11, 12(5) and 16(2), (4) and (6) that change the rules for members who cannot be traced by their 75th birthday are treated as if they had effect from 6 April 2006. So the funds of untraceable members who have reached 75 since 6 April 2006 are treated as if they have not been held under the alternatively secured pension provisions, but have effectively been held in suspense instead.

The amendments made by paras 12(2) and 13 introducing a charge where a member becomes entitled to alternatively secured rights apply on or after 6 April 2007. They do not apply however in respect of members or dependants with alternatively secured pension funds who died before that date.

The amendments made by para 16(3) and (5) to the charity lump sum death benefit rules apply on or after 6 April 2007.

The amendments made by para17 to the provisions for discharging the scheme administrator's liability to the scheme sanction charge came into effect on 6 April 2007.

The amendments made by paras 19 to 27 relating to IHT have effect in respect of deaths, cases where scheme administrators become aware of deaths and cessations of dependency, occurring on or after 6 April 2007.

SCHEDULE 20

PENSION SCHEMES ETC: MISCELLANEOUS

Section 70

GENERAL NOTE

This schedule incorporates amendments to FA 2004, to IHTA 184 and to ITEPA 2003 announced in the Pre-Budget Report of 6 December 2006 increasing the range of persons who may establish a registered pension scheme, countering abuse of the amount subject to tax charges where unauthorised payments are made, giving pension savers additional flexibility, and further clarifying the original pensions tax simplification legislation.

There had been considerable lobbying in the last two or three years to widen the eligibility for those persons wishing to establish registered pension schemes, particularly personal pension schemes. At the same time it was recognised that an element of regulation of these persons would be needed. The amendments cover both of these aspects.

HMRC had been concerned that amounts subject to tax charges where unauthorised payments were made to scheme members or sponsoring employers were being manipulated to avoid tax. Measures are introduced to prevent such manipulation and to counter an avoidance arrangement involving tax-free lump sums from a reduction in an ill-health pension.

Further flexibility is being given to scheme members to allow:

— more frequent reviews of the annual maximum withdrawal from a member's or dependant's unsecured pension fund;

— the payment of a pension commencement lump sum up to six months before the pension commences;

— easing of the administrative requirements for paying winding-up lump sums;

— extension of the time limit for paying lump sum death benefits free of IHT at the trustees' discretion.

The opportunity has also been taken to clarify the pensions tax simplification legislation in certain areas regarding:

— indirect holdings in REITS held by investment-regulated pension schemes;
— lump sum death benefits subject to primary transitional protection;
— the loss of enhanced transitional protection where a new arrangement is made within a registered pension scheme or the terms of a life insurance policy are varied;
— the loss of enhanced transitional protection where transfers take place from occupational pension schemes following corporate mergers or acquisitions;
— the amount to be tested for relevant benefit accrual in relation to a permitted transfer.

Introduction

1 Part 4 of FA 2004 (pension schemes etc) is amended as follows.

GENERAL NOTE

Paragraph 1 makes provision for FA 2004 to be amended by paras 2 to 17 and 20.

Persons by whom registered pension schemes may be established

2— (1) Section 154 (persons by whom registered pension scheme may be established) is amended as follows.

(2) For subsection (1) substitute—

"(1) An application to register a pension scheme may be made only if the pension scheme—

(*a*) is an occupational pension scheme, or

(*b*) has been established by a person with permission under FISMA 2000 to establish in the United Kingdom a personal pension scheme or a stakeholder pension scheme."

(3) After subsection (2) insert—

"(2A) Subsection (1) is to be construed in accordance with section 22 of FISMA 2000, any relevant order under that section and Schedule 2 to that Act."

(4) Omit subsection (3).

(5) In subsection (4), omit "and section 155".

GENERAL NOTE

This amends FA 2004 s 154 by replacing it with new eligibility criteria for a person wishing to establish a registered pension scheme. Any employer may continue to establish an occupational pension scheme, but from 6 April 2007 to establish a new registered pension scheme other than an occupational scheme that person must have permission from the Financial Services Authority (FSA) under FSMA 2000 to establish a personal pension scheme or stakeholder pension scheme. Whilst this has introduced an element of regulation to the provision of personal and stakeholder pension schemes, it has also widened the scope of persons who can establish them from the usual insurance companies, banks and building societies to independent financial advisers who are regulated by the FSA.

3 Omit section 155 (persons by whom scheme may be established: supplementary).

GENERAL NOTE

Paragraph 3 deletes FA 2004 s 155 as it defines terms used in FA 2004 s 154(1) which have been replaced under para 2 above.

4 In section 273 (members liable as scheme administrator)—

(*a*) in subsection (5)(*a*), omit "was established by a person or body specified in section 154(1)(*a*) to (*g*) (insurance companies etc) and", and
(*b*) in subsection (7), omit "was established by a person or body specified in section 154(1)(*a*) to (*g*) and".

GENERAL NOTE

Paragraph 4 amends FA 2004 s 273 to remove references to a person or body specified in the replaced part of FA 2004 s 154(1).

Unauthorised payments reduced by amount of scheme sanction charge

5 In section 160 (unauthorised payments), after subsection (4) insert—

"(4A) If an unauthorised member payment or unauthorised employer payment made to or in respect of a person would have been greater but for a reduction made in respect of the whole, or any proportion, of the amount which the scheme administrator considers may be the amount of the liability to the scheme sanction charge in respect of it, it is to be regarded for the purposes of this Part as increased by the amount of the reduction.

(4B) But if the amount, or that proportion of the amount, of that liability is in fact less than the amount of the reduction, a subsequent payment of an amount not exceeding the difference between that amount and the amount of the reduction made—

(*a*) to or in respect of the same person, and
(*b*) before the end of the period of two years beginning with the date on which the unauthorised member payment or unauthorised employer payment was made,

is not to be regarded for the purposes of this Part as an unauthorised member payment or unauthorised employer payment."

GENERAL NOTE

FA 2004 s 160 is amended by para 5 by adding subsections 4A and 4B which clarify the amount of an unauthorised payment. Provision is made for an unauthorised member or employer payment to be increased by any amount withheld by the administrator of a registered pension scheme to cover all or part of the pension scheme's liability to the scheme sanction charge in respect of that payment.

Provision is also made that if the pension scheme's liability to tax under the scheme sanction charge is less than the amount withheld and subsequently the amount or part of the amount withheld is paid to or in respect of the person originally in receipt of the unauthorised payment, then that payment or subsequent payments, if made within two years of the date of the original payment, is not to be treated as a second unauthorised member or employer payment.

Surrenders

6— (1) Section 172A (surrender) is amended as follows.

(2) In subsection (5), after paragraph (*d*) insert—

"(da) a surrender made as part of a retirement-benefit activities compliance exercise,
(db) a surrender of a prospective entitlement to pension death benefits within section 167(1) or lump sum death benefits within section 168(1) (or both) made in order to comply with the Employment Equality (Age) Regulations 2006 or Employment Equality (Age) Regulations (Northern Ireland) 2006 (or any regulations amending or replacing them),".

(3) In subsection (10), for "An" substitute "For the purposes of this section an".

(4) After that subsection insert—

"(10A) For the purposes of this section a surrender relating to an arrangement under the pension scheme ("the old arrangement") is made as part of a retirement-benefit activities compliance exercise if—

(*a*) it is made in connection with the making of an arrangement under another pension scheme relating to the member ("the new arrangement"),
(*b*) the old arrangement and the new arrangement relate to the same employment,
(*c*) both the rights surrendered and the rights conferred under the new arrangement consist of or include a prospective entitlement to pension death benefits within section 167(1) or lump sum death benefits within section 168(1) (or both),

(*d*) the surrender and the making of the new arrangement constitute or form part of a transaction the purpose of which is to secure that the activities of the pension scheme are limited to retirement-benefit activities within the meaning of section 255 of the Pensions Act 2004 or Article 232 of the Pensions (Northern Ireland) Order 2005, and

(*e*) the rights surrendered and the rights conferred under the new arrangement are not significantly different."

GENERAL NOTE

Paragraph 6 amends the rules in FA 2004 s 172A setting out when the surrender of a right or benefit by a member of a registered pension scheme means that the scheme is treated as making an unauthorised payment to that member. The amendments make additions to the categories of surrender that mean the scheme is not treated as making an unauthorised payment. One instance is where the surrender is part of a retirement-benefit activities compliance exercise (defined below). A further instance is where the surrender is of prospective entitlement to death benefits necessary because the surrendered entitlement fails to comply with age-equality legislation enacted in 2006.

The amendments set out the circumstances where a surrender is part of a retirement-benefit activities compliance exercise. This is where the surrendering arrangement has to provide rights to death benefits and be replaced by a new arrangement relating to the same individual and employment and providing similar rights. These features must be necessary to ensure the provision of benefits by the old pension scheme is limited to the activities referred to in Pensions Act 2004 s 255 or corresponding Northern Ireland legislation.

Scheme pensions where ill-health condition met

7— (1) Schedule 28 (pension rules) is amended as follows.

(2) In paragraph 2(4) (scheme pensions: cases where cessation or reduction of pension is permitted), for paragraph (*a*) substitute—

"(*a*) the reduction of the pension if the member became entitled to it by reason of the ill-health condition being met,".

(3) In paragraph 2A(2) (certain reductions not permitted if part of avoidance arrangements), for "the rate of which is reduced in accordance with paragraph (*b*) of sub-paragraph (4) of paragraph 2 but" substitute "which is reduced in accordance with paragraph (*a*) of sub-paragraph (4) of paragraph 2, or the rate of which is reduced in accordance with paragraph (*b*) of that sub-paragraph, and".

GENERAL NOTE

Paragraph 7 replaces FA 2004 Sch 28 para 2(4)(*a*). It now provides that a reduction of a scheme pension paid on ill-health grounds before normal minimum pension age (50) that includes its cessation, does not preclude it from satisfying the conditions in FA 2004 Sch 28 para 2(3) that the pension is payable for life and the rate of pension cannot be reduced from one year to another.

Paragraph 7 also amends FA 2004 Sch 28 para 2A(2) to provide that a reduction of the scheme pension in accordance with FA 2004 Sch 28 para 2(4)(*a*) (see above) is subject to the provisions of FA 2004 Sch 28 para 2A where that reduction was part of avoidance arrangements.

Unsecured and dependants' unsecured pensions: reference periods

8— (1) Schedule 28 (pension rules) is amended as follows.

(2) In paragraph 10 (reference periods for unsecured pensions), for sub-paragraph (1) substitute—

"(1) Subject as follows, the period of five unsecured pension years beginning with the first unsecured pension year, and each succeeding period of five unsecured pension years, is a "reference period".

(1A) Sub-paragraph (1B) applies if, at any time during a reference period ("the current reference period"), the member notifies the scheme administrator that the member wishes a new reference period to begin on the next day that is an anniversary of the reference date in relation to the current reference period.

(1B) The scheme administrator may determine—

(*a*) that the current reference period is to end immediately before that day (so that sub-paragraph (1) no longer applies), and

(*b*) that (subject to any further operation of this sub-paragraph) the period of five unsecured pension years beginning with that day, and each succeeding period of five unsecured pension years, is to be a reference period.

(1C) The first day of each reference period is, in relation to that period, "the reference date"."

(3) In paragraph 24 (reference periods for dependants' unsecured pensions), for sub-paragraph (1) substitute—

"(1) Subject as follows, the period of five unsecured pension years beginning with the first unsecured pension year, and each succeeding period of five unsecured pension years, is a "reference period".

(1A) Sub-paragraph (1B) applies if, at any time during a reference period ("the current reference period"), the dependant notifies the scheme administrator that the dependant wishes a new reference period to begin on the next day that is an anniversary of the reference date in relation to the current reference period.

(1B) The scheme administrator may determine—

(*a*) that the current reference period is to end immediately before that day (so that sub-paragraph (1) no longer applies), and

(*b*) that (subject to any further operation of this sub-paragraph) the period of five unsecured pension years beginning with that day, and each succeeding period of five unsecured pension years, is to be a reference period.

(1C) The first day of each reference period is, in relation to that period, "the reference date"."

GENERAL NOTE

FA 2004 Sch 28 paras 10 and 24 are amended by para 8 allowing a review of the annual maximum withdrawal from a member's or dependant's unsecured pension fund more frequently than five years. The requirement that the maximum withdrawal should be reviewed at least every five years remains.

The reference period for a member's or dependant's unsecured fund is defined as five unsecured pension years from the first unsecured pension year and each subsequent five year period. Provision is made for the pension scheme administrator to determine ultimately whether to carry out a member's or dependant's wish, having been notified by the member or dependant of the same, and end the five year reference period on the day before the anniversary of an unsecured pension year and start a new five year reference period on the date of the next unsecured pension year.

Pension commencement lump sums

9 In section 166(2)(*a*) (when person becomes entitled to pension commencement lump sum), after "paid" insert "(or, if the person dies before becoming entitled to the pension in connection with which it was anticipated it would be paid, immediately before death)".

GENERAL NOTE

Paragraph 9 amends FA 2004 s 166(2)(*a*), by including in the provisions where a person becomes entitled to a pension commencement lump sum, the situation where a person dies before becoming entitled to the pension in connection with which it was anticipated the pension would be paid immediately before death.

10 In section 219(7) (multiple benefit crystallisation events occurring by reason of payment of lump sum death benefits treated as occurring immediately before death), insert at the end "but immediately after any benefit crystallisation event occurring immediately before the individual's death by virtue of section 166(2)."

GENERAL NOTE

Paragraph 10 amends FA 2004 s 219(7), covering multiple benefit crystallisation events occurring by reason of payment of lump sum death benefits treated as occurring immediately before death, by including the circumstances at para 9 above.

11— (1) Schedule 29 (authorised lump sums) is amended as follows.

(2) In paragraph 1(1) (conditions to be met if lump sum is to be pension commencement lump sum)—

(*a*) for paragraph (*a*) substitute—

"(*a*) the member becomes entitled to it before reaching the age of 75,

(*aa*) the member becomes entitled to it in connection with becoming entitled to a relevant pension (or dies after becoming entitled to it but before becoming entitled to the relevant pension in connection with which it was anticipated that the member would become entitled to it)",

(*b*) in paragraph (*c*), for "of three months beginning with" substitute "beginning six months before, and ending one year after,", and

(*c*) omit paragraph (*e*) (but not including the "and" at the end).

(3) In paragraph 1(6) (power to provide that certain lump sums are to be treated as pension commencement lump sums), for "(1)(*c*) and (*e*)" substitute "(1)(*a*) and (*c*)".

(4) In paragraph 2 ("permitted maximum"), after sub-paragraph (5) insert—

"(5A) But if the member dies before becoming entitled to the relevant pension in connection with which it was anticipated that the member would become entitled to the lump sum, the permitted maximum is the available portion of the member's lump sum allowance."

GENERAL NOTE

Paragraph 11 amends the rules on pension commencement lump sums in FA 2004 Sch 29 paras 1 and 2 to allow a lump sum to be paid, where a member becomes entitled to it before age 75, up to six months before the pension commences as long as a pension scheme is arranging for a pension to commence. This allows schemes and members greater flexibility in arranging a pension. It allows savers time to take advantage of the open market option and choose the most suitable option annuity for them. Paragraph 11(4) provides that if a member dies before becoming entitled to the relevant pension in connection with which it was anticipated that the member would become entitled to the lump sum, the maximum pension commencement lump sum payable is the available portion of the member's lump sum allowance. The amendment applies retrospectively to 6 April 2006 to ensure that those lump sums that have been paid remain tax-free.

Winding-up lump sums

12— (1) Paragraph 10 of Schedule 29 (winding-up lump sums) is amended as follows.

(2) In sub-paragraph (1)(*c*), for "the member's employer" substitute "any person by whom the member is employed at the time when the lump sum is paid, and who has made contributions under the pension scheme in respect of the member within the period of five years ending with the day on which it is paid,".

(3) In sub-paragraph (3)—

(*a*) for "are that the employer" substitute "referred to in paragraph (*c*) of sub-paragraph (1) are that the person mentioned in that paragraph", and

(*b*) omit paragraph (*a*).

GENERAL NOTE

FA 2004 Sch 29 para 10 is amended by para 12 to ease the administrative requirements for paying lump sums where a registered pension scheme is winding-up. Previously the administrators of occupational pension schemes that were winding-up had to make checks and seek an undertaking from all former employers of the member receiving the lump sum. Under the amended provisions the administrator needs only to seek an undertaking from the member's employer at the time when the winding-up lump sum is paid and who has also contributed to the pension scheme in respect of the member in the previous five years.

Lump sum death benefits

13— (1) Schedule 29 (authorised lump sums) is amended as follows.

(2) In paragraph 13(*c*) (defined benefits lump sum death benefit), for "day on which the member died," substitute "earlier of the day on which the scheme administrator first knew of the member's death and the day on which the scheme administrator could first reasonably be expected to have known of it,".

(3) In paragraph 15(1)(*c*) (uncrystallised funds lump sum death benefit), for "day on which the member died," substitute "earlier of the day on which the scheme administrator first knew of the member's death and the day on which the scheme administrator could first reasonably be expected to have known of it,".

GENERAL NOTE

This paragraph amends FA 2004 Sch 29 13(c) so that defined benefit lump sum death benefits can be paid within two years of the earlier of the date on which the scheme administrator could reasonably have known of the member's death and when the administrator first knew of the death.

Paragraph 13 similarly amends FA 2004 Sch 29 para 15(1)(c) so that lump sum death benefits from a money purchase arrangement can also be paid within two years of the earlier of the date on which the scheme administrator could reasonably have known of the member's death and when the administrator first knew of the death.

Taxable property held by investment-regulated pension schemes: indirect holdings in REITs

14— (1) Schedule 29A (taxable property held by investment-regulated pension schemes) is amended as follows.

(2) In paragraph 20(1)(*b*) (indirect holdings: introduction to exception for REITs), for "paragraph 22 makes" substitute "paragraphs 22, 24 and 25 make".

(3) In paragraph 22 (REITs)—

(*a*) in sub-paragraph (1), after paragraph (*b*) insert—

"and paragraph 24 applies to the pension scheme's interest in the vehicle.", and

(*b*) omit sub-paragraph (2).

(4) In paragraph 24(1) (conditions applying for paragraph 23), for "paragraph 23" substitute "paragraphs 22 and 23".

(5) In paragraph 25(2) (provisions supplementing paragraph 24), for "23(1)" substitute "22 or 23".

GENERAL NOTE

Paragraph 14 amends FA 2004 Sch 29A concerning indirect holdings in REITS held by investment-regulated pension schemes. This ensures that the rules on diversity of ownership of vehicles through which investment-regulated pension schemes hold taxable property indirectly apply in the same way for UK REITS as for all other vehicles. The amendment to the legislation is necessary because of a change in the UK REITS legislation restricting corporate shareholders, but not an investment-regulated pension scheme, to holding less than 10 per cent in a UK REIT. So, FA 2004 Sch 29A has been amended to maintain the position that investment–regulated pension schemes, mainly small self-administered and self invested personal pension schemes, cannot hold 10 per cent or more of a UK REIT which holds taxable property, eg residential property, without creating a tax charge. This ensures that an investment in a UK REIT by an investment–regulated pension scheme is not used to hold taxable property for the personal use of scheme members.

Transitional provision: primary protection

15 In paragraph 11D of Schedule 36 (lump sum death benefits to be taken into account as part of individual's pre-commencement rights only if paid under policy not significantly varied since 5th April 2006), after sub-paragraph (2) insert—

"(2A) A variation of the terms of a policy of life insurance made in order to comply with the Employment Equality (Age) Regulations 2006 or Employment Equality (Age) Regulations (Northern Ireland) 2006 (or any regulations amending or replacing them) is to be ignored for the purposes of sub-paragraph (2).

(2B) Where a policy of life insurance held on 5th April 2006 for the purposes of an occupational pension scheme is surrendered and a new one is taken out—

(*a*) as part of a retirement-benefit activities compliance exercise, or

(*b*) to comply with the Employment Equality (Age) Regulations 2006 or Employment Equality (Age) Regulations (Northern Ireland) 2006 (or any regulations amending or replacing them), the new policy is to be treated for the purposes of sub-paragraph (2) as if it were the same as the old.

(2C) For this purpose a policy of life insurance is surrendered and a new one is taken out as part of a retirement-benefit activities compliance exercise if—

(*a*) the surrender of the old policy and taking out of the new policy constitute or form part of a transaction the purpose of which is to secure that the activities of the pension scheme are limited to retirement-benefit activities within the meaning of section 255 of the Pensions Act 2004 or Article 232 of the Pensions (Northern Ireland) Order 2005, and

(*b*) the rights under the old policy and the new policy are not significantly different."

GENERAL NOTE

FA 2004 sch 36 para 11D is amended by para 15 concerning lump sum death benefits to be taken into account as part of an individual's pre-commencement rights only if paid under a policy varied since 5 April 2006, i.e. they are treated as within the total rights subject to primary transitional protection from the lifetime allowance tax charge.

One amendment provides that where the terms of a policy are varied to comply with age equality legislation, the amount of the death benefit do not fall outside the total of transitionally protected rights.

Another amendment provides that where a policy is replaced by another policy, as part of a retirement-benefit activities compliance exercise (see para 6 above) or to comply with age-equality legislation, the new policy is treated as if it were the original policy to which primary protection applies.

A further amendment provides that for a surrender of a policy and its replacement to be part of a retirement-benefit activities compliance exercise, the exercise must be necessary to ensure the provision of benefits by the surrendering pension scheme is limited to the activities referred to in Pensions Act 2004 s 255 or corresponding Northern Ireland legislation. Also the rights under the old and new policies must not be significantly different.

Transitional provision: enhanced protection

16 Schedule 36 (transitional provision) is amended as follows.

GENERAL NOTE

Paragraph 16 makes provision for FA 2004 Sch 36 to be amended by paras 17 to 19.

17— (1) Paragraph 12 (when enhanced protection ceases) is amended as follows.

(2) In paragraph (*c*) of sub-paragraph (2), for "solely for the purposes of a permitted transfer" substitute "in permitted circumstances".

(3) After that sub-paragraph insert—

"(2A) An arrangement is made in permitted circumstances if it is made—

(*a*) for the purposes of a permitted transfer,

(*b*) as part of a retirement-benefit activities compliance exercise, or

(*c*) as part of an age-equality compliance exercise.

(2B) For the purposes of sub-paragraph (2A)(*b*) an arrangement ("the new arrangement") relating to an individual is made as part of a retirement-benefit activities compliance exercise if—

(*a*) it is made in connection with the cancellation of rights under another arrangement relating to the individual ("the old arrangement"),

(*b*) the old arrangement and the new arrangement relate to the same employment,

(*c*) there is a prospective entitlement to pension death benefits within section 167(1) or lump sum death benefits within section 168(1) (or both) under both the old arrangement and the new arrangement,

(*d*) the making of the new arrangement and the cancellation of the old arrangement constitute or form part of a transaction the purpose of which is to secure that the activities of the pension scheme under which the arrangement is made are limited to retirement-benefit activities within the meaning of section 255 of the Pensions Act 2004 or Article 232 of the Pensions (Northern Ireland) Order 2005, and

(*e*) the rights cancelled under the old arrangement and the rights conferred under the new arrangement are not significantly different.

(2C) For the purposes of sub-paragraph (2A)(*c*) an arrangement ("the new arrangement") is made as part of an age-equality compliance exercise if—

(*a*) it is made in connection with the cancellation of rights under another arrangement relating to the individual ("the old arrangement"),

(*b*) the old arrangement and the new arrangement relate to the same employment,

(*c*) there is a prospective entitlement to pension death benefits within section 167(1) or lump sum death benefits within section 168(1) (or both) under both the old arrangement and the new arrangement, and

(*d*) the new arrangement is made, and the old arrangement cancelled, in order to comply with the Employment Equality (Age) Regulations 2006 or Employment Equality (Age) Regulations (Northern Ireland) 2006 (or any regulations amending or replacing them)."

(4) In sub-paragraph (7)—

(*a*) omit paragraph (*a*),

(*b*) in paragraph (*b*), omit "held for the purposes of, or representing accrued rights under, the arrangement", and

(*c*) in paragraph (*c*), for "those" (in both places) substitute "the".

(5) In paragraph (*a*) of sub-paragraph (8), omit—

(*a*) ", or two or more money purchase arrangements that are not cash balance arrangements,", and

(*b*) "or" at the end.

(6) After paragraph (*b*) of that sub-paragraph insert—

"(*c*) where the arrangement is a cash balance arrangement or a defined benefits arrangement relating to a present or former employment, they are transferred in connection with a relevant business transfer so as to become held for the purposes of, or to represent rights under, a cash balance arrangement or defined benefits arrangement made under a registered pension scheme or recognised overseas pension scheme, or

(*d*) where the arrangement ("the old arrangement") is a cash balance arrangement or a defined benefits arrangement, they are transferred as part of a retirement-benefit activities compliance exercise so as to become held for the purposes of, or to represent rights under, a cash balance arrangement or defined benefits arrangement ("the new arrangement") relating to the same employment as the old arrangement and made under a registered pension scheme or recognised overseas pension scheme."

(7) After that sub-paragraph insert—

"(8A) For the purposes of sub-paragraph (8)(*c*) "relevant business transfer" means a transfer of an undertaking or a business (or part of an undertaking or a business) from one person to another—

(*a*) which involves the transfer of at least 20 employees, and

(*b*) in the case of which, if the transferor and the transferee are bodies corporate, they would not be treated as members of the same group for the purposes of Chapter 4 of Part 10 of ICTA.

(8B) For the purposes of sub-paragraph (8)(*d*) sums or assets held for the purposes of, or representing accrued rights under, the old arrangement are transferred as part of a retirement-benefit activities compliance exercise if—

(*a*) there is a prospective entitlement to pension death benefits within section 167(1) or lump sum death benefits within section 168(1) (or both) under both the old arrangement and the new arrangement, and

(*b*) the transfer constitutes or forms part of a transaction the purpose of which is to secure that the activities of the pension scheme under which the old arrangement was made are limited to retirement-benefit activities within the meaning of section 255 of the Pensions Act 2004 or Article 232 of the Pensions (Northern Ireland) Order 2005."

(8) In sub-paragraph (9)—

(*a*) in paragraph (*a*), omit ", or each of the arrangements," and "and" at the end,

(*b*) in paragraph (*b*), after "(8)(*b*)" insert "or (*d*)" and after "15" insert "to 17", and

(*c*) after that paragraph insert "and

(*c*) if the transfer is a permitted transfer by virtue of sub-paragraph (8)(*c*), this paragraph (and paragraphs 13, 15 to 17 and 17A(3)) apply as if the arrangement to which the transfer is made were the same as that from which it is made and (if the employment is transferred) as if the employment with the transferee were the employment with the transferor."

(9) After that sub-paragraph insert—

"(10) The Treasury may by order amend sub-paragraph (8) (and make other amendments consequential on any amendment of that sub-paragraph)."

GENERAL NOTE

Paragraph 17 amends FA 2004 Sch 36 para 12 regarding the circumstances in which enhanced protection ceases. A broadening of the circumstances in which the making of a new arrangement within a registered pension scheme does not result in the loss of enhanced protection is provided for. Provision is made for three circumstances. These are where there is a permitted transfer, where the making of the arrangement is part of a retirement-benefit activities compliance exercise or an age-equality compliance exercise.

For the making of a new arrangement to be part of a retirement-benefit activities compliance exercise, the arrangement must replace a cancelled arrangement providing rights to death benefits. The exercise must also be necessary to ensure the provision of benefits by the pension scheme under which rights are cancelled is limited to the activities referred to in Pensions Act 2004 s 255 or corresponding Northern Ireland legislation.

For the making of a new arrangement to be part of an age-equality compliance exercise, the new arrangement must replace another arrangement providing rights to death benefits, relate to the same individual and employment and provide similar rights, and that this exercise must be necessary to ensure compliance with age-equality legislation.

Paragraph 17(4) amends FA 2004 Sch 38 para 12(7) by removing the requirement that a permitted transfer must involve the transfer of all sums and assets held under an arrangement. This allows the transfer of only some of those sums and assets to be a permitted transfer. In consequence, FA 2004 Sch 38 para 12(8) is amended to remove the reference to a transfer from one arrangement to two or more money purchase arrangements as this wording is no longer necessary for such split transfers to be permitted transfers.

FA 2004 Sch 36 para 12(8) is further amended by inserting two sets of conditions which if satisfied mean that a transfer between one defined benefits or cash balance arrangement and another is a permitted transfer. So the transfer is permitted if it is employment-related and in connection with a relevant business transfer (see below). Additionally, the transfer is permitted if made as apart of a retirement –benefit activities compliance exercise (see paragraph 6 above) and both arrangements relate to the same employment.

Further amendments are inserted into FA 2004 Sch 36 para 8 by para 17(7). These define a relevant business transfer as a transfer of a business or undertaking involving at least 20 employees which takes place between two parties that are not companies within the same group. They also provide that a transfer is part of a retirement-benefit activities compliance exercise if the old and new arrangements both provide rights to death benefits and the exercise is necessary to ensure that the provision of benefits by the pension scheme under which the old arrangement was made are limited to the activities referred to in Pensions Act 2004 s 255 or corresponding Northern Ireland legislation.

Further consequential amendments are made to FA 2004 Sch 36 para 12(9) providing that the new categories of permitted transfer may trigger tests for relevant benefit accrual. They also provide that where there is a permitted transfer in connection with a permitted business transfer, for the purposes of the rules on relevant benefit accrual the arrangement and employment to which the individual is transferred are treated as the arrangement and employment from which the transfers are made.

There is provision for HM Treasury to amend FA 2004 Sch 36 para 2(8) as amended and to make any consequential amendments elsewhere.

18 In paragraph 14 (relevant contributions), after sub-paragraph (3) insert—

"(3A) A variation of the terms of a policy made in order to comply with the Employment Equality (Age) Regulations 2006 or Employment Equality (Age) Regulations (Northern Ireland) 2006 (or any regulations amending or replacing them) is to be ignored for the purposes of sub-paragraph (3).

(3B) Where a policy of insurance on the life of the individual issued, or issued in respect of insurances made, before 6th April 2006 is surrendered and a new one is taken out—

(*a*) as part of a retirement-benefit activities compliance exercise, or

(*b*) as part of an age-equality compliance exercise.

the new policy is to be treated for the purposes of sub-paragraph (3) as if it were the same as the old.

(3C) For the purposes of sub-paragraph (3B)(*a*) a policy is surrendered, and a new policy of life insurance is taken out, as part of a retirement-benefit activities compliance exercise if—

(*a*) the surrender of the old policy and the taking out of the new policy constitute or form part of a transaction the purpose of which is to secure that the activities of the pension scheme under which the arrangement is made are limited to retirement-benefit activities within the meaning of section 255 of the Pensions Act 2004 or Article 232 of the Pensions (Northern Ireland) Order 2005, and

(*b*) the rights under the old policy and the new policy are not significantly different.

(3D) For the purposes of sub-paragraph (3B)(*b*) a policy is surrendered, and a new policy of life insurance is taken out, as part of an age-equality compliance exercise if—

(*a*) the old policy is surrendered, and the new policy is taken out, in order to comply with the Employment Equality (Age) Regulations 2006 or Employment Equality (Age) Regulations (Northern Ireland) 2006 (or any regulations amending or replacing them), and

(*b*) any significant difference between the rights under the old policy and the rights under the new policy is attributable to the need to comply with those Regulations (or any regulations amending or replacing them)."

GENERAL NOTE

This paragraph amends FA 2004 Sch 36 para 14 relating to the definition of relevant contributions that, if made to a money purchase arrangement that is not a cash balance arrangement, would result in the loss of enhanced protection.

One amendment provides that a variation in the terms of a life insurance policy made to ensure compliance with age-equality legislation would not result in a contribution to the varied policy being a relevant contribution. Another amendment ensures that where a policy is surrendered and replaced by another as part of a retirement-benefit activities or age-equality compliance exercise, that the new policy is treated as the old policy and that contributions to the new policy are not relevant contributions.

A further amendment provides that the surrender of a policy and its replacement by another are part of a retirement-benefits activities compliance exercise if the two policies provide similar benefits and the exercise is necessary to ensure that the provision of benefits by the pension scheme from which the old policy is surrendered are limited to the activities referred to in Pensions Act 2004 s 255 or corresponding Northern Ireland legislation.

FA 2004 Sch 36 para 14 is further amended by para 18 providing for the surrender of a policy and its replacement by another to be part of an age-equality exercise if the exercise is necessary to comply with age-equality legislation and the two policies otherwise provide similar benefits.

19— (1) Paragraph 15 (relevant benefit accrual) is amended as follows.

(2) In sub-paragraph (2), after "arrangement" (in both places) insert "which are transferred".

(3) In sub-paragraph (7), for "15 and 16" substitute "16 and 17".

GENERAL NOTE

Paragraph 19 amends FA 2004 Sch 36 para 15 so that where a permitted transfer is a relevant event and triggers a test for relevant benefit accrual, it is the amounts transferred and not the amounts held that are used for the test. The amendment is necessary because partial transfers may now be permitted transfers.

Paragraph 19 also corrects an erroneous cross-reference.

Inheritance tax: lump sum death benefits

20 In section 58 of IHTA 1984 (settlements: "relevant property"), after subsection (2) insert—

"(2A) For the purposes of subsection (1)(*d*) above—

(*a*) property applied to pay lump sum death benefits within section 168(1) of the Finance Act 2004 in respect of a member of a registered pension scheme is to be taken to be held for the purposes of the scheme from the time of the member's death until the payment is made, and

(*b*) property applied to pay lump sum death benefits in respect of a member of a section 615(3) scheme is to be taken to be so held if the benefits are paid within the period of two years beginning with the earlier of the day on which the member's death was first known to the trustees or other persons having the control of the fund and the day on which they could first reasonably be expected to have known of it."

GENERAL NOTE

Paragraph 20 amends IHTA 1984 s 58 which covers the exemption from IHT for settled property held for the purposes of a registered pension scheme or pension schemes formerly approved under TA 1988 s 615(3) (s 615(3) schemes). The amendment ensures that the two year time limit for paying lump sum death benefits free of IHT at the trustees' discretion from a registered pension scheme will now run from the date on which the pension scheme was notified or could reasonably have been aware of the member's death instead of two years from the member's death.

A similar amendment ensures the same extension for paying lump sum death benefits from a s 615(3) scheme and exemption from IHT.

Failure by a registered pension scheme or s 615(3) scheme to meet the extended time limit means that the IHT exemption ceases to apply as at the date of the scheme member's death. Any relevant IHT charges then apply from the date of death.

Benefits under employer-financed retirement benefits schemes

21 In section 393B of ITEPA 2003 (employer-financed retirement benefits schemes: relevant benefits), after subsection (4) insert—

"(4A) Regulations under subsection (3)(*d*) may include provision having effect in relation to times before they are made."

GENERAL NOTE

Paragraph 21 amends ITEPA 2003 s 393B empowering HMRC to make regulations with retrospective effect in relation to benefits paid under employer-financed retirement benefits schemes.

Consequential amendments

22— (1) In section 167(2) of FA 2004 (meaning of "pension death benefit"), for ""Pension" substitute "In this Part "pension".

(2) In section 280(2) of that Act (index of expressions), insert at the appropriate place—

"pension death benefit"	section 167(2)".

GENERAL NOTE

Paragraph 22 makes amendments to FA 2004 s 167(2) and s 280(2). These ensure the term pension death benefit (see paras 6 and 15) is defined for the purposes of the pension provisions of FA 2004.

23— (1) In section 1(1) of the Pension Schemes Act 1993 (c 48) (categories of pension schemes), in paragraph (*b*) of the definition of "personal pension scheme", omit "any of the paragraphs of".

(2) In section 1(1) of the Pension Schemes (Northern Ireland) Act 1993 (c 49) (categories of pension schemes), in paragraph (*b*) of the definition of "personal pension scheme", omit "any of the paragraphs of".

GENERAL NOTE

This paragraph makes consequential amendments to Pension Schemes Act 1993 s 1(1) and Pension Schemes (Northern Ireland) Act 1993 s 1(1) so that the references therein to FA 2004 s 154(1) do not mention the paragraphs removed by para 2 above.

Commencement

24— (1) The amendments made by paragraphs 2 to 4 and 23 are deemed to have come into force on 6th April 2007.

(2) The amendment made by paragraph 5 has effect in relation to payments made on or after 6th April 2007.

(3) The amendments made by paragraphs 6, 7(2), 9 to 11, 15 to 19 and 22 are deemed always to have had effect.

(4) The amendment made by paragraph 7(3) has effect in relation to reductions occurring on or after 6th April 2007.

(5) The amendments made by paragraph 8 have effect in relation to notifications given on or after 6th December 2006.

(6) The amendments made by paragraph 12 have effect in relation to lump sums paid on or after 6th April 2006.

(7) The amendments made by paragraph 13 have effect in relation to deaths occurring on or after 6th April 2006.

(8) The amendments made by paragraph 14 are deemed to have come into force on 1st January 2007.

(9) The amendment made by paragraph 20 has effect in relation to lump sum death benefits paid on or after 6th April 2006.

GENERAL NOTE

This paragraph sets out the date on which the provisions of Sch 20 are effective.

The amendments made by paras 2–4 and 23 that amend respectively the rules for persons who may establish registered pension schemes and make consequential amendments to Pension Schemes Act 1993 and Pension Schemes (Northern Ireland) Act 1993 apply from 6 April 2007.

The amendment made by para 5 where unauthorised payments are reduced by the amount of the scheme sanction charge, has effect in relation to payments made on or after 6 April 2007.

The amendments made by paras 6, 7(2), 9–11, 15–19 and 22, relating respectively to surrenders, reduction of pensions on ill-health grounds, payment of pension commencement lump sums up to six months before the pension commences, transitional provisions for primary and enhanced protection, and inclusion of the definition of pension death benefit, are deemed always to have had effect.

The amendment made by para 7(3) relating to the reduction of pensions on ill-health grounds as part of avoidance arrangements has effect in respect of reductions occurring on or after 6 April 2007.

The amendments made by para 8 relating to members' and dependants' unsecured pensions and reference periods have effect in relation to notifications given on or after 6 December 2006 (the date of the Pre-Budget Report 2006).

The amendments made by para 12 regarding winding-up lump sums have effect in relation to lump sums paid on or after 6 April 2006.

The amendments made by para 13 extending the time for paying lump sum death benefits have effect in respect of deaths occurring on or after 6 April 2006.

The amendments made by para 14 regarding investments in UK REITS are deemed to have come into force on 1 January 2007.

The amendment made by para 20 exempting lump sum death benefits from IHT where the time limit for paying them is extended has effect in respect of such benefits paid on or after 6 April 2006.

SCHEDULE 21

EXEMPTIONS FROM STAMP DUTY AND SDRT: INTERMEDIARIES, REPURCHASES ETC

Section 73

PROSPECTIVE AMENDMENT

This Schedule to be repealed by FA 2007 s 114, Sch 27 Pt 4(2) with effect in accordance with the provisions of FA 1990 ss 108, 110.

Intermediaries

1— (1) Section 80A of FA 1986 (exemption from stamp duty: sales to intermediaries) is amended as follows.

(2) For subsections (1) to (3) substitute—

"(1) Stamp duty shall not be chargeable on an instrument transferring stock of a particular kind on sale to a person or the person's nominee if—

(*a*) the person is a member of a regulated market on which stock of that kind is regularly traded; and

(*b*) the person is an intermediary and is recognised as such by the market in accordance with arrangements approved by the Commissioners.

(1A) Stamp duty shall not be chargeable on an instrument transferring stock of a particular kind on sale to a person or the person's nominee if—

(*a*) the person is a member of a multilateral trading facility, or a recognised foreign exchange, on which stock of that kind is regularly traded;

(*b*) the person is an intermediary and is recognised as such by the facility or exchange in accordance with arrangements approved by the Commissioners; and

(*c*) the sale is effected on the facility or exchange.

(1B) Stamp duty shall not be chargeable on an instrument transferring stock of a particular kind on sale to a person or the person's nominee if—

(*a*) the person is an intermediary who is approved for the purposes of this section by the Commissioners; and

(*b*) stock of that kind is regularly traded on a regulated market.

(1C) Stamp duty shall not be chargeable on an instrument transferring stock of a particular kind on sale to a person or the person's nominee if—

(*a*) the person is an intermediary who is approved for the purposes of this section by the Commissioners;

(*b*) stock of that kind is regularly traded on a multilateral trading facility or a recognised foreign exchange; and

(*c*) the sale is effected on the facility or exchange.

(2) Stamp duty shall not be chargeable on an instrument transferring stock of a particular kind on sale to a person or the person's nominee if—

(*a*) the person is a member of a regulated market, a multilateral trading facility or a recognised foreign options exchange;

(*b*) options to buy or sell stock of that kind are regularly traded on, and are listed by or quoted on, that market, facility or exchange;

(*c*) the person is an options intermediary and is recognised as such by that market, facility or exchange in accordance with arrangements approved by the Commissioners; and

(*d*) stock of that kind is regularly traded on a regulated market.

(2A) Stamp duty shall not be chargeable on an instrument transferring stock of a particular kind on sale to a person or the person's nominee if—

(*a*) the person is a member of a regulated market, a multilateral trading facility or a recognised foreign options exchange;

(*b*) options to buy or sell stock of that kind are regularly traded on, and are listed by or quoted on, that market, facility or exchange;

(*c*) the person is an options intermediary and is recognised as such by that market, facility or exchange in accordance with arrangements approved by the Commissioners; and

(*d*) the sale is effected on a relevant qualifying exchange on which stock of that kind is regularly traded or is effected on a relevant qualifying exchange pursuant to the exercise of a relevant option and options to buy or sell stock of that kind are regularly traded on, and are listed by or quoted on, that exchange;

and in paragraph (*d*) "relevant qualifying exchange" means a multilateral trading facility, a recognised foreign options exchange or a recognised foreign exchange.

(2B) Stamp duty shall not be chargeable on an instrument transferring stock of a particular kind on sale to a person or the person's nominee if—

(*a*) the person is an options intermediary who is approved for the purposes of this section by the Commissioners;

(*b*) options to buy or sell stock of that kind are regularly traded on, and are listed by or quoted on, a regulated market, a multilateral trading facility or a recognised foreign options exchange; and

(*c*) stock of that kind is regularly traded on a regulated market.

(2C) Stamp duty shall not be chargeable on an instrument transferring stock of a particular kind on sale to a person or the person's nominee if—

(*a*) the person is an options intermediary who is approved for the purposes of this section by the Commissioners;

(*b*) options to buy or sell stock of that kind are regularly traded on, and are listed by or quoted on, a regulated market, a multilateral trading facility or a recognised foreign options exchange; and

(*c*) the sale is effected on a relevant qualifying exchange on which stock of that kind is regularly traded or is effected on a relevant qualifying exchange pursuant to the exercise of a relevant option and options to buy or sell stock of that kind are regularly traded on, and are listed by or quoted on, that exchange;

and in paragraph (*c*) "relevant qualifying exchange" means a multilateral trading facility, a recognised foreign options exchange or a recognised foreign exchange."

(3) In subsection (6) (meaning of sale being on an exchange)—

(*a*) after "effected on" insert "a facility or",

(*b*) for "subsection (1) or (2) above" substitute "this section", and

(*c*) for "the exchange" (in each place) substitute "the facility or exchange".

(4) After that subsection insert—

"(6A) The Commissioners may approve a person for the purposes of this section only if the person is authorised under the law of an EEA State to provide any of the investment services or activities listed in Section A 2 or 3 of Annex I to the Directive (execution of orders on behalf of clients and dealing on own account), whether or not the person is authorised under the Directive."

(5) The amendments made by this paragraph have effect in relation to any instrument executed on or after 1st November 2007.

PROSPECTIVE AMENDMENT

This Schedule to be repealed by FA 2007 s 114, Sch 27 Pt 4(2) with effect in accordance with the provisions of FA 1990 ss 108, 110.

2— (1) Section 80B of FA 1986 (exemption from stamp duty on sales to intermediaries: supplementary) is amended as follows.

(2) In subsection (2)—

(*a*) after the definition of "collective investment scheme" insert—

""the Directive" means Directive 2004/39/EC of the European Parliament and of the Council of 21 April 2004 on markets in financial instruments, as amended from time to time;",

(*b*) omit the definition of "EEA exchange", and

(*c*) in the definition of "EEA State", for "means a State which" substitute ", in relation to any time, means a State which at that time is a member State or any other State which at that time" and insert at the end "(as modified or supplemented from time to time)".

(3) After that subsection insert—

"(2A) Each of the following expressions—

"multilateral trading facility", and

"regulated market",

has the same meaning in section 80A above as it has for the purposes of the Directive."

(4) After subsection (5) insert—

"(5A) The Treasury may by regulations amend section 80A above and this section (as they have effect for the time being) in order to extend the exemption from duty under that section."

(5) In subsection (7) (power for regulations to provide for stamp duty to be chargeable at a rate not exceeding 0.1%), for "subsection (1) or (2)" substitute "any of subsections (1) to (2C)".

(6) The amendments made by this paragraph have effect in relation to any instrument executed on or after 1st November 2007.

PROSPECTIVE AMENDMENT

This Schedule to be repealed by FA 2007 s 114, Sch 27 Pt 4(2) with effect in accordance with the provisions of FA 1990 ss 108, 110.

3— (1) Section 88A of FA 1986 (exemption from SDRT: sales to intermediaries) is amended as follows.

(2) For subsections (1) to (3) substitute—

"(1) Section 87 above shall not apply as regards an agreement to transfer securities of a particular kind to B or B's nominee if—

(*a*) B is a member of a regulated market on which securities of that kind are regularly traded; and

(*b*) B is an intermediary and is recognised as such by the market in accordance with arrangements approved by the Commissioners for Her Majesty's Revenue and Customs ("the Commissioners").

(1A) Section 87 above shall not apply as regards an agreement to transfer securities of a particular kind to B or B's nominee if—

(*a*) B is a member of a multilateral trading facility, or a recognised foreign exchange, on which securities of that kind are regularly traded;

(*b*) B is an intermediary and is recognised as such by the facility or exchange in accordance with arrangements approved by the Commissioners; and

(*c*) the agreement is effected on the facility or exchange.

(1B) Section 87 above shall not apply as regards an agreement to transfer securities of a particular kind to B or B's nominee if—

(*a*) B is an intermediary who is approved for the purposes of this section by the Commissioners; and

(*b*) securities of that kind are regularly traded on a regulated market.

(1C) Section 87 above shall not apply as regards an agreement to transfer securities of a particular kind to B or B's nominee if—

(*a*) B is an intermediary who is approved for the purposes of this section by the Commissioners;

(*b*) securities of that kind are regularly traded on a multilateral trading facility or a recognised foreign exchange; and

(*c*) the agreement is effected on the facility or exchange.

(2) Section 87 above shall not apply as regards an agreement to transfer securities of a particular kind to B or B's nominee if—

(*a*) B is a member of a regulated market, a multilateral trading facility or a recognised foreign options exchange;

(*b*) options to buy or sell securities of that kind are regularly traded on, and are listed by or quoted on, that market, facility or exchange;

(*c*) B is an options intermediary and is recognised as such by that market, facility or exchange in accordance with arrangements approved by the Commissioners; and

(*d*) securities of that kind are regularly traded on a regulated market.

(2A) Section 87 above shall not apply as regards an agreement to transfer securities of a particular kind to B or B's nominee if—

(*a*) B is a member of a regulated market, a multilateral trading facility or a recognised foreign options exchange;

(*b*) options to buy or sell securities of that kind are regularly traded on, and are listed by or quoted on, that market, facility or exchange;

(*c*) B is an options intermediary and is recognised as such by that market, facility or exchange in accordance with arrangements approved by the Commissioners; and

(*d*) the agreement is effected on a relevant qualifying exchange on which securities of that kind are regularly traded or is effected on a relevant qualifying exchange pursuant to the exercise of a relevant option and options to buy or sell securities of that kind are regularly traded on, and are listed by or quoted on, that exchange;

and in paragraph (*d*) "relevant qualifying exchange" means a multilateral trading facility, a recognised foreign options exchange or a recognised foreign exchange.

(2B) Section 87 above shall not apply as regards an agreement to transfer securities of a particular kind to B or B's nominee if—

(*a*) B is an options intermediary who is approved for the purposes of this section by the Commissioners;

(*b*) options to buy or sell securities of that kind are regularly traded on, and are listed by or quoted on, a regulated market, a multilateral trading facility or a recognised foreign options exchange; and

(*c*) securities of that kind are regularly traded on a regulated market.

(2C) Section 87 above shall not apply as regards an agreement to transfer securities of a particular kind to B or B's nominee if—

(*a*) B is an options intermediary who is approved for the purposes of this section by the Commissioners;

(*b*) options to buy or sell securities of that kind are regularly traded on, and are listed by or quoted on, a regulated market, a multilateral trading facility or a recognised foreign options exchange; and

(*c*) the agreement is effected on a relevant qualifying exchange on which securities of that kind are regularly traded or is effected on a relevant qualifying exchange pursuant to the exercise of a relevant option and options to buy or sell securities of that kind are regularly traded on, and are listed by or quoted on, that exchange;

and in paragraph (*c*) "relevant qualifying exchange" means a multilateral trading facility, a recognised foreign options exchange or a recognised foreign exchange."

(3) In subsection (6) (meaning of sale being on an exchange)—

(*a*) after "effected on" insert "a facility or",

(*b*) for "subsection (1) or (2) above" substitute "this section", and

(*c*) for "the exchange" (in each place) substitute "the facility or exchange".

(4) After that subsection insert—

"(6A) The Commissioners may approve a person for the purposes of this section only if the person is authorised under the law of an EEA State to provide any of the investment services or activities listed in Section A 2 or 3 of Annex I to the Directive (execution of orders on behalf of clients and dealing on own account), whether or not the person is authorised under the Directive."

(5) The amendments made by this paragraph have effect in relation to any agreement to transfer securities—

(*a*) in a case where the agreement is conditional, if the condition is satisfied on or after 1st November 2007, and

(*b*) in any other case, if the agreement is made on or after that date.

PROSPECTIVE AMENDMENT

This Schedule to be repealed by FA 2007 s 114, Sch 27 Pt 4(2) with effect in accordance with the provisions of FA 1990 ss 108, 110.

4— (1) Section 88B of FA 1986 (exemption from SDRT on sales to intermediaries: supplementary) is amended as follows.

(2) In subsection (2)—

(*a*) after the definition of "collective investment scheme" insert—

""the Directive" means Directive 2004/39/EC of the European Parliament and of the Council of 21 April 2004 on markets in financial instruments, as amended from time to time;",

(*b*) omit the definition of "EEA exchange", and

(*c*) in the definition of "EEA State", for "means a State which" substitute ", in relation to any time, means a State which at that time is a member State or any other State which at that time" and insert at the end "(as modified or supplemented from time to time)".

(3) After that subsection insert—

"(2A) Each of the following expressions—

"multilateral trading facility", and

"regulated market",

has the same meaning in section 88A above as it has for the purposes of the Directive."

(4) After subsection (3) insert—

"(3A) The Treasury may by regulations amend section 88A above and this section (as they have effect for the time being) in order to extend the exemption from tax under that section."

(5) In subsection (5) (power for regulations to provide for SDRT to be chargeable at a rate not exceeding 0.1%), for "subsection (1) or (2)" substitute "any of subsections (1) to (2C)".

(6) In subsection (7) (regulations exercisable by statutory instrument and subject to annulment), for "(4)" substitute "(3A)".

(7) The amendments made by this paragraph have effect in relation to any agreement to transfer securities—

(*a*) in a case where the agreement is conditional, if the condition is satisfied on or after 1st November 2007, and

(*b*) in any other case, if the agreement is made on or after that date.

PROSPECTIVE AMENDMENT

This Schedule to be repealed by FA 2007 s 114, Sch 27 Pt 4(2) with effect in accordance with the provisions of FA 1990 ss 108, 110.

Repurchases and stock lending

5— (1) Section 80C of FA 1986 (exemption from stamp duty: repurchases and stock lending) is amended as follows.

(2) In subsection (1) (application of section), after "conditions set out in subsection" insert "(2A) or".

(3) After subsection (2) insert—

"(2A) The conditions in this subsection are—

(*a*) that A or B is authorised under the law of an EEA State to provide any of the investment services or activities listed in Section A 2 or 3 of Annex I to the Directive (execution of orders on behalf of clients and dealing on own account) in relation to stock of the kind concerned, whether or not A or B is authorised under the Directive; and

(*b*) that stock of the kind concerned is regularly traded on a regulated market."

(4) In subsection (3) (conditions for exemption)—

(*a*) after "The conditions" insert "in this subsection",

(*b*) for "an EEA exchange" substitute "a regulated market, a multilateral trading facility", and

(*c*) after "on that" insert "market, facility or".

(5) In subsection (6) (meaning of arrangement being on an exchange)—

(*a*) after "effected on" insert "a market, a facility or", and

(*b*) for "the exchange" (in each place) substitute "the market, facility or exchange".

(6) In subsection (7)—

(*a*) after "In this section—" insert—

""the Directive" has the meaning given in section 80B(2) above;

"EEA State" has the meaning given in section 80B(2) above;", and

(*b*) omit the definition of "EEA exchange" (together with the "and" at the end of it).

(7) After that subsection insert—

"(7A) Each of the following expressions—

"multilateral trading facility", and

"regulated market",

has the same meaning in this section as it has for the purposes of the Directive."

(8) The amendments made by this paragraph have effect in relation to any instrument executed on or after 1st November 2007.

PROSPECTIVE AMENDMENT

This Schedule to be repealed by FA 2007 s 114, Sch 27 Pt 4(2) with effect in accordance with the provisions of FA 1990 ss 108, 110.

6— (1) Section 89AA of FA 1986 (exemption from SDRT: repurchases and stock lending) is amended as follows.

(2) In subsection (1) (application of section), after "conditions set out in subsection" insert "(2A) or".

(3) After subsection (2) insert—

"(2A) The conditions in this subsection are—

(*a*) that P or Q is authorised under the law of an EEA State to provide any of the investment services or activities listed in Section A 2 or 3 of Annex I to the Directive (execution of orders on behalf of clients and dealing on own account) in relation to securities of the kind concerned, whether or not P or Q is authorised under the Directive; and

(*b*) that securities of the kind concerned are regularly traded on a regulated market."

(4) In subsection (3) (conditions for exemption)—

(*a*) after "The conditions" insert "in this subsection",

(*b*) for "an EEA exchange" substitute "a regulated market, a multilateral trading facility", and

(*c*) after "on that" insert "market, facility or".

(5) In subsection (5) (meaning of arrangement being on an exchange)—

(*a*) after "effected on" insert "a market, a facility or", and

(*b*) for "the exchange" (in each place) substitute "the market, facility or exchange".

(6) In subsection (6)—

(*a*) after "In this section—" insert—

""the Directive" has the meaning given in section 88B(2) above;

"EEA State" has the meaning given in section 88B(2) above;", and

(*b*) omit the definition of "EEA exchange".

(7) After that subsection insert—

"(6A) Each of the following expressions—

"multilateral trading facility", and

"regulated market",

has the same meaning in this section as it has for the purposes of the Directive."

(8) The amendments made by this paragraph have effect in relation to any agreement to transfer securities—

(*a*) in a case where the agreement is conditional, if the condition is satisfied on or after 1st November 2007, and

(*b*) in any other case, if the agreement is made on or after that date.

PROSPECTIVE AMENDMENT

This Schedule to be repealed by FA 2007 s 114, Sch 27 Pt 4(2) with effect in accordance with the provisions of FA 1990 ss 108, 110.

Exemptions from stamp duty and SDRT in cases involving recognised investment exchanges

7— (1) In section 116 of FA 1991 (stamp duty: investment exchanges and clearing houses), subsection (4) is amended as follows.

(2) After "In this section—" insert—

"(*aa*) "the Directive" means Directive 2004/39/EC of the European Parliament and of the Council of 21 April 2004 on markets in financial instruments, as amended from time to time,".

(3) In paragraph (*b*) (definition of "recognised investment exchange"), after "2000" insert ", a regulated market within the meaning of the Directive or a multilateral trading facility within the meaning of the Directive".

PROSPECTIVE AMENDMENT

This Schedule to be repealed by FA 2007 s 114, Sch 27 Pt 4(2) with effect in accordance with the provisions of FA 1990 ss 108, 110.

Consequential repeal

8— (1) In F(No 2)A 2005, omit section 50 (power to extend stamp duty and SDRT exemptions to recognised exchanges).

(2) This paragraph comes into force on 1st November 2007.

PROSPECTIVE AMENDMENT

This Schedule to be repealed by FA 2007 s 114, Sch 27 Pt 4(2) with effect in accordance with the provisions of FA 1990 ss 108, 110.

GENERAL NOTE

Intermediaries

Para 1(2) introduces new s 80A(l) requiring the purchaser, if he or his nominee is to obtain the relief from stamp duty on a transfer, now to be a member of a regulated market (defined by cross-reference to MiFID: see s 80B(2A), inserted by para 2(3) of Sch 21); and to be recognised as an intermediary. Para 3(2) provides for a similar relief from SDRT in respective of otherwise chargeable agreements to transfer chargeable securities in substituted s 88A(1).

New subsection 80A(1A) introduces a similar stamp duty relief where the transferee (whether the transfer is to him or his nominee) is a member of a multilateral trading facility (or MTF, again defined by cross-reference to MiFID) or recognised foreign exchange (or RFE); the stock of that kind is regularly traded on it; the person to be an intermediary; and the sale is effected "on exchange". New FA 1986 ss 88A(1A) contains the equivalent SDRT relief.

New sub-section 80A(1B) provides for relief where the intermediary, if the transfer is to him or to his nominee, is approved by HMRC; and stock of the kind in question in respect of which relief is sought is regularly traded on the regulated market . New s 88A(1B) provides for equivalent SDRT relief.

New sub-section 80A(1C) provides for relief where the transfer is made to a person or his nominee if that person is approved as an intermediary by HMRC; stock of the kind is question is regularly traded on the MTF or RFE ;and effected " on exchange". A similar relief from SDRT is provided in new s 88A(1C).

Option Transactions

Para 1(2) introduces similar reliefs for options intermediaries either who are members of a regulated market, MTF or recognised foreign options exchange (or RFOE) or approved either by HMRC or the market etc; options of the kind in question or stock (to which the option relates) are regularly traded and listed or quoted on the market etc; and the relevant persons are recognised as intermediaries: see the specific requirements of new s 80A(2)–(2C). The equivalent SDRT reliefs contained in new s 88A(2)–(2C) are introduced by para 3(2).

Miscellaneous

Paras 1(3) and (5) and 2(2)–(3) make consequential amendments for stamp duty and paras 3(3) and (5) and 4(2)–(3) are their SDRT equivalent; paras 1(4) (stamp duty) and 3(4) (SDRT) limit the persons that HMRC can approve to those authorised in accordance with MiFID under the law of the relevant Member State; and paras 2(4) and 4(4) confer powers on HM Treasury to amend ss 80A, 80B, 88A and 88B.

Repos and stock-lending

Para 5 (3) of Sch 21 inserts extra conditions for stamp duty relief (in s 80C) relating to authorisation and para 6(3) inserts the equivalent extra conditions for SDRT (and paras 5(2) and 6(2) make necessary consequential amendments). Paras 5(4)–(7) (stamp duty) and 6(4)–(7) introduce consequential extra definitions for the two taxes.

COMMENCEMENT

The stamp duty amendments apply to any instrument executed on or after 1 November 2007 and the SDRT changes to any agreement entered into after 31 October or, if a conditional agreement, that became unconditional on or after 1 November: see paras 1(5) and 2(6) (stamp duty) and 3(5) and 4(7) (SDRT).

Recognised Investment Exchanges

FA 1991 s 116 contains regulation making powers by which HM Treasury can exempt certain transactions from stamp duty, and para 7 merely contains MiFID related definitions. Paragraph 8 repeals F(No2)A 2005 s 50 which contained powers to amend ss 80A and 80C, and s 88A and 89AA, in relation to MiFID as a result of the changes made (including regulation making powers) by paras 1–6. In both cases the changes are with effect from 1 November 2007.

SCHEDULE 22

AMENDMENTS AND REPEALS CONSEQUENTIAL ON EXTENSION OF HMRC POWERS

Section 84

GENERAL NOTE

This Schedule makes various amendments and repeals to provisions concerning HMRC's powers in connection with search warrants and arrests, consequent on the extension of powers introduced by ss 82–83.

They will come into force on a date to be appointed by Treasury Order. Budget Note BN78 indicates that this is likely to be before the end of 2007.

PART 1

AMENDMENTS

1 In section 20D(1) of TMA 1970, for "sections 20A, 20BA and 20C" substitute "sections 20A and 20BA".

2 In section 67 of the Criminal Justice and Police Act 2001 (c 16) and the heading of that section, for "customs officers" substitute "officers of Revenue and Customs".

GENERAL NOTE

Paragraphs 1 and 2 make consequential amendments to ensure that the wording of TMA 1970 s 20D(1) and the Criminal Justice and Police Act 2001 s 67 is consistent with the new rules.

PART 2

REPEALS

3 The provisions listed below are omitted.

4 In TMA 1970—

(*a*) sections 20C and 20CC (search warrants), and
(*b*) in the definition of "tax" in section 118 the word ", 20C".

5 In CEMA 1979—

(*a*) section 118C(3)(*c*) (gaming duty), and
(*b*) the references to "a gaming duty offence" in section 118C(4)(*b*) and (5).

6 In BGDA 1981—

(*a*) paragraph 16 of Schedule 1 (general betting duty: search warrants),
(*b*) paragraph 17 of Schedule 3 (bingo duty: search warrants), and
(*c*) paragraph 17 of Schedule 4 (amusement machine licence duty: search warrants).

7 Section 148(4) of FA 1989 (definition of "business" for purposes of section 20C of TMA 1970).

8 In VATA 1994—

(*a*) section 72(9) (powers of arrest), and
(*b*) paragraph 10(3) to (6) of Schedule 11 (search warrants).

9 In Schedule 7 to FA 1994 (insurance premium tax)—

(*a*) paragraph 4(2) to (5) (search warrants), and
(*b*) paragraph 4(6) and (7) (power of arrest).

10 In Schedule 5 to FA 1996 (landfill tax)—

(*a*) paragraph 5 (search warrants), and
(*b*) paragraph 6 (power of arrest).

11 In Schedule 6 to FA 2000 (climate change levy)—

(*a*) paragraph 97 (power of arrest), and
(*b*) paragraph 130 (search warrants).

12 In FA 2001 (aggregates levy)—

(*a*) paragraph 6 of Schedule 6 (power of arrest), and
(*b*) paragraph 7 of Schedule 7 (search warrants).

13— (1) In the Criminal Justice and Police Act 2001—

(*a*) section 57(1)(*c*) (section 20CC of TMA 1970),
(*b*) section 63(2)(*e*) (section 20C of TMA 1970), and
(*c*) section 65(3) (section 20C of TMA 1970).

(2) In Schedule 1 to that Act—

(*a*) paragraph 13 (section 20C of TMA 1970),
(*b*) paragraph 28 (paragraph 17(2) of Schedule 3 to BGDA 1981),
(*c*) paragraph 29 (paragraph 17(2) of Schedule 4 to BDGA 1981),
(*d*) paragraph 57 (paragraph 4(3) of Schedule 7 to FA 1994),
(*e*) paragraph 58 (paragraph 10(3) of Schedule 11 to VATA 1994),
(*f*) paragraph 61 (paragraph 5(2) of Schedule 5 to FA 1996), and
(*g*) paragraph 72 (paragraph 130(2) of Schedule 6 to FA 2000).

14 Section 36(2) and (3) of the Tax Credits Act 2002 (c 21) (search warrants).

15 Section 323(3)(*e*) and (*f*) of the Proceeds of Crime Act 2002 (c 29) (approval of applications under section 20C of TMA 1970).

16 Part 7 of Schedule 13 to FA 2003 (stamp duty land tax: search warrants).

17 In CRCA 2005—

(*a*) section 13(3)(*b*) and (*c*) (Commissioners' functions not delegable to officers), and
(*b*) section 14(2)(*b*) and (*c*) (non-delegable functions of Commissioners).

GENERAL NOTE

Paragraphs 3–17 list the provisions which cease to have effect. These contain powers that are being superseded so are no longer required, or references to powers that are being repealed.

SCHEDULE 23

EXTENSION OF HMRC POWERS: SCOTLAND

Section 85

GENERAL NOTE

HMRC inherited different criminal investigation powers in respect of former Revenue and Customs responsibilities. Those powers were initially ring-fenced by CRCA 2005 so that they could only be used for their original purposes, and a review was announced of HMRC's powers, deterrents and safeguards, to include the alignment and modernisation of their criminal investigation powers.

One of the principles established during the subsequent consultation was that a single code of investigatory powers should apply consistently throughout the UK, within the separate jurisdictions, to remove the current inconsistency of powers in a criminal investigation which involves more than one country in the UK.

For England and Wales, the existing powers are those in PACE 1984, with parallel legislation applying in Northern Ireland. PACE does not apply in Scotland, and it was suggested during consultation that provisions should be developed which were appropriate to the Scottish legal system and which broadly corresponded to the provisions of PACE.

Schedule 23 introduces new and consistent criminal investigation powers and accompanying safeguards for HMRC to use in Scotland. These provisions, together with ss 82–84, harmonise HMRC's powers across England, Wales, Northern Ireland and Scotland.

Paragraphs 1–3 detail the new powers, introducing new ss 23A–23P into the Criminal Law (Consolidation) (Scotland) Act 1995, whilst paras 4–7 make further amendments to that Act.

Paragraphs 8–13 make amendments to the Criminal Procedure (Scotland) Act 1995 and the Criminal Justice and Police Act 2001 to ensure that existing powers and safeguards apply more consistently to investigations under Scottish law.

The amendments will come into force on a date to be appointed by Treasury Order. Budget Note BN78 indicates that this is likely to be before the end of 2007.

Criminal Law (*Consolidation*) (*Scotland*) *Act 1995* (*c 39*)

1 Part 3 of the Criminal Law (Consolidation) (Scotland) Act 1995 is amended as follows.

GENERAL NOTE

This paragraph introduces the Schedule.

2 The heading to that Part becomes "INVESTIGATION OF REVENUE AND CUSTOMS OFFENCES".

GENERAL NOTE

This paragraph amends the heading of the target legislation (the Criminal Law (Consolidation) (Scotland) Act 1995 Part 3).

3 At the beginning of that Part insert—

"Investigation of offences by HMRC

23A Investigation of offences by Her Majesty's Revenue and Customs

(1) This Part of this Act applies to the investigation of Revenue and Customs offences.

(2) Subject to subsection (3) below, in this Part of this Act, a "Revenue and Customs offence" is an offence which relates to a matter in relation to which Her Majesty's Revenue and Customs have functions other than any matter specified in—

(*a*) section 54(4)(*b*) or (*f*) of; or

(*b*) paragraphs 3, 7, 10, 13 to 15, 19 or 24 to 29 of Schedule 1 to,

the Commissioners for Revenue and Customs Act 2005 (former Inland Revenue matters).

(3) In sections 23B to 23P and 26A of this Act, any reference to a "Revenue and Customs offence" shall be construed as if, in subsection (2) above, there were added at the end the words "and other than any matter relating to the movement of goods which is subject to any prohibition or restriction for the time being in force under or by virtue of any enactment".

Production orders

23B Production orders

(1) The sheriff may, if satisfied on information on oath given by an authorised officer as to the matters mentioned in subsection (2) below, make an order under subsection (3) below (in this Part, a "production order").

(2) Those matters are—

(*a*) that there are reasonable grounds to suspect that a Revenue and Customs offence has been or is being committed; and

(*b*) that a person (in this Part, a "haver") specified by the officer has possession or control of a document which may be required as evidence for the purposes of any proceedings in respect of such an offence.

(3) A production order is an order requiring the haver, before the expiry of the period specified in the order—

(*a*) to deliver the document to an officer; or

(*b*) to—

(i) give an officer access to the document; and

(ii) permit the officer to make copies of or remove the document.

(4) The period specified in a production order is—

(*a*) the period of 10 working days beginning with the day on which the order is made; or

(*b*) such other period as the sheriff considers appropriate.

(5) A sheriff may make a production order in relation to a haver residing or having a place of business in an area of Scotland notwithstanding that it is outside the area of that sheriff and any such order shall, without being backed or endorsed by another sheriff, have effect throughout Scotland.

(6) Subject to section 23J of this Act, a production order has effect in spite of any restriction on disclosure of information (however imposed).

(7) Without prejudice to section 23D(1) of this Act, failure by a person to comply with a production order may be dealt with as a contempt of court.

(8) In subsection (4)(*a*) above, "working day" means any day other than—

(*a*) a Saturday;

(*b*) a Sunday; or

(*c*) any day which is a public holiday in the area in which the production order is to have effect.

23C Production orders: supplementary

(1) The sheriff may deal with an application for a production order ex parte in chambers.

(2) The sheriff may, on the application of a person mentioned in subsection (3) below—

(*a*) vary; or

(*b*) discharge,

a production order.

(3) The persons referred to in subsection (2) above are—

(*a*) the authorised officer who applied for the production order;

(*b*) a person affected by the order.

(4) Without prejudice to section 305 of the Criminal Procedure (Scotland) Act 1995, rules of court made by Act of Adjournal may make provision in relation to—

(*a*) proceedings relating to the making of production orders; and

(*b*) the variation or discharge of such orders.

23D Offences in relation to production orders

(1) A person who intentionally—

(*a*) falsifies;

(*b*) conceals;

(*c*) destroys or otherwise disposes of,

a document to which this section applies, or who causes or permits any of those acts, commits an offence.

(2) This section applies to a document which the person is required, under a production order, to—

(*a*) deliver to an officer; or

(*b*) give an officer access to.

(3) A person does not commit an offence if the person acts—

(*a*) with the written permission of—

(i) an officer; or

(ii) the sheriff who made the order,

after the document has been delivered or the officer has had access to it;

(*b*) subject to subsection (4) below, after the expiry of the period of 2 years beginning with the day on which the order is made.

(4) Subsection (3)(*b*) above does not apply where, before the expiry of the period referred to in that paragraph, an officer gives notice in writing to the person that the order has not been complied with to that officer's satisfaction.

(5) A person who commits an offence under subsection (1) above is liable—

(*a*) on summary conviction, to imprisonment for a period not exceeding 12 months or to a fine not exceeding the statutory maximum or to both;

(*b*) on conviction on indictment, to imprisonment for a period not exceeding 2 years or to a fine or both.

Revenue and Customs warrants

23E Revenue and Customs warrants

(1) The sheriff may, if satisfied on information on oath given by an authorised officer as to the matters mentioned in subsection (2) below, grant a warrant under subsection (3) below (in this Part, a "Revenue and Customs warrant").

(2) Those matters are—

(*a*) that there are reasonable grounds to suspect that a Revenue and Customs offence has been or is being committed; and

(*b*) that evidence of that offence is to be found in or on premises specified in the information.

(3) A Revenue and Customs warrant is a warrant authorising an officer to—

(*a*) enter, if necessary by force, the premises specified in the information; and

(*b*) search those premises,

before the expiry of the period of one month beginning with the day on which the warrant is granted.

(4) The sheriff may, when granting a warrant, impose such conditions as the sheriff considers appropriate.

(5) An officer who enters premises under the authority of a Revenue and Customs warrant may—

(*a*) subject to any condition imposed under subsection (4) above, take with the officer such other persons (including persons who are not officers) as appear to that officer to be necessary;

(*b*) subject to subsection (6) below, seize and remove any document or other thing found in or on the premises which the officer has reasonable cause to believe may be required as evidence for the purposes of proceedings in respect of the offence mentioned in subsection (2)(*a*) above; and

(*c*) subject to subsections (6) and (7) below—

(i) search or cause to be searched any person found in or on the premises whom the officer has reasonable cause to believe may be in possession of any such document or thing; and

(ii) seize and remove any such document or thing found.

(6) An officer acting under the authority of a Revenue and Customs warrant may, if the officer considers it appropriate, makes copies of any document or thing found in or on the premises or on any person searched under subsection (5)(*c*) above.

(7) No person may be searched under subsection (5)(*c*) above except by a person of the same sex.

(8) A sheriff may grant a Revenue and Customs warrant in relation to premises situated in an area of Scotland notwithstanding that it is outside the area of that sheriff and any such warrant may, without being backed or endorsed by another sheriff, be executed throughout Scotland in the same way as it may be executed within the sheriffdom of the sheriff who granted it.

(9) In this section and in sections 23F to 23H of this Act, "premises" includes any place and, in particular—

(*a*) any vehicle, vessel, aircraft or hovercraft;

(*b*) any offshore installation (within the meaning of section 12(1) of the Mineral Workings (Offshore Installations) Act 1971); and

(*c*) any tent or other movable structure.

Orders and warrants: common provisions

23F Procedure where documents etc removed

(1) This section applies where—

(*a*) a document is removed under a production order;

(*b*) a document or other thing is removed under a Revenue and Customs warrant.

(2) An officer who removes any document or thing shall, if requested to do so by a person mentioned in subsection (3) below, provide that person with a record of what that officer removed.

(3) The persons referred to in subsection (2) above are—

(*a*) in the case of a document removed under a production order, a haver;

(*b*) in the case of a document or thing removed under a Revenue and Customs warrant—

(i) a person who is the occupier of any premises from which the document or thing was removed; or

(ii) a person who had possession or control of the document or thing before it was removed.

(4) The officer must provide the record within a reasonable time of the request for it.

23G Access to and copies of documents etc removed

(1) This section applies where—

(*a*) a document is removed under a production order;

(*b*) a document or other thing is removed under a Revenue and Customs warrant.

(2) A person mentioned in subsection (3) below may apply to the officer in overall charge of the investigation to which the order or warrant relates—

(*a*) for access to the document or thing; or

(*b*) for a copy or photograph of it.

(3) The persons referred to in subsection (2) above are—

(*a*) in the case of a document removed under a production order—

(i) a haver; or

(ii) a person acting on behalf of the haver;

(*b*) in the case of a document or thing removed under a Revenue and Customs warrant, a person who had possession or control of the document or thing before it was removed.

(4) Unless subsection (5) below applies, the officer in overall charge of the investigation shall—

(*a*) in a case to which subsection (2)(*a*) above applies, allow the applicant supervised access to the document or thing; or

(*b*) in a case to which subsection (2)(*b*) above applies—

(i) allow the applicant supervised access to the document or thing for the purposes of photographing or copying it; or

(ii) photograph or copy the document or thing (or cause it to be so photographed or copied) and provide the applicant with such a photograph or copy within a reasonable time.

(5) The officer in overall charge need not comply with subsection (4) above where that officer has reasonable grounds for believing that to do so would prejudice—

(*a*) the investigation;

(*b*) the investigation of a Revenue and Customs offence other than the offence for the purposes of the investigation of which the document or thing was removed; or

(*c*) any criminal proceedings which may be brought as a result of any investigation mentioned in paragraph (*a*) or (*b*) above.

(6) In subsection (4) above, "supervised access" means access under the supervision of an officer approved by the officer in overall charge of the investigation.

23H Failure to comply with requirements of section 23F and 23G

(1) This section applies where—

(*a*) a document is removed under a production order;

(*b*) a document or other thing is removed under a Revenue and Customs warrant.

(2) Subject to subsection (3) below, a person who claims that—

(*a*) an officer has failed to comply with the requirements of section 23F(2) or (3) of this Act; or

(*b*) an officer in overall charge of an investigation has failed to comply with the requirements of section 23G(4) of this Act,

may apply to the sheriff for an order under subsection (4) below.

(3) An application under subsection (2) above—

(*a*) relating to a failure mentioned in subsection (2)(*a*) above, may be made only by a person who is entitled to make a request under section 23F(2) of this Act;

(*b*) relating to a failure mentioned in subsection (2)(*b*) above, may be made only by—

(i) a haver;

(ii) a person acting on behalf of a haver but only where that person applied under section 23G(2) of this Act;

(iii) a person who had possession or control of the document or thing before it was removed under a Revenue and Customs warrant.

(4) The sheriff may, if satisfied that—

(*a*) the officer has failed to comply with the requirements of section 23F(2) or (3) of this Act; or

(*b*) the officer in overall charge of the investigation has failed to comply with the requirements of section 23G(4) of this Act,

order the officer or, as the case may be, the officer in overall charge of the investigation to comply with the requirements within such time and in such manner as the sheriff specifies in the order.

23J Confidentiality

(1) Neither a production order nor a Revenue and Customs warrant authorises the seizure, removal or copying of any documents or other things subject to legal privilege.

(2) Subsection (1) above does not apply where the document or thing is held for the purposes of furthering a criminal purpose.

(3) In this section—

"documents or other things subject to legal privilege" means—

(*a*) communications between a professional legal adviser and the adviser's client; or

(*b*) communications made in connection with or in contemplation of legal proceedings and for the purposes of those proceedings,

which would, in legal proceedings, be protected from disclosure by virtue of any rule of law relating to confidentiality of communications.

23K Meaning of "document" etc

(1) In sections 23B to 23J of this Act, references to a "document" include—

(*a*) any thing in which information of any description is recorded; and

(*b*) any part of such a thing.

(2) Where a production order or a Revenue and Customs warrant applies to a document in electronic or magnetic form, the order or, as the case may be, the warrant requires the person having possession or control of the document to deliver or, as the case may be, give access to the information in a form which is visible and legible and, if the officer executing the order or warrant wishes to remove it, in a form which can be removed.

Execution and enforcement of orders and warrants outwith Scotland

23L Cross-border exercise of powers

(1) Section 4 of the Summary Jurisdiction Act 1881 (execution of process of Scottish courts in England and Wales) shall apply to—

(*a*) a production order; and

(*b*) a Revenue and Customs warrant,

as it applies to a process mentioned in that section.

(2) Section 29 of the Petty Sessions (Ireland) Act 1851 (execution of warrants in Northern Ireland) shall apply to—

(*a*) a production order; and

(*b*) a Revenue and Customs warrant,

as it applies to a warrant mentioned in that section.

Detention and questioning of suspects and witnesses

23M Powers relating to suspects and potential witnesses

(1) Where an authorised officer has reasonable grounds for suspecting that a person has committed or is committing, at any place, a Revenue and Customs offence, the officer may require—

(*a*) that person, if found by the officer at that place or at any place where the officer is entitled to be, to give—

(i) the information mentioned in subsection (2) below; and

(ii) an explanation of the circumstances which have given rise to the officer's suspicion;

(*b*) any other person whom the officer finds at that place or at any place where the officer is entitled to be and who the officer believes has information relating to the offence, to give the information mentioned in subsection (2) below.

(2) That information is—

(*a*) the person's name;
(*b*) the person's address;
(*c*) the person's date of birth;
(*d*) the person's place of birth (in such detail as the officer considers necessary or expedient for the purpose of establishing that person's identity); and
(*e*) the person's nationality.

(3) The officer may require the person mentioned in paragraph (*a*) of subsection (1) above to remain with the officer while the officer (any or all)—

(*a*) subject to subsection (4) below, verifies any information mentioned in subsection (2) above given by the person;
(*b*) subject to section (5) below, establishes whether the person may be a person suspected of having committed a Revenue and Customs offence other than the offence in relation to which the officer made the requirement of that person under paragraph (*a*) of subsection (1) above;
(*c*) notes any explanation proffered by the person.

(4) The officer shall exercise the power under paragraph (*a*) of subsection (3) above only where it appears to the officer that such verification can be obtained quickly.

(5) The officer shall exercise the power under paragraph (*b*) of subsection (3) above only where—

(*a*) the person mentioned in paragraph (*a*) of subsection (1) above has given a name and address; and
(*b*) it appears to the officer that establishing the matter mentioned in paragraph (*b*) of subsection (3) above can be achieved quickly.

(6) The officer may use reasonable force to ensure that the person mentioned in paragraph (*a*) of subsection (1) above remains with that officer.

(7) The officer shall inform a person, when making a requirement of that person under—

(*a*) paragraph (*a*) of subsection (1) above, of the officer's suspicion and of the general nature of the offence which the officer suspects that the person has committed or is committing;
(*b*) paragraph (*b*) of subsection (1) above, of the officer's suspicion, of the general nature of the offence which the officer suspects has been or is being committed and that the reason for the requirement is that the officer believes the person has information relating to the offence;
(*c*) subsection (3) above, why the person is being required to remain with the officer;
(*d*) any of the said subsections, that failure to comply with the requirement may constitute an offence.

23N Fingerprinting of persons suspected of offences

(1) An authorised officer may, if the person mentioned in section 23M(1)(*a*) of this Act gives a name and address, require that person to provide—

(*a*) that person's fingerprints; or
(*b*) a record, created by an approved device, of the skin on that person's fingers.

(2) Such fingerprints or record may be used only for the purposes of—

(*a*) verifying the name and address given by the person;
(*b*) establishing whether the person may be a person who is suspected of having committed any other Revenue and Customs offence,

and all record of such fingerprints or record shall be destroyed as soon as possible after they have fulfilled those purposes.

(3) The officer shall inform a person, when making a requirement of that person under subsection (1) above—

(*a*) of the existence of the power to make the requirement and why the officer proposes to exercise it in the person's case; and
(*b*) that failure to comply with the requirement may constitute an offence.

(4) In subsection (1)(*b*) above, an "approved device" is any device approved by the Scottish Ministers under section 13(8) of the Criminal Procedure (Scotland) Act 1995.

23P Offences arising from breach of requirements under sections 23M and23N

(1) A person mentioned in paragraph (*a*) of subsection (1) of section 23M of this Act who, having been required—

(*a*) under that subsection to give the information mentioned in subsection (2) of that section;

(*b*) under subsection (3) of that section to remain with an officer; or

(*c*) under subsection (1) of section 23N of this Act to provide that person's fingerprints or a record such as is mentioned in paragraph (*b*) of that subsection,

fails, without reasonable excuse, to do so, shall be guilty of an offence and liable on summary conviction to a fine not exceeding level 3 on the standard scale.

(2) A person mentioned in paragraph (*b*) of subsection (1) of section 23M of this Act who, having been required under that subsection to give the information mentioned in subsection (2) of that section, fails, without reasonable excuse, to do so, shall be guilty of an offence and liable on summary conviction to a fine not exceeding level 2 on the standard scale.

(3) An authorised officer may arrest without warrant any person whom the officer has reasonable grounds for suspecting has committed an offence under subsection (1) or (2) above."

GENERAL NOTE

Paragraph 3 is important, introducing HMRC's new powers in Scotland. These are to be contained primarily in new Criminal Law (Consolidation) (Scotland) Act 1995 (referred to below as CLCSA) ss 23A–23P.

CLCSA 1995 s 23A

This section details the investigations to which the new powers will apply. A number of specific areas (mainly ex-Revenue matters which have their origins in social security law) fall outside the provisions.

CLCSA 1995 s 23B

This section introduces a new power which will allow a sheriff in Scotland to issue a production order requiring the recipient to make available to HMRC such documents as may be required as evidence in proceedings relating to an HMRC offence. The time allowed for compliance is specified.

CLCSA 1995 s 23C

This section deals with applications for production orders, their variation or discharge. In particular provision is made for the application for an order to be heard *inter partes*. An application for an order may only be made by an officer authorised by the HMRC Commissioners.

CLCSA 1995 s 23D

This section provides sanctions similar to those in certain existing production order powers, e.g. TMA 1970 s 20BB, in that a person who intentionally falsifies, conceals or disposes of a document which is the subject of a production order may commit an offence. The section also sets out the sanctions for committing such an offence.

CLCSA 1995 s 23F

New s 23F introduces a new power for a sheriff in Scotland, where certain conditions are satisfied, to grant a warrant to an authorised HMRC officer to enter and search premises, and details the procedures the officer should follow when entering premises under the authority of a warrant.

These provisions are broadly similar to those which already apply to HMRC. The new power will replace existing legislation, which will be repealed.

CLCSA 1995 s 23G

This section deals with procedural matters relating to compliance with requests for access to, and the removal of documents (or copies) and is based on similar existing provisions eg VATA Sch 11 para 12.

CLCSA 1995 s 23H

This follows on from ss 23F and 23G and sets out the redress procedure where a recipient of a production order claims that an HMRC officer has failed to comply with the requirements of ss 23F–G in relation to either access to documents (or copies thereof) or the removal of documents.

CLCSA 1995 s 23J

This section provides a specific exclusion from the scope of production orders and HMRC warrants for material subject to legal and professional privilege (referred to in Scotland as the law relating to 'confidentiality of communications').

CLCSA 1995 s 23K

This section defines 'document' for the purposes of ss 23B–23J and sets out the position where the production order applies to a document in electronic form.

CLCSA 1995 s 23L

HMRC currently do not have consistent powers where a criminal investigation involves more than one UK country. This section ensures that a production order or HMRC warrant granted in one country may be executed in other parts of the UK. The consultative document *Criminal Investigation Powers: Publication of Draft Clauses and Explanatory Notes* gives the example of where the suspect is to be apprehended in England for a suspected crime committed in Scotland.

CLCSA 1995 s 23M

Powers have recently been given to the police in Scotland to help with the identification of suspects and witnesses (Criminal Procedure (Scotland) Act s 13 as amended by the Police Public Order and Criminal Justice (Scotland) Act 2006 ss 81, 82). Sections 23M–23P extend similar powers to HMRC. The consultative document *Criminal Investigation Powers: Publication of Draft Clauses and Explanatory Notes*, at para 5.11, comments that

> 'these proposals for Scotland were not seen as controversial by those who commented on Scottish matters'

This section details the information that an HMRC officer is allowed to obtain and is entitled to require in connection with a suspected HMRC offence. This power may be used not only where a person is suspected of committing an offence, but also where the officer believes a person has information relating to the offence (ie witnesses). The officer may require specified details of the person's identity and, in the case of a suspected person, detain that person whilst the identity details are verified. Failure to comply may be an offence (see s 23P).

CLCSA 1995 s 23N

In addition to the power of questioning and detention introduced by s 23M is a new power to require a person suspected of an HMRC offence to provide fingerprints in certain circumstances. The prints may be used only to verify the person's name and address, or to establish whether he or she may be a suspect, and all records of the prints must be destroyed as soon as possible once used for those purposes. Once again, failure to comply may constitute an offence.

CLCSA 1995 s 23P

This section sets out the offences and sanctions where a person fails, without reasonable excuse, to comply with the requirements of ss 23M–N and gives authorised officers the power to arrest a person suspected of committing such an offence.

4 In section 24 (detention and questioning by customs officers)—

(*a*) in subsection (1)—

(i) for "an offence punishable by imprisonment relating to an assigned matter" substitute "a Revenue and Customs offence punishable by imprisonment",

(ii) for "a customs office" substitute "an office of Revenue and Customs", and

(iii) for "customs office", in the second place, substitute "office of Revenue and Customs",

(*b*) in subsection (5), for "customs office" (in both places) substitute "office of Revenue and Customs",

(*c*) in subsection (8)—

(i) for "his name and address" substitute "the information mentioned in subsection (8A) below", and

(ii) for "customs office" substitute "office of Revenue and Customs",

(*d*) after that subsection insert—

"(8A) That information is—

(*a*) the person's name;

(*b*) the person's address;

(*c*) the person's date of birth;

(*d*) the person's place of birth (in such detail as the officer considers necessary or expedient for the purpose of establishing that person's identity); and

(*e*) the person's nationality.",

(*e*) omit subsection (9), and

(*f*) the heading accordingly becomes "**Detention and questioning at office of Revenue and Customs**".

GENERAL NOTE

The Criminal Law (Consolidation) (Scotland) Act 1995 s 24 currently deals with the power of questioning and detention by Customs officers. This paragraph extends those provisions to apply to HMRC and amends the information that a person detained can be required to give, in line with new s 23M and recent changes to police powers in Scotland (see para 3 above).

5 In section 25(1) (right to have someone informed of the fact of detention)—

(*a*) for "a customs office" substitute "an office of Revenue and Customs", and

(*b*) for "customs office", in the second and third places, substitute "office of Revenue and Customs".

GENERAL NOTE

The Criminal Law (Consolidation) (Scotland) Act 1995 s 25 currently deals with the right of a person being detained under s 24 to have a solicitor and another person informed. Paragraph 5 makes similar changes to para 4 in that it replaces all reference to Customs' offices with reference to HMRC offices.

6 In section 26 (detention in connection with drug smuggling offences), for "a customs office" (in both places) substitute "an office of Revenue and Customs".

GENERAL NOTE

Consequential changes are made by this paragraph to amend references to Customs in the Criminal Law (Consolidation) (Scotland) Act 1995 s 26 to HMRC. Section 26 relates only to detention in connection with drug smuggling offences: there is no change to the scope or operation of the section.

7 After that section insert—

"Power of arrest

26A Power of arrest

Where an authorised officer has reasonable grounds for suspecting that a Revenue and Customs offence has been or is being committed, the officer may arrest without warrant any person whom the officer has reasonable grounds for suspecting to be guilty of the offence.

General provisions

26B Interpretation of Part 3 etc

(1) In this Part of this Act—

"authorised officer" means an officer acting with the authority (which may be general or specific) of the Commissioners for Her Majesty's Revenue and Customs;
"office of Revenue and Customs" means premises wholly or partly occupied by Her Majesty's Revenue and Customs; and
"officer" means an officer of Revenue and Customs.

(2) In any proceedings (whether civil or criminal) under or arising from this Part of this Act, a certificate of the Commissioners for Her Majesty's Revenue and Customs that an officer had authority to exercise a power or function conferred by a provision of this Part shall be conclusive proof of that fact."

GENERAL NOTE

This paragraph inserts a new s 26A into the Criminal Law (Consolidation) (Scotland) Act 1995 giving an authorised HMRC officer the power to arrest a person without a warrant in certain circumstances (see also General Comment on FA 2007 s 81).

It also inserts a new s 26B defining the terms used in Part 3 of the Criminal Law (Consolidation) (Scotland) Act 1995 (the investigation of HMRC offences) following on from the extension of HMRC powers in Scotland made by FA 2007.

Criminal Procedure (Scotland) Act 1995 (c 46)

8 Section 307 of the Criminal Procedure (Scotland) Act 1995 (interpretation) is amended as follows.

GENERAL NOTE

This paragraph introduces changes made to the Criminal Procedure (Scotland) Act 1995 s 307 by paras 9 and 10.

9 In subsection (1), in the definition of "officer of law", for paragraph (*ba*) substitute—

"(*ba*) subject to subsection (1A) below, an officer of Revenue and Customs acting with the authority (which may be general or specific) of the Commissioners for Her Majesty's Revenue and Customs;".

GENERAL NOTE

The definition of 'officer of the law' in s 307 currently refers to Customs. In line with changes made elsewhere, this is amended to include 'an HMRC officer acting with the authority of the HMRC Commissioners', subject to certain restrictions (see para 10 below).

10 After that subsection insert—

"(1A) The inclusion of officers of Revenue and Customs as "officers of law" shall not have effect in relation to any matter specified in—

(*a*) section 54(4)(*b*) or (*f*) of; or
(*b*) paragraphs 3, 7, 10, 13 to 15, 19 or 24 to 29 of Schedule 1 to,

the Commissioners for Revenue and Customs Act 2005 (former Inland Revenue matters).

(1B) In any proceedings (whether civil or criminal) under or arising from this Act, a certificate of the Commissioners for Her Majesty's Revenue and Customs that an officer of Revenue and Customs had the authority to exercise a power or function conferred by a provision of this Act shall be conclusive evidence of that fact."

GENERAL NOTE

Paragraph 10 specifies that the changes made to s 307 will not apply to certain ex-Revenue matters, mainly those which have their origins in social security law, and is consistent with the scope of the new HMRC investigation powers set out in the Criminal Law (Consolidation) (Scotland) Act 1995 new s 23A introduced by FA 2007 Sch 23 para 3 (see above).

Criminal Justice and Police Act 2001 (c 16)

11 The Criminal Justice and Police Act 2001 is amended as follows.

GENERAL NOTE

This paragraph introduces changes made to the Criminal Justice and Police Act 2001 by paras 12–14.

12 In section 63(2) (powers to obtain hard copies etc of information stored in electronic form), after paragraph (*g*) insert—

"(ga) section 23E(5)(*b*) (as read with section 23K(2)) of the Criminal Law (Consolidation) (Scotland) Act 1995;".

13 In Schedule 1—

(*a*) in Part 1, after paragraph 59 insert—

"*Criminal Law (Consolidation) (Scotland) Act 1995 (c 39)*

59A The power of seizure conferred by section 23E(3) of the Criminal Law (Consolidation) (Scotland) Act 1995 (seizure of evidence of Revenue and Customs offences).", and

(*b*) in Part 2, after paragraph 81 insert—

"*Criminal Law (Consolidation) (Scotland) Act 1995 (c 39)*

81A The power of seizure conferred by section 23E(3) (as read with section 23E(5)(*c*)) of the Criminal Law (Consolidation) (Scotland) Act 1995 (seizure of evidence of Revenue and Customs offences)."

14— (1) The amendments made by this Schedule come into force in accordance with provision made by the Treasury by order.

(2) The power to make an order under this paragraph is exercisable by statutory instrument.

GENERAL NOTE

The provisions in the Criminal Justice and Police Act 2001 concerning whether or not material can be seized in certain situations already apply to both ex-Customs and ex-HMRC powers and are now extended to cover the new provisions for Scotland introduced by FA 2007.

SCHEDULE 24

PENALTIES FOR ERRORS

Section 97

GENERAL NOTE

During the second reading of the Commissioners for Revenue and Customs Bill, which, when enacted as CRCA 2005, established the formation of HMRC, the Paymaster General announced a major review, involving wide consultation, of the powers, deterrents and safeguards that would underpin the new department.

The powers of the Revenue and Customs had evolved over a considerable periods and involved substantial differences between the two departments and between individual taxes and whilst these were initially transferred to HMRC ring-fenced so that they could only apply for their original purpose, it was the Government's wish that these should be aligned and modernised.

One area to be covered by the review was the sanctions that could be applied in cases where complete and accurate information was not provided, and it was said that a central element of HMRC's strategy was to develop further its risk-based approach to compliance work.

HMRC set out their initial plans in a consultative document issued in December 2006 entitled *Modernising Powers, Deterrents and Safeguards: A new approach to penalties for incorrect tax returns.*

FA 2007 Sch 24 introduces the resulting legislative framework which is to come into force on a date to be appointed by Treasury Order. Budget Note BN79 indicates that the new regime is expected to apply to return periods commenced after 31 March 2008 where the return is filed after 31 March 2009. It further indicates that there will be at least 20 months between Royal Assent to the Finance Bill and the implementation of the changes.

HMRC's guidance to their staff on the new approach is to be published in due course.

The provisions are highly significant, representing a new regime for tax-based penalties and a major change in the way that those penalties are applied by HMRC. They create a single penalty framework for the submission of inaccurate documents (broadly, returns and associated documents) and for failure to tell HMRC of an under-assessment, where currently there are different rules, and make explicit that the penalties are behaviour-related. New terms are used to describe that behaviour.

The main concepts in the amended legislation are—

(*a*) a new single penalty regime for incorrect returns will replace all existing penalty systems for incorrect returns for income tax, corporation tax, PAYE, the construction industry scheme and VAT, as well as underpayments of NIC as a result of an error in one of those returns (but there is no mention of other areas such as SDLT and tax credits);

(*b*) the level of penalty will depend on the underlying behaviour giving rise to the incorrect return, with a stepped and differentiated approach leading to a penalty from nil to 100 per cent. There will be statutory maximum and minimum penalties for each behaviour;

(*c*) all penalties are mitigable for disclosure, within a range. There is no provision for mitigation based on either co-operation or the seriousness of the offence;

(*d*) there is a new concept of 'suspended penalties' where the taxpayer can demonstrate that his compliance has improved over a specified period; and

(*e*) all penalties will be subject to the right of appeal.

The new rules do not deal with the fixed and tax-geared penalties and surcharges that are imposed for non-compliance e g for failure to submit a return on time.

PART 1

LIABILITY FOR PENALTY

GENERAL NOTE

Part 1 sets out the grounds for liability to a penalty and defines the degrees of error for penalty purposes.

Error in taxpayer's document

1— (1) A penalty is payable by a person (P) where—

(*a*) P gives HMRC a document of a kind listed in the Table below, and
(*b*) Conditions 1 and 2 are satisfied.

(2) Condition 1 is that the document contains an inaccuracy which amounts to, or leads to—

(*a*) an understatement of P's liability to tax,
(*b*) a false or inflated statement of a loss by P, or
(*c*) a false or inflated claim to repayment of tax.

(3) Condition 2 is that the inaccuracy was careless or deliberate (within the meaning of paragraph 3).

(4) Where a document contains more than one inaccuracy, a penalty is payable for each inaccuracy.

Tax	*Document*
Income tax or capital gains tax	Return under section 8 of TMA 1970 (personal return).
Income tax or capital gains tax	Return under section 8A of TMA 1970 (trustee's return).
Income tax or capital gains tax	Return, statement or declaration in connection with a claim for an allowance, deduction or relief.
Income tax or capital gains tax	Accounts in connection with ascertaining liability to tax.
Income tax or capital gains tax	Partnership return.
Income tax or capital gains tax	Statement or declaration in connection with a partnership return.
Income tax or capital gains tax	Accounts in connection with a partnership return.
Income tax	Return for the purposes of PAYE regulations.
Construction industry deductions	Return for the purposes of regulations under section 70(1)(a) of FA 2004 in connection with deductions on account of tax under the Construction Industry Scheme.
Corporation tax	Company tax return under paragraph 3 of Schedule 18 to FA 1998.
Corporation tax	Return, statement or declaration in connection with a claim for an allowance, deduction or relief.
Corporation tax	Accounts in connection with ascertaining liability to tax.
VAT	VAT return under regulations made under paragraph 2 of Schedule 11 to VATA 1994.
VAT	Return, statement or declaration in connection with a claim.
Income tax, capital gains tax, corporation tax or VAT	Any document which is likely to be relied upon by HMRC to determine, without further inquiry, a question about— (a) P's liability to tax, (b) payments by P by way of or in connection with tax, (c) any other payment by P (including penalties), or (d) repayments, or any other kind of payment or credit, to P.

GENERAL NOTE

Paragraph 1 details the circumstances in which a penalty is payable, and these are extended beyond the submission of an incorrect document to include false or inflated claims to a loss or a repayment of tax. Relevant too is the behaviour giving rise to the inaccuracy (see para 3). A table sets out the returns within the scope of the new regime: broadly, income tax and corporation tax self-assessment returns, PAYE, VAT and CIS returns, together with related documents.

Under-assessment by HMRC

2— (1) A penalty is payable by a person (P) where—

(*a*) an assessment issued to P by HMRC understates P's liability to tax, and

(*b*) P has failed to take reasonable steps to notify HMRC, within the period of 30 days beginning with the date of the assessment, that it is an under-assessment.

(2) In deciding what steps (if any) were reasonable HMRC must consider—

(*a*) whether P knew, or should have known, about the under-assessment, and
(*b*) what steps would have been reasonable to take to notify HMRC.

(3) In sub-paragraph (1) "tax" means—

(*a*) income tax,
(*b*) capital gains tax,
(*c*) corporation tax, and
(*d*) VAT.

GENERAL NOTE

There is provision in para 2, for a penalty where a person fails to take reasonable steps to notify HMRC of an under-assessment. In these circumstances, a penalty in the 'careless action' category (see para 3) will arise.

This provision currently applies only to VAT and reinforces the requirement to provide accurate information to HMRC rather than accepting estimated or incorrect statements, etc from HMRC which are too low.

Degrees of culpability

3— (1) Inaccuracy in a document given by P to HMRC is—

(*a*) "careless" if the inaccuracy is due to failure by P to take reasonable care,
(*b*) "deliberate but not concealed" if the inaccuracy is deliberate but P does not make arrangements to conceal it, and
(*c*) "deliberate and concealed" if the inaccuracy is deliberate and P makes arrangements to conceal it (for example, by submitting false evidence in support of an inaccurate figure).

(2) An inaccuracy in a document given by P to HMRC, which was neither careless nor deliberate when the document was given, is to be treated as careless if P—

(*a*) discovered the inaccuracy at some later time, and
(*b*) did not take reasonable steps to inform HMRC.

GENERAL NOTE

Paragraph 3 is important as it makes explicit that a penalty will be behaviour-related and defines the key terms, clearly distinguishing between different sorts of behaviours, which are divided into categories reflecting the seriousness with which each is viewed (and thus the level of penalty, see para 4). Three categories are identified:

– careless (defined as failure to take reasonable care);
– deliberate but not concealed; and
– deliberate and concealed.

The consultative document *Modernising Powers, Deterrents and Safeguards: A new approach to penalties for incorrect tax returns*, at 5.5–5.11 gives examples of what behaviour HMRC consider to be appropriate to each category. It is recognised that 'reasonable care' must be judged by reference to the capacity of the individual taxpayer.

These definitions apply also to anyone acting on the person's behalf and replace all current terms and concepts, e.g. fraudulent and negligent conduct, misdeclaration, reasonable excuse, dishonest conduct, etc.

The Explanatory Notes to the Finance Act make it clear that where a person has taken reasonable care in completing the return and has taken reasonable steps to notify any errors, no penalty will arise. It can therefore be said that the concept of 'innocent error' will remain under the new rules.

Other penalties that were proposed in the consultative document, eg for taking an unreasonable tax position, and for obstruction, have not made their way onto the statute books.

PART 2

AMOUNT OF PENALTY

GENERAL NOTE

Part 2 covers the amount of the penalty, expressed as a percentage of the potential lost revenue, broadly similar to the current principle. The term 'potential lost revenue' is defined and the reductions for disclosure are detailed.

Standard amount

4— (1) The penalty payable under paragraph 1 is—

(*a*) for careless action, 30% of the potential lost revenue,

(*b*) for deliberate but not concealed action, 70% of the potential lost revenue, and

(*c*) for deliberate and concealed action, 100% of the potential lost revenue.

(2) The penalty payable under paragraph 2 is 30% of the potential lost revenue.

(3) Paragraphs 5 to 8 define "potential lost revenue".

GENERAL NOTE

This paragraph determines the standard maximum penalty payable for each type of behaviour, expressed as a percentage of the potential lost revenue. For the most serious category of 'deliberate understatement with concealment', the maximum penalty is in line with the current maximum rate of 100%. Penalties for the two less serious categories are lower, in steps; for action which is deliberate but not concealed, the maximum is 70% and for the action in the least serious category of 'careless' the maximum is 30%.

This contrasts with the current direct tax position where penalties are expressed as an amount 'not exceeding' a percentage of the tax lost.

Given the steep rise between the levels of penalty, there is potential for disagreement and argument between inspectors and advisers over the degree of culpability.

Potential lost revenue: normal rule

5— (1) "The potential lost revenue" in respect of an inaccuracy in a document or a failure to notify an under-assessment is the additional amount due or payable in respect of tax as a result of correcting the inaccuracy or assessment.

(2) The reference in sub-paragraph (1) to the additional amount due or payable includes a reference to—

(*a*) an amount payable to HMRC having been erroneously paid by way of repayment of tax, and

(*b*) an amount which would have been repayable by HMRC had the inaccuracy or assessment not been corrected.

(3) In sub-paragraph (1) "tax" includes national insurance contributions.

(4) The following shall be ignored in calculating potential lost revenue under this paragraph—

(*a*) group relief, and

(*b*) section 419(4) of ICTA (close company: relief for loans);

(but this sub-paragraph does not prevent a penalty being charged in respect of an inaccurate claim for relief).

GENERAL NOTE

Paragraphs 5–8 define the term 'potential lost revenue', the measure to which the standard amount penalty percentages will be applied. It is a new phrase which replaces the direct tax concept of tax difference and the VAT concepts of amounts which would have been lost, or amounts evaded or sought to be evaded, but is intended to have broadly the same effect.

Paragraph 5 sets out the rule that will apply in 'normal' circumstances, i.e. where the result of the inaccuracy (or underassessment) is that additional tax is due and can be calculated. It makes it clear that the term includes NIC as well as any amounts which were (or would have been) repaid by HMRC in error.

The position relating to any penalty due under TA 1988 s 419 remains unchanged in that the penalty is payable even if the loan is subsequently repaid and the tax becomes repayable. However, in contrast to the current position, 'potential lost revenue' will be calculated before any group relief claim or surrender.

Potential lost revenue: multiple errors

6— (1) Where P is liable to a penalty in respect of more than one inaccuracy, and the calculation of potential lost revenue under paragraph 5 in respect of each inaccuracy depends on the order in which they are corrected—

(*a*) careless inaccuracies shall be taken to be corrected before deliberate inaccuracies, and (*b*) deliberate but not concealed inaccuracies shall be taken to be corrected before deliberate and concealed inaccuracies.

(2) In calculating potential lost revenue where P is liable to a penalty in respect of one or more understatements in one or more documents relating to a tax period, account shall be taken of any overstatement in any document given by P which relates to the same tax period.

(3) In sub-paragraph (2)—

(*a*) "understatement" means an inaccuracy that satisfies Condition 1 of paragraph 1, and

(*b*) "overstatement" means an inaccuracy that does not satisfy that condition.

(4) For the purposes of sub-paragraph (2) overstatements shall be set against understatements in the following order—

(*a*) understatements in respect of which P is not liable to a penalty,

(*b*) careless understatements,

(*c*) deliberate but not concealed understatements, and

(*d*) deliberate and concealed understatements.

(5) In calculating potential lost revenue in respect of a document given by or on behalf of P no account shall be taken of the fact that a potential loss of revenue from P is or may be balanced by a potential over-payment by another person (except to the extent that an enactment requires or permits a person's tax liability to be adjusted by reference to P's).

GENERAL NOTE

This paragraph provides for an order for calculating the potential lost revenue where there are multiple errors arising from different behaviours and the order in which any overstatements are to be set against the understatements, with the most serious understatements being considered last.

This puts on a statutory footing what was previously HMRC's practice.

Potential lost revenue: losses

7— (1) Where an inaccuracy has the result that a loss is wrongly recorded for purposes of direct tax and the loss has been wholly used to reduce the amount due or payable in respect of tax, the potential lost revenue is calculated in accordance with paragraph 5.

(2) Where an inaccuracy has the result that a loss is wrongly recorded for purposes of direct tax and the loss has not been wholly used to reduce the amount due or payable in respect of tax, the potential lost revenue is—

(*a*) the potential lost revenue calculated in accordance with paragraph 5 in respect of any part of the loss that has been used to reduce the amount due or payable in respect of tax, plus

(*b*) 10% of any part that has not.

(3) Sub-paragraphs (1) and (2) apply both—

(*a*) to a case where no loss would have been recorded but for the inaccuracy, and

(*b*) to a case where a loss of a different amount would have been recorded (but in that case sub-paragraphs (1) and (2) apply only to the difference between the amount recorded and the true amount).

(4) Where an inaccuracy has the effect of creating or increasing an aggregate loss recorded for a group of companies—

(*a*) the potential lost revenue shall be calculated in accordance with this paragraph, and

(*b*) in applying paragraph 5 in accordance with sub-paragraphs (1) and (2) above, group relief may be taken into account (despite paragraph 5(4)(*a*)).

(5) The potential lost revenue in respect of a loss is nil where, because of the nature of the loss or P's circumstances, there is no reasonable prospect of the loss being used to support a claim to reduce a tax liability (of any person).

GENERAL NOTE

Paragraph 7 introduces another new concept – that overstated losses can be penalised, even where they have not been used to reduce the amount of tax payable. The same will apply where the inaccuracy is a timing difference.

Where the loss has been used to reduce the amount of tax payable and the tax advantage gained can therefore be ascertained, the penalty will be calculated in the same way as for understated profits or gains. However, where the loss has not been wholly used in this way, there is provision for the potential lost revenue to be deemed to be 10 per cent of any such part of the loss. This rule applies where the inaccuracy creates or increases a loss, and in the case of groups of companies, applies after group relief (in contrast with the normal situation, see paragraph 5 above).

There is provision for a 'nil' penalty in circumstances where there is no reasonable prospect of the loss being used to reduce a tax liability and special provisions are made for groups of companies.

Potential lost revenue: delayed tax

8— (1) Where an inaccuracy resulted in an amount of tax being declared later than it should have been ("the delayed tax"), the potential lost revenue is—

(*a*) 5% of the delayed tax for each year of the delay, or

(*b*) a percentage of the delayed tax, for each separate period of delay of less than a year, equating to 5% per year.

(2) This paragraph does not apply to a case to which paragraph 7 applies.

GENERAL NOTE

A similar provision to that set out in para 7 applies where the inaccuracy is one of timing rather than absolute tax loss. Where payment of tax has been delayed, e g as the result of an inaccurate accounting adjustment, or delay in the recognition of sales, thus resulting in tax being paid for a later period, 5 per cent of the delayed tax is treated as lost revenue and is liable to a penalty. The 5 per cent is charged per annum and is calculated pro rata for part years.

Reductions for disclosure

9— (1) A person discloses an inaccuracy or a failure to disclose an under-assessment by—

(*a*) telling HMRC about it,

(*b*) giving HMRC reasonable help in quantifying the inaccuracy or under-assessment, and

(*c*) allowing HMRC access to records for the purpose of ensuring that the inaccuracy or under-assessment is fully corrected.

(2) Disclosure—

(*a*) is "unprompted" if made at a time when the person making it has no reason to believe that HMRC have discovered or are about to discover the inaccuracy or under-assessment, and

(*b*) otherwise, is "prompted".

(3) In relation to disclosure "quality" includes timing, nature and extent.

GENERAL NOTE

This paragraph determines the framework for reductions that can be made from a penalty for disclosure (the term 'mitigation' is no longer used). There is to be no reduction for size and gravity, as now, because this element will be taken into account in the tax-geared nature of the penalty and the stepped levels of standard amounts for different categories of behaviour, but the definition of disclosure includes the mitigation elements that under the current system would be taken into account for both disclosure and co-operation.

The new definition, however, requires the taxpayer to be more proactive as the amount of the reduction is based on the quality of the disclosure (in terms of timing, nature and extent). As now, a greater reduction will be due for an 'unprompted' disclosure – this term is specifically defined in terms of timing, nature and extent.

10— (1) Where a person who would otherwise be liable to a 30% penalty has made an unprompted disclosure, HMRC shall reduce the 30% to a percentage (which may be 0%) which reflects the quality of the disclosure.

(2) Where a person who would otherwise be liable to a 30% penalty has made a prompted disclosure, HMRC shall reduce the 30% to a percentage, not below 15%, which reflects the quality of the disclosure.

(3) Where a person who would otherwise be liable to a 70% penalty has made an unprompted disclosure, HMRC shall reduce the 70% to a percentage, not below 20%, which reflects the quality of the disclosure.

(4) Where a person who would otherwise be liable to a 70% penalty has made a prompted disclosure, HMRC shall reduce the 70% to a percentage, not below 35%, which reflects the quality of the disclosure.

(5) Where a person who would otherwise be liable to a 100% penalty has made an unprompted disclosure, HMRC shall reduce the 100% to a percentage, not below 30%, which reflects the quality of the disclosure.

(6) Where a person who would otherwise be liable to a 100% penalty has made a prompted disclosure, HMRC shall reduce the 100% to a percentage, not below 50%, which reflects the quality of the disclosure.

GENERAL NOTE

Paragraph 10 sets out the *maximum* reductions that can apply to each level of penalty for a prompted or unprompted disclosure. Thus the reduction can never reduce the penalty below a statutory maximum, as set out in the table below—

type of behaviour	*statutory maximum penalty*	*statutory minimum penalty with unprompted disclosure*	*statutory minimum penalty with prompted disclosure*
careless	30%	0%	15%
deliberate but not concealed	70%	20%	35%
deliberate and concealed	100%	30%	50%

These are the *minimum* penalties assuming *maximum* reduction for disclosure. As now, the reduction will be on a sliding scale and therefore will be a question of judgment. The final amount of penalty in any individual case is therefore likely to be the subject of some negotiation.

The additional discount for an unprompted disclosure is to be 15 per cent for the two lesser behaviours, rising to 20 per cent in a case where it is judged that there has been deliberate error and concealment. This contracts with the current additional discount of 10 per cent.

Special reduction

11— (1) If they think it right because of special circumstances, HMRC may reduce a penalty under paragraph 1 or 2.

(2) In sub-paragraph (1) "special circumstances" does not include—

(*a*) ability to pay, or

(*b*) the fact that a potential loss of revenue from one taxpayer is balanced by a potential over-payment by another.

(3) In sub-paragraph (1) the reference to reducing a penalty includes a reference to—

(*a*) staying a penalty, and

(*b*) agreeing a compromise in relation to proceedings for a penalty.

GENERAL NOTE

This paragraph gives HMRC the discretion to further reduce a penalty in special circumstances e.g. where they consider that a penalty would in some way be inappropriate or disproportionate. The include inability to pay or the existence of an overpayment will not be classed as special circumstances. The Explanatory Notes indicate that it is anticipated that this will be used rarely. The taxpayer would need to demonstrate why his circumstances were special.

Interaction with other penalties

12— (1) The final entry in the Table in paragraph 1 excludes a document in respect of which a penalty is payable under section 98 of TMA 1970 (special returns).

(2) The amount of a penalty for which P is liable under paragraph 1 or 2 in respect of a document relating to a tax period shall be reduced by the amount of any other penalty which P has incurred and the amount of which is determined by reference to P's tax liability for that period.

(3) In the application of section 97A of TMA 1970 (multiple penalties) no account shall be taken of a penalty under paragraph 1 or 2.

GENERAL NOTE

This paragraph makes provision to prevent overlapping and multiple penalties and is consistence with the current position.

PART 3

PROCEDURE

GENERAL NOTE

This part sets out the mechanisms whereby HMRC can assess, notify and enforce penalties. In the past, VAT penalties have been assessed, but direct tax penalties have been determined. FA 2007 simplifies and aligns across taxes the machinery for bringing penalties into charge, using the same machinery as assessments to tax. It also shortens the time limits for assessing penalties, compared to previous regimes, in recognition of the requirements of HRA 1998 Sch 1 Art 6.

Assessment

13— (1) Where P becomes liable for a penalty under paragraph 1 or 2 HMRC shall—

(*a*) assess the penalty,
(*b*) notify P, and
(*c*) state in the notice a tax period in respect of which the penalty is assessed.

(2) An assessment—

(*a*) shall be treated for procedural purposes in the same way as an assessment to tax (except in respect of a matter expressly provided for by this Act),
(*b*) may be enforced as if it were an assessment to tax, and
(*c*) may be combined with an assessment to tax.

(3) An assessment of a penalty under paragraph 1 must be made within the period of 12 months beginning with—

(*a*) the end of the appeal period for the decision correcting the inaccuracy, or
(*b*) if there is no assessment within paragraph (*a*), the date on which the inaccuracy is corrected.

(4) An assessment of a penalty under paragraph 2 must be made within the period of 12 months beginning with the end of the appeal period for the assessment of tax which corrected the understatement.

(5) For the purpose of sub-paragraphs (3) and (4) a reference to an appeal period is a reference to the period during which—

(*a*) an appeal could be brought, or
(*b*) an appeal that has been brought has not been determined or withdrawn.

(6) Subject to sub-paragraphs (3) and (4), a supplementary assessment may be made in respect of a penalty if an earlier assessment operated by reference to an underestimate of potential lost revenue.

GENERAL NOTE

Paragraph 13 details the formal procedures for assessment of a penalty and sets a time limit for notification. Penalty assessments are treated in the same way as tax assessments and are subject to appeal within a specified period.

Suspension

14— (1) HMRC may suspend all or part of a penalty for a careless inaccuracy under paragraph 1 by notice in writing to P.

(2) A notice must specify—

(*a*) what part of the penalty is to be suspended,
(*b*) a period of suspension not exceeding two years, and
(*c*) conditions of suspension to be complied with by P.

(3) HMRC may suspend all or part of a penalty only if compliance with a condition of suspension would help P to avoid becoming liable to further penalties under paragraph 1 for careless inaccuracy.

(4) A condition of suspension may specify—

(*a*) action to be taken, and
(*b*) a period within which it must be taken.

(5) On the expiry of the period of suspension—

(*a*) if P satisfies HMRC that the conditions of suspension have been complied with, the suspended penalty or part is cancelled, and
(*b*) otherwise, the suspended penalty or part becomes payable.

(6) If, during the period of suspension of all or part of a penalty under paragraph 1, P becomes liable for another penalty under that paragraph, the suspended penalty or part becomes payable.

GENERAL NOTE

An approach suggested by HMRC during consultation whereby penalties might take account of previous compliant behaviour was judged not to be practical. However, this paragraph gives HMRC discretion to suspend for up to two years all or part of a penalty for careless action. It sets out the mechanics of how this would happen and how the penalty can subsequently be cancelled or become payable. It does not provide for suspension of penalties for deliberate actions.

The consultative document *Modernising Powers, Deterrents and Safeguards: A new approach to penalties for incorrect tax returns* explains that this new measure is seen as a positive use of the penalty system, as it encourages future compliance rather than just penalising past errors. It will be used where HMRC judge that it will provide an incentive for taxpayers to improve their record keeping and systems to ensure that future returns are correct and before considering suspension, they will need to be satisfied that there is likely to be an improvement in future compliance and that past inaccuracies were not deliberate.

The Explanatory Notes indicate that suspended penalties are not likely to be appropriate for one-off inaccuracies in a return, but are likely to be appropriate for accounting system or record-keeping weaknesses, where the money that would have been spent on a penalty could be used to remedy those defects.

Appeal

15— (1) P may appeal against a decision of HMRC that a penalty is payable by P.

(2) P may appeal against a decision of HMRC as to the amount of a penalty payable by P.

(3) P may appeal against a decision of HMRC not to suspend a penalty payable by P.

(4) P may appeal against a decision of HMRC setting conditions of suspension of a penalty payable by P.

GENERAL NOTE

All HMRC decisions in relation to penalties are to be appealable to an independent tribunal. This paragraph sets out specific appeal rights; the ways in which a taxpayer may appeal against the amount of a penalty, a decision by HMRC not to suspend a penalty or the conditions attached to a suspended penalty.

The option of an informal dispute resolution process was mentioned during the consultation as an alternative to a formal Tribunal hearing. HMRC are currently considering this.

16 An appeal may be brought to—

(*a*) the General Commissioners, in so far as the penalty relates to direct tax, or
(*b*) a VAT and duties tribunal, in so far as the penalty relates to VAT.

GENERAL NOTE

This paragraph provides for appeals to be brought before the General Commissioners or the VAT & Duties Tribunal, although this has been substituted by the Tribunals, Courts and Enforcement Act 2007.

17— (1) On an appeal under paragraph 15(1) the appellate tribunal may affirm or cancel HMRC's decision.

(2) On an appeal under paragraph 15(2) the appellate tribunal may—

(*a*) affirm HMRC's decision, or

(*b*) substitute for HMRC's decision another decision that HMRC had power to make.

(3) If the appellate tribunal substitutes its decision for HMRC's, the appellate tribunal may rely on paragraph 11—

(*a*) to the same extent as HMRC (which may mean applying the same percentage reduction as HMRC to a different starting point), or

(*b*) to a different extent, but only if the appellate tribunal thinks that HMRC's decision in respect of the application of paragraph 11 was flawed.

(4) On an appeal under paragraph 15(3)—

(*a*) the appellate tribunal may order HMRC to suspend the penalty only if it thinks that HMRC's decision not to suspend was flawed, and

(*b*) if the appellate tribunal orders HMRC to suspend the penalty—

(i) P may appeal to the appellate tribunal against a provision of the notice of suspension, and

(ii) the appellate tribunal may order HMRC to amend the notice.

(5) On an appeal under paragraph 15(4) the appellate tribunal—

(*a*) may affirm the conditions of suspension, or

(*b*) may vary the conditions of suspension, but only if the appellate tribunal thinks that HMRC's decision in respect of the conditions was flawed.

(6) In sub-paragraphs (3)(*b*), (4)(*a*) and (5)(*b*) "flawed" means flawed when considered in the light of the principles applicable in proceedings for judicial review.

(7) Paragraph 14 (see in particular paragraph 14(3)) is subject to the possibility of an order under this paragraph.

GENERAL NOTE

Paragraph 17 sets out what the appellate tribunal may do and makes it clear that it may affirm, substitute or cancel HMRC's decision. In certain circumstances however, substitution may only be made if it considers that HMRC's decision is flawed. There are special rules with regard to appeals in connection with the suspension of penalties.

PART 4

MISCELLANEOUS

GENERAL NOTE

This part sets out the circumstances in which a person may be charged a penalty as a result of a careless (not deliberate) action by someone acting on his behalf, and considers three separate sets of circumstances – where an agent is acting, where an officer of a company is acting on behalf of the company and where an inaccuracy in a partnership return affects partners other than the nominated partner.

Agency

18— (1) P is liable under paragraph 1(1)(*a*) where a document which contains a careless inaccuracy (within the meaning of paragraph 3) is given to HMRC on P's behalf.

(2) In paragraph 2(1)(*b*) and (2)(*a*) a reference to P includes a reference to a person who acts on P's behalf in relation to tax.

(3) Despite sub-paragraphs (1) and (2), P is not liable to a penalty in respect of anything done or omitted by P's agent where P satisfies HMRC that P took reasonable care to avoid inaccuracy (in relation to paragraph 1) or unreasonable failure (in relation to paragraph 2).

(4) In paragraph 3(1)(*a*) (whether in its application to a document given by P or, by virtue of sub-paragraph (1) above, in its application to a document given on P's behalf) a reference to P includes a reference to a person who acts on P's behalf in relation to tax.

(5) In paragraph 3(2) a reference to P includes a reference to a person who acts on P's behalf in relation to tax.

GENERAL NOTE

Paragraph 18 makes it clear that a taxpayer is responsible for the accuracy of a document submitted on his behalf and is therefore liable for any penalty for its inaccuracy. Similarly, he is responsible, where a person acting on his behalf fails to take reasonable steps to notify an under-assessment.

However, where the taxpayer can satisfy HMRC that he has taken all reasonable steps to avoid the inaccuracy, no penalty will be due, despite a careless action by someone on his behalf. There have been concerns that this provision could encourage unscrupulous taxpayers to evade the responsibility of providing complete and accurate information to their advisers.

Companies: officers' liability

19— (1) Where a penalty under paragraph 1 is payable by a company for a deliberate inaccuracy which was attributable to an officer of the company—

(*a*) the officer as well as the company shall be liable to pay the penalty, and

(*b*) HMRC may pursue the officer for such portion of the penalty (which may be 100%) as they may specify by written notice to the officer.

(2) Sub-paragraph (1) does not allow HMRC to recover more than 100% of a penalty.

(3) In the application of sub-paragraph (1) to a body corporate "officer" means—

(*a*) a director (including a shadow director within the meaning of section 251 of the Companies Act 2006 (c 46)), or

(*b*) a secretary.

(4) In the application of sub-paragraph (1) in any other case "officer" means—

(*a*) a director,

(*b*) a manager,

(*c*) a secretary, and

(*d*) any other person managing or purporting to manage any of the company's affairs.

(5) A reference to P in this Schedule (including paragraph 15) includes a reference to an officer of the company who is liable for a portion of the penalty in accordance with this paragraph.

GENERAL NOTE

Paragraph 19 provides that where a penalty in chargeable on a company for a 'deliberate action' offence, but the action is attributable to an officer of that company, all or a proportion of the penalty may be recovered from the officer. The position of 'officer of the company' is defined for this purpose.

This provision currently applies only to a VAT civil evasion penalty, but under the new rules is extended to all taxes in respect of penalties for inaccuracies due to deliberate action.

Partnerships

20— (1) This paragraph applies where P is liable to a penalty under paragraph 1 for an inaccuracy in or in connection with a partnership return.

(2) Where the inaccuracy affects the amount of tax due or payable by a partner of P, the partner is also liable to a penalty ("a partner's penalty").

(3) Paragraphs 4 to 13 and 19 shall apply in relation to a partner's penalty (for which purpose a reference to P shall be taken as a reference to the partner).

(4) Potential lost revenue shall be calculated separately for the purpose of P's penalty and any partner's penalty, by reference to the proportions of any tax liability that would be borne by each partner.

(5) Paragraph 14 shall apply jointly to P's penalty and any partner's penalties.

(6) P may bring an appeal under paragraph 15 in respect of a partner's penalty (in addition to any appeal that P may bring in connection with the penalty for which P is liable).

GENERAL NOTE

Paragraph 20 cover the situation where a person is liable to a penalty for an inaccuracy in a partnership return and clarifies that partners other than the nominated partner may be liable for the penalty where they are affected by the amount of tax due. Similarly any suspension of the penalty will apply jointly. For the purposes of the penalty, potential lost revenue is calculated separately by reference to the proportion of each partner's tax liability.

Double jeopardy

21 P is not liable to a penalty under paragraph 1 or 2 in respect of an inaccuracy or failure in respect of which P has been convicted of an offence.

GENERAL NOTE

Paragraph 21 confirms that a taxpayer cannot be both penalised and prosecuted for the same inaccuracy or failure.

PART 5
GENERAL

Interpretation

22 Paragraphs 23 to 26 apply for the construction of this Schedule.

23 HMRC means Her Majesty's Revenue and Customs.

24 An expression used in relation to income tax has the same meaning as in the Income Tax Acts.

25 An expression used in relation to corporation tax has the same meaning as in the Corporation Tax Acts.

26 An expression used in relation to capital gains tax has the same meaning as in the enactments relating to that tax.

27 An expression used in relation to VAT has the same meaning as in VATA 1994.

28 In this Schedule—

(*a*) a reference to corporation tax includes a reference to tax or duty which by virtue of an enactment is assessable or chargeable as if it were corporation tax,

(*b*) a reference to tax includes a reference to construction industry deductions under Chapter 3 of Part 3 of FA 2004,

(*c*) "direct tax" means—

(i) income tax,

(ii) capital gains tax, and

(iii) corporation tax,

(*d*) a reference to understating liability to VAT includes a reference to overstating entitlement to a VAT credit,

(*e*) a reference to a loss includes a reference to a charge, expense, deficit and any other amount which may be available for, or relied on to claim, a deduction or relief,

(*f*) a reference to repayment of tax includes a reference to allowing a credit,

(*g*) "tax period" means a tax year, accounting period or other period in respect of which tax is charged,

(*h*) a reference to giving a document to HMRC includes a reference to communicating information to HMRC in any form and by any method (whether by post, fax, email, telephone or otherwise),

(i) a reference to giving a document to HMRC includes a reference to making a statement or declaration in a document,

(j) a reference to making a return or doing anything in relation to a return includes a reference to amending a return or doing anything in relation to an amended return, and

(k) a reference to action includes a reference to omission.

Consequential amendments

29 The following provisions are omitted—

(*a*) sections 95, 95A, 97 and 98A(4) of TMA 1970 (incorrect returns and accounts),

(*b*) sections 100A(1) and 103(2) of TMA 1970 (deceased persons),

(*c*) in Schedule 18 to FA 1998 (company tax returns), paragraphs 20 and 89 (company tax returns), and

(*d*) sections 60, 61, 63 and 64 of VATA 1994 (evasion).

30 In paragraph 7 of Schedule 1 to the Social Security Contributions and Benefits Act 1992 (c 4) (penalties) a reference to a provision of TMA 1970 shall be construed as a reference to this Schedule so far as is necessary to preserve its effect.

31 In paragraph 7 of Schedule 1 to the Social Security Contributions and Benefits (Northern Ireland) Act 1992 (c 7) (penalties) a reference to a provision of TMA 1970 shall be construed as a reference to this Schedule so far as is necessary to preserve its effect.

GENERAL NOTE

Paragraphs 22–28 contain a series of explanatory provisions for the purposes of Sch 24, as well as defining certain terms.

Paragraphs 22–29 make consequential amendments, setting out the penalty provisions which will cease to have effect from a specified date and which be replaced by the new regime. Previous provisions will continue to apply for earlier periods. It is clarified that Sch 24 will apply to national insurance contributions in the same way as for PAYE.

SCHEDULE 25

AMENDMENTS CONNECTED WITH GAMBLING ACT 2005

Section 105

PART 1

AMENDMENTS OF THE TAX ACTS

Exemption from corporation tax for profits of charitable companies from certain lotteries

1 In section 505(1)(*f*) of ICTA (charitable companies: exemption for profits from lotteries), for the words from "a lottery if" to the end substitute "a lottery if the profits are applied solely to the charitable company's purposes and—

(i) the lottery is an exempt lottery within the meaning of the Gambling Act 2005 by virtue of Part 1 or 4 of Schedule 11 to that Act;

(ii) the lottery is promoted in accordance with a lottery operating licence within the meaning of Part 5 of that Act; or

(iii) the lottery is promoted and conducted in accordance with Article 133 or 135 of the Betting, Gaming, Lotteries and Amusements (Northern Ireland) Order 1985."

Exemption from income tax for profits of charitable trusts from certain lotteries

2 In section 530(2) of ITA 2007 (charitable trusts: exemption for profits from lotteries), for paragraph (*a*) (together with the "or" following it) substitute—

"(*a*) the lottery is an exempt lottery within the meaning of the Gambling Act 2005 by virtue of Part 1 or 4 of Schedule 11 to that Act,

(*ab*) the lottery is promoted in accordance with a lottery operating licence within the meaning of Part 5 of that Act, or".

PART 2

AMENDMENTS OF BGDA 1981

Introductory

3 BGDA 1981 is amended as follows.

Bookmakers: spread bets

4— (1) Section 3 (bookmakers: spread bets) is amended as follows.

(2) In subsection (1), omit paragraph (*b*) (together with the "and" before it).

(3) For subsection (2) substitute—

"(2) A bet is a spread bet if it constitutes a contract the making or accepting of which is a regulated activity within the meaning of section 22 of the Financial Services and Markets Act 2000."

Liability to pay general betting duty

5 In section 5B(3)(*a*) (liability to pay general betting duty), for "bookmaker's permit" substitute "general betting operating licence (in Great Britain), or a bookmaker's permit (in Northern Ireland),".

Bet-brokers

6 In section 5C(5) (bet-brokers: cases where section 5C does not apply), omit paragraph (*b*) (together with the "or" before it).

Definitions for purposes of betting duties

7— (1) Section 12(4) (definitions for purposes of Part 1) is amended as follows.

(2) In the definition of "betting office licence", omit paragraph (*a*) (together with the "and" following it).

(3) In the definition of "bookmaker's permit", omit paragraph (*a*) (together with the "and" following it).

(4) After that definition insert—

""general betting operating licence" has the same meaning as in Part 5 of the Gambling Act 2005 (see section 65(2)(*c*));".

(5) Omit the definitions of "meeting", "totalisator" and "track".

Combined bingo

8 In section 20A(1) (meaning of "combined bingo"), omit paragraph (*a*) (together with the "or" following it).

Definitions for purposes of bingo duty

9— (1) Section 20C(2) (definitions for purposes of Part 2) is amended as follows.

(2) After the definition of "bingo" insert—

""bingo premises licence" has the same meaning as in Part 8 of the Gambling Act 2005 (see section 150(1)(*b*)),".

(3) For the definition of "licensed bingo" substitute—

""licensed bingo"—

(*a*) in Great Britain, means bingo played at premises licensed under a bingo premises licence, and

(*b*) in Northern Ireland, means bingo played at premises licensed under Chapter 2 of Part 3 of the Betting, Gaming, Lotteries and Amusements (Northern Ireland) Order 1985,".

Definition of "gaming"

10 In section 33(1) (interpretation of Act), for the definition of "gaming" substitute—

""gaming" means playing a game of chance for a prize within the meaning of Group 4 of Schedule 9 to the Value Added Tax Act 1994;".

Supplementary provisions as to betting duties

11— (1) Schedule 1 (enforcement) is amended as follows.

(2) Omit paragraph 7 (production of documents etc relating to general betting business or pool betting business).

(3) In paragraph 15 (cancellation of betting office licence)—

(*a*) at the beginning insert—

"(A1) This paragraph applies only in relation to premises in Northern Ireland.",

(*b*) in sub-paragraph (2), omit "in England or Wales or Northern Ireland",

(*c*) omit sub-paragraphs (3) to (4A), and

(*d*) in sub-paragraph (5), omit "in Northern Ireland".

Exemptions from bingo duty

12— (1) Schedule 3 (exemptions from bingo duty) is amended as follows.

(2) For paragraph 2B (and the italic cross-heading before it) substitute—

"Non-profit making bingo

2B— (1) In calculating liability to bingo duty no account shall be taken of non-profit making bingo.

(2) "Non-profit making bingo" means bingo—

(*a*) in respect of the playing of which no charge in money or money's worth is made, and

(*b*) in respect of which no levy is charged on any of the stakes or on the winnings of any of the players (irrespective of the means by which the levy is charged),

and it does not matter whether the charge or levy is compulsory, customary or voluntary.

(3) In sub-paragraph (2)(*a*) "charge" includes an admission charge, but does not include—

(*a*) any payment of the whole or any part of an annual subscription to a club,

(*b*) any payment of an entrance subscription for membership of a club, or

(*c*) any stakes hazarded.

(4) In sub-paragraph (3)—

"club" means a club which is so constituted and conducted, in respect of membership and otherwise, as not to be of a temporary character, and

"membership of a club" does not include temporary membership of a club."

(3) In paragraph 5(1) (small-scale amusements provided commercially)—

(*a*) in paragraph (*a*), for the words from "premises" to the end substitute "family entertainment centre within the meaning of the Gambling Act 2005 (see section 238);", and

(*b*) in paragraph (*b*), for the words from "a permit" to "that Act" substitute "an adult gaming centre premises licence issued under Part 8 of the Gambling Act 2005 (see section 150(1)(*c*))".

(4) In paragraph 10(2) (notification to Commissioners by, and registration of, bingo-promoters), in the second sentence, for "the Gaming Act 1968" substitute "a bingo premises licence".

PART 3

AMENDMENTS OF FA 1993 RELATING TO LOTTERY DUTY

Introductory

13 Chapter 2 of Part 1 of FA 1993 (lottery duty) is amended as follows.

Charge to lottery duty

14 In section 24(4) (lotteries in respect of which lottery duty not chargeable)—

(*a*) in the opening words, for "not chargeable in respect" substitute "not chargeable (in Great Britain) in respect of a lottery which is an exempt lottery within the meaning of the Gambling Act 2005 (see section 258) or (in Northern Ireland) in respect",

(*b*) in paragraph (*a*), omit "the Lotteries and Amusements Act 1976 or",

(*c*) in paragraph (*b*), omit "Act or",

(*d*) in paragraph (*c*), omit "Act or" and "section 5(3) of that Act or", and

(*e*) omit paragraph (*d*).

Disclosure of information

15 In section 37 (disclosure of information to or by the Gaming Board for Great Britain etc)—

(*a*) in subsection (1), for "Gaming Board for Great Britain" substitute "Gambling Commission" and for "or Gaming Board" (in both places) substitute "or Gambling Commission", and

(*b*) in subsection (2), for "Gaming Board for Great Britain" substitute "Gambling Commission" and for "or Gaming Board" substitute "or Gambling Commission".

PART 4

AMENDMENTS OF FA 1997 RELATING TO GAMING DUTY

Introductory

16 FA 1997 is amended as follows.

Charge to gaming duty

17— (1) Section 10 (charge to gaming duty) is amended as follows.

(2) In subsection (3)—

(*a*) in paragraph (*a*), for "section 2(2) of the Gaming Act 1968" substitute "Part 1 of Schedule 15 to the Gambling Act 2005",

(*b*) in paragraph (*b*), for "section 6 of that Act" substitute "section 279 of that Act",

(*c*) omit paragraph (*c*),

(*d*) in paragraph (*d*), omit "section 41 of that Act or", and

(*e*) in paragraph (*e*), for "section 15 or 16 of the Lotteries and Amusements Act 1976" substitute "Part 13 of that Act".

(3) After that subsection insert—

"(3A) This section does not apply to any gaming taking place by means of a machine that is an amusement machine for the purposes of the Betting and Gaming Duties Act 1981.

(3B) This section does not apply to any lawful gaming which consists of games played in Great Britain at an entertainment in respect of which all the payments made by the players (whether by way of entrance fee or stake or otherwise) are, after making permissible deductions from those payments, applied for a purpose other than that of private gain (within the meaning of the Gambling Act 2005).

(3C) For the purposes of subsection (3B), only the following deductions are permissible deductions—

(*a*) deductions on account of reasonable expenses incurred in providing the facilities for the purposes of the games, and

(*b*) deductions for the provision of prizes or awards in respect of the games."

(4) In subsection (4), for the words from "any gaming" to the end substitute "any gaming which takes place on any premises in Great Britain of—

(*a*) a members' club within the meaning of the Gambling Act 2005 (see section 266), or

(*b*) a miners' welfare institute within the meaning of that Act (see section 268)."

Banker's profits from gaming

18— (1) Section 11 (rate of gaming duty) is amended as follows.

(2) In paragraph (*b*) of subsection (10), for "the value, in money or money's worth, of the winnings paid" substitute "the value of the prizes provided".

(3) After that subsection insert—

"(10A) Subsections (2) to (6)(*a*) of section 20 of the Betting and Gaming Duties Act 1981 (expenditure on bingo winnings: valuation of prizes) apply, with any necessary modifications, for the purposes of gaming duty as they apply for the purposes of bingo duty."

(4) In subsection (11), for "(10)" substitute "(10A)".

Definition of "gaming"

19 In section 15(3) (definitions for purposes of the gaming duty provisions), for the definition of "gaming" substitute—

""gaming" has the same meaning as in the Betting and Gaming Duties Act 1981 (see section 33(1));".

Gaming Duty Register

20— (1) Schedule 1 (gaming duty: administration, enforcement etc) is amended as follows.

(2) In sub-paragraph (1) of paragraph 2 (interpretation), before the definition of "the register" insert—

""casino premises licence" has the same meaning as in Part 8 of the Gambling Act 2005 (see section 150(1)(*a*));

"club gaming permit" has the same meaning as in that Act (see section 271);".

(3) In sub-paragraph (2) of that paragraph, for paragraphs (*a*) and (*b*) substitute—

"(*a*) in respect of which a casino premises licence is for the time being in force, or

(*b*) in respect of which a club gaming permit is for the time being in force."

(4) In paragraph 3(4)(*a*) (registrable persons: holders of licences under the Gaming Act 1968)—

(*a*) for "licence under the Gaming Act 1968" substitute "casino premises licence or club gaming permit", and (*b*) after "which the licence" insert "or permit".

(5) In paragraph 6 (notification of premises)—

(*a*) in sub-paragraph (10)(*a*), for "licence under the Gaming Act 1968" substitute "casino premises licence or club gaming permit" and after "of the licence" insert "or permit", and

(*b*) in sub-paragraph (11)(*a*), for "licence under the Gaming Act 1968" substitute "casino premises licence or club gaming permit" and after "of the licence" insert "or permit".

(6) In paragraph 14 (disclosure of information)—

(*a*) in sub-paragraph (1), for "the Gaming Board for Great Britain" substitute "the Gambling Commission", for "that Board" (in each place) substitute "that Commission" and for "that Board's functions under the Gaming Act 1968" substitute "that Commission's functions under the Gambling Act 2005", and

(*b*) in sub-paragraph (2), for "the Gaming Board for Great Britain" substitute "the Gambling Commission" and for "that Board" (in both places) substitute "that Commission".

PART 5

MISCELLANEOUS AMENDMENTS

Provision of FA 1966 relating to repealed law

21 In Schedule 3 to FA 1966 (provision relating to Schedule 1 to the Betting, Gaming and Lotteries Act 1963 (c 2)), omit paragraph 6.

Customs and Excise Management Act 1979

22 In section 1(1) of CEMA 1979 (interpretation), in paragraph (*a*)(ic) of the definition of "revenue trader", for the words from "any gaming" to the end substitute "gaming within the meaning of the Betting and Gaming Duties Act 1981 (see section 33(1))".

PART 6

COMMENCEMENT

23— (1) Paragraphs 3, 4, 6, 7(1) and (5), 11(1) and (2), 13, 15, 16 and 20(1) and (6) and this paragraph come into force on the day on which this Act is passed.

(2) The other provisions of this Schedule come into force in accordance with provision made by the Treasury by order.

(3) The power to make an order under this paragraph is exercisable by statutory instrument.

(4) An order under this paragraph—

(*a*) may make different provision for different purposes, and

(*b*) may contain transitional provision and savings.

GENERAL NOTE

This Schedule makes amendments to the tax legislation for betting, gaming and lotteries that are consequential on, or otherwise connected with, the implementation of the Gambling Act 2005.

Part 1 maintains the existing exemption from tax for charities for the profits from certain charitable lotteries run in accordance with lottery regulations.

Paragraph 1 deals with tax relief for charitable companies contained in TA 1988 s 505(1)(*f*). That provision is amended by this paragraph to ensure that the tax relief is given by reference to the Gambling Act 2005, rather than the relevant provisions of the Lotteries and Amusements Act 1976 which will shortly be repealed. The amendments preserve the original restriction whereby tax relief is given only where the profits are applied solely to the charitable company's purposes. The changes reflect the new regulatory framework for lotteries introduced by the 2005 Act, ensuring that only lotteries which are lawful under the 2005 Act receive tax relief. In particular:

— the tax relief in new sub-paragraph (i) (exempt lotteries by virtue of Part 1 or 4 of Schedule 11 to the Gambling Act 2005) covers lotteries incidental to non-commercial events and small society lotteries, which are run neither for private gain nor for commercial reasons;

— the tax relief in new sub-paragraph (ii) (lotteries promoted in accordance with a lottery operating licence with the meaning of Part 5 of the Gambling Act 2005) covers large society lotteries, which are single lotteries where the proceeds may exceed £20,000, or all of a society's lotteries in a calendar year if the total proceeds are over £250,000; and

— the tax relief in new sub-paragraph (iii) (lotteries promoted and conducted in accordance with Article 133 or 135 of the Betting, Gaming, Lotteries and Amusements (Northern Ireland) Order 1985) is required as it is the Northern Ireland Order, not the Gambling Act 2005, which applies in Northern Ireland.

These amendments will be brought into force in accordance with a Treasury order by virtue of paragraph 23 of this Schedule. It is understood that the effective date will coincide with the introduction of the new licencing regime under the 2005 Act which is due to occur on 1 September 2007.

Paragraph 2 makes similar changes to the tax relief for charitable trusts. This relief is contained in the Income Tax Act 2007 s 530(2), so that provision is amended to ensure that charitable trusts continue to receive the relief.

Parts 2, 3, 4, and 5 of the Schedule make amendments to the Betting and Gaming Duties Act 1981, FA 1993 relating to lottery duty, FA 1997 relating to gaming duty, FA 1966, and CEMA 1979. These amendments are also being made as a consequence of, and in connection with, changes that will be introduced by the Gambling Act 2005. Part 6 of this Schedule contains the commencement provisions.

SCHEDULE 26

MEANING OF "RECOGNISED STOCK EXCHANGE" ETC

Section 109

Meaning of "recognised stock exchange" etc in Tax Acts and TCGA 1992

1 For section 1005 of ITA 2007 substitute—

"1005 Meaning of "recognised stock exchange" etc

(1) In the Income Tax Acts "recognised stock exchange" means—

(*a*) any market of a recognised investment exchange which is for the time being designated as a recognised stock exchange for the purposes of this section by an order made by the Commissioners for Her Majesty's Revenue and Customs, and

(*b*) any market outside the United Kingdom which is for the time being so designated.

(2) An order under subsection (1) may—

(*a*) designate a market by name or by reference to any class or description of market (including, in the case of a market outside the United Kingdom, one framed by reference to any authority or approval given in a country outside the United Kingdom),

(*b*) contain incidental, supplemental, consequential and transitional provision and savings, and

(*c*) vary or revoke a previous order under that subsection.

(3) References in the Income Tax Acts to securities which are listed on a recognised stock exchange are to securities—

(*a*) which are admitted to trading on that exchange, and

(*b*) which are included in the official UK list or are officially listed in a qualifying country outside the United Kingdom in accordance with provisions corresponding to those generally applicable in EEA states.

(4) For this purpose "qualifying country outside the United Kingdom" means any country outside the United Kingdom in which there is a recognised stock exchange.

(5) References in the Income Tax Acts to securities which are included in the official UK list are to securities which are included in the official list (within the meaning of Part 6 of FISMA 2000) in accordance with the provisions of that Part.

(6) In this section—

"recognised investment exchange" has the same meaning as in FISMA 2000 (see section 285), and

"securities" includes shares and stock."

2 For section 841 of ICTA substitute—

"841 Meaning of "recognised stock exchange" etc

(1) In the Corporation Tax Acts "recognised stock exchange" has the same meaning as in the Income Tax Acts (see subsections (1) and (2) of section 1005 of ITA 2007).

(2) References in the Corporation Tax Acts to securities which are listed on a recognised stock exchange are to be read in accordance with subsections (3) and (4) of that section.

(3) References in the Corporation Tax Acts to securities which are included in the official UK list are to be read in accordance with subsection (5) of that section.

(4) In this section "securities" includes shares and stock."

3 In section 288 of TCGA 1992 (interpretation), after subsection (5) insert—

"(5A) References in this Act to shares or securities which are listed on a recognised stock exchange shall be construed in accordance with subsections (3) and (4) of section 1005 of ITA 2007.

(5B) References in this Act to shares or securities which are included in the official UK list shall be construed in accordance with subsection (5) of that section."

Valuation of shares listed on recognised stock exchange for purposes of TCGA 1992 etc

4— (1) In section 272 of TCGA 1992 (valuation: general), for subsections (3) and (4) substitute—

"(3) The Treasury may make regulations as to the manner for determining for the purposes of this Act—

(*a*) the market value at any time of shares or securities which are included in the official UK list, and

(*b*) the market value at any time of shares or securities which are listed on a recognised stock exchange outside the United Kingdom.

(4) The regulations may—

(*a*) make different provision for different cases, and

(*b*) contain incidental, supplemental, consequential and transitional provision and savings."

(2) The amendment made by sub-paragraph (1) has effect where the date of valuation falls on or after such day as may be appointed by the Treasury by order; and different days may be appointed for different purposes.

5— (1) In ITTOIA 2005, for sections 450 and 451 substitute—

"450 Market value of strips etc

(1) The Treasury may make regulations as to the manner for determining—

(*a*) the market value at any time of a strip for the purposes of this Chapter, and

(*b*) the market value at any time of a security exchanged for strips of that security for the purposes of section 445(1).

(2) The regulations may—

(*a*) make different provision for different cases, and

(*b*) contain incidental, supplemental, consequential and transitional provision and savings."

(2) The amendment made by sub-paragraph (1) has effect where the date of valuation falls on or after such day as may be appointed by the Treasury by order; and different days may be appointed for different purposes.

Minor and consequential amendments

6 In section 90(8) of FA 1986 (exceptions to the charge to SDRT), for paragraph (*b*) substitute—

"(*b*) references to anything listed on a recognised stock exchange shall be construed in accordance with section 1005 of the Income Tax Act 2007;".

7— (1) ICTA is amended as follows.

(2) In section 210(4) (bonus issue following repayment of share capital), in the definition of "preference shares", for "listed in the Official List of the Stock Exchange" substitute "included in the official UK list".

(3) In section 312(1E)(*a*) (interpretation of Chapter 3 of Part 7), for "section 841" substitute "section 1005(1)(*b*) of ITA 2007".

(4) In section 415(1)(*b*) (certain quoted companies not to be close companies), for "in the official list of" substitute "on".

(5) In section 576H(2)(*a*) (the unquoted status requirement), for "1005" substitute "1005(1)(*b*)".

(6) In section 587B (gifts of shares, securities and real property to charities etc)—

(*a*) in subsection (9), in the definition of "qualifying investment", for "or dealt in on a recognised stock exchange" substitute "on a recognised stock exchange or dealt in on any designated market in the United Kingdom", and
(*b*) after that subsection insert—

"(9ZA) In paragraph (*a*) of the definition of "qualifying investment" in subsection (9) above, "designated" means designated by an order made by the Commissioners for Her Majesty's Revenue and Customs for the purposes of that paragraph.

(9ZB) An order under subsection (9ZA) above may—

(*a*) designate a market by name or by reference to any class or description of market, and
(*b*) vary or revoke a previous order under that subsection."

(7) In section 704 (prescribed circumstances mentioned in section 703(1)), in paragraph D(2)(*b*), for "listed in the Official List of the Stock Exchange, and are dealt in on the Stock Exchange" substitute "included in the official UK list, and are dealt in on a recognised stock exchange in the United Kingdom".

(8) In section 828(2) (orders and regulations made by the Treasury or the Board), after "conferred by section" insert "587B(9ZA) or".

(9) In section 842(1)(*c*) (investment trusts), for "listed in the Official List of the Stock Exchange" substitute "included in the official UK list".

(10) In paragraph 5 of Schedule 20 (charities: qualifying investments and loans), omit ", or which are dealt in on the Unlisted Securities Market".

8— (1) TCGA 1992 is amended as follows.

(2) In section 130(1)(*a*) (composite new holdings)—

(*a*) for "had quoted market values" substitute "were listed", and
(*b*) omit "in the United Kingdom or elsewhere".

(3) In section 144(8)(*a*) (options and forfeited deposits), for "quoted on" substitute "listed on".

(4) In section 146(4)(*b*) (options: application of rules as to wasting assets), omit "in the United Kingdom or elsewhere".

(5) In section 273(2) (unquoted shares and securities), for "quoted" substitute "listed".

(6) Omit section 285 (recognised investment exchanges).

9 In paragraph 4(2C)(*b*) of Schedule 26 to FA 2002 (derivative contracts: contracts excluded by virtue of their underlying subject matter), for "quoted" substitute "listed".

10— (1) ITEPA 2003 (persons to whom section 421J applies) is amended as follows.

(2) In section 421L (persons to whom section 421J applies)—

(*a*) in paragraph (*b*) of subsection (6), for "or dealt in on a recognised stock exchange" substitute "on a recognised stock exchange or dealt in on any designated market in the United Kingdom", and
(*b*) after that subsection insert—

"(7) In subsection (6)(*b*) "designated" means designated by an order made by the Commissioners for Her Majesty's Revenue and Customs for the purposes of that provision.

(8) An order under subsection (7) may—

(*a*) designate a market by name or by reference to any class or description of market, and
(*b*) vary or revoke a previous order under that subsection."

(3) In section 717(2) (orders and regulations made by Treasury or Commissioners), insert at the end "or section 421L(7) (persons to whom section 421J applies: order in relation to excluded securities)."

11— (1) ITTOIA 2005 is amended as follows.

(2) In section 443(2) (application of Chapter 8 of Part 4 to strips of government securities)—

(*a*) at the end of paragraph (*e*) insert "and", and
(*b*) omit paragraph (*g*).

(3) In section 460(3) (minor definitions in Chapter 8 of Part 4), omit "or 451".

12— (1) ITA 2007 is amended as follows.

(2) In section 143(2)(*a*) (losses on disposal of shares: the unquoted status requirement), for "1005" substitute "1005(1)(*b*)".

(3) In section 151(2) (interpretation of Chapter 6 of Part 4), for "the Stock Exchange" substitute "a recognised stock exchange".

(4) In section 184 (EIS: the unquoted status requirement)—

(*a*) in subsection (3)(*a*), for the words from "the Stock Exchange" to the end substitute "a recognised stock exchange,", and

(*b*) in subsection (6)(*a*), for "1005" substitute "1005(1)(*b*)".

(5) In section 257(5) (minor definitions in Part 5), for "the Stock Exchange" substitute "a recognised stock exchange".

(6) In section 274(2) (requirements for the giving of VCT approval), for "listed throughout the relevant period in the Official List of the Stock Exchange" substitute "included in the official UK list throughout the relevant period".

(7) In section 295(3) (VCTs: the unquoted status requirement)—

(*a*) in paragraph (*a*), for the words from "the Stock Exchange" to the end substitute "a recognised stock exchange,", and

(*b*) in paragraph (*c*), omit "on the Unlisted Securities Market or dealt in".

(8) In section 382(2) (minor definitions in Part 7), for "the Stock Exchange" substitute "a recognised stock exchange".

(9) In section 397(6) (eligibility requirements for interest on loans within section 396), in the definition of "unquoted company", for "listed in the Official List of the Stock Exchange" substitute "included in the official UK list".

(10) In section 432 (gifts of shares, securities and real property to charities etc: meaning of "qualifying investment")—

(*a*) in subsection (1)(*a*), for "or dealt in on a recognised stock exchange" substitute "on a recognised stock exchange or dealt in on any designated market in the United Kingdom",

(*b*) in subsection (2), after "In this section—" insert—

""designated" means designated by an order made by the Commissioners for Her Majesty's Revenue and Customs for the purposes of subsection (1)(*a*),", and

(*c*) after that subsection insert—

"(3) An order under subsection (2) may—

(*a*) designate a market by name or by reference to any class or description of market, and

(*b*) vary or revoke a previous order under that subsection."

(11) In section 691(1)(*b*) (meaning of "relevant company" in sections 689 and 690), for sub-paragraphs (i) and (ii) substitute—

"(i) included in the official UK list, and

(ii) dealt in on a recognised stock exchange in the United Kingdom regularly or from time to time."

(12) In section 989 (list of Income Tax Acts definitions), after the definition of "settlor" insert—

""shares, stock or other securities included in the official UK list" is to be read in accordance with section 1005,

"shares, stock or other securities listed on a recognised stock exchange" is to be read in accordance with section 1005,".

(13) Omit section 1010 (application of Income Tax Acts to recognised investment exchanges).

(14) In section 1014(2)(*g*) (orders and regulations)—

(*a*) after sub-paragraph (ii) (but before the "and") insert—

"(iia) section 432(2) (gifts of shares, securities and real property to charities etc: meaning of "qualifying investment"),", and

(*b*) in sub-paragraph (iii), for "1005(1)(*b*)" substitute "1005(1)".

(15) In Schedule 4 (index of defined expressions), after the entry relating to "share loss relief (in Chapter 6 of Part 4)" insert—

"shares, stock or other securities included in the official UK list	section 1005
shares, stock or other securities listed on a recognised stock exchange	section 1005".

GENERAL NOTE

The key provision is in para 1 of the Schedule. It provides a new definition of the term "recognised stock exchange" for the purposes of the Income Tax Acts. The new definition will substitute that which has been found in ITA 2007, s 1005 since 6 April. The new definition will ensure that UK stock exchanges other than the London Stock Exchange can come within the definition of recognised stock exchange.

The definition will apply, however, for both corporation tax and capital gains tax purposes as well for income tax. This is because para 2 substitutes a new version of TA 1988 s 841 so that the term "recognised stock exchange" for the purposes of corporation tax will follow that in ITA 2007 s 1005. Similarly, TCGA 1992 s 288 is modified to reflect and accommodate the new version of ITA 2007 s 1005 for capital gains tax purposes.

Recognised Stock Exchanges

New s 1005(1) provides that a recognised stock exchange is any market that is so designated by HMRC for the purposes of that section.

For markets in the UK, the market must be a market of a recognised investment exchange. That restriction will not apply to markets outside the UK. The term "recognised investment exchange" has, by virtue of sub-s (6), the same meaning as it does in the Financial Services and Market Act ("FISMA") 2000 s 285.

The designation of a market as a recognised stock exchange will be by HMRC order.

When the new definition was first announced, there was concern that it would have the effect of removing the many tax advantages available to companies (or their shareholders) listed on the Alternative Investment Market (AIM). However, such concerns were unfounded because (at least under the present law) AIM is not a recognised investment exchange. The latest list of recognised investment exchanges is available on the FSA website (http://www.fsa.gov.uk/register/exchanges.do).

HMRC orders (new s 1005(2))

HMRC orders designating markets as recognised stock exchanges may designate a market by name or by reference to any class or description of market.

For markets outside the UK, the designation may be framed by reference to any authority or approval given in another country.

New s 1005(2) also provides that the order has the power:

(*a*) to contain incidental, supplemental, consequential and transitional provision and savings; and

(*b*) to vary or revoke any previous order.

"Securities listed on a recognised stock exchange" (new s 1005(3), (4))

New s 1005(3) defines what is meant by "securities listed on a recognised stock exchange". Such securities are those which are:

(*a*) admitted to trading on that exchange and

(*b*) either:

- (i) included in the official UK list or
- (ii) officially listed in a qualifying country outside the UK in accordance with provisions corresponding to those generally applicable in EEA states.

A country is a qualifying country for these purposes if that country has a recognised stock exchange (new sub-s (4)).

EXAMPLE

Hoederer ZZ has shares which are officially listed in Illyria and are admitted to trading on the Illyrian Stock Exchange. The shares are not included in the official UK list.

The shares qualify as securities listed on a recognised stock exchange if and only if:

(*a*) the listing provisions in Illyria correspond generally applicable in EEA states; and

(*b*) Illyria has a recognised stock exchange.

"Securities included in the official UK list" (new sub-s (5))

New s 1005(5) provides that references to "securities being included in the official UK list" are to securities which are included in the official list (within the meaning of FISMA 2000 Pt 6) and in accordance with the provisions of that Part.

Meaning of "securities" and "recognised investment exchange" (new sub-s 6))

New s 1005(6) makes it clear that shares and stock come within the meaning of securities.

It also ensures (as referred to above) that the term "recognised investment exchange" has the same meaning as it does in FISMA 2000 s 285.

Valuation for capital gains tax purposes (para 4)

At present TCGA 1992 s 272(3) and (4) provide that, for capital gains tax purposes, the market value of quoted shares is generally found using either the "quarter up" method or the halfway point between the lowest and highest recorded normal trade price on the particular day.

Schedule 26 para 4 provides a new version of s 272(3) and (4). The new version provides that the method for valuing listed shares and securities (whether those on the official UK list or those which are listed on a recognised stock exchange outside the UK) may be determined in accordance with Treasury regulations.

New s 272(4) again provides that such regulations may be widely drafted. In particular, they will be able to make different provision for different cases.

The new version of s 272(3) and (4) will come into effect on a date to be appointed by Treasury order (sub-para (2)). As is usual, a different day may be appointed for different purposes.

It must be assumed that the regulations when they come into force will continue to apply the quarter-up and half way methods for Stock Exchange investments and that the regulations will simply be used to introduce new (or similar) methods for other exchanges. However, the Explanatory Notes give no indication about the likely contents of any regulations.

Market value of strips (para 5)

ITTOIA 2005 Part 4 Chapter 8 contains rules treating gilt (Government) strips as deeply discounted securities for the purposes of that chapter.

Section 450 determines the market value for any strip or security quoted on the Stock Exchange Daily Official List based upon the "quarter-up" method.

Paragraph 5 replaces the quarter up method in s 450 by a new rule providing that the method will be determined in accordance with Treasury regulations (new s 450(1)(*a*)). Similarly, these regulations will be applied to determine the market value of any security exchanged for strips of that security for the purposes of s 445(1).

New s 450(2) again provides that such regulations may be widely drafted. In particular, they will be able to make different provision for different cases.

The new version of s 450 will come into effect on a date to be appointed by Treasury order (sub-para (2)). As is usual, a different day may be appointed for different purposes.

Minor and consequential amendments (paras 6–11)

The rest of the Schedule makes minor and consequential amendments.

Paragraph 6 updates FA 1986 s 90(8) (Stamp Duty Reserve Tax).

Paragraph 7 makes consequential amendments to TA 1988, amending ss 210(4), 312(1E)(*a*), 415(1)(*b*), 576H(2)(*a*), 704, 828, 842(1)(*c*) and Sch 20, para 5.

Additionally, sub-para (6) amends ICTA 1988, s 587B(9) which defines a qualifying investment for the purposes of the corporation tax rules relating to gifts to charities. The previous provision that included, as a qualifying investment, shares or securities which are listed or dealt in on a recognised stock exchange, is now replaced. The new s 587B(9) refers instead to shares or securities which are listed on a recognised stock exchange or dealt in on any designated market in the UK.

Designation applies for the purposes of that section by HMRC Order (s 587B(9ZA) as inserted).

New s 587B(9ZB) provides that the HMRC order may designate a market by name or by reference to any class or description of market. Orders may also vary or revoke previous orders.

Paragraph 8 makes consequential amendments to TCGA 1992:

— amending ss 130(1)(*a*), 144(8)(*a*), 146(4)(*b*) and 273(2); and

— omitting s 285 which provided for a definition of "relevant investment exchange".

Paragraph 9 (introduced into the Finance Bill at Committee stage) makes a consequential amendment to the rules on derivatives in FA 2002 Sch 26 para 4(2C)(*b*).

Paragraph 10 makes consequential amendments to ITEPA 2003 s 717(2).

Additionally, sub-para (2) amends ITEPA 2003 s 421L(6)(b) which provides that certain securities are excluded from the requirement to notify HMRC of certain events in connection with employment-related securities and options. The previous version provided an exemption for securities issued by a person other than an employer which are listed or dealt in on a recognised stock exchange. The latter part of that rule is now replaced. The new version refers instead to securities which are listed on a recognised stock exchange or dealt in on any designated market in the UK.

Designation applies for the purposes of that section by HMRC Order (s 412L(7) as inserted).

New s 421L(8) provides that the HMRC order may designate a market by name or by reference to any class or description of market. Orders may also vary or revoke previous orders.

Paragraph 11 amends ITTOIA 2005 ss 443(2) and 460(3).

Finally, para 12 amends other parts of ITA 2007. The amended sections are 143(2)(*a*), 151(2) ,184, 257(5), 274(2), 295(3), 382(2) , 397(6), 691(1)(*b*), 989 and 1014(2)(*g*).

Additionally, sub-para (10) amends s 432 which defines a qualifying investment for the purposes of the rules relating to gifts to charities. The previous provision that included, as a qualifying investment, shares or securities which are listed or dealt in on a recognised stock exchange, is now replaced. The new s 432(1)(a) refers instead to shares or securities which are listed on a recognised stock exchange or dealt in on any designated market in the UK.

Designation applies for the purposes of that section by HMRC Order (section 432(2) as amended).

New s 432(3) provides that the HMRC order may designate a market by name or by reference to any class or description of market. Orders may also vary or revoke previous orders.

Finally, the Table in ITA 2007 Sch 4 is consequentially amended to reflect the new definitions in s 1005.

SCHEDULE 27
REPEALS

Section 114

PART 1
ENVIRONMENT

(1) Exempt Aggregates: Railways etc

Short title and chapter	*Extent of repeal*
Finance Act 2001 (c 9)	In section 17(3), the word "or" at the end of paragraph (*d*).

(2) Climate Change Levy: Reduced-rate Supplies etc

Short title and chapter	*Extent of repeal*
Finance Act 2000 (c 17)	In Schedule 6—

Short title and chapter	*Extent of repeal*
	(*a*) in paragraph 11, in sub-paragraph (1) the words "has, before the supply is made, notified the supplier" and "that he" (in both places), and, in sub-paragraph (3), the words "has, before the supply is made, notified the supplier that" and "he", (*b*) paragraph 45(2) to (4), and (*c*) in paragraph 101, sub-paragraph (1), and, in sub-paragraph (3), the words "notification or"

The repeal of paragraph 45(2) to (4) of Schedule 6 to FA 2000 has effect in accordance with Schedule 2 to this Act.

PART 2
INCOME TAX, CORPORATION TAX AND CAPITAL GAINS TAX

(1) Restrictions on Trade Loss Relief for Partners

Short title and chapter	*Extent of repeal*
Income Tax Act 2007 (c 3)	In section 104(5), the words "(see section 112)". Section 106. In section 107(2), the words "(see section 112)". In section 110(1)(*a*), the words "(see section 112)". Section 112(1) to (5). In section 115(1)(*d*), the words "(see section 112)". Section 116.

These repeals have effect in accordance with Schedule 4 to this Act.

(2) Extension of Restrictions On Allowable Capital Losses

Short title and chapter	*Extent of repeal*
Taxation of Chargeable Gains Act 1992 (c 12)	Section 8(2A) to (2C).
Finance Act 2006 (c 25)	Section 69.

These repeals have effect in accordance with section 27 of this Act.

(3) Avoidance Involving Financial Arrangements

Short title and chapter	*Extent of repeal*
Income and Corporation Taxes Act 1988 (c 1)	Section 347A. Section 660C(4).
Finance Act 1988 (c 39)	Section 36(1).
Capital Allowances Act 2001 (c 2)	In section 228F— (*a*) subsection (4), and (*b*) in subsection (8), paragraph (*b*) (together with the word "and" before it).
Income Tax (Trading and Other Income) Act 2005 (c 5)	In Schedule 1, paragraph 272(4).
Income Tax Act 2007 (c 3)	In Schedule 1, paragraph 52.

These repeals have effect in accordance with Schedule 5 to this Act.

(4) Restrictions on Companies Buying Losses or Gains: Tax Avoidance Schemes

Short title and chapter	*Extent of repeal*
Taxation of Chargeable Gains Act 1992 (c 12)	In section 184A(2), the words "unless the gains accrue to the company on a disposal of a pre-change asset".

Short title and chapter	Extent of repeal
	In section 184B(2), the words "unless the loss accrues to the company on a disposal of a pre-change asset".
Finance Act 2006 (c 25)	In section 70(9)— (*a*) in paragraph (*a*), the words "or 184B", (*b*) paragraph (*d*) (together with the word "and" following it), and (*c*) in paragraph (*e*), the words ", or a qualifying gain for the purposes of section 184B of that Act,".

These repeals have effect in accordance with section 32 of this Act.

(5) Employee Benefit Contributions

Short title and chapter	Extent of repeal
Finance Act 2003 (c 14)	In Schedule 24, in paragraph 9(1), the definition of "the third party".
Finance Act 2004 (c 12)	Section 245(2).
Income Tax (Trading and Other Income) Act 2005 (c 5)	In Schedule 1, paragraph 624(2).

These repeals have effect in accordance with section 34 of this Act.

(6) Schemes etc Designed to Increase Double Taxation Relief

Short title and chapter	Extent of repeal
Income and Corporation Taxes Act 1988 (c 1)	In section 804ZA(8)(*c*), the words "resident in a territory outside the United Kingdom".

This repeal has effect in accordance with section 35 of this Act.

(7) Insurance Companies: Gross-roll Up Business etc

Short title and chapter	Extent of repeal
Taxes Management Act 1970 (c 9)	In section 98, in the Table, the entries relating to section 333B of the Income and Corporation Taxes Act 1988.
Income and Corporation Taxes Act 1988 (c 1)	In section 76— (*a*) in subsection (1), the second sentence, (*b*) subsection (14), and (*c*) in subsection (15), the definition of "capital redemption business". Section 333B. Section 403E(3). In section 431(2), the definitions of "annuity business" and "overseas life assurance fund". In section 431A(3)(*a*), the words "and Schedule 19AA". In section 432A— (*a*) subsection (4), (*b*) in subsection (5), the words "(apart from overseas life assurance business)", (*c*) in subsection (7)(*c*)(i), the word "438B," and (*d*) subsection (9). In section 432AA— (*a*) subsection (3), and (*b*) in subsection (5), the words "(3) or". Section 432AB(6). In section 432B—

Short title and chapter	*Extent of repeal*
	(*a*) in subsection (4), paragraph (*b*) and the word "and" before it, (*b*) in subsection (5), the words "the relevant fraction of", (*c*) in subsection (7), the words "the relevant fraction of" (in both places), (*d*)in subsections (8A) and (8C), the words "the relevant fraction of", and (*e*) in subsection (9), the definitions of "the relevant fraction" and "the section 83 net amount". Section 432D. In section 432E— (*a*) in subsection(3)(*b*), the words "mentioned in subsection (1) above", and (*b*) subsections (5) and (6) In section 432F(2)— (*a*) the words "For each category of business in relation to which section 432E falls to be applied", and (*b*) the words ", after making any reduction required by section 432E(5)," Section 434(6A)(*b*) In section 434A(2)(*a*), the words "the aggregate of" and sub-paragraph (iii) Section 436 Section 438(2) and (4) Section 438B Section 438C Section 439 Section 439B Section 440A(2)(*c*) Section 441 In section 444A(3), paragraph (*b*) and the word "or" before it Sections 458 and 458A Section 460(2)(cb) Section 461(3A) Section 461B(2A) In section 466— (*a*) in subsection (2), the definition of "life assurance business", and (*b*) subsections (2ZA), (2A) and (2B). In section 804B— (*a*) in subsection (2), the words "or section 438B", (*b*) in subsection (4), the words "or 438B", and (*c*) in subsection (6), the words "or 432D" (in both places) Schedule 19AA
Finance Act 1989 (c 26)	In Schedule 8, paragraph 6
Finance Act 1990 (c 29)	In Schedule 6— (*a*) in paragraph 1(2)(*b*), the entry relating to "overseas life assurance fund", and (*b*) paragraph 7 In Schedule 7, paragraphs 3, 6 and 10(2).
Finance Act 1991 (c 31)	In Schedule 7, paragraph 4(1)(*b*) In Schedule 15, paragraph 16
Taxation of Chargeable Gains Act 1992 (c 12)	In section 204(10)(*b*), the word "other"

Short title and chapter	*Extent of repeal*
	In section 210B(6), paragraph (*b*) and the word "or" before it. In section 213(1A), the words following "general annuity business".
Finance Act 1995 (c 4)	In Schedule 8— (*a*) in paragraph 1, the entry relating to "reinsurance business", (*b*) paragraph 3, (*c*) paragraph 5(2), (*d*) paragraph 8, (*e*) paragraph 9(2), (*f*) in paragraph 12(1)(*a*), the words "section 432C(1), section 432D(1) (in both places)and" and "and (6)(*a*)", (*g*) paragraph 13(5), (*h*) paragraph 14, (*i*) paragraph 15, (*j*) paragraph 16(3), (*k*) paragraph 17(2), (*l*) paragraph 27(1) and (2), (*m*) paragraph 51(5), and (*n*) in paragraph 55(1), the word "3,". In Schedule 9, paragraph 1(3).
Finance Act 1996 (c 8)	Section 167(2). Section 168(1) and (3). In Schedule 11— (*a*) in paragraph 3A(5), paragraph (*c*) and the word "and" before it, and (*b*) in paragraph 4, in sub-paragraph (1), paragraph (*b*) and the word "or" before it, and sub-paragraph (16). In Schedule 31, paragraph 7(2).
Finance (No 2) Act 1997 (c 58)	In Schedule 3, paragraphs 3 and 6(3).
Finance Act 1998 (c 36)	Section 77.
Finance Act 2000 (c 17)	Section 108(1). Section 109(3), (4), (7) and (9)(*b*). In Schedule 27, paragraph 8.
Capital Allowances Act 2001(c 2)	Section 255(2).
Finance Act 2001 (c 9)	In Schedule 22, in paragraph 14(10), "or (6)". In Schedule 25, paragraphs 5, 6 and 8.
Finance Act 2003 (c 14)	In section 153(1)(*a*), the words "in Schedule 19AA, paragraph 5(5)(*c*);". In Schedule 33, paragraphs 1(3)(*a*) and (4)(*a*), 6(7)(*a*), 9, 10(2) and 13(6)(*b*).
Child Trust Funds Act 2004 (c 6)	Section 14.
Finance Act 2004 (c 12)	Section 147(1), (2) and (4). In Schedule 7, paragraph 9(1). In Schedule 35, paragraph 22(3).
Income Tax (Trading and Other Income) Act 2005 (c 5)	In Schedule 1, paragraphs 143 and 175.
Finance (No 2) Act 2005 (c 22)	In Schedule 9— (*a*) paragraph 18(5) and (6), and (*b*) paragraph 19(1) to (3).
Income Tax Act 2007 (c 3)	In Schedule 1, paragraphs 78 and 83.

These repeals have effect in accordance with section 38 of this Act.

(8) Insurance Companies: Basis of Taxation etc

Short title and chapter	*Extent of repeal*
Income and Corporation Taxes Act 1988 (c 1)	In section 76—
	(*a*) in subsection (7), Steps 9 and 10, and
	(*b*) subsections (10) and (11).
	Section 439A.
	Section 440B(5).
Finance Act 1989 (c 26)	Section 88(2).
Taxation of Chargeable Gains Act 1992 (c 12)	Section 212(7A).
Finance (No 2) Act 1992 (c 48)	Section 65.
Finance Act 1993 (c 34)	In Schedule 14, paragraph 9.
Finance Act 1995 (c 4)	In Schedule 8—
	(*a*) paragraph 12(3),
	(*b*) paragraph 16(6),
	(*c*) paragraph 20(2),
	(*d*) paragraph 26,
	(*e*) paragraph 28(5), and
	(*f*) paragraph 51(3).
Finance Act 1996 (c 8)	In Schedule 11, paragraph 4(12) to (14).
Finance (No 2) Act 1997 (c 58)	In Schedule 3, paragraph 15.
Finance Act 2002 (c 23)	In Schedule 29, paragraph 36(6).
Finance Act 2003 (c 14)	In Schedule 33, paragraph 7.

These repeals have effect in accordance with section 39 of this Act.

(9) Insurance Companies: Transfers etc

Short title and chapter	*Extent of repeal*
Income and Corporation Taxes Act 1988 (c 1)	In section 12(7B), the definition of "insurance business transfer scheme".
	In section 444A—
	(*a*) in subsection (1), the words "Subject to subsection (7) below," and
	(*b*) subsections (7) and (8)
	Section 444AB(11) (as originally enacted).
	In section 444AC(11) (as originally enacted), the definition of "insurance business transfer scheme"
	Section 444AD
	Section 460(10B)
Taxation of Chargeable Gains Act 1992 (c 12)	In Schedule 10, paragraph 14(25)
Finance Act 1989 (c 26)	Section 82C
	In section 83—
	(*a*) subsection (2A)(*b*),
	(*b*) in subsection (2B), the second sentence,
	(*c*) subsections (3) to (7), and
	(*d*) in subsection (8), the definitions of "add", "demutualisation" and "total reinsurance"
	Section 83AA
	Section 83AB
Finance Act 1996 (c 8)	In Schedule 9, in paragraph 12(9), the definition of "insurance business transfer scheme".
	In Schedule 31—
	(*a*) paragraph 5,
	(*b*) paragraph 9, and
	(*c*) in paragraph 10(2), the words "Subject to paragraph 9 above,"
Finance Act 2000 (c 17)	In Schedule 29, paragraph 30

Short title and chapter	*Extent of repeal*
Capital Allowances Act 2001 (c 2)	Section 560(5)(*b*)
Finance Act 2002 (c 23)	In section 66— (*a*) in subsection (5), the definition of "transfer scheme", and (*b*) subsections (6) and (7) In Schedule 9, paragraph 5(11) In Schedule 22, in paragraph 10— (*a*) in sub-paragraph (4), the definition of "transfer scheme", and (*b*) sub-paragraphs (5) and (6) In Schedule 26, paragraph 28(5) In Schedule 29, in paragraph 89(3), the definition of "insurance business transfer scheme"
Finance Act 2003 (c 14)	In Schedule 33— (*a*) paragraph 2(3), (4) and (6), (*b*) paragraph 5(*b*), (*c*) paragraphs 18 and 19, and (*d*) paragraph 20(4).
Finance Act 2004 (c 12)	In Schedule 7— (*a*) paragraphs 2 to 4, and (*b*) in paragraph 5(2) and (3).
Finance (No 2) Act 2005 (c 22)	In Schedule 9— (*a*) paragraphs 6 and 7, (*b*) paragraph 11, (*c*) paragraph 12(4) and (6), and (*d*) paragraph 20(3) to (5).
Finance Act 2006 (c 25)	In Schedule 11— (*a*) paragraph 3, (*b*) paragraph 4, and (*c*) paragraph 6(2).

These repeals have effect in accordance with Schedule 9 to this Act.

(10) Insurance Companies: Miscellaneous

Short title and chapter	*Extent of repeal*
Taxes Management Act 1970 (c 9)	In section 98, in the Table, in both columns, the words "or 441A(3)".
Income and Corporation Taxes Act 1988 (c 1)	In section 12(7B), the words from the beginning to the end of the definition of "contracts of long-term insurance". In section 76— (*a*) in subsection (7), in Step 3, the entries relating to section 587B(8)(*b*)(i) of ICTA and paragraph 23(2) of Schedule 13 to FA 2002, and (*b*) in subsection (15), the words "and other expressions have the same meaning as in Chapter 1 of Part 12". Section 431A(7). In section 432YA(5), the definitions of "non-profit company" and "non-profit fund". In section 432ZA(6), the definition of "internal linked fund". Section 432A(9A). In section 432E(2A), the words "444ACA(2)," and paragraph (*b*). Section 440(2A), (2B) and (5). Section 442(4).

Short title and chapter	*Extent of repeal*
	Sections 443 and 444. Section 444AB(6) (as originally enacted). In section 444AC(11) (as originally enacted), the words from the beginning to the end of the definition of "fair value" Section 444ACA Section 444AD(5) In section 502H— (*a*) in subsection (2), paragraph (*b*) and the word "and" before it", and (*b*) subsections (8) to (10) In section 587B— (*a*) subsection (8), and (*b*) in subsection (9), the words ""life assurance business" and related expressions have the same meaning as in Chapter 1 of Part 12;" In section 587BA— (*a*) subsection (12), and (*b*) in subsection (13), paragraph (*b*) and the word "and" before it In section 755A(12), the definition of "long-term insurance fund" Section 804F In section 807A— (*a*) subsections (4) and (5)(*b*), and (*b*) in subsection (6)(*a*), the words "or an insurance credit" In Schedule 28AA, in paragraph 14(1), the definition of "insurance company"
Finance Act 1989 (c 26)	Section 82D(5) In section 83(8), in the definition of "fair value", paragraph (*a*) In section 83YA— (*a*) subsection (8), and (*b*) in subsection (11), the definition of "with-profits fund" Section 83YB(5) In section 83A— (*a*) in subsection (1), the words "In sections 82A to 83AB", (*b*) in subsections (2)(*b*) and (3D)(*b*), the words "(see subsection (6))", and (*c*) subsection (6) Section 84(2), (3), (5) and (6) In section 85— (*a*) in subsection (2A), the second sentence, and (*b*) in subsection (3), the words "(including the 1990 component period)". In section 86— (*a*) subsections (3) and (3A), and (*b*) in subsection (10), the words "(including the 1990 component period)". Section 87. In section 89(6), the words from the beginning to "; and". Section 90A.
Finance Act 1991 (c 31)	In Schedule 7— (*a*) paragraph 13(2),

Short title and chapter	*Extent of repeal*
	(*b*) in paragraph 16(7), the words from "and, subject to that," to the end, and
	(*c*) paragraph 17(4A) and (5).
Taxation of Chargeable Gains Act 1992 (c 12)	In section 210B(8), the definition of "internal linked fund".
	Section 212(2A).
	Section 214.
	Section 214A.
	Section 214BA.
	In Schedule 7AC, paragraph 17(5).
	In Schedule 10, paragraph 14(22)(*b*).
Finance Act 1993 (c 34)	Section 91(5) and (6).
Finance Act 1995 (c 4)	In Schedule 8, paragraph 9(3).
	In Schedule 9—
	(*a*) in paragraph 1(2)(*d*), the words "214(11) and 214A(7)", and
	(*b*) paragraph 5.
Finance Act 1996 (c 8)	In section 87A(2), the words ", within the meaning of Chapter 1 of Part 12 of the Taxes Act 1988," and the words "(see section 431(2) of that Act)".
	Section 88(7).
	In section 103(3), the word "or" at the end of paragraph (*a*).
	In Schedule 9—
	(*a*) in paragraph 12(9), the definitions of "contracts of long-term insurance" and "overseas life insurance company", and
	(*b*) in paragraph 20(3)(*b*), the words ", within the meaning of Chapter 1 of Part 12 of the Taxes Act 1988," and the words "(see section 431(2) of that Act)".
	In Schedule 11—
	(*a*) paragraph 1,
	(*b*) paragraph 2(2) and (3) to (5),
	(*c*) paragraph 3A(6),
	(*d*) paragraph 4(6), and
	(*e*) paragraphs 5 and 6.
	In Schedule 14, paragraphs 25 and 63.
	In Schedule 15, paragraph 1(3).
	In Schedule 31, paragraph 6.
Finance Act 1997 (c 16)	In Schedule 12—
	(*a*) paragraph 18, and
	(*b*) paragraph 19(1) to (3).
Finance Act 1998 (c 36)	In Schedule 18—
	(*a*) in paragraph 13(3), the words after "1988", and
	(*b*) paragraph 86.
Finance Act 1999 (c 16)	In Schedule 6, paragraph 4.
Finance Act 2000 (c 17)	In Schedule 30, paragraph 19.
Capital Allowances Act 2001 (c 2)	Section 257(3).
	Section 544(5).
	Section 560(5)(*a*) and (*c*).
Finance Act 2001 (c 9)	Section 87(3) and (4).
	In Schedule 22, in paragraph 31(1), the definitions of "insurance company" and "life assurance business".

Short title and chapter	*Extent of repeal*
Finance Act 2002 (c 23)	In section 66(5), the words from the beginning to the end of the definition of "long-term insurance fund". In Schedule 12, in paragraph 19(1), the definition of "life assurance business". In Schedule 13— (*a*) paragraphs 22 and 23, (*b*) paragraph 25(3), and (*c*) in paragraph 27, the definition of "life assurance business". In Schedule 22, in paragraph 10(4), the words before the definition of "transfer scheme". In Schedule 26— (*a*) in paragraph 12, in sub-paragraph (1), the references to the expressions "Integrated Prudential Sourcebook" and "long-term insurance fund" and sub-paragraphs (15) and (16), and (*b*) in paragraph 54(1), the definitions of "insurance company", "life assurance business", "long-term insurance business" and "contract of long-term insurance". In Schedule 27, paragraph 5. In Schedule 29— (*a*) paragraph 36(4) and (5), (*b*) in paragraph 89(3), the definition of "contracts of long-term insurance", and (*c*) paragraph 138(1).
Finance Act 2003 (c 14)	In Schedule 33, paragraphs 1(2), 26 and 30 to 32.
Finance Act 2004 (c 12)	In Schedule 10, paragraphs 43 and 70.
Finance (No 2) Act 2005 (c 22)	In Schedule 9, paragraphs 4, 8, and 13(5).
Finance Act 2006 (c 25)	Section 134(4)(*c*).
Income Tax Act 2007 (c 3)	In section 442(6), paragraph (*b*) and the word "and" before it. Section 443(6). In Schedule 1, paragraph 137(8).

These repeals have effect in accordance with Schedule 10 to this Act.

(11) Technical Provisions Made by General Insurers

Short title and chapter	*Extent of repeal*
Income and Corporation Taxes Act 1988 (c 1)	Section 804E(3)(*d*).
Finance Act 2000 (c 17)	Section 107.
Finance Act 2003 (c 14)	Section 153(1)(*c*).

These repeals have effect in accordance with Schedule 11 to this Act.

(12) Friendly Societies

Short title and chapter	*Extent of repeal*
Finance (No 2) Act 1992 (c 48)	In Schedule 9, paragraphs 8(3) and 11(2).

These repeals have effect in accordance with Schedule 12 to this Act.

(13) Purchased Life Annuities

Short title and chapter	*Extent of repeal*
Income and Corporation Taxes Act 1988 (c 1)	Section 437(1C)(*c*)(i) and (*d*)(i). Section 656(5) and (6).

Short title and chapter	*Extent of repeal*
	Section 658(1) and (4) to (6).
	In section 828(4), the word "658(3)".
Income Tax (Trading and Other Income) Act 2005 (c 5)	Section 717(3).
	Section 723.Section 724(2).
	Section 873(3)(*b*).
	In Schedule 1, paragraphs 268(3) and 270.
	In Schedule 2, paragraphs 143 and 145.
Commissioners for Revenue and Customs Act 2005 (c 11)	In Schedule 4, paragraph 133(5).

These repeals have effect in accordance with section 46 of this Act.

(14) Sale and Repurchase of Securities

Short title and chapter	*Extent of repeal*
Income and Corporation Taxes Act 1988 (c 1)	In section 231AA(4), the words "or 737A(5)".
	Sections 730A to 730BB.
	In section 731(2A), the words "section 737A(5) below or".
	Sections 737A to 737C.
	Section 737E.
Taxation of Chargeable Gains Act 1992 (c 12)	Section 263A(2).
Finance Act 1994 (c 9)	Section 122.
Finance Act 1995 (c 4)	Section 80(1) and (3).
Finance Act 1996 (c 8)	Section 100(2A).
	In Schedule 14, paragraph 37.
Finance Act 1997 (c 16)	Section 91(5).
Finance Act 2002 (c 23)	In Schedule 25, paragraphs 32 and 52.
Finance Act 2003 (c 14)	In Schedule 38, paragraphs 2, 3, 5, 7 to 14, 16 to 20 and 21(3).
Finance Act 2004 (c 12)	In Schedule 10, paragraphs 44 and 78.
Finance (No 2) Act 2005 (c 22)	In Schedule 7, paragraph 19.
Finance Act 2006 (c 25)	Section 139(5).
	In Schedule 6, paragraphs 5 and 20.
Income Tax Act 2007 (c 3)	In Schedule 1, paragraphs 164 to 166, 173, 174 and 334.

These repeals have effect in accordance with section 47 of this Act.

(15) Controlled Foreign Companies

Short title and chapter	*Extent of repeal*
Income and Corporation Taxes Act 1988 (c 1)	In section 748(1), paragraph (*c*) (together with the word "or" at the end of it).
	In Schedule 25, Part 3.
Finance Act 1996 (c 8)	In Schedule 38, in paragraph 6— (*a*) in sub-paragraph (2), paragraph (*m*) (together with the word "and" before it), and (*b*) in sub-paragraph (5), the words "and (*m*)"

These repeals have effect in accordance with Schedule 15 to this Act.

(16) Venture Capital Schemes

Short title and chapter	*Extent of repeal*
Income and Corporation Taxes Act 1988 (c 1)	In section 297(5A), paragraphs (*b*) and (*c*) and the words after paragraph (*c*).

Short title and chapter	*Extent of repeal*
	In section 312(1), in the definition of "qualifying 90% subsidiary", the words "to (13)".
Finance Act 2000 (c 17)	In Schedule 15— (*a*) in paragraph 15, the word "and" at the end of paragraph (*f*), and (*b*) paragraph 23(10) and (11).
Finance Act 2004 (c 12)	In Schedule 18, paragraph 1(8). In Schedule 20, paragraph 7(*d*).
Income Tax Act 2007 (c 3)	In section 195(6), the definition of "holding company". In section 274(3), the word "and" at the end of paragraph (*c*). In section 284(*d*), the words "for Her Majesty's Revenue and Customs". In section 306(6), the definition of "holding company". In section 327(1), the word "and" immediately before "section 297".

These repeals have effect in accordance with Schedule 16 to this Act.

(17) Real Estate Investment Trusts

Short title and chapter	*Extent of repeal*
Finance Act 2006	Section 107(5), (7) and (7A).In section 115(2), the words "+ Financing Costs". In Schedule 17— (*a*) paragraph 6(2) and (3), and (*b*) in paragraph 14, the words "+ Financing Costs (all)" and paragraph (*b*) of the substituted subsection (2)
Income Tax Act 2007 (c 3)	In Schedule 1, paragraph 617.

These repeals have effect in accordance with section 52 of this Act.

(18) Offshore Funds

Short title and chapter	*Extent of repeal*
Income and Corporation Taxes Act 1988 (c 1)	In Schedule 27, in paragraph 6(1)(*c*), the words "without regard to the provisions of this paragraph,".

This repeal has effect in accordance with section 57 of this Act.

(19) Benefits Code: Whether Employment is "Lower-Paid Employment"

Short title and chapter	*Extent of repeal*
Income Tax (Earnings and Pensions) Act 2003 (c 1)	Section 219(5) and (6).

This repeal has effect in accordance with section 62 of this Act.

PART 3
PENSIONS

(1) Alternatively Secured Pensions etc

Short title and chapter	*Extent of repeal*
Inheritance Tax Act 1984 (c 51)	In section 151C(4), the word "and" at the end of the definition of "dependant". In Schedule 2, paragraph 6A.

Short title and chapter	Extent of repeal
Income Tax (Earnings and Pensions) Act 2003 (c 1)	In section 636A— (*a*) in subsection (1), paragraph (*f*) and the word "or" before it, and (*b*) in subsection (7), the words ""transfer lump sum death benefit",".
Finance Act 2004 (c 12)	Section 168(1)(*g*). Section 172B(5)(*a*). In section 188(5), paragraph (*b*) and the word "and" before it. In section 280(2), the entry relating to transfer lump sum death benefit. In Schedule 28, paragraph 12(3) and (4). In Schedule 29, paragraph 19. In Schedule 34, in— (*a*) paragraph 1(6), and (*b*) paragraph 4(3), the words from "but also" to the end. In Schedule 36, in paragraph 17A— (*a*) in sub-paragraph (1), paragraph (*c*) and the word "or" before it, and (*b*) in sub-paragraph (2), the words ", or to a transfer lump sum death benefit being paid,".
Finance Act 2006 (c 25)	In Schedule 22, paragraph 11.

These repeals have effect in accordance with Schedule 19 to this Act.

(2) Miscellaneous

Short title and chapter	Extent of repeal
Pension Schemes Act 1993 (c 48)	In section 1(1), in the definition of "personal pension scheme", in paragraph (*b*), the words "any of the paragraphs of".
Pension Schemes (Northern Ireland) Act 1993 (c 49)	In section 1(1), in the definition of "personal pension scheme", in paragraph (*b*), the words "any of the paragraphs of".
Finance Act 2004 (c 12)	In section 154— (*a*) subsection (3), and (*b*) in subsection (4), the words "and section 155" Section 155. In section 273— (*a*) in subsection (5)(*a*), the words "was established by a person or body specified in section 154(1)(*a*) to(*g*) (insurance companies etc) and", and (*b*) in subsection (7), the words "was established by a person or body specified in section 154(1)(*a*) to (*g*) and". In Schedule 29— (*a*) in paragraph 1(1), paragraph (*e*) (but not including the word "and" at the end), and (*b*) paragraph 10(3)(*a*) In Schedule 29A, paragraph 22(2). In Schedule 36, in paragraph 12— (*a*) in sub-paragraph (7), paragraph (*a*) and, in paragraph (*b*), the words "held for the purposes of, or representing accrued rights under, the arrangement",

Short title and chapter	*Extent of repeal*
	(*b*) in sub-paragraph (8)(*a*), the words ", or two or more money purchase arrangements that are not cash balance arrangements," and the word "or" at the end, and (*c*) in sub-paragraph (9)(*a*), the words ", or each of the arrangements," and the word "and" at the end

These repeals have effect in accordance with Schedule 20 to this Act.

PART 4
SDLT, STAMP DUTY AND SDRT

(1) Anti-avoidance: Partnerships

Short title and chapter	*Extent of repeal*
Finance Act 2003 (c 14)	In Schedule 15— (*a*) paragraphs 13 and 14(1)(*b*) and (4), and (*b*) in the italic cross-heading before paragraph 14 the words "for consideration"

These repeals have effect in accordance with section 72 of this Act.

(2) Exemptions: Intermediaries, Repurchases etc

Short title and chapter	*Extent of repeal*
Finance Act 1986 (c 41)	In section 80B(2), the definition of "EEA exchange". In section 80C(7), the definition of "EEA exchange" (together with the word "and" at the end of it). In section 88B(2), the definition of "EEA exchange". In section 89AA(6), the definition of "EEA exchange".
Finance (No 2) Act 2005 (c 22)	Section 50.
Finance Act 2007 (c.)	Section 73. Schedule 21.

1 Subject to Note 2, these repeals have effect in accordance with Schedule 21 to this Act.

2 The repeals of section 73 of, and Schedule 21 to, this Act have effect in accordance with sections 108 and 110 of FA 1990.

(3) Certain Transfers of School Land

Short title and chapter	*Extent of repeal*
School Standards and Framework Act 1998 (c 31)	Sections 79 and 79A.
Education and Inspections Act 2006 (c 40)	In Part 3 of Schedule 4, paragraph 20.

These repeals have effect in accordance with section 79 of this Act.

(4) Payment of SDLT

Short title and chapter	*Extent of repeal*
Finance Act 2003 (c 14)	In section 76(3), paragraph (*b*) and the word "and" before it. In section 81(2), paragraph (*b*) and the word "and" before it. In Schedule 10, in paragraph 2(2), paragraph (*b*) and the word "and" before it.

These repeals have effect in accordance with section 80 of this Act.

PART 5
INVESTIGATION, ADMINISTRATION ETC

(1) Criminal Investigations

Short title and chapter	*Extent of repeal*
Taxes Management Act 1970 (c 9)	Sections 20C and 20CC.
	In section 118(1), in the definition of "tax", the word ", 20C".
Customs and Excise Management Act 1979 (c 2)	In section 118C—
	(*a*) in subsection (3), paragraph (*c*) and the word "or" before it,
	(*b*) in subsection (4)(*b*), the words "or in respect of a gaming duty offence", and
	(*c*) in subsection (5), the words from "and "a gaming duty offence" " to the end.
Betting and Gaming Duties Act 1981 (c 63)	In Schedule 1, paragraph 16.
	In Schedule 3, paragraph 17.
	In Schedule 4, paragraph 17.
Finance Act 1984 (c 43)	In Schedule 3, paragraph 7(12).
Police and Criminal Evidence Act 1984 (c 60)	In Schedule 6, paragraph 39(*b*) to (*d*).
Finance Act 1989 (c 26)	Section 146 and 147.
	Section 148(4).
Finance Act 1994 (c 9)	In Schedule 7, paragraph 4(2) to (7).
Value Added Tax Act 1994 (c 23)	Section 72(9).
	In Schedule 11, paragraph 10(3) to (6).
Finance Act 1995 (c 4)	In Schedule 3, paragraph 11(10).
Criminal Procedure (Consequential Provisions) (Scotland) Act 1995 (c 40)	In Schedule 4, paragraph 91(*a*).
Finance Act 1996 (c 8)	In Schedule 5, paragraphs 5 and 6.
Finance Act 1997 (c 16)	In Schedule 2, paragraph 4(3) to (5).
Finance Act 2000 (c 17)	Section 149(4).
	Section 150.
	In Schedule 6, paragraphs 97 and 130.
Finance Act 2001 (c 9)	In Schedule 6, paragraph 6.
	In Schedule 7, paragraph 7.
Criminal Justice and Police Act 2001 (c 16)	Section 57(1)(*c*).
	Section 63(2)(*e*).
	Section 65(3).
	In Schedule 1, paragraphs 13, 28, 29, 57, 58, 61 and 72.
	In Schedule 2, paragraph 13(2)(*d*).
Tax Credits Act 2002 (c 21)	Section 36(2) and (3).
Proceeds of Crime Act 2002(c 29)	Section 323(3)(*e*) and (*f*).
Finance Act 2003 (c 14)	Part 7 of Schedule 13.
Commissioners for Revenue and Customs Act 2005 (c 11)	Section 13(3)(*b*) and (*c*).
	Section 14(2)(*b*) and (*c*).
	In Schedule 2, paragraphs 7 and 9.

These repeals have effect in accordance with section 84(5) of this Act.

(2) Criminal Investigations: Scotland

Short title and chapter	*Extent of repeal*
Criminal Law (Consolidation) (Scotland) Act 1995 (c 39)	Section 24(9).

This repeal has effect in accordance with Schedule 23 to this Act.

(3) Filing Dates for Returns

Short title and chapter	*Extent of repeal*
Taxes Management Act 1970 (c 9)	In section 8—
	(*a*) in subsection (1)(*a*), the words ", on or before the day mentioned in subsection(1A) below", and
	(*b*) subsection (1A).
	In section 8A—
	(*a*) in subsection (1)(*a*) the words ", on or before the day mentioned in subsection(1A) below", and
	(*b*) subsection (1A).
	In section 33A(9), the definition of "filing date".
	In section 93A(8), the definition of "the filing date".
Finance Act 1996 (c 8)	Section 125(3).

These repeals have effect in accordance with section 92 of this Act.

(4) Mandatory Electronic Filing of Returns

Short title and chapter	*Extent of repeal*
Value Added Tax Act 1994 (c 23)	In section 76(3), the word "and" at the end of paragraph (*d*).
Commissioners for Revenue and Customs Act 2005 (c 11)	In Schedule 2, paragraph 12.
	In Schedule 4, paragraph 95(2).

(5) Penalties for Errors

Short title and chapter	*Extent of repeal*
Taxes Management Act 1970 (c 9)	Section 95.
	Section 95A.
	Section 97.
	Section 98A(4).
	Section 100A(1).
	Section 103(2).
Finance Act 1989 (c 26)	Section 163(1)(*a*).
Finance Act 1994 (c 9)	In Schedule 19, paragraphs 27(1), 28 and 32.
Value Added Tax Act 1994 (c 23)	Sections 60 and 61.
	Sections 63 and 64.
Finance Act 1996 (c 8)	Section 36.
	Section 123(12) and (13).
Finance Act 1998 (c 36)	In Schedule 18, paragraphs 20 and 89.
Finance Act 2001 (c 9)	Section 98(3).
	In Schedule 29, paragraph 32.

These repeals have effect in accordance with section 97 of this Act.

PART 6
MISCELLANEOUS

(1) Vat: Non-Business Use etc of Business Goods

Short title and chapter	*Extent of repeal*
Value Added Tax Act 1994 (c 23)	In Schedule 4, paragraph 5(4A).
Finance Act 2003 (c 14)	Section 22.

These repeals have effect in accordance with section 99 of this Act.

(2) Vat: Transfers of Going Concerns

Short title and chapter	*Extent of repeal*
Value Added Tax Act 1994 (c 23)	In section 49(1), paragraph (*b*) (together with the word "and" before it).

This repeal has effect in accordance with section 100 of this Act.

(3) Repeals Connected with Gambling Act 2005

Short title and chapter	*Extent of repeal*
Finance Act 1966 (c 18)	In Schedule 3, paragraph 6.
Betting and Gaming Duties Act 1981 (c 63)	In section 3(1), paragraph (*b*) (together with the word "and" before it). In section 5C(5), paragraph (*b*) (together with the word "or" before it). In section 12(4)— (*a*) in the definition of "betting office licence", paragraph (*a*) (together with the word "and" following it), (*b*) in the definition of "bookmaker's permit", paragraph (*a*) (together with the word "and" following it), and (*c*) the definitions of "meeting", "totalisator" and "track". In section 20A(1), paragraph (*a*) (together with the word "or" following it). In Schedule 1— (*a*) paragraph 7, and (*b*) in paragraph 15, in sub-paragraph (2), the words "in England or Wales or Northern Ireland", sub-paragraphs (3) to (4A), and in sub-paragraph (5), the words "in Northern Ireland".
Finance Act 1986 (c 41)	In Schedule 4— (*a*) paragraph 4(*b*), and (*b*) in paragraph 11, in sub-paragraph (1), the words from "in paragraph 7" to the end, and sub-paragraph (2)(*a*) and (*b*).
Finance Act 1993 (c 34)	In section 24(4)— (*a*) in paragraph (*a*), the words "the Lotteries and Amusements Act 1976 or", (*b*) in paragraph (*b*), the words "Act or", (*c*) in paragraph (*c*), the words "Act or" and "section 5(3) of that Act or", and (*d*) paragraph (*d*).
Finance Act 1997 (c 16)	In section 10(3)— (*a*) paragraph (*c*), and (*b*) in paragraph (*d*), the words "section 41 of that Act or".
Access to Justice Act 1999 (c 22)	In Schedule 13, paragraph 120.
Finance Act 2002 (c 23)	Section 13.

Short title and chapter	*Extent of repeal*
	In Schedule 4, paragraph 10(14).
Finance Act 2003 (c 14)	Section 9(4).
Courts Act 2003 (c 39)	In Schedule 8, paragraph 266.
Income Tax Act 2007 (c 3)	In Schedule 1, in paragraph 94(2)(*e*), sub-paragraph (iii) (together with the word "and" before it).

These repeals have effect in accordance with Schedule 25 to this Act.

(4) Disclosure of Tax Avoidance Schemes

Short title and chapter	*Extent of repeal*
Taxes Management Act 1970 (c 9)	In section 98C(2), the word "or" at the end of paragraph (*c*).

(5) Meaning of "Recognised Stock Exchange" etc

Short title and chapter	*Extent of repeal*
Income and Corporation Taxes Act 1988 (c 1)	In Schedule 20, in paragraph 5, the words ", or which are dealt in on the Unlisted Securities Market".
Taxation of Chargeable Gains Act 1992 (c 12)	In section 130(1)(*a*), the words "in the United Kingdom or elsewhere".
	In section 146(4)(*b*), the words "in the United Kingdom or elsewhere".
	Section 285.
Finance Act 1996 (c 8)	In Schedule 38, paragraphs 7 and 12(1).
Financial Services and Markets Act 2000 (c 8)	In Schedule 20, paragraph 4(6).
Income Tax (Trading and Other Income) Act 2005 (c 5)	Section 443(2)(*g*).
	In section 460(3), the words "or 451".
Income Tax Act 2007 (c 3)	In section 295(3)(*c*), the words "on the Unlisted Securities Market or dealt in".
	Section 1010.
	In Schedule 1, paragraph 227.

FINANCE BILL DEBATES

Committee of the Whole House

30 April 2007	Cl 25
1 May	Cl 81

Public Bill Committee

15 May	Cll 17, 19, Sch 3
17 May	Cll 27, 28, 31, 32, 33, Schs 5, 6
22 May	Cll 52, 54, 56, Schs 7, 8, 9, 10, 11, 13, 16, 17
24 May	Cll 58, 63, 65
5 June	Cll 70, 71, 85, 92, 96, Schs 19, 20, 21
7 June	Cll 97, 98, 105, 106, Sch 26

Report Stage

25 June	New cl 5 (inserted as Finance Act 2007 s 28), cl 97

PUBLISHER'S NOTE

Extracts from the debates have been ordered below according to original Finance Bill clause/Schedule number, for ease of reference. Readers are advised to refer to the above table for details of dates when provisions were debated, and at what stage.

New clause 5, inserted at Report Stage, became Finance Act 2007 s 28. Therefore, all subsequent sections were renumbered accordingly, with previous clause 28 renumbered as section 29, previous clause 29 renumbered as section 30 and so on.

Clause 17 – Corporation tax deduction for expenditure on energy-saving items

(Col 120)

The Chief Secretary to the Treasury (Stephen Timms): "We will lay regulations introducing the same conditions for corporation tax that are already in place under the existing allowance for income tax, and the regulations will set the maximum deduction available at £1,500 per property per year and provide for that deduction to be apportioned in cases of joint ownership. A draft of the regulations has been provided for the Committee ... From 2008, energy performance certificates will be introduced in the private rented sector for every home bought, sold and let in the UK. Those certificates will highlight to landlords and tenants the existing energy efficiency of properties, as well as suggesting affordable ways to improve them. Setting 2015 as the date strikes a good balance between giving landlords enough time to take advantage of the allowance and encouraging them to take steps to improve the energy efficiency of their properties as soon as possible. The extension of the allowance by six years gives them time to take full advantage of the extended allowance and to benefit from the information provided by energy performance certificates."

Clause 19 – SDLT relief for new zero-carbon homes

(Col 126)

The Economic Secretary (Ed Balls): "This is an important part of the Bill, which creates a regulation-making power on which we will consult. In that light, and given that we intend to conclude the consultation by July and publish a further set of regulations, I would be happy—subject to agreement from the business managers—if we could deal with the regulations under the affirmative, rather than the negative, procedure, to ensure that the House has a further opportunity to scrutinise the detail of the regulations before they come into effect."

(Col 135)

The Economic Secretary: "In recent years, we have used building regulations to improve the energy efficiency of new homes. Changes to the building regulations in 2006 achieved a 40 per cent. improvement on pre-2002 standards, and a 70 per cent improvement on pre-1990 standards in the efficiency of new homes. However, this Government want to go further. In part, we will do that through regulations that require that by 2016 new build houses will meet the zero-carbon standard."

(Col 137)

The Economic Secretary: "The clause amends the stamp duty land tax legislation in the Finance Act 2003 by inserting new sections to deal with relief or exemption for the first sale of new zero-carbon homes. They will enable the Government to make regulations to define zero-carbon homes, to quantify the amount of relief or exemption and to deal with administrative matters. The regulations will cease to have effect at the end of a five-year period, on 30 September 2012, unless we decide to extend that relief further."

(Col 138)

The Economic Secretary: "The regulations that we set out are in draft. For reasons of good policy making and wider politics, we welcome the opportunity to have a further debate if the business managers allow. We genuinely intend to consult on the regulations. The Department for Communities and Local Government is currently consulting on the definition of zero-carbon homes by 2016, which is part of the reason why our approach must be consultative. Our regulations are running in parallel, and it desirable that those consultations end up with aligned definitions ... The first exemption will be complete for all new homes priced at less than £500,000; purchases above that level will benefit by £15,000. Stamp duty land tax will be paid only on the balance, which is equivalent to stamp duty at £500,000. The regulations set out a technical definition of a zero-carbon home, but that is in draft and for consultation."

Clause 25 – Managed service companies

(Col 1330)

The Financial Secretary (John Healey): "There is a specific exclusion from the definition of an MSC provider of those merely providing legal and accountancy services in a professional capacity. Let me make it clear that even where this specific exclusion does not apply, the purpose of the legislation is not to include within the definition of an MSC provider accountants, tax advisers, lawyers and company secretaries, who provide advice or other professional services to companies and individual clients. Those parties are not in the business of promoting or facilitating the use of companies to provide the services of individuals. Nor are they regarded as involved with the company in the way that the legislation envisages. In other words, simply because someone is not exempt by virtue of proposed new section 61B(1)(b) does not mean that they are caught by the legislation."

Clause 27 – Extension of restrictions on allowable capital losses

(Col 211)

The Economic Secretary (Ed Balls): "Clause 27 denies tax relief for capital losses where the existence or amount of the losses has been contrived—in other words, where the taxpayer has entered into arrangements of which one of the main purposes is to secure a tax advantage, so that the tax losses that arise do not reflect economic reality. The key principle set out in the statement issued by HMRC on 6 December is that relief for capital losses should be available only where a person has suffered a genuine commercial loss on a real disposal. The legislation will apply only where one of the main purposes of the arrangements is to secure a tax advantage. It will not apply to genuine economic transactions, so the vast majority of disposals—a wide range of innocent transactions—will be unaffected. We need to draw the rule widely enough to prevent further loss-creation schemes, but as I said, the rule will apply only to arrangements of which one of the main purposes is to gain a tax advantage ... It is not our intention to get in the way of proper tax planning, but when the complexity and ingenuity of schemes moves from tax planning to tax avoidance, the Government must respond to protect the taxpayer."

(Col 219)

The Economic Secretary: "I will give two examples to clarify our intentions and to further reassure Opposition Members. A straightforward example of a loss that would not be affected by this measure is a simple arm's length sale of FTSE 100 shares that have genuinely gone down in value. The fact that someone who realises such a loss might be able to set it off against gains that he or she has made on other investments in the year would not mean that the loss would be disallowed by this measure. Similarly, if a husband transfers to his wife, on a no-profit, no-loss basis, shares that are standing at a loss, it is perfectly acceptable for her to sell those shares and set the loss against a gain that she intends to realise on some other

(Col 220)

asset. Those are examples of normal tax planning that would not be captured by the measures."

New Clause 5 – Restriction on expenses of management

(*Note: this clause inserted as FA 2007 s 28*)

(Col 41)

The Financial Secretary (John Healey): "New clause 5 introduces a targeted anti-avoidance rule that tackles the use of tax avoidance schemes designed to generate deductions in respect of 'expenses of management' under section 75 of the Income and Corporation Taxes Act 1988. If left unchecked, those schemes would cost the UK Exchequer—the public

(Col 42)

purse—£1 billion a year. Section 75 of the 1988 Act provides 'companies with investment business' relief for the expenses of managing that investment business. The rules were introduced way back in 1915 and originally applied only to pure investment companies and to insurance companies. The rules remained largely unchanged until the Finance Act 2004. The changes that we made three years ago widened the range of companies able to obtain relief for expenses of management. They also specifically excluded capital expenditure and introduced an unallowable purpose rule in relation to investments not held for a business or commercial purpose. The unallowable purpose rule made no explicit reference to tax avoidance purposes. It was believed at the time that that rule and a tough approach to the construction of the phrase 'expenses of management' derived from case law would be sufficient to stop any abuse. Sadly, the appetite of some for tax avoidance has proved us wrong. In the past two or three years, the disclosure of tax avoidance schemes rules and other inquiries have shown us that there are already a number of avoidance schemes that create deductions for relief as expenses of management which are both substantial and contrived. The latest scheme is an attempt to circumvent other anti-avoidance legislation introduced in the Finance Act 2004. It creates a wholly artificial deduction for management expenses in return for the receipt of a dividend to which the UK company was already entitled before the scheme was put in place. These payments—treated by the companies as management expenses—are made to overseas companies, which are usually located in tax havens and therefore usually outside the UK tax net. The group of companies as a whole suffers no economic loss as the money is effectively flowing in a circular fashion—the loss is actually borne by the UK Exchequer ... The new clause confirms that assets held for a tax avoidance purpose are not held for a business or commercial purpose of the company, and ensures that the scope of the provisions is as wide as possible."

Clause 28 – Life policies etc: effect of rebated or reinvested commission

(Col 243)

The Economic Secretary: " ... clause 28 is an anti-avoidance measure that tackles schemes marketed to wealthy investors who seek to avoid tax on savings. Under a typical scheme, the investor takes out a large, short-term life insurance policy, which is cash-based to guarantee investment performance. The avoidance arises because the financial adviser, who arranges the investment, rebates to the policyholder a significant

(Col 244)

proportion of the commission on the policy, so that in effect all or virtually all the investment return on the policy is made up of commission that is passed on to the policyholder, free of income tax, by the adviser ... Some concern was expressed, which I think was allayed in discussions with the industry, the ABI and others, that this part of the clause might also apply to ordinary commission reinvestment arrangements in which the adviser agrees to take a lower level of commission in return for the insurer enhancing the investor's policy. The clause would not apply in those circumstances, nor is it the intention for it to do so. In ordinary commission reinvestment arrangements of this type, the value of the policy is enhanced, but there is no increase in the premium. Also, the adviser would not have a strict entitlement to the commission that they forgo; they are not rebating any commission to which they would be entitled, and so the clause would not apply. The outcome is that the full amount of premium paid by the policyholder remains allowable in computing any taxable gain, just as it has always been. It would not have to be reduced by the amount of commission that the adviser had forgone and the policy holder would therefore not be taxed on a gain that they have not realised."

Clause 31 – Restrictions on companies buying losses or gains: tax avoidance schemes

(Col 244)

The Chief Secretary to the Treasury: "The main purpose of clause 31 is to close another tax avoidance scheme that has been disclosed to Her Majesty's Revenue and Customs and that could be used to defeat the aim of a targeted anti-avoidance rule introduced in the Finance Act 2006. That rule stops tax avoidance schemes that seek to secure a tax advantage, whereby a company is sold from one group to another primarily to transfer the benefit of capital losses between the two groups, and so reduce tax. We have also taken the opportunity to relax a provision of the 2006 legislation that affects only a small number of groups of companies that realised capital losses before the legislation came into effect. We now realise that the softening of the targeted anti-avoidance rule provided by the clause goes a little too far, and would result in the rule failing to prevent all cases of loss buying involving those protected losses, hence the need for the Government amendments. Amendments Nos. 79 and 80 make the necessary changes to the text of the clause. They remove the protection that the losses enjoy from the effects of the loss buying targeted anti-avoidance rule where the parent company in the group is taken over as part of a loss-buying scheme. The clause still allows relief for the losses within the original group of companies if the takeover is for commercial purposes. It prevents relief

(Col 245)

only where one of the main purposes of the takeover is to secure a tax advantage from the losses for the new group. Amendment No. 81 provides that the changes apply only to assets disposed of on or after 9 May this year, the date when the amendments were laid."

Clause 32 – Lloyd's corporate members: restriction of group relief

(Col 258)

The Economic Secretary: "The clause adds a new section to the special tax rules dealing with corporate members of the Lloyd's insurance market. It aims to counter a loss-buying scheme reported to Revenue and Customs under the avoidance scheme disclosure rules. The scheme involves companies buying tax losses from loss-making corporate members of the Lloyd's insurance market, thus ceasing their underwriting activities. The clause will close that window by requiring that the group relationship between a corporate member and company that claims group relief to exist from the last day of the year in which the insurance business was written to the first day of the year in which the claim to group relief is made. The rule is narrowly targeted and will apply only to losses of a corporate member's final year of writing insurance business. The rule will restore the usual group relief principle that relief for losses incurred in a year will be available only to companies related to the corporate member in that same year, but it will not affect ordinary commercial acquisitions in reorganisations when the newly created group relationship is part of ongoing economic activity. The amendment arose from discussions with Lloyd's. It will refine the definition of "reinsurance to close premium" so that it includes "other consideration". "Reinsurance to close" is the mechanism by which a Lloyd's syndicate closes its account. The commercial definition of "reinsurance to close" has evolved over time and the amendment will ensure that the tax rule will reflect the definition in Lloyd's own rule."

Clause 33 – Employee benefit contributions

(Col 263)

The Chief Secretary to the Treasury: "The new avoidance schemes, known as "employer self trust schemes", attempt to avoid the restrictions introduced in 2003... They seek to allow employers to manufacture deductions artificially without the need to provide real benefits to employees. The Government do not accept that employer self trust schemes bypass the existing anti-avoidance legislation that was put in place in 2003. However, given the scale of activity in that area, we have decided to clarify the position and put it beyond doubt that

(Col 264)

employers are not entitled to a deduction under such schemes."

Clause 52 – Alternative finance investment bond

(Col 354)

The Economic Secretary: "The clause introduces tax rules on a type of Islamic bond known as a sukuk. In the Finance Acts of 2005 and 2006, we introduced legislation that set out the tax treatment of several sharia-compliant financial products, on which interest is not paid, but an alternative financial return is paid instead. The broad principle of the tax rules is that when a return paid to or by a saver or borrower is economically equivalent to interest, it is taxed as though it were interest ... The amendments make small but important technical changes, and were drafted as a result of the consultation. Although sukuk are economically similar to debt securities in law, they are not debts or loans, which gives rise to difficulties with applying the tax rules that normally apply to debts and loans. The interaction of the rules in the clause with certain tax rules was not fully appreciated when the Bill was published, and the amendments deal with some of those interactions."

Clause 54 – Trust income

(Col 358)

The Economic Secretary: "The clause amends a minor omission in last year's trust modernisation legislation concerning payments received by trustees ... The omission in the Finance Act 2006 meant that in a buy-back the whole payment is taxed. The clause corrects the position so that only the whole payment, less the original subscription price, is taxable. Because the legislation that we are correcting came into force on 6 April 2006, we are backdating the clause to take effect from that date to ensure that nobody loses out."

Clause 56 – Offshore funds

(Col 359)

The Economic Secretary: "The clause amends the rules of the offshore funds tax regime, both to enable offshore funds to use popular commercial structures that allow investors access to a range of financial instruments through a single product and to ensure that the offshore fund regime continues to provide a level playing field for onshore funds ... Industry highlighted the fact that one of the changes in the clause would retrospectively affect UK investors in funds that fall within the scope of the clause, as well as compliant funds investing in such funds. Our two amendments will ensure that the legislation will not retrospectively affect any investor and that funds

(Col 360)

investing in other offshore funds or which for commercial purposes hold underlying assets through intermediate holding companies, including funder fund structures, will not be affected by the changes."

Clause 58 – Securitisation companies

(Col 366)

Mrs. Villiers (Conservative, Chipping Barnet): "Proposed new subsection (7B) permits the Government to take a different approach to various types of securitisation companies. Given the importance of the issue, it would be useful if the Economic Secretary could explain how the Government propose to deal with the different types of company and how they will be divided up for the purposes of both the temporary rules and hopefully the new permanent ones? Will he set out the rationale for the differential treatment of the various types of securitisation company and explain the operation of the payments condition that determines whether a company can qualify to use the regime provided for in the December 2006 regulations?"

(Col 368)

The Economic Secretary (Ed Balls): "The hon. Lady asked how the payments condition will work. All cash must be paid out within 18 months, which is similar to the rules for accounts under UK GAAP, to ensure that companies are not cash money boxes. Extensive HMRC guidance will be placed in the public domain to help people through that technical area."

Clause 63 – Armed forces: Operational Allowance

(Col 376)

The Financial Secretary (John Healey): "The purpose of the allowance is to recognise the increased and enduring danger in operational locations over and above that which is already compensated for in a service person's salary. The qualifying areas will be regularly reviewed by the Secretary of State for Defence on advice from the Commander, Joint Operations. That assessment will depend on a review of the nature of the danger to armed forces personnel who are deployed on operations. Any change to the qualifying locations will be approved by Ministers … the exemption will apply retrospectively, and HMRC will not collect tax from any payment of the operational allowance."

Clause 65 – Charge on benefits received by former owner of property: late elections

(Col 385)

The Economic Secretary: "The clause will allow HMRC to use its discretion to accept elections for inheritance tax treatment in cases that would otherwise be too late … the POAT rules provide that an election must be made in a manner prescribed

(Col 386)

by regulations. No such regulations have yet been made, which we regret. That is an oversight on the part of HMRC. However, HMRC has consulted its lawyers about the validity of elections that it has already received. The advice that it has been given is that all timeous elections received—whether using the form that HMRC provided or simply giving all the necessary information—can be accepted as validly made."

Adam Afriyie (Conservative, Windsor): "The Economic Secretary used the words 'can be accepted'. That sounds slightly ambiguous. Will he put on the record now that all such elections will be accepted?"

The Economic Secretary: "Well, as I said, whether elections are made on the form provided by HMRC or by giving all the necessary information, they will be accepted as valid."

Clause 70 – SDLT: anti-avoidance

(Col 409)

The Chief Secretary: "On the Government amendments, we have made it clear that HMRC will only be allowed to use the retrospective taxation powers if it favours the taxpayer. We have clarified that only property investment partnerships are covered by the clause and that, where separate parcels of land are sold on as part of a transaction, we will use apportionment to reduce the amount of tax that purchasers might have to pay."

Clause 71 – SDLT: partnerships

(Col 425)

The Chief Secretary: "… clause 71 amends the Finance Act 2003 to counter known schemes that attempt to avoid stamp duty land tax by moving property tax-free into a partnership—that is, by the ceding of partnerships. The clause will prevent tax avoidance schemes that we initially dealt with by regulations in the pre-Budget report 2006. The two amendments that I am tabling are directly in response to representations from the property sector. The first amendment is merely to rectify an omission from the clause; it is a minor omission, but if it was not rectified we would run the risk of confusing those trying to interpret the law. The second amendment follows some late representations suggesting that the clause could have an adverse effect on investment structures that use partnerships but are not engaged in avoidance. We have been lobbied to include a transitional provision, so that the provisions that will create the change do not apply where all the property in a partnership was acquired before Royal Assent and stamp duty land tax was paid in full on the gross market value of the property, and that is what the amendment does."

Clause 81 – Criminal investigations: powers of Revenue & Customs

(Col 1459)

The Financial Secretary (John Healey): "The phrases "the officer thinks" and "the officer has reasonable grounds

(Col 1460)

for believing" have the same meaning and effect in the circumstances covered by the clause, but I consider that "think" is clearer, simpler and shorter. Under administrative law a public officer must think reasonably; otherwise, his decision would be unlawful …"

(Col 1468)

The Financial Secretary (John Healey): "Some people have argued that the exercise represents a levelling up of old Customs powers to the Revenue. That is not the case. In some instances, the provisions would introduce higher thresholds and stronger safeguards; they also mean a narrowing rather than an extension of the number of HMRC officers who can exercise the powers. The power of arrest would be restricted to authorised officers with the necessary training, who needed to perform an arrest in the course of their duties. That will mean removing the power of arrest from about 18,000 ex-Customs officers who at present have the power but no operational need to use it. Some Members expressed concern that criminal and civil matters would get mixed up. I assure them that the law makes it clear that the powers we are considering can be used only where it is reasonable to suspect that a crime has been committed and only for the purposes of a criminal investigation into that crime. None of the powers can be used for civil matters. No HMRC officer is responsible for both civil and criminal inquiries. The only guidance not yet published by HMRC is on the detail of the training courses officers must complete before they are authorised to use the powers. As promised, the guidance will be published before any powers come into effect."

Clause 85 – Search warrants

(Col 439)

The Financial Secretary (John Healey): "Clause 85 ensures that a search warrant granted in England and Wales under section 8 of the Police and Criminal Evidence Act 1984—PACE—in connection with an HMRC investigation can, when appropriate, be executed in Scotland once suitably endorsed by a court in Scotland. Schedule 23 has similar provisions for warrants granted in Scotland to be executed in England. In a similar way, clause 86 applies some existing provisions that allow various powers of arrest or detention of suspects, and search powers on arrest, to be exercised in another country of the United Kingdom when appropriate. I make it clear to the Committee that the clause does not provide HMRC with new powers, but allows existing provisions to be used appropriately. It will provide greater clarity regarding which provisions can be used and which safeguards apply."

Clause 92 – Mandatory electronic filing of returns

(Col 464)

The Financial Secretary: "Clause 92 extends HMRC's powers to require the use of electronic communications for the delivery of information to all taxes and duties for which it is responsible. In line with Lord Carter's recommendations, the revised power will enable HMRC to make recommendations to require companies to file their company tax returns online, to require employers to file their in-year forms online and to require VAT traders to file their VAT returns online. Those requirements will be phased in from April 2009, in line with the revised timetable that we announced in the Budget."

Clause 96 – Penalties for errors

(Col 468)

The Financial Secretary: "… I come now to the Government amendments, which I pay tribute to the hon. Member for Falmouth and Camborne for prompting. We discussed the issue in Committee of the whole House and I undertook to consider the matter further and to return with my own amendments, which are set out on the amendment paper. She and others reflected a concern about the phrase 'HMRC think', which occurs in a number of places in schedule 24. The Government amendments remove that phrase without replacing it in each instance. Let us be clear. The meaning and effect of the schedule are not changed by the amendments, but they have helped to reassure certain representative bodies, and the CIOT made it clear that it would welcome such an amendment."

Clause 97 – VAT: joint and several liability of traders in supply chain where tax unpaid

(*Public Bill Committee*)

(Col 491)

The Financial Secretary (John Healey): "The provisions on joint and several liability are used when HMRC identifies a company that has traded in a supply chain that has involved MTIC fraud. In those circumstances, HMRC notifies the company, in writing, that it might face an increased risk of being made liable for VAT debts elsewhere in the supply chain. Hundreds of those warning letters are issued and, in many cases, they deter the sort of activity that HMRC is concerned about, such as people turning a blind eye to suspect trading patterns or practices. That is proved by the small number of cases—the number is in single figures—in which HMRC has gone on to issue formal notification letters. It has gone on to issue notices of liability in only four cases. That is largely because of the deterrent effect of the warning letters."

(Col 494)

The Financial Secretary: "Currently, under the Finance Act 2003, HMRC can direct that another person in the supply chain other than the seller is responsible for accounting for the VAT payable, if that person knew or had reasonable grounds to suspect that it would go unpaid. That presumption is rebuttable on proof that the price reduction is due to circumstances that are unconnected with the tax being unpaid. The new power in clause 97 will allow us to change the circumstances under which a person can be presumed to know that the tax will go unpaid. Any such change would also include a provision to lay down how the presumption can be rebutted."

Clause 97 – VAT: joint and several liability of traders in supply chain where tax unpaid

(*Report Stage*)

(Col 76)

The Financial Secretary: "Government amendment No 2 ... changes the procedure for this House in considering Treasury orders relating to joint and several liability provisions for VAT. In future, both types of order will be subject to the affirmative procedure."

Clause 98 – VAT: non-business use etc of business goods

(Col 497)

The Financial Secretary: "It is the Government's intention simply that the clause brings the *Lennartz* accounting period into line with the capital goods scheme. At the same time, it implements the European Court of Justice's judgment in the Wollny case. We intend the regulations to come into effect on 1 September."

Clause 105 – VED: exempt vehicles

(Col 506)

The Economic Secretary (Ed Balls): "The current definition of an agricultural vehicle within the 1994 Act was established when the distinction between vehicles built for purposes relating to agriculture and vehicles with wider utility was starker ... some vehicles are capable of being used on the land although they are not built primarily or solely for that purpose. That leaves the current definitions open to challenge ... the clause provides for an order-making power that will be subject to the affirmative resolution procedure. The intention is to use the power to achieve firmer definitions and legislative concurrence between the vehicle excise duty exemption and eligibility under the Hydrocarbon Oil Duties Act 1979 for agricultural vehicles to use duty rebate diesel. That will ensure greater clarity, as those who are entitled to license their vehicles as exempt within the agricultural machine taxation class will also be eligible to use red diesel."

Clause 106 – Limitation period in old actions for mistake of law relating to direct tax

(Col 511)

The Chief Secretary to the Treasury (Stephen Timms): "Our purpose here is to ensure that the limitation period in which to make a claim for the recovery of direct tax paid by reason of mistaken law is six years from the date of payment. That follows a House of Lords judgment on 25 October last year in Deutsche Morgan Grenfell Group plc v. Her Majesty's Revenue and Customs. The Lords held that in certain circumstances the limitation period for claims does not begin until the claimant has discovered the mistake, which means that restitution is due in some cases for payments made more than three decades ago ... That judgment leaves the Government facing potential repayments of very large sums in other cases

(Col 512)

which means that the general populace might pay a price through higher taxes or reduced public spending for a disproportionate benefit to a small number of groups and companies. In 2004, legislation was introduced to protect the Exchequer from new claims arising on or after 8 September 2003. We are acting now on claims made before that date to protect the wider public interest. The clause ensures that a six-year limitation period applies from the date of payment. In other words, the payment groups affected will still be entitled to six year's worth of repayments. That strikes a fair balance, familiar to other parts of the legislation, as the hon. Lady rightly said, between the general interest of the community and the protection of the rights of claimants."

Schedule 3 – Managed service companies

(Col 171)

The Financial Secretary (John Healey): "Proposed section 61B(1) sets out the four conditions that must be met for a company to be defined as an MSC. They are, in summary: that the business consists wholly or mainly of providing the services of an individual to others; that payments made to the individual are equal to the greater part or all of the consideration for the provision of the services; that the way in which those payments are made would result in them receiving

(Col 172)

net of tax and national insurance, an amount exceeding that which they would have received if the payment were employment income; and that an MSC provider is involved with the company ... Turning to the fourth of the conditions in proposed new section 61B(1), it is essential that this subsection is read carefully and in its entirety. It may be that we keep coming back to the point that I wish to make now. Proposed new subsection (1)(d) states that a company is an MSC provider if 'a person who carries on a business of promoting or facilitating the use of companies to provide the services of individuals ...is involved with the company'. The first element that must be satisfied is that a person is carrying on a business of promoting or facilitating companies to provide the services of individuals, not a business to promote or facilitate companies generally. For that reason, those promoting or facilitating companies generally—for example, company formation agents—are not MSC providers. The same would be true of training providers and a number of companies that may provide advice. Some have asked whether a person who promotes their business and who provides services to those working through service companies is an MSC provider. The answer is no. There is a clear distinction between a person who promotes themselves or their business and someone who is, as a business, promoting the use of companies to provide the services of individuals. Even if a person fulfils the criterion of being an MSC provider, it does not automatically follow that their client companies are MSCs. That depends on the nature of their relationship with their client companies—namely, whether they are involved with the client companies. The word "involved" is separately defined in the legislation ..."

(Col 173)

The Financial Secretary: " ... MSC providers seeking to circumvent the legislation will claim that each relationship with their thousands of client companies is unique and does not constitute being involved. Let me try and be clear about how HMRC will approach this. First and foremost, it will look at the nature of the

(Col 174)

product provided by an MSC provider. Where it is clearly a standardised product constituting the MSC being involved with client companies, it will take the starting view that all client companies are MSCs. The onus will then be on the individual companies to demonstrate no involvement."

(Col 175)

The Financial Secretary: "… proposed section 61B(2) sets out five tests of involvement. If one of these tests is met, the company is an MSC. It is important to emphasise that this measure needs to be considered only if there is an MSC provider. For example, a tax adviser providing tax advice is not an MSC provider and therefore the tests set out in proposed section 61B(2) are not considered. The five activities defining "involved" go beyond the services provided by accountants. Some have suggested that the word "influences" in proposed section 61B(2) captures all the advice given by accountants and advisers, but there is a distinct difference—I think that hon. Members would accept that there is a difference—between a person who provides independent, tailored advice to a client, who is then able to consider that advice before accepting it or rejecting it, and the person who simply supplies a client with a standard solution or product that the client accepts. It is not the intention that the former situation—the provision of advice—be considered to be influencing in this context. However, the latter situation—supplying a standard solution or product—is regarded as influencing."

The Financial Secretary: "… a person who merely provides legal or accountancy services in a professional capacity is not an MSC provider involved with their client. There is a specific exclusion—this is the point about which the hon. Lady is concerned—from subsection (1)(d) for those who provide such services. Let me try to make this absolutely clear: even when the specific exclusion does not apply, the purpose of the legislation is not to include within the definition of MSC provider accountants, tax advisers, lawyers and

(Col 176)

company secretaries who provide advice or other professional services to companies in general. Those persons are not in the business of promoting or facilitating the use of companies to provide the services of individuals, nor are they regarded as involved with the company in the way in which the legislation envisages … When an individual asks a tax adviser for help or advice in setting up a business to provide that individual's services to end users, the tax adviser considers the individual's position and might recommend a corporate structure that includes the payment of dividends to the individual as a shareholder worker. The tax adviser is not acting as an MSC provider."

Mrs. Villiers (Conservative, Chipping Barnet): "I am grateful to the Financial Secretary. Let us take a different example, where an accountant specialises in giving advice to freelance workers and contractors. Day in, day out, contractors come to that accountant to get advice on the best way in which to run their business. The accountant regularly sets up companies and carries out services in relation to them. Do they not fall within the scope of paragraph (d), so that there is a danger that they might be construed as being in the business of promoting or facilitating the use of companies to provide the services of individuals?"

The Financial Secretary: "Freelancers or agency workers who are engaged directly by any agency or who are in some way in business on their own account and run their own affairs, either through a personal service company or some sort of umbrella company, are simply not affected by the legislation. Only those freelancers or agency workers who operate through managed service companies will be affected by the changes that we propose."

(Col 177)

The Financial Secretary: "I apologise to the Committee for a mistake in the explanatory notes, which we published on 29 March. The note on clause 25 and schedule 3 contained an error in paragraph 24, which provides the explanation of proposed new section 61B(3)… Unfortunately, the original note misquoted the text, by referring to the 'business of promoting and facilitating', rather than the 'business of promoting or facilitating'. Clearly the hon. Member for Chipping Barnet also spotted that. Just to reassure the Committee, we have amended the explanatory notes on our website, although we have not published a new printed version. Before turning to some other points, I should like briefly to mention Government amendment No. 97. I said in the Committee of the whole House that employment agencies and businesses have an important and legitimate role to play in the temporary labour market and we would not want to disrupt that. To ensure that employment agencies are not caught by the definition of MSC provider, we have provided an exclusion in proposed

(Col 178)

new section 61B(4). However, given the potential for MSC providers simply to re-badge themselves as employment businesses or agencies, the exclusion in proposed new section 61B(4) was restricted, to the extent that employment businesses and agencies do no more than would be expected from such businesses. Our amendment No. 97 corrects a technical flaw in the legislation, which, if left unchanged, would have resulted in the exclusion being too narrow and therefore bringing employment businesses back within the scope of the definition, which was clearly not our intention. Our amendment will allow an employment business or agency to influence a worker's company or its finances to the extent that that relates to the placing of the individual with an end client. That will mean that such businesses can carry on their normal activities, as intended."

(Col 190)

The Financial Secretary: "We have found that when a PAYE or national insurance contributions debt is established, the MSCs frequently escape from making payment by winding up or ceasing to trade and moving workers into a new company, and because MSCs are simply a vehicle through which workers' income is routed, they often have no assets and so HMRC is unable to recover the unpaid tax and national insurance contributions. Proposed new section 688A contains provisions to enable regulations to transfer PAYE debts to appropriate third parties when the MSC does not pay. It sets out, of course, who those third parties are. As respondents to the consultation confirmed, the provision for the transfer of debts is essential to ensure that the wider aims of the legislation are achieved. Without it, those promoting and benefiting from the schemes could carry on without any financial risk ... I am aware that concerns remain about the scope of the transfer provisions, so the three remaining Government amendments represent our considered response to dealing with those concerns ... Government amendment No. 98 will remove the word "facilitated" from proposed new section 688A(2)(c) so that only those who have encouraged or been actively involved in the provision by the MSC of the services of the individual will fall within its scope. Both tests require the third party to have an active role, so those who simply use MSC workers will not be caught. If an end client did more than simply use MSC labour, for example by telling those who it employed that they must move to an MSC, it would fall within the scope of the measure as that would be regarded as encouragement—the hon. Lady asked about that point. That was the reason why we included the word "actively", which I am glad she welcomed. She asked for clarification of whether the tax clock is ticking from April. I confirm that debts can be transferred only for PAYE or national insurance contributions from August or January, depending on which third party is considered, not from April ... Proposed new section 688A does not provide for HMRC to create a PAYE debt, but for regulations to enable the transfer of debts that have been created by virtue of existing legislation. Government amendments Nos. 99 and 100 reflect the consideration that we have given to concerns that employment businesses or agencies might be within the scope of the debt transfer provision, simply as a result of carrying on their normal business of placing individuals. We have considered the risk that such

(Col 191)

activity might be regarded as "actively involved" under proposed new section 688A(2)(c), and have decided to remove that risk by expanding the exclusion, as set out in proposed new section 688A(3), so that the mere placing of individuals with clients is not within the scope of the provisions. An employment business will be within that scope where it is involved beyond such activity, perhaps by advising workers to use an MSC."

The Financial Secretary: "The hon. Lady was rightly concerned about the position of those she termed "ordinary employees" of MSCs. Let me make it clear that we do not intend ordinary employees of MSCs or third parties to be caught by the debt transfer provision. Defining an ordinary employee would be difficult, however, and her attempt to do so made that point for me. Except for MSC directors, providers and associates, the debt transfer provisions cover only those who have encouraged or been actively involved with the supply of labour services through MSCs. It is important to recognise that the transfer of debt regulations include a specific right of appeal on the grounds that 'the amount specified in the transfer notice does not have regard to the degree and extent to which the transferee ...has encouraged ...or been involved'. On those grounds, the special commissioners may reduce the amount specified in the transfer notice to a level that, in their opinion, is just and reasonable."

Schedule 5 – Avoidance involving financial arrangements

(Col 246)

The Economic Secretary: "The amendments will make a slight extension to the scope of one of the anti-avoidance provisions in schedule 5 to stop avoidance scheme promoters introducing even more contrived arrangements to circumvent the effect of the measure. Paragraph 15 of the schedule is aimed at schemes that create artificial losses from a company's holdings in offshore funds or similar collective investment schemes. The losses are generated by the scheme making an investment that is bound to decline in value. Shortly after the Bill was published, disclosure was made to HMRC of a scheme that attempts to get round the provisions by arranging for the collective investment scheme to take on a liability for the same purpose, ensuring that the value of the fund declines. The amendments will frustrate such an attempt by broadening paragraph 15 so that it refers to a liability as well as to an investment. The rule in paragraph 15 as a whole will have effect from 6 March, when the measure was announced, but the extension brought about by the amendments will apply from 9 March."

(Col 248)

The Economic Secretary: "I was tempted to intervene on the hon. Member for Chipping Barnet to ask her whether she thought paragraph 23 of schedule 26 to the 2002 Act is framed in the most apposite way … We have been persuaded to act by the number of avoidance schemes that have come to our attention. In the judgment of HMRC, most schemes are covered by paragraph 23. However, the judgment of HMRC experts is that that measure does not cover all potential schemes or those that are already in operation. The Bill gives us confidence that we will cover all such schemes in the future. We are ensuring that the gaps in paragraph 23 are well and truly closed. Most schemes hit by the schedule are being challenged in court, but not all. Whether we litigate will depend on legal advice. The changes will mean that any gaps in paragraph 23 will be comprehensively closed."

Schedule 6 – Companies carrying on business of leasing plant or machinery

(Col 251)

The Chief Secretary to the Treasury (Stephen Timms): "… schedule 6 introduces anti-avoidance legislation in response to disclosures that we have received about avoidance schemes being used that are designed to get round measures in the Finance Act 2006 to combat the loss of tax from the sale of companies leasing out plant or machinery. In the early years of a profitable lease, lessor companies generated losses but in the later years the situation reversed: the lease became profitable, but tax was being lost because groups were selling lessor

(Col 252)

companies to loss-making groups at just the time that the leasing transaction was about to become tax-profitable. The relevant provisions in the 2006 Act prevent a loss of tax when a lessor company leaves a profit-making group and becomes a member of a loss-making group by bringing into charge an amount that prevents the loss of tax when a lessor company is sold. The disclosures that we received indicated that groups were avoiding the rules in two ways. One type of scheme was using legislation that enables a group to transfer leasing businesses without tax effect, rather than selling the lessor company and the other manipulated the balance sheet value of leased assets in a way that would reduce or eliminate the charge that should be brought into account to prevent the loss of tax. Schedule 6 stops both types of scheme. First, it makes changes to the rules allowing groups to transfer businesses without tax effect; those rules are in section 343 of the Income and Corporation Taxes Act 1988. Changes to section 343 will mean that only transfers of assets between subsidiaries of the same parent company—and certain transfers involving consortium companies and partnerships—will benefit from tax neutrality. Where the new rules apply so that a transfer falls outside the existing section 343 provisions, the disposal of the assets of the business is treated as taking place at a value equal to the value of the asset unencumbered by the lease: that is, as if the lease did not exist. That creates a charge broadly equivalent to the effect of schedule 10 to the Finance Act 2006. Secondly, the schedule adds two new paragraphs to schedule 10 on the sale of lessors. New paragraph 38A requires a company to ignore the consequences of arrangements entered into to secure a tax advantage, and new paragraph 38B requires a company to ignore liabilities when determining the value of its assets. Those changes will ensure that the sale of lessors legislation works as intended."

Schedule 7 – Insurance companies: gross roll-up business etc.

(Col 302)

The Economic Secretary (**Ed Balls**): "Amendment No. 129 is a good example of the openness and trust between the industry and the Government that has been built up during the course of this major consultation on life insurance company taxation. As drafted in the Finance Bill, new section 444ABD of the Taxes Act 1998 gave what commentators described as an over-generous treatment of certain losses, which could lead to double counting. We are removing the part about losses, but that is not the end of the story. HMRC and the industry are continuing to discuss the tax treatment of transfers of business ... If a revised or more focused rule about losses is needed, it can be done in the regulations."

Schedule 8 – Insurance companies: basis of taxation etc.

(Col 305)

The Economic Secretary: "Schedule 8 and clause 38 carry on the process of simplification ... In particular, the measures abolish what is known as the Crown option—the ancient rule under which an HMRC officer can, even in these days of self-assessment, decide whether a life insurance company should pay tax on a trading profits basis or on the I minus E basis that nearly always applies to such companies. The current system has been part of the life insurance tax rules since 1915. When HMRC published its technical consultation document in May 2006, there was a small passage about the Crown option. It became clear from the responses to the document that the uncertainty of not knowing when the Crown option would be exercised was causing problems for the life insurance industry, especially in the calculation by a company's actuaries of its embedded value profits. There are ways for insurance companies to show more realistic profit figures than those that are given by the regulatory accounting rules of the Financial Services Authority. They require the actuary to predict the tax treatment of the business over the coming decade or so. The complete change of basis that is caused if the Crown option is exercised plays havoc with those calculations. HMRC and the industry have together devised a new approach to replace the Crown option, to which schedule 8 gives effect. The schedule sets out unequivocally, with no element of choice for either HMRC or companies, the circumstances in which a company will be assessed on the trading profits basis. They are restricted to two types of specialist business. Pure reinsurers—companies that do reinsurance business only in the market—will, as they are now, always be taxed on the trading profits basis. The same will apply to companies whose only business is gross roll-up business, which we discussed in relation to schedule 7. All other business that is not gross roll-up business, such as ordinary life assurance business with UK residents, will be taxed only on the I minus E basis. Schedule 8 sets out how changes between the two bases will be handled, which is particularly relevant for any change of basis that is caused by the schedule itself. There are a number of transitional provisions. As part of the agreed package, the schedule improves the mechanism for ensuring that the I minus E basis of taxation results at least in the taxation, at mainstream corporation tax rates, of the life insurance company's profits that are not being accrued for policy holders."

Schedule 9 – Insurance companies: transfers etc.

(Col 306)

The Economic Secretary: "Where a transfer of business took place before Budget day the repeal is intended to be effective for any period beginning in 2007. However, the life insurance industry has said that there is some doubt about whether the measure has that effect. To deal with that uncertainty, Government amendment No. 89 puts matters beyond doubt."

(Col 307)

The Economic Secretary: "Transfers of business are a common feature within the insurance industry, particularly as the industry consolidates and reorganises. A merger of companies within a group can reduce the cost of capital significantly and make operations more efficient. The Government do not want in any way to stand in the way of such important transactions. Indeed, we are keen to facilitate them and to reduce the administrative and compliance burdens associated with genuine commercial transfers. Transfers of business have also, however, presented opportunities for some to try to extract profits in untaxed form, against the intentions of Parliament. It has therefore been necessary for the Government to introduce a number of complex measures over recent years to block a succession of schemes designed to avoid tax on a transfer of life insurance business. That has led to the tax rules for transfers of insurance business becoming the most complex part of this very complex area, and there is anecdotal evidence that that complexity is inhibiting genuine commercial transactions. It will come as no surprise, therefore, that simplifying the transfer rules was an important objective for the industry in the consultation process. We want to facilitate that if we can. Schedule 9 is designed to achieve those twin objectives by facilitating commercially driven transfers and protecting the tax base. The basic principle on which we worked in producing the legislation is that transfers of business should be tax neutral, but only where assets and liabilities pass from the long-term insurance fund of the transferor to the long-term insurance fund of the transferee. Schedule 9 achieves that by clarifying the existing rules and by adding new rules where previously there was only guidance. To sit alongside those clarified and simplified rules, there is a targeted anti-avoidance rule. That will not affect 'plain vanilla' commercial transfers, but it will protect the tax base where there is any attempt to reduce profits or create artificial losses during the transfer process."

(Col 308)

The Economic Secretary: "... The TAAR will operate in association with a clearance process, so that where Her Majesty's Revenue and Customs is satisfied that obtaining a tax advantage is not a main purpose of a proposed transaction, the TAAR will not be invoked. In addition, the TAAR will not apply where a group can show that one company in that group may have got a tax advantage but there is a corresponding tax disadvantage to another company."

Schedule 10 – Insurance companies: miscellaneous

(Col 313)

The Economic Secretary: "... where structural assets are held in a company's long-term insurance fund, inappropriate tax rules can arise, because the life insurance tax rules assume that all assets held in a long-term fund are held

(Col 314)

or sold in the course of the company's insurance business. For example, dividends from insurance subsidiaries through structural assets are subject to corporation tax, whereas dividends from structural subsidiaries of other types of trading company are exempt. As taxation of life insurance companies is based on their regulatory returns, it follows that write-downs can result in a tax deduction where there is no economic loss. Following consultation with the life insurance industry, we have introduced paragraph 3, which will reform the taxation of structural assets, treating them as capital assets rather than trading assets. Dividends from structural assets will be exempt from tax, giving the insurance industry parity with other traders. A further measure in paragraph 4 will remove the restriction on use of capital losses where a life insurance company sells holdings in an authorised unit trust or an open-ended investment company to the manager of that trust or company, and that manager is a member of the same group of companies as the life insurer. The capital gains rules impose restrictions on the use of capital losses on all disposals between connected parties, such as members of the same group. The policy reason is that connected parties have opportunities to manipulate the circumstances of the disposal that are not available to independent parties. However, where a life insurer disposes of holdings in unit trusts or open-ended investment companies, both Financial Services Authority rules and life insurance tax rules ensure that the disposal is at market value and minimise opportunities for manipulation, regardless of who acquires the assets. For that reason, the life insurance industry has argued that it is unfair to restrict any losses arising. The Government accept its argument, and schedule 10 will remove the restrictions. The remainder of the schedule comprises a general tidying up of life insurance tax rules, modernising definitions, removing duplication by putting all definitions in one place and repealing spent or obsolete provisions ... The amendments will modify the new provisions in response to our consultation. Paragraph 3 will reform the taxation of structural assets, treating them as capital assets rather than trading assets. Dividends from structural assets will now be exempt from tax, giving the insurance industry parity. The schedule defines structural assets initially as shares in and loans to subsidiaries of insurance companies that themselves write insurance business. The measure also includes a regulatory power to add to or amend the list of structural assets; however, the life insurance industry will be consulted before that power is exercised."

Schedule 11 – Technical provisions made by general insurers

(Col 321)

The Economic Secretary: "The Government amendments to the schedule arise from discussion with Lloyd's. Government amendments Nos 76 and 77 will substitute for 'reinsurance to close contracts' the term 'reinsurance to close amounts'. Reinsurance to close is a mechanism by which a Lloyd's syndicate closes its accounts. The commercial definition of reinsurance to close has evolved over time. The amendments ensure that the tax rule reflects the definition in Lloyd's rules and that the schedule has its intended scope. Government amendment No. 78 is a response to the concern of Lloyd's that the schedule could have unintended unfair results in particular circumstances. It will enable the making of regulations to deal with those circumstances, which include members leaving syndicates and members having their own reinsurance arrangements in addition to arrangements that the syndicate may have. Officials are discussing with Lloyd's an appropriate solution to the issue, so draft regulations are not yet available to us or to the Committee. Any regulations that are passed under the new power would reduce or eliminate the effects of adjustments that would arise under the schedule. They will be discussed in detail with Lloyd's before they are laid."

Schedule 13 – Sale and repurchase of securities

(Col 322)

The Economic Secretary: "The three Government amendments make a minor modification to schedule 13. They correct a defect that might have led to loss of tax. The new rules for charging sales and repurchase agreements to corporation tax provide that where a company sells securities under a repo, it is to be taxed on income arising on the securities as if the sale had not taken place. That is subject to the requirement that the company must recognise the income in its accounts during the period of the repo. That requirement may result in income falling out of the charge to tax in which the borrower is taxed on a receipts basis in respect of income arising on the securities. For accounts purposes, it recognises that income before entering into the repo. In that case, it will not recognise the income again during the repo. If the amendments were not made, the income could not be charged to tax. The amendments, therefore, omit the requirement that recognition of the income for accounts purposes must take place in the same period in which the arrangement is in force. That ensures that companies remain taxable on the income, provided that that is reflected in their accounts."

Schedule 16 – Venture capital schemes, etc.

(Col 340)

The Financial Secretary (John Healey): " ... the amendments would enable venture capital trusts to dispose of investments that they have held as qualifying holdings for a period of at least six months for cash without jeopardising their approval status for the following six months ... The amendments would widen the scope of the disregard rules to cover disposals made wholly or partly for consideration other than cash and have again been warmly and widely welcomed by representatives from the sector."

Schedule 17 – Real Estate Investment Trusts

(Col 345)

The Economic Secretary: "The Government amendments will ensure that schedule 17 provisions relating to demergers within UK REITs apply where a demerged property or subsidiary is transferred to a new company that then becomes a UK REIT itself. The amendments will ensure also that the terminology used to describe the demergers is consistent with that used elsewhere in UK REITs legislation by using the word "disposal" rather than "transfers". Amendment Nos. 138 to 148 will mean that the provisions in paragraph 11 of schedule 17 will apply to a company that acquires a subsidiary company to which the ring-fenced assets have been transferred. The amendments allow also the company time to satisfy the conditions for entry to the UK REITs regime. That extends the same flexibility to disposals of ring-fenced assets by a single company UK REIT, as paragraph 16 proposes already for demergers from group UK REITs ... Amendments Nos. 149 to 158 will mean that the provision in paragraph 16 of schedule 17 will apply where a demerged company becomes a member of a new group UK REIT, rather than, as originally provided for, a parent of such a group. In summary, the amendments ensure that schedule 17 provisions relating to demergers from UK REITs have their intended scope and include additional flexibility. Just to be clear, amendments Nos. 138, 142, 146 and 147 substitute "disposal" for "transfer", which will mean that the terminology in that part of the Bill is

(Col 346)

consistent with other sections of UK REITs legislation … "

Schedule 19 – Alternatively secured pensions and transfer of lump sum death benefits, etc.

(Col 393)

The Chief Secretary to the Treasury (Stephen Timms): "Amendment No. 134 clarifies the fact that there will be no further charge to inheritance tax on the death of a dependant where the left-over funds in an alternatively secured pension—ASP— were chargeable to inheritance tax on the death of a scheme member. Amendment No. 135 ensures that the changes to remove an option to transfer funds on death from an ASP fund will not affect any members with ASPs who died before 6 April 2007."

Schedule 20 – Pension schemes, etc: miscellaneous

(Col 406)

The Chief Secretary: "… amendment No. 137, on the rules of pension commencement lump sums, will allow lump sums to be paid up to six months before the pension commences so long as a pension scheme is arranging for a pension to commence. That will allow schemes and pension members greater flexibility in arranging a pension. It will allow savers time to take advantage of the open market option and choose the most suitable option annuity for them, and it meets principles underlying pensions tax relief. The amendment will apply retrospectively to A-day to ensure that those lump sums that have been paid remain tax-free."

Schedule 21 – Exemptions from stamp duty and SDRT

(Col 432)

The Chief Secretary: "Our amendments will remove an unnecessary condition from the stamp duty and stamp duty reserve tax intermediary reliefs. From 1 November, intermediaries will be able to benefit from MIFID, the new regulatory regime. As MIFID contains provisions for making public transactions in shares that are admitted to trading on regulated markets, we have decided that it is no longer necessary for such provisions to be a condition for intermediary relief. The amendments remove the requirement to make public transactions in regulated market shares for shares that are admitted to trading only on a multilateral trading facility. Transactions will still qualify for relief only if reported to the market, so the changes are consistent with the written ministerial statement of 20 February. We are also taking the opportunity to make a technical amendment to the definition of a European Economic Area State to ensure that it has the same meaning as the definition in the Interpretation Act 1978."

Schedule 26 – Meaning of 'recognised stock exchange', etc.

(Col 513)

The Economic Secretary: "Amendment No. 118 will ensure that all known consequential amendments have been made. As I said, the legislation's aim is to ensure competition for markets and to modernise the terminology used. This consequential amendment, which was omitted from the original list, should now be included. If it is not added to the list, it could create uncertainty for the industry and unnecessary administrative burdens in clarifying that there is no essential difference between "quoted" and "listed" for the purpose of Schedule 26."

INDEX